1

The 2016 Hampton Reader

SELECTED ESSAYS, ANALYSES AND
COMMENTARIES FROM THE HAMPTON
INSTITUTE: A WORKING-CLASS THINK
TANK

Hampton Institute Press

www.hamptoninstitution.org

ISBN: 0-9913136-4-X
ISBN-13: 978-0-9913136-4-8

CONTENTS

WEEDS IN THE HOLY GARDEN

WOMEN'S ISSUES ... 660

WOMEN'S RIGHTS ACTIVISM 101

LATINA FEMINISM

IS THERE ROOM FOR DECOLONIAL, TRANSNATIONAL, AND RADICAL FEMINIST DISCOURSE IN POP CULTURE FEMINISM?

GENTRIFICATION IS A FEMINIST ISSUE

*EXCLUSIVE ESSAY ONLY AVAILABLE IN THE READER

Criminal Justice

Policing the Blacks
Ferguson and Past Histories

Dr. Jason Michael Williams

The continuing protesting efforts in Ferguson are a constant reminder that democracy left unchecked is totalitarianism disguised as freedom and inclusivity. The protestors in Ferguson, who represent all walks of life, are protesting in defense of a mentality and ideal that is unable to conceive inequality and mistreatment as a normative function within American democracy. They understand that no American citizen should have to face differential treatment within a society that allegedly claims to be among the leaders of the world and yet is not whole. How could it be 2014 and yet, still, as a society, brutalization against Black bodies is tolerated and, in many cases, quickly justified by those who have yet to accept Blackness as their equal within the human family, let alone within American democracy. Yes, the problem is largely race-based, and America should accept this truth however hard it might be to fathom. Many critics on this subject rush toward politically correct speaking points that overwhelmingly discount a truth that is knowable and historic. The politically correct orientation of Ferguson is one based in the fantasy of colorblindness. It attempts to shield the hard historical fact that policing in America has always been one of color/class-consciousness. Thus, American policing at its foundation is inherently protective of the status quo. Regarding Blacks, this reality dates back to plantation justice-a time within which Black bodies were brutality policed at the behest of White domination. Sadly, almost 400 years later, this would still be the dominant thinking behind policing the Blacks, whether known consciously or not.

Given the history of American social control and its relationship to Black bodies, there could be not a single question of doubt against the general inquiry of those in Ferguson-police accountability. America has long tolerated and justified the brutalization of Black bodies (even when the culprit is Black) and, because of this historic hard fact, it is hard to fathom how some are unable to conceive the possibility that police officers might be engaging in the same activity that was once legal or customary within American society. Police officers are not somehow disconnected from the broader American ethos as they too are socially conditioned and therefore susceptible to the biases, prejudices, and misperceptions that ought to be *checked* given the amount of power they hold over the lives of citizens.

The answer lies in the stark racial contrast regarding the value of life and how certain lives are legitimated to the detriment of others. An example of this contrast was eloquently and expectedly showcased at a Cardinals game where pro-Brown protestors were met face to face with an all-White crowd of pro-Wilson responders. Thus, the racial make-up of this incident speaks volumes to the impact that histories of racial control and exclusion have had on modern day social-racial discourses.

Figure 1.

Teenage White Men
1 million

Teenage Black Men
1 million

1.5 in 1 million reported   31 in 1 million reported

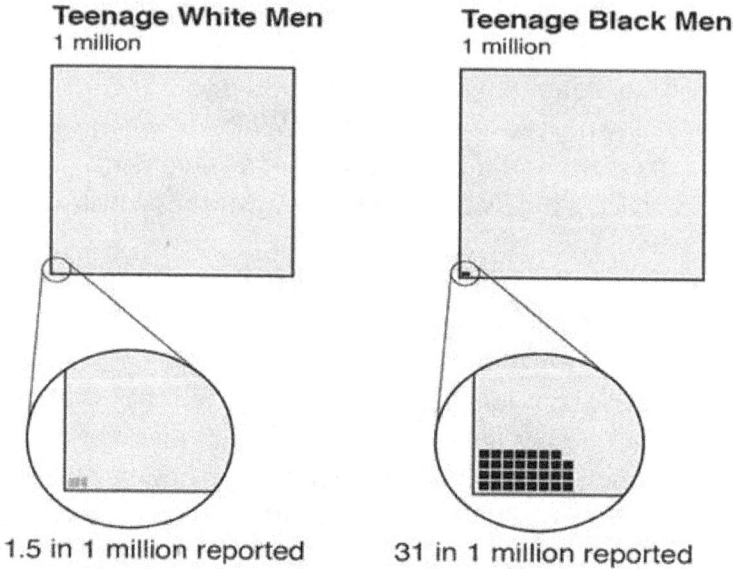

Reported killings by police during 2010-2012
21 times as likely for black vs. white teenage men
(Source: ProPublica)

Why are people surprised by the fact that Black men, in particular, are the quintessential victim of police brutality and violence, again, given the history of brutalization in America? For example, a study published by ProPublica, recently found that Black teens were 21 times more likely to be murdered by police than White teens from 2010-2012 (see figure 1). Yet, most will inevitably fail to realize the deep importance of this study as it situates, clearly, the level of vulnerability that Blacks must still face in 2014.

Moreover, the revelations noted in this study and *many* others like it, is what compels those in Ferguson to protest. The revelations in studies like these also give power to the significance of past histories; for example, the often quoted words of Chief Justice

14

<u>Taney</u> in the United States Supreme Court Dred Scott decision regarding Africans:

"In the opinion of the court, the legislation and histories of the times, and the language used in the Declaration of Independence, show that neither the class of persons who had been imported as slaves nor their descendants, whether they had become free or not, were then acknowledged as a part of the people, nor intended to be included in the general words used in that memorable instrument...They had for more than a century before been regarded as beings of an inferior order, and altogether unfit to associate with the white race either in social or political relations, and so far inferior that they had no rights which the white man was bound to respect, and that the negro might justly and lawfully be reduced to slavery for his benefit. He was bought and sold, and treated as an ordinary article of merchandise and traffic whenever a profit could be made by it. This opinion was at that time fixed and universal in the civilized portion of the white race. It was regarded as an axiom in morals as well as in politics which no one thought of disputing or supposed to be open to dispute, and men in every grade and position in society daily and habitually acted upon it in their private pursuits, as well as in matters of public concern, without doubting for a moment the correctness of this opinion."

Given the rampant amounts of blatant and hidden discrimination in the American administration of justice, how could anyone argue that Taney's words are not as important today in reflexive contexts as they were when they were written? Like Mr. Scott, the protestors in Ferguson are asking for inclusion and the humanity of *all* to be respected. History serves as a constant reminder on the extent to which their simple requests have not been met, but when will this nightmare end? Moreover, how can America continue to be the mediator of world problems when it continues to ignore domestic issues like police brutality? It is the inconsistencies in American democracy that hinders U.S. imperialism in the Middle East and beyond. Even before Ferguson the international community knew that the U.S. does not always practice what it preaches.

15

One of the last bastions of pre-sixties white supremacy is, in fact, the criminal justice system itself. For instance, the use of the criminal justice system as a post-sixties tool of racialized social control begun with the state's hampering down on resistance movements and groups in the '70s and later with the war on drugs, which targeted Blacks. It is the ultimate tool because most people (especially the majority) do not question the law as a result of being taught to respect it at all costs. Thus, judicial mistreatment is justified via majoritarian trickery masquerading as justice. Also, people are taught that justice in America is colorblind, albeit easily debunked by decades of social science research. The result is a recipe for judicial deceit and betrayal because it complicates what is essentially in plain sight, at least to the non-majority.

Nevertheless, Ferguson is an excellent test case on which to examine race and criminal justice. For example, many pundits are arguing for better training, community relations, and the inclusion of people of color on police forces, all of which has been tried before with little difference. On the contrary, however, the solution is simply *police accountability*. Officers of color are equally guilty, at a lesser rate, though, of some of the same questionable behavior predominately exhibited by White officers. Therefore, more training and diversity, although probably useful, is not a panacea. Like Taney, rogue officers understand the Constitution very well, and they recognize that racial profiling and excessive force is inappropriate even though they *choose* (like any ordinary criminal) to engage in those kinds of behavior. Yet, at the same time, these officers also know that there are very little consequences for poor decision making that is often life changing and ending.

Therefore, the solution to problems like these must be akin to the same kinds of consequences faced by civilians. The people in Ferguson are tired of the term, "justifiable homicide" they instead would like to see investigations and consequences as opposed to having to witness two different forms of justice. They see no difference between the extrajudicial murders of yesterday and so-called justifiable homicides today, which Blacks are accounted disproportionately. They are tired of subjective citizenship when they deserve full citizenship. They are tired of having to respect the rights of others while their rights are unacknowledged. They are tired of being guilty until proven innocent unlike Darren Wilson (and other White males) who seem to never be guilty first of criminal behavior because they are likely perceived as innocent and non-dangerous. Finally and perhaps more *important*, their tiredness falls on the backdrop of *histories of racial discrimination* (legal and custom), brutalization of their bodies via systems of social control/criminal justice, and outright democratic exclusion. The only fix to this problem is *police accountability*. No other fix will work. Those in Ferguson and beyond must believe that they too matter and that the death of their *bodies* will be met with *swift justice*. The Ferguson movement is essentially proposing that *now* is our society's chance to prove Taney wrong.

The Brutes in Blue
From Ferguson to Freedom

Andrew Gavin Marshall

The protests resulting from events in Ferguson and New York have spurred a nation-wide anti-police brutality and social justice movement. This movement is addressing issues related to the realities of institutional racism in the United States, a colonial legacy born of slavery. Policing itself has a history and institutional function that is relevant to current events. This part in the series, 'From Ferguson to Freedom' examines the institution of policing and 'law enforcement', designed to protect the powerful from the people, to punish the poor and enforce injustice.

A Primer on Policing

Many social divisions erupt when it comes to discussing the issues of police and policing. Many accept the police and state-propagated view of police as being there 'to serve and protect', and that the 'dangerous' jobs of ensuring 'peace' and 'safety' are deserving of respect and admiration. Others view police as oppressors and thugs, violent and abusive, the enforcers of injustice. Here, as with the issue of racism itself, we come to the dichotomy of individual and institutional actions and functions. As individuals, there are many police who may act admirably, who may 'serve and protect', who serve a social function which is beneficial to the community in which they operate. But, as with the issue of racism, individual acts do not erase institutional functions. The reality is that as an institution, policing is fundamentally about *control*, with cops acting as agents of 'law and order'. They enforce the law and punish its detractors (primarily among the poor), they 'serve and protect' the powerful (and their interests) from the people.

When individuals in poor black neighborhoods are caught with illegal substances, such as drugs, the police are there to arrest them and send them into the criminal justice system for judgment and punishment. When Wall Street banks launder billions in drug money, police are nowhere to be seen, the law is ignored, justice is evaded, and the rich and powerful remain untouched. Crime is subject to class divides. Crimes such as mass murder, crimes against humanity, war crimes, slavery, ethnic cleansing, money laundering, mass corruption, plundering and destruction are typically committed (or decided) by those who hold the power, have the money and own the property. These crimes largely go unpunished, and very often are even rewarded.

Crimes committed by the poor, the oppressed, and especially those which take place in communities of colour are the main focus of the criminal injustice system. It is the poor and exploited who are policed and repressed, punished and sentenced, beaten and executed. The criminal rich and powerful are largely untouchable. The police enforce the law, so far as it applies to the poor, and are primarily there to serve the interests of the powerful. This is not new.

Like with all institutions, to understand their functions, one must turn to their origins and evolution through the years. In the United States, the history of 'policing' pre-dates the formation of the country itself, when it was a collection of European colonial possessions. From the late 1600s onward, just as racism was itself

19

becoming institutionalized in the slave system, the social concept of policing increasingly emerged. The European colonial system was dependent upon the exploitation of slave labour, which since the late 1600s had become increasingly defined along racial lines.
In the 1700s, colonial societies began forming "slave patrols" to keep the slaves in line, to capture escapees, and to maintain "law and order" in an inherently unjust and exploitative social system of domination. As black slaves increasingly outnumbered the local white colonists, paranoia increased (especially in the wake of slave rebellions), and so the "slave patrols" and other locally organized 'vigilante' groups would be formed to protect the white colonizers against the local indigenous populations and the enslaved black African population.

The slave patrols defined the early formation of the modern " law enforcement" institution in the United States, which extended into the 19th century, up until the Civil War. The slave patrols also had other functions within the communities they operated, but first and foremost, their primary purpose was "to act as the first line of defense against a slave rebellion."

Following the processes of industrialization and urbanization, cities became crowded, immigrants became plenty, and poverty was rampant as the rich few became ever more powerful. Thus, throughout the 19th century, the slave patrols began evolving into official "police forces," with their concern for "order" and "control", largely via the policing of poor communities of colour.

The evolution of policing in America since the 19th century has largely maintained its focus on the policing of the poor, acting as soldiers in the "war against crime" (which J. Edgar Hoover declared in the 1930s), though, of course, this applies almost exclusively to crime committed by the poor, by immigrants and 'minority' groups, as the rich and powerful are able to continue plundering and stealing wealth, waging wars and killing great masses of people, engaging in institutional corruption and even participating in war crimes and crimes against humanity, almost always with impunity and beyond the reach of police or justice.

In the past few decades, police forces across America have become increasingly militarized, with the rise of what has been called the " warrior cop." Police forces get military equipment, tanks, rocket launchers, and even wear military outfits and get military training. Militaries are of course designed to be institutions of force, to kill, to destroy, to occupy and oppress. They are fundamentally, and institutionally, *imperial*. So as police forces become increasingly militarized, their function becomes increasingly aligned with that of the military. While the military secures the interests of the rich and powerful abroad, the police secure the interests of the rich and powerful at home. The domestic population is treated increasingly like an "enemy population," with poor communities (especially poor black, Hispanic and indigenous communities) treated like occupied populations.

The origins of the modern police force began as a distinctly colonial structure, to enforce the injustice of slavery, to protect the colonizers as they expanded their territories and committed genocide against the indigenous population. Colonization, ethnic cleansing, slavery and genocide are *inherently* wrong and unjust. As such, these policies must be protected *by force*. The legal system has always been far more concerned with the protection of property (belonging to rich white men) than it has been with the protection of the population from the abuses of an inherently unjust social system. In a slave society, human beings become property. The law protects private property, but does so often through the oppression of populations. Property becomes more important than people, even when people *are* property.

The Global Reality of the Brutes in Blue

Think, for a brief moment, of the images, videos and realities of protests, revolutions, resistance movements and rebellions around the world in the past several years. From the Arab Spring in Tunisia and Egypt, to Indigenous movements in Canada and Latin America and Africa, to the peasant and labour unrest across Asia, to the anti-austerity movements across Europe, with social unrest reaching enormous heights in Greece, Spain, Italy and Portugal, from the Indignados to Occupy Wall Street, to the student movements in Quebec, the UK, Chile, Mexico and Hong Kong, to the urban rebellions in Turkey and Brazil, and now to the civil unrest in the US sparked by Ferguson. What do you see, in all of these cases? In each and every case, there are large or significant segments of populations who are rising up in resistance to oppressive structures, against dictatorships, state violence and repression, against poverty, racism and exploitation. In each case, there are populations struggling for dignity and opportunity, for freedom and democracy, for justice and equality. These populations, those who protest and resist, those who struggle and strive for the realization of democracy and justice, are historically the main reason why society has in any meaningful way ever been able to advance, to civilize itself, for rights and freedoms to be won and realized. Progress for people as a whole has always been accompanied by mass struggle and resistance against the forces of oppression and to upset the 'stability' of the status quo.

And, both historically and presently, without exception, the struggle and resistance of populations at home and abroad has always been met with the blunt, brute force of police, there to beat the people back down into subservience and to maintain "law and order." In the youth-led rebellions from Egypt to Spain to Indonesia, from Brazil to Mexico to Quebec, from Hong Kong to Turkey to Ferguson, Missouri, the police are there with batons, pepper spray, tear gas, rubber bullets, *real* bullets, beatings and brutality, mass arrests and murder, all in the name of preserving 'stability'.
This is the true institutional function of the police. It cares not whether there are good or decent individuals within police forces, no more than the institutional reality of militaries cares whether individual soldiers are good or decent. Their *job* is to protect the powerful, police the poor, and punish those who threaten the stability of this unjust system. This is an institutional function which has been a *lived reality* for the black community in the United States since the origins of slavery and policing. The protests resulting from

22

Ferguson are a reflection of this reality, regardless of the opinions of white people who have been largely spared the blunt truth of batons and bullets wielded and shot by the Brutes in Blue.

Black and Blue

According to a study published in 2012, every 28 hours in the United States, a black man, woman or child is murdered by a law enforcement official, security guard or "vigilante." In 2011, murder was listed as the number one cause of death for black males between the ages of 15 and 34 . In the month prior to Michael Brown's murder, three other unarmed black men were killed by police, with data from police forces across the country revealing that black males are far more likely to be shot and killed by police than any other demographic group.

According to data from the Department of Justice, between 2003 and 2009, roughly 4,813 people were killed in the process of being arrested or while in the custody of police officers. In 2012 alone, 410 people were killed by police in the United States. Between 1968 and 2011, data from the CDC reveals, black Americans were between two and eight times more likely to be killed by police than white Americans. On average, black Americans were 4.2 times more likely to be murdered by police than whites.

Between the murder of Michael Brown in August and the delivery of the verdict in November of 2014, police in the United States killed roughly 14 other teenagers, at least six of them black. Two days before the Darren Wilson verdict was reached, 12-year-old Tamir Rice was murdered by police in Cleveland, Ohio, for holding a BB gun.

In late December, however, a mentally ill man in New York shot and killed two NYPD police officers in Brooklyn, after which he shot and killed himself. New York mayor Bill de Blasio, who has attempted to navigate between placating protesters and police, has made himself hated by many in the NYPD, who view anything but absolute and unquestionable loyalty as unforgivable betrayal. The head of the NYPD's union commented on the two killed cops, saying that many had "blood on their hands", which "starts on the steps of City Hall, in the office of the major."

Attempting to placate the police, mayor de Blasio called for the protests to end until the funerals for the two cops had passed, saying, "It's time for everyone to put aside political debates, put aside protests, put aside all of the things that we will talk about in due time." Of course, this and other statements made by de Blasio are designed to keep his own police force under his control; however, the hypocrisy of the statement should not go unnoticed. After all, hundreds of unarmed black Americans are *murdered by police* every year, and now, people have had enough, have reacted, taking to the streets to protest. Yet, when *two cops* are killed, the mayor calls for the protests to end out of some misplaced form of 'respect' for the police. Clearly, murdered black Americans are not given the same type of respect, even if it is guided by political pandering. That should speak volumes.

The backlash against the protesters and the emerging social justice movement has been palpable, and the police have been (as they often are) on the front lines of social regression. There was even a small protest in New York held in support of the NYPD, attended mostly by white men (and cops), some wearing shirts declaring, "I *can* breathe," mocking the final words of Eric Garner as he was choked to death by a NYPD officer, repeating, "I can't breathe." At the same time, there was a counter protest on the other side of the street, attended largely by black and Hispanic New Yorkers, chanting, "Whose streets? Our streets!" with the pro-NYPD crowd responding, "Whose jails? Your jails!" When the crowd chanted "hands up, don't shoot!" the pro-police crowd chanted, "Hands up, don't loot!" The pro-NYPD protest was largely made up of retired or off-duty police officers and their supporters, which along with the assembled on-duty police, media and counter-protesters, did not amount to more than 200 people.

Following the shooting deaths of the two NYPD officers, the head of an NYPD union declared that, "we have, for the first time in a number of years, become a 'wartime' police department. We will act accordingly." So the NYPD has declared 'war', but against who? Well, they place the blame for the two deaths not only on the mayor, but more so on the protesters and the anti-police brutality movement itself. Thus, the largest police force in the United States, made up of 35,000 people, has essentially declared 'war' on a significant part of the population. It's worth remembering that the previous New York mayor, billionaire oligarch Michael Bloomberg, once declared during a press conference, " I have my own army in the NYPD, which is the seventh biggest army in the world."

In light of the two killed cops, many who had previously been pleading for people to respect the police and remember 'that they are there to protect us' and have 'dangerous jobs' suddenly feel vindicated. However, as the *Washington Post* reported back in October of 2014, " policing has been getting safer for 20 years ," with 2013 being the safest year for police since the end of World War II. Indeed, as the *Post* noted, "You're more likely to be murdered simply by living in about half of the largest cities in America than you are while working as a police officer." According to the U.S. Bureau of Labor Statistics, policing is not even on the list of the top ten most dangerous jobs in America. Some of the jobs which appear on the top ten list include loggers, fishermen, pilots, garbage collectors, truck drivers, farmers and ranchers.
However, it *IS* dangerous to be an unarmed black man, woman or child in America. And while the NYPD union boss has declared a "war" on the people, the realities of that war have been felt and suffered by black and Hispanic Americans for years and decades. For over a decade, New York City has implemented a "stop and frisk" policy whereby police are given the illegal 'authority' to stop and frisk citizens without reasonable suspicion or probable cause, an obvious violation of constitutional rights. Between 2004 and 2012, New York City cops conducted 4.4 million 'stops', with 88% resulting in no further action (arrest or court summons). In roughly 83% of 'stop and frisk' cases, those stopped by the police were either black or Hispanic.

A study published in the American Journal of Public Health in 2014 revealed that young men who were subjected to stop and frisk by police, particularly young black men, "show higher rates of feelings of stress, anxiety and trauma." In over 5 million stop and frisks that took place during the 12-year tenure of New York mayor Michael Bloomberg, a billionaire oligarch, young black men accounted for a total of 25% of those targeted , yet accounted for 1.9% of the city's population, according to the New York Civil Liberties Union. In over 5 million stops, police found a gun in less than 0.02% of the cases.

In late 2014, with a new mayor (de Blasio) and following increased public outrage against the policy as well as legal rulings against it, the 'stop and frisk' policy declined in its implementation. However, as the New York Times noted, "police officers today remain ever-present in the projects," with a "new strategy" for policing the projects slowly forming. Police stand at posts on the perimeters of housing blocks, "officers park their cars on the sidewalk and turn on the flashing roof lights," and, at night, "the blue beams illuminate the brick of the projects for hours on end, projecting both a sense of emergency and control."

Black communities remain under 'military' occupation by the Brutes in Blue, the modern manifestation of the 'slave patrols'. The rich and powerful are protected and served, the poor are punished, the descendants of African slaves are slain, their communities under 'control,' as the police walk their beat, and beat black lives back down. From Eric Garner and Michael Brown, to the mass protests and civil unrest, the institutional function of the police is, as always, about maintaining stability and order in an inherently unjust social system.

The institutionalization of racism, slavery, and policing predates the formation of the United States itself. And while these things have evolved and changed over the years, decades and centuries, they remain relevant and present. If they are not addressed in a meaningful or substantial way, the America that many imagine or believe in will fade away, leaving only racism, slavery and repression here to stay.

Gangs of the State
Police and the Hierarchy of Violence

Frank Castro

Hierarchy of Violence: A system of oppression in which those with power, existing above those without, enact and enforce a monopoly of violence upon those lower on the hierarchy. Violence done by those higher on the hierarchy to those lower is normal and is accepted as the order of things. When violence is attempted by those lower on the hierarchy upon those higher, it is met with swift and brutal repression.

December 15th, after the killings of Officers Liu and Ramos of the NYPD , New York City mayor Bill de Blasio tweeted "When police officers are murdered, it tears at the foundation of our society. This heinous attack was an attack on our entire city." On July 18th, the day after Eric Garner, a longtime New Yorker and father of six, was choked to death by NYPD officer Daniel Pantaleo, the mayor of of the Big Apple had only this to say: "On behalf of all New Yorkers, I extend my deepest condolences to the family of Eric Garner."

In his condolences there was no mention of a " heinous attack" against the actual people of New York City. There was no mention of the "tearing at the foundation of our society" either. Still further, in the case for the police officers, de Blasio went as far as to use the word "murdered" long before a shred of evidence was provided. Yet in the face of video footage (that pesky thing called evidence) of Eric Garner's actual murder at the literal hands of an NYPD officer, de Blasio showed no "outrage", only platitudinous sentiment.

Such reactions are typical, but there is nothing shocking about them when we understand that our society operates on a clearly defined, yet often unarticulated, hierarchy of violence, and that the function of politicians and police is to normalize and enforce that violence. Thus, as an institution, police act as state-sanctioned gangs charged with the task of upholding the violent, racist hierarchy of white supremacist capitalism and, whenever possible, furthering a monopoly of power where all violence from/by those higher on the hierarchy upon those lower can be normalized into business as usual.

Any deviation from this business as usual, any resistance-the threat of force displayed in massive protests after Garner's death, or any displacement of state power whatsoever-by those lower on the hierarchy upon those higher is met with brutal repression. This is why cops are always present at protests. It is NOT to "Keep the peace." We have seen their "peace"-tear gas, rubber and wooden bullets, mace, riot gear, sound cannons, and thousands of brutal cops leaving dead bodies. They are not there for peace, but rather to maintain at all times the explicit reminder of America's power hierarchy through the brutalization of black and brown bodies above all others.

This is why de Blasio offered worthless platitudes to Eric Garner's family instead of outrage or solidarity. To him, as heinous as choking an unarmed black person to death is, it was business as usual.

Normalizing the Hierarchy of Violence

By framing this power dynamic as business as usual or "just how things are", it follows that the deployment of violence by police is always justified or necessary. This framing takes a myriad of forms almost always working in tandem to control how we think about the violence enacted by the state and its domestic enforcers, the police. Below are just a few of the tactics employed 24/7, 365 days a year.

Cop Worship & the Criminalization of Blackness. In this hierarchy of violence a cop's life matters infinitely more than a black person's life, and Americans, like NYC mayor Bill de Blasio, are expected to demonstrate sympathy with the lives of police officers. By contrast, Americans are encouraged to scrutinize and question the humanity of black and brown people murdered by police before questioning the lethal force used in otherwise non-lethal situations. This social reality illustrates how power is coordinated and wielded unilaterally, directed against the masses by a specialized minority within the population.

Police repression is framed in the mainstream media in such a way that when police commit violence against black and brown communities, it appears to white Americans as if they simply are protecting white communities from black criminality. This is the active dissemination of white supremacy. From it police accrue social capital and power within a conception of black bodies that perpetuates their dehumanization and murder. Completing the cycle, racist white Americans, after participating in the process of dehumanizing black people slain by police, then offer their sympathy, material support, and privilege to killer cops.

For example: George Zimmerman and Darren Wilson received over a million dollars for their legal defense funds. Both were either acquitted or not indicted by majority white juries. Officers Liu and Ramos of the NYPD, their families' mortgages are being paid. And thousands of other (white) officers are awarded paid time off (vacation) and non-indictments for what would otherwise be brutal crimes.

Ultimately, cops are praised because they enforce violence on behalf of the moneyed class. They protect existing power, wealth, and the right to exploit for profit, while simultaneously appearing to exist primarily for public safety. Straddling this paradoxical position, cops are worshiped because they are explicitly and implicitly attached to the rewards of privilege under capitalism.

Victim Blaming (Lynching the Dead). Seeking to justify hierarchical violence, the police collude directly with the mainstream media to exalt those who "uphold the law," while eroding the humanity of those whom have had their lives stolen by the police. Most often in the extrajudicial killings of black and brown people this has happened through a process of character assassination, or the process by which authorities and the media dredge up every possible occurrence of a "bad deed" of the victim's to discredit their innocence. It is effective considering dead people cannot defend themselves.

Erasure & Decontextualization. Time and time again police and the mainstream media will attempt to divert attention from the violence of the state by focusing on the retaliation of an oppressed group. This purposeful refocusing is a method of erasing the previous violence visited upon oppressed peoples in order to delegitimize any resistance to police domination. If those higher on the hierarchy can erase the history of those lower on the hierarchy, they effectively erase the oppression they themselves committed and make invisible the power they obtain from it.

We have seen this in the establishment's constant prioritization of defending private property over black and brown lives. As an example, after Mike Brown was slayed in the street by killer cop Darren Wilson the media headlined stories about "looting" instead of the fact that an unarmed 18 year old child's life was snuffed out. The role of "looting" rhetoric served to remove the context of a white supremacist power structure, its history, and to allow for a game of moral equivalence to be played-one where property damage was as heinous as killing a black child.

In addition it served to usurp the fact that America's justice system has always been and continues to be racist. From its racist policing built on profiling, to its war on drugs which dis-proportionally incarcerates black (and brown) people, to its sentencing laws that increase in severity if you are black, to the fact that a black person is killed by cops or vigilantes every 28 hours. It is murderous and racist to its core, but the neither the mainstream media nor the state will ever admit it.

Narrative Restriction. To build off what Peter Gelderloos said in his piece *The Nature of Police, the Role of the Left*, discussions in America operate by fixing the terms of debate firmly outside any solutions to the problem. This happens by first establishing "fierce polemics between two acceptable "opposites" that are so close they are almost touching". Surrounding the national "discussion" about police terror, this has manifested as a polemic between "good cops" versus "bad cops". Second, encourage participants toward lively debate, and to third "either ignore or criminalize anyone who stakes an independent position, especially one that throws into question the fundamental tenets that are naturalized and reinforced by both sides in the official debate."

By creating a limited spectrum of discourse an ideological foundation is created for the hierarchy of violence. The end result is a set of normalized choices (reforms) which restrict or repress any competition an actual solution to the problem might bring. What is valued as acceptable within this limited spectrum then is only that which reflects the range of needs of those higher on the hierarchy of violence (reforms which gut radical resistance in order to maintain status quo power structures) and nothing more. In the current "discussion", the prevailing and unapproachable axiom is that the police represent protection and justice, and therefore they are a legitimate presence in our lives. Anyone who says otherwise is an agent of chaos.

This narrowing of the discourse never allows us to deconstruct the fact that policing in our society has nothing to do with justice and everything to do with punishment.

As _Against Hired Guns_ put it, "Regardless of laws that claim we are all innocent until proven guilty, the results of wrongdoing and office referral, investigation and trial, always start and end in punishment. Our society takes this punishment as justice, and even though it is the nature of this system to attempt to prevent crime by deferment regardless of circumstance, many of us still cling to the idea that at its core the system means well. Many of us think to ourselves that aberrations of this are merely "bad apples" and we must expunge or punish them, but the reality is that this is not a unilateral system of justice at all. The police enforce a steady system of punishment on our streets, and punishment is specifically and intentionally directed at Black or Brown people."

The Law & the (In)Justice System. Institutions designed exclusively for punishment, primarily the Prison Industrial Complex (PIC), expose the inability of a penal system to produce justice and the conditions for liberation. Here, the deliberately narrowed discourse concerned only with crime and punishment fabricates a perceived necessity for police that appears undeniable. This is an exploitative deception obscuring the socio-economic conditions that produce poverty and suffering within oppressed communities. On its own terms, the mechanisms of hierarchical violence fail to provide the resources and opportunities necessary for assimilation into a white supremacist capitalism. The ultimate limitation of capitalism is that it will always need an exploitable class of people to produce profit for an insignificantly small wealthy population.

The System Isn't Broken, It Was Built This Way

Since its formative days as an institution of slavery, policing in America has always been about the maintenance of this country's racist power structure. The major difference today has been an increased technological and military capacity for politicians, the media, and the police to march locked in step with each other in controlling the narrative we see. Politicians like Bill de Blasio still make laws informed by white supremacy. The police still enforce them through the same hierarchy of violence. The media still kowtows to the powered elite's depiction of violent oppression. And we the oppressed are still fighting for our liberation. Thus by now we ought to know that police, as the Gangs of the State tasked with the preservation of white supremacy and capitalism, can only be abolished by a movement which has correctly identified and been equipped with the tools to dismantle the hierarchy of violence.

On the Unasked Question of Morality in Police Shootings of Black Bodies

Dr. Jason Michael Williams

In the past year much has happened regarding police shootings of Black bodies, and the majority of these shootings go unpunished. They go unpunished due to defensive statements such as, "I followed procedure" or "I feared for my life". Nevertheless, these two quintessential defense statements are disproportionately applied to instances where Blacks are killed by police, yet as a society the United States does or says very little to contextualize the impact such defensive statements have on our collective consciousness and morality. However, it should be noted that this silence is deliberate, historical, and quintessentially American. Thus, morality, to many on the margins, is nonexistent at the foundation of the criminal justice system and many of the laws that govern society specifically laws that disproportionately target the poor.

There is a social-historical pathology attached to the ways in which the American public responds to the killing of Black bodies. Just as police officers claim fear today, so did white mobs during Jim Crow. Black men were hunted and killed countless times out of so-called fear due to often false allegations of rape, murder, and a myriad of other unreasonable accusations. Black women were often murdered for trivial reasons too. Nevertheless, these false and unreasonable accusations were justifiable to the American public whose barbarity knew no measures when directed at Black bodies. This pathology exists today, in the hearts and minds of many mainstreamers who dare utter "#AllLivesMatter", as if to suppose that the murdering of Black bodies is somehow contemporary. Some mainstreamers have considered #BlackLivesMatter as a form of reverse racism. Thus arguing that the statement is somehow exclusive to other people who are killed, but this is, of course, a testament to the lack of critical thinking and historical intelligence writ large in America.

In modern society, this pathology is played out most vividly via the tumultuous relationship between Blacks and police officers. There had been countless murders of Black citizens by police, and yet many of them have been legally justified-that is, these cases have gone through the investigative processes of so-called fact-finding and rendered permissible. However, every so often, there are cases that wreck the consciousness of even the greatest conformers to the social order. For example, the case of Eric Garner, to many Americans of all colors was a *prima facie* case of wrongdoing, and yet the officer involved in Mr. Garner's death faced no punishment. Another case in Cleveland where two Black bodies were shot 137 times by police officers has too failed to accomplish moral justice. Cleveland police officer, Michael Brelo cried as he heard his verdict of not-guilty. Brelo was accused of firing 49 shots of which 15 were shot while on the hood of the victims' car. In clear opposition to an increasingly irritated public regarding police brutality, Judge John P. O'Donnell uttered, "I will not sacrifice him to a public frustrated by historical mistreatment at the hands of other officers." If the judge were truly neutral to the concerns of the irritated public, such a reckless and defining statement would not have been made.

Nevertheless, the Judge's rationale coexists with the feelings of many throughout the country. Whether one is scrolling through social media commentary, internet articles or watching mainstream media, the mainstream narrative is quite clear: Black lives don't matter! And the insistence of this reality is cemented each time a Black is immorally murdered by the state. These *ceremonial constants* have caused many people throughout the nation to lose faith in the American justice system, including mainstreamers. Although Judge O'Donnell in the Cleveland case believed that the evidence was not solid to convict Officer Brelo, like the Garner case, many feel discontent. This discontentment is the *proper* manifestation of people realizing that justice in America isn't always the *moral outcome,* a concept that a true justice system would strive to achieve. In fact, when "fact-finding" exist within an adversarial system easily corrupted by extralegal factors (race, gender, wealth, power, etc.), justice will undoubtedly fail those who aren't privy to the game. Thus, American justice isn't always about siding with moral rights, but rather it often swings on the side of barbarity and injustice as it falsely masquerades as one of the world's most advanced and civilized systems.

The countless cases of police officers walking free from killing American citizens who happen to be Black is a testament to the limitations of American justice. Black lives don't matter. As a result, demonstrators of late have continued to take to the streets against the immorality of American justice. They have continued to expose lady justice for the two-faced symbolism that she represents, as the global community pays witness. For these courageous individuals, the legality of justice and the majoritarian trickery invested in trying fact does not seem to fit within a moralistic frame. To these people, lives were unjustly lost, and police officers can get away with murder for simply stating what White men were able to hide behind since slavery: Fear of a Black body.

The Black lives matter movement at best should force the public to question the *purpose* of the criminal justice system seriously, and whether or not the processes that are currently embraced serve the interest of justice. The subjective citizenship of Black Americans should be the next topic of discussion. For instance, are Blacks to be treated as human beings, citizens, and, therefore, worthy of the right to live, breathe, and seek justice? These are key discussions that must begin to happen if justice is to be taken seriously in America. This conversation should also be raw, wide-reaching, and aided by both historical and contemporary facts. Certain acts of "justice" should be studied as violence. For example, the deliberate mass incarceration of minorities and poor people is, in fact, violence. Mass incarceration breaks up families (much like how slavery did), predisposes people to crime, destroys communities (politically, economically, and ecologically) thus pushing these spaces further beyond the margins, and render most to a life of poverty and outcast. The effects of so-called justice seem to perpetuate further inequality. In a real democracy, the state would not engage in such violence.

Furthermore, the creation of immoral laws like the war on drugs that create the contexts for Michael Browns are inhumane and violent. Such laws are neither safe for its targets (predominantly Black and Brown although now increasingly White) nor police officers. Also, the over policing of the poor is violent and extremely telling for a nation that considers itself a democracy. Over policing is violent, repressive, and undemocratic, as it mandates surveillance for the bottom and liberty for those at the top. While many people advocate for community policing in America's ghettos, such arguments should be met with extreme caution, as community policing furthers the paternalistic mindset that the poor must be governed. Meanwhile, there are zero discussions regarding the need for community policing or surveillance programs on Wall Street or within other corporate spaces that are obviously privileged against the criminal justice system. These basic statements are more than enough for a conversation to be had on the *purpose* of the criminal justice system. Who does it serve? Who is most affected by it? What are the collateral consequences? Is a system of violence capable of delivering justice? Is the system

37

morally bankrupt? Does there need to be a revolution regarding the criminal justice system?

Doing Ferguson and Baltimore at the Intersection of Racial Oppression and Hopelessness

Dr. Jason Michael Williams

This summer (2015), I made several trips to Ferguson and Baltimore, not only as one in great solidarity with protesting efforts but as a researcher, too. My several trips to both locations have impacted me tremendously as a criminologist. Though I have had perfect training in critical theory and, not to mention, my biography, which informs me (as it does anyone else), I have been more enriched by stepping into the intersectional realities of others whom are like myself (in racial heritage, etc.), but who exist in different social categories and spaces. While matriculating through these very racially oppressed and hopeless spaces, I was suddenly awakened to my privilege-to the fact that my academic credentials have allowed me to ascend my previous status, which in many ways was akin to what I am now studying in Ferguson and Baltimore. The combination of my experiences and the life-stories of those whom I interviewed have forced me to drift away into a deeply induced state of introspection. At this moment, I was forced to recognize that I was angrier now than I was before-that me being able to achieve self-determination and actualization was not enough so long as others were still being oppressed and left hopeless.

I began my research in Ferguson long before I decided to include Baltimore in my study. My first trip to Ferguson was deeply revolutionary. I was amazed at the organizing that had been going on, and the unification (albeit sometimes shaky) that I was observing. A unique caveat, however, was that the organizing was largely being done by millennials, a generation within which I belong. Seeing all of this was deeply revolutionary and impressive to me, as millennials are typically stereotyped as apolitical and unbothered by government and its goings-on. However, in this moment, they were coming together to resist state violence, an undemocratic function of the US government that many of them (and their forebearers) have long had to experience. In this intersectional and educative moment, the true complexity of American injustice and inequality is captured. While mainstreamers would prefer a one-size-fits-all conception of what was going on, protestors in Ferguson and beyond were taking the narrative back and sticking to their humanity and their right to tell their story. Ferguson and the shock surrounding Brown's death for me, and many of those whom I interviewed, highlighted many inconsistencies within the administration of American democracy and justice. While many congregated there in defense of Michael Brown, several people were also making interconnections between Brown and a myriad of others (especially Black women) killed due to state violence. These expressions helped to jump start a larger-scaled movement, #BlackLivesMatter, which would later shock the *moral consciousness* of America and beyond.

Moreover, the mainstream narrative surrounding these instances of state violence is that the victims (disproportionately of Color) somehow deserved their deaths, that the protestors are just lawbreaking "troublemakers" who have no respect for authority; and therefore, are not deserving of participation in American democracy let alone humanity. Thus, the underpinnings of

American democracy and justice, as shown now and throughout history, are to always other those who are excluded, and legitimate the majority's indifference to outsiders whenever possible and at all costs. These tactics are the foundation that keeps oppressive ideologies like white supremacy alive and well. The irony in what appears to be a battle of legitimacy and power is that the protestors are, in fact, well knowledgeable of power dynamics and governance. They regularly make very sensible arguments against the status quo which often highlights countless inconsistencies in the mainstream image of America. It is these heartfelt first-hand kind of experiences living in the belly of the beast that compels mainstreamers to immediately move to discredit the excluded, much like past government counter-initiatives such as *COINTELPRO,* for example.

While Ferguson and Baltimore are two very different locations, they both exist within *manufactured*oppressed and hopeless spaces at the behest of white supremacy. Genuinely stepping into these spaces as one looking to understand the residents' experiences forces one to stand at the *intersection of racial oppression and hopelessness.* As I walked the streets of Baltimore and witnessed racialized abject poverty, despair, and disorganization, I had to ask myself, "why America?" This country can waste money on imperialism overseas but it cannot make its inner cities and other oppressed areas whole. Through my research narrators (participants/interviewees), I experienced lots of vicarious traumas. For example, from talking to some individuals whose family members were killed by state agents, to talking to struggling forgotten and stigmatized single mothers, and seemingly desperate, detached, and unemployed yet able-bodied young men, the dominant theme was clear-hopelessness was the end result, and whether this was *intentional*or *unintentional*, mainstreamers, to many of my narrators, do not seem to care. Thus, the underlying assumption is that those occupying these manufactured oppressed spaces operate under subjective citizenship.

Moreover, the everyday reality for those residing in these *manufactured* spaces of oppression and hopelessness is one of constant a) delegitimization (physically, mentally, economically, and socially), b) state-sanctioned surveillance via *manufactured* police occupation due to intentional non-preventative crime measures that ensures crime and disorganization and, c) facing of *othered apathy*-a maxim of*excluded versions* of American democracy and justice. For many of my narrators, getting through life is a day-by-day traumatic experience of not knowing what may happen tomorrow, or if one's child is going to make it to adulthood, or whether or not one can afford to provide for his/her family. Though my narrators are what Joe Madison would call "underestimated, undervalued and marginalized," many still find it necessary to believe that total inclusion is just around the corner; after all, for many of these individuals, hoping for a better future is all they have to hold on to besides engaging in the sometimes more advertised *self-fulfilling prophecy and trap* laid out by mainstreamers.

Ecology & Sustainability

The Age of Fever

Jeriah Bowser

Once upon a time, there was a Great Rock that hurtled through space. The conditions on the surface of this Rock were just right to allow various life-forms to evolve and flourish, and flourish they did. Many, many distinctive life-forms began to explore and find their unique role on the Great Rock. Some life-forms were very small and found their niche in decomposing organic matter and maintaining the processes of life on a very small scale. These came to be known as Fungi, Bacteria, Protozoa, Algae, and others. Other life-forms chose to spend their life in one spot and play a role in bringing up minerals from deep within the Soil of the Great Rock, converting the Sun's energy into fruits and seeds with which to feed others, and providing an invaluable resource to any who might need shade from the Sun, branches to nest in, or a leaf to form a cocoon under. These became known as Plant people, and their kind spanned the width and breadth of the Great Rock; some living for thousands of years and some for only a year; some climbing hundreds of feet into the air, and others living humbly underneath the oceans; some grew thick and strong, while others were thin and flexible. Other life-forms became mobile and decided to spend their lives roaming the surface of the Rock on limbs, wings, and fins. These became known as the Animal people, and their variety was incredible. Some Animals were very small and lived short lives in burrows in the ground, others soared the Sky and lived on Mountain tops, others took to the Water and explored the great Seas with their giant shells, some grew great necks with which to eat leaves from tall trees, and yet others developed strong muscles and teeth with which to kill and eat other Animals.

It was a dazzling orchestra of life, an entire world made up of unique and varied creatures that somehow all worked together and found a role and purpose on the surface of the Great Rock they called Mother. This only worked because everyone observed the one Noble Truth: the Truth of Connectedness. This Truth states that what happens to you is also what happens to me. What is bad for you is also bad for me. What happens to a tiny Protozoa on a remote island is what happens to a Macaw Parrot in the Jungle is what happens to a Yellow Bell Clematis Vine in the Rainforest is what happens to Ocean is what happens to Air is what happens to the tiny Protozoa. All life on the Great Rock is connected, in a physical and metaphysical way. This does not mean that there cannot be killing and death and sadness, as these are all an integral part of life on the Rock. This does mean that all life-forms, from the tiny Zooplankton to the Sneaky Cape Fox to the majestic Giant Sequoia, are constantly aware of their role and function in the web of life known as the Ecosystem. Observing this Noble Truth, the Great Rock Mother and all her inhabitants lived peaceably for a very, very long time... some say millions and millions of years. Then, one day, around 12,000 years ago, a particularly funny-looking and clever little animal known as Human had a particularly funny and seemingly clever idea: it thought that it could make its conditions a little bit better by breaking the one Noble Truth and taking a few Plant people: Flax, Barley, Wheat, Lentil, Pea, Chickpea, and Bitter Vetch, and forcibly cultivating them in the area around where Human lived. This seemed like an innocent experiment at the time, as Human was not smart enough to realize

45

the horrible chain of events it had set in place. The Plant people tried to warn Human, but Human would not listen. The Soil tried to warn Human, but Human would not listen. Even when the Soil was tired and could give no more, even when the River stopped flowing and dried up the land, even when the Great Rock Mother herself began to get sick from the salinization and topsoil depletion, the stubborn little hairless ape called Human would not listen. Only when Humanity was no longer able to live in the place where they first began their terrible experiment - due to the desertification of their former paradise - did they realize that something might be wrong. Instead of abandoning their fateful experiment, however, they simply relocated to a healthier part of the surface of the Rock in order to repeat the process all over again. The Great Rock hoped that Humanity would abandon its foolhardy endeavor soon, and yet knew that the Humans must learn the hard lesson themselves. Humanity had forgotten the one Noble Truth and had accepted the one Great Lie: the Lie of Disconnection. And so, the Great Rock Mother, the Plant people, the Water, the Air, the other Animal people, and all the other life-forms living on the surface of the Rock were involuntarily taken as victims while this foolish and dangerous experiment played itself out.

Once Humanity accepted the Lie of Disconnection with the Plant people through the process of agriculture, it became easier to accept the Lie in regards to the other Animal people, the Water, the Air, the Soil, and ultimately with themselves. Humanity became increasingly intoxicated with the notion of disconnection and superiority over the other inhabitants of the Great Rock and, due to its cleverness, invented many ways in which to carry out its theory of hierarchy. The male Humans thought themselves superior to the female Humans; the Humans who had more grain and tools thought themselves superior to those with less grain and tools; the Humans with lighter skin thought themselves superior to those with darker skin; and the Human animals as a whole thought all the other Animal and Plant people to be less important than them. This pattern continued for thousands and thousands of years, as the Humans who believed the Great Lie killed and enslaved the remaining Humans who had not broken the one Noble Truth, killed and enslaved many Animal and Plant people, and slowly began killing the Great Rock Mother herself. Huge expanses of land that were once fertile habitats for many thousands of life-forms gradually became barren Deserts; great stretches of Water called Rivers dried up and disappeared; enormous Forests were cut down and burned or turned into tools of destruction; and many noble and beautiful Animals and Plants were killed needlessly. Humanity had created an insatiable monster that continually fed off of the abundance of the Great Rock. Gradually, Humanity turned its back on its great Mother. As they took from the Great Rock without honoring the one Noble Truth, they ceased to become a contributing member to the whole and instead became a Parasite - an organism that receives life from the Host without giving anything in return. Humanity created a Great Beast that took on a life of its own, that couldn't be stopped and wouldn't be satiated - and they called that Great Beast "Empire".

The Parasite - the Great Beast Empire - grew until it reached the boundaries of the great Oceans, yet it was not satisfied with that. The Beast built great ships out of dead Plant people and explored the Oceans until it found new, healthy parts of the Great Rock to devour. There were many great wars where different heads of the Great Beast Empire would attack each other, realizing that the resources of Air, Water, Soil, and Animal and Plant people were slowly dwindling; realizing that there was not enough to go around if they continued their ways, if they continued on the path of disconnection, if they continued to believe the Great Lie.

As the amount of healthy Soil grew smaller and smaller, as the Great Rock became used up more and more quickly, the Great Beast became more desperate in its attempts to feed, entertain, and satiate itself. The Stomach of the Beast was enormous: it could eat of hundreds of thousands of Animal and Plant people every day while drinking entire Rivers dry. Great expanses of Forests and fertile Grasslands were consumed in a few years, and huge Mountains were leveled and digested. The Beast had a particular fondness for Oil, a vital fluid of the Great Rock, and began

47

consuming it at an alarming rate, belching out huge clouds of poisonous gases and expelling rivers of toxic waste. Some Humans saw the foolishness and destruction of the Beast and tried to stop it, but they were either killed or silenced by the others. Some Humans - the few remaining old ones who had never believed the Great Lie and remembered the one Noble Truth - tried to warn the others by reminding Humanity of the agreement we all had with the Great Rock, but they too were killed and silenced by the Beast. Slowly, and with great sadness, the Great Rock realized that she was dying. Her child, Human, had turned from her, had broken the one Noble Truth, and was slowly killing her. The Parasite of the Great Beast Empire was growing stronger every day. The Great Rock Mother had given Humanity thousands of years to return to the Noble Truth, thousands of years to realize their mistake and return to the old ways of living in harmony and respect with the rest of the inhabitants living on the surface of the Rock. The Great Rock had sent many messengers: some Human messengers, some non-Human Animal messengers, some Plant messengers, some Air, Water, and Soil messengers - but no one listened. Sadly, many of the messengers, the great teachers and prophets of old, were killed and their teachings were distorted to reinforce the logic of Empire. The Great Mother Rock tried to visit Human in dreams, tried to speak directly to Human through spiritual connection, but Human was always distracted with either the fascinating array of Empire's gadgets and toys or the difficulty of surviving in the cruel world run by the Beast. The Great Rock Mother was sick, and no one was taking care of her.

As with many of her Animal children, when the Great Rock Mother became sick with the parasitic Virus, she naturally began to fight it by raising her body temperature high enough to kill the Virus and restore her body to a healthy state. This was known as the Age of Fever. The heat of the Fever had to be raised high enough to completely eliminate any trace of the Parasite, and so, sadly, it killed many living things along with it. The Age of Fever was a terrible time for all beings living on the surface of the Great Rock, as there was great suffering and loss. Many species of Animal and

Plant people died, and the body of the Great Rock bore many deep wounds and scars from the effects of the Fever. When the Age of Fever had finally passed and the parasitic Great Beast of Empire had been killed, the time of healing and restoration began. The few remaining members of Humanity returned to the one Noble Truth and realized the terrible mistake they had made. They returned to the old ways and once again lived at peace with the Great Rock Mother and all her children, although they never, ever forgot the lesson they had learned and the terrible price the World had paid for them to learn it.

******

Right now, we are entering the Age of Fever. The temperature on the surface of the planet is increasing exponentially. The increase in the amount of heat in the oceans over the last thirty years amounts to 17 x 1022 Joules. That measure of heat is equal to exploding a Hiroshima bomb in the ocean every second for the last thirty years.[1] Averaging over all land and ocean surfaces across the Earth during the past 134 years, global temperature has increased roughly 1.53°F (0.85ºC) [2], and is still increasing at an ever-alarming rate. Rising global temperatures are speeding the melting of glaciers and polar ice caps, many of which feed the world's greatest rivers. The thickness of the Arctic ice cap has decreased 40% since the late 1960s.[3] The great Himalayan glaciers which feed such mighty rivers as the Indus, the Brahmaputra, the Mekong, the Yangtze, the Yellow, and the Ganges, are rapidly melting and could cease to maintain an annual flow as early as 2035.[4] The percentage of Earth's land area stricken by serious drought more than doubled from the 1970s to the early 2000s due to increased evaporation caused by rising temperatures. [5] There is no question that we have seriously affected the Earth's temperature due to Industrial Civilization and its various appendages.

However, I do not believe that this is the end. Contrary to both the doom and gloom apocalyptic scenarios presented by many, and the optimistic 'buy greener things and save the planet' option presented by others, I believe that we as a species need to face the cold, harsh reality that we have rejected the one Noble Truth and wandered deep into a world of disconnection, destruction, and death. We have transitioned from a symbiotic relationship with our Host to a parasitic one, and the Host is much stronger than us. I believe, tragically, that there is almost no hope of turning back the wheels of Empire. Many have tried, and yet it is stronger today than ever.

Yet, instead of throwing our hands into the air and 'giving up', we need to turn away from the logic of Empire, release our disconnected, linear concept of time and return to the old ways by accepting the cyclical, holistic view of time as it is seen by the few remaining survivors of Empire in the world today - the indigenous peoples of the world. From the Hopi to the San, from the Tarahumara to the Yanomami, from the Zapotec to the Bororo, from the Oirats to the Jarawa, these few remaining specimens of an ancient age speak with one voice as they reveal ancient wisdom, prophecies and warnings to the rest of humanity. They uniformly speak of a coming age of destruction, death, suffering, and fever which we must go through in order to cleanse ourselves of the parasite known by such various names as Empire, Civilization, Hierarchy, Agriculture, Domination, Exploitation, Patriarchy, Capitalism, Fascism, Racism, Sexism, Genocide, Ecocide, Ethnocide, and ultimately, Disconnection.

Those of us willing to listen to the ancient warnings must ready ourselves as well as anybody who will listen for this coming age. We must be willing to enter the heat of the Great Fever and let it purify us of any notions of the old way, as Humanity once again enters into the fold of the Great Mother Rock called Earth and re-learns how to follow the one Noble Truth by engaging all of life with respect, reverence, interdependence, and humility. The Great Lie of Disconnection must die, and the Great Fever must continue until the funny-looking, clever little animal called Human discards its

12,000-year-old experiment with Empire and humbly returns to living on the surface of a big Rock hurtling through space.

Notes

[1] http://www.realclimate.org/index.php/archives/2013/09/what-ocean-heating-reveals-about-global-warming/
[2] https://www2.ucar.edu/climate/faq/how-much-has-global-temperature-risen-last-100-years
[3] http://www.nrdc.org/globalwarming/fcons/fcons4.asp
[4] "*Himalayan Glaciers: Climate Change, Water Resources, and Water Security*" The National Academies Press (2012)
[5] http://www.ucar.edu/news/releases/2005/drought_research.sht ml

From Rust Belt to Blue Belt
Water, Climate Change, and the Reordering of Urban America

Sean Posey

Taking a drive down State Route 224 through Northeast Ohio is in many ways akin to taking a trip back through time. At one point, before the interstate highway program, US 224 was an all-important route for truckers. Small towns and farms thrived along its edges. The construction of the expressway ultimately diverted much of the economic lifeblood of 224. And though much has been said about the subsequent decline of the small communities on the route, much less talked about is the disappearance of the farms. Vast stretches of fallow farmland are a common sight, not just around 224, but also around cities and towns of all varieties in Ohio Indiana, Pennsylvania, New York, and Michigan. However, that's likely to change-as is the position of these declining states. The exodus from the Great Lakes region, so lamented by many, will likely reverse itself in the coming decades. It won't be smart shrinkage, tech belts, or tax incentives that will arrest the region's decline, but the vagaries of climate change and the natural gift of fresh water.

In his monumental study of the most underappreciated resource on earth, investigative journalist Charles Fishman paints a picture of the price we will pay for our having taken water for granted: "We are entering a new age of water scarcity-not just in traditionally dry or hard-pressed places like the U.S. Southwest and the Middle East, but in places we think of as water wealthy, like Atlanta and Melbourne. The three things we have taken to be the natural state of our water supply-abundant, cheap, and safe-will not be present together in the decades ahead."[1] This will hold especially true for the fastest growing regions of the United States.

California's Central Valley today is perhaps the most agriculturally important region in the country. Four out of the top five counties in total agricultural sales are in the valley, and a good portion of America relies on produce grown in and then shipped from California. The Central Valley, however, faces a growing number of problems that threaten its future as an agricultural mainstay. Increasing sprawl and population growth in Northern California is now moving into the San Joaquin Valley, threatening water supplies in an area already suffering from problems linked to increased salinity. If salinity rates continue on their present course for the next sixteen years, California will start to lose billions of dollars a year in revenue. Combine that with an estimated 131 percent increase in population in the San Joaquin Valley by mid-century, and you have an enormous threat to one quarter of the nation's domestic food supply.[2]

States in the American West and Southwest exist as they do today by the grace of two things: the Bureau of Land management and irrigation. A monumental governmental effort made the semi-arid and desert regions of the country habitable. Yet the habitability of these regions rests on the shakiest of foundations. As Mark Reisner, who in 1986, authored perhaps the most important book on water and the American West, puts it "...this water, which has turned the western plains and large portions of California green, will be mostly gone in one hundred years." [3] In Las Vegas alone, nearly 60,000 residents arrive annually, which necessitates an extra 100 million gallons of water per week.[4]

One of the most important rivers in America is also under siege after decades of mismanagement. The existentially threatened Colorado River is a ticking time bomb for Arizona, California, Colorado, New Mexico, Nevada, and Wyoming. Damns, diversions, aqueducts, and climate change have taken a heavy toll on a waterway that supports around 36 million people. Increased salinity is also destroying the river. With continued population growth and development in areas supported by the Colorado, the future of the river as a viable water source is questionable.

The disappearance of surface water sources like Lake Mead and the Colorado River aren't the only major concerns for states. Water tables across America, many of them formed hundreds of thousands or millions of years ago, are being over-pumped to compensate for out of control population growth and droughts linked to climate change. One of the most crucial of these is the Ogallala Aquifer. South Dakota, Nebraska, Wyoming, Colorado, Kansas, Oklahoma, New Mexico, and Texas all rely on the Ogallala. Irrigated agriculture has long been a mainstay in these states, especially in Kansas, often known as the "Breadbasket of the World." If drastic steps are not taken to reduce pumping of the Ogallala, it's estimated that 70 percent of the aquifer will be gone just past mid-century.[5] And in Texas, fracking-related industries are trying to acquire water resources even as municipal water levels plummet.

What is actually being described is what Lester Brown of the Earth Policy calls "peak water." From now on, water supply will be outstripped by demand. Already states like Georgia and Florida are fighting over access to dwindling water supplies. But this is not the case for the Great Lakes region, home to nearly one-fifth of the planet's surface freshwater supply. The region is now seeking to capitalize on the situation by creating something called the "Blue Economy." Michigan has already benefited from increased tourism, especially fishing in its abundant lakes and streams. Fishing alone is worth $2.5 billion a year for the state, wildlife-related tourism accounts for another $2 billion, and the boating industry in Michigan, sure to grow, supports thousands of jobs.[6] Businesses and universities throughout the region are financing start-ups and water-related services. Milwaukee has already invested almost $100 million to attract and grow water-intensive businesses and industries. The Milwaukee Water Council is at the forefront of much of this type of work. Last year they opened the Global Water Center for research related to Blue Economy initiatives.[7]

A green economy is gradually growing in the region as well. Already, fallow farmland is being revived across Michigan and now in the Buckeye State. Ohio and other states in the Great Lakes region won't just be providing food domestically either. China, with a fast-growing population, a lack of arable farmland, and increasing desertification, is eyeing agricultural imports from the United States. China lacks the corn and feedstock necessary to nourish cattle for the country's rapidly expanding meat-eating population. Former Ohio State agricultural economist, Dr. Allan Lines, sees Ohio in a position to take advantage of China's issues with groundwater and arable land. Export markets to China could provide a huge boon for the state, especially as other agricultural centers in America face growing water problems.[8]

The decline of one other scarce resource will eventually bring back even the struggling cities clinging to the banks of the Great Lakes. As we are facing peak water, so will we eventually face peak oil. America's current fracking boom cannot and will not last. When gasoline prices eventually rise to the $16 a gallon range, America's system of growing food far from markets will be over; an economic model dependant on over-the-road shipping will collapse. The end of cheap gas will also mean the revitalization of urban areas, as density again becomes desirable-indeed, necessary. In his book *$20 Per Gallon*, civil engineer Christopher Steiner outlines how the end of cheap oil will revitalize cities everywhere, but he states that especially "cities such as Detroit, Pittsburgh, St. Louis, will see their stocks rise the fastest."[9] The end of cheap oil will itself end the moniker "Rust Belt," as production and manufacturing again become localized.

Texas and California in particular dominate the Sun Belt as the two most populous states with the largest economies. Much of the discussion surrounding their future trajectory of late has centered on taxes, regulation, housing, and energy, but less attention is paid to the very problematic climate future they both face. The changing climate is already disrupting (much sooner than expected) large swaths of the Sun Belt, especially in California and Texas. The amount of acreage burned every year by wildfires in the U.S. could increase by as much as 100 percent in the next three decades. Much of this will likely occur in the ever-drier western states.[10] Drought, the close cousin of the wildfire, is now seemingly a permanent condition for both the Golden State and the Lone Star State. The worsening situation of the Colorado River poses enormous problems for the ballooning Texas population. Six of the lowest inflows ever recorded for the lower Colorado River basin have occurred since 2006.[11] This is a real problem for the Highland Lakes of Texas, which were formed from the damning of the Colorado and are now well below maximum levels; they provide for recreational water activities and serve as an important buffer when drought hits. And drought has hit with a vengeful-like force. In 2011, a dry spell of Biblical proportions descended-the worst in Texas history. Over three quarters of the state entered a period of "exceptional drought." El Paso received only slightly more rainfall than Baghdad in 2011. By April of 2012, well over $5 billion in agricultural losses had been sustained.[12]Hapless Governor Rick Perry even resorted to declaring prayer days dedicated to beseeching the divine for precipitation. Some communities came to close to running out of water altogether. Climatic events like the 2011-2012 drought are likely to increase as overall climate patterns shift, and studies conducted during the recent drought show that increased periods of aridity could radically impact organic matter in the soil and the ability of ecosystems to survive in the future. [13] Prolonged dry spells will imperil important urban centers like Austin, destabilizing their ability to grow and their economic base.

In his seminal work, *The Ecology of Fear: Los Angeles and the Imagination of Disaster,* Mike Davis describes the grossly unsustainable landscape that is modern Southern California: *For generations, market driven urbanization has transgressed environmental common sense. Historic wildfire corridors have been turned into view-lot suburbs, wetland liquefaction zones into marinas, and floodplains into industrial districts and housing tracts. Monolithic public works have been substituted for regional planning and responsible land ethic. As a result, Southern California has reaped flood, fire, and earthquake tragedies that were as avoidable, as unnatural, as the beating of Rodney King and the subsequent explosion in the streets. In failing to conserve natural ecosystems it has also squandered much of charm and beauty.* [14]

And the ever-growing urban footprint of Southern California has recently been caught in an epic drought on par with the disaster in Texas. The years 2011 and 2012 saw well-below average rainfall for the state, but 2013 marked the beginning of a record-breaking water crisis. It also saw the driest year in history in Los Angeles. By fall of 2014, the state had already witnessed over 1,000 more wildfires than average. Now, a deluge of record-breaking rain is causing extreme mudslides and erosion in areas denuded by wildfires. The state's troubled Sacramento-San Joaquin Delta faces a myriad of extraordinary problems: levees are weakening, wetlands are drying up, and native species face extermination from habitat destruction. All of this has ominous portends for cities like Los Angeles, San Jose, and Sacramento.[15]

The climate of the future will rearrange the fortunes of urban America. Rising temperatures will scorch most of the Sun Belt even as drought and increasing storms batter economies in the mostly poorly planned boom cities of the South and West. Depressed industrial cities like Milwaukee and Detroit will shed their rust and become sought-after metros, positioned next to the natural wealth of the Great Lakes. Environmental economics professor Matthew Kahn predicts, "millions of people will be moving to these areas."

57

According to Kahn, as the climate radically shifts, Detroit, in particular, will become "one of the nation's most desirable cities."[16]

The Great Lakes region has come to represent failure in the eyes of many over the past fifty years, but it could easily come to represent revitalization over the next half-century. The Sun Belt's pressing water problems, and the country's changing climate, will turn the pendulum back to the Great Lakes, remaking it in new and unexpected ways. In the meantime, careful stewardship of the lakes, restoration projects, planning for the contingencies of global warming, and a skeptical look at natural gas drilling will be necessary. But the day will come when the fallen urban giants of old industrial belt reawaken to take their place back at the forefront of a nation undergoing the painful transition to a new environmental reality.

Notes

[1] Charles Fishman, *The Big Thirst: The Secret Life and Turbulent Future of Water* (New York: Free Press, 2009), 9.

[2] Water Education Foundation, "Salinity in the Central Valley: A Critical Problem" http://www.watereducation.org/post/salinity-central-valley-critical-problem (Accessed December 1, 2014).

[3] Marc Reisner, *Cadillac Desert: The American West and its Disappearing Water* (New York: Viking Penguin, 1986), 5.

[4] Fishman, 55.

[5] **PNAS Plus - Physical Sciences - Sustainability Science:** David R. Steward, Paul J. Bruss, Xiaoying Yang, Scott A. Staggenborg, Stephen M. Welch, and Michael D. Apley. Tapping unsustainable groundwater stores for agricultural production in the High Plains Aquifer of Kansas, projections to 2110, PNAS 2013 110 (37) E3477-E3486; published ahead of print August 26, 2013.

[6] E regulations, "Michigan Fishing Guide" http://www.eregulations.com/michigan/fishing/general-information-2/

[7] See Gunter Pauli, *Blue Economy-10 Years, 100 Innovations, 100 Million Jobs* (Boulder: Paradigm Publishers, 2010).

[8] Christina Nelson, "The Ten States Exporting the Most Goods to China," *China Business Review,*May 10, 2103. (Accessed December 3, 2014). http://www.chinabusinessreview.com/the-10-states-exporting-the-most-goods-to-china/

[9] Christopher Steiner, *$20 a Gallon: How the Rising Cost of Gasoline Will Radically Change our lives*(New York: Grand Central Publishing, 2009), 55.

[10] Peter Howard, *Flammable Planet: Wildfires and the Social Cost of Carbon* (Environmental Defense Fund, 2014).http://costofcarbon.org/files/Flammable_Planet__Wildfires_and_Social_Cost_of_Carbon.pdf (Accessed December 3, 2014).

[11] LCRA "Texas Drought" http://www.lcra.org/water/water-supply/drought-update/Pages/default.aspx

[12] Texas Comptroller of Public Accounts, *The Impact of the 2011 Drought and Beyond*, Susan Combs, Austin, Texas, 2012. http://www.window.state.tx.us/specialrpt/drought/pdf/96-1704-Drought.pdf(Accessed December 5, 2014).

[13] Jon Cotton, T. Gardner, Jennifer Moore Kucera, Veronica Acosta Martinez and David Wester, "Soil Enzyme Activities During the 2011 Texas Record Drought/Heatwave and Implications to Biogeochemical Cycling and Organic Matter Dynamics," *Elsevier*, Applied Soil Ecology 75 (2014) 43-51.

[14] Mike Davis, *Ecology of Fear: Los Angeles and the Imagination of Disaster* (New York: Vintage Books, 1999), 34.

[15] Alexis C. Madrigal, "American Aqueduct: The Great California Water Saga," *The Atlantic*, February 24, 2014.

[16] Jennifer A. Kingston, "On a Warmer Planet, Which Cities will be Safest?" *The New York Times,*September 22, 2014.

The First Kill

Jeriah Bowser

You never forget your first kill. Mine happened on a desolate stretch of backcountry gravel road several miles outside of a tiny town in Utah that nobody has ever heard of. I remember the day clearly; it is permanently etched into my memory like a hot ember on the back of my eyelids. It was mid-March in the desert, which means stifling hot days and bitter cold nights. The sun was high in the sky and there was a slight haze which tinted the landscape in hues of red and orange, an appropriate palette for the scenario which was to soon unfold. The wind was unusually strong that day, blowing tumbleweeds and clouds of dust across the barren and desolate terrain and kicking up dust-devils, or *Chindi.* According to the indigenous Diné peoples of this area, Chindi are the spirits of departed peoples, and they carry either positive or malicious messages, based on the direction they are spinning. Some, if sent by a witch, are messengers of death or sickness. Since it is hard to determine the intention or direction of a Chindi, it is best to just avoid them at all costs.

My first sign that something important was going to happen that day came in the form of a Chindi that blew right over my sleeping bag as I woke up that frosty morning in the desert. As I didn't have time to look at which direction it was spinning or sense its intention, I tried to ignore it and move on with my day, which consisted of a lot of driving around back roads and transporting some supplies for my employer. I had already been driving and doing errands for several hours that day when I thought I saw out of the corner of my eye a large form lying on the side of the road. I didn't pay much attention to it the first time I drove by, as I was distracted with the wind and the radio. I drove by about an hour later and saw the form again. It looked like a young woman. This time, I pulled the truck over and got out to see what had happened. She was young, attractive and thin, with striking brown eyes and light brown hair. She was lying on the side of the road quietly, not moving as I walked up to her. I gently asked her, "Hey, are you ok? Can you hear me? Hello? Are... are you alive?" No response or movement. I assumed she was dead. I knelt down and laid my hand on her neck, to try to feel her pulse, and she suddenly jumped and kicked with a ferocity that sent me reeling backwards into the dirt. I was completely startled, as I was not expecting that. "You... you're still alive! Oh my God!" I said as I shook the fright off of me and went back to her side, asking her, "Are you ok? What happened to you?" She did not respond. From a quick assessment, it was clear that despite her powerful movement a second ago, she was not doing well at all. Her legs were broken and she appeared to have a concussion. But now she was awake, and she was staring around with wild eyes, terrified and angry and not ready to die without a fight. It was immediately clear to me what I had to do. I sprinted back to my truck and grabbed my knife, a hardy five-inch piece of Damascus steel, and sprinted back to her side. I pulled the knife out with my right hand and stared down into her eyes, her ferociously beautiful eyes which spoke louder and clearer than any word in any language could have ever communicated. She stared at me, then at the knife in my hand, then back at me, not yet accepting her fate. My mind briefly played with scenarios of first-aid and a possible recovery, hoping that there was another way, but then just as quickly returned to the reality of the situation. I closed my eyes,

61

swallowed the rising swell of emotion in my throat, and said as clearly and compassionately as I could manage, "I'm sorry you have to die like this," as I plunged my knife into her throat, quickly sawing back and forth to sever the jugular and the windpipe as quickly and painlessly as possible. Hot, thick blood poured over the blade and the hand holding it, gushing onto the dusty gravel and quickly forming a thick brown puddle around her head. Her young, powerful body reacted violently; kicking, twisting, and refusing to accept the reality that her life was slowly ebbing away from her. Her mouth gasped for air that wasn't coming, her heart beat frantically for blood that was leaking out onto the gravel road. Her eyes still stared around fiercely, as if trying to take in as much of the world around her as she could before leaving. After a couple of seconds, when it appeared that the most intense convulsions were over, I gently laid my hand across her eyes with my right hand to block the hot sun from her eyes and to help ease her transition into the next world. I laid my left hand on her side, gently stroking her and trying to be as kind and reassuring as one can be after you just slit someone's throat. I spoke soft, gentle words to her, sometimes praying, sometimes singing, sometimes just talking. I told her that she deserved a better life and a better death. I told her that I would never forget her or how she died. I told her that I would honor her death and make it meaningful, somehow. I sat with her for what seemed like several hours, softly rubbing her side and covering her eyes and talking to her. As the life slowly ebbed out of her, as her gasps for air became more strained and faint, and as her strong body gave way the earth, I continued sitting with her, hoping that I was providing some comfort and meaning to her death. It was how I would want someone to remove me from this world.

By the time she finally died, there were tears streaming down my face. Her death had not been quick, sanitized, or painless, but rather long, dramatic, and terrible. I knew it had to be done, but I wasn't quite ready for the emotional intensity and involvement of the situation. I sat there quietly crying for a few seconds after I knew she was gone, and said one last prayer for her as I stared into her now lifeless eyes; fixed in an eternal glare of defiance. I then heaved her body into the back of my truck and drove deep into the desert, found a road that led to a secluded area with a stream nearby, and parked by a tall male Juniper tree, probably at least four hundred years old. I picked a tall, sturdy branch at least nine feet high, tied a rope around it, and went back to the truck to pick her dead body up and carry her over to the Juniper tree. I looped the other end of the rope around her neck and hoisted her into the air, until her face was a little higher than my own and her feet dangled slightly off of the ground. Using a piece of chert, a very hard sedimentary rock that was as sharp as glass, I began the long process of taking her skin off, cutting all the muscles from her body, cleaning out her internal organs to use for sausage casings, removing her brain to use during the tanning process, and taking her bones to craft into tools. Over the next five hours I slowly removed each part of her body and carefully washed the various parts in the stream which quietly flowed by. I slowly and intentionally turned her body into various foods and tools, a sort of ghastly alchemy. By the time the Sun was finally setting deep into the western sky, I was putting the finishing touches on my work, wrapping her brain in a section of the gut, pulling the long tendons off of her back and legs to use for making a bow, and finally burying the remains of her, including her beautiful eyes, in a hole under the great Juniper. I hoped that the little bit of her that I was not able to use would nourish him and she would live on in his gnarled bark, massive limbs, and delicate fingers. I hoped that her eyes would continue that intense gaze under the soil, and that they would eventually become part of the soil once they had seen all they wanted to see. I carried the results of my alchemy back to the truck, a pile of bones to be used for tool-making, her skin folded up neatly, several sections of intestines and internal organs wrapped up in a bag, her brain wrapped in her own gut, and several plastic bags of her muscles to be used for food.

Before I left, I said one last prayer and performed a simple ceremony honoring her life and death. I washed my hands and the now dull piece of chert in the stream, and headed home. I spent the next week continuing the alchemy, transmuting her muscles into steaks, sausages, and jerky, reconstructing her skin and brain into a rich, supple piece of leather, and converting her bones into fish-hooks, needles, scrapers, and jewelry. Whenever I ate her flesh over the next several months, I felt a deep connection to her life and death, and remembered her sacrifice and the way her eyes stared deeply into mine. I was intentionally taking a part of her and putting her into my own body, a deeply intimate and vulnerable process. I shared her flesh with some friends of mine around a campfire, and told them the story of her life and death as they too received a part of her into their bodies. Whenever I wear the leather or use the tools I made from her corpse, I tell her story. Even though I never even knew her name, my Deer sister had become a part of me, and I of her.

There are some who would call my actions heartless, disgusting, cruel, and vicious. They would have me believe that my consuming the flesh of a Deer is unethical and is participating in oppressive violence towards non-human animals. In many circles of progressives and radicals, being a vegan or vegetarian is almost a requirement, a rite of passage, in order to prove your commitment to the cause. Eating the flesh of a non-human animal or wearing her skin is considered barbaric and immoral. Yet to hold this belief is to ignore over 200,000 years of human interactions with non-human animals and to not understand the most basic principle of ecology - that matter cycles continually through the web of life. Life cannot exist without death. In order for something to live, something else must die. Whether we are talking about microorganisms, phytoplankton, insects, rodents, cows, pigs, deer, or humans, the principle remains the same. The most strident vegan on the planet is conducting a mass genocide everyday if one considers the amount of plants, insects, and microorganisms which had to die in order to allow him to continue existing on this planet.

Yet the other end of the spectrum is ignorant and ill-informed to a much greater degree, as is illustrated by the average consumer in the Western world who blindly shovels as much life into his mouth as will fit at one time. The average American consumer is responsible for the deaths of over 600 non-human animals every year, from such various industries as meat, dairy, eggs, seafood, leather, fur, feathers, medical research, and cosmetic testing. By now, scenes from factory farms are somewhat common knowledge, as several documentaries have shown the grotesquely violent and profane ways in which millions of non-human animals are kept and slaughtered. Incredibly, whatever images you may have seen are not even close to the actual levels of horror which happen in industrial factory farms every day. The worst footage of animal abuse and their living conditions is so terrible to watch that laws have recently been passed banning the videotaping or recording of conditions inside these factories, due to the incredibly emotional and violent reactions they elicit from viewers; ignoring the fact that many of the actions are technically illegal and the perpetrators should be prosecuted, rather anyone who films the illegal actions taking place in these factories will be prosecuted, so as to not create any more animal rights activists or informed citizens. If you manage to watch one of these non-human animal snuff films, it will be a much more difficult experience than you might think; by the end of them you look upon the grossly disrespectful and painful deaths with relief, knowing that at least the suffering is over, for that one. This wanton destruction of non-human animal life in order to satiate the hyper-inflated lust for flesh which the Western diet has created can no longer be allowed to exist. It is immoral and unsustainable on every level, and has led to the needless deaths of billions of beautiful, intelligent, thoughtful, and compassionate creatures simply because Joe 'Murica wants his super-sized cheeseburger with a side of Chicken nuggets.

The problem lies not in the fact that humans need to consume other life in order to survive, but the way in which we participate in consuming. Veganism/Vegetarianism is not a practical, sustainable solution for many people in the world, and it is actually an incredibly privileged position to be able to survive solely off of plants. The Standard American Diet (SAD) is also incredibly unsustainable and immoral, and must not continue. Both of these lifestyles are missing something incredibly important, something that humans have known for 98% of our existence and have only just recently forgot.

All life on this planet is connected. What you do to a Chicken is what you do to yourself. How you treat a dying Deer on the side of the road is how you treat yourself. One day, your body will stop breathing and your death will nourish other life. This simple awareness can lead to a fundamentally different way of viewing the act of eating life. If we are not connected to other living creatures, then it doesn't matter what we put in our mouths, it's just food. If we are connected to other living creatures, then it matters deeply what we put in our mouths, for it will become a part of us. All living creatures must kill other creatures in order to survive. We are no exception. What matters is *how* we participate in this cycle of life and death.

We can choose to participate callously and ignorantly, consuming unnecessarily large amounts of life with no awareness or intention put into the process. We can choose to act like we are not participating, by advocating a strict Vegan diet and shaming those who do not do likewise. Or, we can choose to participate intentionally, with respect and awareness of the necessary cycle of life that we must all go through.

Non-human animals must sometimes die in order for humans to eat them and continue our lives. This is an incredibly serious and sacred act which must be treated as such, and must be only done when absolutely necessary. Plants must sometimes die in order for humans to eat them and continue our lives. This is also a serious and sacred act, and should be done with the same amount of intention as with an animal. Grubs, insects, the honey of bees, the milk of animals, and the eggs of birds must sometimes be harvested with respect and an awareness of the cost of the food which we are eating, and must be eaten with gratitude and ceremony. To deny this reality is to ignore the way that humans have interacted with other living beings for hundreds of thousands of years and the ways that many indigenous peoples continue to interact with the Earth today.

Instead of claiming a certain diet as your identity or committing to eating a certain way for the rest of your life, a more appropriate and ultimately effective plan would be to simply start interacting and engaging with the lives that you eat in order to sustain your own life. If you do choose to abstain from the consumption of meat or all animal products, that is definitely a respectable decision, and one that I have followed for the past several years. However, it is important that you recognize that lifestyle choice as a privileged one, which not everyone can make, and that you recognize the important thing is not the abstaining from the taking of lives, which is innately impossible, but to honor the sacredness of all living things. Try to become aware of the great sacrifices which were made in order to place dinner on your table. Become intimately familiar with every death that sustains your life. If possible, try to hunt your own non-human animals and experience the real cost of eating another animal. Try to grow a small garden and experience the joys and trials of nurturing a small plant, killing it, and eating it. As you become more aware of the true cost of life-nourishing food, you will naturally seek to minimize the amount of death which your existence necessitates, and you will begin to understand the many powerful ways that food affects you and becomes you. Once someone has experienced the act of taking a life, you can never treat life the same way again. Once you have experienced your first kill, you will hopefully understand how humans have been killing life for hundreds of thousands of years, why they have participated in the process of death in the way that they do, and why it matters.

Weeds in the Holy Garden
A Wildist Review of the Laudato Si'

Jeriah Bowser

When Pope Francis published his second encyclical letter in May earlier this year, it was almost immediately regarded as one of the most controversial encyclicals in the history of the Catholic church.[1] Previous encyclicals have touched on social issues such as war, birth control, racism, and poverty, but this latest letter is a radical departure from any of its precedents. In this 180-page message to the Catholics of the world (some 1.2 billion humans), Pope Francis attempts to take on what he perceives as the greatest problems of our time: climate change, mass extinction, modernism, neoliberalism, capitalism, technology, scientism, globalization, consumerism, individualism, and anthropocentrism. This is an admittedly daunting task, made all the more daunting when one considers the fact that the Catholic Church has been the vanguard of these very same ideas for the past two millennia.

Although the *Laudato Si'* has garnered widespread criticism from conservatives, politicians, and corporate media outlets for its seemingly radical stance on social and environmental issues, the letter falls short of any real critique of our species and its relationship to the rest of the world. Couched in reformist language, religious doublespeak, and a social-ecology dialect that reeks of Bookchin, Pope Francis truly channels his namesake as he subtly conflates relationship with domination, dignity with work, respect with paternalism, creativity with technology, and freedom with moral relativism. On the other hand, the letter carries some very valid critiques of modernism, technology, social alienation, and the Judeo-Christian legacy of de-sacralizing and dominating the natural world that are commendable and quite impressive, considering its source. Despite its numerous shortcomings, the letter is significant in that it is daring to question some truisms of civilization, namely the Myth of Progress and radical anthropocentrism. The simple fact that a powerful symbolic figurehead is willing to pause for a second on his Ascent of Humanity, this tiny crack in the logic of Logic, is noteworthy and begs to be examined fully by those interested in the state of wildness on our planet.

The relationship between Pope Francis and his namesake, Francis of Assisi, is notable if nothing else, so a brief history of the much-revered saint is relevant here. The historical account of Giovanni di Pietro di Bernardon (nicknamed Francesco by his father and shortened to Francis by his peers) is lost to the annals of time, but the mythology is what's really important anyways. Giovanni was most likely born at the end of the 12th century in Assisi, Italy to a wealthy merchant family. His early life was marked with privilege, wealth, and revelry, until a brief stint in war and prison introduced him to the darker side of human existence. Later experiences with poverty and disease made a profound impact on him as a young man, as he became deeply involved with the outcasts of his society-lepers. Lepers were the lowest social caste in early 13th century European culture; they filled the social role that our "mentally insane" serve today, as Foucault pointed out.[2] In Jungian terms, lepers and leper colonies represented the shadow side of civilization, the objectified "other" upon which domesticated and repressed humans were allowed to project all their hatred and fear of all that is wild, feral, and free.[3]Engaging with this cultural fear had a profound effect on this young Italian aristocrat, and he lost all desire to pursue his family trade, preferring instead to spend his days praying, sleeping, walking through the forest, and building relationships with lepers and other social outcasts. His rejection of domestication famously culminated in an incident where, when confronted with his anti-social choices and given an ultimatum, he chose the path of wildness: he stripped off all his clothes, renounced his nobility and wealth, and walked away from his family into the wilderness. Giovanni eventually found an old abandoned church, restored it, fashioned clothes for himself out of natural materials, and foraged for food for years, fully embracing the "wild-man" archetype. Eventually he gathered followers from among both the poor and the wealthy of Italy, the only requirements being a vow of poverty and a commitment to following the teachings of Yeshua, the dissident rabbi more commonly known as Jesus. His wilderness cult grew as he began teaching his simple gospel to anyone who would listen, abandoning traditional religious teaching for more informal, open-air messages that advocated prayer and contemplation, animism, simplicity, voluntary poverty, and resistance.

The Catholic Church was quite adept at dealing with dissent at this point, having only very recently finished its massacres of the Cathars/Albigensians in France and the Bogomils in Macedonia. However, for whatever reason, they decided that co-optation would be a more strategic move for young Giovanni and his wilderness cult, and Pope Innocent established the "Franciscan Order" in 1210 with Giovanni at the head. Their strategy worked, as the now-christened Francis spent the rest of his life working within the confines of the church, turning his focus towards pacifism and monasticism; he even made a journey to Egypt in a quixotic attempt to convert the sultan al-Kamil to Catholicism. The re-domesticated Giovanni abandoned his nomadic lifestyle and, settling into a friary, became an avid gardener. His famous gardens, in which he dutifully tamed wild soil in hopes of growing food with which to feed his followers and the poor, had one feature which made them unique among gardens of the day: Giovanni would always leave a small section of the friary garden untouched, letting wild plants take over and live in relative peace. This "weeds in the garden" tradition carries on today, not only in Franciscan monasteries around the world, but also in various "green" ideologies which acknowledge importance of the environment while still assaulting it at full bore.

The Franciscan Order quickly became another safe outlet for empire to let off steam, as individuals drawn towards wildness and resistance were instead drawn towards this officially sponsored (and tightly controlled) group which posed no real threat to Progress. In the words of Perlman, "Francis himself becomes aware of this ruse only at the end. He dies marked by the stigmata of an earlier resistor, thereby trying to communicate with his last act that his whole life has been as deflected and betrayed as the life of his Judaean forerunner." [4]

The legacy of Francis was even further corrupted after his death, as is often the case with resistors, and today over 30,000 men are members of Franciscan orders around the globe. It remains remarkable, however, that such a revolutionary figure is not only enshrined and sanctified within the Catholic church, but is currently being held aloft as an example and inspiration for the Catholics of the world. It is intensely appropriate that this figure should provide the setting and context for the *Laudato Si'*, for this intellectual garden with a touch of wildness creeping in around the edges. Pope Francis opens up the letter with a verse from Giovanni's "Canticle of the Creatures," a famous Catholic hymn which is imbued with animist undertones, as the hymn addresses Brother Sun, Sister Moon, Brother Wind, Sister Water, Brother Fire, Sister/Mother Earth, and Sister Death with a level of respect, humility, and tenderness that is foreign to much of the Judeo-Christian tradition.[5] This language sets the tone for the remainder of the letter, as Pope Francis continually refers to the Earth in tones of sisterly affection, and even lends her a voice, imploring us to listen to her as she, "cries out to us because of the harm we have inflicted on her by our irresponsible use and abuse of the goods with which God has endowed her."[6] This seemingly wildist/animist perspective is tempered by the fact that it is always placed within the context of a masculine, monotheistic, anthropocentric, time-and-space transcendent Sky-God; our Sister is still subject to the whims and designs of the Father. This subtle conflation remains consistent throughout the text, as the Pope attempts to craft a new ecological language for the church within the confines of catholic monotheism; he is indeed attempting to pour new wine into old wineskins.

Of course, what remains unstated and unexamined in the *Laudato Si'* (and just about everywhere else throughout the history of organized religion) is that as long as there is a God, there will be a priest-class - those who claim to have special access to the thoughts of God and who see it as their duty to inform the rest of us what they are. Even if one were to accept the existence of a monotheistic deity, there remains the question of: What does (s)he want from us? Pope Francis assures us that he knows what God wants, but how do we know this to be true? How do we know what anybody says about God is true? Maybe if we allowed God to speak for her/himself, we could transcend this problem of the mediating priest-class, but we all know what happens to those who attempt to pursue direct relationship with the "other," via mysticism (hint: crucifixion and burning at the stake come to mind).

By far the most critical aspect of the letter is its indictment of modernism (scientism, technology, Progress, anthropocentrism etc.) While managing to avoid exploring into the roots of these phenomena (as that would be talking himself out of a job), the Pope manages to provide an impressive understanding of the history and philosophy of modernism and its implications. Beginning in the first chapter of the letter, he begins critiquing reductionism, "the world cannot be analyzed by isolating only one of its aspects... the book of nature is one and indivisible. [7]" He questions the sanctity of technology many times when he urges that we should, "look for solutions not only in technology but in a change in humanity; otherwise we would be dealing merely with symptoms, [8]" when he states that, "Technology, which, linked to business interests, is presented as the only way of solving these problems, in fact proves incapable of seeing the mysterious network of relations between things and so sometimes solves one problem only to create another,[9]"as well as, "Life gradually becomes a surrender to situations conditioned to technology, itself viewed as the principal key to the meaning of existence." Yet he again lapses into reformism when he differentiates between "beneficial" and "destructive" technologies, and argues for "well-directed technoscience. [10]"

The theme continues, as the Pope brings up scientism, globalization, anthropocentrism, and other truisms of civilization, even going so far as to criticize those who uphold the myth of Progress[11], yet this astounding level of insight is always mitigated only a few sentences later with a reaffirmation of monotheism and a dogged belief that forward is the only way.

Pope Francis is apparently able to pull off these philosophically acrobatic feats due to a simple formula: by working from a monotheistic narrative which desacralizes all that is not of God, he is able to attribute the evils of civilization to "humanism," "worldliness," and "moral relativism," which makes God and his followers solely responsible for all that is true, beautiful, and free in the world. This depiction of humanity completely ignores the realities of pre-civilized human existence, which the Pope is, unfortunately, uneducated in. By drawing from this Hobbesian worldview, he is able to offer God as the only force capable of acting as a restraining force on us vicious and depraved humans, determined to destroy ourselves and our planet at a moments notice. Only by listening to God and obeying his instruction will we find the way forward, saving ourselves from our fallen state. The Pope is clearly either naively unaware or wilfully ignorant of the history of catholicism and monotheism, for it is carved in the flesh of those who have fought and died trying to protect our environment from monotheists, those who have resisted civilization's death march and died in the process.

The enshrinement of Work is reiterated throughout the letter, with the Pope even going so far as to call Work a basic human right and using it as a placeholder for relationship, "Underlying every form of work is a concept of the relationship which we can and must have with what is other than ourselves, [12]" and when he compares Work to spiritual practice, "Personal growth and sanctification came to be sought in the interplay of recollection and work.[13]" This deification of Work is perhaps the most honest part of the letter, as there is little need for deconstructing or analyzing this theme. Work is indeed a placeholder for relationship; in a (civilized) world where all relationships have been desacralized and commodified, we seek solace in repetitive, isolated tasks and services for one another, as Manicardi said, "Life does not consist anymore in what we *are*, but in what we represent for the civilized world - in the function we must learn to perform through the years.[14]" It is unfortunate that for all his (limited) criticisms of modernity, the Pope never questions the validity or sanctity of Work. Perhaps it was a simple oversight, or perhaps the Pope realizes that in the absence of Work, there would be relationships, there would be play, there would be healing, there would be wildness, there would be no profane "world in need of development,[15]" and there would be no need for an "other" to measure ourselves against... truly not an environment hospitable to monotheism or popes.

On the opposite end of the spectrum is a fascinating idea that the Pope considers in his letter: the conception of the self which is reflected into the world and vice versa, known as "soul alchemy" to New Age gurus, "internal alchemy" or "Neidan" to esoteric Taoists [16], the "parabola" or "philosopher's stone" to depth psychologists and Jungian analysts, and to ecopsychologists, it is the eighth and final principle of ecopsychology: "there is a synergistic interplay between planetary and personal well-being.[17]" Simply stated, this concept states that whatever is done internally is also done externally, and whatever is done externally is also done internally. The Pope alludes to this principle throughout the letter, without ever specifically naming, describing, or elaborating on it, when he refers to, "the violence present in our hearts, wounded by sin, is also reflected in symptoms of sickness evident in the soil, in the water, in the air and in all forms of life, [18]" when he notes the connection between alienation and consumerism, "When people become self-centered and self-enclosed, their greed increases. The emptier a person's heart is, the more he or she needs things to buy, own, and consume, [19]" when he draws a parallel from desertification and disconnection, "The external deserts in the world are growing, because the internal deserts have become so vast [20]," and when he later argues that, "no one can cultivate a sober and satisfying life without being at peace with him or herself. An adequate understanding of spirituality consists in filling out what we mean by peace, which is more than the absence of war. Inner peace is closely related to care for ecology and for the common good because, lived out authentically, it is reflected in a balanced lifestyle together with a capacity for wonder which takes us to a deeper understanding of life. [21]"

The presence of this self-other parabola is curious, as it does not conform to the form or style of the rest of the letter and it is a radical departure from the philosophical assumptions of civilization. To acknowledge that what is done to you is also done to me speaks to the fluidity of the Self and Other; it acknowledges a basic level of connectivity and interdependency of all things, which is a principle that exists in direct opposition to the logic of civilization. Civilization (and its various appendages) can only exist in an environment of objectification, disconnection, competition, alienation, and atomization. The Pope seems to understand the philosophical implications of this self-other parabola, at least to an extent, as he also directly addresses the issue of connectivity when he speaks of an "intimate relationship between the poor and the fragility of the planet, the conviction that everything in the world is connected,[22]" when he urges for more thorough ecological research to be done because "all creatures are connected, each must be cherished with love and respect, for all of us as living creatures are dependent on one another, [23]" and when he insists on a "loving awareness that we are not disconnected from the rest of creatures, but joined in a splendid universal communion.[24]"

Without the context of the remainder of the letter (and the history of the Catholic church), these statements could be placed in any radical environmental journal, anarcho-primitivist lecture, or animal/earth liberation communique without raising eyebrows, but of course the context does not allow for such an ideological leap to take place. For every nod to connectivity, there is a bow to disconnection as evidenced in subtle anthropocentric bias and human utilitarianism, as the Pope implores us to halt the destruction of our environment because "human life is itself a gift which must be defended from various forms of debasement,[25]" when he defends clean water because "it is indispensable for human life... necessary for health care, agriculture, and industry,[26]" when he laments the loss of biodiversity because certain species, "may constitute extremely important resources in the future, not only for food but also for curing diseases and other uses. Different species contain genes which could be key resources in years ahead for meeting human needs, [27]" when he warns of the dangers of industrial fishing practices because, "marine organisms which we tend to overlook, like some forms of plankton... represent a significant element in the ocean food chain, and species used for our food ultimately depend on them[28]" and when he outrageously states that animal testing is morally permissible, "when it pertains to the necessities of human life."

This cleverly modernistic doublespeak really is at the core of the *Laudato Si'*; and it finally begins to crystallize into an ideology which the Pope calls, "integral ecology." Although he never specifically defines integral ecology, he describes it as, "an openness to categories which transcend the language of mathematics and biology, and take us to the heart of what it means to be human, [29]" and, "a vision capable of taking into account every aspect of the global crisis... one which clearly respects its human and social dimensions,[30]" as well as, "a unifying principle of social ethics.[31]" For those familiar with Bookchin's writings on "social ecology," this is beginning to look all too familiar, to the extent that one almost wonders if "Pope Bookchin" might have been a more suitable papal name for the author of this letter. For those unfamiliar with Bookchin's social ecology model, it is essentially an attempt to understand that ecological problems are also social problems, while somehow steering clear of both deep ecology (the belief that all forms of life are of equal value; interspecies egalitarianism) and anarchism (the belief that all humans are of equal value; anthropic egalitarianism). Pope Bookchin, I mean Francis, again manages to couch this essentially reformist critique of society within with the language of monotheism, crafting an ideology which posits that although hierarchy, domination, scientism, and anthropocentrism might be destructive and unsustainable, there are no other options worth exploring or critiquing and should therefore be carried out.... more responsibly.

In order to effectively carry out this "integral-ecology," the Pope imagines a globalized authoritarian power structure that will regulate environmental destruction in an ethical and responsible manner, that will assist in "planning a sustainable and diversified agriculture, developing renewable and less polluting forms of energy, encouraging a more efficient use of energy, promoting a better management of marine and forest resources, and ensuring universal access to drinking water,[32]" and that will help manage the oceans with "an agreement on systems of governance for the whole range of so-called "global commons" [33]." He minces no words when he ultimately states that, "there is urgent need of a true world political authority.[34]"

At this point in the *Laudato Si'*, all the poignant critiques of modernism, technology, scientism, and objectification are completely overshadowed by this sweeping endorsement of the whole mess, as the Pope, unable to see past his blinders of domestication, naively falls for the oldest hustle around - more Progress will fix Progress. More control, more regulation, more authoritarianism, more technology, more democracy, more science, etc.

Rather than letting wildness take over the garden that is our planet, abandoning our futile quest for control, domination, and the domestication of all of life, the Pope Francis miraculously believes that letting a small patch of weeds and wildflowers grow in a corner will somehow remind us to practice restraint and sustainability in our daily dealings with civilization. For those of us who are less optimistic about such miracles, there is the daily reality of resistance to domestication. While it is encouraging that the Pope is at least validating the existence of wildness and is cautiously questioning the truisms of civilization, he has a long way to go in understanding the roots of our present crisis and the incredibly limited options we face as we look forward to the collapse of civilization.

Notes

[1] https://laudatosi.com
[2] "Madness and Civilization" - Michel Foucault (1964)
[3] "Jung on Evil" -C.G. Jung (1996)
[4] "Against His-story, Against Leviathan!" - Fredy Perlman (1983)
[5] "Francis of Assisi - The Saint: Early Documents, vol 1" - Regis J.Armstrong (1999)
[6] Laudato Si, verse 2
[7] Laudato Si, verse 6
[8] Laudato Si, verse 9
[9] Laudato Si, verse 20
[10] Laudato Si, verse 103
[11] Laudato Si, verse 60
[12] Laudato Si, verse 125
[13] Laudato Si, verse 126
[14] "Free From Civilization" - Enrico Manicardi (2012)
[15] Laudato Si, verse 170
[16] "Foundations of Internal Alchemy: The Taoist Practice of Neidan" - Wang Mu (2011)
[17] "The Voice of the Earth" - Theodore Roszak (1992)
[18] Laudato Si, verse 2
[19] Laudato Si, verse 204
[20] Laudato Si, verse 217, quoting the "Homily for the Solemn Inauguration of the Petrine Ministry" - Pope Benedict XVI (2005)

[21] Laudato Si, verse 225
[22] Laudato Si, verse 16
[23] Laudato Si, verse 220
[24] Laudato Si, verse 70
[25] Laudato Si, verse 5
[26] Laudato Si, verse 28
[27] Laudato Si, verse 32
[28] Laudato Si, verse 40
[29] Laudato Si, verse 11
[30] Laudato Si, verse 137
[31] Laudato Si, verse 156
[32] Laudato Si, verse 164
[33] Laudato Si, verse 174
[34] Laudato Si, verse 175, quoting Pope Benedict XVI's encyclical letter *Caritas in Veritale* (2009)

Education

Internationalizing Educational Resistance
On Identifying a Common Enemy from Standardized Testing to the War on Libya

Derek R. Ford

On April 15, 1986, under the orders of U.S. president Ronald
Reagan 66 U.S. warplanes began a deadly bombing campaign
against the independent and sovereign state of Libya, killing at least
100 civilians, including Libyan leader Muammar Gaddafi's adopted
daughter, Hana. It was the second attack against the nation in as
many months: on March 24, U.S. warships and aircraft carriers
entered Libyan air and water territories and attacked Libyan patrol
boats and ground targets. Both acts of war were unprovoked and,
particularly in the second set of strikes (which intended to
assassinate the leader of a sovereign head of state), in complete
violation of international law. Reagan, of course, attempted to
portray at least the April 15 bombing campaign as "retaliatory,"
although it was soon revealed that the entire campaign had been
set in motion nine months earlier. At that time, in July of 1985,
Robert MacFarland, Reagan's National Security Advisor, drew up
plans for an attack and in October of that year the U.S. military ran

an attack simulation. This hostile orientation toward Libya continued for decades, and culminated in a full-scale war in 2011. Three years before the 1986 bombing campaign, in April of 1983, *A Nation at Risk* was published by Reagan's National Commission on Excellence in Education. This report embedded the goals and purposes of education within a nationalist framework of economic and technological productivity, called for "rigorous" standards and accountability mechanisms and technologies, and placed teachers in the crosshairs of reform efforts, among other things. The report itself flowed from previous stabs at educational "reform by commission" (Ravitch, 2003). Yet it is the 1983 report that in many ways inaugurated the winding path of neoliberal education reform that is currently treading us today, coming as it did just after the 1978-1980 neoliberal turn.

Although separated in time and space, it is absolutely crucial to understand these two events-the attack on Libya and the publication of *A Nation at Risk*-as part of the same global neoliberal agenda, which is to say that both of these assaults shared the same broad underlying logic and overarching goals. Indeed, they both were produced by-and productive of-a protracted war in which we are still engrossed. The reason why such an understanding is necessary is quite simple: There is currently a burgeoning and promising movement against educational privatizations in the U.S. Across the country students, teachers, parents, and workers are waging often militant struggles against standardized testing, accountability regimes, attacks on teachers unions, school closures, scripted curricula, the Common Core, and so on.

Yet these movements have tended to be constrained to either the local or - at their most expansive - national level. They have not, in other words, been articulated within an international context. This is a problem for a few reasons. First, one of the primary historic drags on social and resistance movements in the U.S. has been national chauvinism. One of the primary domestic ideological affects of U.S. imperialism has thus been a silencing of popular movements, which are halted or dispersed, as they are absorbed into nationalist rhetoric. Consider, for example, the way in which the near-revolutionary anti- or alter-globalization movement virtually vanished after the 9/11 attacks, when George W. Bush's approval rating skyrocketed to 92 percent. Second, without examining the relationship between the current educational "reform" movement in the U.S. and broader structures of imperialism we miss important opportunities to link resistances and establish alliances.

The thread running through both of these reasons is an appropriate identification of the enemy. And, since the figure of the enemy is absolutely fundamental to any sort of politics, a correct politics requires a correct conception of the enemy.

The *internal* accumulation of capital

The central drive behind the current round of U.S. educational reforms is the logic of the market: educational processes and institutions run more effectively if they are subject to the free market, and this, in turn, will advance the national free market, as schools churn out a workforce tailored to the demands of capital. As an example, consider Race to the Top (RttT), introduced by and passed under the Obama administration as part of the American Recovery and Reinvestment Act of 2009. RttP is a cash-prize contest that rewards states for falling into line with neoliberal education policies. Carr and Porfilio (2011) delineate several aspects of RttT that help facilitate the privatization of education, or the transfer of capital away from the public and into the hands of corporations and other private interests.

First, the program expedites the expansion of charter schools by encouraging states to remove or raise caps on the percentage of charter schools that can operate in the state. Carr and Porfilio note, "New York State passed a law specifically to increase the amount of charter schools in the state, which gave them a better chance to net federal dollars" (p. 11). Charter schools, of course, allow corporations and wealthy individuals to capture federal and state moneys destined for education through operating the school and exploiting the labor-power of non-unionized and precarious teachers and staff. This is particularly true of "for-profit" charter schools, although "non-profit" charter schools also run on similar logic. In addition to charter schools, there are also voucher programs. Under a voucher system, the government provides a voucher to family that can be spent at a private educational institution. Additionally, there are performance-contractors, groups that contract with school districts to run or otherwise manage schools within the district for a definite period of time.

Kenneth Saltman (2010) provides a list of some of the forms that educational privatizations take: "'performance-contracting,' for-profit charter schools, school vouchers, school commercialism, for-profit online education, online homeschooling, test publishing and textbook industries, electronic and computer-based software curriculum, for-profit remediation, educational contracting for food, transportation, and financial services" (p. 17). Carr and Porfilio (2011) emphasize the profits to be made through the production and purchase of "standardized curricula, textbooks, and test preparation materials" (p. 12). Through commercialism in schools, children are placed in the crosshairs of corporate marketing campaigns, as advertisements for candy and toys appear in tests and textbooks, and corporations "partner" with school districts.

Pedagogically speaking, however, RttT also allows for the production of particular types of workers, notably those that will fill precarious and flexible positions in the service-sector of the economy. Because charter schools are publicly funded but privately owned and run, they represent a guaranteed market for business interests, both in terms of their ability to realize values and their ability to produce a suitable workforce. Part and parcel of this latter effect of privatization is an attack on critical pedagogy, or critical thinking skills more broadly. Standardization, testing, and accountability grants corporations and private interests "the power to subvert teachers' ability to implement pedagogies that guide students to reflect critically about self and Other, knowledge and power, and the role they and their students can play to eliminate oppression in schools and their communities" (p. 12).

The *external* accumulation of capital

Educational reforms are about the private expropriation of public goods, services, and social relations. Moreover, they are about attacking one of the most entrenched public rights, and in this respect they provide a crucial ideological tool for neoliberalism more generally. Yet this must be seen as a process of the *internal* or *domestic* accumulation of capitals. And here is the link between educational reforms and the U.S. war against Libya: this war - which entailed the reconquering of a former colony and the privatization of a highly nationalized economy - was about the *external* accumulation of capitals.

Libya suffered under colonial rule until it achieved "formal independence" in 1949. This is most often attributed to an act passed by the United Nations, but it was also no doubt attributable to sustained resistance by the Libyan people. In 1951, a monarchy was established and power was granted (by the United Nations, not the Libyans) to King Idris. Britain stepped in as the neo-colonial overseer, and it as well as the United States established and maintained military and air bases in the country; "For Gaddafi and his fellow officers who led the overthrow of King Idris, the monarch had sold out Libya to foreign, imperial powers" (Forte, 2012, p. 37). Thus, when Gaddafi led a 1969 coup that ousted the colonial powers and inaugurated a period of national liberation, one of the first acts of the new government was to close all foreign military bases, including the U.S. Wheelus Air Force Base on the outskirts of Tripoli.

Although the new Jamahriya government was not socialist, it existed in antagonism with imperialism and, later, neoliberalism. The government would be defined best as "national-bourgeois," a somewhat contradictory social formation that is progressive in that it defends the formerly colonized country against imperialism and possesses nationalized social systems, but regressive in that it protects a system of class rule. Indeed, Libya under the Jamahriya government was characterized by a high standard of living.[1] As Brian Becker (2011, Aug. 22) notes,

Because of Libya's economic policies, living standards for the population had jumped dramatically after 1969. Having a small population and substantial income from its oil production, augmented with the Gaddafi regime's far-reaching policy of social benefits, created a huge advance in the social and economic status for the population. Libya was still a class society with rich and poor, and gaps between urban and rural living standards, but illiteracy was basically wiped out, while education and health care were free and extensively accessible. By 2010, the per capita income in Libya was near the highest in Africa at $14,000 and life expectancy rose to over 77 years, according to the CIA's World Fact Book.

These radical improvements that came as a result of social spending, including free tuition through higher education, were made possible because the state exerted tight control over oil production, and hence did not allow unrestricted foreign access, which was more than irksome to Libya's foreign colonizers. Additionally, the financial, military, and symbolic support that Libya gave to national liberation struggles across the globe was particularly threatening to imperialism and the burgeoning neoliberal order. The Jamahriya government helped the South African fight against apartheid, the Palestinian struggle against the Israeli settler-colonial state, and the Irish Republican Army struggle against British colonialism, just to name a few. This support was instrumental to many resistance movements.

While the Libyan government was forced to make concessions to global capital after the fall of the Soviet Union and the wave of counterrevolution that began in 1989-1991, Libya under the Gaddafi government was never a neoliberal state; goods and services like housing, education, and healthcare were non-privatized and considered free and public. Additionally, there are signs that the neoliberal policies adopted by the Gaddafi government in the 1990s were being turned back. For example, one cable from the U.S. Embassy in Tripoli to the U.S. State Department in 2007 warned, "there has been growing evidence of Libyan resource nationalism. The regime has made a point of putting companies on notice that 'exploitative' behavior will not be tolerated" (U.S. Department of State, 2007/11/15). The public services and institutions that were built from nationalization policies became direct targets in the war against Libya, including schools. During the second month of the bombing campaign, for example, a NATO missile took aim at and destroyed the Libyan Down's Syndrome Society, an elementary school that helped transition young students with Down's Syndrome into the general public school system (Noueihed, 2011, Apr. 30).

Conclusion

We are enduring through a period of intense reaction. We might even call it *counterrevolutionary*. To be sure, there are promising sparks of uprisings routinely occurring, flickers of protest and social movements, and sustained flames of resistance across the globe. In some parts of the world, resistance movements even hold dominant political, military, social, and economic power. But compared to the circuit of socialist and national liberation struggles that swept the world during the 20th century, it is clear that international capital is winning. The neoliberal agenda could even still be in an infantile stage.

As we study and fight against neoliberal rule in the U.S. educational arena and elsewhere domestically, we must look abroad for allies and supporters. We must also recognize and address our relatively privileged position in an oppressing, imperialist, and settler-colonial nation (with all of the contradictions involved for the various sectors of the working-class). Thinking through how current war on public education in the U.S. and the war on Libya are embedded within the same neoliberal logic of capital accumulation and production can address both of these pressing, practical needs. This step also entails surveying the world scene and drawing lines of demarcation. In so doing, we might be surprised who and what forces we find on our side. This does not mean that we have to be in complete political agreement. Indeed, as Peter McLaren and Ramin Farahmandpur (2001) note, "Revolutionary movements can succeed on a global basis only when differences over ideological interests and political goals can be put aside" (p. 147).

Despite facing a concerted military attack by a consortium of the most well-funded and deadly militaries, which continuously bombed Libyan cities and villages for a nine-month period, the Libyan people resisted heroically. This included both armed resistance and organized protest movements. For example, in July of 2011, as the bombing campaign was intensifying, 2 million Libyans-*about one-third of the entire population*-hit the streets of Tripoli in a protest against the bombing.[2] The line between "civilian" and "military" became increasingly blurred and, as the war progressed, obliterated. In March, as the rebels first tried to advance to the central coastal city of Sirte, they were repelled not by government forces but by armed civilians, primarily those belonging to the Warfalla tribe. In July, as NATO bombing intensified, the government distributed 1.2 million weapons to civilian volunteers, many of them women (Londono, 2011, Jul. 1).[3] Unfortunately, in the U.S. there was a relative absence of an anti-war protest movement, especially when viewed in light of the massive movement against the war in Iraq. [4] Even worse, many activists, left organizations, and alternative media outlets actually supported the NATO-backed rebels, in deed if not also in word (see Becker and Majidi, 2013 for a sharp polemic about this).

It could be argued that the movement against the neoliberal rule in U.S. schools should focus its energy and momentum on one issue only. Once we locate this trend as an internal manifestation of a global system, recognizing the tight connection between neoliberalism and imperialism, however, then the stakes of the struggle change. More accurately, the stakes of the struggle and the battle lines that define that struggle-and the enemy-become sharper. The neoliberal war on U.S. public education becomes one facet in a broader neoliberal war against the public everywhere. This is particularly important for movements operating in the U.S., given the debilitating impact of patriotism and national chauvinism, which often channel popular struggles into nationalist campaigns for global domination. For any social movement-let alone revolutionary movement-to succeed in the U.S., this legacy has to be countered, and this can only be done through an unapologetic and firm anti-imperialist stance.

Acknowledgments: This article is an amended version of a book chapter, "From standardized testing to the war on Libya: The privatization of U.S. education in international context," in Brad Porfilio & Mark Abendroth's forthcoming edited volume, *School against the neoliberal rule: Understanding neoliberal rule in PK-12 schools*. Charlotte: Information Age Publishing.

References

Becker, B. (2011, Aug. 22). The truth about the situation in Libya: Cutting through the government propoaganda and media lies. *Liberation News*. Retrieved from: http://www.pslweb.org/liberationnews/news/truth-about-situation-libya.html.

Becker, B., & Majidi, M. (2013). *Socialists and war: Two opposing trends*. San Francisco: PSL Publications.

Carr, P.R., and Porfilio, B.J. (2011). The Obama education files: Is there hope to stop the neoliberal agenda in education? *Journal of Inquiry & Action in Education*, 4(1), pp. 1-30.

Forte, M. (2012). *Slouching towards Sirte: NATO's war on Libya and Africa*. Montreal: Baraka Books.

Londono, E. (2011, Jul. 1). In Libya, women brace for battle. *Washington Post*. Retrieved from:

http://articles.washingtonpost.com/2011-07-01/world/35236634_1_moussa-ibrahim-women-brace-libya-specialist.

McLaren, P., & Farahmandpur, R. (2001). Teaching against globalization and the new imperialism: Toward a revolutionary pedagogy. *Journal of Teacher Education*, 52(2), pp. 136-150.

Noueihed, L. (2011, Apr. 30). Libya disabled children school hit in NATO strike. *Reuters*. Retrieved from: http://www.reuters.com/article/2011/04/30/libya-school-idAFLDE73T0AG20110430.

Ravitch, D. (2003). The test of time. *Education Next*, 3(2), pp. 32-38.

Saltman, K.J. (2010). *The gift of education: Public education and venture philanthropy*. New York: Palgrave MacMillon.

U.S. Department of State. (2007/11/15). Growth of resrouce nationalism in Libya. U.S. Embassy Cable, Tripoli, Libya. Retrieved from: http://wikileaks.org/cable/2007/11/07TRIPOLI967.html.

Notes

[1] For example, life expectancy increased by 20 years between 1980 and 2000.See http://www.earthtrends.wri.org/ for more information.

[2] Video footage of the protest can be seen here: http://www.youtube.com/watch?v=jWzNhk3zv4U.

[3] The fact that the Libyan government felt confident distributing over 1 million arms to volunteers speaks to the popular support that they enjoyed in the fight against the international neoliberal order.

[4] The primary, and perhaps only, exception to this was a united front formed by the Nation of Islam and the ANSWER Coalition (Act Now to Stop War and End Racism), which organized nation-wide protests and a nation-wide speaking tour featuring Cynthia McKinney, who led an international delegation to Libya in May-June, 2011.

Schooling and Education
Indoctrination Versus Empowerment

Boyce Brown

The reigning social delusion is that schooling and education are synonymous, both designed to impart knowledge, skills, and dispositions; foster critical rationality; enhance economic opportunities; and foster democratic engagement among the pupils being taught. Many critics describe the many ways in which this is not the case and that, in fact, the educational system operates to thwart those noble ideals.

For example, Ivan Illich compares the school with "a global madhouse or global prison in which education, correction, and adjustment become synonymous" (1975, 44). He goes on to discuss the social mechanisms by which this hypocrisy is camouflaged. In "rich countries" people "cannot learn much" because the cultural environment is "highly programmed" (Illich, 1975, 47). Furthermore, the media "exclude(s) those things they regard as unfit to print," "secrets are guarded by bureaucracies" and "facts that could serve them" are kept from "entire classes of people" by the political and professional structure of global society (Illich, 1975, 47). He explicitly blames this gatekeeping function and the grotesque hypocrisy and deceit it generates on the class structure in imperialist and capitalist societies (Illich, 1975, 49).

The editors of *Rethinking School Reform* suggest that the power elite use the educational system to inculcate certain means, mores, and assumptions to reproduce the existing class structure of society. They blame schools that "foster narrowly self-centered notions of success" and "making it" in the context of a "me-first, dollar driven culture (that) undermines democratic values, and seems to invent daily new forms of alienation and self-destruction" (Karp and Christensen, 2003, 3). Similarly, Jean Anyon cites numerous thinkers who concur that knowledge and skills leading to social power and reward (e.g. medical, legal, managerial) are made available to the advantaged social groups but are withheld from the working classes, to whom a more practical curriculum is offered (e.g. manual skills, clerical knowledge) (1980, 253).

The hidden curriculum consists of the implicit cues given off by society and its bureaucracies and institutions regarding how one can navigate the educational system to achieve success in the "me-first dollar driven" culture. In essence, those students bright, savvy, and ambitious enough, and unduly burdened by scruples for humanity, the planet, and the future realize early on in their educational careers the key requirements for "success" (e.g. money and prestige). They are simple enough: obedience to authority figures, willingness to jump through any institutional hoops no matter how asinine, and an acceptance of (or at least silence towards) the conventional wisdom and the towering infrastructure of hypocrisy, lies, deception, and fraud that is the very bulwark of modern techno-consumerist society.

For letting themselves be incorporated into the suicidal logic of the market economy, they are rewarded handsomely by sequentially increased use value, certified by credentials from elite schools and universities. These credentials typically lead to highly remunerative positions in law, finance and medicine. As they gradually assume positions of ever-greater responsibility, they know implicitly that their ongoing careerism necessitates they assume the duties of maintaining the hypocrisies that got them to their positions of wealth and prestige in the first place.

92

In countries that brand themselves as democracies - which today includes virtually all nation-states - this cannot be a closed system with the rich staying rich and the working class staying the working class ad nauseum. This is because the notion of class mobility is one of the most crucial lies that must be maintained in order to maintain democracy as a functioning brand name. Hence, a limited number of working and middle class will be allowed to ascend to the upper class as technocrats to the power elite if they show the appropriate obeisance to the lies of society, if they demonstrate themselves adequately accommodating to power. This is more likely to occur if these individuals are able to get into the elite K-12 institutions that routinely funnel their "successful" graduates into elite colleges, universities, and professional schools. Barack Obama, a graduate of Punahou Preparatory Academy, is a fine example. Society is built upon a creaking edifice of the most disgusting and transparent lies. Among the most durable of these are that the nation-state exists to provide a forum for the peaceful resolution of competing social and economic interests, and that it has the people's interest at heart. Instead, I would contend that the nation-state exists to allow a tiny group of clinical psychopaths to lie, murder, steal and swindle on an unimaginably vast scale, without restraint or consequence. It is the function of law, politics, the media, and education to (paraphrasing Churchill) protect that dire truth with "a bodyguard of lies" and make sure a critical mass of the general public never acquire the critical rationality and empathy needed for them to see that deception for themselves, which would be the death knell for the nation-state and its endless cavalcade of crimes.

This can be seen quite starkly in the United States Supreme Court Case of Wisconsin vs. Yoder. Some Amish in Wisconsin wanted to pull their kids out of public schools before the state's allowable age. Although the court actually ruled in their favor, as an anarchist, I find the decision a nauseating, albeit illuminating, read. The court points to "the state's interest in universal education." (United States Supreme Court, 1972, 214)

There is no doubt as to the power of a State, having a high responsibility for education of its citizens, to impose reasonable regulations for the control and duration of basic education (United States Supreme Court, 1972, 213).

Since the state is a massive, ongoing and duplicitous criminal entity, I recognize no state interest in universal education whatsoever. Rather, I agree with what anarchist and school teacher Max Stirner wrote in *The Ego and his Own*: "state, church, people, and society have to thank for their existence the disrespect I have for myself" (1907, 376-377).

The court found in favor of the defendants in part because of religious freedom and a sense that the informal, community-based vocational education of the Amish was an adequate substitute for the additional year or two of the compulsory schooling that they would otherwise be missing.

What I found more illuminative of the state's interest in universal education, however, was the courts repeated stress on the economic self-sufficiency and law-abiding nature of the Amish. The state would not be burdened by Amish education because their adherents tend to stay off of the dole and out of jail.

Here we see the hidden pedagogy of the court case. Sure, the state would be spared the expense of paying for welfare or incarceration but this is a narrow, instrumental benefit. Lurking behind it is the assumption that Amish education does not train its children to question unjust laws designed to maintain an oppressive social system or to question their humble place in an economic system designed to consolidate wealth into what George H.W. Bush has called "ever higher, tighter, and righter hands" (Martin, 2010, para. 1).

Thus, a philosophical accommodation to the consensus reality - intensified by the Amish's preference for actual physical separation from the broader society - ensure that their system of education is no threat to the lies that glue "democratic capitalism" together. Curiously, these lies are even hinted at in the court decision by its reference to the "requirements of contemporary society exerting a hydraulic insistence on conformity to majoritarian standards" (United States Supreme Court, 1972, 217).

Not being revolutionaries, the Wisconsin Amish can be allowed their insular program. What is needed, however, is a radical, sustained and ongoing engagement with the early education, K-12 and higher education systems by philosophers, teachers, and administrators for freedom of conscience, as the basis for all else. This seems highly unlikely to ever occur, as long as the oligarchic and militaristic interests in control of the Amerikkkan nation-state continue to maintain that control.

Compulsory mass schooling reproduces the existing class structure of society. Education has the potential to create free men and women.

References

Anyon, J. (1980). Social class and the hidden curriculum of work. *Journal of Education, 162,* 67-92.

Illich, I. (1975). *The deschooled society.* New York: Jeffrey Norton.

Karp, S., & Christensen, L. (Eds.). (2003). *Rethinking school reform: Views from the classroom.* Milwaukee, WI: Rethinking Schools Press.

Martin, A. (2010, June 28). The end of capitalism: The era of post-Bushonomics. Retrieved fromhttp://www.conspiracyplanet.com/channel.cfm?channelid=49&contentid=7023 .

Stirner, M. (1907). *The ego and his own.* New York: Benjamin R. Tucker Publisher.

United States Supreme Court. (1972). 406 U.S. 205. *Wisconsin v. Yoder.* Retrieved fromhttp://www.law.cornell.edu/supremecourt/text/406/205.

Reading *'Pedagogy of the Oppressed'* Together as Critical Public Pedagogy

Michael B. MacDonald

On my morning bus ride I noticed two words I had not seen in a while stenciled on the back of a black jacket:*Occupy Edmonton*. I was reminded of the encampments, the excitement, the incessant twitter traffic and the buzz in the classroom as students and faculty debated whether a movement needed a message, whether Occupy Wall Street (Occupy) was effective, whether the 99% was a rhetorical strategy or economic and political reality. It is remarkable now that so much of that radical energy has dissipated. In fact, most undergraduate students in the classes I teach have little idea what Occupy was all about. But it is not only their lack of information that troubles me, there is something else. It is as if they were enrolled in an anti-political public education campaign and I wonder how this campaign looks like, how it operates?

Critical theorists have a lot to say on this subject. Walter Benjamin's voice would be the loudest. He taught us in *The Work of Art in the Age of Mechanical Reproduction* that a political education is wrapped up in popular aesthetic education. Stuart Hall would interject that, building on Gramsci, he spent a career documenting the ways hegemonic power structures naturalize power differences, making inequality seem natural, even necessary. Althusser would add that ideology is not an idea that floats above us but is what we do, how we behave, and how we interact with each other in society.

I can see these lessons at work in shocking clarity. Our entertainment industry insists that products do not represent the views of the corporation producing them. They entertain, that's it. That's all they do. But is it? In Niki Minaj's video for _Only_, there is an open and unapologetic celebration of nazi/authoritarian aesthetics; the centralization of power in a culture-cabal that celebrates a racist, violent, surveillance state. Henry Giroux calls this public pedagogy. It highlights educational activities that governments and corporations utilize for the production of consent.

I felt a deep bitterness as I watched the young man exit the bus because, just yesterday, (Jan. 20, 2015) Oxfam released _Working for the Few_ a sobering and terrifying document which shows that, "Almost half of the world's wealth is now owned by just one percent of the population" and that, "The bottom half of the world's population owns the same as the richest 85 people in the world," and that this already extreme economic disparity is getting worse. There should no longer be any doubt that Occupy emerged as a political response to growing inequality. But nowhere in the coverage of the report was a connection made to Occupy or other political movements against the increasing inequality caused by the proper functioning of capitalism.

The problem is striking because there is nothing wrong with the system. It is working properly. The problem is that we operate a system that is producing unbelievable inequality. But instead of recognizing this, the opposite is occurring. Popular culture references to Occupy, like its caricature in Aaron Sorkin's American Television Series _News Room_, is dismissive. This is an ongoing educational campaign to obscure the economic inequality that both Occupy and Oxfam illuminate. It is further troubling that, ultimately, what is being ridiculed in *News Room* is public participation in democracy.

Occupy was not a political party; it was democracy. Political parties and corporate media challenged the legitimacy of Occupy by comparing it to a political party, and then expecting it to perform as such. When it did not, when there was no set of issues, it was denounced by both the left and right. But Occupy was not this; it was a complex political emergence and not a naïve and leaderless mess the way it is continuously characterized by media. This unfortunate characterization is a neoliberal public pedagogy to belittle any public reaction meant to limit the increasing power of capital, evident in the centralization of wealth into the hands of 85 individuals.

In the context of the Oxfam report, Occupy can be seen as a sensible response to growing inequality, the separation of community from government, the loss of representative governance, and perhaps the shrinking of democracy. I'm not going to respond to *News Room* because it has been done very well elsewhere. I am going to suggest that it's time to consider developing a critical public pedagogy to the neoliberal public pedagogy of corporate media.

"You can't evict an idea whose time has come"

For most of us today it is hard to imagine working class public learning. That from the 1800s to the 1970s labour movements, churches, political parties, social movements, unions, and even some universities were actively involved in community education. All of these movements had the interests of communities at the center of their educational philosophy. Education was the responsibility of community and not solely the professional educator. As Paulo Freire pointed out in his famous*Pedagogy of the Oppressed,* communities already possess knowledge and methods of teaching and learning, the professionalization of educators risks the oppression of learners.

In the wake of the Oxfam report it is clearly not a matter of whether or not learners are oppressed or incorporated into methods of oppression, it is now very clear that the economic system that Felix Guattari calls "Integrated World Capitalism" functions as a machine to efficiently produce inequality. That capitalism produces inequality and that it must be resisted by a political community education was already well known in Marx's time and incorporated both into Marxist and anarchist political organizations. There are still traces of this, of course. But we are no longer in the 19th century, and no longer struggling against the factory boss as the center of power. Public pedagogy in the digital era requires nuanced methods of critical public pedagogy. Adbusters was created as precisely this form of critical public pedagogy, and Occupy might be understood as a contemporary form of critical community education.

What is critical public pedagogy and how does it work?

My hometown, Glace Bay, Nova Scotia, in the early part of the 1900s was under the control of coal mining companies. The coal miner worked for "the company" lived in houses owned by "the company" and purchased groceries at "the company" store. Miners were extended credit against their pay that often left workers and families indebted to "the company". If injured or sick miners families could be evicted as there was nothing to protect the worker from the dictates of capital.

Cooperatives and adult education programs were developed as a way of struggling against the expansive reach of exploitative capital. Building on developments that stretched back to the 1800s a collection of priests and educators called the Antigonish Movement were moved to resist the economic oppression suffered in mining communities. The realization that community learning was essential to increased economic equality led priests to stop giving prayers at confession and start handing out manuals to build community development capacities. These priests politicized their pedagogy and shared books and supported the creation of study groups. Cooperatives developed, international relationships of mutual support grew and slowly workers organized and won rights. The foundations of the liberation of my hometown was a democratic community learning movement with community development as its goal.

Before we can explore contemporary critical public pedagogy we need to understand the form of capitalism that we are engaging. It is no longer the capitalism of the Antigonish Movement with the forms of repression embodied in "the company". It is no longer Marx's *Capital*. It is also no longer Freire's economic development sketched out in *Education for Critical Consciousness*. It is something else. As Italian Autonomist Marxists have pointed out Capitalism is no longer simply operations of production that occur on the marketplace and the factory floor, it is the production of capitalist society, a social factory. As we have learned from Italian autonomism the *factory worker* of capitalism is now a *social worker*, making social life with products, *cultural workers* producing capitalist-cultural life within *culture centres.*

Capitalism is not only a system of exchange but also an epistemological factory producing knowledge that conforms to the laws of profit as surely as scientists conform to scientific laws in the production of scientific knowledge. It is not simply enough to point to neoliberalism-as if it can be pointed out-as Freire has shown in *Pedagogy of the Oppressed*, the oppressor-oppressed is a binary produced by a system that captures both, which we call capitalism. Freire argues for critical consciousness, conscientization, or *conscientização* as the process by which we collectively produce critical awareness of the functioning system. Critical consciousness alone, however, is insufficient if it doesn't lead to critically informed action. Education does this. This is why public pedagogy is so important to identify, why *News Room*'s account of Occupy, or Niki Minaj's celebration of authoritarianism requires critique. Without critique of public pedagogy, and without critical action to build community solidarity, the public pedagogy of contemporary capitalism remains unchallenged. W.E.B. DuBois, Franz Fanon,

Michel Foucault, Gilles Deleuze, Felix Guattari, Fred Hampton, bell hooks, and Angela Davis have all taught us that political liberation is a community-self activity.

What I find most interesting is that capitalism not only functions as exchange but through exchanges produces subjectivities that are properly developed for capitalism. The priests in the Antigonish Movement first had to convince coal miners that their lives, at this moment, were not all they could be and that the world could be better through learning, commitment and community development. Our struggle is no different. Today's educators and activists need to articulate a critical public pedagogy capable of working against the radical inequality described in the Oxfam report.

The first step is to understand how public pedagogy shapes capitalist epistemology and leads our society to instantly notice the growth of inequality while allowing the production of inequality to remain invisible in plain sight. Maurizio Lazzarato describes this phenomenon, capitalism as a system of knowledge production:

The semiotic components of capital always operate in a dual register. The first is the register of "representation" and "signification" or "production of meaning", both of which are organized by signifying semiotics (language) with the purpose of producing the "subject", the "individual", the "I". The second is the machinic register organized by a-signifying semiotics (such as money, analog or digital machines that produce images, sounds and information, the equations, functions, diagrams of science, music, etc.), which "can bring into play signs which have an additional symbolic or signifying effect, but whose actual functioning is neither symbolic nor signifying". This second register is not aimed at subject constitution but at capturing and activating pre-subjective and pre-individual elements (affects, emotions, perceptions) to make them function like components or cogs in the semiotic machine of capital. (Lazzarato 2006)

Machinic enslavement first introduced by Gilles Deleuze and Felix Guattari, in a two-part analysis of contemporary capitalism called *Anti-Oedipus,* is developed on a cybernetics notion that systems function by controlling their component parts. Cybernetics, being the study of control systems, looks at enslavement within a control system not as slavery in the older notion of blatant oppression, but as systems of control that allow actors to operate freely but within a predetermined range. It has been noted that contemporary philosophers, like Luciana Parisi, describe contemporary capitalism as second-order cybernetics that "constitutes the dominant interactive paradigm of capitalism today, revolves around the idea that the observer is also part of the system and concerns notions of reflexivity, self-organisation, autopoiesis, the contingency of environmental factors, and the indeterminacy of living systems."

Capitalism is not simply, or not only, the distribution of capital for profit it is a productive and semiotic operator that creates resources, producers and consumers as much as products. Capitalism is a knowledge system and public pedagogy is how that knowledge is taught.

What about community development and social economy initiatives, are these not steps forward, and don't these offer solutions to reduce inequality, to combat poverty while using the mechanisms of capitalism? The short answer is I don't know. But I do know that we need to create systems of research and evaluation that critically interrogate not only the rhetoric but also the impact of proposed solutions. Oxfam has shown that economic inequality has increased since Occupy and that capitalism produces inequality. And here we find ourselves in what Gregory Bateson called a double bind: a) engagement in capitalism produces economic inequality and b) community development requires capitalism. Freire found himself in just such a double bind in Brazil in the 1950s. Brazil was industrializing and Freire was tasked to support indigenous communities develop the literacy skills necessary to participate in community economic development. But he also realized that teaching Portuguese in indigenous communities advanced colonization. The double bind: a) teaching Portuguese literacy advanced colonization and increased inequality b) not teaching literacy left indigenous communities out of industrialization and increased inequality. The solution was a method of political literacy education that helped communities identify forces of inequality and to develop the capacities necessary to create projects, programs, activities, and agencies that would produce a more equal society. We are tasked with the same double bind. The Oxfam report has begun to sketch out the nature of inequality, Occupy has provided a model of networked community learning, Henry Giroux has provided us a way of understanding the teaching and learning functions of capitalism and now it's our turn to develop a critical pedagogy of our time.

Working towards this I have started a reading circle in Edmonton, Canada, on Freire's *Pedagogy of the Oppressed*. Borrowing a model from David Harvey's *A Companion to Marxist Capital*, we are going to produce a series of essays to help support collective readings of *Pedagogy of the Oppressed* wherever they might develop. This is our response to the Oxfam report and we will share our essays with you in the hopes that we might move towards a critical public pedagogy of capital.

References

Althusser, Louis. (2014) On the Reproduction of Capitalism: Ideology and Ideological State Apparatuses. London: Verso.
Bateson, Gregory.(2000). Steps to an Ecology of Mind. Chicago: University of Chicago Press.
Benjamin, Walter. (1968). "The Work of Art in the Age of Mechanical Reproduction." In Illuminations, edited by Arendt Hannah. New York: Harcourt Brace & World.
Deleuze, Gilles and Felix Guattari. (2009) Anti-Oedipus: Capitalism and Schizophrenia. London, UK: Penguin.
Foucault, Michel. (2004).The Hermeneutics of the Subject: Lectures at the College de France 1981-1982. New York: Picador.
Foucault, Michel. (2010). The Government of Self and Others: Lectures at the College De France 1982-1983. New York: Palgrave MacMillan.

Foucault, Michel. (1988). "Technologies of the Self." In Technologies of the Self, edited by Luther H. Martin, Huck Gutman, Patrick H. Hutton. Boston: University of Massachusetts Press.

Freire, P. (1974). Education for critical consciousness. New York: Bloomsbury.

Freire, P. (2000). Pedagogy of the oppressed. New York: Bloomsbury.

Fuentes-Nieva, Ricardo, and Nicholas Galasso. (20 Jan 2014) Working for the Few: Political capture and economic inequality. Oxfam International Briefing Paper.
See,http://www.oxfam.org/en/research/working-few

Giroux, Henry A. (2000). Public Pedagogy As Cultural Politics: Stuart Hall and the 'Crisis' of Culture. Cultural Studies 14 (2): 341-60.

Giroux, Henry A. 1997. Pedagogy and the Politics of Hope: Theory, Culture, and Schooling, The Edge: Critical Studies in Educational Theory. Boulder, CO: Westview Press.

Giroux, Henry A. 2003. The Abandoned Generation: Democracy Beyond the Culture of Fear. New York: Palgrave MacMillan.

Giroux, Henry A. 2004. "Public pedagogy and the politics of neo-liberalism: Making the political more pedagogical." Policy Futures in Education, 2 (3-4): 494-503.

Giroux, Henry A. 2009. Youth in a suspect society: Democracy or disposability? New York: Palgrave MacMillan.

Guattari, Felix.(2008). Molecular Revolution in Brazil. Los Angeles: Semiotext(e) Foreign Agents Series

Hall, Stuart. (1997). Representation: Cultural Representations and Signifying Practices. Thousand Oaks, CA: Sage Publications

Harvey, David. (2005). A Brief History of Neoliberalism. New York: Oxford University Press.

Harvey, David. (2013) A Companion to Marxist Capital. New York: Verso.

Harvey, David. (2014). Seventeen Contradictions and the end of Capitalism. New York: Oxford University Press.

hooks, B. (1990). Yearning: Race, gender, and cultural politics. Boston, MA: South End Press.

hooks, bell. (1994). Teaching to Transgress: Education as the Practice of Freedom. New York: Routledge..

hooks, bell. (2003). Teaching Community: A Pedagogy of Hope. New York: Routledge.

hooks, bell. (2010). Teaching Critical Thinking: Practical Wisdom. New York: Routledge.

hooks, bell. (2013). Writing Beyond Race: Living Theory and Practice. New York: Routledge.

Lazzarato, Maurizio. (2014) Signs and Machines: Capitalism and the Production of Subjectivity. Los Angeles: Semiotext(e)

Marx, Karl. (2013) Capital. Ware, UK: Wordsworth Editions.

Parisi, Luciana. (2013) Contagious Architecture: Computation, Aesthetics, and Space. Cambridge, MA: MIT Press.

Falsehoods and Shattered Dreams
The Dark Side of For-Profit Colleges

Devon Douglas-Bowers

For-profit colleges are a phenomenon that have grown over time and make up the "fastest growing segment of higher education."[i] While it may seem like a positive occurrence that more people are getting access to a college education, there are serious problems with for-profit colleges, many of which leave student unemployed and jobless, while having fleeced them of extremely large amounts of money.

In order to get a handle on for-profit colleges (FPCs), it would be prudent to examine the history of the institution. FPCs began making headway in the late 1800s, known as commercial colleges, and grew quite quickly. "By 1871, more than 150 commercial colleges were operating across the U.S., and by the early 1890s, estimates went as high as 500."[ii] While such colleges taught a variety of skills, from bookkeeping and stenography to operating mock banks and stock exchanges, success and quality of instruction varied from school to school. "Some schools were reputable establishments offering 'able commercial lectures and thorough training,' but others were, as the U. S. commissioner of education put it in 1872, "purely business speculations."[iii]

Like today's FPCs, commercial colleges back then also aided people who couldn't get into traditional colleges. Such schools, "played a particularly important role in opening up education to women, people of color, Native Americans, and those with disabilities, especially blind and deaf people."[iv] FPCs continued to have a small stake in the college market accounting for only 0.2 percent of college students in the US in the 1970s.

However, it should be noted that FPCs grew following World War II as federal financial assistance for student increased, especially under the GI Bill and the Higher Education Act of 1972 which allowed for federal funds such as the Pell Grant to be used at for-profit universities.[v]

Yet, there is a serious problem with for-profit universities and federal and state governments as it relates to financial aid. With regards to state aid it was noted in 1999 that FPCs were getting a sliced of state aid as "About half of the states [awarded] some money to students enrolled at for-profit institutions. In New York, for example, nearly 26,000 students at for-profit colleges received about $85-million in need-- based aid from the state's huge assistance programs, which totaled $640-million in 1996-97"[vi] and they were actively attempting to get more state aid, arguing that they met all the needed standards and yet weren't getting increased aid. In the current day, the situation has changed with FPCs being granted state aid and even fighting to keep it[vii] in some states while losing it in others.[viii]

With federal funds, the problem revolves around Title IV eligibility. Title IV is granted by the Department of Education and requires that the college in question must be accredited by at least one of the department's approved accrediting agencies, be registered by one of the states, and meet other requirements on a regular basis. In order to get such eligibility, a for-profit school "must either provide training for gainful employment in a recognized occupation or provide a program leading to a baccalaureate degree in the liberal arts."[ix]

The problem is that most currently existing colleges have Title IV eligibility as they make the majority of their funds from federal aid. However, due to that fact, what is occurring is not only an effective subsidizing of FPCs, but also students often get buried under debt due to the high prices of these schools and the universities themselves walk away consequence free.

This situation is made all the worse when one examines the default rates of students who go to for-profit colleges (which are higher than those students who go to non-profit colleges[x]), but also the fact that such universities harm certain groups of people more than others, namely veterans.

An FPC can only receive a maximum of 90 percent of its revenue purely from federal student aid[xi], however, that doesn't "include military educational benefits provided to veterans and active service members, which do not count towards the limit of 90 percent federal Title IV student aid revenues."[xii] Also, it was reported in 2014 that GI Bill funds were going to for-profit colleges that failed state aid standards.[xiii] So veterans are having their financial futures put in jeopardy by attending for-profit universities. There are further problems with FPCs when the question of degree completion comes up. It was noted in 2010 that "among first-time, fulltime, bachelor's degree-seeking students who enroll at for-profit institutions, only 22 percent earn degrees from those institutions within six years. By contrast, students at public and private nonprofit colleges and universities graduate at rates two to three times higher—55 and 65 percent, respectively."[xiv] This is compounded by the fact that many student go into massive debt in order to finance their education and creates an even worse situation where they are now burgeoning large amounts of debt and don't even have a degree to show for it. This results in students having higher default rates than their peers who go to non-profit colleges.[xv]

However, all of this shouldn't be surprising as FPCs run themselves like businesses. They are *for-profit* after all. A 2012 Senate investigation found that "many for-profit colleges set and raise tuition based on the internal financial projections of the company, rather than the cost of educating students." Two major examples of this are that

The [CFO] of National American University emailed senior executives and campus presidents that 'the university (as a system) was not successful in achieving its summer quarter profit expectations and 'as a result' a mid-year tuition increase' and change in how the company bills students was necessary to hit these expectations.

In 2008 Westwood conducted pricing experiments to see if reducing tuition could increase revenue by attracting more students. An internal presentation showed that the company reduced tuition for a small number of its programs, but determined that the reduction had 'no discernible impact' on recruitment. As a result, the presentation recommended a tuition increase between 3.5 and 4 percent for the following year.[xvi]

For-profit universities also mislead students, such as with Heald College which "misled students and accreditation agencies about graduates' employment rates."[xvii] There are also racial aspects that aren't much talked about. Specifically, many Black and Latino students go to FPCs as they are unable to get into more traditional colleges due to barriers such as cost, resulting in, for example, a disproportionate number of Black students winding up in for-profit universities.[xviii]

Finally, even if students do get a degree, it likely doesn't mean much as employers have low views of for-profit colleges. *CNN* noted the story of Rosalyn Harris, a unemployed 23-year old single mother who enrolled in a for-profit university in an attempt to get a criminal justice degree, however, "all she ended up with was more than $22,000 in student loan debt. She said classes were terrible, she didn't receive any of the training she needed, and as a result, she spent months after graduation searching for criminal justice jobs without ever getting a call back."[xix]

The Center for Analysis of Postsecondary Education and

Employment did a study in October 2014 which showed that "Employers are less likely to call back job applicants with business degrees from online, for-profit colleges than those with degrees from nonselective public universities"[xx] while another study found that "Employers treated people with high school diplomas and coursework at for-profit colleges equivalently."[xxi] Thus, going to a for-profit institution is an endeavor which will leave an individual much worse off than they already were.

With the success of the Corinthian College debt strike[xxii], possibly more students at these colleges will organize and fight back against the ruining of their futures. Yet, the best advice would be to not go at all.

Notes

Eduardo Porter, "The Bane and Boon of For-Profit Colleges," *New York Times*, February 25, 2014 (http://www.nytimes.com/2014/02/26/business/economy/the-bane-and-the-boon-of-for-profit-colleges.html)

Caitlin Rosenthal, "The Long and Controversial History of For-Profit Colleges," *Bloomberg View*, October 25, 2012 (http://www.bloombergview.com/articles/2012-10-25/the-long-and-controversial-history-of-for-profit-colleges)
Ibid

Emily Hanford, *A Brief History of For-Profit Education in the United States*, American Radioworks, http://americanradioworks.publicradio.org/features/tomorrows-college/phoenix/history-of-for-profit-higher-education.html

Daniel L. Bennett, Adam R. Lucchesi, and Richard K. Vedder, *For-Profit Higher Education: Growth, Innovation, and Regulation*, Center for College Affordability and Productivity (July 2010), pg 9
Jeffrey Selingo, "For-Profit Colleges Aim to Take a Share of State

Financial Aid Funds," *The Chronicle of Higher Education*, September 24, 1999

Tim Post, "For-Profit Colleges Fight Effort To Ban State Aid To Students," *Michigan Public Radio News*, March 25, 2009 (http://www.mprnews.org/story/2009/03/25/for_profit_schools_loans)

Judy Lin, "Most California For-Profit Colleges Lose State Grants," *San Jose Mercury News*, August 1, 2012 (http://www.mercurynews.com/ci_21208286/most-california-profit-colleges-lose-state-grants)

David J. Deming, Claudia Goldin and Lawrence F. Katz, "The For-Profit Postsecondary School Sector: Nimble Critters or Agile Predators," *The Journal of Economic Perspectives* 26:1 (Winter 2012), pg 145
Steven Salzberg, "For-Profit Colleges Encourage Huge Student Debt," *Forbes*, July 12, 2015 (http://www.forbes.com/sites/stevensalzberg/2015/07/12/for-profit-colleges-encourage-huge-student-debt/)

FinAid, *90/10 Rule*, http://www.finaid.org/loans/90-10-rule.phtml

Bennett, Lucchesi, Vedder, pg 150
Aaron Glantz, *GI Bill Funds Flow To For-Profit Colleges That Fail State Aid Standards*, The Center for Investigative Reporting, http://cironline.org/reports/gi-bill-funds-flow-profit-colleges-fail-state-aid-standards-6477 (June 28, 2014)

Jose L. Cruz, Jennifer Engle, Mamie Lynch, *Subprime Opportunity: The Unfulfilled Promise of For-Profit Colleges and Universities*, The Education Trust (November 2010), pg 3
Clive R. Belfield, "Student Loans and Repayment Rates: The For-profit Colleges," *Research in Higher Education* 54:1 (February 2013), pgs 18, 26

U.S. Senate, Senate, Committee on Health, Education, Labor, and Pensions, *For Profit Higher Education: The Failure to Safeguard the Federal Investment and Ensure Student Success*, 112th Congress, 2nd Session, July 30, 2012 (Washington D.C.: GPO, 2012) pg 42

Shahien Nasiripur, "Heald College Fined For Misleading Students About Job Prospects," *Huffington Post*, April 14, 2015 (http://www.huffingtonpost.com/2015/04/14/heald-college-fine-jobs_n_7067056.html)

Hannah Appel, Astra Taylor, "Subprime Students: How For-Profit Universities Make a Killing By Exploiting College Dreams," *Mother Jones*, September 23, 2014 (http://www.motherjones.com/politics/2014/09/for-profit-university-subprime-student-poor-minority)

Blake Ellis, "My College Degree Is Worthless," *CNN*, November 2, 2014 (http://money.cnn.com/2014/11/02/pf/college/for-profit-college-degree/)

Capsee, *Employers Value For-Profit Degrees Less, New Study Finds*, The Center for Analysis of Postsecondary Education and Employment, http://capseecenter.org/employers-value-for-profit-degrees-less/ (October 6, 2014)

Lisa Wade, "In Many Employers' Eyes, For-Profit Colleges Are Equivalent to High School," *Pacific Standard*, September 3, 2014 (http://www.psmag.com/business-economics/many-employers-eyes-profit-colleges-equivalent-high-school-89940)

Tamar Lewin, "Government to Forgive Student Loans at Corinthian Colleges," *New York Times*, June 6, 2015 (http://www.nytimes.com/2015/06/09/education/us-to-forgive-federal-loans-of-corinthian-college-students.html)

Communist Pedagogy and the Contradictions of Capital

Curry Malott

As each day passes the gap between labor and capital becomes wider and deeper. Generally speaking, for example, in the aftermath of the 2007 recession the capitalist class in Britain is 64% richer and the poor are 54% poorer. Similarly, in the U.S., the amount of total wealth going to the top 1% has more than doubled since 1979. As general poverty escalates, racialized inequality also tends to expand. With growing immiseration spontaneous working class uprisings and rebellions occur with more frequency. But without a scientific understanding of the society we live in and a theory and method of organization, embryonic proletarian resistance is not likely to shift the paradigm therefore leaving the root cause of suffering in tact.

In this context critical approaches to education have a lot to gain from Marx. That is, while the consequences of capitalism, such as massive wealth and poverty, are readily visible to the untrained eye, their dialectical relationship and root causes are not. Whereas bourgeois propaganda, what they call *education*, would have people believe that wealth and poverty reflect natural or socially constructed differences in ability, intelligence, perseverance and so on, Marx, on the other hand, would have us see labor and capital as part of a contradictory whole, each requiring the other to exist as such. Even though both parts of the whole live an alienated existence, capital lives in opulence whereas labor is plagued with uncertainty and growing poverty. While Marx's contributions here are vast, complex and largely counter-intuitive, I will summarize a few points that I think are most closely related to an anti-capitalist, critical education, what we might call communist pedagogy.

First of all capitalism is not a static system. It is developmental. It is its own internal contradictions that drive its developmental change.

Arguably capitalism's most central contradiction is that in its unlimited quest for the self-expansion of capital, that is, for profit, it not only disrupts the lives of workers, but it disrupts itself. In other words, the process of capitalist production is disruptive to capitalist production.

Think of the Great Depression and the Stock Market Crash of 1929. Not only were an unusually large number of workers thrown out of work, but thousands upon thousands upon thousands of capitalist enterprises also went belly up. U.S. workers' experience of living this contradiction allowed socialist workers to recruit heavily and swell the ranks of the Communist Party USA from 8 thousand members to over 100,000 members during the 10 years of the Great Depression. While the bourgeois state's response to this working class agency was savage and deadly crushing the communist rebellion, workers still won many concessions under attack to this day, from a series of new labor laws and social security to more autonomy in the classroom, which was allowed only after all the communists were purged from schools.

Similarly, the housing market crash of 2007 not only disrupted the lives of millions of workers by destroying the use-value of their homes, but the wave of foreclosures disrupted mortgage lenders' ability to realize the exchange value in their investments. This led to a ripple effect disrupting capitalism in general. Of course the capitalist state bailed out their capitalist masters, externalizing the cost to labor through crushing austerity. In education this has meant even more budget cuts and rollbacks. Following Lenin critical educators can use these crises as schools of war, because the bailouts make it increasingly obvious that the state works not for labor, but for capital. This can foster a class consciousness amongst labor, including teachers, conducive to the movement needed to develop capitalist production relations into socialist ones, and to transform the state into an apparatus that represses not working class resistance, but that represses bourgeois domination and capitalist exploitation.

Disruptions, of course, are nothing new to capital. Capitalism, as Marx explores in volume 1 of *Capital*, began with a series of deadly disruptions he referred to as the chief moments of primitive accumulation, from the expropriation of European peasants from the soil, beginning in England, to the genocidal African slave trade, to the discovery of gold and the genocidal colonization of the Americas. There are no areas of the world safe from the disruptive and devastating effects of capitalism.

The first disruption was a prerequisite for the development of the rest. That is, before the process of the augmentation of capital could begin, a class of people needed to be created who had no way to support themselves but by selling their ability to work on the market for a wage. History has shown us that the peasant will not do this voluntarily and must therefore be violently expropriated from the soil. In the process the conditions necessary for capitalism to take hold, such as the creation of private property, become its consequences as the dependency of labor on capital proceeds on an extending scale through the system's development.

While regulations and organized labor can slow down this process, only working class agency can push capital to become its own dialectical, communist opposite. Critical education can play a fundamental role here. While this formulation of dialectical change should not be interpreted to suggest a clean or linear process, it is a process with a definite direction nonetheless.

The next fundamental insight for a critical education against capital is the understanding that within every hour of paid labor there contains an unrequited or an unpaid portion.

At its most basic level we can understand this, as Marx did, by dividing the workday into two distinct portions: necessary labor time and surplus labor time. Necessary labor time is the material basis of the minimum wage. It is the equivalent value of the bare minimum cost of reproducing ones existence for a 24-hour period. The minimum wage today in this country is far below what is socially necessary. While explaining the specific ways capital pushes wages below what is socially necessary is beyond the scope of this introduction, it is driven by the same internal logic as capitalism in general. If it takes 6 hours of labor to reproduce the value of ones daily existence, then every hour the laborer works after that is surplus labor time, the material basis of surplus value or profit. Because the products of labor power go to the buyer of this commodity and not the seller, the extra value created goes to the capitalist and not the laborer.

Again, this is the basis of capital's exploitation of labor. This exploitation is disguised or hidden by the money relation. That is, if you have a job, when you receive your paycheck, it appears that every hour of work is paid, because every hour of work is typically accounted for right there on your pay stub. Consequently, the relationship between labor and capital appears to be fair. If workers are unhappy with the paychecks they receive, we are told it is their own fault for not working harder for the kind of results they desire. What we are *not* told is that there is no escape from exploitation within capitalism. Without some degree or rate of exploitation, the owner of wealth cannot expand his or her money, and they cannot therefore create new value. Without exploitation, in other words, the capitalist cannot exist as such. Money, in other words, is not necessarily capital. Capital is the product of a self-expansive process based upon the exploitation of human labor power. Just being wealthy does not make one a capitalist. This is another counter-intuitive characteristic of capitalism.

Reflecting on this larger context of capitalism, one of the purposes of a critical education is to help students understand their true class position within it, and develop the collective revolutionary agency necessary to transform it. There is no substitute for this. Even as poverty escalates and the consequences of capitalism become more obvious—over-the-top opulence on one hand, and extreme poverty on the other—the internal mechanism of how new value is created capitalistically remains hidden, and so do realistic solutions. That is, without a scientific understanding of capitalism, solutions are doomed to be focused on tinkering with the rate of exploitation: such as the current movement for the 15 dollar an hour minimum wage, the movement to grow unions, the movement to tax capitalists more, and the movement to increase public spending on things like education. While all of these interrelated movements are important and tend to be supported by socialists, they leave the basis of capitalistic exploitation itself untouched. The history of education in capitalist society is, in large part, the history of how attention on the root, capitalist cause of poverty has been diverted away from the economic structure and to the individual.

For example, dating back to the mid nineteenth century the moral crusade for Common Schooling, led by Massachusetts lawyer turned secretary of education, Horace Mann, has tended to be conceptualized as placing the hope for social improvement, that is ending poverty and suffering, on the individual, ignoring the internal drive of capital itself. The more feudalistic model of educating or socializing workers was based on the Christian concept of original sin, where education served the function of keeping the inherent evil within the poor at bay. With the development of capitalism this theory of education was being replaced with the more nineteenth century concept of the blank slate, where the immoral laborer had to be molded into the proper citizen. In this context poverty is the result of improperly molded workers, rather than on the drive to accumulate surplus labor hours. Schooling in capitalist society has therefore always tended to be based on the assumption that poverty is an individual problem, and that capitalism offers individuals the freedom to overcome it. Today's rhetoric argues that unaccountable schools with low standards, created by teachers' unions that protect incompetence, has failed to mold the individual into the type of worker that is competitive on the 21st century international labor market. Of course unions cannot protect workers who do not do their jobs, they can only work to ensure dismissals are not arbitrary. What is more, the individual cannot be held responsible for the poverty created by capitalism's limitless quest for surplus value.

As the enrollment of school-aged children continued to increase through the Great Depression, the curriculum steadily moved away from the common schooling approach where rich and poor children were schooled together as a way to ensure workers did not grow up to hate their exploiting bosses. As capitalism expanded and developed technologically, the children of the elite were more and more groomed for leadership and the children of labor were trained for specialized jobs through a differentiated, or socially efficient, vocational education.

Traditional educational historians argue that the emergence of vocational education was an example of how schools were providing what workers wanted, therefore operating as a progressive, democratic institution. Responses to this narrative argued that social efficiency was really about dumbing workers down to snuff out radicalism and quell the revolutionary potential within labor as alienated existence.

The social control argument is easy to understand given the logic of social efficiency. That is, the assumption was that educating future machine minders, for example, with luxuries such as philosophy, literature, political science, etc. was a waste of resources, and thus not efficient. Another interpretation of social efficiency was that wasting educational resources on say public speaking and debating skills not required for the future mechanic was taking time away from producing better mechanics, for example. In the years before and after WWI it was argued that inefficient, common methods of education were putting America at an international competitive disadvantage.

But capital and its state apparatus, also under false allusions about the fairness of the exchange between labor and capital, have tended to be ignorant to how the competitive advantage of individual capitalists is always only temporary, and its cumulative effect, actually, tends to shift the general composition of capital so it takes less labor hours to transform a given quantity of raw materials into useful products, and therefore leads to a tendency toward the falling rate of profit.

Let me explain:

Because the price of individual products is determined by the average amount of labor time it takes to produce them, the capitalist ahead of the technology race will yield a greater surplus from his products than his competitor until the new more efficient or productive technology is integrated into that branch of industry generally, and the average amount of time it takes to produce a given commodity is lowered. This tendency drives down the price of products, the value of labor, and the rate of the capitalists' profit. This is another one of capital's central driving contradictions.

This internal drive of capital therefore, while enriching certain capitalists in the short term, ultimately erodes its own desired effect. That is, if the only way to expand capital is by exploiting human labor power, then the capitalist is always searching for ways to put more labor hours into motion. If advances in production decrease the amount of labor hours needed to convert a particular quantity of raw materials into useful products, then the capitalist faces an internal contradiction threatening the objective of his existence as personified capital (i.e. the capitalist).

Bourgeois education policy makers fail to either acknowledge or realize that the real key to increases in the efficiency in production is not necessarily in the training of laborers, but in the means of production itself. The real threat to workers is therefore not their own immoral character, but the internal drive of capital, and what the capitalist is compelled to do to counter the falling rate of profit.

For example, the measures capitalists enact to counter the falling rate of return are always at the expense of labor. Such measures include increasing the intensity of work, extending the length of the working day beyond all natural limits, expanding imperialistically into new regions, and when there remain no new regions to expand into, turning to each other, imperialist nations to imperialist nations, in a military competition for existing colonies sending working class youth of one empire to kill and be killed by the working class youth of another empire. And when the most exploited and degraded hands of an internal or external colony resist and especially when they engage in national liberation struggles, they are called terrorists and ruthlessly destroyed, collectively or individually.

Thinking about what this means for education Marx challenges communist pedagogy to resist attempts to reduce the necessity of transforming concrete material conditions into an exercise in transforming consciousness alone. Marx also challenges critical educators, as already suggested, to resist utopian conceptions of a new society emerging magically separate and disconnected from the one that exists. Marx is correct, I believe, that new social arrangements can only emerge out of existing ones.

In this context of uncertainty, deadly state racism, oppression, exploitation, and contradiction more and more organized struggle is in fact emerging. The resistance is developing not only outside of the U.S., but it is happening within the U.S. as well. With the Soviet Union unfortunately gone and the fog and bigotry of anti-communism in the U.S. slowly dissipating, a new socialist movement, a new anti-capitalist movement, is emerging. The Occupy movement, the Black Lives Matter movement, and the Sanders campaign, despite some significant socialist critiques, have been contextualized as harbingers of what is to come.

In the context of teachers' unions, the recent strike of the Seattle Education Association sent shock waves across the country and embodies the spirit of the largely forgotten history of socialism in the U.S. That is, the Seattle teachers strong connection and solidarity with students, their care givers, and other unions gave them strength, leverage, and a real ability to achieve largely unprecedented concessions including the removal of the "Student Growth Rating" clause that links teacher evaluations to student test scores. They were also able to achieve the establishment of 30 "race and equity teams" charged with identifying examples of institutional racism and recommending ways to address them. It is not perfect, but it is a great beginning. The Seattle Education Association's concrete support and victory for these and other social justice issues might be viewed as a reminder of what workers can win through their organizations and leadership.

Of course, this does not mean we can sit back and wait for things to get better. It means we have to fight harder than we ever have. It means we have to be more disciplined and organized than we ever have. It means we have to be smarter than we ever have. It means we have to be fiercer and more committed than we ever have. The future is not guaranteed, but any means. While it may be hard to imagine, things could take a turn for the worse, and it is up to us to ensure that it does not.

Revolutionary Critical Pedagogy and the Struggle against Capital Today
An Interview with Peter McLaren

Derek R. Ford

Peter McLaren is an internationally renowned revolutionary activist and teacher, and one of the founders of critical pedagogy. He has written over 45 books and hundreds of scholarly articles, and his writings have been translated into dozens of languages. He is currently Distinguished Professor of Critical Studies at Chapman University.

*Peter is also a close friend, comrade, and mentor of mine. He generously agreed to engage in a dialogue with me amidst his busy summer schedule (he has a terrible time saying "no" to young scholars and activists). In this dialogue we speak about his personal, scholarly, political, and activist journey, address some of the themes in his forthcoming book, **Pedagogy of Insurrection**, explore the internationalization of critical pedagogy, and examine what's next for critical pedagogy and the revolutionary left.*

Derek Ford: Greetings, Peter! Thanks so much for taking the time out of your schedule for this interview with *The Hampton Institute*. I wonder if we can start the conversation with where you are right now, in China. Can you tell us a bit about what you are doing there, and how and why it is that your activist and academic work has increasingly brought you to the international arena?

Peter McLaren: Thanks for starting this conversation, Derek, it's always a pleasure. To answer your question I'll have to dig back a bit. For even as a slatternly and relatively untutored youth the question of oppression and exploitation was of grave discernment to me. I trace this concern to the economic fate suffered by my father, who as a working-class wallpaper salesman before he went overseas for 6 years to fight the Nazis during WWII, found himself on the dole after he was fired from a managerial position he landed in an international electronics firm once the war ended. The severe trauma suffered by my family during this period stayed with me from my teenage years into my early twenties, and after my first marriage fell apart due, partly, to financial pressures, I decided that teaching offered me a chance to test my interpersonal skills and creativity, clear some pedagogical space for examining alarming social trends of the day, as well as try to make a positive difference in the lives of young people-and at the same time enjoy some financial security. That was 1974.

I had always perceived as banal most of what was meant to provoke my interest and attention in the world of commodity culture and for the most part refused to answer invitations to participate in the suburban dream. So in 1968, I made the decision to hitchhike to San Francisco and Los Angeles in 1968, a year after the storied the "summer of love", and participate in demonstrations against the Vietnam war, as well as take advantage of the chemical and cultural offerings of the psychedelic age that was in full blossom at the time. That was my first international trip, no pun intended. It gave me the opportunity to meet and explore interior space with Timothy Leary, and to have my poetry mentored by Allan Ginsberg. I returned to Canada to finish my university

123

degree in Elizabethan drama, and eventually found myself teaching elementary school in the largest public housing complex in Canada, located in Toronto's Jane-Finch Corridor.

After publishing a book about my teaching experiences in 1980, which rose to number 7th on the better-seller lists in Canada, and finishing my Ph.D. in 1984, I tried out university teaching for a year, but my contract wasn't renewed the following year, for political reasons that you can likely imagine. Fortunately, Henry Giroux had seen some of my writings and invited me to join him at Miami University of Ohio (Henry had been fired from Boston University in 1983 by reactionary university president, John Silber, in a landmark tenure case) to create the first cultural studies center in education in the U.S. at the time. So in 1985, I head for the U.S. where I have been based ever since. My first formal invitation to speak internationally came from one of my mentors, the renowned educator, Paulo Freire, who not only gave my work early support but provided opportunities for me to travel outside of the U.S. Paulo invited me in 1987 to speak in Havana, Cuba, at an international conference, and it was there that I made friends with scholars and activists in Cuba as well as with visitors from Brazil and Mexico. My work eventually caught the eye of some radical educators in northern Mexico and they established Instituto McLaren de Pedagogia Critica y Educacion Popular in 2007. From there I went on to present my work and build connections and networks, in Colombia, Argentina, Brazil and Puerto Rico mostly, and then around the mid 1990s my work began to capture the attention of Marxist educators in the United Kingdom, and later on in Turkey, Greece, Taiwan, Poland, Hungary, Germany, Pakistan, India, Occupied Palestine (known also as "Israel"), Palestine proper, Croatia, Serbia and other countries who had constituencies, large and small, interested in critical pedagogy. One of my books, *Life in Schools,* was translated into Russian as an award for coming in 11th place in an international poll conducted in Moscow regarding the 12 most significant education books written to date.

Ford : And you have also worked closely with the Bolivarian Revolution in Venezuela, correct?

McLaren : Yes, eventually, I was invited to help critical pedagogy become more integrated into the Bolivarian revolution in Venezuela. After meeting with Hugo Chavez in Miraflores Palace, I began to realize that no revolution could exist in isolation. That meeting further inspired me to establish as many relationships with radical groups as I could with the idea of turning critical pedagogy into a transnational social movement. Eventually my work drew interest from northeast China, where I was to meet my wife Wang Yan, and I have been invited to serve as honorary director of a center for the study of critical education, which we hope to get off the ground this fall.

I retired from UCLA in order to take up a position in Orange County (yes, behind the Orange Curtain) when a group of Freirean educators at Chapman University invited me to try to make a difference in their doctoral program in this very conservative part of California. As somebody whose life has always been an uphill battle, I relished the opportunity. To be honest, I can't tell you how that struggle is going yet; it's much too early. I've spent time as faculty and in visiting capacities in various academic institutions for over forty years. I've met great scholars and activists from all over the world who I admire greatly who have managed to do good work within the academy. During this time I have also heard plenty of horror stories that were documented in a book I co-edited with Richard Kahn, Steve Best and Tony Nocella called *Academic Repression*. But I can tell you that being at Chapman has revived my faith that academic life can be more than just swimming with the sharks and being morally suffocated by a group of self-aggrandizing, self-righteous and power-harvesting egos fueled by a rampant careerism and willing to do anything to enhance their power and prestige, including selling out their colleagues.

Ford : It seems to me that this process of internationalization has been accompanied by a radicalization of your thinking and activism. Can you speak a bit about that? In particular, I am wondering what the historical, material, and theoretical factors are that have contributed to this radicalization.

McLaren : Of course much of my journey and formation has to do with developing a theoretical framework and political line of march. I will discuss that road shortly. But traveling and meeting activists far more courageous and politically astute than I afforded me moments of clarity and reflection. And meeting individuals-some renowned and some unknown-who had forged their lives in the heat of struggle gave me pause to think about how much you can really learn from books alone.

Ford : Are there particular moments that you recall?

McLaren : Absolutely: visiting East Germany shortly after the wall came down when the universities were firing Marxist professors and replacing them with West German critical theorists; visiting Russia during its formal transition to capitalism and watching people scavenge through the garbage bins to find food; staying in Cuba with the Soviet boxing team at the old Capri Hotel; visiting the Museum of the Revolution in Old Havana and spending hours talking to Aleida Guevara about her father (with the help of a translator since my Spanish is atrocious); Paulo Freire attending one of my lectures in Brasil and trying to assist a frustrated translator who was struggling with my unorthodox prose; meeting Hugo Chavez in Miraflores Palace and listening to him encourage an office secretary to return to university; speaking to 25,000 protesting teachers in Morelia, Michoacan; meeting Lopez Obrador in Mexico; weeping alongside the sons and daughters of los desaparecidos in Rosario, Argentina, casualties of La Guerra Sucia; listening to Ernesto Cardinal call Hugo Chavez a prophet during a live broadcast of Alo Presidente outside of Caracas; flying in a

Venezuelan National Guard airplane as part of a tour of support for the revolution and watching the two young pilots, their machine guns on the floor of the cockpit, trying to figure out where the landing strip was located; singing Hasta Siempre Comandante along with factory workers on buses roaring through the Venezuelan countryside in support of La Revolucion Bolivariana; meeting Las Madres de la Plaza de Mayo who visited me during a ceremony in Buenos Aires; speaking at a conference in Morelia when La Familia Michoacana attacked the city, setting passenger buses on fire to block the exits out of the city and being saved from danger by a radical taxi driver who was able to get me safely to the airport; suddenly finding myself listed as "the most dangerous professor at UCLA by a rightwing organization backed with Republican dollars that offered to pay students 100 dollars to secretly audiotape my classes and 50 dollars to provide notes from my lectures (there were 30 professors who were targeted) and finding few official condemnations of this action by North American teacher groups in contrast to vigorous defense of my work by Latin American educational organizations; conversing with the head of a teachers union in Bogota about how former leaders of the union had been assassinated and that he was fully prepared to die in the struggle to help educate the young people of Colombia; being asked to speak at a school outside of Medellin, Colombia, and using a very ultra leftist discourse in my talk, and then being gently reprimanded that such a militant language could get both students and teachers killed as when the community in which the school was located was attacked several years earlier by helicopter gunships, thousands of troops, followed by a wave of paramilitary assassinations; being humbled by the dedication of activists all around the world who risk life and limb everyday while I am able to return to the comfort of my job and home back in the United States.

Those moments congeal in the memory and become part of the emotional strata of my work. They form their own pathways to the heart and of course are entangled with the theoretical work-in a type of dialectics between the head and heart-that has persuaded me over the years that we are faced with no other choice than a socialist alternative to capitalist value production. However, in citing these examples, I am aware of the danger of falling into an oversimplified and uncritical euphoria often linked to the politics of memory that can override contradictions that I observed in many of these settings.

When I was a teenager I was inspired by the works of William Blake, Dylan Thomas, Shakespeare, Milton, Chaucer, the new criticism of Northrop Frye. In the late 1960s and early 1970s I become influenced by the Beat Poets, the Harlem Renaissance and works by James Baldwin and W.E.B. Du Bois. Then of course, there was the Black Power Movement and the works of Angela Davis, Malcolm X, Amiri Baraka (Leroy Jones) and others. The writings of Margaret Randal were certainly an influence. Now, Derek, you need to understand that this shift from classical literature to more radical works was not easy. My parents were very conservative. My dad was in the Royal Canadian Engineers during WWII and was a member of the conservative party in Canada. My uncle, Terry Goddard, was a hero in the Royal Navy and flew his Fairey Swordfish off the Arc Royal and disabled the German Battleship Bismark with a torpedo strike. I was disparaged for turning into a hippie, and I was an outcast among my larger family of cousins, uncles and aunts (which isn't to say that I wasn't proud of my father's service in the war, or my uncle's Distinguished Service Medal pinned on him by King George VI (The King's Speech)--I was very proud of both of them). My two best friends committed suicide during those years of rebellion, and for the longest time I felt guilty that I had survived the tumultuous 1960s without my closest friends.

Ford : Yes, the political and the personal...

McLaren : Certainly. There are always personal struggles that shadow shifts in political perspectives. I think it is important to recognize, too, that theory doesn't just come to you through books alone but through an engagement with the authors, if you are fortunate enough to do so. I was fortunate that in my early formation there were individual scholars who took time out to acknowledge my interest in their work-I was impressed, for instance, that Michel Foucault gave me the time of day during a class of his that I audited while a doctoral student in Toronto; there were others, too, that were courteous and hospitable and patient with my naïve quesitons: Jean Francois Lyotard, Anthony Wilden, and Ernesto Laclau stand out. That they were willing to engage with me, however briefly, in person, while I was a young scholar certainly influenced my early "critical postmodernism" period from the mid-1980s to early 1990s since I was more inclined to gravitate to their work after having conversations with them. Henry Giroux was another scholar who befriended me early on when I was a doctoral student and later I had the fortunate opportunity to work with Henry for eight very productive years at Miami University of Ohio. Stanley Aronowitz's mentoring was significant in my early leftist formation. So I owe a great deal of my orientation-both in my postmodern period and in my current Marxist work-to the kindness of individuals who were humble and gracious enough to befriend a relatively unknown scholar from el norte.

One of the biggest influences on my work other than Paulo Freire and the life and legacy of Che Guevara has been the formidable Marxist scholar and activist, Peter Hudis. Peter was secretary to Raya Dunayevskaya, who served as the Russian language translator for Leon Trotsky in 1937, returning several years before his assassination in Coyoacán, Mexico in 1940. Raya's theory of state capitalism had a big impact on my work. So did the writings of Mas'ud Zavarzadeh and Teresa Ebert. I should mention, in passing, one other moment that stands out for me. Three Marxist educators in the UK-Mike Cole, Dave Hill, and Glenn Rikowski-saw potential in my early critical postmodernist work but were also highly critical of it from their own Marxist perspectives. They took time to engage my work personally and eventually we became close comrades. I learned a great deal from them. E. San Juan is another scholar whom I was fortunate enough to meet on a number of occasions and his critique of cultural studies has certainly had a considerable impact on my work. While I was in Venezuela, I had the opportunity to spend time with Marta Harnecker and Michael Lebowitz and found much to admire in their work. Instituto McLaren de Pedagogia Critica has brought both Marta Harnecker and Peter Hudis to address our annual Volver a Marx conference that we hold in different cities throughout Mexico each year, along with scholars such as Atilio Boron and Enrique Dussel. The internet has now made it much easier for scholars and activists to connect with each other in person, but given the volume of queries that I receive each day, I can fully understand how difficult it is to respond personally to every budding young leftist with a bucket full of pressing questions.

Ford : Given this political and personal journey, how do you now identify yourself?

McLaren : I describe myself as Marxist humanist and share an affinity with the International Marxist Humanist organization. I also work in the field of liberation theology and more recently this influence has begun to surface in my work. Some have described my work as Christian communism and this is not an inaccurate description. What my work attempts to do is develop a philosophy of praxis, grounded in a Hegelian-Marxist understanding of history and politics. This is the deep undercurrent that drives my revolutionary critical pedagogy, and works very well with a Freirean approach which was very much influenced by Karel Kosik's dialectics of the concrete. It works well with Marx's understanding of revolutionary praxis.

Ford : I would say that your thinking has also radicalized in response to the depoliticization of foundations of education. One of the battle fronts in your work has been within the field of foundations of education, and one of the main lines of demarcation has been between post-structuralism and Marxism, or historical materialism. This is why scholars like Ebert and Rikowski were so important to your development as a scholar and, as you said, to your break from critical postmodernism. I am wondering what theoretical or political

130

tendencies you see as our main adversaries in foundations of education today?

McLaren : Derek, I prefer the term adversity to adversaries, since I believe the problems in the foundations of education is a condition that can be found not just among the poststructuralists or postmodernists but embedded within the axial question: What social class do the central theorists studied in foundations courses represent?

Ford : Yes, that phrasing certainly emphasizes more appropriately the structural nature of this manifestation of the class struggle.

McLaren : So, in education there are three fundamental approaches in philosophical reasoning: essentialism, perennialism, and progressivism, and the focus today among the educational left is mainly on progressivism-romantic progressives and pragmatic progressives (to use terms developed by Richard Quantz), and in my observations over the years, Marxism usually comes into the picture during discussions of the various political-economic ideologies within the progressive coalition. It is therefore important for me to address the following question to students of education: To what extent do these progressive thinkers believe their work rises above the reigning class antagonisms of transnational austerity capitalism?

Most students likely believe that the theories that they study are relatively free of class determinations, and that should be a signal to us as critical educators, a warning about how and why certain theories have made their way into the official curriculum. For me, the immediate challenge is to locate theoretical and philosophical work politically within a larger vision or project of emancipation. Ideas-which under certain conditions can certainly exert a material force-are always situated in particular settings. These settings are always conditioned by the ideological and political superstructure, the historical conjuncture in which they were produced and in which they are now studied, and the economic and social structure.

We need to understand how possibilities unleashed by the theories we study can be transformed into necessities and for that to happen we need to examine our present conjuncture dialectically, because social conditions and ideologies reciprocally inform each other; they are entangled and to a large extent mutually constitutive, and clearly they are never static or eternal. That being the case, we need to ask ourselves: What are the objective possibilities at this certain historical moment for socialism to become a viable possibility? As a socialist educator, that becomes the fundamental question. That means helping our students navigate beyond false dualisms and abstractions, between thought and action, theory and practice and it is here that a Marxist dialectic becomes important, especially the concept of praxis.

One of the primary goals could be put thusly: How can we help the working-class become conscious of itself and its universal role in a permanent revolution? The really important consideration here is what standpoint we take when we move from merely interpreting the world to changing it, when we move from the indicative to the imperative. All of this, of course, is fueled by commitment and commitment relies on being able to assume the standpoint of the oppressed, the subaltern. Do we educate our teachers by discussing authors that place themselves in the class perspectives of the proletariat, the cognitariat, or the precariat? Paulo Freire, Howard Zinn, Frantz Fanon and Che Guevara all do. But does that mean we only read working-class authors or authors sympathetic to the working-class? Of course not. But we need to teach students to consider how an author's own class positionality influences his or her work. Over time, and during years of deliberation, I came to understand postmodern thought and reformist liberalism embedded in the work of some critical theorists such as Habermas and in the work of John Dewey as insufficient for challenging the behemoth of transnational capitalism. Rousseau's voluptuous protest was against the vile and iniquitous social institutions dominated by capitalists. He wagered that if the social contradictions stemming from these institutions could be abolished

132

or severely attenuated, then there would be greater possibility for liberty and sovereignty.

Yet as Istvan Meszaros pointed out, Rousseau could not abstain from idealizing the very conditions against which he provided alternatives since it was clear that the contradictions that he condemned were integrated within the objective conditions of capitalist society itself. After all, Rousseau considered private property to be one of the ultimate foundations of civilized life. Many well-intentioned theorists idealize the very conditions of alienation and atomization that they rail against, affirming what they originally intended to negate and they do this by employing abstract moral ideals to challenge what are essentially economic systems of exploitation and thus fail to mediate their ideas to the material base of society (i.e., the social relations of production as well as determinate human relations). The only way out of this impasse in which one interest is set up against another in permanent struggle is through a dialectical materialist analysis. We see a similar predicament in the later Marcuse when he became more interested in the development of Hegel's ontology than his dialectics, which forced him into an aesthetic ontology marked by an antinomial (neo-Kantian) cul-de-sac in which his critique vacillated between poles regarded as independent rather than internally related, preventing Marcuse from forging a path forward to transformation.

While Marcuse's earlier Great Refusal was rooted in the Hegelian notion of negativity where a positive is constituted as the old is being negated, Marcuse tended at times to separate the normative and the descriptive, thus remaining in the thrall of the Kantian ought or an indeterminate rather than a determinate negation, lacking in the final instance the concrete emancipatory universals of Marx. This, of course, relates to Dunayevskaya's critique of Marcuse, when she accuses Marcuse of viewing Hegel's Absolute Idea as a closed totality when Dunayevskaya saw it as containing the highest opposition within itself, a dialectic of negativity that served as the lifeblood of transcendence, a place of self-movement where contradictions cannot be adventitiously dismissed or harmlessly reconciled or cancelled. For Dunayevskaya, absolute negativity constituted important new beginnings for revolutionary thought. But this is not to dismiss the important work of Marcuse. As Charles Reitz points out, Marcuse's work importantly contributed to a philosophy of labor, which recognizes labor's central and transformative role in human life. The point I am trying to make is that even within the field of critical pedagogy there is a studied reluctance when it comes to confronting the transformation of surplus labor into private capital. Again, we come back to my earlier question: What do educational theorists represent by their ideas? This is no small matter at a time when we are witnessing the gargantuan rise of transnational state apparatuses, interlocked networks of nation states and supranational and transnational institutions that fuels the new global ruling class, a class that is intent on superceding national accumulation. Or, as William I. Robinson points out, at a time of capitalist restructuring, reorganization and refurbishing, producing a new transnational class based on deregulation, informalization, deunionization and the flexibility of labor, creating vast armies of precariats and new strategies by the transnational elites to contain real and potential rebellion by the immiserated masses.

Ford : And so it is the two irretrievably connected questions of how we understand and combat this new transnational capitalist class, yes?

McLaren : Right, and right now colleges of education courses that attempt to be radical usually follow through with hefty doses of Foucault, Holloway, Deleuze, Hardt, Negri and Said. Such foundation courses in schools of education tend to focus on autonomous Marxism, post-colonialism, and the strategic importance of the self-limiting revolution. Taken together, this constitutes a rejection of Marxism and revolution and the affirmation of a position that supports labor reform but does not advocate overthrowing state power. Here, the utopian horizon of Marxism is often conflated with repression, something that is likely to lead to the gulag. Kevin Anderson and Peter Hudis have written about this and I am in agreement with them. There is a serious problem with Foucault's rejection of the Marxist conception of false consciousness in favor of a view in which power is productive and enabling rather than repressive; power is something that, according to Foucault, produces alternative realities.

Marx's humanism is held in suspect as Promethean within which a colonial hubris is embedded. With Foucault there exists no main locus of power that must be challenged, and therefore no concept of liberation or emancipation is possible, only the more truncated possibility of challenging power as forms of micro-resistance. Kevin Anderson maintains that a similar position is reflected in Hardt and Negri's politics of difference where global struggles are viewed as incommensurable to the extent that they can only be challenged in terms of localized bio-power absent of any unified philosophy or organization. Anderson notes that Hart and Negri posit a one-sided alternative by choosing to remain on the plane of immanence or within the given social reality as a point of resistance, preferring to take their inspiration from a pre-Hegelian world cut off from the dialectic and thereby sidelining the positive contained within the negative. While I may agree that the working-class is immanent to capital, I also maintain that it can also become a force for transcendence, as the future is always contained in the present. This does not mean that I reduce everything to proletarian class struggle. Marxist humanists vigorously embrace struggles around race, disability, gender and sexuality but they do so within a revolutionary praxis that is capable of overcoming capitalism and building a social universe outside of the value form of labor. I have faith that people can overcome capitalism through their own emancipatory praxis, as people change society and change their own consciousness at the same time.

Ford : And this brings us to the question of consciousness, which has always been a central concern of critical pedagogy. What is your position here, in regards to the role of consciousness in struggle and as an educational object of transformation?

McLaren : Here, I concur with Che's stress on the struggle of human consciousness against alienation and believe that this is necessary in order to create a more human, radical and egalitarian world. I am not reluctant to say that the creation of socialism is a heroic act. After all, the capitalist regime is brutal, as social life throughout the US now reflects the imprint of austerity capitalism and the world is being brought to an ecological tipping point as quantitative changes are transforming into qualitative changes. Garry Leech called capitalism a form of genocide--so we are fighting against the triple threat of genocide, ecocide, and epistemicide--the latter referring to the destruction of indigenous communities and their languages and way of life, their cosmovisions, their ecologies of the mind. A friend of mine at Instituto McLaren de Pedagogia Critica was talking to an indigenous group leader who told him the community has decided not to reproduce new members, they want to become extinct, life is too difficult, to unremittingly devastaing for them to keep going. Capitalism has assumed the jeering rictus of the Grim Reaper as we move ineluctably towards a militarized surveillance state and its fatal degeneration into forms of authority that can only be compared to fascism.

We must roundly reject the so-called economic laws of a system oriented to growth, where all activity is reduced to profit calculations and all life is quantified and turned to stone. Hence, we choose not replace capitalist market ecology. Our focus is on use value, not exchange value. The historical totality is not static, conjunctures change and because history is not independent of human will and action we must resolve at each moment of history to turn the spontaneity of the masses into consciousness, into critical consciousness, taking socialism as an idea-force to create conditions for ecological revolution, for economic equality, for a social universe outside of capital's value form where we can create a society free from necessity and absent of racism, sexism, patriarchy, white supremacy and militarism. We do this by reaching out to the people, by taking their individual and personal concerns about family life such as health insurance, job security, violence, racism and meaningful coexistence with their neighbors, and connecting their personal struggles to the larger structures of oppression and exploitation in today's austerity capitalism.

Ford : Rewinding slightly to your remarks on understanding and combatting the current manifestations of capital, let's shift now to your recent work. Don't you have a new book that is about to hit the presses?

McLaren : Yes, I do, it's titled *Pedagogy of Insurrection: From Resurrection to Revolution*, and it is central to my ongoing project of developing a transnational pedagogy of revolution. I offer an analysis of the impact of transnational capitalism on education, particularly U.S. education, including the devastating effects of various corporate initiatives to privatize schools. I discuss what I believe to be the most pressing issues and debates in education today, including advances in ecopedagogy, expanding and deepening ideas that I have been developing under the name "revolutionary critical pedagogy". Included is a chapter in which I engage in a spirited critique of new digital technologies. I also discuss historical figures that have been crucified in the U.S. media but who merit a more serious and sympathetic consideration for their contributions to the liberation and emancipation of humanity-Paulo Freire, Che Guevara, Fidel Castro, and Hugo Chavez. But the centerpiece of the book is a chapter called Comrade Jesus, which concludes with a discussion of violence.

Ford : Interesting. I am sure that some people might at first blush be a bit surprised to see you speaking about Jesus. Can you talk more about your interest there and the theoretical and practical work that it does?

McLaren : Absolutely. My basic premise, and it is certainly not an original one but one that is consistently abominated by the corporate media-is that there has been an egregious betrayal of doctrine in much Christian teaching, a profound transgiversation when it comes to the most authentic logia of Jesus, that of teaching communism. There have been some exceptions to this betrayal-for instance, liberation theology and critical spirituality. But to me it is clear from reading the bible that communism is identified with being a Christian. Jesus, in fact, taught communism to the first Christians. In fact, the renunciation of property is a primary condition for entering the kingdom of God. I draw on numerous sources of biblical exegesis but rely a great deal on the work of Jose Porfirio Miranda. The kingdom of God is not an otherworldly place that exists in some supernatural realm but rather founded by Jesus here on earth, where it is unequivocally impossible for the rich to enter the kingdom. Mark (10:21) tells us, "Go sell everything you have and give it to the poor" and that "It is easier for a camel to pass through the eye of a needle than for a rich person to enter the kingdom of God" (Mark 10:25).

According to Miranda, Jesus is not against wealth in the absolute sense, but in the relative sense, in the way that such wealth contrasts with the poor, the destitute, the immiserated so that we can safely say that Jesus was against differentiated wealth, against inequality. Money made through profit is considered to be iniquitous. The rich have already received their comfort and are refused entry into the kingdom of God, something that is made clear in Luke 6:24. The fact that some are rich and others are poor is indefensible, according to Jesus. The moral reprobation of Jesus with respect to the rich is undeniable. In fact, Jesus' condemnation of relative wealth is consistent with the teaching of the Old Testament, with Moses and the prophets. It is undeniably the case that the rich deserve to be punished for remaining rich in the face of the poverty, as Psalm 34:11 makes clear. It is impossible to accept one's self-enrichment at the expense of the exploitation of others. The price of labor in the capitalist marketplace is imposed on the laborer-the differentiating social position of the rich is predicated on the unfreedom of the poor, whose only alternative to exploitation by the rich is unemployment, hunger and destitution. Differentiating wealth is the fruit of injustice. Chapter 24 of Job explains how the poor suffer at the hands of the rich, as this really is the problem of evil. Evil is a social condition. It is incorrect to interpret Jesus as saying that the poor will always be with us, and that we are never going to the change the world and rid it of poverty. I discuss this translation problem in my book. Jesus was saying that the poor are with us continuously-not forever, not always.

The prosperity evangelical Christians will likely curse me as they exit their tents and put their serpents back in their baskets, but I believe that what I have to say is backed by careful scriptural exegesis. Since the election of Pope Francis, there have appeared in the mainstream media some interesting articles about a revival of liberation theology, or the social gospel of Jesus Christ, and I found it interesting that Raoul Castro recently said he may return to the Catholic church as a result of conversations he has had with Pope Francis. I think this is a very good time for the book to become available to teachers, educators and theologians. The conditions for such a debate are ripening. It's time that people of faith who do freedom-work in the interest of social justice make their voices heard.

Ford : Peter, I know that you are spread quite thin right now, and so I don't want to keep you too much longer. But, as we are Marxists, we have to end with a note on the future. In your opinion, what work is there to do for critical pedagogues to contribute most effectively toward the intensification of resistance to capitalism? What theorists and movements should we be investigating and engaging?

McLaren : Well, Derek, honestly the first thing that comes to mind is your book with Curry Malott,*Marx, Capital and Education: Towards a Critical Pedagogy of Becoming*, which is a glowing testament to generation of scholars who have discovered Marx and are using his work in politically innovative ways, opening up new options for living and laboring freely and creatively. The difficulty I think is that the organization, the culture, and the climate of universities today, with their emphasis on harvesting corporate grants, and focusing on instrumental and technocratic skills to prepare students for positions within the capitalist marketplace, is less hospitable to leftists whose research, teaching, or personal activism is driven by a socialist agenda. You can be center-left and survive but it is much more difficult if you are on the revolutionary left. Some leftists I know who populate the universities remain very cautious in the classrooms and relegate their political work to their free time outside of the campus. It's a kind of self-monitoring, self-censorship.

In the years to come, what spaces will be available for Marxist scholarship and a Marxist politics, especially in very conservative places such as colleges of education? There will always be spaces for identity politics, but fewer spaces for what Angela Davis calls identity in politics. As long as educators rewrite economic problems as moral problems or cultural issues and see class as simply just one other "ism" along with racism, sexism, speciesism or ableism, then the crisis of capitalism will not be regarded as a strategic priority. And I think that deserves to be seen as such. Don't misunderstand me, Derek, I believe identity politics is very important, questions of inclusion are important, questions about making our curricula culturally responsive and appropriate are important, and examining culture as a site of contestation is also extremely important. I've written books about the importance of interculturality and have created many anti-racist and anti-sexist and anti-homophobic initiatives through my work. And I think that you and Curry address the relationship between race and class quite productively in your chapter on the Ferguson rebellion, which if I recall correctly was actually first published on *The Hampton Institute*.
I believe we should struggle for cognitive justice, and that we should be engaging in decolonizing pedagogies, and learning from epistemologies that have been developed over the centuries by indigenous groups, including those from America Latina. I am a big proponent of the concepts of "buen vivir" and "communalidad" (you can find these terms written into the constitutions of Venezuela, Bolivia and Ecuador)and recently spent time in Chiapas in communities supporting the Zapatistas. There is much to be

learned from these autonomous communities. But our struggles against racism, for example, can also be deepened by seeing the role that capitalism plays and has played since the cotton industry of the early Virginia plantations. I sometimes wonder in my less optimistic moments if the few Marxists, anarchists and revolutionary socialists that currently fleck the landscape of teacher education will be replaced in the years to come mostly by part-time contingent labor, functionaries who will only be able to survive on their grit and food stamps. But what I am seeing now is a resurgence of interest in Marx, at least among the youth, and they need to demand more critical scholarship in the universities. Otherwise they will be contributing to a longer and more resilient school-to-prison pipeline, to more integration of universities into the military industrial complex and to more control over education by corporate investors.

The young people need to start a new political party with a clear cut socialist agenda, a party that can make transnational alliances with left parties in Latin America and elsewhere, and chart out a new global future for humanity. The difficulty is that there are very few outlets for critically literate media to challenge the lies, deceptions and the commonsense ignorance of the corporate media. We need to win the war of position, which means, of course, that the left needs to create a viable alternative to austerity capitalism-a socialist alternative-that the majority of people can invest in both rationally and emotionally, something that can build and reinforce their protagonistic agency and will for change. In Venezuela, the state media outlets were overwhelmingly owned and controlled by the rich and favored the ideas of the ruling class, and still do. And still, the people prevailed and elected Hugo Chavez and his successor, Nicolas Maduro to power. In most countries the rich celebrate and the poor protest while in Venezuela the poor celebrate and the rich protest. Perhaps something like this can happen here. Let's hope the situation here does not have to get as desperate as it did in Venezuela, in order for that to happen.

Ford : I think that we are both in a sort of grounded agreement in respect to the revolutionary potential that is bubbling over across the U.S.

McLaren : Indeed, and this comes from our activism no doubt.

Ford : Peter, I promise that I will let you go now. I know that you are anxious to start writing your keynote speech for this year's International Conference on Critical Education in Poland for next week. And I also don't want to keep you from reading and responding to the first draft of my dissertation! But I do want to thank you again. Your willingness to collaborate and your readiness to engage in dialogue are really inspiring to young scholars and activists like me. I am looking forward to digging into your new book when it's out later this summer, and I am sure we will be seeing each other soon.

McLaren : We definitely will be. It's great to contribute to *The Hampton Institute*, so thanks for that opportunity. Solidarity!

The Neoliberal Banking Model of Education

Michael B. MacDonald

In Pedagogy of the Oppressed Paulo Freire described negative impacts on student imagination by a process he famously called the banking model of education. Critical Pedagogy has used the banking model as a point of critical departure. But I have recently become concerned that the banking concept no longer fully describes our current challenges. While Freire's original critical analysis still stands there is another layer of oppression requiring critique, the financialization of student life in neoliberalism. I see this form of oppression as having a different texture than the banking model, emerging from post-Fordist economic transformations and the rise of the financial sector. Post-Fordist finance is not the mode of banking Freire drew upon. His banking model was located at the local savings and loan where a community of people deposits money and expects interest before withdrawing. Contemporary banking has a new and more dangerous, in fact murderous, layer.

What's more, Freire's banking model drew upon a shared understanding of industrial capitalist production and its embedded forms of alienation. This alienation occurred in the capitalist mode of production in industrial capitalism where profit emerged from the exploitation of workers, and resistance was enacted through organized labor. Today, we seem to neither know where value is produced nor how to organize resistance. It feels to me that when I meet with activists, community organizers and critical scholars we have a difficult time figuring out where power and resistance are located in the post-Fordist period. Yet, examples of exploitation abound. We read daily about market turmoil, economic bubbles, growing personal debt, reduced government support, the reduction of the state, and the school to prison pipeline. While these issues may seem a long way from the banking model of education, I argue that they are not in fact separate, but are examples of a system of modern oppression, the *neoliberal banking model of education*.

We need to build upon and update Freire's critique. The neoliberal banking model of education builds upon Henry Giroux's extremely important work on public pedagogy that blurs any distinction between education and the marketplace and any distinction between labor/work, political power, media and language illustrated by Christian Marazzi and Franco Berrardi. These studies have shown that in neoliberalism there no longer a distinction between language production and value production, education and industry. Public pedagogy is the process of learning (power) that organizes all bodies (politics). Capitalist valorization is no longer just produced through the exploitation of working bodies at work, but also by exploitation through debt. Public pedagogy normalizes unchecked accumulation of lifestyle purchasing even if you don't have the money. As anyone who has ever watched Friends will note, the normalization of lifestyles supports the development of lifestyle expectations funded by a steady stream of credit, turned into ever-increasing debt. The neoliberal banking model of education, supported by the mechanisms of public pedagogy, prepares all bodies to acquire debt, to find citizenship through consumption, and to value debt. Debt is the factory floor of the contemporary production of value. Those who can accumulate and carry debt are the exploited bodies of financial factories that do not have locations; they are embedded in the mechanism of lifestyle consumption, student loans, car loans, and mortgage loans. Those who cannot accumulate and carry debt are marginalized, pushed into high-risk lifestyles that are leading rapidly to increasing numbers of incarceration bodies. Modern incarceration is the process by which bodies that could not previously hold debt are converted into a debt bearing commodities, where public money and the money of relatives is converted into prisoner debt.

I will warn you at the outset of this article, I have no happy ending. I do not provide any solutions, suggestions, nor words of comfort. Instead, I present a totalizing neoliberal banking model of education that shows little opportunity for escape. My intent is not to produce hopelessness, but to displace naive humanistic optimism in transcendental liberation with sober political analysis. Only through reinvigorated analysis can we hope to develop pedagogical and curricular strategies to break into the public pedagogy that supports and extends the neoliberal banking model of education.

Part One: Freire's Banking Concept of Education

Freire describes the damaging effects of the banking concept of education in a three part process: a) a teacher disseminates information to students; b) students memorize information; c) with the intent to later cash out the information for grades and advancement. The student is the bank and the teacher the source of intellectual capital. The banking concept does damage because it contributes to two forms of alienation. The first occurs when learning moves from the material experience of learning in and withcommunity-anthropological and evolutionary human learning-to the *virtual* learning of industrialized and professionalized education. Virtual learning's most common mode is the teacherly performance of talking in front of the class. In community

145

embedded learning, students learn from practice that leads to the (often informal) production of locational praxis, the production of knowledge emerging from the struggle to understand and predict (therefore theorizing) lived reality. In virtual learning students collect information by way of transcription to later be returned as data on an exam sheet. What has transpired is a circuit of exchange. In this circuit information is transferred from teacher to student and back. Learning is assessed by a calculation of the difference between data loaned out against what is returned on exam day. The rate of return is given a percentage evaluation called a grade. Students with a high rate of return warrant a high percentage later used to organize student bodies into hierarchies of intelligence. Low rates of return equal a failure of learning, understood as the personal failing of the student or teacher, but almost never as a failure of the banking concept.

The second form of alienation is "narration sickness" (Freire 2013, 71) caused when the semiotic connections between sign-signifier and signified are dissolved. The sign-signifier connection comprises the symbolic representation of the socially produced meaning that is supposed to point to the signified, the world. Narration sickness breaks the sign-signifier from the signified. It is like lecturing about democracy without creating an environment for students to self-organize. It is very possible to lecture and test about the mechanics of democracy without students ever learning to self-organize. In this model the lived experience of students is not a subject for analysis and this is made worse by the use of learning to discipline the collective bodies and minds of students. During the democracy lecture students are made to raise their hands to ask a question, are required to sit still in rows, and are provided no input on how the class is going to proceed, nor how the testing and evaluation are going to unfold. The power of narration sickness is related to Michel Foucault's biopower and biopolitics.

Alienation occurs when people are separated from their own labor. Marx locates this break in the purchasing of proletarian labor by the capitalist class. Freire contributes to the Marxist theorization of alienation by locating the beginning of the process in education. It seems to me that Freire is innovating on Marx's theory of alienation by introducing narration sickness as a mode of semiotic alienation, the divorce of sign-signifier from signified. Pedagogical alienation separates learning from lived experience, and submerges learning in the production of workers. In this way the banking concept shares with Althusser an interest in theorizing the reproduction of capitalist ideology, social formation, and modes of capitalist exploitation.

Freire ingeniously argued that alienation caused by narration sickness emerges from a learning environment colonized by a marketplace of signs. The semiotic triangle of sign-signifier-signified is replaced in the classroom with sign-sign-sign and students' tests are the recall of signs. The biopolitical power of education occurs in the break from the signified-community knowledge-that locates the authority of schools in the closed circulation and valuation of signs. The teacher distributes and collects signs in the name of learning. Students and teaching provide a material example of this in the oft-repeated distinction between school and the "real world". The *real* is not a philosophical game, an inaccessible unmediated *real*, a la Zizek, but is the fully constituted semiotic triangle that points to the material and conceptual aspects of human lives. To break the triangle is to reduce learning to the virtual and to participate in a flight from the social, cultural, environmental and economic crises occurring in our communities. Freire's banking concept helps explain why so many educational institutions seem to renounce the world. While there is still much to learn from Freire's conception of the banking model, in the years of its popularization much has changed. The soaring increase in both student debt and student panic, read as existential crisis, must be understood in respect to the financialization of student life, fear of an uncertain future, and overwhelming debt.

Part Two: The Neoliberal Banking Model

The *neoliberal* banking model of education begins in 1971 when Richard Nixon broke with The Bretton Woods System, a financial agreement put in place to ensure economic stability following 1944. Until this moment, the American dollars was connected to the nation's gold reserves. By disconnected the dollar monetary value entered into the world of socially produced linguistic value. In theory the neoliberal model "should favour strong individual private property rights, the rule of law, and the institution of freely functioning markets and free trade" (Harvey 2005, 64) but the "main substantive achievement of neoliberalization has been to redistribute, rather than to generate, wealth and income" (ibid., 159). Wealth began consolidating in the upper 10 percent of the population, with highest consolidation in the upper .1 and .01%. David Harvey calls the transfer of capital from the middle classes to the upper .1%, accumulation by dispossession. In *A Brief History of Neoliberalism* he explains that accumulation by dispossession has four main features: 1) privatization and commodification, 2) financialization, 3) the management and manipulation of crisis and 4) state redistributions (ibid., 160-165). Franco 'Bifo' Berardi has argued that neoliberalism has led to the elimination of "legal norms and social regulations" and has led to the transformation of "every domain of social life into an economic space (including health care, education, sexuality, affects, culture, etc.) where the only valid rule is that of supply and demand within an increasingly absolute privatization of services" (2009, 189). The current neoliberal banking model is characterized by: a) value determined by the exchange of fluctuating signs; b) production that is no longer only material production by wage labor but immaterial production (knowledge and creative capital) and; c) labor only as wage labor (and not community work for instance). As Franco Berardi has explained:

In the Fordist era, the fluctuations of prices, salaries, and profits were founded on the relation between the time of socially necessary labor and the determination of value. With the introduction of micro-electronic technologies, and the consequent intellectualization of productive labor, the relationships between existing units of measure and the different productive forces entered a regime of indeterminacy. (2009, 184)

Baudrillard described the transition from a banking model that "corresponded to a certain stage of the law of value" to a neoliberal banking model where the "whole system [is] swamped by indeterminacy, and every reality is absorbed by the hyperreality of the code and simulation" (1993, 2). Learning fully absorbed by the rules of capital means that each exchange between teacher and student is framed by economic rules. Students learn to evaluate the amount of intellectual labor they will expend based on the quantity of grade points that can be "earned". But it is incorrect to say earned here, because students are trading effort for grades at an expected rate of exchange. Intellectual labor is disconnected from the goals of humanist enlightenment (a la Kant and Foucault) and reduced to communicative wage labor. It is necessary to update Freire's banking concept with the neoliberal banking model so as to work through the micro and macro impacts brought about by post-Fordism and neoliberalism.

The neoliberal banking concept makes it necessary to engage in a political economy of learning, to analyze student apathy from the perspective of the alienation of the working class from their labour, in this case intellectual labor (mental/scholastic development) that has been drawn into economic exchange. Neoliberalism is the process that has led not only to macroeconomic transformations like deregulation and the domination of financial sector but to microeconomic transformation that have turned learning into a form of wage labor, an aspect of a new form of semiotic or language capitalism: *semiocapitalism*.

Semiocapitalism is a political economy of debt and privatization, where value is separated from concrete production and is located in the economic valorization of thoughts, communication, human organization, and symbols. It is the perfect companion to the virtual learning of the banking model, plunging symbols into financial markets in a way that makes it impossible to separate information and capital. The potential destructive force of semiocapitalism is difficult to articulate, not because we do not see its impacts but because we are in the early stages of articulating it theoretically. The neoliberal banking model is the confluence of the banking model *with* the public pedagogy of debt that justifies the financing of language exchange in the creation of newly emerging forms of economic oppression.

Part Three: Semiocapitalism, debt, prison and the reorganization of life

Semiocapitalism does not add another layer of oppression to institutionalized schooling but makes imperceptible alterations to social interactions and modes of thought. Students evaluate intellectual effort based on rates of exchange, with non-classroom time considered 'off the clock' negatively impacting both classroom participation and out of classroom discussions with fellow students. But it is not enough to stop here because most student investment is not conceptualized as an investment of effort, nor necessarily of intellectual energy, but of accruing debt.

In Canada, students owe over $15 billion in federal student debt, increasing at a rate of $1 million a day, with an additional 5 billion in provincial debt, and ever increasing credit card debt. Student debt increases are not magical and can be traced to the reduction of government support for higher education. In the 1970s governments looked after 90% of the costs but today it is down to 57%. As governments pay less, students pay more. This means that governments instead of socializing costs for the good of the entire community are privatizing debt. Christian Marazzi (2011, 2011b) has pointed out that governments are not seeing these costs as necessary infrastructure investments into the post-Fordist knowledge economy but are instead treating it as expense to be reduced from the public books. Youth are asked to shoulder investment into the state knowledge economy in a period of economic transformation. This is like asking workers to build the factory that will exploit their labor.

In this privatization of economic transformation working class youth are especially hard hit. Their debt burden is amplified by punishing interest rates and by asset inflation on houses, cars, and clothes that is leading to greater and greater debt contributing to increasing inequality. Economists complain about the economic risk of high debt lifestyle spending but at the same time know that 70% of the US GDP is made up of consumption. The economy is not located on the factory floor, but on our lifestyle spending. The knowledge economy creates the communication resources that produce economic value, while governments rush to reduce taxation and therefore education spending instead of seeing it as direct investment into an expanding lifestyle economy.

In Anya Kamenetz's 2006 book *Generation Debt*, she argued that debt is a "new model of subjugation" (Berardi 2009, 141). It is easy to understand why students invest in their education, higher education has for a long time been a trusted pathway to a better life. But there is something sinister here. The privatization of education investment, turned into student debt, becomes a commodity sold by government to banks for their profit. This is counter-intuitive. As governments decrease social support of learning, private business benefits through the packaging and sale of student debt to financial markets. Reduced investment into education becomes a way to create and support financial speculation that becomes the vehicle by which money is redistributed from the middle class to the upper .1% who have the capital to loan out in the first place.

The picture for youth in Alberta, Canada, where I live and work, is not rosy. First off, 50.4% of income in the province is earned by 10% of the population. If a student has been putting money in a bank account preparing for university interest rates have been so low (1%) that there is no chance of generating any wealth from savings.

151

Asset inflation is making home-owning less likely, causing Canadian household debt to reach record levels at 162.6% of disposable income , while "household debt increased to $124,838 in 2014, up 40 percent from the previous year, and the highest in the country." Food and fuel costs are increasing and Alberta's percentage of GDP spent on Education is currently at4.7% GDP, below the OECD average of 6.1%. In fact, Alberta's percentage of GDP to education is the lowest in the country (8.1% in Ontario). Alberta has the highest population growth at27.3% but only 17% university enrollment, the lowest higher education enrollment in the country. One of the reasons given for low university enrollment is the surplus of employment opportunities readily available in Alberta. And it is true that while youth unemployment nationally is at 13-14% in Alberta it is only 9-10%. But 10% youth unemployment is high when adult unemployment is only 5.2%. Comparing this to Germany where the adult unemployment rate is 4.7%, German youth unemployment is only 7.1%, much lower than Alberta's 10%. And there are worrying signs that the recent drop in oil prices may increase youth unemployment making it more difficult for university students to find summer work. It has been argued that "the stark difference in youth unemployment between the U.S. and many European countries may, in fact, have quite a lot to do with that high school-to-college transition, which Americans have traditionally viewed as leading to good jobs and financial security." It seems that students have learned that speculation on their university education is a model of success and perhaps this is part of the new neoliberal banking model of education. This new model not only degrades communication resources and the connection of learners with the material world but also degrades student's futures and contributes to precariousness "not a particular element of the social relations, but the dark core of the capitalist production in the sphere of the global network where a flow of fragmented recombinant info-labor continuously circulates" (Berardi 2009, 191). But this is to mistake what is actually occurring. The neoliberal banking model of education is not interested in youth success, but in the creation of debt across the entire society.

In higher education this translates into a dangerous ideology of investment through debt and economic individualism - a collective system of theft of the future and an erosion of traditional democratic forms of sociality expressed in citizenship, the public good, and the welfare state. The public good now finds expression in the creation of individual debt, not the socialization of debt. Youth are in debt to themselves for their education while provincial and federal governments sell off increasing debt loads to banks. What makes matters worse is that consumption is not real growth when it is powered by debt. Long-term growth is powered by education, quality of workers, the capacity of communities to build social bonds, cohesion, inclusivity, and innovation of social life not financial enterprise alone. The most worrying form of neoliberal banking model of education is enacted upon youth unable to carry debt. They are excluded from the social bonds of debt production and are entered into the school to prison pipeline, a vicious mode of neoliberal model of education.

Vulnerable youth are pushed into this pipeline by insufficient access to debt production. The reduction of school funding, caused by reductions of corporate taxes and reduced tax rates of the highest earners, creates a cascade of problems for under resourced schools. That these schools are located in poor neighborhoods is not an accident. Middle class and upper middle class families are able to carry the large mortgage debts and pay the companion property taxes that organize school funding. Children who come from families that cannot maintain large debts are converted into criminals. The ACLUargues that

Overly harsh disciplinary policies push students down the pipeline and into the juvenile justice system. Suspended and expelled children are often left unsupervised and without constructive activities; they also can easily fall behind in their coursework, leading to a greater likelihood of disengagement and drop-outs. All of these factors increase the likelihood of court involvement.

But this needs to be read as the entry point into an increasingly private prison system that produces debt, the new mode of profit production. While most money is made by corporations who profit off of incarcerating prisoners on behalf of states, prisons also produce debt by shifting the costs of maintaining prisoners from the state to families. Predatory companies like JPay specializing in family to inmate financial transfers that handle "7 million transactions in 2013, generating well over $50 million in revenue. It expects to transfer more than $1 billion this year" (Time Magazine). Incarceration produces debts that already poor families need to pay while making money for the owners and managers of prisons and the prison industrial complex.

Vice has reported that George Zoley, the CEO of GEO Group, the second-biggest [sic] investor in the incarceration industry made nearly $6 million last year through salary and bonuses alone, but the real money is in stocks-he owns more than 500,000 shares in GEO, and he has made $23 million in stock trades during one 18-month period. But you can't accuse him of not earning his pay, exactly. GEO saw a 56 percent spike in profits in the first quarter of 2013, and the company's executives reassured investors that the incarceration rate wouldn't be dropping any time soon when announcing its earnings. Zoley will be mega rich for years to come.

This is a start at sketching out the neoliberal banking model of education. The banking model of education unhitched the sign-signifier from the signified turning learning into a virtual exercise that produced narration sickness. The banking model produced a marketplace that was further transformed post-Fordist developments and neoliberal rationality. The neoliberal banking model began locating knowledge value in debt, and debt as the sole product of value. That students graduate into failing sectors with precarious jobs is no longer a problem for economic growth. The proletariat is reduced to precarious labor, becoming the precariate. With debt as the central location of value production, failure is success for financial elite. We need to theorize the mechanics that produce and normalize growing debt to explain how youth are being converted from humans to debt bearing bodies.

Works Cited

Baudrillard, Jean. (1993). *Symbolic Exchange and Death*. London, UK: Sage Publications.

Berardi, Franco. (2009). *The Soul at Work: From Alienation to Autonomy*. Los Angeles: Semiotext(e).

Freire, P. (2013). *Pedagogy of the Oppressed*. New York, NY: Bloomsbury.

Giroux, H. A. (1997). *Pedagogy and the politics of hope: Theory, culture, and schooling: A critical reader*. Boulder, CO: Westview Press.

Giroux, H. A. (2000). "Public pedagogy as cultural politics: Stuart Hall and the 'crisis' of culture".*Cultural Studies*, 14(2), 341-360.

Giroux, H. A. (2003). *The abandoned generation: Democracy beyond the culture of fear*. New York, NY: Palgrave Macmillan.

Giroux, H. A. (2004). "Public pedagogy and the politics of neo-liberalism: Making the political more pedagogical". *Policy Futures in Education*, 2(3-4), 494-503.

Giroux, H. A. (2009). *Youth in a suspect society: Democracy or disposability?*. New York, NY: Palgrave MacMillan.

Harvey, David. 2005. *A Brief History of Neoliberalism*. New York: Oxford University Press.

Marazzi, Christian. (2008) *Capital and Language: From the New Economy to the War Economy*. Los Angeles: Semiotext(e)

Marazzi, Christian. (2011a) *Capital and Affects: The Politics of the Language Economy*. Los Angeles: Semiotext(e)

Marazzi, Christian. (2011b) *The Violence of Financial Capitalism (New Edition)*. Los Angeles: Semiotext(e)

The Common Core of Being
A Conversation about the Philosophical Foundations of "Common Core" in Education

Tod Desmond and Boyce Brown

"I forgot, said I, that we were jesting, and I spoke with too great intensity...Nothing that is learned under compulsion stays with the mind...Do not, then, my friend, keep children to their studies by compulsion but by play. That will also better enable you to discern the natural capacities of each" (Plato 1994, 536c-537a).

"Do people know the two most popular forms of writing in the American high school today? It is personal writing. It is either the exposition of a personal opinion or it is the presentation of a personal narrative. The only problem, forgive me for saying this so bluntly... the only problem with those two forms of writing is that you grow up in this world and you realize people really don't give a shit about what you feel or what you think" (Coleman 2012).

The first quote is from Plato's *Republic*. The second is from David Coleman, widely regarded as the architect of Common Core. They exemplify opposite ends of the spectrum: how much coercion should exist in education? Plato explicitly says coercion should be minimal. Coleman implicitly says it should be maximal. When Coleman says that "people really don't give a shit about what you feel or what you think," one is instantly led to wonder which "people" he is referring to. Given Common Core's obsessive mantra of "college and career readiness" in an age of neoliberal authoritarianism, it is not unreasonable to infer that Coleman is suggesting that education should be used to bend students into conformity with an ideology of global economic competitiveness and a regime of transnational corporate socialism, in which the power of the nation-state is used to socialize the costs and privatize the benefits, a system in which corporations exercise the predominant influence on virtually every major institution of society in America. In this context, Coleman's demonization of personal writing makes sense, as personal writing is a crucial means of fashioning

A radical imagination that foregrounds the necessity for drastically altering the material and symbolic forces that hide behind a counterfeit claim to participatory democracy (Giroux 2014, para. 4).

Standards-based education is the most influential educational policy reform model of the last several decades. Common Core is its latest and most pervasive iteration. The overarching tendency of standards-based education is to establish a set of general performance guidelines that dictate the skills each student should have in each subject at each grade. Common Core nationalizes this impulse. At its peak it was adopted by 46 states. This trend was accelerated when states were incentivized to adopt it to gain points in their applications for federal Race to the Top education funding. Three of the 46 states that had previously adopted it have since dropped out. These are South Carolina, Indiana and Oklahoma. Louisiana is pursuing a lawsuit against it and several other states have or are considering legislative action to withdraw from it.

Criticism of the model stems from a variety of reasons, pedagogical, philosophical and political (right and left). The *statewide longitudinal data systems*program of the United States Department of Education, began in fiscal year 2005 and reauthorized with the American Recovery and Reinvestment Act *of 2009 couple "big data" to Common Core through* "grants to states to design, develop, and implement statewide P-20 longitudinal data systems to capture, analyze, and use student data from preschool to high school, college, and the workforce" (United States Department of Education 2009, para. 1). Although legally distinct initiatives, they must be considered as acting in tandem with one another for all practical purposes. Common Core must also be considered as a major shift in four centuries of American tradition in the local control over education, yet another extension of compulsory mass schooling.

In this context, there are several salient questions to be asked. Will Common Core and big data in education lead us to a dystopian nightmare of tracking and surveillance from cradle to grave? Or will it lead to the wise and equitable distribution of economic resources in support of individual learning and differentiated instruction? Perhaps both visions are true? Perhaps neither? At the classroom level, data can help teachers adjust teaching strategies to best reach the multiple intelligences and differing developmental stages of their pupils. At the school level, it helps an administrator or teacher see where their school fits in in comparison with others, to also help see where room for improvement lies. At the legislative and policy-making level, it helps tell where resources can be best allocated. Without question, big data has an important and valuable place in education. Nevertheless, numerous concerns must be raised as well. These concerns center largely around the facts that 1) there are so many data points being collected, 2) they are being held for such a long period (typically of P-20), and 3) this robust set of data on individuals is vulnerable to state or non-state actors assaulting it in cyberspace.

These are complicated questions to phrase and still more difficult to answer. Given these difficulties, we should develop a framework for the conversation about the philosophical basis behind Common Core first. This must be a conversation that is simultaneously as comprehensive and focused as possible (and solution-oriented) and also capable of providing the foundations for any educational policy regime that may seek to supplant it.

Considering the paralyzing effects of our nation's ideological divide, we cannot hope to engage one another in a conversation about these issues until we first agree upon definitions for the terms of debate. It must be clearly understood that all attempts to define abstractions such as "the good" in Plato's *Republic* and "college and career ready" in Common Core are rooted in cosmological assumptions. These assumptions must be articulated. To establish common definitions for basic terms related to public education, we must first agree upon a common cosmology within a well-defined historical context. With all this in mind, we suggest that a national dialogue on Common Core would be most productively convened in the context of Plato's *Republic* - the prototypical western treatise on education and politics - and James Dator's theory of four generic images of the future. These four images are:

(1) continuation; (2) collapse; (3) disciplined society; and (4) transformational society. The first - continuation - is essentially the official ideology espoused by much of the media, government, academia and other key agenda-setters. It posits that society and the economy can, should and will continue to operate indefinitely into the future just as they have in the past. The collapse scenario says "that continued economic growth is inherently destructive - whether from a social, cultural, environmental, or economic standpoint" - and that "collapse today, unlike in the past, may be global instead of simply local." The disciplined society sees a type of continuation, albeit one that focuses beyond a "static and passive notion of sustainability." Transformational society anticipates technological and/or spiritual breakthroughs from as yet largely unknown sources, which will significantly alter the present condition of society (Dator 2006, para. 9-11; cited in Brown 2013, 483).

Dator concludes that

From our years of work in futures studies we firmly believe that "futures of education" should never be undertaken until the alternative futures of the societies in which future graduates will live have been identified. Then, after a careful consideration and evaluation of the full array of alternatives has been made, plans, policies, and actions that will make educational institutions robust over all futures (rather than only one, mistakenly assumed to be "the most likely") should be undertaken (2014, 3).

Plato's *Republic* provides an appropriate lattice upon which the vines of this discussion can grow. It summarizes key aspects of the original curricula in the original Academy. It defines fundamental philosophical terms by framing them in a cosmology with many similarities to contemporary academic cosmology. It is an ur-text, the original normative future studies exercise in educational and political design in the western context.

References

Brown, B. (2013). *The assumptions and possible futures of standards-based education.* Policy Futures in Education 11: 481-489.

Coleman, D. (2014). *Bringing the Common Core to life.* Retrieved from http://www.youtube.com/watch?v=Pu6lin88YXU.

Dator, J. (2006). *Campus futures.* Planning for Higher Education 34: 45-48.

Dator, J. (2014). *Education fit for the futures.* UNESCO. Retrieved from http://www.unescobkk.org/education/apeid/news/news-details/article/education-fit-for-the-futures/.

Giroux, H. (2014). *Beyond Orwellian nightmares and neoliberal authoritarianism.* Truthdig. Retrieved from http://www.truthdig.com/report/item/beyond_orwellian_nightmares_and_neoliberal_authoritarianism_20141018.

Plato. (1994). *The collected dialogues of Plato, including the letters.* New Jersey: Princeton University Press.

United States Department of Education. (2009). *Statewide P-20 longitudinal data systems. Author: Washington, DC.* Retrieved from http://www2.ed.gov/programs/slds/factsheet.pdf.

Geopolitics

The West Marches East, Part One

The U.S.-NATO Strategy to Isolate Russia

Andrew Gavin Marshall

In early March of 2014, following Russia's invasion of Crimea in Ukraine, the *New York Times* editorial board declared that Russian President Vladimir Putin had "stepped far outside the bounds of civilized behavior," suggesting that Russia should be isolated politically and economically in the face of "continued aggression." John Kerry, the U.S. Secretary of State, lashed out at Russia's "incredible act of aggression," stating that: "You just don't in the 21st century behave in 19th century fashion by invading another country on [a] completely trumped up pre-text." Indeed, invading foreign nations on "trumped up pre-texts" is something only the United States and its allies are allowed to do, *not Russia*! What audacity!

Even Canada's Prime Minister, Stephen Harper, proclaimed Russia's actions in Ukraine to be "aggressive, militaristic and imperialistic ," threatening "the peace and stability of the world." This is, of course, despite the fact that Russia's invasion and occupation of Crimea took place without a single shot fired, and "faced no real opposition and has been greeted with joy by many citizens in the only region of Ukraine with a clear majority of ethnic Russians."

Indeed, Russia can only be said to be an "aggressive" and "imperial"   power so long as one accepts the unrelenting hypocrisy of U.S. and Western leaders. After all, it was not Russia that invaded and occupied Afghanistan and Iraq, killing millions. It is not Putin, but rather Barack Obama, who has waged a "global terror campaign," compiling "kill lists" and using flying killer robots to bomb countries like Afghanistan, Pakistan, Iraq, Yemen, Libya, Somalia, and even the Philippines, killing thousands of people around the world. It is not Putin, but rather, Barack Obama, who has been sending highly-trained killers into over 100 countries around the world at any given time, waging a "secret war" in most of the world's nations. It was not Russia, but rather the United States, that has supported the creation of "death squads" in Iraq, contributing to the mass violence, civil war and genocide that resulted; or that has been destabilizing Pakistan, a nuclear-armed nation, increasing the possibility of nuclear war.

All of these actions are considered to be a part of America's strategy to secure 'stability,' to promote 'peace' and 'democracy.' It's Russia that threatens "the peace and stability of the world," not America or its NATO and Western allies. That is, of course, if you believe the verbal excretions from Western political leaders. The reality is that the West, with the United States as the uncontested global superpower, engages the rest of the world on the basis of 'Mafia Principles' of international relations: the United States is the global 'Godfather' of the Mafia crime family of Western industrial nations (the NATO powers). Countries like Russia and China are reasonably-sized crime families in their own right, but largely dependent upon the Godfather, with whom they both cooperate and compete for influence.

When the Mafia - and the Godfather - are disobeyed, whether by small nations (such as Iraq, Syria, Libya, et. al.), or by larger gangster states like China or Russia, the Godfather will seek to punish them. Disobedience cannot be tolerated. If a small country can defy the Godfather, then any country can. If a larger gangster state like Russia can defy the Godfather and get away with it, they might continue to challenge the authority of the Godfather.

For the U.S. and its NATO-capo Mafia allies, Ukraine and Russia have presented a complex challenge: how does one punish Russia and control Ukraine without pushing Russia too far outside the influence of the Mafia, itself? In other words, the West seeks to punish Russia for its "defiance" and "aggression," but, if the West pushes too hard, it might find a Russia that pushes back even harder. That is, after all, how we got into this situation in the first place.

A little historical context helps elucidate the current clash of gangster states. Put aside the rhetoric of "democracy" and let's deal with *reality*.

The Cold War Legacy

The end of the Cold War and the collapse of the Soviet Union between 1989 and 1991 witnessed the emergence of what was termed by President George H.W. Bush a 'new world order' in which the United States reigned as the world's sole superpower, proclaiming 'victory' over the Soviet Union and 'Communism': the age of 'free markets' and 'democracy' was at hand.

The fall of the Berlin Wall in 1989 prompted the negotiated withdrawal of the Soviet Union from Eastern Europe. The 'old order' of Europe was at an end, and a new one "needed to be established quickly," noted Mary Elise Sarotte in the *New York Times*. This 'new order' was to begin with "the rapid reunification of Germany." Negotiations took place in 1990 between Soviet president Gorbachev, German Chancellor Helmut Kohl, and President Bush's Secretary of State, James A. Baker 3rd. The negotiations sought to have the Soviets remove their 380,000 troops from East Germany. In return, both James Baker and Helmut Kohl promised Gorbachev that the Western military alliance of NATO would not expand eastwards. West Germany's foreign minister, Hans-Dietrich Genscher, promised Gorbachev that, " NATO will not expand itself to the East." Gorbachev agreed, though asked - and did not receive - the promise in writing, remaining a "gentlemen's agreement."

The U.S. Ambassador to the USSR from 1987 to 1991, John F. Matlock Jr., later noted that the end of the Cold War was not 'won' by the West, but was brought about "by negotiation to the advantage of both sides." Yet, he noted, "the United States insisted on treating Russia as the loser ." The United States almost immediately violated the agreement established in 1990, and NATO began moving eastwards, much to the dismay of the Russians. The new Russian President, Boris Yeltsin, warned that NATO's expansion to the East threatened a 'cold peace' and was a violation of the " spirit of conversations " that took place in February of 1990 between Soviet, West German and American leaders.

In 1990, President Bush's *National Security Strategy for the United States* acknowledged that, "even as East-West tensions diminish, American strategic concerns remain," noting that previous U.S. military interventions which were justified as a response to Soviet 'threats', were - in actuality - "in response to threats to U.S. interests that could not be laid at the Kremlin's door," and that, "the necessity to defend our interests will continue." In other words, decades of justifications for war by the United States - blaming 'Soviet imperialism' and 'Communism' - were lies, and now that the Soviet Union no longer existed as a threat, American imperialism will still have to continue.

Former National Security Adviser - and arch-imperial strategist - Zbigniew Brzezinski noted in 1992 that the Cold War strategy of the United States in advocating "liberation" against the USSR and Communism (thus justifying military interventions all over the world), " was a strategic sham, designed to a significant degree for domestic political reasons... the policy was basically rhetorical, at most tactical."

The Pentagon drafted a strategy in 1992 for the United States to manage the post-Cold War world, where the primary mission of the U.S. was "to ensure that no rival superpower is allowed to emerge in Western Europe, Asia or the territories of the former Soviet Union." As the *New York Times* noted, the document - largely drafted by Pentagon officials Paul Wolfowitz and Dick Cheney - "makes the case for a world dominated by one superpower whose position can be perpetuated by constructive behavior and sufficient military might to deter any nation or group of nations from challenging American primacy."

This strategy was further enshrined with the Clinton administration, whose National Security Adviser, Anthony Lake, articulated the 'Clinton doctrine' in 1993 when he stated that: "The successor to a doctrine of containment must be a strategy of enlargement - enlargement of the world's free community of market democracies," which "must combine our broad goals of fostering democracy and markets with our more traditional geostrategic interests."

Under Bill Clinton's imperial presidency, the United States and NATO went to war against Serbia, ultimately tore Yugoslavia to pieces (itself representative of a 'third way' of organizing society, different than both the West and the USSR), and NATO commenced its Eastward expansion . In the late 1990s, Poland, Hungary and the Czech Republic entered the NATO alliance, and in 2004, seven former Soviet republics joined the alliance.

In 1991, roughly 80% of Russians had a 'favorable' view of the United States; by 1999, roughly 80% had an unfavorable view of America. Vladimir Putin, who was elected in 2000, initially followed a pro-Western strategy for Russia, supporting NATO's invasion and occupation of Afghanistan, receiving only praise from President George W. Bush, who then proceeded to expand NATO further east .

The Color Revolutions

Throughout the 2000s, the United States and other NATO powers, allied with billionaires like George Soros and his foundations scattered throughout the world, worked together to fund and organize opposition groups in multiple countries across Eastern and Central Europe, promoting 'democratic regime change' which would ultimately bring to power more pro-Western leaders. It began in 2000 in Serbia with the removal of Slobodan Milosevic. The United States had undertaken a $41 million "democracy-building campaign" in Serbia to remove Milosevic from power, which included funding polls, training thousands of opposition activists, which the *Washington Post* referred to as "the first poll-driven, focus group-tested revolution," which was "a carefully researched strategy put together by Serbian democracy activists with the active assistance of Western advisers and pollsters." Utilizing U.S.-government funded organizations aligned with major political parties, like the National Democratic Institute and the International Republican Institute, the U.S. State Department and the U.S. Agency for International Development (USAID) channeled money, assistance and training to activists (Michael Dobbs, Washington Post, 11 December 2000).

Mark Almond wrote in the *Guardian* in 2004 that, "throughout the 1980s, in the build-up to 1989's velvet revolutions, a small army of volunteers - and, let's be frank, spies - co-operated to promote what became People Power." This was represented by "a network of interlocking foundations and charities [which] mushroomed to organize the logistics of transferring millions of dollars to dissidents." The money itself "came overwhelmingly from NATO states and covert allies such as 'neutral' Sweden," as well as through the billionaire George Soros' Open Society Foundation. Almond noted that these "modern market revolutionaries" would bring people into office "with the power to privatize." Activists and populations are mobilized with "a multimedia vision of Euro-

Atlantic prosperity by Western-funded 'independent' media to get them on the streets." After successful Western-backed 'revolutions' comes the usual economic 'shock therapy' which brings with it "mass unemployment, rampant insider dealing, growth of organized crime, prostitution and soaring death rates."
Ah, *democracy*!

Following Serbia in 2000, the activists, Western 'aid agencies', foundations and funders moved their resources to the former Soviet republic of Georgia, where in 2003, the 'Rose Revolution' replaced the president with a more pro-Western (and Western-educated) leader, Mikheil Saakashvili, a protégé of George Soros, who played a significant role in funding so-called 'pro-democracy' groups in Georgia that the country has often been referred to as 'Sorosistan'. In 2004, Ukraine became the next target of Western-backed 'democratic' regime change in what became known as the 'Orange Revolution'. Russia viewed these 'color revolutions' as "U.S.-sponsored plots using local dupes to overthrow governments unfriendly to Washington and install American vassals."

Mark MacKinnon, who was the *Globe and Mail*'s Moscow bureau chief between 2002 and 2005, covered these Western-funded protests and has since written extensively on the subject of the 'color revolutions.' Reviewing a book of his on the subject, the *Montreal Gazette* noted that these so-called revolutions were not "spontaneous popular uprisings, but in fact were planned and financed either directly by American diplomats or through a collection of NGOs acting as fronts for the United States government," and that while there was a great deal of dissatisfaction with the ruling, corrupt elites in each country, the 'democratic opposition' within these countries received their "marching orders and cash from American and European officials, whose intentions often had to do more with securing access to energy resources and pipeline routes than genuine interest in democracy."

The 'Orange Revolution' in Ukraine in 2004 was - as Ian Traynor wrote in the *Guardian* - " an American creation, a sophisticated and brilliantly conceived exercise in western branding and mass marketing," with funding and organizing from the U.S. government, "deploying US consultancies, pollsters, diplomats, the two big American parties and US non-governmental organizations."

In Ukraine, the contested elections which spurred the 'Orange Revolution' saw accusations of election fraud leveled against Viktor Yanukovich by his main opponent, Viktor Yuschenko. Despite claims of upholding democracy, Yuschenko had ties to the previous regime, having served as Prime Minister in the government of Leonid Kuchma, and with that, had close ties to the oligarchs who led and profited from the mass privatizations of the post-Soviet era. Yuschenko, however, "got the western nod, and floods of money poured into groups which support[ed] him." As Jonathan Steele noted in the *Guardian*, "Ukraine has been turned into a geostrategic matter not by Moscow but by the US, which refuses to abandon its cold war policy of encircling Russia and seeking to pull every former Soviet republic to its side."

As Mark McKinnon wrote in the *Globe and Mail* some years later, the uprisings in both Georgia and Ukraine "had many things in common, among them the fall of autocrats who ran semi-independent governments that deferred to Moscow when the chips were down," as well as being "spurred by organizations that received funding from the U.S. National Endowment for Democracy," reflecting a view held by Western governments that "promoting democracy" in places like the Middle East and Eastern Europe was in fact "a code word for supporting pro-Western politicians ." These Western-sponsored uprisings erupted alongside the ever-expanding march of NATO to Russia's borders.

The following year - in 2005 - the Western-supported 'colour revolutions' hit the Central Asian republic of Kyrgyzstan in what was known as the 'Tulip Revolution'. Once again, contested elections saw the mobilization of Western-backed civil society groups, "independent" media, and NGOs - drawing in the usual funding sources of the National Endowment for Democracy, the NDI, IRI, Freedom House, and George Soros, among others. The *New York Times* reported that the "democratically inspired revolution" western governments were praising began to look " more like a garden-variety coup ." Efforts not only by the U.S., but also Britain, Norway and the Netherlands were pivotal in preparing the way for the 2005 uprising in Kyrgyzstan. The then-President of Kyrgyzstan blamed the West for the unrest experienced in his country.

The U.S. NGOs that sponsored the 'color revolutions' were run by former top government and national security officials, including Freedom House, which was chaired by former CIA Director James Woolsey, and other "pro-democracy" groups funding these revolts were led by figures such as Senator John McCain or Bill Clinton's former National Security Adviser Anthony Lake, who had articulated the national security strategy of the Clinton administration as being one of "enlargement of the world's free community of market democracies." These organizations effectively act as an extension of the U.S. government apparatus, advancing U.S. imperial interests under the veneer of "pro-democracy" work and institutionalized in purportedly "non"-governmental groups.

By 2010, however, most of the gains of the 'color revolutions' that spread across Eastern Europe and Central Asia had taken several steps back. While the "political center of gravity was tilting towards the West," noted *Time Magazine* in April of 2010, "now that tend has reversed," with the pro-Western leadership of both Ukraine and Kyrgyzstan both having once again been replaced with leaders " far friendlier to Russia." The "good guys" that the West supported in these countries, "proved to be as power hungry and greedy as their predecessors, disregarding democratic principles... in order to cling to power, and exploiting American diplomatic and economic support as part of [an] effort to contain domestic and outside threats and win financial assistance." Typical behavior for vassal states to any empire.

The 'Enlargement' of the European Union: An Empire of Economics

The process of European integration and growth of the European Union has - over the past three decades - been largely driven by powerful European corporate and financial interests, notably by the European Round Table of Industrialists (ERT), an influential group of roughly 50 of Europe's top CEOs who lobby and work directly with Europe's political elites to design the goals and methods of European integration and enlargement of the EU, advancing the EU to promote and institutionalize neoliberal economic reforms: austerity, privatizations, liberalization of markets and the destruction of labour power.

The enlargement of the European Union into Eastern Europe reflected a process of Eastern European nations having to implement neoliberal reforms in order to join the EU, including mass privatizations, deregulation, liberalization of markets and harsh austerity measures. The enlargement of the EU into Central and Eastern Europe advanced in 2004 and 2007, when new states were admitted into EU membership, including Bulgaria, Romania, Poland, the Czech Republic, Hungary, Slovakia, Latvia, Estonia and Lithuania.

These new EU members were hit hard by the global financial crisis in 2008 and 2009, and subsequently forced to impose harsh austerity measures. They have been slower to 'recover' than other nations, increasingly having to deal with "political instability and mass unemployment and human suffering." The exception to this is Poland, which did not implement austerity measures, which has left the Polish economy in a better position than the rest of the new EU members. The financial publication *Forbes* warned in 2013 that "the prospect of endless economic stagnation in the newest EU members... will, sooner or later, bring extremely deleterious political consequences ."

In the words of a senior British diplomat, Robert Cooper, the European Union represents a type of "cooperative empire." The expansion of the EU into Central and Eastern Europe brought increased corporate profits, with new investments and cheap labour to exploit. Further, the newer EU members were more explicitly pro-market than the older EU members that continued to promote a different social market economy than those promoted by the Americans and British. With these states joining the EU, noted the *Financial Times* in 2008, "the new member states have reinforced the ranks of the free marketeers and free traders," as they increasingly "team up with northern states to vote for deregulation and liberalization of the market."

The West Marches East

For the past quarter-century, Russia has stood and watched as the United States, NATO, and the European Union have advanced their borders and sphere of influence eastwards to Russia's borders. As the West has marched East, Russia has consistently complained of encroachment and its views of this process as being a direct threat to Russia. The protests of the former superpower have largely gone ignored or dismissed. After all, in the view of the Americans, they "won" the Cold War, and therefore, Russia has no say in the post- Cold War global order being shaped by the West.

The West's continued march East to Russia's borders will continue to be examined in future parts of this series. For Russia, the problem is clear: the Godfather and its NATO-Mafia partners are ever-expanding to its borders, viewed (rightly so) as a threat to the Russian gangster state itself. Russia's invasion of Crimea - much like its 2008 invasion of Georgia - are the first examples of Russia's push back against the Western imperial expansion Eastwards. This, then, is not a case of "Russian aggression," but rather, Russian *reaction* to the West's ever-expanding imperialism and global aggression.

The West may think that it has domesticated and beaten down the bear, chained it up, make it dance and whip it into obedience. But every once in a while, the bear will take a swipe back at the one holding the whip. This is inevitable. And so long as the West continued with its current strategy, the reactions will only get worse in time.

The West Marches East, Part Two
Georgia Starts a War, Russia Draws a Line

Andrew Gavin Marshall

In Part 1 of this series - 'The West Marches East' - I examined the circumstance that while Russia has received the majority of the blame for the more than six-month-crisis in Ukraine, these events did not take place in a vacuum, and, in fact, the Western powers and institutions - notably the United States, NATO and the European Union - have broke promises made at the end of the Cold War to expand NATO - a Western military alliance that was created *in opposition* to the Soviet Union - to Russia's borders. Simultaneously, the European Union has expanded eastwards, bringing Eastern and Central European countries within its orbit and in adherence to its economic orthodoxy. Further, many NATO powers had worked together to promote 'colour revolutions' across much of Eastern Europe over the previous decade or so, helping to overthrow pro-Russian leaders and replace them with pro-Western leaders.

After nearly a quarter-century of Western expansion - militarily, politically, economically - to Russia's borders, Russia has had enough. But Ukraine was not the first instance in which Russia has been provoked by the West into a response that the West subsequently declared as an act of imperial "aggression." In 2008, the small Caucasus nation and former Soviet republic of Georgia started a war with Russia, leading to Russia's invasion of the tiny country, effectively ending nearly two decades of NATO and Western expansion. This report examines the 2008 war in Georgia and the roles played by Russia and the NATO powers.

Setting the Stage

As documented in part 1, Georgia was - in 2003 - subjected to a NATO sponsored 'Colour Revolution' which removed the previous leader and replaced him with a pro-Western (and Western-educated) politician, Mikeil Saakashvili. In December of 2003, Georgian defense officials met with the U.S. Secretary of Defense Donald Rumsfeld to discuss enhancing military cooperation between the two countries. The US had sent roughly 60 military trainers to Georgia in 2002, but the Georgians had been lobbying for a US military base in their country.

Instead, the Pentagon decided to " privatize its military presence in Georgia" through a security contractor, Cubic, which signed a three-year $15 million contract with the Pentagon to support the Georgian ministry of defense. The team from Cubic would engage in training and equipping the Georgian military, as well as protection for the oil pipeline that was to take oil from Baku, Azerbaijan, to Turkey through Georgia. Western diplomats suggested that the country could become a "forward operations area" for the US military, "similar to support structures in the Gulf." In return for the program, Georgia agreed to send 500 soldiers to Iraq.

As the *BBC* reported in 2006, Georgia was discarding its ties with Moscow and instead, leading "westwards - towards NATO, and perhaps eventually the European Union." US military instructors were in the country "to drive that change," training Georgian soldiers to manage checkpoints in US-occupied Iraq. Georgia was largely uneasy with Russia due to the fact that Moscow provided - since the early 1990s - moral and material support to the country's two breakaway regions of South Ossetia and Abkhazia. A Georgian corporal deployed in Iraq was quoted in the *New York Times* in 2007 saying, "As soldiers here [in Iraq], we help the American soldiers... Then America as a country will help our country." This reflected the implicit thinking within Georgia up until the 2008 war. In early April of 2008, U.S. President George W. Bush said he "strongly supported" Ukraine and Georgia's bids to join NATO, despite the enormous objections from Russia, which would then see NATO powers located directly on its borders. Bush made the comments following a NATO meeting, where France, Germany, Italy, Hungary, Belgium, the Netherlands and Luxembourg all opposed the U.S. position of fast-tracking Georgian and Ukrainian membership into NATO, seeing it as " an unnecessary offense to Russia." Shortly after Bush made his announcement, a former Russian armed forces chief of staff said that Russia would " take military and other steps along its borders if ex-Soviet Ukraine and Georgia join NATO," claiming that "such a move would pose a direct threat to its security and endanger the fragile balance of forces in Europe."

Within Georgia and its separatist regions, which were home to Russian soldiers, tensions were increasingly flaring over the summer months of 2008. With both sides undertaking provocative measures, there was a growing awareness that war could break out. In July of 2008, following her visit to the Czech Republic where she signed an agreement to base part of a new U.S. missile defense system in the country, U.S. Secretary of State Condoleezza Rice traveled to Georgia to meet with the country's leadership. At that time, U.S. military forces in the region had begun joint exercises with soldiers from Georgia, Armenia, Ukraine and Azerbaijan. The exercises were taking place less than 100km from Russia's border, with roughly 1,000 U.S. soldiers and an equal number of Georgian troops. As Rice arrived in Georgia, the Russian foreign ministry issued a statement accusing Georgia "of pushing the region towards war through actions openly supported by the United States." Then-Russian President Dmitri Medvedev later explained that as tensions escalated into July of 2008, he was in contact with his Georgian counterparts. However, following Secretary Rice's July 2008 visit to Georgia, he claimed, "my Georgian colleague simply dropped all communication with us. He simply stopped talking to us, he stopped writing letters and making phone calls. It was apparent that he had new plans now. And those plans were implemented later."

Indeed, as the *New York Times* noted, when Rice went to Georgia, she had two different goals, one private, and one public. Privately, she reportedly told the Georgians "not to get into a military conflict with Russia that Georgia could not win." However, in public, standing alongside the Georgian president, Rice spoke defiantly against Russia and in support of Georgia and its "territorial integrity" in the regions of South Ossetia and Abkhazia. Standing next to the president, Rice declared that Russia "needs to be a part of resolving the problem... and not contributing to it." The *NYT* claimed that these public statements of support for Georgia - and antagonism toward Russia - not to mention the fact that the US was engaging in large-scale military exercises with Georgians, expanding military installations all across Eastern Europe and providing Georgia with military advisers, had the combined effect of sending the small country "mixed messages " about U.S. support for a war with Russia.

No doubt contributing to these 'mixed messages' was when - at the very same news conference with President Saakashvili - Rice was asked a question about a potential conflict with Iran, to which she replied that, "We will defend our interests and defend our allies... We take very, very strongly our obligations to defend our allies and no one should be confused of that." Apparently, Georgia was a little confused.

When the Soviet Union collapsed and Georgia declared independence, the two regions of South Ossetia and Abkhazia gained de facto independence in the early 1990s following conflict between the breakaway regions and the central state. Following this brief period of fighting, tensions were largely reduced, though Russian 'peacekeepers' were on the ground monitoring the fragile balance. That balance was upset when Saakashvili became president in 2004, making one of his pledges "national unification." By 2008, when tensions were reaching a breaking point, there were over 2,000 American civilians in Georgia, according to the Pentagon, with over 130 U.S. military trainers and 30 Defense Department civilians.

Another facet to the increased tensions was the fact that Georgia was an important conduit for a major pipeline, bringing oil from Baku in Azerbaijan through Georgia and to the Turkish port of Ceyhan on the Mediterranean. When the pipeline was completed in 2006, it was the second-longest pipeline in the world, and its construction and use was specifically designed to "bypass Russia, denying Moscow leverage over a key resource and a potential source of pressure." As Jonathan Steele wrote in the *Guardian*, the resulting war was about more than pipeline politics, however, as it represented "an attempt, sponsored largely by the United States but eagerly subscribed to by several of its new ex-Soviet allies, to reduce every aspect of Russian influence throughout the region, whether it be economic, political, diplomatic or military."

The *Wall Street Journal* reported that the Baku-Tbilisi-Ceyhan pipeline was built by a consortium of major Western energy corporations, and was "the first pipeline on former Soviet territory that bypasse[d] Russia," which "was strongly backed by the US as a way of loosening Moscow's grip on the Caspian's oil wealth."

When War Broke Out

On August 7, 2008, war broke out. Georgia claimed that it was responding to an attack on the country by separatists in South

Ossetia and Russian aggressors. However, independent military observers from the Organization for Security and Cooperation in Europe (OSCE) who were deployed in the region refuted the Georgian government's claim, and instead reported that, "Georgia's inexperienced military attacked the isolated separatist [South Ossetian] capital of Tskhinvali on Aug. 7 with indiscriminate artillery and rocket fire, exposing civilians, Russian peacekeepers and unarmed monitors to harm." While Georgian President Saakashvili presented the Georgian military actions as "defensive," in response to separatist and Russian shelling of Georgian villages, the OSCE monitors were unable to confirm that such villages had been attacked, with no shelling heard in the villages prior to the Georgian bombardment of Tskhinvali. Two senior Western military officials who were stationed in Georgia, working with the Georgian military, told the*New York Times* that, "whatever Russia's behaviour or intentions for the enclave, once Georgia's artillery or rockets struck Russian positions, conflict with Russia was all but inevitable."

A year after the war, an EU-commissioned report which took nine months to compile concluded that despite much of the blame at the time of - and since - the war being directed at 'Russian aggression,' the conflict began "with a massive Georgian artillery attack." The "damning indictment" of Georgia, however, blamed both Georgia and Russia for committing war crimes during the conflict, and noted that the conflict resulted from months and years of growing conflict. However, the report flatly stated: "There was no ongoing armed attack by Russia before the start of the Georgian operation... Georgian claims of a large-scale presence of Russian armed forces in South Ossetia prior to the Georgian offensive could not be substantiated... It could also not be verified that Russia was on the verge of such a major attack." However, Vladimir Putin stated in 2012 that Russia had drawn up plans to counter a Georgian attack as far back as 2006 and 2007, when he was president. Still, while the Russians were clearly aware - and preparing - for a war, it was ultimately Georgia that fired the first shots.

Months before the war broke out, according to documents and interviews obtained by the *Financial Times*, senior U.S. military officials and U.S. military contractors were inside Georgia training special forces commandos. The two contractors, MPRI and American Systems, both of which are based in Virginia, were responsible for training the Georgian special forces as part of a program run by the Pentagon. The Pentagon had previously hired MPRI to train the Croatian military in 1995, just prior to the Croatian military's invasion of the ethnically-Serbian region of Krajina, "which led to the displacement of 200,000 refugees and was one of the worst incidents of ethnic cleansing in the Balkan wars." MPRI, of course - in both cases - denied "any wrongdoing." The first phase of the training in Georgia took place between January and April of 2008, and the second phase was due to begin on August 11, with the trainers arriving in Georgia on August 3, four days before the war broke out.

Just prior to the outbreak of war, as U.S. diplomatic cables showed, the U.S. Embassy in Georgia knew and reported about the fact that Georgian forces were concentrating their forces near South Ossetia, "either as part of a show of force or readiness, or both." The U.S. ambassador reportedly told Georgian officials "to remain calm, not overreact, and to de-escalate the situation." As the diplomatic cables from Georgia revealed, unlike in neighboring countries, U.S. diplomats in Georgia "relied heavily on the Saakashvili government's accounts of its own behavior" and embraced the "Georgian versions of important and disputed events." Whereas in other regional countries, U.S. diplomats would report to Washington on their "private misgivings" about their host countries' claims, in Georgia, the Saakashvili government's "versions of events were passed to Washington largely unchallenged."

The five-day war between Russia and Georgia lasted from August 7 - 12, leading to a decisive Russian victory and a humiliating defeat for the US-puppet regime in Georgia. Months of 'mixed messages' and indecision and divisions within the Bush administration directly led to the conflict, inflaming internal confrontations within the Bush administration itself. A *New York Times* article tells this brief story based upon interviews with diplomats and senior officials in the US, EU, Russia and Georgia. Five months before Georgia started the war - in March of 2008 - President Saakashvili had gone to Washington to lobby for NATO membership at Congress, the State Department and the Pentagon. Bush promised the Georgian president " to push hard for Georgia's acceptance into NATO."

In early April, President Bush flew to the Russian resort city of Sochi where he met with President Putin. Putin delivered Bush a message: "the push to offer Ukraine and Georgia NATO membership was crossing Russia's 'red lines'." The United States, however, clearly underestimated Russia and Putin's determination to adhere to those 'red lines'. Meanwhile, Vice President Dick Cheney saw Georgia as a "model" for the administration's "democracy promotion campaign," and continued to push for selling Georgia more arms and military equipment "so that it could defend itself against possible Russian aggression." Opposing Cheney were Secretary of State Rice, National Security Adviser Stephen J. Hadley and Undersecretary of State for Political Affairs William J. Burns, who were arguing that " such a sale would provoke Russia, which would see it as arrogant meddling in its turf."

While the official line of the Bush administration after the war broke out was to blame Russia, quietly and internally, top U.S. officials noted that Georgia was largely to blame, and that U.S. officials had contributed to that process by sending confused messages. Indeed, as some administration officials reported, the Georgian military had created a "concept of operations" plan for a military operation in South Ossetia which "called for its army units to sweep across the region and rapidly establish such firm control that a Russian response could be pre-empted." As early as January of 2008, Georgia's Ministry of Defense laid out plans in a "strategic defense review" which "set out goals for the Georgian armed forces and refers specifically to the threat of conflict in the separatist regions." U.S. officials had reportedly warned the Georgians that, " the plan had little chance of success."

Indeed, as the war was under way, debates were raging within the Bush administration regarding the possible US response. In particular, tensions started to erupt between Bush and Cheney, as Cheney's office felt that when Bush had previously met Putin in April, his silent response to Putin's warning "inadvertently gave Russia the all-clear to attack." There was discussion within the administration (from Cheney's side of the debate) of launching air strikes to halt the Russian invasion. After four days of talks with the National Security Council (NSC), George Bush "cut off the discussion," siding with his somewhat more rational advisers, as there was "a clear sense around the table that any military steps could lead to a confrontation with Moscow."

Putin had also spoken with Georgian president Saakashvili in February of 2008, where he warned the Georgian president: "You think you can trust the Americans, and they will rush to assist you?" Putin then reportedly claimed that, " Nobody can be trusted! Except me." Interestingly, in this respect, Putin happened to be correct.

European governments were not big fans of Saakashvili, either, seeing him as "an American-backed hothead who spelled trouble." During the five-day war, French President Nicolas Sarkozy shuttled between Russia and Georgia attempting to negotiate a ceasefire. Sarkozy reportedly told the Georgians: "Where is Bush? Where are the Americans?... They are not coming to save you. No Europeans are coming, either. You are alone. If you don't sign [the ceasefire], the Russian tanks will be here soon."

The day after the war began, the Russians called an emergency session at the United Nations to find a resolution to the conflict. The Russian's proposed a short, three-paragraph draft resolution calling on all parties to "renounce the use of force." This phrase ran into opposition from the United States, France and Britain, who claimed the phrase was "unbalanced" because it "would have undermined Georgia's ability to defend itself." The US, British and French opposition to "renounce the use of force" led to a collapse of diplomatic attempts at the UN to end the fighting, according to the *New York Times*. When the French President eventually negotiated a ceasefire on August 12, at least one senior U.S. official (presumably Cheney) was reportedly "appalled" by the ceasefire text.

Erosi Kitsmarishvili, a former Georgian diplomat and ambassador to Moscow (and confidante of President Saakashvili) caused controversy within Georgia when he testified at a parliamentary hearing in Georgia in November of 2008 that Georgian officials were responsible for starting the war. He said that he was told by Georgian officials in April of 2008 that they had "planned to start a war in Abkhazia," saying that they "had received a green light from the United States government to do so." However, he added, the officials later decided to start the war in South Ossetia instead, believing that "United States officials had given their approval." He discussed the July 2008 meeting between Georgian officials and Secretary of State Rice, saying, "Some people who attended the meeting between Condoleezza Rice and Saakashvili were saying that Condoleezza Rice gave them the green light for military action," though U.S. and Georgian officials "categorically denied this information."

When the war broke out, the United States military airlifted Georgian troops from Iraq back to Georgia to participate in the fighting against Russia. In the Pentagon, a 28-year-old junior staffer, Mark Simakovsky, "almost overnight... became a key policy adviser" to Secretary of Defense Robert Gates and other top administration officials. Serving as the Pentagon's country director for Georgia, he "used his expert knowledge and contacts throughout the government and in Georgia to quickly gather information about developments on the ground." He was pivotal in shaping the Pentagon's response to the crisis, including the coordination of airlifting 2,000 Georgian soldiers from Iraq back to Georgia.

Aftermath

Within a week of the Georgian war ending on August 12, Secretary of State Condoleezza Rice declared that the United States "would not push for Georgia to be allowed into NATO" during an upcoming emergency meeting of the NATO countries in Brussels, in what the *New York Times* reported as, "a tacit admission that America and its European allies lack the stomach for a military fight with Russia."

However, NATO foreign ministers were expected to reaffirm that they would eventually like to see both Georgia and Ukraine join NATO, but not to fast-track the process through the Membership Action Plan (MAP), for which Georgia and the US had previously been lobbying. In November of 2008, Rice affirmed that the US was no longer attempting to fast-track Georgian and Ukrainian membership into NATO, largely due to opposition from France and Germany. In 2011, Russian President Dmitri Medvedev stated that if Russia hadn't invaded Georgia in 2008, NATO would have expanded already to include Georgia as a member.

In late August, Russian commanders were reportedly "growing alarmed at the number of NATO warships sailing into the Black Sea." The U.S. said it was delivering "humanitarian aid on military transport planes and ships," though the Russians suspected that the Pentagon was shipping in weapons and military equipment "under the guise" of humanitarian assistance.

Weeks following Georgia's defeat, officials at the White House, Pentagon and State Department were "examining what would be required to rebuild Georgia's military." The U.S. Chairman of the Joint Chiefs of Staff, Admiral Mike Mullen, stated during a news conference that Georgia was "a very important country to us" and that the U.S. would continue to pursue a "military-to-military relationship." Both Democrats and Republicans proclaimed their unyielding support for Georgia, as both the John McCain and Barack Obama presidential campaigns had "cultivated close ties" to President Saakashvili. John McCain's wife and Senator Joe Biden (who would become Obama's Vice President) had gone to visit Georgia in August of 2008, just following the end of the war. In early September, President Bush promised $1 billion in "humanitarian and economic assistance" to help rebuild the country following the war, making Georgia one of the largest recipients of U.S. foreign aid, after Israel, Egypt and Iraq. Comparatively, in the previous 17 years, the United States had provided a total of $1.8 billion in aid to the country. The European Union also pledged to contribute funds to Georgia, as did the International Monetary Fund (IMF), declaring its intention to provide the country with a $750 million loan.

In September of 2008, Vice President Dick Cheney flew to Georgia "to deliver a forceful American pledge to rebuild Georgia and its economy, to preserve its sovereignty and its territory and to bring it into the NATO alliance in defiance of Russia." Cheney, who arrived in Georgia a day after the U.S. announced a $1 billion rescue package to help the country, then flew to Ukraine to deliver a similar message. Russia, meanwhile, was entrenching its control over the breakaway regions of South Ossetia and Abkhazia, recognizing their independence from Georgia and keeping military units stationed within them.

Cheney's visit, which began in Azerbaijan, then to Georgia and Ukraine, was orchestrated to confirm that the U.S. had "a deep and abiding interest" in the region, and notably in terms of ensuring that these and neighboring countries remained "free from a new era of Russian domination." Cheney was the highest-ranking U.S. official to visit Azerbaijan since it gained independence in 1991. Underscoring the importance of the BP-led pipeline transporting oil from Azerbaijan through Georgia to Turkey, Cheney's first meetings in Azerbaijan were not with political officials, but with representatives from BP and Chevron.

In the last weeks of the Bush administration, Condoleezza Rice and the Georgian Minister of Foreign Affairs signed the U.S.-Georgian Charter on Strategic Partnership. This was followed up by the Obama administration, holding the first meeting of the Strategic Partnership Commission meeting in Washington on June 22, 2009, marking the launch of four bilateral working groups on "democracy, defense and security, economic, trade and energy issues, and people-to-people cultural exchanges." The Strategic Partnership reflected U.S. commitment "to deepening Georgia's integration into Euro-Atlantic institutions and enhancing security cooperation," including eventual membership into NATO.

The Obama administration sent Vice President Joe Biden to Georgia in July of 2009, with Saakashvili lobbying for the U.S. to sell the country weapons, which Russia strongly opposed, considering the rearmament of Georgia to be "more serious than whether Georgia enters NATO."

In 2010, Georgia began a "serious push" to lobby the U.S. for "defensive weapons," notably air defense and anti-tank systems. To help achieve this objective, Georgia spent roughly $1.5 million at four top Washington, D.C. lobbying firms over the course of the year. Meanwhile, Russia had been "intimidating" many of Georgia's past arms suppliers, including Israel and other Eastern European nations, not to resume arms sales to the country.

In 2010, the United States also resumed its military training exercises in Georgia, which have continued in recent years, much to Russia's displeasure. However, Saakashvili lost the 2012 elections and was replaced with a billionaire Bidzina Ivanishvili, who had made his fortune in Russia, leading to slightly improved relations with Putin. In 2013, Russia accused the U.S. of "putting peace at risk" by holding joint military exercises in Georgia.

Bidzina Ivanishvili was the Georgian Prime Minister from 2012 to 2013, during which time Saakashvili was still president. As the *Economist* reported in October of 2013, weeks before the Georgian presidential elections to replace him, Saakashvili, who came to power through the U.S.-sponsored 'Rose Revolution' in 2003, had, in the following decade, "fought and lost a war with Russia, cracked down on the opposition, dominated the media, interfered with justice and monopolized power ." No wonder Cheney saw him as an ideal representation of America's "democracy promotion" project.

The billionaire oligarch prime minister, Ivanishvili, Georgia's richest man, had put his weight behind a presidential candidate, Giorgi Margvelashvili, who subsequently won the October 2013 elections. Under reforms implemented by Saakashvili, the role of president would become "largely ceremonial, with the bulk of power resting with the prime minister." Ivanishvili proclaimed his intention to turn Georgia into a "perfect European democracy." In May of 2014, months into the Ukrainian conflict, NATO announced its intentions to find ways of bringing Georgia " even closer" to the military alliance. Just days earlier, both France and Germany "assured Georgia that a deal bringing it closer to the European Union would be sealed soon."

Georgian officials were holding "extensive discussions" with US and German and other NATO members seeking ways to accelerate the country's membership into NATO. Whereas previously, the US and NATO powers had decided to put Georgia's NATO membership on the backburner, the conflict in Ukraine had changed the situation. Georgia's Defense Minister stated: "Clearly, what's happening in Ukraine impacts the thinking in Europe... Now it's very different." The Defense Minister went to Washington in May 2014 to visit with Vice President Biden and U.S. Secretary of Defense Chuck Hagel.

And so, in the more than ten years since Georgia's U.S. and NATO-supported colour revolution, the West - particularly the United States - have increased Georgia's military capabilities, armed and trained its forces, all the while aggravating Russia as NATO and Western military, political and economic influence spread ever-closer to its borders. This ultimately resulted in a war. Though, since then - and with the recent conflict in Ukraine - it is clear that rearming Georgia and further aggravating Russia is back on the agenda.

The hypocrisy and imperious expansionism of the West in Georgia is but a minor reflection of a similar process which has been taking place across much of Eastern Europe, and most especially in Ukraine. Thus, despite the never-ending proclamations of "Russian aggression," it is once again the Western powers, NATO, the EU, the IMF and especially the United States that are the most to blame for the current conflict in Ukraine.

The 2008 war in Georgia had seemingly put an end - or a halt - on NATO's eastward expansion. Russia had - after 18 years of NATO expansion - finally drawn a line in the sand over how much it was willing to put up with. It was clear, then, that a similar process with Ukraine, a much larger and more strategically significant country than Georgia, was sure to incur a military response from Russia. If anything, the only surprise is that Russia's military response has been so minimal, comparatively speaking; at least, for the time being. But as this process continues in response to Ukraine's crisis, and as NATO and the U.S. military, the EU and the IMF accelerate their advance eastward, future conflict is seemingly all but inevitable.

No doubt, when that conflict comes, we will once again hear the amnesic proclamations of "Russian aggression" and Western benevolence.

From 'God's Wrath' to 'Protective Edge'
Israel's Four-Decade-Long Assault on Palestine

Derek Alan Ide

In Beirut on July 8, 1972, thirty-six year old Ghassan Kanafani entered into his Volkswagen for the last time. The prolific writer and editor of *Al Hadaf* ("The Goal") was headed to the newspaper's office. His seventeen year old niece Lamis Najm was with him. Not long before, he had penned these words to her:

"Dearest: You are rising now, while we start to fall. Our role is almost complete. The role of this generation was the shortest for any generation in history. We live in crucial times for the history of humanity and people are divided between participants and spectators... The battle is harsh and human capacity cannot tolerate this much. I, young one, chose not to be a spectator. It means that I chose to live the crucial moments of our history, no matter how short..."[1]

It was around 11 a.m. that Saturday when the explosion occurred, judging from the watch later found on what remained of

190

Lamis' hand. [2] Kanafani was a leading member of the Popular Front for the Liberation of Palestine, the heart of the left-wing secular opposition to Israel. He was a noncombatant, and although pictures of Ho Chi Minh and Che Guevara adorned his office, he never personally picked up a gun against his Zionist enemies, despite having every right to resist to the ongoing occupation by whatever means necessary. Yet, he still became a victim of Israeli terror.

The car bomb attached to Kanafani's vehicle killed him and his teenage niece on July 8, 1972. The assassination was part of a secret operation known as God's Wrath. The plan, carried out under the tutelage of Prime Minister Golda Meir, was intended to murder leading militants and officials within the Palestinian resistance movement and was executed by Israel's "Institute for Intelligence and Special Operations," more commonly known as *Mossad*.

Operation God's Wrath was a covert operation that utilized methods, such as car bombs, akin to what Arundhati Roy once referred to as the "privatization of war."[3] Forty-two years later, to the day, after the car bomb killed Ghassan and Lamis, the terrorist state of Israel began a new public operation of a different sort. On Tuesday, July 8, 2014 Israel unleashed Operation Protective Edge onto Gaza, a much more *hasbara*-friendly initiative. This spectacle of sheer force - conventional terrorism, it might be called - had indiscriminately slaughtered nearly 200 Palestinians within the span of one week.[4] Seven days in and Israel's casualties had reached a stunning zero.

Unlike the names of the three Israeli teenage settlers who were kidnapped and murdered not long before Operation Protective Edge was initiated, the names of the 192 victims of Israeli aggression have not yet been plastered on the front pages of every newspaper or the headlines on every television set. Sa'ad Mahmoud al-Hajj was 17, the same age as Kanafani's niece Lamis, was murdered along with seven members of his family when an Israeli bomb destroyed their home in Khan Younis. Sa'ad's brother Tarek, age 18, and his sister Fatima, age 12, died with him. Ziad

Maher al-Najjar, 17 years old, was also killed in Khan Younis days later. 17-year-old Anas Youssef Kandil was murdered by Israeli terror in Jabalia, and 17-year-old Mohammed Isam al-Batash was killed in Gaza city. 10-year-old Bassim Salim Kawareh, 11-year-old Maryam Atieh Mohammed al-Arja, 12-year-old Qassi Isam al-Batash, all victims of this most recent terrorist attack. These names may not find their way onto the pages or television screens of major news outlets in the west, where Palestinian blood has always been worth less than Israeli blood, but they, along with all the other names of victims of Israeli barbarity, should grace the lips and enter the hearts of those engaged in the struggle for a free Palestine. Thus, forty-two years after the terrorist state martyred Kanafani, its reign of terror continued. The world is a different place from 1972, however, and the voice of worldwide opposition is growing. Just as the movement against apartheid South Africa took decades to build, so did the opposition to the settler-terrorist state of Israel. Today, however, the movement for boycott, divestment, and sanctions (BDS), put forward by Palestinian civil society in 2005, is growing at an even more rapid pace than did its predecessor. Across US campuses, student governments have passed resolutions calling for divestment, and victories in the name of a free Palestine have been on the rise.[5] While the puppet Arab leaders, sheikhs and Israeli pawns wring their hands, donate a pittance of their enormous wealth to clean up the aftermath, and send fighters off to die in Iraq or Syria, they cannot be the face of the Palestinian resistance.

As Ghassan Kanafani explained: "If we are failed defenders of the cause, it is better to change the defenders, not to change the cause." Since his time, the defenders have changed more than once, but Kanafani's cause lives on. For those of us who live outside the "harsh battle," we too should "choose not to be a spectator." Let us, like Kanafani, "choose to live the crucial moments of our history" and contribute to the struggle for a free Palestine. For those of us who face no imminent threat of retaliation, no fear of bombs dropping onto our homes while we eat with our families, no chance of a car bomb detonating as we head to our offices, it should not only be our choice, but our obligation, our duty, to support the movement to boycott and divest from the terrorist state of Israel. As Alice Walker, who refused an Israeli publisher's offer to publish "The Color Purple," once said, "Activism is my rent for living on this planet." Indeed, when it comes to Palestine, it is time for Americans to pay some rent.

Notes

[1] http://english.al-akhbar.com/node/20505
[2] Ibid.
[3] http://www.isreview.org/issues/38/Arundhati_roy.shtml
[4] http://hummusforthought.com/2014/07/12/names-of-the-victims-in-gaza-continuously-updated/
[5] http://electronicintifada.net/blogs/nora/bds-roundup-victories-2012

World Economic Forum 2015

Global Governance In a World of Resistance

Andrew Gavin Marshall

The annual meetings of the World Economic Forum (WEF) in Davos, Switzerland, bring together thousands of the world's top corporate executives, bankers and financiers with leading heads of state, finance and trade ministers, central bankers and policymakers from dozens of the world's largest economies; the heads of all major international organizations including the IMF, World Bank, World Trade Organization, Bank for International Settlements, UN, OECD and others, as well as hundreds of academics, economists, political scientists, journalists, cultural elites and occasional celebrities.

The WEF states that it is "committed to improving the state of the world through public-private cooperation," collaborating with corporate, political, academic and other influential groups and sectors "to shape global, regional and industry agendas" and to "define challenges, solutions and actions." Apart from the annual forum meeting in Davos, the WEF hosts regional and sometimes even country-specific meetings multiple times a year in Asia, Latin America, Africa and elsewhere. The Forum is host to dozens of different projects bringing together academics with corporate representatives and policy-makers to promote particular issues and positions on a wide array of subjects, from investment to the environment, employment, technology and inequality. From these projects and others, the Forum publishes dozens of reports annually, identifying key issues of importance, risks, opportunities, investments and reforms.

The WEF has survived by adapting to the times. Following the surge of so-called anti-globalization protests in 1999, the Forum began to invite non-governmental organizations representing constituencies that were more frequently found in the streets protesting against meetings of the WTO, IMF and Group of Seven. In the 2000 meeting at Davos, the Forum invited leaders from 15 NGOs to debate the heads of the WTO and the President of Mexico on the subject of globalization. The participation of NGOs and non-profit organizations has increased over time, and not without reason. According to a poll conducted on behalf of the WEF just prior to the 2011 meeting, while global trust in bankers, governments and business was significantly low, NGOs had the highest rate of trust among the public.

In an interview with the Wall Street Journal last September, the founder and executive chairman of the WEF, Klaus Schwab, was asked about the prospects of "youth frustration over high levels of underemployment and unemployment" as expressed in the Arab Spring and Occupy Wall Street movements, noting that the Forum was frequently criticized for promoting policies and ideologies that contribute to those very problems. Schwab replied that the Forum tries "to have everybody in the boat." Davos, he explained, "is about heads of state and big corporations, but it's also civil society - so all of the heads of the major NGOs are at the table in Davos." In reaction to the Occupy Wall Street movement, Schwab said, "We also try... to put more emphasis on integrating the youth into what we are doing."

So, what exactly has the World Economic Forum been doing, and how did it emerge in the first place?

It began in 1971 as the European Management Forum, inviting roughly 400 of Europe's top CEOs to promote American forms of business management. Created by Schwab, a Swiss national who studied in the U.S. and who still heads the event today, the Forum changed its name in 1987 to the World Economic Forum after growing into an annual get together of global elites who promoted and profited off of the expansion of "global markets." It is the gathering place for the titans of corporate and financial power. Despite the globalizing economy, politics at the Forum have remained surprisingly national. The annual meetings are a means to promote social connections between key global power players and national leaders along with the plutocratic class of corporate and financial oligarchs. The WEF has been a consistent forum for advanced "networking" and deal-making between companies, occasional geopolitical announcements and agreements, and for the promotion of "global governance" in a world governed of global markets.

Writing in the Financial Times, Gideon Rachman noted that more than anything else, "the true significance of the World Economic Forum lies in the realm of ideas and ideology," noting that it was where the world's leaders gathered "to set aside their differences and to speak a common language... they restate their commitment to a single, global economy and to the capitalist values that underpin it." This reflected the "globalization consensus" which was embraced not simply by the powerful Group of Seven nations, but by many of the prominent emerging markets such as China, Russia, India and Brazil.

Indeed, the World Economic Forum's main purpose is to function as a socializing institution for the emerging global elite, globalization's "Mafiocracy" of bankers, industrialists, oligarchs, technocrats and politicians. They promote common ideas, and serve common interests: their own.

Geopolitics, Global Governance and the Arrival of the "Davos Class"

The World Economic Forum has been shaped by - and has in turn, shaped - the course and changes in geopolitics, or "world order," over the past several decades. Created amidst the rise of West Germany and Japan as prominent economic powers competing with the United States, the oil shocks of the 1970s also produced immense new powers for the Arab oil dictatorships and the large global banks that recycled that oil money, loaning it to Third World countries.

New forums for "global governance" began to emerge, such as the meetings of the Group of Seven: the heads of state, finance ministers and central bank governors of the seven leading industrial powers including the U.S., West Germany, Japan, U.K., France, Italy and Canada, starting in 1975. When the debt crisis of the 1980s hit, the International Monetary Fund and the World Bank achieved immense new powers over entire economies and regions, reshaping the structure of societies to promote "market economies" and advance the interests of domestic and international corporate and financial oligarchs.

Between 1989 and 1991, the global power structure changed dramatically with the fall of the Berlin Wall and the collapse of the Soviet Union. With that came President George H.W. Bush's announcement of a "New World Order" in which America claimed "victory" in the Cold War, and a unipolar world took shape under the hegemony of the United States. The ideological war between the West and the Soviet Union was declared victorious in favor of Western Capitalist Democracy. The "market system" was to become globalized as never before, especially under the presidency of Bill Clinton who led the U.S. during its largest ever economic expansion between 1993 and 2001.

During this time, the annual meetings of the World Economic Forum became more important than ever, and the role of the WEF in establishing a "Davos Class" became widely acknowledged. At the 1990 meeting, the focus was on Eastern Europe and the Soviet Union's transition to "market-oriented economies." Political leaders from Eastern Europe and Western Europe met in private meetings, with West German Chancellor Helmut Kohl articulating his desire to reunify Germany and cement Germany's growing power within the European Community and NATO.

Helmut Kohl laid out his strategy for shaping the "security and economic structure of Europe" within a unified Germany. Kohl's "grand design" for Europe envisioned a unified Germany as being "firmly anchored" in the expanding European Community, the main objective of which was to establish an "internal market" by 1992 and to advance toward an economic and monetary union, with potential to expand eastward. Kohl presented this as a peaceful way for German power to grow while assuaging fears of Eastern Europeans and others about the economically resurgent country at the heart of Europe.

At the 1992 WEF meeting, the United States and reunified Germany encouraged "drastic steps to insure a liberalization of world trade," and furthered efforts to support the growth of market economies in Eastern Europe. The German Economics Minister called for the Group of Seven to meet and restart global trade talks through the 105-nation General Agreement on Tariffs and Trade (GATT). At that same meeting, the Chinese delegation included Prime Minister Li Peng, who was the highest-level Chinese official to travel internationally since the 1989 Tiananmen Square crackdown.

Of great significance also was the attendance of Nelson Mandela, the new president of South Africa. When Mandela was released from prison in 1990, he declared the policy of the African National Congress (ANC) was to implement "the nationalization of the mines, banks and monopoly industries." When Mandela attended the January 1992 meeting of the WEF just after becoming president, he changed his views and embraced "capitalism and globalization." Mandela attended the meeting alongside the governor of the central bank of South Africa, Tito Mboweni, who explained that Mandela arrived with a speech written by ANC officials focusing on nationalization. As the week's meetings continued, Mandela met with leaders from Communist Parties in China and Vietnam, who told him, "We are currently striving to privatize state enterprises and invite private enterprise into our economies. We are Communist Party governments, and you are a leader of a national liberation movement. Why are you talking about nationalization?"

As a result, Mandela changed his views, telling the Davos crowd that he would open South Africa up as a market economy and encourage investment. South Africa subsequently became the continent's fastest growing economy, though inequality today is greater than it was during apartheid. As Mandela explained to his official biographer, he came home from the 1992 WEF meeting and told other top officials that they had to choose: "We either keep nationalization and get no investment, or we modify our own attitude and get investment."

At the 1993 meeting, the main consensus that had emerged called for the U.S. to maintain its position as a global economic and military power, and for it to take the lead encouraging greater "co-operation" between powerful nations. The major fear among Davos participants was that while economies were becoming globalized, politics was turning inward and becoming "renationalized." Later that year, Anthony Lake, Bill Clinton's National Security Adviser, articulated the "Clinton Doctrine" for the world, explaining: "The successor to a doctrine of containment must be a strategy of enlargement - enlargement of the world's free community of market democracies." Lake explained that the United States "must combine our broad goals of fostering democracy and markets with our more traditional geostrategic interests." No doubt, the Davos crowd welcomed such news.

At the 1994 meeting, the director-general of GATT, Peter D. Sutherland, declared that world leaders needed to establish "a new high-level forum for international economic co-operation," moving beyond the Group of Seven to become more inclusive of the major "emerging market" economies. Sutherland told the assembled plutocrats that "we cannot continue with the majority of the world's people excluded from participation in global economic management." Eventually, the organization Sutherland described was formed, as the Group of 20, bringing the leading 20 industrial and economic powers together in one setting. Formed in 1999, the G20 didn't become a major forum for global governance until the 2008 financial crisis.

In 1995, the Financial Times noted that the new "buzzword" for international policymakers was "global governance," articulating a desire and strategy for updating and expanding the institutions and efforts of international co-operation. The January 1995 World Economic Forum meeting was the venue for the presentation of an official UN report on global governance. President Clinton addressed the Davos crowd by satellite, stressing that he would continue to push for the construction of a new "economic architecture," notably at meetings of the Group of Seven.

In 1997, the highly influential U.S. political scientist Samuel Huntington coined the term "Davos Man," which he described as a group of elite individuals who "have little need for national loyalty, view national boundaries as obstacles that are thankfully vanishing, and see national governments as residues from the past whose only useful function is to facilitate the elite's global operations." An article that year in The Economist came to the defense of the "Davos Man," declaring that he was replacing traditional diplomacy which was "more likely to bring peoples together than to force them apart," noting that the WEF was "paid for by companies and run in their interests."

Samuel Huntington presented a thesis, summarized in a 1997 Financial Times article, that outlined a world that "would be divided into spheres of influence," within which "one or two core states would rule the roost." Huntington noted that the "Davos culture people," while extremely powerful, were only a tiny fraction of the world's population, and the leaders of this faction "do not necessarily have a secure grip on power in their own societies." The Financial Times, however, noted that while the "Davos culture people" did not constitute a "universal civilization" being such a tiny minority of the world's population, "they could be the vanguard of one."

Russian Oligarchs and the Rise of China

In fact, at the previous year's meeting in Davos, the World Economic Forum functioned precisely as the vanguard for seven Russian oligarchs to take control of Russia and shape its future. At the 1996 meeting of the WEF, the Russian delegation was made up largely of the country's new oligarchs who had amassed great fortunes in the transition to a market economy. Their great worry was that Russian President Boris Yeltsin would lose his re-election later that year to the resurgence of the Communists. At the WEF meeting, seven Russian oligarchs, led by Boris Berezovsky, formed an alliance during private meetings, where they decided to fund Yeltsin's re-election and work together to "reshape their country's future." This alliance (or cartel, as some may refer to it), was the key to Yeltsin's re-election victory later that year, as they held weekly meetings with Yeltsin's chief of staff, Anatoly Chubais, the architect of Russia's privatization program that made them all so rich.

Berezovsky explained that if the oligarchs did not work together to promote common ends, it would be impossible to have a transition to a market economy "automatically." Instead, he explained, "We need to use all our power to realize this transformation." As the Financial Times noted, the oligarchs "assembled a remarkable political machine to entrench and promote the market economy - as well as their own financial interests," as the seven men collectively controlled roughly half the entire Russian economy.

Anatoly Chubais commented on this development and the role of the oligarchs, saying: "They steal and steal and steal. They are stealing absolutely everything and it is impossible to stop them... But let them steal and take their property. They will then become owners and decent administrators of this property."

In the 1990s, with the spread of global markets came the spread of major financial crises: in Mexico, across Africa, East Asia, Russia and then back to Latin America. At the WEF meeting in 1999, the key issue was "reform of the international financial system." As the economic crises spread, the Group of Seven nations, and the Davos Class, told the countries in crisis that in order "to restore confidence [of the markets], they should adopt politically unpopular policies of radical structural reform," promoting further liberalization and deregulation of markets to open themselves up to Western corporate and financial interests and 'investment.'

The major emerging markets have been frequent participants in annual Davos meetings, providing a forum in which national elites may become acquainted with the global ruling class, with whom they then cooperate and do business. China has been a major feature at Davos meetings. China started sending more high-level delegations to the WEF in the mid-1980s. During the 2009 meeting, two prominent speakers were President Putin of Russia and the Chinese Prime Minister Wen Jiabao. Both leaders painted a picture of the crisis as emanating from the centers of finance and globalization in the United States and elsewhere, with the "blind pursuit of profit" and "the failure of financial supervision" - in Wen's words - and bringing about what Putin described as a "perfect storm." Both Wen and Putin, however, declared their intentions to work with the major industrial powers "on solving common economic problems."

In 2010, China's presence at Davos was a significant one. Prime Minister Wen Jiabao, who attended the previous year, was not to return. In his stead, his chosen successor, Li Keqiang, attended. China's economy was performing better than expected as its government was coming under increases pressure from major global corporations.

Kristin Forbes, a former member of the White House Council of Economic Advisers and an attendee at Davos, commented, "China is the West's greatest hope and greatest fear... No one was quite ready for how fast China has emerged... Now everyone is trying to understand what sort of China they will be dealing with." China sent its largest delegation to date to the World Economic Forum, with a total of 54 executives and government officials, many of whom were intending to "go shopping" for clients among the world's elite. Li Keqiang, the future Chinese prime minister, told the Davos audience that China was going to shift from its previous focus on exports and turn to "boosting domestic demand," which would "not only drive growth in China but also provide greater markets for the world." Li explained that China would "allow the market to play a primary role in the allocation of resources."

In 2011, The New York Times declared that the World Economic Forum represented "the emergence of an international economic elite" that took place at the same time as unprecedented increases in inequality between the rich and poor, particularly in the powerful countries but also in the fast-emerging economies. Chrystia Freeland wrote that "the rise of government-connected plutocrats is not just a phenomenon in places like Russia, India and China," but that the major Western bailouts reflected what the former chief economist at the IMF, Simon Johnson, referred to as a "quiet coup" by bankers in the United States and elsewhere.

Davos and the Financial Oligarchy

The power of global finance - and in particular, banks and oligarchs - has grown with each successive financial crisis. As the financial crisis tore through the world in 2008, the January 2009 meeting of the World Economic Forum featured less of the Wall Street titans and more top politicians. Schwab declared, "The pendulum has swung and power has moved back to governments," adding that "this is the biggest economic crisis since Davos began." Goldman Sachs, which in past years was "renowned for hosting one of the hottest parties at the World Economic Forum's glittering annual meeting in Davos," had cancelled its 2009 party. Nonetheless, Jamie Dimon, CEO of JPMorgan Chase, decided to continue with his plans to host a Davos party.

In 2010, thousands of delegates assembled to discuss the "important' issues of the day. And despite the reputation of banks and bankers being at all-time lows, top executives of the world's largest financial institutions showed up in full force. The week before the meeting, President Obama called for the establishment of laws to deal with the "too big to fail" banks, and European leaders were responding to the anger of their domestic populations for having to pay for the massive bailouts of financial institutions during the financial crisis.

Britain and France were discussing the prospect of taxing banker bonuses, and Mervyn King, governor of the Bank of England, suggested the possibility of breaking up the big banks. Several panels at the WEF meeting were devoted to discussing the financial system and its possible regulation, as bankers like Josef Ackermann of Deutsche Bank suggested that they would agree to limited regulations (at least on "capital requirements").

More important, however, were plans for a series of private meetings of government representatives and bank chiefs, who would meet separately, and then together, in Davos. Roughly 235 bankers were to attend the summit - a 23% increase from the previous year. Global bankers and other corporate leaders were worried, and warned the major governments in attendance against the financial repercussions of pursuing "a populist crackdown" against banks and financial markets. French President Nicolas Sarkozy spoke to the Forum's guests about a need for a "revolution" in global financial regulation, and for "reform of the international monetary system."

The heads of roughly 30 of the world's largest banks held a private meeting at Davos "to plot how to reassert their influence with regulators and governments," noted a report on Bloomberg. The "private meeting" was a precursor to a later meeting at Davos involving top policymakers and regulators. Brian Moynihan, CEO of Bank of America, said of the assembled bankers, "We're trying to figure out ways that we can be more engaged." According to Moynihan, a good deal of the closed-door discussion "was about tactics, such as who the executives should approach and when."

The CEO of UBS, a major Swiss bank, commented that "it was a positive meeting, we're in consensus." The bankers said they were aware that some new rules were inevitable, but they wanted to encourage regulators and countries to coordinate the rules through the Group of 20, revived in 2009 as the premier forum for international cooperation and "global governance."

Josef Ackermann, CEO of Deutsche Bank, suggested that "we should stop the bank bashing," and affirmed that banks had a "noble role" to play in managing the economic recovery. Christine Lagarde, France's Finance Minister and current Managing Director of the IMF, encouraged a "dialogue" between governments and banks, saying, "That's the only way we're going to get out of it." Later that week, the bankers met "behind closed doors with finance ministers, central bankers and regulators from major economies." The key message from finance ministers, regulators and central bankers was a political one: "They [the banks] should accept more stringent regulation, or face more draconian curbs from politicians responding to an angry public." Guillermo Ortiz, who had just left his post as governor of the central bank of Mexico, said, "I think banks have misjudged the deep feelings of the public regarding the devastating effects of the crisis." French President Sarkozy stated that "there is indecent behavior that will no longer be tolerated by public opinion in any country of the world," and that bankers giving themselves excessive bonuses as they were "destroying jobs and wealth" was "morally indefensible."

As the 2011 Davos meeting began, Edelman, a major communications consultancy, released a report that revealed a poll conducted among 5,000 wealthy and educated individuals in 23 countries, considered to be "well-informed." The results of the poll showed there to be a massive decline in trust for major institutions, with banks taking the biggest hit. Prior to the financial crisis in 2007, 71% of those polled expressed trust in banks compared with a new low of 25 percent in 2011.

Despite the lack of public trust in banks and financial institutions, Davos remains devoted to protecting and expanding the interests of the financial elite. In fact, the Foundation Board of the World

Economic Forum (its top governing body) includes many representatives of the world of finance and global financial governance. Among them are Mukesh Ambani, who sits on advisory boards to Citigroup, Bank of America and the National Bank of Kuwait; and Herman Gref, the CEO of Sberbank, a large Russian bank. Ernesto Zedillo, the former President of Mexico who is also a member of the board, currently serves as a director on the boards of Rolls Royce and JPMorgan Chase, international advisory boards to BP and Credit Suisse, an adviser to the Bill & Melinda Gates Foundation, and is a member of the Group of Thirty and the Trilateral Commission as well as sitting on the board of one of the world's most influential economic think tanks, the Peterson Institute for International Economics.

Also notable, Mark Carney, the governor of the Bank of England, is a member of the Foundation Board of the World Economic Forum. Carney started his career working for Goldman Sachs for 13 years, after which he was appointed as Deputy Governor of the Bank of Canada. After a subsequent stint in Canada's Ministry of Finance, Carney returned to the Bank of Canada as governor from 2008 to 2013, when he became the first non-Briton to be appointed as head of the Bank of England in its 330-year history. From 2011 to present, Carney has also been the Chairman of the Financial Stability Board, run out of the Bank for International Settlements in Basel, Switzerland.

Apart from heading the FSB, Mark Carney is also a board member of the BIS, which serves as the central bank for the world's major central banks. He is also a member of the Group of Thirty, a private and highly influential think tank and lobby group that brings together dozens of the most influential economists, central bankers, commercial bankers and finance ministers. Carney has also been a regular attendee at annual meetings of the Bilderberg Group, an even more-exclusive "invite only" global conference than the WEF.

Though there are few women among the WEF's membership - let alone its leadership - Christine Lagarde has made the list, while simultaneously serving as the managing director of the IMF. She previously served as the French finance minister throughout the course of the financial crisis. Lagarde also attends occasional Bilderberg meetings, and is one of the most powerful technocrats in the world. Min Zhu, the deputy managing director of the IMF, also sits on the WEF's board.

Further, the World Economic Forum has another governing body, the International Business Council, first established in 2002 and composed of 100 "highly respected and influential chief executives from all industries," which "acts as an advisory body providing intellectual stewardship to the World Economic Forum and makes active contributions to the Annual Meeting agenda."
The membership of the WEF is divided into three categories: Regional Partners, Industry Partner Groups, and the most esteemed, the Strategic Partners. Membership fees paid by corporations and industry groups finance the Forum and its activities and provide the member company with extra access to meet delegates, hold private meetings and set the agenda. In 2015, the cost of an annual Strategic Partner status with the WEF had increased to nearly $700,000. Among the WEF's current strategic partners are Bank of America, Barclays, BlackRock, BP, Chevron, Citi, Coca-Cola, Credit Suisse, Deutsche Bank, Dow Chemical, Facebook, GE, Goldman Sachs, Google, HSBC, JPMorgan Chase, Morgan Stanley, PepsiCo, Siemens, Total, and UBS, among others. Depending on its finances from these sources, as well as being governed by individuals from these and others institutions, it is no surprise that Davos promotes the interests of financial and corporate power above all else. This is further evident on matters related to trade.

Davos and "Trade"

Trade has been another consistent, major issue at Davos meetings - which is to say, the promotion of powerful corporate and financial interests has been central to the functions of the WEF. As the Wall Street Journal noted, "it is pretty much a tradition that trade ministers meet at Davos with an informal meeting." At the 2013 meeting, U.S. Trade Representative Ron Kirk explained at Davos that the Obama administration was "committed to reaching an agreement to smooth trade with the European Union," saying in an interview that "we greatly value the trans-Atlantic relationship." The week's meetings suggested that there "were signs of progress toward a trade accord." Thomas J. Donohue, the president of the U.S. Chamber of Commerce, who was present at Davos, commented that "half a dozen senior leaders in Europe are ready to move forward."

In fact, at the previous Davos meeting in January 2012, high level U.S. and EU officials met behind closed doors with the Transatlantic Business Dialogue (TABD), a major corporate grouping that promotes a U.S.-E.U. "free trade" agreement. The TABD was represented at the meeting by 21 top corporate executives, and was attended by U.S. Trade Representative Kirk, WTO Director-General Pascal Lamy, the European Commissioner for Trade, Karel De Gucht, other top technocrats, and Obama's Deputy National Security Adviser for International Economic Affairs, Michael Froman (who is now the U.S. Trade Representative). The result of the meeting was the release of a report on a "Vision for the Future of EU-US Economic Relations," which called "to press for urgent action on a visionary and ambitious agenda." The meeting also recommended the establishment of a "CEO Task Force" to work directly with the "High Level Working Group" of trade ministers and technocrats to chart a way forward.

Just prior to the 2013 meeting in Davos, the TABD corporate group merged with another corporate network to form the Transatlantic Business Council (TBC), a group of top CEOs and chairmen of major corporations, representing roughly 70 major corporations. The purpose of the TBC was to hold "semi-annual meetings with U.S. Cabinet Secretaries and European Commissioners (in Davos and elsewhere)." At the Davos 2013 meeting, the TBC met behind closed doors with high level officials from the U.S. and EU. Michael Froman, who would replace Ron Kirk as the U.S. Trade Rep, spoke at the meeting, declaring that "the transatlantic economy is to become the global benchmark for standards in a globalized world."

The following month, the U.S. and EU "High Level Working Group" released its final report in which it recommended "a comprehensive trade and investment agreement" between the two regions. Two days after the publication of this report, President Obama issued a joint statement with European Council President Herman Van Rompuy and European Commission President José Manuel Barroso, in which they announced that "the United States and the European Union will each initiate the internal procedures necessary to launch negotiations on a Transatlantic Trade and Investment Partnership," or TTIP. At the announcement, Kirk declared the sectors that will fall under the proposed agreement, stating that, "for us, everything is on the table, across all sectors, including the agricultural sector."

The World Economic Forum in a World of Unrest

Perhaps most interestingly, the World Economic Forum has been consistently interested in the prospects of social unrest, protests and resistance movements, particularly those that directly confront the interests of corporate and financial power. This became particularly true following the mass protests in 1999 against the World Trade Organization, which disrupted the major trade talks taking place in Seattle and marked the ascendency of what Davos called the "anti-globalization movement."

These issues were foremost on the minds of the Davos Class as they met less than two months later in Switzerland for the annual WEF meeting in 2000. The New York Times noted that as President Clinton attempted to address the issue of restoring "confidence in trade and globalization" at the WEF, global leaders - particularly those assembled at Davos - were increasingly aware of the new reality that "popular impressions of globalization seem to have shifted" with growing numbers of people, including the protesters in Seattle, voicing criticism of the growing inequality between rich and poor, environmental degradation and financial instability. The head of the WTO declared that "globalism is the new 'ism' that everyone loves to hate... There is nothing that our critics will not blame on globalization and, yes, it is hurting us."

The guests included President Clinton, British Prime Minister Tony Blair and Mexican President Ernesto Zedillo, along with the leaders of South Africa, Indonesia, Malaysia and Finland, among others. The head of the WTO and many of the world's trade ministers were also set to attend, hoping to try to re-start negotiations, though protesters were also declaring their intention to disrupt the Forum's meeting. With these worries in mind, the Swiss Army was deployed to protect the 2,000 members of the Davos Class from being confronted by protesters.

As the World Economic Forum met again in January of 2001 in Davos, "unprecedented security measures" were taken to prevent "hooligans" from disrupting the meeting. On the other side of the world, in Porto Alegre, Brazil, roughly 10,000 activists were expected to converge for the newly-formed World Social Forum, a counter-forum to Davos that represented the interests of activist groups and the Third World. As the Davos Class met quietly behind closed doors, comforted by the concrete blocks and razor wire that surrounded the small town, police on the other side of the fence beat back protesters.

In the wake of the financial crisis, the WEF meeting in 2009 drew hundreds of protesters to Davos and Geneva where they were met by riot police using tear gas and water cannons. Inside the Forum meeting, French Finance Minister Christine Lagarde warned the assembled leaders, "We're facing two major risks: one is social unrest and the second is protectionism." She noted that the task before the Davos Class was "to restore confidence in the systems and confidence at large." Protesters assembled outside held signs reading, "You are the Crisis."

The January 2012 WEF meeting took place following a year of tumultuous and violent upheavals across the Arab world, large anti-austerity movements across much of Europe, notably with the Indignados in Spain, and the Occupy Wall Street movement just months prior in the United States and across much of the world. As the meeting approached, the WEF announced in a report that the top two risks facing business leaders and policy makers were "severe income disparity and chronic fiscal imbalances." The report warned that if these issues were not addressed it could result in a "dystopian future for much of humanity." The Occupy Movement had taken the issue of inequality directly to Davos, and there was even a small Occupy protest camp constructed at Davos.

As the Financial Times noted, "Until this year [2012] the issue of inequality never appeared on the risk list at all, let alone topped it." At the heart of it was "the question of social stability," with many Davos attendees wondering "where else unrest might appear." Beth Brooke, the global vice chair of Ernst & Young, noted that "countries which have disappearing middle classes face risks - history shows that."

With citizens taking to city streets and protesting in public squares from Cairo to Athens and New York, the Financial Times noted that discontent was "rampant," and that "the only consistent messages seem to be that leaders around the world are failing to deliver on their citizens' expectations and that Facebook and Twitter allows crowds to coalesce in an instant to let them know it." For the 40 government leaders assembling in Davos, "this is not a comforting picture."

In Europe, democratically elected leaders in Italy and Greece had been removed and replaced with economists and central bankers in a technocratic coup only months earlier, largely at the behest of Germany. Mario Draghi, the head of the European Central Bank (ECB), was perhaps "the most powerful leader in Europe," though an Occupy movement had sprung up at the headquarters of the ECB in Frankfurt as well.

During the Forum, Occupy protesters outside clashed with police. Stephen Roach, a member of the faculty at Yale University and a chairman of Morgan Stanley Asia, wrote an article in the Financial Times describing his experiences as a panelist at the "Open Forum," held on the last day of the Davos gathering, in which citizens from the local community could participate along with students and

Occupy protesters. The topic he discussed was "remodeling capitalism," which, Roach wrote, "was a chance to open up this debate to the seething masses." But the results were "disturbing" as "chaos erupted immediately" with chants from Occupy protesters denouncing the forum and calling for more to join them. Roach wrote that it was "unruly and unsettling" and he "started thinking more about an escape route than opening comments." Once the discussions began, Roach found himself listening to the first panelist, a 24-year-old Occupy protester named Maria who expressed anger at "the system" and that there was a "need to construct a new one based on equality, dignity and respect." Other panelists from the WEF included Ed Miliband from the U.K., a UN Commissioner, a Czech academic and a minister from the Jordanian dictatorship. Roach noted that compared to Maria from Occupy, "the rest of us on the panel spoke a different language." Having spent decades as a banker on Wall Street, Roach confessed that "it as unsettling to engage a hostile crowd whose main complaint is rooted in Occupy Wall Street," explaining that he attempted to focus on his expertise as an economist, "speaking over hisses." He explained that all of his "expert" insights on economics "hardly moved this crowd." Maria from Occupy, Roach wrote, got the last word as she stated, "The aim of Occupy is to think for yourself. We don't focus on solutions. We want to change the process of finding solutions." As "the crowd roared its approval," Roach "made a hasty exit through a secret door in the kitchen and out into the night." Davos, he wrote, "will never again be the same for me. There can be no retreat in the battle for big ideas."

In October of 2013, The Economist reported that "from anti-austerity movements to middle-class revolts, in rich countries and in poor, social unrest has been on the rise around the world." A World Economic Forum report from November 2013 warned of the dangers of a "lost generation" that would "be more prone to populist politics," and that "we will see an escalation in social unrest." Over the course of 2013, major financial institutions such as JPMorgan Chase, UBS, HSBC, AXA and others were issuing reports warning of the dangers of social unrest and rebellion. JPMorgan Chase, in its May 2013 report, stated that Europe's "adjustment" to its new economic order was only "halfway done on average," warning of major challenges ahead. The report complained about laws hindering the advancement of its agenda, such as "constitutional protection of labor rights... and the right to protest if unwelcome changes are made to the political status quo." The 2014 meeting of the World Economic Forum drew more than 40 heads of state, including then-president of Ukraine, Viktor Yanukovich, as well as Mexico's Enrique Pena Nieto, Japanese Prime Minister Shinzo Abe, British Prime Minister David Cameron, Brazilian Presient Dilma Rousseff, Iranian President Hassan Rouhani, Israeli Prime Minister Benjamin Netanyahu and Nigeria's Goodluck Jonathan. U.S. Treasury Secretary Jacob Lew and prominent central bankers such as Mario Draghi and Mark Carney also attended alongside IMF Managing Director Christine Lagarde and World Bank president Jim Yong Kim.

As the meeting began, a major report by the World Economic Forum was published, declaring that the "single biggest risk to the world in 2014" was the widening "gap between rich and poor." Thus, income inequality and "social unrest are the issue[s] most likely to have a big impact on the world economy in the next decade." The report warned that the world was witnessing the "lost generation" of youth around the world who lack jobs and opportunities, which "could easily boil over into social upheaval," citing recent examples in Brazil and Thailand.

Brazilian President Dilma Rousseff is due to attend the annual Davos meeting this week. But just prior to that meeting, violent protests erupted in the streets of Brazil in opposition to austerity measures imposed by President Rousseff, recalling "the beginnings of the mass street demonstrations that rocked Brazil in June 2013." One wonders whether Rousseff will be attending next year's meeting of the WEF, or whether she will still even be president. Indeed, the growth and power of the Davos Class has grown with - and spurred - the development of global unrest, protests, resistance movements and revolution. As Davos welcomes the global plutocrats to 2015, no doubt they'll be reminded of the repercussions of the "market system" as populations around the world remind their leaders of the power of people.

Indigenous Rights

The Stolen Generations of Australia

Debra Hocking

Perhaps one of the most brutal government policies to impact on the lives of Aboriginal Australians was the Child Removal Policy, which stemmed from the previous failed policy of Assimilation in the 1930s. The Assimilation Policy was clearly defined. It stated that all Aboriginal people should attain the same manner of living as other Australians, enjoying the same rights and privileges, accepting the same responsibilities, observing the same customs and being influenced by the same beliefs, hopes and loyalties. (Lippman, 1981) The policy of Assimilation was also promoted through a continuation of restrictive laws and paternalistic administration. The 'Stolen Generations' are the generations of Aboriginal children taken away from their families by governments, churches and welfare bodies to be brought up in institutions or fostered out to white families. Removing children from their families was official government policy in Australia until 1969. However, the practice had begun in the earliest days of European settlement, when children were used as guides, servants and farm labour. The first 'native institution' at Parramatta, Sydney in 1814 was set up to 'civilise' Aboriginal children.

The Aborigines Protection Board was established and oversaw the mass dislocation of Aboriginal people from their traditional lands onto reserves and stations. Aboriginal girls in particular were sent to homes established by the Board to be trained for domestic service. In 1909 the Aborigines Protection Act gave the Aborigines Protection Board legal sanction to take Aboriginal children from their families. In 1915, an amendment to the Act gave the Board power to remove any child without parental consent and without a court order. (Department of Aboriginal Affairs NSW, 1998)
It was believed that by placing Aboriginal children in non-Aboriginal homes, and preventing contact with their families their Aboriginality (Aboriginal identity) would cease to exist. It was also thought that this process would eventually 'breed out' the cultural inheritance and identity of the children. In many cases this worked, but there were also a good percentage that resisted this process, and retained their heritage under the most extreme attempts to remove it. This was indeed true resilience. What was not taken into account was the inherent cultural knowledge and understandings that could not be visualised by the white authoritarians and so were not considered to be relevant. To understand Aboriginality, one must understand the significance of cultural identity, what it is made up of and what it stems from.

The other issue associated with the Child Removal Policy is that it was the fairest skin babies who were born of intercultural marriages to be the priority of removal. This was a reflection of emerging theories of the mixing of races. The Bringing Them Home Report stated that:

By the late nineteenth century it had become apparent that although the full descent Indigenous population was declining, the mixed descent population was increasing. In social Darwinist terms they were not regarded as near extinction. The fact they had some European 'blood' meant that there was a place for them in non-

Indigenous society, albeit a lowly one. (Human Rights Commission, 1997)

The issue of being fair-skinned at times poses a problem, not necessarily for Aboriginal people but for non-Aboriginal people. It may be that fair-skinned Aboriginal people are a stark reminder of the colonisation process and the fact they have retained their cultural identity regardless of attempts to assimilate by white authorities.

To restore personal and cultural identity can be most of the hurtful and painful parts of healing. The question many Stolen Generations ask is 'Where do I fit in?' After perhaps being raised by a non-Aboriginal family and your life having been shaped by the values, understandings and knowledge within that family, sometimes the individual strength and spirituality is suppressed for a long time.

I have no doubt as a Stolen Generation survivor that perhaps one of the most profound and meaningful gestures of reconciliation ever undertaken in this country, was the Formal Apology to the Stolen Generations by former Prime Minister Keven Rudd in 2008 on behalf of the Federal Government. This was to address the injustices of the past and attempt the healing of our nation. The Apology was one of the fifty four recommendations of the Bringing Them Home Report which was tabled and accepted in Australian Parliament in 1997. Being present that day in Parliament as a Stolen Generation survivor was indeed the end of a long fight for justice and retribution to be done and for a formal acknowledgement of the pain and suffering experienced by the Stolen Generations.
It is not known precisely how many Aboriginal children were taken away between 1909 and 1969, when the Aborigines Welfare Board (formerly the Aborigines Protection Board) was abolished. Poor record keeping, the loss of records and changes to departmental structures have made it almost impossible to trace many connections. Almost every Aboriginal family has been affected in some way by the policies of child removal. Taking children from their families was one of the most devastating practices since white

settlement and has profound repercussions for all Aboriginal people today. The fact that the term 'generations' is in the plural implicates that this misguided Government policy was not just relative to a particular period of Australia's history, but has had a continuing effect on the lives of undoubtedly most. The overwhelming evidence is that the effects do not stop with the children removed; their children and families inherit them. The effects on family and structure have been documented in the context of war-related trauma, or even family terrorism.

In this huge human experiment I have no doubt that identity was the last thing on the minds of governments when removing the children from their families and communities. The practice of Britain sending it's convicts to Australia in the hope that they would be rid of the 'criminal' class - and if possible to forget about them, too - was similar to the situation in Australia and the Stolen Generations. The difference was that most of the children removed could not be sent to another country, but had to be displaced within their own country. The effects of trauma on Aboriginal Australians have therefore been widespread and enduring, recurring across generations. (Bessarab and Crawford, 2013) Although these Policies were introduced decades ago the impact still remains. 'We' are often told that we live in the past, but in fact, the past lives in us.

References

Bessarab, D & Crawford, F. R (2013). *Trauma, grief and loss: The vulnerability of Aboriginal families in the child protection system.* In B. Bennet, S, Gilbert & D. Besserarb (eds), *Our voices: Aboriginal and Torres Strait Islander Social Work.* (pp. 93-113) Melbourne: Palgrave Macmillan.

Department of Aboriginal Affairs NSW (1998) - *Securing the Truth -* NSW Government Submission to the Human Rights and Equal Opportunities Commission Inquiry into the Separation of Aboriginal

and Torres Strait Islander Children from their families. Sydney,
Australia
Human Rights and Equal Opportunities Commission
(1997). *Bringing Them Home: A guide to the findings and
recommedations of the National Inquiry into the separation of
Aboriginal and Torres Strait Islander children from their
families.* Canberra, Australia:AIATSIS.
Lippman, L (1981). *Generations of Resistance: The Aboriginal
struggle for justice.* Melbourne, Australia: Longman Cheshire.

Entrance and Deportation as Social Control Mechanisms
A Look at U.S. Immigration Historiography

Derek Alan Ide

As the hegemonic world system today, all social relations must be understood within the framework of global capitalism. This is particularly true for the transnational movement of migrants across borders and their experiences with modern state immigration systems. The experience of migrants vis-à-vis the US capitalist state is a subject of vital importance for understanding the leading role of the United States in securing and fostering a global capitalist network that extends to every corner of the world. These experiences, which are both shaped by and shape the US economic order, are deeply gendered, racialized, and stratified by class. Thus, the US state plays a formative role in disciplining migrants to serve the global capitalist order, an order which the US serves as both the apex and nexus of in the modern era. The mechanisms which sustain global capitalism are varied, but migration and the laws structuring it compose a fundamental aspect of capitalist order. As such, the variety of ways in which the US and other capitalist states discipline and regulate migrants within the migration process become an important area of analysis, especially for those interested in challenging the myriad forms of oppression which exist under the capitalist mode of production. The regulation of entrance and the power of deportation are both mechanisms of social control that characterize the immigration system. While the immigration system serves domestic and geopolitical objectives as a whole, these two mechanisms are fundamental to its functioning. Through both the *entrance mechanism* and the *deportation mechanism*, class, race, gender, political ideology, and sexual orientation become inextricably bound components in a collective system of oppression intended not only to incorporate migrants into the dominant economic order but to perpetuate the existence of that economic order. Thus, class exploitation and all the manifestations of oppression stemming from it are not simply the result of arbitrary policy choices, but are essential to an imperialist system rooted in capitalist expansion.

Three books, representing some of the most recent historiographical trends in immigration history, together form a cogent and coherent exploration of these mechanisms in depth. All three suggest in different ways that a primary function of US immigration policy is to discipline and regulate the migrant in order to serve the interests of the global economic order. Such a narrative can be seen in Amy L. Fairchild's *Science at the Borders: Immigrant Medical Inspection and the Shaping of the Modern Industrial Labor Force (2003)*, Carl J. Bon Tempo's *Americans at the Gate: The United States and Refugees during the Cold War (2008)*, and Daniel Kanstroom's *Deportation Nation: Outsides in American History (2007)*. Fairchild, as both a historian and Professor of Sociomedical Sciences at Colombia University, has explored the role of the state in addressing health issues and how such policies intersect with disease, class, and race. *Science at the Borders* is both a continuation of this theme and a timely addition to the historiographical record on US immigration. Bon Tempo, Assistant

Professor of history at the University of Albany, focuses on public policy history, immigration history, and the history of American foreign policy. His work neatly blends these three areas of interest together. Finally, Kanstroom is a Professor of Law at the Boston College of Law, as well as the Director of the International Human Rights Program and an Associate Director of the Boston College Center for Human Rights and International Justice. Both his scholarship and activism center on human rights and social justice, specifically insofar as it pertains to US immigration law. All three scholars possess strong credentials which both provide nuance and reinforce one another's analysis through the intersection of their studies.

Fairchild's book, which explores how the medical examination was a tool to inculcate arriving immigrants into the emerging industrial-capitalist system of power from the late 19th to the early 20th century, provides an in-depth analysis of what might be called the *entrance mechanism* for migrants entering the US. The second book by Bon Tempo, which explicates upon US refugee policies from the mid-20th century until the present, also illuminates how the entrance mechanism has functioned, but does so in a fundamentally different way. While Fairchild emphasizes the role of entrance in disciplining, conditioning, and regulating the body and mind of migrants who would form a key component of US industrial labor, Bon Tempo explores the geopolitical interests which underline and motivate US refugee policies in the US. Thus, the entrance mechanism maintains both domestic and imperial functions, even if, as Bon Tempo argues, these imperial functions are sometimes blunted or softened by domestic pressures. Lastly, Kanstroom's monograph, covering an immense chronological span, adds to the portrait of US immigration by exploring what will be referred to as the *deportation mechanism*. Both the entrance and deportation mechanisms are powerful tools of social control. These broad conceptual frameworks will be explored in turn, alongside the contributions of each book to understanding these frameworks and their role in maintaining US capitalist hegemony.

Both Fairchild and Bon Tempo focus on the importance of the entrance mechanism in maintaining the machine that is US capitalism. Fairchild convincingly argues that "two distinct imperatives" emerged with regard to the role of science at the border: "to discipline the working class, and to exclude groups that did not make a decidedly positive contribution to the industrial workforce."[1] However, she successfully reconstructs the dominant Ellis Island narrative from one primarily of exclusion to one of inclusion. For her, the primary purpose of the medical examination was to inculcate arriving immigrants into the emerging industrial-capitalist system of power. Dealing roughly with the period 1899 to 1930, she posits that the process of "Americanization" begins at the medical exam and takes on a very specific role. The disciplining of migrants, who are to form the backbone of the U.S. industrial working class, becomes far more important than exclusionary measures to keep the "unwanted" out. The disciplinary function "was a normative expression of power intended not simply to prevent deviant behavior but to promote adoption of core industrial values, to create a cadre of good industrial citizens."[2] While the process of exclusion is maintained as a symbol of power, and functions differently at each port in accordance with various regional concerns, it was ultimately an ancillary goal. Thus, the medical exam served both as an introduction to US capitalism and as a form of indoctrination through which the immigrant must successfully pass to become an "industrial citizen." Here the entrance mechanism, in particular the medical examination, was an inclusionary tool of social control "shaped by an industrial imperative to discipline the laboring force in accordance with industrial expectations."[3] As is seen through Bon Tempo's work, similar exclusionary and inclusionary functions are manifest in the various incarnations of the refugee entrance process.

While Fairchild emphasizes the role of shaping and disciplining the migrant working class, *Americans at the Gate* directs attention to the entrance mechanism aimed at refugees and how it functions to bolster US foreign policy and global capitalism. Bon Tempo contends that "refugee policies, laws, and programs in the post-World War II era were a product of interactions between foreign policy imperatives and domestic political and cultural considerations."[4] In other words, "refugee affairs clearly demonstrate that the United States' domestic and international histories should not-and indeed cannot-be disaggregated."[5] While the actual administrative process allowed for a significant level of arbitrariness, most of US refugee policy after World War II was driven by admitting refugees who adhered to a mix of political anticommunism and what Bon Tempo calls "apolitical" characteristics, including particular gender roles, industriousness, and consumption. [6] For nearly three decades, the "refugee equals anticommunist European" paradigm was dominant. According to Bon Tempo, "anticommunism bonded foreign policies, domestic politics and culture, and refugee affairs."[7] Bon Tempo juxtaposes a variety of refugee crises, drawing out an important narrative that emphasizes the role of geopolitical considerations in shaping refugee policy. For instance, the decision to take in half a million Cuban refugees between 1959 and 1973 and fund their resettlement advanced ruling class US interests with an anti-Castro and anticommunist campaign. This stands in stark contrast with the contempt brought upon Haitian refugees as they fled the US-backed François "Papa Doc" Duvalier dictatorship. Similarly, the Ford administration only reluctantly, and after the advent of a "human rights" campaign by significant segments of US civil society, set up a small parole program for 400 Chilean refugees fleeing the neoliberal dictatorship of Augusto Pinochet in 1975.[8] This was a full two years after the CIA had backed the brutal military coup which overthrew the democratically elected government of Salvador Allende and brought a reign of terror to Chile in which leftists, students, community organizers, and trade unionists were persecuted. In this way the refugee entrance mechanism of the state became intricately bound up with and central to establishing US hegemony and capitalist dominance across the planet.

In contrast with both Fairchild and Bon Tempo, Kanstroom fills a large void by detailing the post-entry mechanism upon which the immigration system is built: deportation. Kanstroom posits that "deportation is now, and always has been... a powerful tool of discretionary social control, a key feature of the national security state, and a most tangible component of the recurrent episodes of xenophobia that have bedeviled our nation of immigrants." [9] He continues by elucidating upon the two basic types of deportation laws: extended border control and post-entry social control. Deportation, in both of its manifestations, serves the goal of social control through "scapegoating, ostracism, family and community separation, and, of course, banishment."[10] This social control function serves not only to enervate the power of migrant labor directly; it also is a powerful tool in maintaining capitalist hegemony through control of citizen ideology. For instance, Kanstroom argues that the deportation system "facilitates irrational discrimination against the noncitizens who live, work, pay taxes, raise children, and participate in communities alongside citizens every day."[11] Indeed, this "irrational discrimination" serves to undermine the material class interests that working people, regardless of ethnicity or citizenship, share with one another. For the capitalist system, this "irrational discrimination" is a rational way of maintaining class power and disparity through racial oppression. Kanstroom concludes by arguing that "extended border control deportation... has functioned primarily as a labor control device, a kind of extra tool in the hands of large businesses... to provide a cheap, flexible, and largely rightless labor supply."[12] Thus, the deportation mechanism has been a tool in the hands of capitalists not only to maintain ideological conformity, but to regulate the supply and condition of labor.

It must be noted that both Fairchild and Bon Tempo engage the deportation mechanisms of immigration policy. However, for both authors this is an ancillary mechanism that does not occupy a central role in their argument. For Fairchild, the deportation mechanism is evidenced by the symbol of exclusionary power, through which, in a very public process, migrants deemed unfit for the US industrial order are excluded from entrance and deported. Bon Tempo engages the social control mechanism by focusing both on the propaganda and settlement initiatives undertaken by the US government for specific refugee groups. He also explores the exclusionary function of refugee policy when he juxtaposes the treatment of "unacceptable" refugees, such as Haitians fleeing US-backed dictators, and "open door" refugees, such as Hungarians or Cubans leaving Communist countries.

In terms of organization, *Science at the Borders* is split into two parts, each consisting of three chapters. The first deals with what Fairchild labels the "story of large numbers," or the inclusionary function of the Public Health Service medical exam. In this part she argues that the changing needs of the industrial order in post-Civil War U.S. society required a large influx of migrant labor. As such, the medical exam served to "discipline the laboring body." This was accomplished both physically, manifest in "the line" and the public spectacle known as the "medical gaze," and figuratively, as immigrants were introduced to the bureaucratic principles of scientific management which they were expected to acquiesce to as the new proletariat. In the second part, Fairchild addresses the exam's exclusionary function, which has been the main focus of the medical exam in historiographical literature. Calling this the "story of small numbers," given the relatively low deportation rate, she addresses how race and class intersect with interpretation and identification of disease. Fairchild addresses the various points of entry for immigrants, explicating how regional needs and pressures affected conceptions of race, class, and disease. In this way she compliments Bon Tempo's argument that domestic pressures were important in shaping the entrance mechanism. Finally, Fairchild adumbrates the patterns of medical exclusion, as well as the cooperation and, at times, tension which existed between the Public Health Service (PHS) and the Immigration Service (IS) in the exclusionary process.

Fairchild utilizes an incisive theoretical framework buttressed both by an exhaustive statistical analysis of immigration and exclusion patterns. Alongside her data, a plethora of primary source material is woven in to form a cohesive narrative that draws on a variety of sources. Such primary sources include the testimony, diaries, and written works of PHS and IS officials, eugenicist literature and public policy debates, laws concerning immigration, as well as stories, poems, and memories of immigrants passing through various entry points. In an exceedingly detailed manner, Fairchild utilizes this wide array of source material to compose a compelling and convincing argument.

While *Science at the Borders* is organized thematically, *Americans at the Gate* is organized chronologically. Including an introduction, seven chapters, and an epilogue, Bon Tempo takes the reader through the continuities and convolutions of US refugee policies as geopolitics and domestic pressures each exert their own pressures. Chapter one deals with the "failure" of the US to develop any sort of refugee program from 1900 to 1952. Indeed, it was not until after World War II that the US began, amidst the Cold War's incessant need for propaganda victories, that a refugee program came into being. Chapter two and three explore the "refugee equals anticommunist European" equation, dealing in large part with the Hungarian refugee campaign in the 1950s. By 1957, the battle between what Bon Tempo labels liberalizers and restrictionists is in full swing, and the contours of refugee policy can be attributed partly to domestic pressures from these groups. This battle forms the focus of chapter four. Chapter five explores the dynamics of the Cuban refugee period from 1959 to 1966, another example where geopolitical and class considerations were paramount. In chapter six, Bon Tempo addresses the shift from the Cold War paradigm to a "human rights" paradigm. Chapter seven shows how the Cold War paradigm continues to shape US policy during the Reagan era, even as civil society organizations push for change. Finally, Bon Tempo closes with a discussion of post-Cold War refugee policy, making a plea for an "open door" policy in which "men, women, and children from all around the globe who suffer from violence, persecution, and terror." [13] Bon Tempo draws on wide array of sources to make his argument. He explores refugee policy itself, as well as the role of administrators in handling the policy. Memoirs of and debates amongst refugee administrators, public opinion polls, newspaper articles, propaganda material for resettlement campaigns, and a variety of other sources are utilized. Bon Tempo adequately shows that how the entrance mechanism in refugee policy was driven by the need to secure geopolitical imperatives. This was in spite of the efforts of some segments of civil society attempting to ameliorate or negate the worst manifestations of such imperatives.

Deportation Nation, like *Americans at the Gate*, is organized chronologically. After the introduction, Kanstroom begins with his longest chapter, drawing on antecedents to the modern deportation system. Here he develops an analytically broad notion of deportation which encompasses the conventional expulsion of migrants as well as the removal of American Indians and the repatriation of freed slaves to Africa, among others. Kanstroom moves on in the third chapter to analyze Chinese Exclusion, adumbrating the roots of the conceptual framework he calls "post-entry social control." In chapter four he outlines what he refers to as the "second wave" of deportations in the early 20th century. During this period deportation as a political tool of social control became refined, with labor activists, trade unionists, socialists, communists, anarchists, and dissidents of all sorts being deported or threatened with deportation. This chapter temporally overlaps with Fairchild's scope. For the US ruling class, just as disciplining incoming migrants was a vital function of the entrance mechanism, Kanstroom shows how the deportation mechanism was a tool for "regulating a new society," exercising post-entry social control over a diverse body of immigrant labor.[14] Kanstroom analyzes the "third wave" of deportations from 1930 to 1964 in his fifth chapter. This period was characterized by a "highly technical, bureaucratic system" with "harsh post-entry social control crackdowns on 'criminal aliens' and ideological dissidents," as well as attempts to "control the southern border."[15] This period, with its characteristic erosion of constitutional rights, set the stage for the modern deportation system, which he deals with in chapter six. Arguably his weakest chapter, Kanstroom deals with the period from 1965 to 2006 and concludes by adumbrating a variety of forms of "discretion" exercised by immigration officials. Kanstroom makes use of a wide array of sources, including deportation hearings, laws and legal rulings, and case law. He also draws rather artfully on music, poems, writings, and other materials from those who engaged the deportation system, either as its victims or as opponents of it.

The contributions that each text makes to US immigration historiography cannot be underestimated. Fairchild's analysis of the complex medical inspection process brilliantly reconfigures the narrative of Ellis Island from one of exclusion to one of inclusion into the emerging industrial order. Even while nativism ran high, exclusion was never the primary objective of the medical inspection during the early 20th century. This novel approach to understanding both the inclusionary and exclusionary functions of the entrance mechanism within the US immigration system elucidates upon the state's role in directing and strengthening the capitalist economic order. Bon Tempo's contribution to the historiography is equally important. He positions his work within the "new immigration" history of scholars such as Mai Ngai, Gary Gerstle, Dan Tichenor, and Aristide Zolberg, emphasizing the transnational nature of migration across borders. He provides the reader with a glimpse into the ways in which US refugee policy facilitated geopolitical goals and augmented global capitalism with the US at the helm. While his monograph allows for significant nuance, indicating the complex ways in which domestic pressures either buttressed or enervated the state's ability to pursue their geopolitical and economic prerogatives. This was especially true of the 1960s liberation struggles and the human rights movement of civil society during the 1970s. Bon Tempo's work is not without its drawbacks, however. At times he provides too much leniency to the US state's function as a humanitarian tool, such as when he laments Clinton's decision not to militarily intervene in Rwanda. [16] He also fails to adequately situate refugee policy within a larger theoretical framework of capitalist social relations. Despite the weaknesses inherent in a liberal critique such as his, the work is well-researched and compelling. Finally, Kanstroom provides a persuasive humanitarian and political argument against the US deportation system, a system that has functioned as both a tool in the hands of business and a social control mechanism to de-democratize political culture. Another significant way in which his work contributes to the historiography is its emphasis on the antecedents of deportation. He constructs a broad definition of deportation with roots extending far beyond the construction of the official deportation mechanisms that came with Chinese exclusion. This approach, drawing on past precedent to inform the future, is a welcome one for historians and activists seeking to understand the development of the US state and how it has bolstered capitalist hegemony here and abroad.

Fairchild's *Science at the Borders*, Bon Tempo's *Americans at the Gate*, and Kanstroom's *Deportation Nation* are all vital and valuable contributions to the scholastic record on US immigration history. However, they are not just sterile academic tracts to be read and discussed in elite circles. They are, in one way or another, all passionate pleas for a humanizing, democratic alternative to the model of immigration which currently dictates the lives of millions of people, both inside and outside of US borders. Fairchild and Bon Tempo's explications upon the function of the entrance mechanism, as well as Kanstroom's emphasis on the deportation mechanism, form a cohesive narrative that facilitates understanding of the state's role in disciplining labor, enforcing social control, and maintaining US capitalist hegemony. These three books come together in an eloquent tripartite attack on the injustices of US immigration policy. All three ought to be on the reading lists of those who wish to change US immigration policy for the better or challenge the state-capitalist model of social relations which places profit over people.

Notes

[1] Amy L. Fairchild, *Science at the Borders: Immigrant Medical Inspection and the Shaping of the Modern Industrial Labor Force* (Baltimore: John Hopkins, 2003), 8.

[2] Fairchild, 15.

[3] Ibid., 16.

[4] Carl J. Bon Tempo, *Americans at the Gate: The United States and Refugees during the Cold War*(New Jersey: Princeton University Press, 2008), 3.

[5] Bon Tempo, 3.

[6] Ibid., 7.

[7] Ibid., 8.

[8] Ibid., 143.

[9] Daniel Kanstroom, *Deportation Nation: Outsiders in American History* (Cambrdige: Harvard University Press, 2007), 5.

[10] Kanstroom, 5.

[11] Ibid., 18.

[12] Ibid., 245.

[13] Bon Tempo, 206.

[14] Kanstroom, 132.

[15] Ibid., 162.

[16] Bon tempo, 198.

Sorry, We Didn't Hear You
On Owning up to History and Moving Forward

Debra Hocking

One could be forgiven if thinking that an Apology to the Native Americans has not happened. Well, apparently it has. Deceptively President Barack Obama signed off on the Native American Apology Resolution Dec. 19, 2009 as part of a defense appropriations spending bill. The resolution originated in Congress and had passed the Senate as stand-alone legislation. The House ended up adding the resolution to their version of the defense bill in conference. It was somewhat hidden in the 67-page Defense Appropriations Act of 2010 (H.R. 3326) on page 45 in between the sections which outlined how much money the U.S. military would spend on what. The version signed by President Obama became diluted, not making a direct apology from the government, but rather apologising "on behalf of the people of the United States to all Native peoples for the many instances of violence, maltreatment, and neglect inflicted on Native peoples by citizens of the United States". The resolution also included a disclaimer: Nothing in it authorises or supports any legal claims against the United States, and the resolution does not settle any claims. The interesting point here is that the Apology was not made public, so the question is, what was the agenda was behind that. However, a public reading of the Apology was held on May 20, 2010, when Sen. Brownback read the resolution during an event at the Congressional Cemetery in Washington, D.C.

There were five tribal leaders present, representing the Cherokee, Choctaw, Muscogee (Creek), Sisseton Wahpeton Oyate and Pawnee nations.

So one has to wonder, by signing the document as part of the defense spending bill, has the resolution by Obama been fulfilled? Or, is there an obligation to say the apology out loud and to let tribes know how the resolution was signed? There should be a moral, if not ethical obligation to offer this apology to the people and not just congress. Surely one would think that if such an initiative was taken, public and press should be involved.

On February 13, 2008 The Honorable Kevin Rudd M.P. offered a very public apology to the Stolen Generations of Australia. The Prime Minister used the word " sorry" three times in the 360 word statement read to parliament. Thousands of Aboriginal Australians gathered in Canberra to watch the historic apology, which was televised around the nation and shown at special outdoor settings in remote indigenous communities. Kevin Rudd stated there came a time in history when people had to reconcile the past with their future and believed Australia had reached such a time and that was why the Parliament was there on the day assembled. This was to deal with the unfinished business of the nation. His intention was also remove a great stain from the nation's soul and in the true spirit of reconciliation to open a new chapter in the history of Australia.

The media frenzy that occurred before, during and after this event gave true testament that the nation's leader was prepared to offer what no other leader would be bold enough to do. The previous leader of the nation John Howard MP utterly refused to offer an apology. He had a certain language of defensiveness justifying the actions of past governments and those who played a part of the forcible removal of Aboriginal children from their families. It was suggested that those involved in this process believed they were 'doing the right thing'. This attitude fed the racism of many Australians who agreed with John Howard. The concept of compensation was also used by the Howard Government to scare Australians and sparked much unproductive debates around Australia.

The colonisation of Australia was underpinned by the concept of Enlightenment. Cassirer (1979: 19) cites the argument of Condillas who states that no particular class of citizen should disturb the harmony of the whole due to their unique societal requirements or prerogatives, all special interests should, for the good of all, be subjugated and should essentially contribute to the good of the whole. This may to some extent be considered as a foundation to the assimilationist policies that John Howard would not apologise to the Stolen Generations for on behalf of the Australian people present and past.

John Howard embraced an Australian history written by the colonisers and that suited a conservative Australian electorate. Walker (2008) reported that "Howard cited concerns that acceptance of wrongdoing by previous governments that enforced assimilation policies would unfairly imply wrongdoing by present generations who were not involved in removal policies". Wolfe (2009) cites Hage (2003) in stating that the threat posed by Australian Aborigines is that they signify a strong memory that contradicts the coloniser version upon which Australian citizenship and homogenous society is predicated. Is there dispute regarding the political existence of an 'other' in Australia? Does this then signify that the State (Australia and its government) has historically supported a political agenda that covertly had a plan to eliminate the minority political 'other'?

Would an apology that included compensation address the wrongs of such an agenda, but most importantly would it open up and apportion blame to political agenda's that have been supported by Australia until and including the 21st Century? Of course, to agree with compensation for the Stolen Generations, the question of sovereignty must be addressed. There would never be a case for compensation in Australia without the question of sovereignty arising. Therefore there is no reflection on the possibility that the nature of government power or the extent of the sovereignty of Australia may be in question. Sovereignty has always been assumed and there is an inherent belief in the absolute sovereignty of the coloniser in Australia.

I'm beginning to wonder if this idealology is the thinking of President Obama. This may explain why the apology to Native Americans was offered in such a contentious way. Is the fear of formally apologising to the people underpinned by the same notion as John Howard? Would there be a possibility of sending the country 'broke' through compensation claims? This certainly was a scare tactic by the Howard government and many Australians believed that not only would it financially ruin Australia but the issue of sovereignty would see much of the land apportioned back to Aboriginal people.

This notion was overturned by Kevin Rudd, and he successfully offered an apology with meaningful gusto. Although President Obama has offered a tokenistic apology to the Native Americans, it would appear that transgenerational injustice remains. My hope is that one day Native Americans can experience what Aboriginal people experienced with the offer of a meaningful apology. Maybe President Obama should speak to Kevin Rudd!

References

Cassirer, E. 1979. *The Philosophy of Enlightenment.* Ed. J.C.B Mohr 1932. Trans. J.C.B. Mohr 1951. Princeton: Princeton University Press.
Walker, C. 2008. 'Apology to the Stolen Generations welcomed, compensation the next step.
http://www.foe.org.au/good-news/inspiration/aunty-betty-king-vic/ . Accessed 2 April 2015

Wolfe, P. 2009. "*The inherent limits of the apology to the Stolen Generation.*" University of Adelaide Law School research Paper No. 2009-002. Adelaide: University of Adelaide.

Labor Issues

The Way We Work Matters for Democracy

Dr. Nicholas Partyka

The way we work matters for democracy. Or, more technically, the nature of the labour-process under capitalism matters for democracy. This is because the way we work affects who we are, how we see the world, and how we make decisions in it. Work transforms those who labour. Human capacities, or talents, are largely learned. If they are practiced they develop and grow, if not they wither and atrophy. Human beings never stop learning. The workplace is a site of learning. Leaving the formal school grounds does not mean one stops learning. One other way to look at learning is training. Education, especially in philosophy, history, and science, is training in how to see the world, how to think about it critically and independently.

The workplace is, no less than the schoolhouse, a site of learning, or as we might say, training. Workers are constantly being trained. Indeed, one need look no further than Samuel Bowles' & Herbert Gintis' classic study on the connection between training in school and training in the workplace. [1] The structure of their activity creates a force pushing workers toward a specific transformation.

The nature of the specific transformation depends on which and how many of an individual's talents the latter structure inhibits or develops. In *A Theory of Justice*, John Rawls explains,

"the social system shapes the wants and aspirations that its citizens come to have. It determines in part the sort of persons they want to be as well as the sort persons they are. Thus an economic system is not only an institutional device for satisfying existing wants and needs but a way of creating and fashioning wants in the future. How men work together now to satisfy their present desires affects the desires they will have later on, the kinds of persons they will be."[2]

If we want to have a thriving and vibrant democratic society, then we need forms of work that encourage the development of democratic skills. Where else but the workplace, where adults will spend - or at least aim to spend- a great deal of time for several decades of their lives, can the training in these skills be more effectively delivered? If the way we work inhibits the development of important democratic skills in the majority of workers, then the quality of democracy can only be diluted. As history shows, a real democracy is a very hard thing to keep going. Depending on the rigor one applies, there have only ever been short outbursts of democracy, which have typically been violently suppressed. If the structure of most workers' jobs transforms them in a way that makes them less capable, less effective, citizens, then we need to find a better way to work. At least if we are truly concerned about living in a democratic society.

Democracy

Democracy. A word we often and easily take as all too well understood. For all its historical warts, there may yet be a kernel of emancipatory potential in this well worn lexicon of 'democracy'. So I will be assuming throughout that the reader is committed to democracy as method of collective self-government. Democracy will serve here as a kind of ideological anchor. The argument I want to present turns on exposing a problem for a healthy democracy. I take a healthy democracy to be one win which citizenship is universal for adults, and citizen participation is robust, widespread, and as direct as possible. Without this commitment, what follows will fall flat. Democracy can mean a lot of things to a lot of different people, and a democratic society has many aspects. I cannot go into detail on all of them. So, we cannot do justice to the notion of democracy we'll appeal to here. But a simple sketch might be enough.

When we talk of democracy, most of the U.S. understand something like the following institutions or policies; universal adult suffrage regardless of race, gender, ethnicity, LGBTQIA identity, disability; "free" elections, in that voters have no undue burdens on their capacity to in-practice exercise their right to vote, and that any and all interested citizens have the ability to stand for public office; public legislative bodies make decisions by the majority of votes among its members; an informed deliberative process precedes voting; freedom of speech, assembly, and of the press; the right to petition the government for redress of grievances; equal treatment of all citizens before the law; right to a trial by jury of one's peers; detention only for a legitimate charge; punishments only for rightful conviction for a legitimate offense; among many others.

It is true that in all of its historical incarnations this ideal of democracy has failed to describe the reality. Society's calling themselves democratic, right up to the 20th century, excluded large sections of their population from participation in the political process. This is the very limited sense in which most "democratic" societies throughout history have been democratic. More often as not such democratic societies were only democratic among the elite. From ancient Greece to modern America 'democratic' societies excluded ethnic and racial minorities, women, and anyone who was a slave. Only in the 20thcentury did racial minorities and women in the United States gain the right to vote, even if they did not secure the practical ability to cast that vote.

Nonetheless, the idea of democracy, of what the ancients -and even early moderns- would call radical democracy, provides a handy model for the polity we seek. One that is inclusive, tolerant, and committed to the things we mentioned above. Those who are looking for a kind of society based on social justice, and participatory collective self-government still quite often find 'democracy', and its lexicon, the best available way to express their vision. So we'll stick with this word, despite its legacy, and look to the vision of a society grounded on liberty, equality, and solidarity that the word can still invoke. Its real-world failings do not need tarnish the emancipatory vision this vocabulary inspires.

The Typical Capitalist Firm

The place to begin is with a bit of terminology. The business of any firm can be described as a list of tasks that have to be accomplished in order for the firm to reproduce itself, for it to continue to exist. This includes everything from sweeping the floors and restocking materials, to sending out invoices and collecting payments. Individual tasks like sweeping the floor we'll call job-tasks. The "job" of any particular worker in the firm is made up of many job-tasks. This latter construction we'll call a job-complex. This distinction will help us be clear in the discussion that follows. In short, the job-complexes of most workers in a typical capitalist firm leaves them deformed in politically significant ways.
The most appropriate name for the kind of economic system in operation in the US and across most of the world is capitalism. Most all of the proponents of the current economic order universally employ this term. That we live in capitalist socio-economic reality should not be controversial. So, in discussing the dominant way that firms are structured in a capitalist economy, we are discussing the nature of a typical firm under capitalism. As Martin Weitzman has written, "the firm is the economy in a microcosm. So anyone who wants to comprehend the functioning

of an economic system should begin with a thorough understanding of how a typical firm operates".[3]

Typical capitalist firms are organized predominantly by hierarchical power relations between employers, or their proxies, and employees. [4] Those on top of this hierarchy have the power to fashion a division of labour within the firm that best suits their pecuniary aims or their ideological fancies. Since the employer needs to extract a sufficient amount of labour-itself from his or her workforce, and knows that the wage relation produces an antagonistic relationship with that same workforce, the employer must decide on a model of workplace organization, a division of labour, that achieves the former goal in light of the latter constraint.

The first thing to notice about the typical firm is the labour contract it makes. Once this contract is made there emerges a basic opposition of interests on either side of it. The labourer primarily desires access to the means of subsistence, i.e. wages, while the employer is ultimately looking to make a profit and to accumulate capital. The labourer trades control over both the product and the process of his or her labour for a specific rate of wage remuneration. Thus, even before the contract is made, both parties know that the worker will have an incentive to provide as little labour-itself as possible for the most remuneration possible. The employer, on the other hand, will have an incentive to extract as much labour-itself for as low a payout of wages as possible. The employer and the wage worker thus meet in the labour market as opponents from the first instant. This is one of the foundations of the Labour Discipline Problem (LDP) as this market dynamic is often called.[5]

To see the other foundation of the LDP we have to look more closely at the employment contract, specifically what it is that is exchanged. When employer and worker meet in the market, what they contract for is the worker's labour-power, that is the worker's potential to do work. However, when the employer and worker meet in the workplace, after the contract is made, the employer must extract actual work in order to make a profit. [6] The rate of profit the employer earns is largely dependent on how much labour she is able to extract out of her workforce. The need to extract labour-itself from those who have only contracted for labour-power, and who have interests opposite from, or at least not entirely aligned with, that of their employer, is what causes employers to implement models of workplace organization which they hope will successfully extract a sufficient amount of actual labour from workers so as to make their enterprise a profitable one. These profit-driven models of workplace organization produce very important political side-effects because of the way they organize workplaces.

The ability of the employer to control the labour-process, combined with the incentive structure associated with being an owner, produces a significant incentive for employers to embrace one or another style of management control in the family of such systems known as Taylorism, or Scientific Management. The Labour Discipline Problem poses a dilemma to the employer about how to extract not only the necessary amount of labour-itself, but more importantly an additional or surplus amount of labour-itself, to which the employer responds with methods of organization inspired by the principles of Scientific Management. These principles involve breaking tasks down into simple sub-parts that can be easily learned and repeated.

This problem of Taylorism is not a problem of by-gone epochs.[7] Taylorist methods have endured, and even dominated, until the present day in the workplaces of not only developing but also developed economies. It has been fashionable at several points to declare the end of Taylorism, and yet these periodic obituaries notwithstanding we can see a great many examples of Taylorist forms of work organization still alive and well in the workplaces of the twenty-first century.[8] Despite growth in high-technology, high-skill, and professional service sectors in the economies of most developed countries, the large majority of types of jobs are still organized around production methods that are easily recognized as Taylorist, in that they rely on machine pacing, fragmented job-complexes, routinized job-tasks, and are geared toward large-scale production.

Taylorism is also a management ideology as much as it is a set of business practices.[9] Taylorism made conscious and explicit what had been, according to Braverman, an unconscious tendency in capitalist economies. As we have seen, the fact of inter-capitalist competition drives each capitalist to examine the labour process as a natural place to increase surplus through control. The views espoused by F.W. Taylor and his later disciples made clear the dynamics which had been the motivating force behind the development of the dominant systems of work organization.[10] Taylor sees the LDP, or as he calls it the problem of "soldiering", as the source of the need for his new efficiency-increasing scientific methods aimed at measuring labour-itself. By being able to more accurately measure and quantify the work done by workers, employers are able to more closely control the process of turning labour-power into labour-itself. Control over this process helps employers gain further control over the process of turning workers' labour-itself into their own profits. The imperative towards profit means that the organization of production from the point of view of the employer leads unconsciously toward workplace methods and practices that Taylor made explicit in describing them more systematically and scientifically. Taylorism inevitably results in job fragmentation and simplification as a result of management's attempts to assert control over the labour-process. The system of Scientific Management is an attempt by management to acquire the job-specific knowledge that workers have and use it to further reorganize the labour process in the name of greater efficiency. According to Braverman, Taylorism has two basic principles: first, acquire knowledge through measurement; second, concentrate that knowledge in the hands of management.[11] The next step in this process would be to use this knowledge to organize, or re-organize, the labour process in more efficient ways, that is, ways that increase the amount of labour-itself extracted from workers. This dynamic ultimately results in what Braverman calls the separation of conception and execution, or the separation of mental work from manual work.

The LDP poses a difficulty to management in having to extract labour-itself from a workforce whose effort-reward structure works at cross purposes with employers' desire for surplus. To successfully extract the desired amount of labour-itself from the workforce, management must acquire the knowledge that workers have of the labour-process, so that they can use this knowledge toward their own purposes of increasing the enterprises' profits. In the hands of workers, this knowledge would help them regulate output in a way that maximizes their effort-reward bargain, usually to the employer's detriment. Workers' jobs become fragmented and simplified in the process of re-organization, so that management can exert control over the labour-process in the form of prescribing job-tasks, often down to precise movement patterns. This dynamic, where employer control of the labour-process leads to job fragmentation, also helps produce that separation of conception and execution, that is, the design and planning of work from the doing of work.

How Work Transforms Workers

Under the current capitalist-imposed division of labour, the owner or his agent, usually the manager, has the right to group job-tasks into job-complexes and then assign them to hired workers. Under the system of division of labour best described as Taylorist, we see that the job-tasks that lead one to engage one's higher cognitive faculties are grouped into one class of job-complex typically assigned to managers, i.e. to brain workers. Manual workers, on the other hand, are typically assigned job-complexes composed of job-tasks that are mundane and repetitive, and that fail to consistently - if at all - engage workers' higher cognitive faculties. The main difference between these two distinct kinds of job-complexes is that the ones assigned to managers allow for some perhaps large measure of self-direction in one's work, while the job-complexes assigned to non-managerial labourers allows for very little if any self-direction in work. This method of constructing job-complexes within the firm is the source of the alienation that poses a problem for workers' democracy.

As it turns out, research done by Seeman, as well as other research done by Melvin Seeman; Carmi Schooler *et al*, supports the use of the conception of alienation as powerlessness and its link to the labour-process. A study of male workers in Malmo, Sweden, conducted by Seeman found that a feeling of powerlessness is indeed strongly correlated with low expectancies for control, that is, low expectation that one's own action will deliver the outcome sought.[12] Moreover, research on American workers done by Melvin Kohn & Carmi Schooler*et al* has shown that alienation is significantly correlated with a worker's opportunity for the exercise of self-direction at work. [13] The opportunity for what Kohn & Schooler *et al* call "occupational self-direction" (OSD), or the "use of initiative, thought, and independent judgment in work", is negatively correlated with worker's feelings of powerlessness or alienation. [14] According to the results of their research,
"all three of the conditions determinative of the degree of occupational self-direction are related to powerlessness, all of them, in the expected direction: close supervision, routinized work, and work with little substantive complexity are all related to feelings of powerlessness". [15]

We saw already that the opportunity for self-direction is largely, if not entirely, a product of the particular division of labour in the firm. As Kohn & Schooler *et al* understand it, opportunity for occupational self-direction is correlated with one's "social-stratification position" within the firm. We observe this correlation because the firm is organized hierarchically according to a division of labour that sharply separates conception and execution, that is, that radically unequally apportions the range of opportunities for the exercise of self-direction available to workers with different job-complexes. The results of their analysis make it extremely "plausible to think that the psychological impact of social-stratification position might result in good part from the close relationship between social stratification and occupational self-direction". [16] The social stratification system within the firm, i.e. the division of labour, is structured such that opportunities for occupational self-direction are consolidated in the hands of a minority of management or supervisory workers. The result is that the majority of workers, whose job-complexes do not afford room for much if any occupational self-direction, are alienated, or have experiences of powerlessness forced on them, precisely *because* they lack the opportunity to exercise self-direction.

Workers who have a wide range of occupational self-direction do substantively complex work, perform non-routine job-tasks, and are not subject to close supervision. The most important of the three elements of occupational self-direction, according to Kohn & Schooler *et al*, is the "substantive complexity" of the work.[17] Again, as we saw earlier the division of labour of the typical capitalist firm is such that for most employees the main trend is toward the reduction of the level of substantive complexity in their job-complexes. At the same time, the vast majority of substantively complex work, which of necessity cannot be closely supervised, nor is it very often routine, is reserved for those higher up in the firm's organizational hierarchy.

That this is so can be gleaned from the description on the kind of work that makes for substantive complexity according to Kohn & Schooler *et al*. As they put it, "occupational self-direction is probable when men spend some substantial amount of their working time doing complex work with data or with people".[18] Thus, as we just saw, social-stratification position correlates strongly with alienation because of the intervening influence of capitalist division of labour and its unequal distribution of working conditions as regards the substantive complexity of work, the closeness of supervision, and the degree of routinized job-tasks.[19]

The results generated by Kohn & Schooler *et al*'s research very importantly demonstrate that there is a psychological impact on workers from their level of occupational self-direction. The job-complexes assigned to individual workers have an important impact on workers' individual psychological functioning through the variable degree of occupational self-direction or substantive complexity present in different job-complexes. [20] Kohn & Schooler *et al* point to "intellectual flexibility", or "ideational flexibility", as the main indicator in workers of their level of psychological functioning. This indicator, as the data bears out, is directly correlated with the substantive complexity of work, which is itself directly correlated with occupational self-direction, which is again negatively correlated with alienation. In their words, "Jobs that facilitate occupational self-direction increase men's ideational flexibility...jobs that limit occupational self-direction decrease men's ideational flexibility".[21] So we can see now very clearly that the structure of firm has important consequences for workers' personalities.

Because the division of labour in the typical capitalist firm is structured in a pyramidal fashion, such that the degree of substantive complexity in one's work increases as one ascends the power hierarchy, the firm's structure serves to reduce the intellectual flexibility of non-supervisory workers, who are still usually the majority in most firms, by restricting access to the most important dimension of occupational self-direction. [22] It is for precisely this reason that Kohn & Schooler *et al* notice a correlation between social stratification position and psychological functioning. One's position within the firm, that is one's job-complex, dictates how much self-direction one will be able to exercise, and thus the direction of change in one's intellectual flexibility. The research done by Kohn & Schooler *et al* thus shows clearly that there is a very real connection between workers' workplace conditions, i.e. their job-complexes, and their personality. They show further that that the kinds of workplace conditions that predominate in the modern economy subject workers to daily experiences of powerlessness through alienating job-complexes.

Alienation Influences Change in Workers' Values and Orientations

Kohn & Schooler *et al*'s research shows that social stratification position is significantly correlated with workers' values and orientations. By "values" Kohn & Schooler mean exactly what is colloquially understood by that term. Values are things that are of importance to individuals. What are being considered are traits of character, and thus, "values" are understood as those traits of character that persons esteem for themselves, and hence for others as well. "Orientations", on the other hand, is a more non-standard term. Kohn & Schooler *et al* understand "orientations" as persons' "conception of the external world and of self...emphasizing that they serve to define men's stance toward reality". [23]Workers' values and orientations, just like their psychological functioning, are affected by their experiences in the workplace.

Kohn & Schooler *et al* begin by marking a distinction between what they call "self-direction" and "conformity". The former regards internal standards of behavior, while the latter regards external standards of behavior. The contrast turns on whether "one thinks for oneself", or whether one gives "obedience to the dictates of authority".[24] What they observed is that the value of each of these varied according to social-stratification position. The results of several studies showed that parental values for children varied along white- and blue-collar lines, that is, along lines based on access to occupational self-direction. White-collar workers place a high value on self-direction, while blue-collar workers place a high value on conformity. The results of their work go on to show that values are related to orientations.

Indeed, what was found was that those with higher social-stratification positions tend to have personality traits like tolerance of non-conformity and open-mindedness, while those with lower social-stratification positions tend to be more authoritarian, and less tolerant of non-conformity. [25]Consonant with our discussion of alienation, Kohn & Schooler *et al* note a correlation between self-conception and social-stratification position.[26] The higher one's social-stratification position the more one tends to see their actions as efficacious to their ends, that individual action is a useful and practicable way to achieve one's ends. Persons with lower social-stratification positions, on the other hand, tend to see adherence to external authority as the best course of action, they tend to see the achievement of ends as largely a product of external circumstance rather than individual initiative.

These results about orientations suggest a qualitative difference between the type of persons associated with higher and lower social-stratification positions. Kohn & Schooler *et al*'s study measured four dimensions of social orientation, namely authoritarian conservatism, trustfulness, stance toward change, and standards of morality. They found that, "Social-stratification position is linearly related to all four aspects of social orientation".[27] Those with higher social-stratification positions tend to be more tolerant of non-conformity, more trustful, more open to change, and tend to see morality as about the spirit of the law. Those with lower stratification positions on the other hand tend to be more rigid with non-conformity, less trustful, more resistant to change, and to see morality as about the letter of the law.

So, we can see now, the higher one's social-stratification position, the more substantively complex is their work, and the more they exercise self-direction at work. As a result they have higher intellectual flexibility, are more likely to value self-direction for themselves and their children, and they are more likely to have personal traits like being open-minded and tolerant. Kohn & Schooler *et al* highlight the critical role played by job-complexes, substantive complexity of work, and hence the range of opportunity for occupational self-direction in this causal chain. They summarize this role as follows,

"men's positions in the larger socioeconomic structure affects their values, orientations, and cognitive functioning, in large part

251

because of the close link between socioeconomic position and the opportunity to be self-directed in one's work".[28]

What makes these consequences for worker's personality especially problematic is that these workers will leave the workplace and take their workplace experiences with them. Workers carry the effects of workplace relations into every other social role they have, very importantly including the political realm. Indeed, "in industrial society, where occupation is central to men's lives, occupational experiences that facilitate or deter the exercise of self-direction come to permeate men's views, not only of work and their role in work, but also of the world and of self". [29] The direction of this transformative effect is very simple, "Occupational experiences that limit worker's opportunities for self-direction in their work are conducive to feelings of powerlessness".[30] We saw in the last section that the dominant trend in self-direction for most workers is downward, at the very least it is not increasing in most places. This implies directly that experiences of powerlessness are increasing, or at least not decreasing for the majority of workers.

Alienation, Control-Relevant Knowledge, Adaptive Preferences, & Political Withdrawal

Kohn & Schooler *et al* go on to show that in addition to effects on workers' values and orientations, labour-process organization also has an impact on workers' non-occupational preferences. This comes out clearly in their study of the intellectuality of workers' leisure time pursuits. After constructing a measure of the intellectuality of individuals' leisure time activities, Kohn & Schooler *et al* find that substantive complexity of work has a direct and statistically significant correlation with the intellectuality of leisure time activity. [31] This research shows plainly that work organization affects workers' personality by altering workers' non-occupational preferences. Feelings of powerlessness learned on the job thus spill over into workers' non-occupational lives. These feelings are manifested in this case are an adaptive preference for leisure time activities with low intellectual content.

According to the results generated by survey research done by Melvin Seeman, workers who experience high levels of alienation selectively avoid control-relevant knowledge. Control-relevant knowledge, as it is understood by Seeman, is that body of knowledge specific to each different form of organization, that if possessed by an individual member of the organization, would enable him or her to most effectively pursue his or her own unique goals within the organization's structure. In democratic polities this selective avoidance of control-relevant knowledge is manifested in highly alienated workers having low political knowledge, as well as in their selective withdrawal from political life.

In his Malmo study, Seeman confirmed internationally results obtained in America in two other studies where he argued that one's level of alienation in large part determines one's level of control-relevant learning.[32] Alienation, for Seeman, means a sense of powerlessness, and the main characteristic of this sense of powerlessness is the low expectancy for control. Those who are alienated are made to feel powerless because they are conditioned to expect to have little control over their external environment. We also saw this in Kohn & Schooler et al in their distinction between the value of self-direction and conformity. They argued that in order to value self-direction one must see their ability to act as an effective means to accomplish desired ends. If one does not think that one's own purposive action will be a practical means to realize one's ends, then one will very likely not place a high value on self-direction.

In his study of workers in Sweden, the results of Seeman's research showed that alienation as powerlessness was indeed significantly correlated with low expectancies for control in workers. These expectancies for control he finds are in turn directly correlated with individual's acquisition of control-relevant knowledge. For example, one study conducted in a reformatory identified control-relevant information for prisoners as the body of

253

knowledge about the parole system. In another study, which Seeman and Evans conducted in a hospital, control-relevant information for tuberculosis patients was identified as the body of medical knowledge related to their health matters.[33]

In Seeman's Malmo study, control-relevant knowledge for workers was understood as political knowledge. Thus, a battery of questions, within the survey given to a random sample of Swedish workers, was designed to measure workers' knowledge of both political and non-political topics. According to Seeman's results, "those who are high in powerlessness are less interested in political activities", which confirms his more general theoretical claim that "those who are low in expectancy for control are not interested in and do not absorb control-relevant knowledge". [34] The Malmo workers who were in the high alienation group scored worse on the political knowledge test than on the cultural knowledge test. Importantly, scores on the cultural knowledge test were consistent across the high and low alienation groups. Thus, low political knowledge is correlated with high powerlessness, i.e. high alienation. Workers who experience high alienation evidence a selective aversion to control-relevant knowledge, i.e. political knowledge. This is because they have low expectancies for control in the democratic political arena.

This aversion is specifically political, because the results indicate no significant change in workers' level of interest in non-political issues, regardless of whether the workers are in the high or the low alienation group. As we have seen in the previous chapter, many workers have this low expectancy for control as a result of the organization of the labour-process imposed on workers by employers. These low levels of learning, conditioned by the structure of workplace relations in the capitalist firm, further degrades workers' political skills by creating an adaptive preference against intellectual leisure time activity as well as for specifically avoiding political issues.

In addition to the lower scores on the survey designed to gauge political knowledge, Seeman's research provided one further, highly suggestive piece of evidence that highly alienated workers selectively avoid politics. After dividing the sample into high and low alienation groups, the time taken to return the two separate surveys was used a proxy measure of avoidance behavior by the alienated. The expectation was that those high in alienation would either not return or take more time in returning the survey gauging political knowledge than returning the survey on cultural knowledge. This expectation was confirmed, even after researchers excluded all the surveys returned within the first five business days after the deadline. They did this so as to attempt to control for Swedes' cultural pressures toward cooperation with researchers' requests. As Seeman himself acknowledges, this evidence is hardly conclusive, though it is highly suggestive.[35]

Conclusion

The reason the effects on workers' psychological functioning and personality are so problematic for democracy is that they undercut two important buttresses of public deliberation. The transformations of workers' personalities and skills brought about by the structure of the labour-process in the typical capitalist firm undermines the mechanisms designed to develop in citizens more active forms of character. Firstly, the dominant mode of capitalist work organization tends toward de-skilling for the majority of workers. This decreases the quality of the deliberative mechanism in that participants are less able to articulate their own reasons for policies, and are less capable as critics. This is because these same persons are low in political knowledge.

Secondly, the alienating effects of capitalist work organization lead to a specifically political withdrawal by the alienated, that is, a selective avoidance of control-relevant knowledge. This leads to an increased likelihood of class-based legislation since those who are most affected by current policies decide not to participate in deliberation about these policies. This degrades the quality of the deliberative mechanism in that it makes it easier for those who do participate in deliberation to lose sight of the general welfare and pass laws designed to advance the interests of some one particular group in society.

Worker exit from political life as citizens degrades the quality of democracy by undermining the quality of the deliberation, the process of which is supposed to help us arrive at policies that promote the general welfare. Without vigorous opposition, the marketplace of ideas will not as nearly approximate the general welfare as it will the private interests of those who continue to participate in the deliberative process. Exit, because it undermines voice in this case, it also disarms the deliberative mechanism by diminishing the competitive rigor of the deliberative process. This highlights the important difference between political institutions and private institutions. Whether or not one chooses to participate in the democratic political process the outcomes of that process are legally binding on all citizens, oneself included.

Withdrawal from the political process also degrades the quality of deliberative democracy by disabling the transformative process of participation from becoming a virtuous cycle. If citizens choose not to participate in the political process then the transformative process of which participation is the key component cannot begin. It is only by participation that one's preferences and sentiments can be changed. If one could as easily opt out of work as out of politics, then work organization would be equally ineffective at changing individual's preferences and sentiments. Mill as we saw had high hopes for the transformative power of participation to improve workers in ways that would make them better more effective citizens. Yet if worker-citizens are being subjected to forces which shape their preferences in ways that disincline them to participate in the political process when not at work, then the virtuous cycle of participation and transformation never begins.

Notes

[1] Bowles & Gintis. Schooling in Capitalist America: Education Reform and the Contradictions of Economic Life. 1977. Haymarket Books; 2011.

[2] Rawls, John, A Theory of Justice. 1971. Belknap Press of Harvard University Press, 2003: 229. (Emphasis Added)

[3] Weitzman, Martin L.. The Share Economy. Harvard University Press, 1984: 11-12.

[4] The most prominent place I have found this view seriously contested is in Armen Alchain and Harold Demsetz 1972 article, "Production, Information Costs, and Economic Organization". *American Economic Review*. Vol.62 (1972): 777-795. Also see, Jensen, Michael C. & William H. Meckling, "Theory of the Firm: Managerial Behavior, Agency Costs, and Ownership Structure", *Journal of Financial Economics*. Vol.3 (1976): 305-360.

[5] We owe this terminology, the "Labour Discipline Problem", to Samuel Bowels & Herbert Gintis' article, "A Political and Economic Case for the Democratic Enterprise". *Economics and Philosophy*. Vol.9 no.1 (1993):75-100.

[6] This Labour Discipline Problem can be considered a kind of Principal-Agent problem in that it is about how inefficiency can be created when the interests or incentives of two collaborating groups diverge. The Agent may have interests that do not align with those of the Principal, from whose perspective the Agent's rational but nonconforming behavior is "inefficient".

[7] This worry about the deadening effects of Taylorism features prominently in Braverman's Labour and Monopoly Capital. 1974. Following Braverman there has developed a large literature both quantitative and theoretical addressing the question of what effects Taylorism has on worker's skills and personality.

[8] The death, or obsolescence, of Taylorism has been proclaimed in the 1960s for example by Robert Blauner (1964). It was later

declared surpassed by Piore and Sabel (1984) in the 1980s. It was once again overcome in the 1990s according to more than one commentator as Grugulis and Lloyd (2010) note.

[9] See Thompson, Paul. The Nature of Work 2nd Ed. Pelgrave MacMillan (1989):74.

[10] For thorough discussion of Taylorism and Scientific Management see Braverman (1974), & Edwards (1979).

[11] Thompson 1989, 75.

[12] Seeman, M. "Alienation, Membership, and Political Knowledge: A Comparative Study". *The Public Opinion Quarterly*. Vol.30 no.3 (1966): 361 & Seeman, M. "Powerlessness and Learning: A Comparative Study of Alienation and Learning". *Sociometry*. Vol.30 no.2 (1967): 118-121.

[13] Kohn, Melvin & Carmi Schooler et al. Work and Personality: An Inquiry into the Impact of Social Stratification. Ablex Publishing Corporation (1983): 82-97.

[14] Kohn 1983, 2.

[15] Kohn 1983, 90.

[16] Kohn 1983, 164.

[17] Kohn 1983, 64.

[18] Kohn 1983, 22.

[19] Although Kohn and Schooler's study encompassed only male workers I think it very plausible to think that the same results would obtain for women. So, when male pronouns appear in quotations from Kohn and Schooler it should be read to imply the same things for female workers.

[20] Kohn 1983, 118-122

[21] Kohn 1983,152.

[22] For a good description of the hierarchical structures of capitalist firms and their historical evolution see Richard Edwards Contested Terrain. (1976).

[23] Kohn 1983, 6.

[24] Kohn 1983, 10.

[25] Kohn 1983, 15.

[26] Kohn 1983, 20.

[27] Kohn 1983, 16.

[28] Kohn 1983, 189.

[29] Kohn 1983, 33.

[30] Kohn 1983, 96.

[31] Kohn 1983, 225.

[32] Seeman, Melvin. "Powerlessness and Knowledge: A Comparative Study of Alienation and Learning". *Sociometry*. Vol. 30 no.2 (1967)B: 105-123.

[33] Seeman, M. "Alienation and Social Learning in a Reformatory". *American Journal of Sociology*. Vol.69 (1963): 270-284 & Seeman, M. & John W. Evans. "Alienation and Learning in a Hospital Setting". *American Sociological Review*. Vol. 27 (1962): 772-782.

[34] Seeman, M. "Alienation, Membership, and Political Knowledge: A Comparative Study". *The Public Opinion Quarterly*. Vol.30 no.2 (1966): 361.

[35] Seeman 1967 B, 119.

The Problem of the Backward-Bending Supply Curve of Labour

Dr. Nicholas Partyka

The backward bending supply curve of labour is a phenomenon well known to economists. This curve models a situation where workers choose to substitute leisure time for work time, ie. wages, thus reducing the pool of labour available. Let us think through this "problem", and consider in what sense, and for whom, it is problematic. Why indeed should there not exist a backward bending supply curve for labour, especially if capitalism allows for workers to truly improve their station in life? If workers are empowered, and achieve a certain level of material independence, and can thus make their own decisions about how to allocate their time, they will strike a balance between consumption of leisure time and labour time. The problem is that the balance of these that is optimal for the worker will likely be sub-optimal for capitalists, in that it reduces the supply of wage-labour for sale on the market. A glut of supply of labour-power on the market is what enables the capitalist to control bargaining with workers, and thus also to control the product of labour. Control over workers' labour, and the product of that labour is the foundation of capitalists' surpluses. In the traditional supply & demand model of a competitive market the supply of any commodity, be it wheat, snow tires, nuclear bombs, or labour-power, should increase as the price of it increases. If there is a large degree of aggregate demand for some good or service, the ensuing volume of business for the existing firms will bid up the price of that good or service. The more money being made by firms in this market should attract new firms, also hungry for profits, into this market. New firms should be attracted to this new industry until the combined output of all the firms meets the level of aggregate demand in the community, and prices then stabilize, ie. reach their competitive equilibrium position. When the total combined output of the industry outstrips the level of aggregate demand in the community, then the glut of output over demand will lead producers to bid-down the sale price of their particular good or service.

For workers this same story implies much tumult and insecurity. As demand rises for the good or service in question, existing firms expand production and new firms attempt to enter the market, and both scramble to hire workers, whose labour-power will animate their entrepreneurial designs. As firms compete among themselves for workers, they bid-up the price of labour-power, ie. the wage rate. However, the reverse happens when the productive output of the whole industry exceeds the level of aggregate demand in the community, firms seek to shed workers whose productive energy is no longer required given the lowered level of output of the firm. As the price for their product drops, producers restrict output to match the new level of aggregate demand. The increasing scarcity of jobs works to bid-down the price of labour, that is, the wage rate. The surplus of supply of labour over demand for it results in a declining rate of wages.

In the traditional picture, workers' pay rate can move up with a higher equilibrium positions, and it can move down with a lower equilibrium position, and these oscillations in the price of labour move in line with the business cycle. However they move, up or down, the supply curve in the traditional model remains a linear progression; just as it is for every other commodity in the market. This implies that workers act on their "rational" market incentives and their budget constraint in making their decisions about employment and their labour-leisure tradeoff. This is to say, that workers choose to supply more hours of labour-power as the price of labour-power rises. This requires, moreover, that workers act this way regardless of the particular moment in the business cycle. Yet, when the business cycle is in the upswing, when wages are increasing relative to the price level, workers are most likely to want to substitute consumption of leisure for labour. And conversely, when the business cycle is in its down-swing, workers are likely to supply many many more hours of labour than can be profitably consumed by capitalist entrepreneurs.

The situation modeled by the backward bending supply curve for labour is one in which workers choose to reduce their "consumption" of labour time and increase their consumption of leisure time, that is all time not devoted to laboring for wage remuneration. Indeed, in a market economy dominated by wage labour, one can understand the choice to work for wages as basically the same as the choice to consume labour time. What this situation entails is one in which worker's wages are increasing in real terms, ie. their actual purchasing power is increasing. Workers are thus getting richer in the sense that they can either maintain their current standard of living for less money, and save the surplus. Or, they can get richer by using the increasing value of their wage remuneration to increase their present level of consumption, either by consuming more expensive versions of products they already consume, or increasing the range of products they consume. This situation is thus one in which quality of life, and/or standard of living, is increasing for workers. In the context of an economy in which the value of workers' wages are rising workers will choose at a certain point to work less, and consume more leisure.

Though workers desire to do many things with their lives, they can only legally access these things by exchanging cash (and now increasingly credit) payment for them, and acquiring cash implies working for wages. Though workers would rather spend more time with their families, ie. not working for wages, because they love their families very much, or they detest their work conditions very much, they must continue to trade their labour-power for wages. The structure of an economy based on free wage-labour inherently attaches a "cost" to not working. One must sleep; it is an essential activity, if one may call it that, in reproducing one's labour-power. But, in pure economic terms, sleeping has a cost. This cost to the worker is whatever the total amount one would have earned if one had worked at the prevailing wage rate in a particular industry for as many hours as one slumbers. This is, again in economic terms, a type of loss to the worker. The same goes to time devoted not to wage remuneration, but to the social reproduction of the individual and his/her family. Economically speaking, this time is also "lost" because it prevents one from doing what is in their interest, ie. earning wages. Living one's life, the ostensible reason most individuals work in the first place, costs money under capitalism. This situation is a result of the fundamental monetization of time under capitalism. The structure of opportunity costs, and the constant presence of scarcity and uncertainty, incentivizes workers to work more than they would ideally prefer. That is, workers might prefer to work fewer hours if they were not forced to obtain the means of subsistence through monetary transactions, the means for which one can get only through "voluntarily" selling one's labor-power for wages, or by living on the charity and benevolence of willing others.

When workers are getting wealthier, when the economy is working for workers, when it empowers them to make decisions based on their own needs and situation and not on the need to earn remuneration to reproduce one's own existence, they will choose to supply less labour once a certain threshold of wealth is passed. Workers' rising wages relative to prices enables them to make a choice trading off consuming more, and or working less. One of the ways that workers will choose to increase their consumption is through increased leisure, ie. non-work time, since as we saw all time in monetized under capitalism. This increased "leisure" time, as mentioned above, may not necessarily be what one immediately conceives on when one hears the word 'leisure'.

This time spent not working is likely, at least for the majority of workers, to be occupied with activities related to reproduction; eg. laundry, cooking, care giving, sleep, medical care, *et cetera*. With some combination of increased material consumption and leisure time most workers lives could very reasonably be said to be improved. If one had more and/or better quality goods, as well as more time to both do necessary work related to social reproduction as well as some potential 'free time' in which to indulge in hobbies, or relaxation. This increased leisure time amounts to the increased ability of workers - of the persons that workers are in reality, in addition to aspects of the apparatus of production- to live their lives, to be and become the people they want to be, and to have and to cultivate relationships of their choosing.

The Problem of the Backward-Bending Supply Curve for Labour

How is this scenario a problem? From the above it might seem like there is no problem here. Workers getting wealthier, and living lives in which more of their time is their own seems like a very desirable situation. And indeed it is, for workers, for most people in society. However, this is indeed a problem, and a big one, for the capitalist class. Above the threshold at which workers chose to substitute more leisure for labour there is less labour supplied overall. A smaller labour pool shrinks the labour market. A labour market with less labour to offer tilts the balance of power inherent to supply/demand based relations in favor of suppliers of labour, that is workers.

Those workers remaining in the labour market receive increased bargaining power relative to employers. This increased bargaining power puts employers in a position to have to compete against each other for the remaining labourers. This competition bids up the price of labour, ie. the level of wages. Or, as may also be the case, keep wages hovering around a relatively high level, a level which enables workers to save, and maintain the real value of those savings. This situation is problematic for the capitalist class, the employers, because the increased price of labour erodes the profit margin of the employer. A lower rate of exploitation reduces the level of profit received by the employer. It is not necessarily the case that the increased cost due to higher wages will lead a particular industry to collapse from being uneconomically inefficient. In some situations a reduction in profit might be unpalatable to the capitalist, but nonetheless something that would not ruin the industry. This loss of some profit is very likely in most cases to not lead the enterprise to be to no longer be productive or worthwhile on the whole.

This situation, which is unfavorable to the capitalist class, is forestalled by the devious tactics of the ruling capitalist class. These are explained by economists with technical sounding explanations that do little more than obfuscate the economic reality. "Wage pull" inflation is a concept well-known to economists. What this claims is that the price level will rise because wages have risen. When workers make more money in real (not just nominal) terms, firms respond by increasing the price of their products, thus eroding the real gains made by workers. What is going on here then? Noticing that certain economic actors, ie. workers, have increased purchasing power firms respond by charging more for their products. Increased purchasing power for workers will lead to increased consumption, which in turn will lead to increased prices. An increase in demand in the market signals to producers that they can 'afford' to charge more since the level of demand in the market will bear an increase. Of course, one must concede that different markets will function differently due to factors like elasticity of demand, among others.

Inflation dilutes the value in real terms of the increase in workers' wages. This helps the capitalist class keep the supply curve for labour from bending backwards. This is a boon for the capitalist class since a larger pool of labour means more competition among labourers for existing jobs, and hence a declining wage rate. A declining share of production costs going to labour increase the profit margin of the producer. This is of course directly in the interest of the capitalist class. As the wage rate dips further and further, more and more labour-power is thrown onto the market as workers, aware of the scarcity of employment, vie ever more aggressively for the few opportunities that arise. The supply curve for labour is straightened in this way by the force of economic compulsion.

Given the relative levels of consumption and standard of living in the society and economy in question, the level of wages at which a majority of people could reproduce themselves and their families will vary. We should expect that where laboring conditions are low, where workers labour for the private benefit of others, ie. the capitalist class, that workers will begin to substitute leisure for labour at the earliest possible opportunity. Under conditions of alienated labour we should expect workers to choose not to labour as soon as they can afford materially to do so. By diluting the value of saving through inflation, which is normal during the upswing in the business cycle, the capitalist class works to keep the supply curve for labour for bending backwards.

In the case of the backward bending supply curve of labour, what we can see is that in a situation in which workers are economically empowered, ie. materially liberated, to make free choices about their time, they will choose to not consume any more alienated labour than is necessary for the reproduction of their desired level of material consumption. This is telling considering that as the price of labour increases, so too do the opportunity costs of not working. The higher the wage rate, the more value one foregoes in deciding not to work for wages. Leisure time becomes more expensive in this sense as the wage rate increases. That workers would continue to buy increasingly expensive leisure time testifies to the aversion workers have to their workplaces, and the way they are organized. I have discussed the way the typical capitalist firm is organized in another article for The Hampton Institute.

One of the main assumptions of most capitalist economic models is that workers choose their hours. Free employment or free labour is one of the most essential conditions for defining the nature of the competitive market. Workers in capitalist economies are technically free to dispose of the commodity they possess, ie. labour-power, in whatever way they find most conducive to their individual advantage. When workers actually have this choice what we see is a rejection of the conditions of labour in the form of a decreased supply of labour. What devices like wage pull inflation serve to do is help to create and recreate a situation in which workers never attain the material bases of the freedom to make a free choice about how much time to devote to labour versus leisure.

Now we can see the answer to an old question, Why do workers continue to work in conditions they would never consent to if they bargained with employers like equals? The brief answer is that they're forced to. First, they do not at all bargain with employers as equals. Second, the monetization of time in a system based on exchange, as well as the dominance of wage-labour as the form of work makes reproduction costly in terms of one's time. And third, producer-initiated market dynamics straighten out the supply curve for labour by preventing accumulation in real terms by the working class. In this way, among others, workers are forced to submit to working conditions that are unsafe, unhealthy, inhumane, or degrading.

What this shows us is that there is indeed little free about "free labour" in the history of capitalism.

Emergence of a Market for Labour-Power

The development of a labour market has an inherently historical aspect, in that a ready pool of labour power that is available for purchase did not always exist, and hence had to be created. As Polanyi asserts, "No market economy was conceivable that did not include a market for labor". [i] We saw in the case of feudalism, that large quantities of labour-power were not readily available for entrepreneurs because of the pervasiveness of social obligations, combined with an economy centered around more or less self-sustaining socio-economic units. It was necessary then, that a transformation take place as a result of which emerged a class of labourers unattached to the land, and possessing only their labour-power, and this could only occur over time. The pace of this historical process of labour market formation was marked by uneven development across physical regions as well as in time.

The transformation of society from feudalism to that of the market was long and turbulent. Traditional modes of social organization were undermined by state intervention designed to help unleash the productive, capacities of the implements of production. [ii] This is specifically the case with the main means of production, land, labour, and capital. As Heilbroner observes, the rise to dominance of market relationships "hinges on the appearance of a class of workers who are dependent for their livelihood on access to the tools and land that can legally be denied to them by their owners".[iii] So it was that peasants' traditional privileges, regarding access to the commons, were increasingly restricted and eventually abolished entirely. While at the same time, large landowners were transitioning away from the peasant self-production model and toward larger scale production. This required large amounts of formally free labourers, and more importantly their labour-power, to be available for hire.

The Enclosure movements in England in the 18th and 19th centuries, progressive consolidation of landholdings in the hands of a wealthy elite, was also a process of excluding precisely such labourers from access to the means of production, forcing them to seek remuneration which could subsequently be turned into the means of subsistence. This process of exclusion and consolidation destroyed the traditional ways of life of large sections of the population. The destruction of these traditional patterns of social reproduction was thus coextensive with the process of labour market formation. This process culminated with the establishment of a modern labour market in England in 1834. [iv]

This process of expropriation was successful, in the main, because of government intervention in society and the economy. [v] Governments secure the fundamental pre-conditions of market activity, e.g. legal enforcement of the system of property rights, building and maintaining infrastructure that facilitates commercial economic activity, among other functions. Governments, as agents in civil society, historically achieved, and then deployed a social apparatus based on a monopoly on the coercive use of force. This enabled governments to play the central role in securing and maintaining the basic social conditions necessary for the market pattern to be the dominant mode of production.[vi]

The individual worker faces a redoubtable situation bargaining with employers over acquiring a remunerative position, salary, and work conditions. This is, in the first instance, because one is required, in a capitalist market economy, to use money to legally obtain the things one wants and needs; including importantly the very means of subsistence.[vii] This applies also to things wanted or needed by family members, or other loved ones, who may not be able to obtain wage remuneration. One is also forced, in a market economy, to find employment which pays wages in order to obtain the money needed for satisfying one's needs and hopefully some portion of one's desires. [viii] The very nature of a market economy forces those who don't own enough capital to trade to meet their basic needs to seek wages in return for the one valuable commodity one always possesses, i.e. labour-power.

The kinds of communal subsistence production that dominated among European peasants, as well as the poor in many places of the world today, are no longer viable options for denizens of more advanced industrial economies. Cutting the masses of poor people off from these bases of production is exactly what characterized the processes of urbanization and proletarianization that occurred in western industrialized nations during their industrial revolutions.[ix] Former peasants were turned, sometimes violently, into industrial workers, disrupting the traditional flow of peasant life. However, this process was important for entrepreneurs, who needed a source of readily available labour-power for hire to combine with other elements of production in their pursuit of profit.

Enforced Competition among the Working Class

In addition to finding themselves constrained by the nature of a market economy, workers find themselves in a position of mutual antagonism among themselves, because there is an enormous surfeit of labourers over and above the remunerative positions currently available in the economy. [x]This dynamic has increasingly characterized industrialized nations since at least the middle of the nineteenth century. The abundance of the supply of labour-power over demand for it applies a downward pressure on workers' wage and benefit demands. This means that workers as a class are highly vulnerable to employers.

The existence of an enormous reserve of unutilized, or underutilized, labour-power means that, in the employment contracting situation, workers will be forced to lower their reservation prices in regards to the level of wages and working conditions.[xi] Workers will do this for fear of losing out on a potential source of income to a more desperate worker willing to accept less in order to get something at all. Employers take advantage of this enormous surplus of labour-power to decrease wages, and exploit a vulnerability workers face primarily as a result of the creation of labour as a commodity.

In a market economy, capitalist employers are always competing with each other, and this reality quite naturally leads the entrepreneur to look to the site of production itself as a place to economize and attempt to out-compete his or her rivals. Employers' focus on the labour-process is thus the result of a systemic force in market economies. This is because the employer has all the appropriate rights and powers which due the owner of any legal property in a market economy. Since the entrepreneur is this common contracting agent, he or she becomes responsible for organizing the actual work that goes on during the production phase of the circuit of capital.

In a market economy, production begins with money, which buys the means of production, which then produces products that are sold, i.e. turned into money.[xii] This means that each competitor in a market has an interest in finding ways to reduce costs wherever possible. One of the first ways that efficiencies of this type are pursued is to contrive machines that replace human labour, or make human labour more productive. The fact of inter-capitalist competition also means that innovations of this sort are likely to be diffused widely throughout a particular industry as competitors adopt, or even steal, the innovation in order to avoid being left behind. The effect of these technologies is often to reduce the need for human labour, which is or can be expensive. Even when labour is not expensive, it always constitutes a savings to the firm to spend less on labour, and hence there is a strong systemic force pushing firms toward automation where feasible. The reduction in the need for labour-power also has an advantageous consequence for the firm, in that any increase in the amount of surplus labour-power available only further depresses wages as inter-worker competition correspondingly increases.

Inequality

Further compounding this problematic situation are the "prior distributions" of wealth the parties to the potential employment contract bring to the contracting situation.[xiii] As a result of structure of the distribution of wealth and resources prior to a specific transaction, employers enjoy a special advantage when bargaining with workers on employment contracts. This is the idea of "threat advantage" that Alan Wertheimer discusses.[xiv] In real life, there comes a point at which material necessity presses up against the weaker party and forces that party to either die or capitulate.[xv] In a capitalist labour market, both employer and worker know that labourers will be the ones that must eventually relent. Individual workers face homelessness and starvation without wages, and it is precisely this threat that forces the class of labourers to seek wage remuneration for their labour-power from employers as a class. This is the condition of vulnerability that characterizes labourers as a class.

Employers are able to achieve sometimes extremely large profits because they are able to control the workplace, and with it the labour process. Employers obtain this control through the terms of the employment contract they make with workers. The content of the employment relationship is what is being bargained about in the contracting situation. Employers take advantage the vulnerability of workers in the labour market to make employment contracts in which they acquire the control needed to generate a profit.[xvi] The structure of a market economy, the existence of a reserve army of unemployed persons, and persistent basic needs all conspire to undermine to bargaining position of workers relative to employers in the labour market, and thus the employment contracting situation that occur within it.

As a result, individual employers, as well as employers as a class, possess a credible threat of exit from the contracting situation. The worker seeking employment, in most cases, possesses no similarly credible threat. This is because the worker most likely does not possess the means to physically subsist until a more favorable contract can be struck. Because the employer can credibly hold out longer, she obtains a superior bargaining position, and can thence make a contract more favorable to her own interests than to the workers'.

This superior bargaining position of employers is only enhanced by the differential mobility of capital and labour. In a market economy, especially with developed credit and banking systems, capital can much more easily be moved across great distances than can labour. The threat advantage of employers is thus bolstered by the credible threat to relocate their capital, and or their productive business enterprises. This is an instance of employers using inter-worker competition to leverage a more advantageous deal with labourers by pitting geographically dispersed pools of labour-power against each other. Given the often limited ability of labour to move to new locations, where employment is more abundant, workers are further pressured into making employment contracts they would otherwise reject because their access to the means of subsistence, and perhaps that of their families as well, is at stake.

Threatened with loss of access to the very means of subsistence, workers are routinely forced to accept wage levels and work conditions that they would otherwise very likely judge inadequate, or even totally unacceptable. The employer as owner also has the ability, as a last recourse, to choose to not employ any of her assets productively at all. The owner, given the market capitalist conception of the right of ownership, is perfectly within his rights to shut his business down, if the local labour force expects too high a level of either wages or work conditions.

Conclusion

The power asymmetry between employer and worker artificially alters the structure of reservation prices to the workers detriment by forcing the worker to lower, often very substantially, his or her reservation price as regards wages and work conditions in the employment contracting situation. This power asymmetry enables employers to offer workers a lower level of wages, work conditions, and control over labour or the product of it than the latter would likely be inclined accept in a labour market situation where the structure of worker's reservation prices more accurately reflected their actual preferences.

So we can see now that the notion of free wage labour in capitalism is a myth. There has never been much free about the freedom of the wage labourer in capitalism. Force has been applied to the worker at almost every stage so that he or she must continue to need to consume many hours of labour. Only by creating a situation in which workers have to be willing to consume a great many hours of wage work can the capitalist class maintain the kind of competition between workers than puts downward pressure on wages, and thus upward pressure on profits. As we saw technological innovation is one key driver of the creation and expansion of the reserve army of labour. The existence of a massive supply of unused but readily available labour-power is, and has been for some time, an important structural feature of our capitalist economy.

Notes

[i] Polanyi 2001, 81.

[ii] Examples of the kind of turbulence to be found in the transition of peasants into wage labourers can be found in Stephen Marglin's excellent article "What Do Bosses Do? The Origins and Functions of Hierarchy in Capitalist Production". *Review of Radical Political Economics*. Vol.6 (1974): 60-112. Also see Polanyi (2001).

[iii] Heilbroner 1986, 41.

[iv] This date of birth for the modern labour market comes from Polanyi (2001: 87).

[v] For an excellent discussion of the role of governments in creating and sustaining the conditions for successful markets see Neil Fligstein The Architecture of Markets. Princeton, Princeton University Press: 2001.

[vi] For a closer look at this historical process see Beaud, Michel. A History of Capitalism. 1981.Tr. Dickman, Tom & Anny Lefebvre. New York, Monthly Review Press: 2001. Also see Arrighi, Giovanni.The Long Twentieth Century. 1994. New York, Verso Press: 2006

[vii] This is of course lest one should find some way to persuade others to provide all one's essentials as free gifts.

[viii] Government sponsored welfare programs, and access to the means for subsistence farming, or independent wealth for example can effect whether or not and to what extent one must seek remunerative employment.

[ix] For an excellent discussion of this process in the context of experience of England see Thompson, E.P. The Making of the English Working Class. Vintage Books, 1963.

[x] This is sometimes not the case for bounded periods of time in specific industries in specific countries at specific times. On the macro-level, the persistence of unemployment in developed industrialized countries testifies to the permanent surplus of labour-power available over the demand of employers for it.

[xi] A "reservation price" is the lowest price at which the owner of commodity is willing to sell that commodity. In this case, the reservation price is the wage rate below which the worker would reject the offer of employment.

[xiii] We owe this terminology to Charles Lindblom (2001). He describes "prior distributions" as the pattern of ownership of valuable resources that obtains in society prior to, i.e. temporally before, any individual instance of bargaining between economic agents over a potential transaction. These 'prior distributions' are what specific economic agents bring to any particular transaction, and what helps define the bargaining situation between them.

[xiv] Wertheimer 1996, 67.

[xv] Or perhaps revolt.

[xvi] To see the link between employer control and their ability to produce benefits for themselves, i.e. profits, see Stephen Marglin's article in Review of Radical Political Economics. Vol.6 (1974): 60-112.

Adjuncts Organize
An Interview with St. Rose (NY) Professor, Bradley Russell

Daniel J. Kelly

In late September, 2014, something happened at the College of Saint Rose in Albany, NY that hasn't happened often enough in recent years. Eighty percent of the approximately 300 adjunct professors at the private, liberal arts college turned out to vote to unionize. When the results were tallied the professors had voted by a margin of 175 to 61 to join Local 200 United of the Service Employees International Union. Local 200 is part of S.E.I.U's Adjunct Action, a nationwide project to organize adjunct professors. As many of our readers will know, the adjunct professor phenomenon is just another neoliberal strategy to disempower the workforce. By a policy of no benefits, no job security, and no raises the employing class atomizes another subset of workers. In other words, if they can fool them into thinking they're independent contractors they will be less inclined to act collectively to secure power in the workplace. This has been part of the neoliberal agenda for nearly forty years and for much of that time that agenda has worked, but not at the College of Saint Rose in 2014.

To get a better idea of how this unionization process unfolded, I met with Dr. Bradley Russell on Oct 2nd of this year. Dr. Russell was the chief instigator of this organizing campaign and the organizer who, along with help from S.E.I.U., pushed it to a successful outcome.

Bradley Russell is a man in his early forties with a strong personality. He earned a PhD in anthropology, with a concentration in archeology, from the State University of New York about a decade ago; his dissertation focused on the importance of Mayan incense burners. He has taught for several years as an adjunct professor at St. Rose where he also teaches a class called "Creating Social Justice." As a husband and, father of an elementary school age child, he has a personal interest in improving the working conditions of the adjunct community. He has also made a name for himself locally as an activist; (full disclosure: Russell and I met when we were both participating in the Occupy Albany movement in 2011 and I have since been a guest speaker in his "Social Justice" class).

I set aside an hour to speak with Dr. Russell at a coffee shop near the College of Saint Rose. When he walked into the shop he was immediately recognized by several people there including a professor from the State University and a local labor activist who congratulated him on the recent organizing campaign victory. With all the congratulations, it was a bit difficult at first to get his undivided attention but, we did finally settle down to the interview. It is my hope that the things he and I discussed that morning will be of some help to others who are exploring organizing campaigns in their own workplaces.

DK: So, let's start with a simple question: how did you come to the conclusion that organizing a union was a workable strategy for solving the problems of adjunct professors?

BR: I'm not sure I concluded it was a workable solution per se. I kind of concluded it was the only viable option. Basically, it was a function of doing things I'd always been told to do to get myself out of the conditions I was in: getting publications out there, getting grant money, ongoing research, getting a terminal degree. And then going beyond that by talking to my immediate supervisors, my department chair, my dean over and over again, semester after semester, and being told by them; yeah, we understand that the situation is really, really bad, and we feel terrible about it, but our hands are tied by the administration-we can't do anything. Finally, I just said something's got to change and as you know, having been one of those labor organizers in my "Social Justice" class, I started talking to people in the labor community, thinking about collective bargaining as a way to get the administration to actually listen to us. There was no way to get the provost or the president of the college to meet with us or consider any of our changes. So, bringing hundreds of voices to the table was the only way I could see for getting any of that done.

What were the first steps you took?

The very first thing I did, back in February, 2013, was to send out an article to our college listserv, actually two articles--links to two articles--on the national state of things in academia and the conditions adjuncts across the board were facing. I didn't comment on them. I didn't say much of anything. I just put these two links out and pretty soon we had 15 or 20 responses from adjuncts saying; "yeah, this is a real problem," and then I used those as a springboard to form an organizing committee. Based on the responses I'd gotten, I started emailing people saying, look I'm considering the collective bargaining option. Do you want to get on board with helping make that happen? So, really, I reached out through our school listserv as the first thing.

How did you eventually reach out to S.E.I.U.?

It was kind of a fluke actually. I just happened to be friends with one of the organizers working with the Adjunct Action campaign they're running. He and I were chatting about totally unrelated things and I brought it up the fact that I'm an adjunct over at St. Rose and he said, "Oh really, we've been looking to talk to someone at St. Rose. Do you have any interest in a union?" I responded, "As a matter of fact we're already discussing forming one so, let's get together." It was really a function of having a friendship with someone and having it pop up in conversation.

Did see any sort of discernable pattern form in the organizing process?

What do you mean a pattern?

Were there any specific steps, for instance, a step you had to take before you could take the next one, then another one you had to take before proceeding further?

The biggest thing was getting information on how to find adjuncts. We're such a transient population that it was pretty impossible to track us all down at any one point. We went through the semester to semester class lists to see who was teaching and compare those to the website to see how many of those had been eliminated or were now full time. We'd reach out to the ones how didn't seem to be full time. The outreach by far was the biggest thing we had to do. Pretty quickly we moved to a point where we publically announced what we were doing. That made the outreach easier because we could just go ahead and make big public announcements across the listserv and encourage people to contact us. The biggest thing by far was definitely getting ahold of this transient population of professors. Once we did that the sell was really easy. Our conditions were so dismal--ARE so dismal--that we had very few people who didn't express interest right away. There were a few people who were just ideologically opposed to unions and rejected our overtures but, for the most part, 75-80% of people were clearly supportive from the get go.

Were there any other obstacles besides outreach and ideological resistance?

Well, there were really two forms. The people who did resist weren't interested, let me put it that way. There were really two classes: There were the people who were just ideologically opposed. Unions just did not fit their politics, but there were also a lot of people who were just fundamentally afraid. We have no job security at all. We can be removed from our jobs any semester that comes along. They just don't offer us a contract and, that's it, we're done. A lot of people were afraid there would be push back from the administration, their department chairs, or their deans would retaliate against them despite labor laws that protect them. You have a certain amount of protection but, if a violation occurs you're still out of that job until you can get some legal finding that puts you back on the job. That's a huge hassle; some people were simply not willing to stick their neck out like that. The thing that I think offset that the most, that did the most good in that area, was that we had really solid support from our full time faculty and, they posted regularly to the listserv encouraging unionization and encouraging people to step up. They clearly supported us and made it clear that there were whole departments voting in favor of supporting unionization so, the likelihood of retaliation on the individual level seemed to decline for a lot of people as the campaign went on.

My next question is kind of an opinion question. Would you say adjuncts are exploited? I'm going to clarify that by saying clearly adjuncts as underpaid and administrators have rather large salaries. Would you characterize that as exploitation and, if so, how would you go about communicating that to other sectors of the workforce?

It's definitely exploitative. In the business model that colleges across the country are using right now they've clearly decided that there is a class of workers--they have frankly created a class of workers--that have little job security, and are so desperate to work they will accept unbelievably low pay, no benefits, no respect, limited access to offices, other facilities, photocopying, printing. A lot of this stuff is coming out of pocket for us which is absurd when we're paid so little to start with. It's definitely an exploitative model. A lot of people have referred to it as the academic caste system. I think that's a pretty good descriptor because people end up in a situation where they're locked in. There are so few full time jobs left at this point. They've eliminated so many of them that there's nowhere to go. There's no movement upwards. There are no options for promotions, no options for raises. We didn't get a raise at St. Rose for well over a decade--still haven't. We'll get one with our first contract. They've clearly created an underclass with a tiered system of pay and it's absolutely absurd. We're essentially doing the same work; we're not doing the committee work, we're not doing the same advising necessarily but in terms of the teaching it's exactly the same. As a matter of fact, a teacher takes a sabbatical or paid time off and an adjunct invariably fills in for their class. They're the same exact classes in some cases but we do it for a tiny fraction of what they pay the full time faculty.

What did you say to colleagues who thought that because they are professionals they don't need a union?

We didn't really hear that much. In the discussion nationwide you hear that position and I think, to some degree, generally that might be an attitude. I can't say that I can think of anybody [at St. Rose] who said that to me. What we got much more often was people who would say, "I'm afraid this is going to change the tone of our relationship with the administration," which was funny since there was no relationship with the administration. It didn't exist as any type of communication, so I'm not sure what relationship they were worried about. There were people worried that some sort of adversarial relationship would develop. But I think that was mostly just rhetoric. There were a certain amount of people that did buy into the administration lie that we have a new president and now that we've gotten to the point where they've heard us, (because we've mobilized like this), we don't have to keep mobilizing because now they've heard us and they'll take care of it. I think that was a weirdly hypocritical stance to take because it was predicated entirely on the fact that we were already taking collective action. Somehow because we've taken collective action we don't need collective action! So, I pushed back pretty strenuously on that notion on the basis that if we hadn't stepped up like this we wouldn't see them acknowledging that there's a problem, more or less talking about maybe finding solutions, but we needed those solutions to be in writing, so we could count on them occurring and not just trust that they'll do it. Those were really the biggest lines of resistance we had from the people who were "anti."

Were any of the classic union busting strategies coming from the College itself?

They hired a lawyer that promotes himself as representing the management side of labor disputes, working to defeat unionization. He played a very predictable playbook. Our provost put out a series of memos and each one was essentially right out of the traditional playbook: "they're going to charge you dues. Why do you need dues?" They played the third party, "You don't need a third party. Why don't we have a direct relationship with each other? Why do you want to interject this third party?" All the kinds of things that you would expect. They tweaked it a little bit and they followed the tactics that were used at St Thomas [College] where they recently defeated a unionization effort. Their [St. Thomas'] argument was very similar to this one that I already mentioned; that "we have a new president. She's really concerned about this. You've just got to give us some time. Trust us." The trust thing; they played that trust card a lot. It went very poorly for them because every time they would try this the full time faculty, who aren't unionized, would push back and say; "look, we've been told we need to trust this deal you offered. We took that deal. You failed to live up to that. You offered us that deal. We took that deal. You failed to live up to that one. Trust is not the answer. The answer is a contract-a binding contract". So, I don't think that the trust thing went well. The other thing they tried was a phrase that we don't even use any more. It used to be one of the school's official slogans; *The St. Rose difference*. "What about the St. Rose difference?" It got to be kind of laughable because they would say, "What about the St. Rose difference?" and we would say, "What St. Rose difference? We're in the same boat as adjuncts at every other school. If there was a St. Rose difference wouldn't it already have fixed this?" This notion that we're somehow fundamentally different than the other schools was played up all the time. It was like saying, "Where is you school spirit?" That's essentially what the argument was, "where is your school spirit?" I don't give a crap about "school spirit". I give a crap that we're being exploited and used while, at the same time, administrative salaries continue to go up. The number of positions in the administration continues to rise. They continue to build incessantly on campus-new dorms, new offices, etc. Meanwhile they're telling us there's no money; we have to tighten our belts. They seem to find money for all their priorities but none for ours and, it was just time for them to stop.

What sorts of things are students saying in response to this process? Also, have you found that the attitudes of students toward what the adjuncts have done since you first started organizing has changed?

I think if there's one thing I wish we had done better is to educate the students about what adjuncts are. This is really a huge problem in academia and one of the reasons it's been allowed to persist is that students and their parents really don't know this is happening. They don't know that a huge percentage of the professors at the colleges are part time, low paid, with no benefits. I've encouraged other adjuncts to explain this their students every chance they get. In the cases where I've explained that to my students they're clearly outraged. They can't believe what they're hearing and it's a real eye opener for them.

I actually tried to show Megan Fulwiler's and Jen Marlow's film; "Con Job: Stories of Adjunct & Contingent Labor," that deals with this, [Fulwiler and Marlow are English Composition instructors at St. Rose]. It's a fifty minute film and I had a fifty minute class window to show it. I got 20 minutes of it shown because there were so many questions from the students--hands just kept popping up. If there's one thing that I wish we had done better, it would be to do outreach directly to students. That wasn't feasible because a lot of the organizing we did was over the summer when they weren't around. The vote came so soon that there wasn't a lot of time to do that direct outreach. It cases where we were able to do that it was very effective. People were really surprised to find out about the conditions we were operating in and wanted to see a change.

Have you begun organizing the committee that will negotiate for a contract yet?

We haven't yet. We're having our first membership meeting on the 15th [of October] and we will take nominations at that point for the three officers; chair, vice chair, and shop steward. We're also going to be looking for representatives from each of the schools who will be direct liaisons with adjuncts in their departments to bring their concerns and issues to the forum for when we're putting together the negotiating objectives

Do you see yourself becoming an officer of the local?

I think so. I've clearly been a major voice up to now. I was sort of the person who got the ball rolling in the first place and I feel like I need to see that through at least to a contract and I am going to be looking to have that chairman position. I've been discussing with some of the other people on the organizing committee about the vice chair and shop steward position. I think we're the people who've been here along and I think we're the best people to carry the movement forward at this point. That said, I do look forward to a little bit of peace and quiet at some point so, once we actually negotiate a contract and get it ratified, I might be prepared to step aside and give that position up to somebody else. I might even be eager to do that. We'll see.

Do you see contract negotiation unfolding in an easy way or do you think the college might dig in its heels?

From the kind of language that was coming from the memos I think they've telegraphed that their plan is to dig in, drag it out as long as possible, and make it as difficult as possible. The tone that they took in their messages was sort of twofold. First, there was that trust issue that we talked about "trust us, we'll fix it. We understand we hear there are real problems." Yet, simultaneously they were saying; "These union contracts, they're adversarial and they take a year at least to negotiate and, we don't have to give anything that we don't want to give." So, it was a carrot on a stick: on one hand don't vote for the union and we'll give you raises and we'll fix the situation, (in whatever ways they deem appropriate), or if you vote for the union we're going to make as difficult as humanly possible.

Last question, what kind of support would you like to see from the local organized labor community as well as from the local activist community as a whole?

That's a really tough question. It's going to depend on how the negotiations are working out. If there is the kind of resistance that I'm anticipating I expect that we might be doing informational picketing and applying other types of pressure to the administration to bargain in good faith. If it comes down to those kinds of efforts then definitely some on the ground presence from other members in the area would be much appreciated. Logistical and negotiating advice from people who have a little more experience with negotiating contracts would definitely be appreciated. General solidarity is always appreciated. It kind of depends on how the campaign plays out as we get to the negotiating table. We really hugely appreciate the amount of support we've already gotten from the local labor community, from the full time faculty, from our students, and in a lot of cases, from local community leaders such as the mayor, state senators, and state assembly members. That's really made all the difference in this campaign and made it successful.

LGBTQ Rights

Rediscovering Dialogue
An Interview with Son of Baldwin

Devon Douglas-Bowers

The following is an interview with the founder and facilitator of Son of Baldwin: "The literary, socio-political, sexual, pop culture blog. Live from Bedford-Stuyvesant."

Why have you named the page Son of Baldwin? What kind of impact has James Baldwin had on you personally?

James Baldwin was the first black gay male intellectual I had ever encountered. His work was really the first time I had seen myself, my identity (as a black gay male), and my point of view represented in art and public discourse in a way that was not meant to be mocked, dismissed, minimized, or dehumanized. His was the first work that started me on the path to thinking critically about myself, the world around me, and my place in it. In tribute to that consciousness raising (which may have come much later, if at all, had it not been for him) and in an effort to answer his final call to dig through the wreckage and use what he left behind to continue the work of trying to make the world a more just, livable, peaceful place, I named the blog "Son of Baldwin." I have been told by friends of Baldwin's family that the family is quite pleased by the work being done and they believe that I am indeed honoring his legacy. That is overwhelming and I am overjoyed.

What made you want to make a Facebook page in the first place?

Son of Baldwin originally started out as a blog via blogspot. But that space wasn't really conducive to conversation. Facebook allows for a kind of direct and extended interaction and dialogue that many other sites, including other social media, don't. And for me, the conversation is the most important part. Despite how I may sometimes come across, this isn't about me. This isn't about being able to proselytize from on high and have everyone applaud the pronouncement. This is about starting conversations and engaging other people in various communities about these causes and concerns in the effort of finding solutions to some of our most pressing social justice issues.

You talk about a number of topics, from LGBTQ rights to racism, through a critical progressive lens. How did you come to this political awakening of sorts?

I think this awakening started in my childhood. I grew up during the 70s, 80s, and 90s-a child of both Black Southern Baptist and Nation of Islam traditions-in a section of Brooklyn called Bensonhurst (infamous for the racist attack against and murder of Yousef Hawkins in 1989).
Bensonhurst, at least at that time I grew up there, was a neighborhood of primarily Italian and Irish first- and second-generation immigrants. In this neighborhood, I lived in a housing

project of mostly black and Latin@ peoples right in the middle of things. We were thus surrounded, if you will, in hostile enemy territory. This made everything tenuous.

As a child and a teen, I had to plot routes home from school that would help me avoid running into the mobs of white children, teens, and adults who--with bats in hand, violence in heart, and death in mind--made a regular ritual of chasing kids of color back to the projects.

What was different for me when I got back to the projects, having often but not always escaped the battering from racists, is that the battle didn't end there. I had to then contend with the other black and Latin@ peoples who wanted to pound on my head because they perceived me as gay.

When you are not safe in any of the worlds you inhabit, you sort of don't have a choice but to become politicized. You kind of don't have a choice but to "wake up" because if you don't, you'll be murdered. Reading the works of authors like Baldwin, Toni Morrison, Alice Walker, Ralph Ellison, Zora Neale Hurston, Richard Wright, Octavia Butler, Audre Lorde, and others helped to direct these concerns and grievances, and made me feel less alone and more empowered to do something about my circumstances.

Something that I have noticed about you is that you actively allow yourself to be called out by others and acknowledge when you messed up and allow yourself to be corrected. Why do you think that this does not exist in larger political circles, especially liberal or progressive spheres?

My opinion is that this willingness to be wrong and be corrected doesn't happen in larger political circles and spheres because many of the people working within those areas actually think this work is about them. They believe that in order to be trusted and effective, they have to feign perfection and position themselves as above reproach. Can you imagine?

291

Many people doing this work think that in order to be trusted they have to lie. The truly sad thing about this contradiction of a strategy is how often it works, and how often complicit audiences are willing to believe the lie if it confirms their system of reality. I guess what I'm saying is that many people doing this work are politicians in the most cynical sense of the word, and that occupation is not something I have any interest in whatsoever. I'm a writer by purpose, training, and profession, and I've never pretended to be anything other than that.

In short, I think ego is at the center of this unwillingness to be incorrect.

You recently made it a requirement that people who post photos on the page to provide a written description. What prompted this?

This comes from a desire to ensure that as many people as possible are able to participate, as fully as they can, in the conversations and discourses happening in the space. Blind and Deaf/Hard of Hearing people are active members of the Son of Baldwin community and this policy makes it possible for them to be even more vibrant participants in discussions. This is one of the ways I'm trying to address my own collusion in institutionalized ableism/disableism.

What are your thoughts on online social justice work? Do you think that it can make a serious difference in people's lives and on a larger scale? (I often hear people saying that tweeting or writing doesn't really do anything.)

For starters, I think online social justice work has been a blessing in the sense that it has given a voice to many peoples and communities whose voices were often missing, excluded, or silenced in sociopolitical discussions. Additionally, the Internet has made it possible for many more people to have access to these debates and discussions, such as disabled people/people with disabilities who are often unable to access on-the-ground events because many organizers are unwilling to make accommodations, or poor peoples who simply cannot afford to travel to these events. There are many absolutely amazing and brilliant online social justice activists doing work that honestly, truly matters, and are, despite narratives to the contrary, affecting the discourse and changing minds.

But like everything else, there is a deeply disturbing dark side to online social justice work.

One of the things I deeply dislike about much of the social justice activism and social justice spaces I've encountered is how intentionally vicious they are. And I'm not talking about viciousness between social justice activists and trolls. I'm talking about the viciousness between peoples with the same goals, but who might have different strategies for obtaining those goals. I've seen some really hateful, ugly, deeply dishonest and self-serving stuff happening in conversations in these spaces-including my own. I'm not talking about disagreements or even heated disagreements. I'm talking about full-on attempts at destroying each other-from credibility to personhood. I'm talking about people who truly get off on making others feel as small as possible so they can feel big. I'm talking about intentionally committing violence against and silencing other people. I'm talking about people lying and slandering others with the intent of spiritually murdering them as though they were opposing a concept rather than a person. The Internet often helps with the depersonalization of people. When you think you're arguing with, and trying to obliterate, digitized images and typed words instead of a living being, it's easier to be joyfully inhumane, spiritually toxic, and intellectually genocidal, then reward yourself by calling it "social justice." It's easy to be gleeful about shitting on an opponent (an opponent that you, yourself, manufactured for your own dubious purposes, by the way) and high-five each other about the havoc you wreaked when you can treat the carnage as a concept rather than reality.

I'm talking about people who wear the cloak of victimhood like a Trojan horse in order to sneak into the village, get close to you and-surprise- become the victimizers you never expected. There are people who use their marginalized identities and communities not for the purposes of liberation, but as a hustle, as masturbation, as a way to elevate themselves to a place where they are above reproach. I'm talking about the people who have the audacity to use "trigger" not as a real expression and sign post of lived trauma, but as a strategic pretense to silence any opinions they don't like. It's like they play this game where the more marginalized identity boxes they can check off, the more they can't be criticized for any behavior they engage in, no matter how abusive and counterrevolutionary. Therefore, the goal is to check off as many marginalized identity boxes as they can-even if they have to invent them or pretend to belong to them. Whoever has the most, wins. To me, that's the original pimp strategy and I guess what I'm saying is that I don't like pimps. But I have discovered that there are so many of them in this arena. Some folks are out here big pimpin' and calling it "radical" of all things.

I don't know why, but that shocked me. I did some research to determine whether this was a new phenomenon brought on by the anonymity of the Internet. What I discovered is this behavior pre-dates the Internet. Shirley Chisholm, for example, was the target of disgusting attacks by people who should have been in solidarity with her. Richard Wright and Ralph Ellison said such despicable things about James Baldwin that it would make your skin crawl. Much to my dismay, I learned this in-fighting and hostility isn't novel in any respect.

Sometimes, I've been accused of being egotistical, which, okay, fine if that's your opinion. But the truth of the matter is that I'm not trying to be a pimp at this stuff. Part of why I don't do public speaking gigs, etc. is because I'm not trying to become some kind of object of celebrity or fame. I'm not trying to become some kind of some kind of commercial figure or commodity.
I'm not trying to be that person who maneuvers themselves closer to the president in group photo opportunities because they are

trying to climb some political ladder. Those people want to be "The One." Not me, though. I'm not trying to be the "go-to" expert. I'm not trying to be in the spotlight. I'm not trying to be anyone's leader. I'm not trying to make money off of this work. I'm not trying to play like I'm perfect and have all the answers. I'm learning right alongside everyone else. I'm not here to be worshiped like some god-thing, but regarded as a human being who is growing and evolving, falling down and getting back up again with increased knowledge. I'm a participant in this conversation.

But increasingly, these aren't conversations anymore. Increasingly, these are encounters with people with not-always-legit agendas trying to push those agendas as liberation strategies. These people are about switching places with the oppressor and will use whichever of the"master's tools" (as Audre Lorde called them) is necessary to do so. However, I'm not interested in being chained and I'm not interested in chaining anyone else. That, for me, is the politics of inertia and I'm interested in progress. I want everyone to be liberated.

Part of the genius of this violence-strategy that some people who call themselves marginalized employ is that it's difficult for the victim of the violence to discern whether the violence is legitimate or illegitimate. Because many of the people in this work are so committed to justice, they err on the side of it being legitimate even when it isn't. So they endure the emotional, psychic, psychological, spiritual, and sometimes even physical abuse because they're afraid if they don't, they will be labeled as a part of the problem. Speaking for myself, I've allowed people to abuse me, even flat-out lie about me on an ongoing basis, just so I wouldn't be perceived as an oppressor and anti-justice (because of the ways in which my identities intersect, in and out, with privilege and oppression and marginalization). To save my "reputation" among the social justice crowd, I've been a masochist. It's so incredibly complicated. And I do not have the answers for it. But I do have the bruises.

So, I'm no longer engaging the brutality. I'm moving away, not from the difficult and needed conversations, but from the egotistical violence. If your concept of social justice is about amassing power at the expense of other victims of hegemonic abuse, I cannot be down for your cause. And if that makes me "bad" at doing this social justice stuff, then so be it. If you need me to be the villain so you can feel like the hero in your own story, play on playa. But you'll be playing sans me. I won't give you the attention you're seeking. I will absolutely refuse to see you no matter what tricks you employ. I've got other work to do.

You are quite critical of the race and class politics of the mainstream LGBT community. Due to this split on multiple levels, from racism to ignoring transgender people, would you say that there is even a real LGBT community? How can people work towards having more inclusive spaces for marginalized LGBT members?

I would say, currently, that there may be LGTBQIA communities, plural. But the singular community that is commonly addressed in media and conversations is one that is actually serving the needs of one particular subset of the communities-namely, white, middle-to-upper class, cisgender, non-disabled, gender conforming men. James Baldwin said back in 1984 that the gay movement was really about white people who lost their white privilege struggling and petitioning to get it back. I see no lies in that statement if the national platforms and conversations, if the faces of the movement are any indication.

I witness tons of conversations about why "black people are so homophobic" (which we can actually trace, ironically, to white colonial intervention) but relatively few to none about why "why white gay people are so racist." The answer, as Baldwin surmised, was because white gay people are still, at heart, white and Whiteness, which is inextricably linked to the idea of racial superiority, is at the root of most of our problems.

To get to a more inclusive space, people (of all races and creeds) have to give up their addiction to Whiteness and white supremacy.

People (or all genders and sexualities) have to give up their addiction to patriarchy and narrow-minded views of masculinity, femininity, gender identity, and sexuality. People of all physical realities have to give up capitalism and incessant materialism, which are commodifications of humanity, and stop treating human bodies as machines that are valuable only for what they can produce for the State-a deeply ableist point of view.

The problem is convincing people to give up the things that define their current comforts. We have to get people to be willing to be uncomfortable, at least for a while, until we can figure all of this out. This may be a continuous journey, rather than a destination.

At the end of the day, what do you want people to get out of your Facebook page?

My dream for Son of Baldwin is that it serves as a place where we can have uncomfortable conversations about social justice issues without dehumanizing one another. We might occasionally yell at one another. We might occasionally have to be corrected for our errors and apologize for them. But I hope out of the consternation come viable solutions and a greater respect for each other's humanity.

Internalizing Black Lives Matter

A Queer Project in Loving Blackness (Part 1)

Dr. Jonathan Mathias Lassiter

Black lives matter. And #BlackLivesMatter, a movement founded after the death of Trayvon Martin in 2012, is bringing this fundamental truth to the masses. As cited on the movement's website, "Black Lives Matter affirms the lives of Black queer and trans folks, disabled folks, black-undocumented folks, folks with records, women and all Black lives along the gender spectrum. It centers those that have been marginalized within Black liberation movements. It is a tactic to (re)build the Black liberation movement." #BlackLivesMatter's mission is a radical one. The mission takes seriously the plight of the "least of these" to which Jesus often referred. This makes sense given that the movement was founded by three Black queer women (Casper, 2014). Black queer women live intersectionality and must often challenge a world that regards them as subordinate in androcentric, heteronormative, and ethnocentric paradigms that privilege white heterosexual males. It is also womanist in that Black women, central to the movement, are working to not only improve their lives but *all* Black lives.

Challenging oppressive systems requires an intersectional framework that is cross cutting and examines the ways in which several oppressive forces act interdependently at the microlevel to impact people's lives structurally. We have had centuries, since the start of European colonialism, of people of color being assaulted by deadly oppressive forces. In societies structured by imperialistic, capitalist, white supremacist, and heteropatriarchal ideas, Blackness is deviance that must either result in profit or death, or both. The implementation of this ideology is seen in America through racial/ethnic disparities in such domains as housing, education, incarceration, and healthcare that leave Black people inadequately housed, under-educated, imprisoned, and dying. Meanwhile, predominately white-controlled corporations overwhelming commodify Black cultural creations, profit from Black prisoners' labor, and bill "supposed" Black deviance. Although, intersectionality begins with an examination of how the microlevel influences the structural level, the inverse relationship is also of interest. Anti-Black ideology and its manifestations not only impacts Black lives at the structural level, it also infects the psyches of Black people.

Anti-Black ideology has serious negative implications for Black people's mental health. Many Black people have internalized, explicitly and implicitly, Black inferiority myths promoted by structural forces. At the other end of the spectrum, some have adopted Black superiority myths which promote white values in Blackface while confessing Afrocentricity. Such internalization has resulted in psychological trauma in various forms, ranging from the exaltation of white beauty aesthetics to Black-on-Black crime. While there is a substantially large literature on the psychological ramifications of anti-Blackness, as a psychologist, I am becoming less interested in pathology and more invested in the affirmation and optimization of Black mental health. What are the possibilities for Black people's psychological well-being when they internalize the truth that Black lives matter? Such internalization would take effort and I imagine it would be a revolution of self-love. That revolution would require a queering of the status quo through the disruption of what it means to be Black in a white supremacist paradigm that dictates anti-Black relations across the globe.

Black psychologists have forged a rich body of knowledge that defines, analyzes, and critiques the contours and composition of a Black-affirmative psychology. This literature is mainly classified into three schools of thought: traditional, reformist, and radical (see Karenga, 1993 for more information on Black Psychology's history). The radical school of thought within the field of Black Psychology most informs my ideas about what an internalization of "Black Lives Matter" would look like. It privileges Black lives through centering an African worldview and promoting self-consciousness. It is less concerned with the white gaze and more focused on defining Black lives in relationship to an African cosmology. This is the promise of the radical school of Black psychology at its best (although it sometimes does not reach this height and recasts heteropatriarchy and other oppressive ideologies, which are most detrimental to Black people who are not able-bodied heterosexual men, through a Black lens). At its best, radical Black psychology is intersectional. It provides a framework for shaping Black people's mental health in a way that promotes healing and optimization through reclamation of an African personhood. This personhood is grounded in a spirituality that permeates all aspects of the Black being (Piper-Mandy & Rowe 2010). Black people who embody this African personhood are integrated in spirit, mind, and body and connected to all else that is spirit. Consequently in this paradigm, Black people are *whole* people and all parts of them (i.e. gender, sexual orientation, ability-status, class, educational level, etc.) are equally essential in their optimal functioning.

If Black people are to internalize "BlackLivesMatter," we must start by accepting, privileging, and integrating all of ourselves. If we are to internalize and live "BlackLivesMatter" for ourselves, beyond the structural efforts (which is a physical manifestation of love in public), we must start by doing four things:

1) Resist myths of inferiority and superiority
2) Engage in reflexivity to understand ourselves and the reality of our diverse and intersecting realities
3) Accept ourselves as we are: multifaceted, fallible, gifted, and beautiful
4) Privilege our personhood without oppressing others

These four actions have the potential to transform a people who have, in significant numbers, internalized death as executed through imperialist, capitalist, white supremacist heteropatriarchal forces into beings that understand and cultivate their own worthiness and wholeness as people. These actions also allow us to nurture the worthiness and wholeness of all Black people and Black creations through emotional and social uplift at the interpersonal level and activism for pro-Black policy at the structural level. In this way, the actions at the microlevel have positive implications for progress at the interpersonal and structural levels.

#BlackLivesMatter, the movement, was birthed from the ideas of three queer women. It often articulates queer, intersectional, and womanist critiques of oppression. While the much-needed push for Black lives to matter at the structural level is ongoing, I hope the psychological work needed for Black lives to matter is also happening. As a psychologist and activist, I believe helping Black people internalize "BlackLivesMatter" is essential to any structural work being effective and sustainable.

References

Casper, M. (December, 2014). *Black Lives Matter / Black Life Matters: A Conversation with Patrisse Cullors and Darnell L. Moore.* Retrieved from http://thefeministwire.com/2014/12/black-lives-matter-black-life-matters-conversation-patrisse-cullors-darnell-l-moore/
Karenga, M. (1996). Black psychology. In K. Monteiro (Ed.). *Ethnicity and Psychology: African-, Asian-, Latino-, and Native-American*

Psychologies-Revised Printing, pp. 21-39. Dubuque, IA: Kendall/Hunt. Retrieved from http://www.radford.edu/jaspelme/minority-groups/past_courses/Karenga_Black_Psychology.pdf

Piper-Mandy, E., & Rowe, T. (2010). Educating African-centered psychologists: Towards a comprehensive paradigm. *Journal of Pan African Studies, 3*(8), 5-23. doi: Retrieved from http://www.jpanafrican.com/docs/vol3no8/3.8EducatingAfrican.pdf

Internalizing #BlackLivesMatter
A Queer Project in Loving Blackness (Part 2)

Dr. Jonathan Mathias Lassiter

In Part 1 of this essay, I emphasized the need to internalize #BlackLivesMatter. This need is both specific and universal. The internalization of the fact that Black lives matter must occur within Black people[1] and all people if humanity is to survive. The internalization of #BlackLivesMatter requires an appreciation and internalization of Blackness. In this essay, I put forth a definition of Blackness and detail how to effectively internalize it and thus actualize Black lives mattering.

Blackness is an integrative state of being that firmly aligns the spiritual with the physical realm. Linda James Meyers, a psychologist in the radical school of thought of Black Psychology, articulated that an optimal Afrocentric belief system emphasizes holistic-spiritual/unity, communalism, and proper consciousness (Meyers, 1988). Along these lines, Blackness is an embrace of wholeness, universal and local kinship, and active movement toward a higher understanding of self and the world. Blackness is not egocentric but harmonious. People who internalize Blackness are in tune with their spirit and understand that their existence and potential is not finite. They understand their purpose and, thus, who they are. They understand that part of who they are is connected to every other living being. They are not suspicious of others because they know that giving love to others is a nurturing of themselves. There is no zero-sum mentality. People who internalize Blackness are able to integrate themselves into a whole greater than their parts.

Blackness wrests against systems of oppression (i.e. white supremacy, imperialism, capitalism, and heteropatriarchy) that seek to sever the spiritual, communal, and physical ties that people innately possess. Oppressive systems tie one's key life values (i.e. self-worth, peace, happiness) solely to materialism (Karenga, 1995). Materialism focuses on not only earthly possessions but also fosters a neglect of one's spirit that connects humans with a consciousness beyond their current state of existence. Such ideologies convince its converts to define life narrowly to encompass only the physical (i.e. what can be seen or measured) and to believe that a "good" life can only be achieved through possession of things and people. Blackness frees one from the confines of owned or owner through its emphasis on communalism instead of commerce.

Oppression and materialism thrive because of miseducation. Black people have been miseducated to believe that 1) we have no innate worth, and 2) worth can only be gained through status and respectability. This mentality has led to many Black people endorsing "pull-up-your bootstraps" or "new Black" ideologies and alternatively fatalism. Preoccupation with propriety pits those deemed respectable against those deemed unrespectable (e.g. same-gender loving, gender nonconforming, poor, formally incarcerated people) and vice versa. It has separated them from meaningful and affirming relationships with each other. We must unlearn these ideas and move towards unity and relating to each other across differences. We must approach each other with a proper consciousness that perceives each other as connected spirits in physical embodiments. Blackness demands this from us.

Moving toward an internalization of Blackness and thus an actualization of #BlackLivesMatter requires that we:

1) Resist myths of inferiority and superiority
2) Engage in reflexivity to understand ourselves and the reality of our diverse and intersecting experiences
3) Accept ourselves as we are: multifaceted, fallible, gifted, and beautiful
4) Privilege our personhood without oppressing others.

The first process is a rejection of inferiority and superiority myths. Black people have been assaulted not only physically but also mentally. A popular stereotype aligned with inferiority myths is that Black people are innately criminal. While such a myth may sound ludicrous, it is widely believed by most people in western societies. However, it is hard to recognize its existence and act upon because it is mostly implicit, activated outside of conscious awareness, and contributes to remarkably quick cognitive processing biases. For example, researchers have found that non-Black people automatically misidentify hand tools as guns when shown pictures of Black faces (Payne, 2001, 2006) and that Black people with stereotypically Black facial features are more likely to be sentenced to death (Eberhardt, Davies, Purdie-Vaughns, & Johnson, 2006). The consequences of such inferiority myths can be seen in contemporary lynchings by cops who descend on Black people whom they perceive as "menacing" and "life threatening" and kill them although these people possess no weapons or have broken no laws (e.g. Eric Garner). Inferiority myths are deadly.

Superiority myths are also detrimental. When Black people believe superiority myths about themselves, elitism and disconnection are engendered. An example can be found in a myth held by some Black nationalists and religious groups that a sociopathic, genius Black scientist named Yacub and his followers invented white people through a 600 year scientific process of breeding out all the Black genetic traits from people on the island of Pelan (Deutsch, 2000). These white people, or devils-as the myth designates them-were considered to be natural born liars and murders (Deutsch, 2000), who eventually took over the world and enslaved Black people through "tricknology" (Curtis, 2006, p. 11). This myth, credited to Wallace Fard Muhammad (Allen, 2000), recasts supremacy myths with Black people at the top and white people at the bottom. Black people in this myth are considered the original people and only natural embodiment of humanity while white people are imagined as test-tube experiments of sociopathic Black geniuses. Such recasting may provide some Black people with a sense of esteem but ultimately it amounts to the adaptation of oppressive narratives instead of fostering liberation. Adherence to such Black supremacy myths perpetuates a system of domination rather than promote a world beyond oppression. In this way, adoption of superiority myths amount to a rejection of Blackness and still places Black people within the confines of whiteness.

Blackness is integrative but we must be aware of and critically consider our various intrapersonal components before we can integrate them. Awareness of ourselves requires that we engage in reflexivity to understand our diverse and intersecting experiences. Reflexivity is the process of "questioning our own attitudes, thought processes, values, assumptions, prejudices and habitual actions, to strive to understand our complex roles in relation to others" (Bolton, 2010, p. 13). Reflexivity is difficult to engage in because it requires that we confront our pain and give up illusions of power. Systems of oppression connect self-worth to attainment of power over ourselves and others, even to our own detriment. Reflexivity demands that we look closely and embrace the parts of us that have been defined as faggoty, niggerish, etc. It requires that we question the assertion of our pathology, the very terms used to describe us as pathological, and the people and institutions that perpetuate such notions. These people may be non-Black people and they may also be our mothers and pastors. Reflexivity requires that we interrogate the status quo definitions that keep us, as Black people, trying to prove our worth to ourselves and others. We must embrace the fact that some of us are same-gender loving. We same-gender loving Blacks must embrace the fact that some of us inhabit (dis)abled bodies. All of us must embrace that struggling with issues of self-worth does not make us worthless. Reflexivity will help us more fully integrate all such things into ourselves and accept them in others. This integration will allow us to move more freely and begin to explore ways of existing outside systems of oppression that chain our worth to being as close as possible to white, powerful, rich, and heterosexual men.

Acceptance fostered through reflexivity will allow us to call ourselves into existence as human beings that are multifaceted, fallible, gifted, and beautiful. The act of calling ourselves into existence is critical. African-centered psychologists have elaborated:

The central characteristic of what a person does and the central problematic of African identity in the West is the same - the distinction between who we think we are and who we really are. We need a way of conceptualizing identity that is consonant with the cosmic reality in which identities were framed. No one can call a person into existence that did not bring that person into existence. If others who did not generate the person, names that person, that person will not be named in a way that sets her/him free; others name us to imprison us in the power and the construct of the symbol - meme - the name. (Piper-Mandy & Rowe, 2010, p. 14).

Part of acceptance is letting go of the things that keep us stagnant. If a definition of us does not serve us, we must be willing to let it go, regardless of its origin (e.g. relatives, teachers, community members). Black people and Blackness have been attacked globally as criminal, flawed, and inferior. Many of us have internalized these pathological definitions and let them influence us consciously and subconsciously. We either try to disprove them by "going against the norm" or adhere to them out of fatalistic impulses. Regardless, our being is negotiated in the context of definitions meant to imprison us. We must learn to accept these definitions for what they are: the projections of others. They are the characteristics that others see when they look at us that stem from their view of themselves. Others' definitions of us are seldom rooted in a comprehensive understanding of us. That is our work. Through reflexivity, we can develop a comprehensive understanding of ourselves-as described above-and accept our complexity. We also must learn that while Blackness is universal, it is also specific. No two people will embody and express Blackness in identical ways. That is expected. The acceptance of pathological definitions of Blackness as simply unrealistic projections does not negate the fact that as humans we are fallible. We do not always accomplish our highest human potential in each moment. We must learn to accept our personal shortcomings while still remaining grounded in our truth and never forgetting our beauty.

The beauty of Blackness is its embodiment of spirit-body integration. When we embody and express Blackness, we are at our most human. Humanity would benefit from privileging Blackness. The privileging of the integrative nature of Blackness is essential for all people regardless of skin color or recent ancestry. As stated before, Blackness focuses on wholeness, community, and proper consciousness (i.e. clear thinking forged out of love and not fear). Living life in a paradigm of Blackness is living a life of more connectedness with others, consciousness of self, and communion with spirit. Such an existence should be privileged rather than one based on fear, paranoia, emptiness, loneliness, and ignorance. It is even more important for those of us who are of recent African descent and culturally characterized as Black to privilege Blackness. Baby Suggs in Toni Morrison's (1987, p. 88) *Beloved* points out the critical nature of loving and privileging ourselves. She stated:
Yonder they do not love your flesh. They despise it... No more do they love the skin on your back. Yonder they flay it. And O my people they do not love your hands. Those they only use, tie, bind, chop off and leave empty. Love your hands! Love them! Raise them up and kiss them. Touch others with them, pat them together, stroke them on your face 'cause they don't love that either. *You* got to love it,*you*! And no, they ain't in love with your mouth. Yonder, out there, they will see it broken and break it again. What you say out of it they will not heed...What you put into it to nourish your

body they will snatch away and give leavins instead. No they don't love your mouth. *You* got to love it.

This lack of love for Blackness necessitates that Black people not only love Blackness but put it first. The effect of anti-Blackness is that Blackness is relegated to the bottom rungs of global society in every domain. As discussed earlier, inferiority myths are internalized by Black people as well. In order to fully internalize #BlackLivesMatter, we must privilege ourselves. Anti-Black and white supremacist ideologies put Blackness last but it must be first in our lives.

Internalizing #BlackLivesMatter is a complex but essential task; it is the internalization of Blackness. The #BlackLivesMatter movement must advance across the globe. The physical, civic, and socioeconomic threats to Black lives will continue to negatively impact Black people's survival if Black lives are not valued. The parallel process of internalizing Blackness at the psychological level must also be seriously undertaken if the threats of anti-Blackness and white supremacy are ever to be overcome in our own psyches. There remains work to do.

References

Allen, E. (2000). Identity and Destiny: The Formative Views of the Moorish Science Temple and the Nation of Islam. In Haddad & Esposito (Eds.). *Muslims on the Americanization Path?*, pp. 163-214. New York, New York: Oxford University Press.

Bolton, G. (2010). *Reflective practice: Writing & professional development.* Thousand Oaks, CA: Sage Publications, Inc.

Curtis, E. (2006). *Black Muslim Religion in the Nation of Islam, 1960-1975.* Chapel Hill, NC: University of North Carolina Press.

Deutsch, N. (2000). The proximate other: The nation of Islam and Judaism. In Chiereau & Deutsch (Eds.). *Black Zion: African American Religious Encounters with Judaism*, pp. 91-117. New York, New York: Oxford University Press.

Eberhardt, J., Davies, P., Purdie-Vaughns, V., & Johnson, S. (2006). Looking deathworthy: Perceived stereotypicality of Black defendents predicts capital-sentencing outcomes. *Psychological Science, 17*(5), 383-386.

Karenga, M. (1995). Black psychology. In K. Monteiro (Ed.). *Ethnicity and Psychology: African-, Asian-, Latino-, and Native-American Psychologies-Revised Printing*, pp. 21-39. Dubuque, IA: Kendall/Hunt. Retrieved from http://www.radford.edu/jaspelme/minority-groups/past_courses/Karenga_Black_Psychology.pdf

Meyers, L. (1988). *Understanding an Afrocentric world view: Introduction to an optimal psychology.* Dubuque, IA: Kendall/Hunt.

Morrison, T. (1987). *Beloved.* New York, New York: Knopf.

Payne, B. (2001). Prejudice and perception: The role of automatic and controlled processes in misperceiving a weapon. *Journal of Personality & Social Psychology, 81, 181-192. doi: 10.1037//0022-3514.81.2.181*

Payne, B. (2006). Weapon bias: Split-second decisions and unintended stereotyping. *Current Directions in Psychological Science, 15,* 287-291. doi: 10.1111/j.1467-8721.2006.00454.x

Piper-Mandy, & Rowe, (2010). Educating African-centered psychologists: Toward a comprehensive paradigm. *The Journal of Pan African Studies, 3* (8), 5-23.

Footnote

[1] Black people are conceptualized in this essay as people of recent African descent or who are treated as socially or culturally Black in their environments. This designation is thought to be applicable regardless of one's personal identification as Black, African, Caribbean Black, Black Latino, or any other self-definition of Blackness. People who are judged to be Black and treated as Black in their societies are subject to the global discrimination and pathologizing of Black people and thus are shaped by their Blackness in real and perceived ways.

Politics & Government

Days of Darkness, Sparks of Hope
Examining Unlikely Political Alliances

Devon Douglas-Bowers

Currently in the United States, we live in an extremely polarized political sphere. People not only seek out news and op-eds that reinforce their own viewpoints, but also associate mainly with those who align with them politically in order to collectively and viciously demonize 'the other side.' The situation has gotten to the point where people view the policies of the opposing party as a threat to the nation. Globally, it seems that the landscape is even worse with problems arising in the Ukraine, the West once again embroiled in a war in the Middle East, and the knowledge that we've already seen irreversible damage due to climate change and are getting ever-closer to the 2017 deadline where climate change will truly be permanent. These are dark days; however, there is room for optimism. Around the world, we have seen unlikely political alliances that are working to fight for a better future.

The 'Cowboy-Indian Alliance'

The 'Cowboy-Indian Alliance' made waves back in April 2014 when they led a five-day 'Reject and Protect' campaign in Washington D.C. against the proposed Keystone XL pipeline. The action was quite prominent, although the origins of the alliance haven't fully been brought to light, nor has the historical importance of such an alliance.

Art Tanderup, a Nebraska farmer who has actively protested against Keystone XL, stated in an April 2014 interview that the alliance formed years ago due to the "common interests between farmers, ranchers and Native Americans in northern Nebraska and southern South Dakota. We've come together as brothers and sisters to fight this Keystone XL pipeline, because of the risk to the Ogallala Aquifer, to the land, to the health of the people."

The pipeline is a common threat to both communities, as the Ogallala Aquifer, a water tablet located beneath the Great Plains, provides water for 2.3 million people. The pipeline also "threatens the Missouri River, which provides drinking water for probably a couple 'nother million," bringing the grand total to about five million people whose clean water supply is under threat due to the proposed construction. In addition, the aquifer also provides water for animals, livestock, and irrigation. All of this means that the pipeline threatens the health and economic stability of the Midwest.

For the Rosebud Sioux Tribe and the Great Sioux Nation, there is historical significance as well. Tanderup stated in the interview that part of the pipeline's route, as well as part of his farm, "is on the Ponca Trail of Tears from back in the 1870s, where Chief Standing Bear and his people were driven from the Niobrara area to Oklahoma."

The extraction processes, such as tar sands mining and the refining and dilution processes, used to obtain the oil are extremely dangerous. Gary Dorr noted in the same interview that, before the oil extraction started, Fort Chip in Canada had "a negligible cancer rate" and now "[has] a cancer rate 400 times the national Canadian per capita average" and that "every single family [in Fort Chip] has cancer in their families."

The alliance, while appearing unlikely on the surface, is rooted in history. It actually isn't new, but is rather "a later incarnation of an alliance that was first formed in 1987 to prevent a Honeywell weapons testing range in the Black Hills, one of the most sacred sites in Lakota cosmology - where, in the 1970s, alliances successfully fended off coal and uranium mining." This current movement is the continuation of a fight for the environment that protects people rather than profits.

This is also affecting Native American-White relations. Take the story of Mekasi Horinek, a member of the Ponca Tribe of Oklahoma who is a Native rights and environmental activist. When first hearing of the Cowboy-Indian Alliance, he was rather skeptical, saying "I've always been a little bit bitter toward white society" and "I've experienced a lot of racism-growing up on the res, living on the res. When I went to town, I was always treated differently than others." However, with a little convincing from his mother, he eventually joined, realizing the cowboys "have that love and respect for the land the same that we do."

This alliance is having far-reaching effects that go beyond just an environmental coalition. It "is beginning the dialogue not just about broken treaties, but about the long history of colonization, the effects of which are ongoing among some of the United States' poorest populations." This can be shown by the fact that both sides "hope the pipeline, which has caused them both much distress, will be a catalyst for reconciliation," and that they "sense the reconciliation their work is a part of has a historic importance, something healing for both settlers and natives-and both feel that it is, in some way, destined to happen."

Does this mean that everything will be smooth sailing between Native Americans and settlers from here on out? Not in the slightest. However, it does offer some hope that a sort of reconciliation and reckoning will take place, changing the views of many so that they will aid the Native Americans in their fight for equal rights, as well as undo the damage done by over a century of mistreatment and cultural destruction.

Fighting For Peace in Palestine

The Israeli-Palestinian conflict has been ongoing since 1948, with both groups claiming the same land, and there is currently no end in sight. While the media promotes the narrative that both Palestinians and Israelis hate each other, there has been a large amount of support for the Palestinian cause as of late from Israelis and Jews.

For example, the International Jewish Anti-Zionist Network took an ad out in the New York Times, which was "signed by 40 Holocaust survivors and 287 descendants and other relatives" and "[called] for the blockade of Gaza to be lifted and Israel to be boycotted." More specifically, the ad stated thatthey were "alarmed by the extreme, racist dehumanization of Palestinians in Israeli society, which has reached a fever-pitch. In Israel, politicians and pundits in The Times of Israel and The Jerusalem Post have called openly for genocide of Palestinians and right-wing Israelis are adopting Neo-Nazi insignia." The ad concluded by arguing for collective action, reading: "We must raise our collective voices and use our collective power to bring about an end to all forms of racism, including the ongoing genocide of Palestinian people."

Actions such as these are greatly important as they prove that not all Jewish people support the Israeli war machine and the wanton slaughter of innocent Palestinians.

There were also solidarity actions in Israel itself. However, it seems that it is increasingly dangerous to be anti-war in Israel as there have not only been attacks by right-wing nationalists, but the Israeli government itself cracked down on anti-war demonstrations. It even went so far as to attempt to use the IDF to ban anti-war protests , proclaiming that the police must obey IDF Home Front

Command orders. These orders "[do] not permit large gatherings in public during times of conflict," which results in people being unable to protest.

There is also increasing support for an end to the conflict in Palestine as well. In June, it was notedthat most Palestinians wanted a unity government and a narrow majority favored "peace talks and peaceful coexistence with Israel." An August 2014 poll in Gaza revealed that a majority supported a long-term truce with Israel, even as they opposed the disarmament of the strip. While the fight for an end to the conflict and the creation of a fully sovereign Palestinian state will continue to be a long and arduous one, it is still good to know that people support peace and are able to reach across lines to form solidarity movements.

Solidarity of the Suppressed

Around the world, minority communities are subject to unjust persecution in many societies - persecution which can range from discrimination and a lack or nonexistence of a political voice to outright brutalization and murder by security forces and intense repression. While oppressed groups have fought for their rights individually, rarely have we seen such groups show solidarity with one another and provide support for each other. With help from social media, this seems to be changing.

Black-Palestinian Solidarity

An inspiring alliance has formed between Black people in the US and Palestinians in Gaza, each of whom have shown solidarity with one another in their struggles.

To make the situation much more relatable for African-Americans, in May 2014, Kristian Davis Bailey penned the article *Why Black People Must Stand With Palestine* in which he noted that police brutality faced by Blacks and other minorities is directly related to the violence in Palestine as "Since 2001, thousands of top police officials from cities across the US have gone to Israel for training alongside its military or have participated in joint exercises here." Both communities experience systemic mass incarceration as well: "Forty percent of Palestinian men have been arrested and detained by Israel at some point in their lives. (To put this in perspective, the 2008 figure for Blacks was 1 in 11.) Israel maintains policies of detaining and interrogating Palestinian children that bear resemblance to the stop and frisk policy and disproportionate raids and arrests many of our youth face." The problems of Black people in the US and Palestinians in Gaza are intimately related as the security forces of both countries work together to develop tactics to oppress and brutalize our communities.

In 2012, Jemima Pierre of Black Agenda Report took a historical look of the situation that is still relevant today, noting that many black leaders spoke out in support of the Palestinian cause. Specifically she made mention that

"Palestine was an important issue during the Black Power years as radicals identified with and embraced the anti-colonial struggle against Israel. Huey Newton, even under allegations of anti-Semitism, stated, "...we are not against the Jewish people. We are against that government that will persecute the Palestinian people...The Palestinian people are living in hovels, they don't have any land, they've been stripped and murdered; and we cannot support that for any reason."

Alice Walker made the direct connection of the Palestinian plight to the Black experience: "Going through Israeli checkpoints is like going back in time to the American Civil Rights struggle." By supporting the Palestinian people, Black people today are only continuing the pro-human rights legacy that has been set by many black leaders before them.

Palestinians have reciprocated in the form of supporting the people of Ferguson in their protests against the police. Al Jazeera reported that "Local authorities in Ferguson have begun responding to nightly protests with tear gas and rubber bullets.

Palestinians on Twitter could relate, and shared words and images of support with the US protesters."

The Popular Front for the Liberation of Palestine issued a statement of support with Black people, saying that the organization "salutes and stands firmly with the ongoing struggle of Black people and all oppressed communities in the United States" and quoted Khaled Barakat, a Palestinian writer and activist, as saying the fight against US brutality around the world is linked, and that, "When we see the images today in Ferguson, we see another emerging Intifada in the long line of Intifada and struggle that has been carried out by Black people in the US and internationally." Solidarity between Palestinians and Blacks is important and noteworthy as it shows international solidarity against oppressive social structures and governments as well as forms a space where the two groups can discuss and interact with one another, from promoting awareness about each other's plights to exchanging resistance tactics.

Black-Asian Solidarity

The National Council of Asian Pacific Americans issued a statement of solidarity with Ferguson, saying, in part that, "our own communities' histories in the United States include violence and targeting, often by law enforcement." While a statement may not seem like much, it is rather important as it notes the history of white supremacy and how that ideology is an enemy of all non-whites, no matter their actual skin color.

Soya Jung argued that what is going on in Ferguson mattered to Asian Americans as while Asians "do not move through the world in the crosshairs of a policing system that has its roots in slave patrols, or in a nation that has used me as an 'object of fear' to justify state repression and public disinvestment from the infrastructure on which my community relies," the situation is still important due, firstly, to*han*.

Jung explains *han* as a word in Korean culture that "loosely means 'the sorrow and anger that grow from the accumulated experiences of oppression" that has been "expressed in protests against Japanese colonial rule in 1919, in the struggle for self-determination as the Korean war broke out in 1950, during student protests against the oppressive U.S.-backed South Korean government in 1960, and again during the democratic uprising in Kwangju in 1980." This anger against a racist system of oppression and its importance to Jung's identity is partly what connects the histories of Black and Asian America.

She then notes that Black rage "serves as a beacon when faced with the racial quandary that Asian Americans must navigate" with regards to "the invisibility of Asian death and the denial of any form of Asian American identity that doesn't play by the model minority rulebook."

Jaya Sundaresh took a broader view of the subject, in part discussing anti-blackness in the Asian community, writing that South Asian Americans must "work towards change in our own communities so that we do not inadvertently work to reinforce anti-black racism in this country, which is at the root of the police brutality which murdered Michael Brown." She urged others to talk with their "South Asian friends and families about Ferguson, why it is important that we stop perpetuating or staying silent on racist views in our communities, why we should vocally support those in the African-American community who are working towards change, and why we should stop keeping silent when our white friends and colleagues find ways to justify Darren Wilson's murder of Michael Brown."

The solidarity between Blacks and Asians serves as an important avenue to hash out problems and tensions that exist between the communities, with hopes of eliminating those tensions and working together to strike back against racist oppression.

Conclusion

Do all of these solidarity actions and statements mean that things are now okay? That Native Americans and settlers will get along, that the Israeli-Palestinian conflict will end anytime soon, or that institutionalized and internalized racism will be dismantled? Unfortunately not. However, what these alliances do represent are sparks of hope that suggest we, as people, can put aside superficial differences and come together in an attempt to radically change the situation we currently find ourselves in.

These alliances, whether they are in the form of solidarity statements or marches, articles or tweets, should give people courage and nourishment to continue the fight for freedom and equality.

The world constantly seems like it is going to hell, and many feel that they may give up at any moment, but, to quote Welsh poet Dylan Thomas, "do not go gentle into that good night" instead one must "rage, rage against the dying light."

The light is almost dead and the clock has nearly struck midnight, but this is the chance for everyone to give it their very best. If we are going to go down, let's go down swinging. Let's give 'em hell!

Anarchism and Political Non-Engagement

Jordan Shanti

"there must be some way out of here!", said the joker to the thief.
"there's too much confusion. i can't get no relief.
businessmen, they drink my wine. plowmen dig my earth. none of
them along the line know what any of it is worth."

As an anarchist, being politically engaged looks very little like the way most people understand political engagement. Political engagement typically brings to mind all kinds of activism, handshakes with the rich and powerful, and emotional speeches about why some candidate or policy is the ultimate good, but anarchists don't like to play that game. It's a losing game for all parties and for every living being on this living planet.

Anarchism precludes something wholly different from political engagement, and that is political non-engagement. Under a system which dominates and oppresses all aspects of our lives, all acts have been rendered political. Where you buy your food, who you bank with, what clothes you wear, what shoes you wear, where you work, how you worship, these basic aspects of life are all deeply political - perhaps even a great deal more political than the ballot you cast or the petitions you sign.

"In the slave wage economy, who will your master be?" is the question that politics asks. Politics never asks you if you'd like to be a slave, or suggests that you may not have to be one. The question of politics is indeed a loaded question, as the questions of "which slave masters will you serve" and "what color would you like your shackles painted?" are presupposing that you have consented to being a slave and are more concerned with the particulars of your slavery.

The anarchist ideal is grossly misunderstood because it presents the idea of walking away from the ballot box and, discontent to live shackled by an abusive system, declaring "No gods! No masters!" Yet, for those who have never thought that there may be another way, who believe that one of those ballot boxes must be checked, they look at the anarchist's empty ballot in confusion, for they can't seem to understand why someone wouldn't want to choose how they would be dominated. The anarchist makes little distinction between the patronizing master and the domineering master. She says that she will have no master.

Good cop, bad cop. Left wing, right wing. Your abuser in a good mood and your abuser in a bad mood. It's all part of the same psychological or sociological game. Two faces of the same system, oppressing and dominating the souls of humanity and our nonhuman sisters and brothers.

But sometimes the abuser goes too far, and the formerly weak and ignorant victim finally conjures up the strength and the courage to walk away. Only once they've begun to walk away do they begin to realize the extent of the abuse that they'd been living in. It often takes years - decades even - for a victim to fully understand how abusive the relationship was. Victims of ongoing abuse are usually the blindest to their own abuse, to the horror of the victim's friends and family who can see the situation so clearly. In the same way, the human victims of the abuse of society are largely blind to the abuse and even believe that they are happy within it.

Finally, we're at a point in our human history where the abuse has gone too far. The masters have taken every freedom away from nearly all of humanity and have violently oppressed every living thing they've encountered, to the point where victims are now beginning to wake up in mass numbers and, fed up with replacing fascist dictators with fascist presidents, and iron shackles with paper ones, have begun removing the shackles altogether and walking out of this prison built of human bodies.

However, every person has endured a different level of abuse and oppression. Some have had more skillful abusers who blocked out all hope of life outside the prison. Most people, in their desire to please and their ignorance of the possibility of life beyond the dark walls, have deeply internalized the abuse and hold it as an integral part of themselves. Some are still open to the call of the wild and will fight to save themselves, their species, and their planet, and still others have been pushed too far, where they may never in this incarnation find the heartbeat of mother earth and follow it to freedom.

"no reason to get excited," the thief, he kindly spoke, "there are many here among us who feel that life is but a joke.
but you and i, we've been through that - and this is not our fate. let us not talk falsely now. the hour is getting late."

The revolution happens when an individual somehow breaks past the illusion and decides to live in freedom. This prison, built from human flesh, is weakened every time someone, declaring that they will no longer play their part in oppressing the community of life, their human family, and even the life force within them, walks away from their post, walks away from the ballot box, walks away from the capitalist slave economy. The walls, the bars, the fences, the guard posts, the guards, and even the warden, are all humans who have somewhere inside of them this animal drive for freedom and for life. The good news is that the revolution is inevitable, because the prison complex itself is comprised of living beings with a propensity towards freedom.

. . .

Political non-engagement, therefore, is not a specific thing. It's everything that makes us human- running wild and naked through fields of wild and naked flowers, making love at midnight under the sensual blue moon, splashing paint on a canvas, flinging words into a poem, gazing into the eyes of children, swinging from vines high in the trees of an old-growth forest. It is gardening, meditating, making music. Anarchists are those humans who feel that mother earth created us just like every other living being she supports, that we may live free and part of nature. That is our political stance. That we may live as though the ultimate purpose of life is simply to live - and live to the fullest.

all along the watchtower, princes kept the view. while, all the women came and went. barefoot servants, too. outside, in the distance, a wildcat did growl. two riders were approaching. and the wind began to howl...

Yet for those who have decolonized their hearts and live free as the flowers, there is a voice on the wind which cries that we are all one, we are each cells of a single living organism, and as such, we can never be fully free until our sisters and our brothers are also freed. The wind whispers that we were freed that we may return in order to, in the ultimate act of sedition, tickle those who still bear upon their shoulders the weight of this great poisonous system, that they will, one by one, shrug the weight of oppression off of their backs, withdraw from their role in maintaining its structure, and come to join the world of the free, the world of love, the world of life.

When someone inquires as to the political and societal role of an anarchist, what can be said? We've quit the world of roles and politics and society altogether, in favor of just being human. We've quit in favor of following our own hearts and our own dreams. And we're finding as we follow our own hearts, that we're actually listening to the collective heart. We're going somewhere together.

As humans.
As earth.
As life.

So, the next time someone asks you what you do for a living, what your role is in society, or how you're politically engaged...
Throw your head back in wild laughter and start tickling them!

Disproportionate Representation
A Look at Women Leadership in Congress

Cherise Charleswell

Political representation is defined as the election of officials, who then stand in for, and speak for a group of their constituents in the legislature, for a set period of time. Unfortunately, moneyed interests, the threat of being "primaried" by the tea party lunatic fringe, and other factors have dismantled this process. Over the last few years, and certainly for most of the Obama Administration, Congress has had a low approval rating - so much so that they have been nicknamed the "Do Nothing" Congress. These elected officials have been voting in lock-step with each other, and often opposite the opinions and desires of the American people. Consider the public's desire to implement some degree of regulations on gun use in this country (In 2012, 54% wanted more strict laws, and 90% wanted to expand background checks), and Congress's unwillingness to even deliberate on the matter. Thus, the questions have to be asked - *Who are these congressional members really representing? What values do they represent? Who do they really speak for? What issues do they advocate for? What segment of the American populace do they look like?*

One merely has to take a glance at the collective members of the United State Congress to realize that there is, and has always been, a glaring problem. That problem has to do with representation, and not just political representation. In short, Congress, like The Academy of Motion Pictures and Arts, is not an equal-opportunity employer, and yes #CongressSoWhite. Women make up 50.8% of the U.S. population but only 19.4% of the current 114th U.S. Congress. In fact, Congress resembles a frat house where young intoxicated men are replaced with middle age men, and the type of policies voted upon, discussed, and proposed by the recently out-going, also Republican controlled Congress, reflects the group think that occurs with members of a fraternity. In 2010, Senate Republican Majority Leader, Mitch McConnell, made a statement and put out a call for action for members of his party -- who are overwhelmingly white, male, and old -- to make their primary focus obstruction in order to ensure that President Obama would not serve a second term. They Tried It, but failed. However, their actions and historic "obstructionism" have succeeded in impeding the passing of progressive policies such as the Paycheck Fairness Act, which was unanimously voted against by all Republican Senators, with women among them. And it is this same level of obstructionism that has allowed the United States to be one of the few nations that has not ratified the United Nations Convention on the Elimination of All Forms of Discrimination Against Women (CEADW), despite the document being signed in 1978 by President Carter. Out of 194 U.N. member nations, 187 countries have ratified the document. When considering this, one has to be realistic about whether the election of Senator Elizabeth Warren, or 2016 Democratic front runner Hillary Clinton, to the U.S. presidency, would bring about the passage and ratification of these proposed legislations. The realistic answer would be NO. What we should have learned after the past 6 years of the Obama Administration - and his failed attempts to "reach across the aisle" and utilize bipartisanship in order to pass legislation, instead of having to continuously rely on Executive Orders - is that we have to set our eyes on far more than the Presidency if we want to effect change. And the first step of this process will have to involve addressing the issue of disproportionate representation. Here we will discuss what this looks like in terms of gender.

Snapshot: What Leadership Currently Looks Like in the U.S. CONGRESS?

So, what does the current representation of women in Congress look like?

We can begin with the fact that, despite women (and girls) making up 50.8% of the U.S. population, women currently make up only 19.4% of the 114th U.S. Congress, which took office in January 2015.[1]In terms of each chamber of Congress, women make up 20.0% of the Senate and 19.3% of the House of Representatives. [1] A closer look of the 2015 Congress reveals the following:

19.4% of Congress means that women only hold 104 seats out of 535[1]
20.0% of the Senate means that women hold 20 seats out of 100[1]
19.3% of the House of Representatives means that women hold 84 seats out of 435[1]
In the 114th Congress, women have been sent from 31 of the 51 states as members of the House of Representatives[1]

The Intersections -- Women of Color leadership in the 2015 Congress and Other Elective Offices

Of the 104 women serving in Congress in 2015, 33 are women of color (18 African American women, 6 Asian/Pacifi Islander women, and 9 Latinas)[2]
31.7% of the women in Congress are women of color[2]
Women of color only constitute 6.2% of the total 535 members of Congress[2]
There is only 1 women of color in the Senate [2]
Of the 77 women serving in statewide elective executive offices, 9, or 11.7% are women of color. [2]
Women of color constitute 2.8% of the total 318 statewide elective executives[2]
Women of color constitute 5.3% of the total 7,383 state legislators. [2]
In the United States's 100 largest cities, 5 women of color serve as mayor[2]

A Historical Overview

Women, and certainly women of color, have essentially been denied adequate representation in Congress since the founding of the United States. This reality was of course worse for African American women, who were denied their freedom until 1965, and other women of color -- Indigenous, Asian, Latina, who were denied citizenship despite many of their ancestors being on North American soil for centuries. Since 1917, when Representative Jeannette Rankin of Montana became the first woman to serve, a total of 307 women have served in the U.S. Congress; with the vast majority serving in the House of Representatives.[1] In fact, since 1917, 35 women have served as Senators, 261 as representatives, 11 as both Senators and Representatives, and 6 as Delegates to the House. [1] When considering the span of 98 years, these numbers may seem like there has been a great deal of progress. However, the problem of disproportionate representation persists. Further, real progress is only being carried out by a few states within the Union. While California has sent the most women to Congress than any other state (39 to date), followed by New York (27 to date), no other state has sent more than 17 women to Congress; and some states, such as Delaware, Mississippi and Vermont, have yet to send a woman to serve in the House or Senate. [1]

Past vs. Current Representation

1992 was dubbed the "Year of the Women" due to a surge in the number of female candidates running and eventually being elected to office. However, this exalted year did not change the status quo greatly, as the problem of disproportionate representation has persisted. 4 out of 11 women running for the U.S. Senate were elected, and those victors included Senator Barabara Boxer (D-CA), who recently announced that she will be retiring from the U.S. Senate in 2016, at the end of her term. 24 females were elected to the House during the Year of the Women, and this election increased the percentage of women in the House from 6% to 11%. 1992 thus remains a high mark in terms of the rate of growth assessed by the number of women elected versus incumbents. While 24 new women were elected in 1992, 13 were elected in 2010, and 19 in 2012. However, there are some small signs of progress. In the short period of 2010 to 2015, the number of women who have served in the U.S. Congress went from 260 to 307.

2013 was also celebrated as a year of high achievement for women in Congress, and again the 2015 114th Congress shows signs of small progress. Women make up 19.4% of the 114th Congress, compared to 18% of the 113th Congress. Further, 79 women were members of the House of Representatives, accounting for 17.9% of the body. While the numbers in the Senate have remained constant with 20 - or 20% - of the members of the Senate being women. Still, the following 2013 infographic shows how small this "progress" is in the larger scope of things by illustrating the problem of disproportionate representation.

In terms of inclusion of women of color there has also been minute progress. In the 113th Congress, women of color only made up 4.5% of the total members of Congress, and 30.6% of women serving in Congress. While the 114th has seen a slight increase, where women of color make up 6.2% of the total members of Congress, and 31.7% of the women serving in Congress. Again, the following 2013 Infographic helps to convey that these nominal increases will not be enough to mitigate the problem of disproportionate representation.

The Standouts: Female Firsts in Congress and Feminist Leadership

For much of US history, women were not a part of the legislative system or process. This did not change until the 20th century (144 years later) with the success of the women's suffrage movement, where women of color like Sojourner Truth and Mary Church Terrell were actively involved. The 19th Amendment passed in 1920 officially granted women in the United States the right to vote. However, the right to vote was not safeguarded for women of color, particularly Black women in the Southern United States, until the passage of the 1964 Voting Rights Act; which the predominantly White and male, U.S. Supreme court is currently dismantling. In 2014, the court invalidated key parts of the legislation. A critical legislation that many sacrificed, suffered, and gave their lives for. The following is a brief overview of some of these trailblazing women in U.S. politics:

In 1917 **Jeanette Rankin** of Montana, a Republican prior to the beginning of the parties "Southern Strategy", became the first woman in Congress, where she served in the House of Representatives. In 1916 she noted that, "I may be the first woman member of Congress, but I won't be the last".[3] She went on to serve again from 1941-1943, but did not win re-election due to her anti-war stance, where she voted vote against both World War I and World War II; proving that she was ahead-of-her-time; speaking out against the military industrial complex, well before it had grown to its current size and influence. In terms of feminist leadership, Rankin was a former lobbyist for the National Woman Suffrage Association (NAWSA), and her speaking and organizing efforts help to secure the right to vote for women in Montana in 1914. In her campaigns she ran as a Progressive, and during her time in Congress she focused on social welfare issues.

While many remember and praise Ronald Reagan, despite the horrific result of Reaganomics, there was another stage star from California, who made a greater impact on policy and U.S. society, and she was **Helen Gahagan Douglas**, a New Deal liberal. Gahagan served in the House for three terms, from <u>1945 - 1951</u>, where she spoke about a range of topics including: equal rights for women, civil rights for African Americans and other people of color, labor rights and the protection of the American worker, food subsidies (all prior to the 1964 Food Stamps Act being signed into law by President Lydon B. Johnson), affordable housing, unemployment insurance for returning GIs, a revitalized farm security program, as well as income-based taxation for farmers and small business owners. Where President Johnson needed to be pushed to act on removing the barriers to the ballot for African Americans in the South, Helen Douglas openly attacked the practice of poll taxes. [4-5] Her political viewpoint was progressive in ever since of the word. Even more remarkable was the fact that she was a White women of wealth and status, who focused on the intersectional issues of the working class and women of color. In fact, many of these issues that she championed remain relevant today, and are those that were widely discussed in the *Occupy* movement.

Julia Hansen, served as a Democratic Representative from the state of Washington from 1959-1975, was the first woman to chair an Appropriations subcommittee. Appropriations committees are of a great deal of importance, in that they are responsible for setting specific expenditures of money by the government of the United States. In other words, they literally hold the purse strings of

Congress. Their actions decide whether a particular legislation, agency, etc. is actually funded, and able to carry out its purpose. Martha Griffiths served as a Democratic Representative from Michigan from 1955 to 1975, and her tenure in office spanned a period that was swept with great social changes, brought about by the implementation of federal policies. Martha was very much part of that process, and she is known as the "Mother of the ERA". Representative Griffith championed the sexual discrimination clause of Title VII of the 1964 Civil Rights Act and the 1972 Equal Rights Amendment. Her career was groundbreaking in another way: being the first woman to secure a seat on the influential Ways and Means committee.[2] The Ways and Means committee is the oldest committee in the U.S. Congress, and it is the chief tax-writing committee, having jurisdiction over revenue and related issues such as tariffs, reciprocal trade agreements, and the bonded debt of the United States, as well as revenue-related aspects of the Social Security system, Medicare, and social services programs.

Bella Abzug, served as a Democratic Representative from the state of New York from 1971-1977, running on an antiwar and pro-feminist platform. Bella openly and apologetically identified as a feminist, and was a staunch civil rights advocate; working to combat the ISMs -- racism, sexism, ableism, etc. -- in American society. During her time in Congress she introduced legislation demanding the withdrawal of U.S. forces from Vietnam and authored an institution to end the draft. She was referred to by the epithet Battling Bella, and some would say that it was due to her tenacity and confrontational demeanor. However, it may be more likely due to the fact that she had the audacity and courage to be an assertive woman. Battling Bella actually called for an investigation of the competence of J. Edgar Hoover, the notorious Director of the Federal Bureau of Investigation, and founder of the counterintelligence program (COINTELPRO).[6] Representative Abzug also introduced groundbreaking legislation, which called for the amending of the Civil Rights Act of 1964, to prohibit discrimination on the basis of sexual or affectional preference.[7] In 1988, a former aide to Representative Abzug, shared these comments about her legacy, "It wasn't that she was the first woman in Congress. It was that she was the first woman to get in Congress and lead the way toward creating a feminist presence".[8]

Patsy Takemoto Mink should truly be a household name. Being of Japanese descent, she was the first woman of color to serve in Congress. She was a Democratic Representative from the state of Hawaii, serving in the house from 1965-1977 and again from 1990-2002. A documentary film, Patsy Mink: Ahead of the Majority, profiles the Representative; covering her battles with racism and sexism, and highlighting how she helped to redefine American politics. She participated and pushed for the passage of the 1960s Great Society legislation. During her time in the House she served on the Committee on Education and Labor, and it was there that she introduced or sponsored the first childcare bill and legislation establishing bilingual education, student loans, special education, and Head Start. Clearly setting the foundation for a more diverse and inclusive educational system in America. She championed many women's issues, which garnered her the title, Mother of Title IX, which passed in 1972, and has recently became part of contemporary discourse, as the federal government tries to grapple with the epidemic of rape culture and sexual violence on university campuses; including the most recent assault to garner the attention of the press, involving a student claiming that he was merely acting out scenes from the movie 50 Shades of Grey . Another one of Representative Mink's great legislative triumphs was the Women's Education Equity Act, which provided $30 million a year in educational funds for programs to promote gender equity in schools, to increase educational and job opportunities for women, and to excise sexual stereotypes from textbooks and school curricula. She was certainly a visionary thinker, and thus was one of the first to raise concern about the establishment of the Department of Homeland Security (DHS) in 2002; which was hastily created in response to terrorist attacks in the United States in 2001. Ultimately, she feared that "the DHS might undermine civil liberties by violating the privacy of American citizens in the name of national security. In favor of full disclosure of government attempts to safeguard the nation from international threats, she proposed that no secrets be kept from the public". Ultimately she feared that the DHS might undermine civil liberties by violating the privacy of American citizens in the name of national security.[6]

Shirley Chisholm, was a community activist who went on to serve as a Democratic Representative from the state of New York from 1969 to 1983. She was the first African American woman in Congress. In 1972 she became the first woman, first African American, and the first person of color to run for the United States presidency. She was also a founding member of the Congressional Black Caucus. She focused on a variety of causes that impacted the poorest and most marginalized people in the nation. These causes included increases in federal funding to extend the hours of day care facilities, pointing out early on that Child Care was not just a women's issue; and these sentiments were echoed by President Obama in his 2015 State of the Union address. Her other caucuses included: guaranteed minimum annual income for families and assistance for education.

Pat Schroeder, served as a Democratic Representative from the state of Colorado from 1973-1997. She served on the Armed Services Committee, who became a household name after telling Pentagon officials that if they were women, they would always be pregnant, because they never said "no".[9] And when asked on how she could be a mother of two small children and a Member of Congress at the same time, she replied "I have a brain and a uterus and I use both".[10] With statements such as these, there should be no doubt that Representative Schroeder was a feminist. In fact, much of Schroeder's career was dedicated to women's rights and reforms affecting families; and these issues included: women's health care, child rearing, expansion of Social Security benefits, and gender equity in the workplace. Her contributions include the following: founding of the Congressional Women's Caucus, helping to pass the 1978 Pregnancy Discrimination Act, which mandated that employers could not dismiss women employees simply because they were pregnant or deny them disability or maternity benefits (yes these rights and benefits were not secured until

1978!), created and chaired the Select Committee on Children, Youth, and Families (which was subsequently dismantled in 1995, and should rightfully be reinstated), her biggest successes were the passage of the Family and Medical Leave Act and the National Institutes of Health Revitalization Act.

Carolyn Mosley Braun was the first African American woman elected to the Senate in 1992, during the *Year of the Women*, and she previously served as a Democratic Representative for the State of Illinois. During her time in office she was referred to as a women's rights activist and civil rights activist; and she even dared to campaign for gun control. However, her career was marred by a scandal involving misconduct and mismanagement of funds.

Nancy Pelosi serves as a Democratic Representative from the state of California. She was also the first woman Speaker of the House of Representatives, and is now the minority leader.

In 2012, **Mazie Hironon** became the first Asian American to serve in the Senate, after previously serving in the House and as the Lieutenant Governor of Hawaii. During her time in office she has cosponsored a number of Bills that focus on safeguarding human rights, women's rights, labor rights, and the rights of marginalized populations. These bills include: S/2687-Access to Contraception for women service members and dependents, S.2625-Access to Birth Control Act, S.2629-Preventative Care Coverage Notification Act, S.2599-Stop Exploitation Through Trafficking Act of 2014, S.2578-Protect Women's Health From Corporate Interference Act of 2014, S.2223-Minimum Wage Fairness Act, S.2199-Paycheck Fairness Act, and the S.2472-International Women Act of 2014. However her cosponsoring of S.2472 comes with a great deal of irony, being that she cosponsored a number of bills upholding the United States' support of the state of Israel, despite the nation's human rights violations that it carries out against the Palestinian people.

Barbara Lee is a Progressive voice in Congress, who was first elected to Congress in 1998 as a Democratic Representative from California. She advocates for social and economic justice, international peace, and civil & human rights. She is a founding member and Vice Chair of the Congressional LGBT Equality Caucus, a member of the Pro-Choice Caucus, receiving a 100-percent rating from Planned Parenthood and NARAL Pro-Choice America; and is a founding member of the Congressional Out of Poverty Caucus, a coalition of the Congressional Black Caucus, Asian Pacific American Caucus, and Hispanic Caucus. She gained national attention and notoriety in 2001 for being the ONLY member of Congress to vote against the Authorization fro Use of Military Force, following the terrorist attacks on September 11th; showing that she is not afraid of sticking to her ideals and convictions. Unfortunately the other members of Congress gave George Bush what he later proclaimed was a "mandate" to rage war in the Middle East - in Afghanistan and Iraq, killing millions (on both sides), and creating new enemies for the nation, leading to networks such as the Islamic State of Iraq and Syria (ISIS); all while being the major contributing factor for the current recession that the U.S. is still trying to dig itself out of. Yet, when pundits speak about the failure of this war that has persisted for 14 years, many do not bother to mention the courage and foresight of Representative Barbara Lee. Even more interesting is that many speak about Hilary Clinton, or freshmen Senator Elizabeth Warren, both Caucasian, being frontrunners for the 2016 Democratic ticket; without even considering Barbara Lee, the African American progressive and feminist.

Is the United States Really a World Leader?

American exceptionalism is a theory that the United States is qualitively different from other nations, and the implication is often that the United States serves as a model first world nation; and thus Americans are able to take on a strangely passionate patriotic pride in this exceptionalism. When it comes to many social issues and political institutions, America is indeed exceptional. It is the only post-industrial nation that lacks universal healthcare and paid sick leave, and continues to be one of two hold outs in ratifying a human rights treaty, the United Nations Convention on the Elimination of All Forms of Discrimination Against Women

(CEDAW), despite the treaty being signed in 1979 by President Carter. The aforementioned Progressive Congresswoman Barbara Lee is co-sponsor of current legislation urging Congress to ratify the CEDAW.

Further, when it comes to the representation of women in the government, especially at the Federal level, there is certainly a great deal of American exceptionalism. So much so that, in 2014, the United States ranked 84th in worldwide female leadership. In the past several years, there has actually been a steady decline in the status or leadership positions of women in the U.S. government, as outlinedbelow:

· In 2002, the United States ranked 57th in worldwide female leadership; out of 188 countries
· In 2008, the United States ranked 69th in worldwide female leadership.
· In 2009, the United States ranked 71st in worldwide female leadership.
· In 2010, the United States ranked 72nd in worldwide female leadership.
· In 2012, the United States ranked 80th in worldwide female leadership.
· In 2013, the United States ranked 77th in worldwide female leadership.
· In 2014, the United States ranked 84th in worldwide female leadership.

Snapshot: A Look at Women Legislators around the World

The 1952 United Nations Convention on the Political Rights of Women brought forth a number of provisions, but did not diminish the concerns of equal access to political participation for women. Thuss it was restated in the Article 7 of the CEDAW, which again the

U.S. government has failed to ratify. Under this article, women are guaranteed the rights to vote, hold public office, and to exercise public functions. Under Article 8 of the CEDAW, these rights are expanded to include equal rights for women to represent their countries at the international level.

However, despite this well-meaning legislation, women are still underrepresented in governments around the world. Only 21.9% of national parliamentarians were female as of December 1, 2014. Here are some other disheartening statistics:

· As of January 2014 only 10 women have served as Head of State and 15 as Head of Government
· Globally there are 37 States in which women account for less than 10% of parliamentarians in single or lower houses, as of December 2014
· As of January 2014, only 17% of government ministers were women, with the majority overseeing social sectors, such as education and the family

When considering these statistics and the global problem of disproportionate leadership, the U.S. does not seem too exceptional, in that it is merely upholding the status quo. Among the Millennium Development Goals (MDG) is goal Number 3 - *Promote Gender Equality and Empower Women*. This will not be achieved without the full participation of women in government. Additionally, without achieving this, demanding and enforcing gender equality in other sectors will prove to be hypocritical and impossible.

Still, there have been some achievements for women's participation in government, globally. While the United States continues to be "exceptional" and has never elected a woman as head of State/government, many other nations have. In recent years, these nations include:

Federal Chancellor Angela Merkel, Germany (Elected 2005)
• Executive President Ellen Johnson-Sirleaf, Liberia (Elected 2006)

- Executive President Michelle Bachelet Jeria, Chile (Elected 2006)
- Minister President Emily de Jongh-Elhage, Nederlandse Antillen (Self-governing Part of the Kingdom of the Netherlands) (Elected 2006)
- Prime Minister Portia Simpson-Miller, Jamaica (Elected 2007)
- Prime Minister Han Myung-sook, South Korea (Elected 2007)
- President Pratibha Patil, India (Elected 2007)
- Executive President Cristina Fernández de Kirchner, Argentina (Elected 2007)
- Acting President Dr. Ivy Matsepe-Casaburri, South Africa (Elected 2008)
- Leader of the Government Antonella Mularoni, San Marino (Elected 2008)
- Prime Minister Sheikh Hasina Wajed, Bangladesh (Elected 2009)
- Prime Minister Jóhanna Sigurðardóttir, Iceland (Elected 2009)
- Prime Minister Jadranka Kosor, Croatia (Elected 2009)
- President Dalia Grybauskaitė, Lithuania (Elected 2009)
- President of the Confederation Doris Leuthard, Switzerland (Elected 2010)
- President Roza Otunbayeva, Kyrgyzstan (Elected 2010)
- President-Elect Laura Chinchilla Miranda, Costa Rica (Elected 2010)

One nation to take note of is Rwanda. Although it may be deemed a developing nation, and had suffered economic and social setbacks during the 1994 Genocide, Rwanda proves to be progressive in terms of government. Due to the fact that the country's constitution provides for Ombudsman who act as public advocates, the nation has some of the lowest levels of corruption relative to other African nations. Transparency International actually ranked Rwanda as the 8th cleanest out of 47 countries is sub-Saharan Africa, and the 66th cleanest out of 178 in the world. The nation also ranks first in female leadership worldwide, where it has the highest number of women parliamentarians. These women hold63.8% of the seats in the lower house of government.

Why Are Numbers Not Enough?

In advocating for the increase in number of women holding political office in governments, we must be cognizant of the fact that numbers are not enough. There is no benefit in having women holding positions of leadership if these women do not advocate for women's human rights and other socioeconomic issues -- racism, police brutality, labor rights, health care access, affordable housing, consumer protections, environmental regulations -- from a progressive standpoint. Electing women who are unwilling to take the necessary stand on these issues - and this is greatly represented by their voting record, and not the lip service that they pay in the media - would only hold up the status quo of gender inequity.

For example, while many celebrate Rebecca Latimer Felton, of the State of Georgia, as being the first woman in the U.S. Senate, one cannot ignore the fact that she was an ardent racist and would certainly not have been an ally to women of color. Take for example her comments from an 1897 speech regarding lynching, "The biggest problem facing women on the farm was the danger of the black rapists. If it takes lynching to protect women's dearest possession from drunken, ravening beasts....then I say lynch a thousand a week". As a Southerner, Latimer Felton condemned anyone who dared to question the South's racial policies, and one can be certain that her discussion about women did not include the Black or indigenous women living in the State of Georgia at that time, who were also subjected to lynchings and mob violence.

Now, take a look at some of the photos of The Texas Federation of Republican Women, which boasts that it is the most powerful women's political organization in Texas, and ask yourself whether this organization and the candidates that it supports and funds look like they consider women of color and the intersecting issues that impact their lives?

Again, it is not enough to have a woman elected to office if she is a racist, blinded by white privilege, or finds some reason to view another group of people - particularly women as "The Other" -

341

outside her scope of representation. It is beliefs like this that later helped usher in the era of Reganomics, with the falsehood of the Welfare Queen and the War on Drugs, which was a nothing more than a War on the Poor and an Attack on the Middle Class. The Welfare Queen story essentially incited, and continues to incite, racial animosity, where Black women (and other women of color) are viewed as being lazy and constantly looking for government handouts when the truth of the matter is that most welfare recipients are white and do not live in urban settings. Yet, the stereotypical view persists and is still used to cut social safety net programs.

Consider the 2014 Paul Ryan Plan, a budget proposal that would get 69 of its budget cuts from programs for people with low or moderate incomes, according to the Center on Budget and Policy Priorities. This was a hypocritical move coming from the Chair of the House Ways and Means committee considering his dependency on government entitlements, public education, etc. The plan, which would see cuts of $3.4 trillion over ten years (2015-2024) predictably does not include any cuts to the defense budget. Defense contractors and their political allies would not have to be concerned about a loss in profits, which they acquire from the military industrial complex - something President Eisenhower warned Americans about. Of course, the 2014 plan was not Ryan's first attempt at putting forth this budget proposal; it is just more worrisome given the current make-up of the U.S. Congress. In 2012, Ryan put forth a similar plan which was famously rejected by women.
Ultimately, having the wrong women in office only contributes to these disastrous effects of wedge politics and social inequity. Finally, there is no greater example as to why numbers are not enough than the case of the Paycheck Fairness Act, a proposed law that would make it easier for employees to talk about wages - and thus potentially help women learn whether they earn less than their male colleagues. The law would also force employers to explain or justify why two similarly qualified workers earn different wages. However, it was unanimously voted against by the

Republican members of the Senate in 2014, including these four Republican women:

New Hampshire's Kelly Ayotte (left) thinks that it would prohibit merit-based pay. She also voted against it because Democrats opposed her amendment to the legislation.

Maine's Susan Collins (second from left) thinks that the Civil Rights Act the 1963 Equal Pay Act are enough protection to provide equal pay. According to Collins, the proposed law would "impose a real burden ... on small businesses." She thinks that women get paid less because of their own choices.

Nebraska's Deb Fischer (second from right) accused Democrats of politics for putting the bill forward for the second time, this time one week before the congressional recess for midterm elections.

Alaska's Lisa Murkowski is on the Right.
You can read these Senators comments and attempts to justify their actions online .

It was the third time since 2012 that the GOP has voted down the bill. The legislation required 60 votes to move on to debate but received only 52, a unanimous vote from Democrats. Clearly the numbers were not enough, as having these additional women - and votes- in the Senate was not enough, because these women care more about their political party affiliation than advancing women's human rights and social equality. One can make the case that they would not be members of the Republican party if they cared about these things. Their voting record exemplifies why we need to focus on much more than increasing the number of women in Congress. The Paycheck Fairness Act is of course not the first legislation that elicited a unanimous vote against it by Republicans (and of course Republican women) in Congress. In 2013, GOP members in the House voted unanimously against The Fair Minimum Wage Act (H.R. 1010) which would have raised the nation's minimum wage to

$10.10 per hour by 2015, and the rate would have been indexed to inflation each year thereafter. Well, here we are in 2015 and the U.S. minimum wage is still $7.25 per hour. Now, compare that to other post-industrial nations:

When looking at women in government and political candidates, we must realize that their being a woman is not enough for our support. We must consider their agenda, look at their affiliations, determine whether they have a feminist platform or one that is at least pro-women's human rights, and review their voting record. For instance, consider the voting record of Republican Senator Kelly Ayotte of New Hampshire. Here are few highlights:

- Jan. 29, 2015 S 1 A Bill to Approve the Keystone XL Pipeline Yea
- Jan. 6, 2015 S 1 A Bill to Approve the Keystone XL Pipeline Co-sponsor
- Nov. 18, 2014 S 2280 A Bill to Approve the Keystone XL Pipeline Yea
- July 30, 2014 S 2569 Bring Jobs Home Act Nay
- July 16, 2014 S 2578 Protect Women's Health From Corporate Interference Act of 2014 Nay
- June 11, 2014 S 2432 Bank on Students Emergency Loan Refinancing Act Did Not Vote
- May 1, 2014 S 2280 A Bill to Approve the Keystone XL Pipeline Co-sponsor
- April 30, 2014 S 2223 Minimum Wage Fairness Act Nay
- April 9, 2014 S 2199 Paycheck Fairness Act Nay

What's At Stake?

The reason why we must advocate for the inclusion of 'pro-women's human rights' women in Congress and other houses and government is because there is truly much at stake. The War on women is welldocumented and has been discussed thoroughly. There are attempts to take agency over our bodies, to categorize rape and talk about "legitimate rape", decrease access to birth control and safe abortions, and the list goes on; including the continued rape and degradation of the environment, which are exemplified by ongoing fracking and attempts to approve the proposed Keystone XL pipeline. From an economic standpoint, there is also the Trans Pacific Partnership trade agreement that will have the greatest and most negative impact on women and children, the groups most marginalized and impoverished in society.

Still, there is the need to ensure the enforcement of Title IX on college campuses as well as investigate the once-silent rape epidemic in the U.S. military. The Convention on the Elimination of all Forms of Discrimination against Women (CEDAW) still awaits ratification, and American workers are still not guaranteed paid sick leave, extended maternal leave, and child care aid; all of which directly impacts women and children. Thus, legislation such as the Affordable Care Act, despite its flaws and avoidance of the single-payer option, should be protected. The act ensures that all women have access to preventative care such as mammograms and pap smears.

We must keep in mind that there is much at stake, and there are attempts to erode women's human rights. Within literally weeks in office, the newly minted Republican-majority Congress attempted to push through an anti-abortion measure, the "Pain Capable Unborn Child Protection Act", which was surprisingly defeated due to the moderate members of the GOP. House GOP members actually broke rank with their party, protesting the language of the bill that required women who seek an exception to the ban due to being raped, having to back up their claim with a formal police report. Although this defeat is welcome news, it does not mean that there will not be even more attempts to curtail the reproductive rights of American women. Which makes the efforts of Democratic Senators Jeanne Shaheen (NH) and Jackie Speier (CA) seem even more important. On February 4, 2015, the two introduced the Access to Contraception for Women Service-members and Dependents Act. In applauding the efforts of the Senators, the National Women's Law Center described the legislation as such: A critical piece of legislation that will ensure all women who rely on the military for health care receive comprehensive contraceptive coverage and counseling. The bill will give these women equal access to the same comprehensive birth control coverage, education and counseling at no cost that all other federal employees and tens of millions of other women now enjoy, thanks to the Affordable Care Act. The bill also ensures that servicewomen will receive comprehensive family planning counseling and are provided the information they need to plan if and when to have a child.

Strategies to Increase Women's Political Leadership

There is certainly no easy way to increase women's political leadership, and that is one of the reasons why much has not changed since Jeannette Rankin entered Congress 99 years ago. However, the United States cannot continue to claim that it is a world leader while ignoring this disparity in representation that threatens the status of women in this country. This disparity is shown with the constant attempt to legislate what a woman can and cannot do with or to her body, as well as with social policies that continue to allow gender-based wage discrimination. Here are just a few strategies that should be implemented to increase participation and improve the political representation of women in the U.S.:

346

Encourage more women, especially women of color, to become more interested and involved in politics and governance in order to cultivate more viable candidates for office. According to the Center for Women and Politics of Rutgers University, in 2008, 60.4% of eligible females voted (70.4 million) while 55.7% of eligible men voted (60.7 million), compared to 48.6% of women, and 46.9% of men in 2006. The fact of that matter is that more women vote in U.S. elections than men, however there only option are only male candidates.

CHECK voting records and hold women in office accountable. Let them know that we are paying attention and that we expect them to vote in a matter that truly represents the needs of women. During the 2010 midterm elections, female (mostly White) voters shifted to the Republican party despite the horrific anti-woman legislation and attacks on social programs, depended upon by many women, that the party was proposing. This shift speaks to the issue of White privilege, where White women voters who are not burdened with stereotypes and racist propaganda such as the Welfare Queen or illegal immigrant worker coming for American jobs, and who do not have to cope with a myriad of intersecting issues, often and more readily shift their votes between the two parties without giving much thought to the detrimental effects of their "swing" vote.

VOTE and support the right women candidates; and this includes voting at the local level where the candidates who eventually seek national office begin their careers and decided upon legislation that would most directly impact your lives

Country	Required Quota
Angola	Quota for women must not be less than 30% for charter of political parties
Rwanda	Women granted at least 30% of positions in all "decision-making organizations"
Korea	PR elections have a 50% quota for women for 56

	positions. Majority elections 30% for 243 seats
Uzbekistan	30% quota for women candidates for political party elections
Albania	30% quota for women on a candidate list; one of the first three names on the list must be from each gender
Armenia	Candidate lest must be 20% women, or parties cannot register
Belgium	Candidate lists must be equal
Bosnia & Herzegovina	33% of candidates must be of the underrepresented sex
Macedonia	On candidates list, one out of 3 must be a woman
Poland	On candidates list, the total number of either gender must not be lower than 35%
Portugal	On candidate lists, minimum 33% of each gender
Spain	On candidate lists minimum 40% and maximum of 60% of each gender
Costa Rica	Candidate lists must be 40% of women
Panama	30% quota for women in party and general elections
Argentina	30% quota for women on party lists
Brazil	30% quota for women on candidate lists
Guyana	Candidates must be one-third women
Peru	30% quota for women

Source: Catalyst. Catalyst Quick Take: Women in Government. New York: Catalyst, 2012.

It is perhaps time to follow the lead of countries such as Rwanda, Angola, Korea, Albania, France, Macedonia, Belgium, Uzbekistan, Poland, Portugal, Spain, Costa Rica, Panama, Argentina, Brazil, Peru, and many others in post-industrial nations, as well as those in the Global South, and put in place legislation to increase the representation of women in national government. Yes, this would be a quota that would ensure that a minimum number of seats in the national government be reserved for women. Doing so may be the only way to ensure that women are represented in a manner which closely reflects their concerns and numbers in society; and to also ensure that women's issues are not debated over by a room full of men.

References

1. Center for American Women and Politics (CAWP). Eagleton Institute of Politics. Rutgers, State University of New Jersey. Fact Sheet. Women in the U.S. Congress 2015
2. Center for American Women and Politics (CAWP). Eagleton Institute of Politics. Rutgers, State University of New Jersey. Fact Sheet. Women of Color in Elective Office, 2015
3. Winifred Mallon, An Impression of Jeannette Rankin" The Suffragist (March 31, 1917)
4. Congressional Record, House, 79th Cong., 1st sess. (12 June 1945): 5977
5. Congressional Record, House, 79th Cong., 2nd sess. (2 August 1946): 10771-10772.
6. Karen Forestel, Biographical Dictionary of Congressional Women (Westport, CT: Greenwood Press, 1999): 19
7. Congressional Record, House, 94th Congress, 1st sess. (25 March 1975): 8581
8. Susan Baer, "Founding, Enduring Feminist Bella Abzug is dead at 77, 1 April 1998, Baltimore Sun: 1A
9. Llyod Grove, Laying Down Her Quip; For Rep. Pat Schroeder, A Hard-Hitting Decision, 1 December 1995, Washington Post: F1
10. Current Biography, 1978: 368

American Gracchi

Dr. Nicholas Partyka

The crisis of 133 B.C. certainly seemed highly significant to those involved in it and those observing it. However, it was to take on much larger significance as time went on. For this crisis signaled the rising momentum of social, political, and economic forces that would undermine the Roman republic within a century. For only thirty years after the crisis of 133 B.C. (and even fewer years after the crisis of 121 B.C.) would be born the man who ride highest on the tide of these forces, and who would ultimately kill the republic, Gaius Julius Caesar. Thus, the crisis of 133 B.C. has come to be seen as the opening salvo in the process the results in the fall of the Roman republic, and the rise of the Roman Empire.

The great crisis of the 20th century, the Great Depression, also seemed a momentous event to those caught up in it. Might it not also come to take on a higher historical significance in decades not too distant from our own? Might not future generations of Americans come to see the first third of the 20th century A.D. as similar to the last thirty years of the 2nd century B.C.? Might perhaps a future American Marius look back and see in the Roosevelts, Teddy & Franklin, the American Gracchi?

When we look at the political careers of the Gracchi and the

Roosevelts in parallel we will notice some striking similarities. Similarities that I think illuminate important aspects of the contemporary political landscape. Often, it is only with the clarity in hindsight afforded by examination of history, that large features of contemporary political reality can be put in a spotlight. Though analogies can, and should, only be pushed so far, the commonalities we will see ought to be somewhat unsettling, that is, if one is concerned for the fate of democracy and democratic citizenship in America.

I must note here the perilous nature of comparisons between modern America and Ancient Rome. Such comparisons are made often, and usually quite poorly. Most often such comparisons come down to a very broad analogy between the political, economic, and military hegemony each possessed in its era of dominance. We must, with Marx, emphasize the important differences between capitalist and pre-capitalist economic formations. Though a model of class struggle may be applicable to the ancient world, as G.E.M de St. Croix adroitly demonstrates, the Roman Empire is not capitalist. Though it may contain capitalistic elements, as indeed Marx was clear that some features of capitalist economies pre-date capitalism, one must not confuse the oligarchy of the wealthiest Romans with a bourgeoisie.

This note of caution registered, I must point out that what is at issue here is not a comparison between modern American and Ancient Rome as empires, or as the international hegemon, or even the nature of that hegemony. What I want to focus our attention on here is a comparison between economic and social dynamics, and the political forces they create or unleash. We'll see that in different eras, dissimilar as they undoubtedly are, interesting similarities emerge that might incline us to see ourselves, and our modern conflicts, in the history of Ancient Rome. It is upon noting these similarities that we come to the unsettling questions about the future of democracy in America. If the Roosevelts are the American Gracchi, then is an American Marius, or more ominously an American Sulla, in our future? Indeed, just like Marius and Sulla, many former US Presidents have parlayed military success in wartime into political careers; perhaps most notably, Washington, Jackson, Taylor, Grant, and Eisenhower. And, in the heart of the Great Depression many Americans wondered aloud whether or not an American Mussolini, a man who modeled himself on Roman strong-men of the past, could lift the nation out of depression. Is the American republic declining? Do the similarities of the economic and political forces at play, and underlying, the crises of 133-121 B.C. & 1929-1945 A.D., signal that our republic is as sickened as the Roman republic? Is there a cure for what ails our republic?

I must pause here to make an important note. Though I have spoken of the "Roman republic", and of "American democracy", one must recognize that these terms are highly problematic. Ancient Rome was indeed a republic of free citizens, but, of course, citizenship was very heavily restricted. Modern America is a democracy, which co-exists with high levels of economic inequality, racial and gender injustice, widespread socio-political exclusion and alienation. I will continue to employ this terminology throughout, but always cognizant of the limited scope of their meaning within the economic and political contexts of their respective epochs.

Lex Sempronia Agraria

Yes, 133 B.C. was an eventful year for the Roman republic. But the crisis that was ignited that year, and which smoldered until flaring up again in 123-121 B.C., and then again from 50-44 B.C., did not just spring into existence. Rather, the crisis that erupted was the result of years, decades, of slowly accumulating forces and pressures. It will do us well then to take some stock of the situation the Romans faced in the years before, and leading up to, 133 B.C.. If we are to understand the political career of Tiberius Sempronius Gracchus, then we must know something of the texture of the economic and political scene into which he inserted himself.[xxiii]

The source of the economic and social problems that created

such political tumult was, in a word, the *latifundia*. These very large, slave-worked estates owned by the wealthy Patrician elite of Rome. The growth of these displaced many small farmers, Plebians, who typically would re-locate to the city of Rome itself. Outside of the resident plebian population of Rome and the freedmen, the major contributing source of the classical *Plebs Urbana*. As part of the severance package from military service, troops were usually given land to farm as small farmers. The Roman ideal was that a Roman man would produce enough in the way of agricultural products on his small-farm to meet his families' consumption needs, and hopefully a surplus to sell.

However, many former soldiers turned out to be terrible farmers; others found out they hated farming; others were pushed off their land against their will by more powerful neighbors; others lost their farms while away on extended military service in the Punic wars or the subsequent Roman wars of conquest. In any event, more and more good Roman land in the Italian peninsula was being consolidated in the hands of fewer and fewer land-owners. This was all in spite of the *Lex Lincinia Sextia*, passed circa 367 B.C., which limited Roman citizens to the possession of not more than five hundred *jugerum* (one *jugerum* is approximately ½ acre). Aside from the illegal dispossession and displacement of small-holders, the *latifundia* grew larger and larger as a result of the illegal appropriation of public lands, the *ager publicus*, by wealthy aristocrats.

Thus, in the years up to 133 B.C. what one sees in Roman society is the growth of the large, slave-worked plantations, which causes increasing unemployment among a class of persons who are Roman citizens and veteran soldiers, and who flock in increasing numbers to Rome itself, swelling the ranks of the "urban mob". These are the folks who come more and more to make up the ranks of the Plebian Assembly, the *Concilium Plebis*. This group became increasingly restive as their economic plight worsened. The spoils of military hegemony brought a flood of slaves into Rome, while Patricians used their social and legal privileges to illegally acquire very large, very profitable estates. As has been common throughout history, the tumult and disorder engendered by a century of warfare from the First Punic war in 264 B.C., through the end of the Third Punic war and the Roman conquest of Greece in 146 B.C., provided the opportunity for many wealthy Romans, Patricians and Plebians, to become even wealthier. In the wake of these wars, which saw Rome rise to preeminence in the Mediterranean world, it looked to many Roman citizens not among the Roman Patrico-Plebian oligarchy that the benefits of the conquests were going mainly to the elites, not to those who did the fighting and the dying.

This then is the environment into which Tiberius Gracchus emerges when he is elected Tribune of the Plebs in 133 B.C. But who is this Tiberius? First, he is of an old and distinguished Patrician family. His mother, Cornelia, was the daughter of the great Scipio Aemilianus, victorious general of the Third Punic war who destroyed Carthage. Thus, to be elected Tribune was deeply shocking to many, especially other Patricians. Remember that to be elected Tribune one must be a Plebian, and so Tiberius had to legally renounce his Patrician status in order to stand for the position at all. Had he been older he could have run for Consul, a more traditional position for someone of his background, but he apparently decided he could not wait to begin his political career, so urgent were the problems facing Roman society.

Second, he is a *Popularis*, that is, one of the *Populares*. This is to say that Tiberius' political base was among the Plebians in the Assembly, and not among the *optimates* in the Senate. This was a fairly new development in Roman political life. Cynical observes will dismiss Tiberius as a political "adventurer", a power-seeker. The upper-class bias found in much of the writing of and on classical history reaffirms this perception of the elder Gracchi. And yet, in fragments of the speech with which he introduced his bill paint a different picture. In describing the plight of dispossessed Roman citizens he says,

"Hearthless and homeless, they must take their wives and families and tramps the roads like beggars...They fight and fall to serve no other end but to multiply the possessions and comforts of the rich. They are called masters of the world but they possess not a clod of earth that is truly their own".[xxiv]

As Tribune in 133 B.C. Tiberius undertook political action to address what he saw at the crisis in Roman society. In seeking solutions to this crisis he enacted measures that directly challenged the power of the established Senatorial elite. As a *Popularis*, he acted to bring more legal and political rights, economic benefits, and social privileges to Roman citizens, as well as working to extend citizenship rights to more of Rome's Italian allies. He also acted to directly attack the basis of aristocratic power, land ownership. In the ancient world, when land was the main means of production, as well as the basis of economic independence, and with it social prestige. Tiberius was able, through much resistance, to pass his *Lex Sempronia Agraria*. This was a land-reform measure designed to break-up the illegal *latifundia* and redistribute land to dispossessed Roman citizens. Knowing that the aristocrats in the Senate would be hostile to his proposals Tiberius, much as a *Popularis* would, took the unorthodox action of appealing his case to the Plebian Assembly, which was much more receptive to his ideas. As a result of *Lex Hortencia*, passed circa 287 B.C., legislation passed by the Plebian Assembly was binding on Patricians too; which it had not been up to that point.

Then, late in the year, Tiberius caused a constitutional crisis with his appropriation of the legacy of Attalus III of Pergamum. Attalus, King of Pergamum, died without an heir and bequeathed his entire estate to the Roman people. Traditionally, this kind of matter was handled by the Senate. It was one thing to redistribute land, which even many elites grew to accept, but in order to give the re-settled farmers a chance they would need capital to stock the farms with the necessaries of farming. In order to pay for this, Tiberius decided to appropriate the Attalus' legacy. He got the Plebian Assembly to vote to do so, and as a result of *Lex Hortencia*, there was nothing the Senate could do. This was, even for a person like Tiberius Gracchus, a stretch of constitutional authority, and indeed for many it was an outright breach. Tiberius had already acted haughtily in - probably illegally- dismissing a fellow Tribune, a man named Octavius, in order to remove the last obstacle to the passage of his land-reform bill.

In order to see why Tiberius' appropriation of Attalus' legacy caused a constitutional crisis we must take a look at the institution of the Roman Senate. In the period directly after the kings, the Roman senate, which had been merely an advisory body, seized control of the reigns of the Roman state. The Patrician and the Plebians had together expelled the odious Lucius Tarquinius Superbus, or Tarquin the Proud, the last king of Rome, and circa 509 B.C. founded what we now call the Roman republic. The slogan around which this new regime coalesced was "SPQR", which translated into English means in essence, "the Senate and the Roman people are one". On one level it announces the fact Patrician and Plebian unity drove out the hated kings, and that their combined strength under-pinned the new regime, whose legitimacy was predicated on preventing kings from ever returning. On another level it very clearly announce that the Patricians, the Senatorial class, were a group separate from and superior to the "people of Rome", i.e. the Plebians and freedmen. It also very clearly announces the order of precedence in the new regime. The Senate and the Roman people are one, but the Senate comes first. Thus, the Senate, or the Senatorial class, came to dominate all or most of the major positions in government, especially the consulship. Until the time of Tiberius Gracchus the political primacy of the Senate was little in doubt.

So, when news of Attalus' bequest reached Rome in late 133 B.C., the Senate took its time discussing what to do at its own leisurely pace. It never occurred to them that someone would do what Tiberius Gracchus was about to do. They were just as shocked as they were earlier when Tiberius renounced his Patrician status to become Tribune, something it never occurred to anyone, Patrician or Plebian, that anyone would even think of doing. So, while the Senate dithered, Tiberius acted. But his action directly challenged the Senate's traditional prerogatives, threatening to take away some, perhaps in the long term all, of their power. By the time of Tiberius Gracchus the example of democratic Athens was well known. Pericles, Ephialtes, and others had successfully broadened to scope of the power of the Assembly at the direct expense of that of the Athenian version of the Senate, the *Areopagus*, stripping it all functions save adjudicating murder trials by 462 B.C..

By these actions, and others, Tiberius Gracchus made plenty of enemies for himself, enemies with important positions in the Roman state. Once Tiberius was no longer Tribune, his enemies could, and in all likelihood would, exact some revenge on Tiberius; the direct and obvious implication being that they might murder him. As Tribune, Tiberius' person was constitutionally sacrosanct. All Plebians swore an oath to protect the tribune from any physical attacks. So, when his term of office expired he would be vulnerable to his enemies, many of whom would likely be able to legal use state powers to pursue their ends. Thus, Tiberius forced further constitutional crisis on the Senate by running for re-election, the legality of which was by no means settled and obvious. Roman law at this time prohibited certain senior magistrates from being immediately re-elected to their post. Tiberius' argument was that since the office of Tribune was an office of the Roman people, i.e. the plebs, not of the Roman state, i.e. the patricians, and thus this prohibition did not apply to him. Despite vigorous resistance to his re-election campaign from the *optimates* it looked likely that Tiberius would be re-elected Tribune.

On election-day, Tiberius was allegedly seen pointing to his head. This news was carried to the Senate, which was meeting close by, where it was universally agreed that Tiberius was attempting to make himself king. For, again, per *Lex Hortencia*, any bill the Plebian Assembly passed, was law. So, if they voted Tiberius king, the he would be king. And if "SPQR" meant anything, it very much meant, "no more kings". Now Tiberius' supporters have claimed that his pointing to his head was a pre-arranged signal to some of his closest allies that he felt his life in danger, and they should rally to him. In any event, the Senate was so enraged, and perhaps after under-estimating Tiberius more than once already, they decided to

357

act swiftly to prevent the *sentina urbis* (the bilge or dregs of the city) from destroying **their** republic. The Senators broke up their furniture to make bludgeons, and stormed off as a group, around 300 persons armed with rocks and clubs, towards where Tiberius and his supporters were. They felt they had little choice as the sitting Consul refused to lead the Senatorial army against a sitting Tribune. When the dust cleared, Tiberius and hundreds of his followers, those who had not successfully fled the scene, had been clubbed to death in the street by the Senate.

The bitter irony is that, as provocative as Tiberius' actions may have seemed to the *optimates*, the best men, the terms of his *Lex Sempronia Agraria* were fairly generous towards them. In fact, Tiberius inserted a compensation clause in his bill. He was going to have the state pay some of the illegal holders of public land to give it up. Senatorial elites, who monopolized land ownership, especially land in and around Rome itself, were going to be paid for land they had stolen in the first place. Not too bad a deal. And in hindsight, taking it might have been preferable to the century of internecine civil strife and violence that followed from not taking it.

Theodore Rex

Theodore Roosevelt was the first United States President to be born in a city, to go by his initials, first to leave the country during his term of office, he was the youngest President, he was the first to win the Nobel Peace prize, first American to win any Nobel Prize, first President to own and automobile, first to do down in a submarine, first to use transatlantic cable to send diplomatic messages, first to grasp the potential of publicity and the burgeoning mass media, and first to dine with an African-American in the White House, among many other firsts. He was an author, naturalist, historian, conservationist, hunter, imperialist, and progressive, among other things. Clearly, these were revolutionary times, and clearly Theodore Roosevelt represented a new force in American politics. The world was changing, that is, being changed, ever more radically and seemingly at an increasing pace, by the economic and political forces of capitalism and liberalism. The early part of the 20th century saw the emergence of a unified national market in America, mostly through the agency of the consolidation of firms. The world most of us today consider "modern" was quickly coming into being, with all the attendant social dislocation and duress for those on the bottom o the social hierarchy.[xxv]

Teddy, like Tiberius Gracchus, had a Patrician upbringing, enjoying the benefits of upper-class privileges. They both entered politics in a time of high corruption, high economic prosperity, as well as constitutional transformation and crisis. Both also had a popular political orientation. Teddy Roosevelt championed many progressive causes during his tenure as President, resulting in many important benefits for working-class Americans. Teddy fought corrupt political machines, tired to get a "Square Deal" for the American people, who he saw as too often being taken advantage of by predatory capitalists. Lastly, like Tiberius Gracchus, Teddy's main political nemesis can be summed up in a single word, trusts. This was the height of the age of the Robber Barons, and of the monopolistic consolidation of America's largest industries. Much like the times of Tiberius Gracchus, the era of T.R. was one of economic prosperity, but mainly for the wealthy. There was a widespread sentiment that the benefits of industrial capitalist society were accruing principally to one class, namely, the capitalists. The predations and manipulations of the giant trusts, reported often in the increasingly frenzied world of competition between newspapers, were perhaps the most glaring symbols to many of this fact. That this problem of trusts and their growing power was recognized can be seen in the passage of the Sherman Anti-Trust Act in 1890.

After the close of the Civil War, American capitalism came increasingly into maturity.[xxvi] It was in this period that some of the most famous as well as infamous names of American business history tread the scene. This was the era when the likes of Carnegie, Rockefeller, Morgan, Fisk, Gould, Vanderbilt, and later Ford, dominated the business world, and constructed their corporate empires. As American capitalism continued to mature, this process of maturation quickly became characterized by the large-scale consolidation of firms in many of the nations' largest, and most important, industries; e.g. railroads, steel, banking, and oil. By the turn of the twentieth century this process was far along in its work, and yet still not finished. The consolidation of individual wealth at the apex of the income scale, and of the ownership of firms via ownership of stock, in the hands of the so-called "captains of industry" gave these men near total control of the American economy from top to bottom. These new large-scale monopolistic firms were able to determine, almost at will, workers' wage hours, and benefits; they determined the prices consumers —especially urban ones- paid for almost everything they bought; they set the rates the farmers had to pay to ship their produce to market, thus determining in large part the earnings of farmers.

Theodore Roosevelt was without a doubt America's most popular President since Abraham Lincoln. Not only did the development of mass media, and a national market for such media, make whomever was going to be a President in this era more accessible to journalists, and thus to the American people, but Teddy in particular connected with the American people in deeper way. Perhaps it was his blend of east and west, or his combination of patrician background and working-class energy, that endeared him so much to the populace. His legacy in the American imagination testifies to the lasting impact he made on the American social and political psyche. The sheer volume of his personal correspondence over his life also testifies to the interest, and indeed fascination, he inspired in many. His landslide victory in the 1904 election also shows how taken Americans, from all across the nation, were with Roosevelt.

And yet, Roosevelt was an avowed patrician. He was a seventh generation New Yorker whose family originally immigrated to New Amsterdam in the middle of the 17th century and prospered. Over generations Theodore's forebears made a fortune, which they successfully passed on to their descendants. This money was made by practices, or in industries, which would be dis-tasteful modern sensibilities, to say the least. In particular, the trade in sugar was the source of much profit for the early Roosevelts. The almost unfathomable human suffering entailed in the production of sugar on European sugar plantations in the Caribbean is well-documented.[xxvii] Teddy was educated at Harvard, where he had a servant to attend to him, and was elected to one of its most prestigious clubs. He was quite conscious of his elite status, refusing to allow journalists to photograph him playing tennis as he thought it a rich man's pastime, or at least, thought voters would see it that way.

And, just like Tiberius Gracchus, this deeply patrician individual took up a popular political orientation, and challenged the political and economic power of established elites. Now, Roosevelt did not have to legally renounce his social status as Tiberius did, but he nonetheless faced vigorous resistance from elites whose power he was threatening. In the New York State Assembly, as Governor of New York, and as President of the United States, T.R. fought often for reforms which would benefit working-class people, often in the face of opposition from bosses in his own party. During his time in the New York State Assembly, that Roosevelt could be so aloof from the bosses that controlled the party political machines testifies again to his patrician status, as he did not need the pecuniary favors and inducements party bosses used to maintain discipline and loyalty. After his tenure in the Assembly Teddy served as a civil service commissioner by Benjamin Harrison, where he fought the spoils systems. So scrupulously did he do his work that Grover Cleveland asked him to stay on at his post, despite Roosevelt being a Republican. In 1895 he appointed one of three commissioners charged with reforming the NYPD. In 1897 party bosses facilitated his appointment as Assistant Secretary of the Navy so as to prevent him from returning to politics in Albany.

As President, Roosevelt continued to champion progressive causes, and win important victories for those not of elite backgrounds, and with elite means. This was the essence of the "Square Deal" he campaigned on in 1904, favoring neither the rich nor the poor, neither capital nor labor. He thought that the government should certainly not redistribute wealth or property, but it also should not align itself with the elite and aid them in preying on the poor. It is in this spirit one can see his efforts towards legislation like the expansion of the national parks system and the creation of the United States Forrest Service, the Pure Food & Drug Act, the Antiquities Act, the Meat Inspection Act, and the Hepburn Act. Also in this spirit one must see T.R.'s trust-busting actions. During his term in office the old Rough Rider initiated at least forty anti-trust actions, the most notable of which being his break-up of J.P. Morgan's Northern Securities Trust, which effectively controlled the nation's railroads, and Rockefeller's Standard Oil trust, which effectively controlled the refining of oil. Lastly, and very importantly, Roosevelt was the first President to formally recognize organized labor, by including the voice of organized labor in labor disputes; something which appalled the more patrician elements in American society.

Of course, Roosevelt's progressivism had limits. He was not anti-business, not in principle against the large corporations. Roosevelt thought that large-scale firms, like the trusts, might be useful, but needed to be regulated so that they did not take advantage of consumers. He was a friend to business, and to transnational capital insofar as he successfully completed the Panama Canal, the importance of which to modern capitalist globalized world-economy cannot be overstated. Roosevelt's actions in the case of Brownsville riots demonstrate the limits of his racial progressivism. He may have invited Booker T. Washington to dine with him in the White House, but he discharged all the black soldiers accused despite a Texas grand jury not returning indictments against any for lack of evidence. T.R. was also an unabashed imperialist; fighting in Cuba during the Spanish-American war, supporting the subsequent U.S. occupation of the Philippines and Puerto Rico, as well as supporting the annexation of Hawaii, and announcing the Roosevelt Corollary to the Monroe Doctrine.

Also, similarly to the elder Gracchi brother, Theodore Roosevelt would resort to the threat of constitutional crisis to achieve his ends. One must note that unlike Tiberius, Teddy only threatened constitutional crisis, never quite pushing beyond the bounds of constitutional legality and forcing a full-blown political crisis. And, like Tiberius, Teddy was accused of expanding executive authority at the expense of more constitutionally appropriate bodies. The title of Edmund Morris' biography, *Theodore Rex*, testifies in part to this perception of Teddy as a usurper of Congress' powers, as someone acting more like a classical Greek *Tyrannos*, as opposed to a *Basileus*. One salient example is found in the Coal Strike of 1902. Heading into the winter coal miners' went out on strike for better wages and hours, and recognition of their union. The mine owners refused to meet with the miners, or even listen to their demands. A national crisis of immense proportion was clearly in the offing if no resolution could be found.

Expanding the role of government, Teddy decided to intervene in the dispute. Intervening at all in a labor dispute in this era meant doing so in support of the workers, as the *lassiez-faire* policy which had dominated was an implicit, if not sometimes very explicit, choice to side with owners. Thus, intervention at all in this case meant the *de facto* recognition of organized labor's political legitimacy. In the face of the owners' continued recalcitrance T.R. threatened to turn an economic and political crisis, into a full-blown constitutional crisis. If the mine owners would not accede to Teddy's request to submit the dispute to federal mediation, Teddy claimed he would take over the mines and use the army to run them. Roosevelt did not have the explicit constitutional power to do this, even if he could have in practice carried out this threat, which he probably could have. The issue with this move was the appropriation of private property for public purposes without due process, or without just compensation, as required by the constitution. Whether or not Roosevelt could have gotten away with this move if it had made it to the Supreme court, which it almost certainly would have had Teddy followed through on his threat, is unclear and beside the point.

In the face of Roosevelt's threat, the mine-owners caved in and accepted federal mediation. The resulting settlement averted a national crisis, and saw the workers win a 10% pay increase and a nine-hour day. In the end, the threat of a constitutional crisis was enough for Teddy to achieve what wanted despite the organized resistance of an economically, and thus also politically, powerful group. Two years later, after Roosevelt's re-election, he once again threatened a constitutional crisis, but not intentionally. His resounding victory in 1904, and his continuing national popularity, gave many observers a good reason to think he could handily win another election in 1908. The issue in this case being that of the political precedent of Presidential term limits, which was an informal constitutional practice until codified into law after the death of Franklin Roosevelt. Roosevelt could have argued that since he merely finished out the term of the assassinated William McKinley, his first term was not really his, and thus he could run for President in 1908 perfectly legally. Whether this argument would have stood up with the Supreme Court, or with American voters, we will never know. Rather than force such a constitutional crisis, Roosevelt committed political suicide by announcing on election-night that he would not seek another term as President.

During his 1912 run for President there was an attempt on Teddy's life, but unlike that against Tiberius Gracchus in 133 B.C., it was not was not organized, lacked elite support, and thus was not successful; indeed, the attempted assassination was carried out by a man, John Flammang Schrank, who claimed to be inspired by the ghost of William McKinley. The potential mental instability of the would-be assassin notwithstanding, he was angered by what he saw as Roosevelt's tyrannical hunger for power, as evidenced in his bid for an unconstitutional third term. Despite having certainly made enemies among the wealthy and propertied elite of America, however, as much as he stretched the law or the limits of his powers, he didn't push the existing order into full-blown crisis. Like most other early 20th century 'progressives', Teddy was for gradual reform as a way of preventing a larger, potentially disastrous, social revolution. Though he fought against the abuses of the capitalist system, its replacement was nowhere on his agenda. Like Tiberius Gracchus with his land reform, Theodore Roosevelt sought not to radically alter an economic and social system, but to alter it so as to make it generate a more broadly-based prosperity. This was the aim of T.R.'s anti-trust actions, as well as the progressive items on his domestic policy agenda.

Facing the Forum

In 123 B.C., ten years after the assassination of his brother Tiberius, Gaius Sempronius Gracchus embarked on a political career by following closely in his brother's footsteps. Gaius renounced his Patrician status, by a legal process called *transitio ad plebem*, in order to be elected Tribune. As Tribune, just like his brother, Gaius was a *Popularis*, continuing Tiberius' un-finished programme of land re-distribution. Also like Tiberius, Gaius' actions as Tribune made for him many enemies among the *optimates* of the Senate, whose distaste for Tiberius would have ill-disposed them to Gaius from the beginning. And lastly, just like his brother, when Gaius pushed the Senate too far, threatened their power and privilege too much, they accused him of trying to become king, *Rex*, and they assassinated him.

Picking up the political legacy established by Tiberius, Gaius was a reform-minded politician who advocated for the needs of 'the Roman people', the same people referenced in the slogan "SPQR". Gaius supported increasing the rights of Plebian Roman citizens, as well as granting citizenship rights to more of the Italian allies. He continued to work of the land commission established by his brother. That Gaius could make political hay with the same economic and political issues as Tiberius had, shows that the fundamental problems in Roman society had not be addressed in the decade between the Tribunates of the Gracchi brothers. Indeed,

"The ten years which separate the tribunate of Tiberius Gracchus from his brother form a sort of twilight interval, such as sometimes separates two important periods of history, full of half-articulate cries, broken lights, and shadows of great events to come. Much is begun, nothing is ended, and the course of events seems to hang in suspense, as if in waiting for some master-hand to give the decisive impulse".[xxviii]

Gaius popular political orientation can be seen in his effort to found a colony on or near the site of the former Carthage, a colony he was to call Junonia, after the goddess Juno. While Tiberius mostly confined himself to the issue of the monopolization of land, and his programme of land redistribution, Gaius was far more wide-ranging in his attempts at reform. He introduced significant reform measures into the judiciary, the military, and the economy. He tried to limit the power of the Senatorial class by transferring some of their judicial powers to the *Equites,* or Knights, trying to drive a wedge between these classes. In the military, Gaius passed laws requiring the state to clothe and equip soldiers, reduce their term of service, and he forbade the conscription of boys under the age of seventeen. He also introduced price –controls for wheat, in effort to limit and regularize the price of bread, the main staple of the diet of the *Plebs Urbana*. Indeed, as if the Senate would not be hostile to Gaius already on account of their disgust with his brother, as well as the reforms he himself proposed, Gaius introduced what seems to us on its face a minor reform. This was a reform whereby, against long-established custom, speeches would now be delivered while facing leftward instead of rightward. By having speeches delivered while facing the *Forum*, the meeting place of the Plebian Assembly, instead of the *curia*, the Senate's meeting house, Gaius was delivering a none too subtle message to the Senate about where he thought power in the Roman state resided.

That the Senate felt threatened by Gaius after his first term as Tribune can be seen clearly in their recruitment of a political stooge to do their bidding in the Plebian Assembly, one Marcus Livius Drusus. It can also be immediately perceived in their use of propaganda – a new development at this time- against Gaius Gracchus by the *optimate* class, while he was away supervising his colony at Junonia. In the first case, the Senate used Drusus to out-do, or one-up any legislation proposed by Gaius Gracchus. If, for example, Gaius proposed to get increased rights for the Italian allies, the Drusus would propose a bill with even more generous rights and privileges, e.g. immunity from 'scourging', i.e. flogging, by a Roman military commander, or ability to appeal the sentence of a Roman magistrate. If Gaius wanted to settle 1,000 people in colonies, then Drusus would propose settling 3,000 people in colonies, *et cetera*.[xxix] Drusus even passes a law cancelling rents.

In the second case, the Senate's hostility to Gaius can be seen in the malicious rumors playing on Romans' superstitions that were spread far and wide in effort to cast Gaius' colony, as well as his person, as cursed. Gaius' enemies wanted to try to turn the people away from Gaius, to make him less popular, and therefore less powerful, by making him out to be impious, by insinuating that the many ill omens surrounding Junonia were clear signs of the disfavor of the Gods. One might see this aggressive push against Gaius by the Senate as their having learned something of a lesson in under-estimating Tiberius' audacity and ambition, and being conscious about not making the same mistake with Gaius. They feared, and perhaps not so unreasonably, that Gaius might be planning to use his new North African colony to stage and then launch an invasion of Rome, in revenge for the Senate's murder of his brother; for which only a few nominal executions of relatively minor Senators took place.

Gaius, like his brother Tiberius, pushed the Senatorial elite too far, and forced a violent reaction from them. Arch-Patrician Scipio Aemilianus intervened in the early part of Gaius career to undermine the Gracchan land commission by transferring the commissions' powers to the Consul, effectively ending land redistribution. Senatorial hostility and use of propaganda rendered the long-term success of the Gracchan colony at Junonia doubtful at best; indeed, the colony only survived for 30 years. Questions about the feasibility of practicability of Drusus' proposals notwithstanding, for it is unclear where he would or could have acquired the land necessary to settle such a large number of colonists, the people took the bait, and Gaius found that his power had been diminished. Upon his return to Rome, Gaius mis-read the political climate and took the provocative action of moving his residence to the Aventine hill in Rome, the well-known long-time strong-hold of the *Populare* faction. After he failed to win a third Tribunate, largely through the machination of his political enemies, many of whom held important political posts, the stage was set for a confrontation.

After his return to Rome in 121 B.C., and the deterioration of his political position, Gaius became increasingly wary about his personal safety and hired a bodyguard. The Senate would have seen both Gaius' moving to the Aventine and his hiring a body-guard as highly provocative actions. To the Senate, they were certainly not the kind of honorable actions befitting an up-standing and law-abiding Patrician Roman citizen. They looked like the action of a dangerous radical, who, like his brother before him, threatened to cause disruption to the pattern of business as usual for the Senatorial aristocracy. For Gaius, cognizant of his brother's fate, these were reasonable measures of self-protection. Unfortunately for Gaius, his bodyguard got into a drunken fight with a slave, who happened to be a servant of the sitting Consul, as a result of which the slave was killed. The Senatorial elites lost no time in spinning this incident into a conspiracy to kill the Consul which had only barely missed its target. This obviously could only further exacerbate the hysterical paranoia among the Senate directed against Gaius Gracchus, and deepened the elite's sentiment that this was a dangerous individual.

With a number of his political enemies elected to prominent political positions, including one Lucius Opimius elected Consul, in addition to Livius Drusus as Tribune, the time had come for the elites to try to un-do the mischief wrought by Gaius Gracchus. On the day set for the repeal of much of his reforms, this Opimius sent an attendant to perform a sacrifice. Let us not forget that religion and politics were far less divorced than they are now. On his way back this servant, Quintus Antyllius, carrying the entrails of the sacrifice tried to push his way through a crowd. Most accounts agree that it was Quintus Antyllius' efforts to get through the crowd, composed of supporters of both Gaius Gracchus' faction and

Opimius' faction that sparked a row between the groups resulting in Quintus' death. On Plutarch's account, it was Quintus' rudeness in pushing through the crowd that caused the Gracchan supporters to attack him. According to Appian, Gaius' supporters misunderstood his dis-approving countenance when approached by Quintus as a sign to act.

The death of Quintus Antyllius gave Opimius and his *optimate* faction all the pre-text they needed to mobilize against Gaius Gracchus. Here was a man who, like his brother before him, had renounced his Patrician status to obtain a political career pandering to the Plebians and freedmen. He had rocked the boat by continuing his brother's land reform project, but then moved much beyond that issue to make sweeping changes to the Roman constitution in many areas. He had founded a colony on cursed land and persisted in building it despite many ill omens - a potential staging point for an invasion aiming at an anti-Senatorial *coup de etat*. Gaius had shown his contempt for the Senate in giving speech facing left, and moving to the Aventine hill. He had acted openly, through his political reforms, to acquire power for himself at the expense of the Senate. He had allegedly plotted to kill the Consul with his bodyguard, was rumored to be involved in the death of Scipio Aemilianus, had appeared to sanction the impious action of his followers in killing Quintus Antyllius. In the eyes of the Senatorial aristocracy, Gaius Gracchus was clearly a very dangerous man, from a now suspect family.

The Senate mobilized the next day behind the Consul Opimius, to pass a declaration of martial law, called a *senatus consultum ultimum*, and to seize Gaius Gracchus and put him on trial; the eventual outcome of which no one, least of all Gaius, would have been in doubt about. After a few unsuccessful attempts at making peace, unsuccessful largely because the Senatorial faction refused anything but unconditional surrender, Opimius led a well-armed group to confront Gaius and his supporters, who had barricaded themselves on the Aventine hill. After a brief skirmish most of Gaius' supporters fled or were killed. The encounter was so brief largely because Gaius' supporters were mostly Plebians, and they were very likely to be less well armed, and especially less well-armored, than their opponents. We are told that Gaius' supporters were armed mainly with the spoils of the Gallic campaign of the former consul, and Gracchi supporter, Marcus Fulvius Flaccus. Having not taken part in the fighting, and having refused to arm himself with anything but a small dagger, Gaius fled the scene. After being hotly pursued as he tried to make a desperate escape across the Tiber River, and with no options remaining, Gaius instructed his slave to kill him rather than be taken alive by his enemies; suicide being a more honorable death in the eyes of an upper-class Roman like Gaius Gracchus.

A final note about the Gracchi is important. Like many popular politicians there are questions about whether the Gracchi were real reformers, or whether they were simply using the power of the Plebian Assembly to advance their own political careers and objectives. Are the Gracchi simply power-seekers, or were they more akin to social revolutionaries? Most likely, there are somewhere in between. The Gracchi provide another first in this regard. They form one of the earliest links in a long chain of aristocratic elements taking the lead in the fights of slaves, serfs, and proletarians over the ages for a society based on the principles of liberty, equality, and fraternity. Individuals in this lineage have always faced such charges. For example, Fidel Castro and his revolutionary cohort in Cuba faced such charges in the 20th century.

A New Deal and a Second Bill of Rights

We could easily imagine, and not unreasonably so, that Gaius Gracchus looked up to and was inspired by his elder brother Tiberius and his political career. We know for certain, thanks to documentary evidence, that Franklin Roosevelt looked up to and was inspired by his fifth cousin Theodore and his political career. And, just as the younger Gracchi took up the spirit of his brother's political ideals, so too did the younger Roosevelt adopt the spirit of his cousin's progressive political ideals. Where T.R. offered Americans overwhelmed by the size, scope, and pace of modern industrial society and the enormous corporate entities that controlled and profited from it a "Square Deal", F.D.R. offered Americans crushed under the weight of the most colossal episode of market failure yet recorded, the Great Depression, a "New Deal". The metaphorical deal had to be new with F.D.R. since the political and economic environment had changed so dramatically in the interval between his cousin's Presidency and his own. In offering such a deal, Franklin became the most popular President since his cousin; even winning the largest electoral victory in American history up to that point in 1936, taking forty six out of forty eight states.

Like his cousin Theodore, Franklin Roosevelt had a distinguished Patrician pedigree. He was raised on his family's aristocratic country estate, Springwood, in Hyde Park New York. Franklin received the kind of education one expects for the scion of a Patrician family. He was first educated by private tutors at home, then attended the prestigious Groton School, and after that, Harvard. His ancestors on his mother's side, the Delano family, were a very wealthy Huguenot family that had been in, and prospered in, America even longer than the Roosevelts. Even his childhood pastimes, much like T.R., bear the marks of upper-class privilege. The young Franklin collected stamps, coins, and books; did photography; hunted and collected bird specimens. And yet, also like his cousin Teddy, Franklin adopted a distinctly popular political orientation, challenging the power of elites, and threatening constitutional crises in order to push through legislation he thought necessary. The many public works and employment programs enacted, and experimented with, during the New Deal era demonstrate this concern for the plight of working Americans. F.D.R.'s lasting political legacy, adored by some and loathed by others, testifies to the significance of his impact on American society. It was under his watch that Congress passed, for example, the Wagner Act, the Social Security Act, the Glass-Steagall Act, the Wealth Tax Act, the Fair Labor Standards Act, and the National Industrial Recovery Act.

He also created the Federal Deposit Insurance Corporation, as well as the Securities and Exchange Commission, and the Federal Reserve Board.

Franklin Roosevelt, idolizing his cousin T.R. as he did, followed closely in his political footsteps, just as the younger Gracchi brother had. Franklin was elected to the New York State Assembly in 1910, where tried to emulate his cousin's anti-establishment politics, fighting the Tammany Hall machine bosses that still dominated New York politics. He followed Teddy again when he was appointed Assistant Secretary of the Navy by Woodrow Wilson in 1913. Then in 1920 he was tapped by the Democratic Party to be the nominee for Vice President. As his political career was gathering much momentum, despite the Democrats losing the 1920 election, F.D.R. was to leave the scene, much as T.R. had done after the death of his mother and wife. Where Teddy headed west to be a cattle rancher, Franklin was to be afflicted with polio. In this way, Franklin once again imitated his cousin and hero by enduring a period of, metaphorical, political exile. F.D.R emerged again later to win the Governorship of New York in 1928. It was in part his term as Governor, and part the effects of the Great Depression, that positioned Franklin Roosevelt to be the Democratic Party's nominee for President in 1932.

In 1929, the Great Crash, as it came to be known, changed the political and economic landscape of America in ways no one was prepared for. In the aftermath of the Crash there was however near universal agreement about who had caused it, and who was to blame. Wall-Street, the banks, and speculators were all the target of a raging torrent of public obloquy. The scope of this tsunami of condemnation is in its own way a measure of the scope of the crash itself, and the social an economic dislocation that followed in its wake. In 1929 unemployment in the US was about 3%; by the later part of 1932 it was 25%. Gross Domestic Product (GDP) declined precipitously. It was $87.4 billion in 1929, but by 1933 it had fallen to $39.7 billion. Workers' earning fell from $50.8 billion in 1929, to 29.3 billion in 1933. In 1929 there were 25,000 banks in the US, but by 1933 there were less than 15,000. Between 1929 and 1932 farmers lost about 2/3rds of their income. Most strikingly 3/4th of the people eligible for assistance were unable to obtain any.[xxx] Homelessness, starvation were widespread, suicide rates rose dramatically. These figures provide some idea of the scale of the crisis produced by the Crash of 1929 and its aftermath.

As if the economic crisis was not enough, Roosevelt also had to confront the growing threat posed by fascism. This threat posed more than one problem for Roosevelt. Not only did the militarism of Italy, Germany, and Japan threaten peace and security, but their example threatened further political instability in America. At a time when the American economy was in dire straits, as were many of the leading European industrial economies, the economies of fascist Germany and Italy, and of the communist Soviet Union, were performing much better. These examples, combined with the economic and political tumult brought on by the effects of the Depression, made fascism and communism, seem like very real alternatives for America. The idea of dictatorship, or of dictatorial powers, was not universally, or unambiguously negative in the eyes of many Americans. Before the out-break of the war, Italy and Germany were not reviled enemies, but potent competitors with a radical new model of political-economic organization, one that was turning in a better performance than the economies of the leading democracies in a time of globalized economic depression. A reporter is said to have commented to F.D.R. about the New Deal that because of it he'd go down in American history as the best President or the worst President. F.D.R. is said to have replied something to the effect of, "no, if I fail, I'll be the last President". This statement provides some insight into how real the threat of fascism and communism felt, even in the highest reaches of American government.

As President, Franklin Roosevelt inherited a chaotic, and indeed dire, social and economic situation. In response, he undertook decisive, and in the eyes of critics radical, action in order to lift the economy out of the depression. In so doing he saw himself as trying to save American capitalism from itself, and thereby save American democracy. Though in the end it was war production that brought the American economy back to life, and to prosperity, Roosevelts' pre-war efforts to combat the Great Depression are not one bit less heroic. Though he enjoyed unprecedented popular support, he also faced much resistance to his proposals from established elites. Like his cousin, Franklin was accused to over-reaching executive authority, of radically altering the constitutionally ordained relationship between the state and the economy, and between the state and its citizens. Many in the American aristocracy felt that the "New Deal" Franklin Roosevelt was offering the American people was far too generous, and involved far too much government intervention, to the point that he was accused of being a communist, or a dictator. This is especially true in regards to the National Labor Relations Act, which created the National Labor Relations Board, and the Social Security Act. The first provided a federal guarantee of workers' right to organize and to bargain collectively, the second provided important benefits for the retired and the unemployed. This conviction that Roosevelt was a despotic tyrant was only confirmed when he stood for and won a third, and then later a fourth, term as President, in contravention of one of America's most revered informal political traditions.

Under the influence of new thinking in economics, especially in macro-economics, in particular the work of John Maynard Keynes, Roosevelt and his advisors designed a myriad of programs and initiatives designed to prime the economic pump by putting money in the hands of workers. Where T.R.'s "Square Deal" aimed only to prevent business from unfairly trampling the consumer, Franklin's "New Deal" aimed beyond just assuring fairness, and towards more directly improving workers' level of material welfare. The alphabet soup of New Deal agencies and administrations testifies to the extent of the efforts undertaken by the Roosevelt administration to fight-off the Great Depression. Thus we have, for example, the T.V.A., the P.W.A. the W.P.A., the C.C.C., the F.E.R.A., the C.W.A., the F.S.A., and the R.E.A., among many others. Some programs or policies were more successful than others, and F.D.R. showed a great deal of pragmatism in moving from one to another, and when one failed, he simply tried something else. His radical expansion of government, in terms of its size, the scope of its powers, and the fields of its action, earned Roosevelt and his "New Deal" the undying enmity of many American capitalists. They saw his expansion of the scope and scale of government intervention in society as unconstitutional, as un-American, and even as a communist take-over. His New Deal employment programs were seen as re-distribution of wealth and his push for increased regulation as an abrogation of private property.

In order to enact his reform programme F.D.R. had to threaten a constitutional crisis, his well-known "court-packing" plan, that is, formally, the Judicial Procedures Reform Bill of 1937. The Supreme Court had been working to undermine his attempts to enact the kind of legislation needed to being economic recovery, relying heavily on its decision in *Adkins v. Children's Hospital*. In response, Roosevelt threatened to add several new justices to the court, one for every current justice over 70 years of age. The implication was very clear. If the court did not stop undermining Roosevelt, he would pack the court with judges who would vote the way he wanted, and thus over-ruling the recalcitrant conservative jurists. If seems very clear that Roosevelt could have followed through on his threat, and had such legislation passed through the Congress if he needed to. The issue in this case is less Roosevelts' ability to do what he threatened, or even the legality of this tactic. The issue has more to do with the spirit of democracy and of the constitution. The threat Roosevelt made certainly appears inconsistent with the spirit of democratic governance, and respect for its mechanisms. His ends may have justified his means in this case, as the threat of fascism was indeed very real at the time, but his threat certainly would seem to violate the spirit of fair play in a democratic polity. We will never know now what might have happened if Roosevelt had carried out his threat. The Supreme Court would no doubt have weighed in, and thus the stage would have been set for a confrontation between the executive and legislative branches and the judicial branch.

Out of this experience, both his own and the nation's, with the

Depression and then the war, came Roosevelt's commitment to the idea of a second Bill of Rights. This would have been Roosevelt's most significant reform to the U.S. constitution, the introduction of social and economic rights into the American constitutional order. Had he lived longer he might have seen more of his idea brought to life. As it is, several aspects of his proposal for a second Bill of Rights have become part of the American constitutional order in the form of what Cass Sunstein calls "constitutive commitments. For example, social security is not a constitutional right, and yet any politician, from any either current party, would be hard pressed to get elected calling for such a policy, or, if elected, to get such a policy passed through the Congress. Discrimination on the basis of sex, for instance, is not explicitly forbidden in the Constitution. However, the constitution has been so interpreted that such a prohibition is today considered consistent with, necessary for, or even implied by, the rights enumerated in it. Indeed, as Sunstein argues, if not for the election of Richard Nixon in 1968 the American constitutional order would contain social and economic rights. Nixon, as President, was able to appoint several justices to the Supreme Court, and as a result, to stop the Warren Court's momentum toward recognition of the kind of social and economic rights outlined in Roosevelt's Second Bill of Rights.

Part of Roosevelt's vision with the second Bill of Rights was to guarantee the exercise of democratic citizenship. The age-old republican principle that economic dependence make for political subjugation, was clearly at work in F.D.R.'s thinking.[xxxi] "Necessitous men are not free men" Roosevelt once said, thus, providing for all citizens to have access to the most basic necessaries of life is the essential pre-requisite for the exercise of democratic citizenship.[xxxii] In order for a democracy to truly flourish, citizens must be liberated from what F.D.R. called "fear" and "want".[xxxiii] Persons who do not enjoy the freedom from fear or freedom from want could never fully realize the ideal of democratic citizenship. Such a Bill of Rights, the inclusion of social and economic rights in the constitutional order, would very obviously be anathema to American oligarchs, who would deride such an inclusion as socialist re-distribution of wealth, as the subsidization of the idleness of the lazy by the industriousness of the productive. That many American aristocrats, and *optimate* politicians, still decry the New Deal as the death of the American republic, shows just how radical were Roosevelt's actions, and how radical they were perceived as being by contemporaries. We know, for example, how shocked and traumatized the Athenians were during the Second Peloponnesian War, because in the surviving literary sources, it is constantly referred to as the worst thing to have ever happened to anyone.[xxxiv] The continuing enmity against Franklin Roosevelt and his New Deal from some elite quarters likewise demonstrates the depth of feeling of people at the time. The same could be said about Southern elites in regard to Abraham Lincoln and his actions during the war and for imposing the Reconstruction regime.

Legacies

In thinking about the political legacies of both the Grachhi and the Roosevelts, one, I think, very striking similarity that jumps to mind is that all of them left their political work unfinished. All envisioned, and attempted to enact —with varying success- significant changes in the constitutions of their societies. All reacted strongly against large concentrations of wealth and power —both economic and political- that left the vast majority destitute and all but formally disenfranchised. In the case of the Gracchi since the problem was caused by the *latifundia* their reforms was focused first on land redistribution, and only later on about issues like extension of citizenship rights.

In the time of the Roosevelts, the problem was the trusts, the large corporations, and the immense concentrations of financial and productive assets they controlled; and also with the social, political, and economic power that control bestowed. Thus, the Roosevelts' reforms were focused in the first phase on trust-busting and consumer protections, and then in the second phase on unemployment relief, social security, and labor rights. While Theodore Roosevelt was the first President to give organized labor a voice at the bargaining table. Franklin Roosevelt formally codified labor rights into law as President. Yet, despite the success both pairs of politicians undoubtedly did have, they all left – or were forced off- the scene before their work could be completed.

We know Tiberius' work was left undone, given that he was violently assassinated, and his land commission effectively neutered after his death. Moreover, that his brother Gaius could make a political career, ten years later, on many of the same issues, shows very clearly that the same problems existed, and that Tiberius' reforms were not sufficient to address the full scale of the problem. Much of the reason for this was that Tiberius' reforms were systematically undermined by the *optimate* faction after his assassination. Though it would have been politically dangerous for the elites to immediately abolish Tiberius' land commission, they did the next best thing, they defunded the project. The Senate was able to deprive Tiberius of sufficient funds to effectively administer the project while he was alive, and then to tighten the purse strings even further after his murder. Later on, in 129 B.C., most of the powers of the commission were transferred to the Consul. The dithering allowed by this maneuver enabled the Senatorial elites to in-practice halt the work of the land commission.

That Gaius was forced, in the end, to choose between suicide and a violent assassination, shows that he was also forced off the scene while his reforming project was not fully consolidated, let alone finished with its work. Again, moreover, that Gaius Julius Caesar later on also made a political career with many of the same political issues as the younger Gracchi, shows once again that the underlying dynamics causing the problem had not been remedied. Perhaps, if the Gracchi had been successful their reform project, there never would have been a Caesar. Nonetheless, it was not until 118 B.C. that Tiberius' land commission was formally dissolved. Then in 111 B.C. even the rents that owners of public land were supposed to pay were abolished, effectively completing the privatization of the *ager publicus*. Thus the legislation of both the Gracchi was in the main repealed formally, or informally undermined. All Gracchan reforms were ultimately cancelled under the ultra-conservative constitution imposed by Sulla and his proscriptions, and enforced by his client-army.[xxxv]

Teddy Roosevelt himself thought he left his work unfinished, and that he quit the scene too soon. He regretted almost immediately his decision on election-night in 1904 to not seek another term. In exchange, his party did allow him to pick his successor. T.R. had much confidence in William Howard Taft when the latter took office. Taft would however prove a disappointment to Teddy. This was one reason, among others, that Theodore Roosevelt decided to run for President again in 1912, his now famous "Bull Moose" campaign. T.R. may be remembered as a trust-busting President, and indeed he was quite active; at least relative to other Presidential administrations, both before and after. However, T.R. was not an anti-business politician, not even an anti- corporate politician. He was a progressive, and fought business leaders, and the "captains of industry", but he was not anti-capitalist. He may have busted some trusts, may have slowed the development of some others for a time. But, that the Crash of 1929 happened shows very clearly that the reforming work of T.R. was not finished; even if it was capable of adequately addressing the problems in the American economy that ultimately caused the Crash.

That right-wing politicians today continue to gripe about the New Deal, and the "welfare state" it created, demonstrates without a doubt that F.D.R.'s work was left unfinished. Towards the end of his Presidency he advocated for a second Bill of Rights, which would include social and economic rights. Though this proposal formed one the major bases of the United Nation's Universal Declaration of Human Rights, and as a result an important part of dozens of national constitutions around the world, only small parts were adopted in the United States. His experience with the Great Depression had convinced Franklin Roosevelt that these social and economic rights were essential. They were needed to alleviate the massive human suffering caused by Depression induced unemployment and deprivation. They also necessary to guarantee a secure foundation upon which citizens could depend, and thus achieve the kind of liberty needed to exercise democratic citizenship. This, very obviously, has not developed; quite the opposite in fact. But that the legacy of the New Deal and the proposal for a second Bill of Rights are still controversial shows that the transformative work F.D.R. begun had also not yet been fully consolidated, and was not yet fully finished.

Conclusion

The crisis of 1929-1945 was a watershed event, not only in American history, but in world history. It was responsible for unleashing perhaps the largest wave of suffering the human world has ever seen; I am including in this wave the Cold War of the subsequent period, and its attendant proxy wars and "disappeared" dissidents; I am also including in this wave the undeclared war of "underdevelopment" that kills through malnutrition and treatable diseases. This crisis occasioned some of the largest movements and exchanges of populations, both voluntary and involuntary, and their attendant cultural mixing. These were extraordinary times, unprecedented times, to the people living through them.

In 1932 A.D. Franklin Delano Roosevelt began a project of radical constitutional change, expanding the powers of the federal government and the executive branch, in response to an extreme crisis. This is much the same as what Tiberius Gracchus did in 133 B.C. in response to the economic crisis of the Roman republic after the Punic Wars. Both were derided as dictators during their careers. Both had their work attacked by factions of the aristocratic elites of their societies. In the long-run, both had big parts of the work undone by political opponents. Like the Grachhi then, could the Roosevelts' political careers be the signal of a new phase in the development of the American republic? Are we heading, like the Romans of the Gracchi's era, towards the destruction of the republic?

If we can venture one broad conclusion, it is that plutocracy and extreme concentrations of wealth foment crisis. And, it is out of moments of crisis that revolutions emerge. Often times, revolutions which are not successful are followed by reaction. Reaction, especially in the ancient world, could be extremely cruel, as the aftermath of the repression of the Gracchan revolution demonstrates. Worries about vast accumulations of wealth undermining democracy also underlay the 'progressive' political agendas of both Roosevelts. And, just like the Gracchi, attacking these concentrations brought unceasing scorn upon both Teddy and Franklin Roosevelt from the elites, but adoration from the masses.

Ancient historians like Plutarch, Livy, Dio Cassius, Cicero, Appian, Tacitus, and Polybius all have distinct upper-class biases. And all roundly condemn the Gracchi as political 'adventurers', as radicals using unconstitutional methods, and as largely responsible for getting themselves murdered. Modern historians, who typically share an upper-class bias, differ more in opinion, but there remain many who decry the Roosevelts as closet-socialists who radically changed the American constitutional order for the worse, in effect undermining the American republic. Conversely, just as the Roman people had erected statutes of the Gracchi brothers throughout Rome, so too during the Depression did people –often with few material possessions and living in ramshackle housing- hang up pictures of F.D.R.. Moreover, Franklin Roosevelt's role as victorious wartime leader – in a war that made his nation a super-power – blunted much of the vitriol some had had toward Roosevelt because of his New Deal policies before the war.

This bring us back to our original question, or questions: Are the Roosevelts the American Grachhi?; If they are, What does this mean for the American republic?; Should we be looking out for an American Marius, or an American Sulla? What would either of these even look like in the 21st century? It was less than a century after the death of Gaius Gracchus that Caesar was himself assassinated, and we are now drawing up closely towards a century since the New Deal era. Perhaps the ancient world and the modern world are too different to draw meaningful parallels? I don't necessarily have the answers to these questions. My main goal was simply to pose the first question about the American Gracchi. I leave the rest of the questions be conjectured about by the reader.

Notes

For excellent resources on Roman history for this period see; Havell. H.L.. Republican Rome. 1914. Oracle Publishing, 1996. Also see; Scullard, H.H.. From the Gracchi to Nero. 1959. 5th edition. Routledge, 1982. Also see; Parenti, Michael. The Assassination of Julius Caesar. The New Press, 2003. Also see; Titchener, Frances. "To Rule Mankind and Make the World Obey". Portable Professor Series. Barnes & Noble Audio; 2004.

Quoted in; Parenti (2003), 61.

For excellent resources on the life and political career of Theodore Roosevelt see; Morris, Edmund. Theodore Rex. Random House, 2002. Also see; The Roosevelts: An Intimate History. Dir. Ken Burns. PBS, 2014. Also see; Brands, H.W.. T.R.: The Last Romantic. Basic Books, 1998.

For an excellent history of this period, up to 1900, see Brands, H.W.. American Colossus. Anchor Books, 2011.

See; Abbott, Elizabeth. Sugar: A Bittersweet History. The Overlook Press, 2011.

Havell (1914), 367.

Colonies were a great tool for the Romans to relieve social pressure accumulating among the *Plebs Urbana* at Rome. Being re-settled in a colony gave the colonist a second chance, which many wanted, even at the cost of re-settlement far from Rome, the idea of which would have abhorred a true Roman. This was thus an easy way for politicians to win acclaim and popularity with the people.

These stats come from Sunstein, Cass. The Second Bill of Rights. Basic Books, (2004): 36-38.

I mean "republican" in the classical political sense here. The republican tradition has a long history in political philosophy.

Excellent modern work in this tradition has been done by Philip Petit. See Republicanism. Oxford University Press, 1997.

Sunstein (2004), 90.

These are two of F.D.R.'s "four freedoms". See Sunstein (2004), 80.

See; Hanson, Victor Davis. The Other Greeks. 1995. University of California Press,1999. Also see; Hanson, V.D.. Warfare and Agriculture in Classical Greece. University of California Press, 1998.

Proscription is a process whereby Roman citizens were declared 'outlaws', 'traitors', or 'criminals' by the state, i.e. the Senate. Once a citizen was declared a criminal they effectively had a bounty put out on their head. If one was a victim of proscription, one would have twenty hour hours to either flee or face trial; the outcome of this trial would not be much in doubt. In response to proscription many Roman citizens chose suicide. This was because if they either fled or were convicted in court their property would be forfeited to the state. Thus, in order to keep property in the family, many proscribed individuals chose suicide to exile or execution.

Race & Ethnicity

Ferguson Revolts and Beyond
Is Property worth More than Black Life?

Devon Douglas-Bowers

"I think that we've got to see that a riot is the language of the unheard. And, what is it that America has failed to hear? It has failed to hear that the economic plight of the Negro poor has worsened over the last few years."

- Martin Luther King Jr., Interview with Mike Wallace, September 27, 1966

"Now, let's get to what the white press has been calling riots. In the first place don't get confused with the words they use like 'anti-white,' 'hate,' 'militant' and all that nonsense like 'radical' and 'riots.' What's happening is rebellions not riots[.]"

- Stokely Carmichael, "Black Power" speech, July 28, 1966

Many people are telling the people of Ferguson that they should not riot, that it is only hurting their community and they should instead engage in peaceful protests. However, this is deeply problematic as it ignores a number of issues.

People's main concern regarding the riots in Ferguson come from a concern about private property. One could say that people are more concerned about the theft and destruction of private property than human life, but this needs to be made much clearer. People are more worried about the smashing and theft of inanimate objects than they are about human life. But it isn't specifically human life; it's black human life that many of these people could care less about.

On a deeper level, this is where capitalism and racism intersect. One of capitalism's main tenets is the dominance of private property and how it must be protected. We can see that this has been transcribed in law, such as with the Stand Your Ground laws. Yet, also within the larger society, there is a lack of caring for black life. In any situation, the media and general public regularly engage in victim blaming and look for anything - anything at all - to assassinate the character of those who died at the hand of the police. This can be seen even today, when the media brings up Akai Gurley's criminal record when discussing his death at the hands of a police officer. These two ideas have come together in Ferguson, creating a situation where people are more concerned about private property destruction than they are about the death of Michael Brown.

Many argue that the people of Ferguson are destroying their own community. Yet this is false. To quote Tyler Reinhard: "we don't own neighborhoods. Black businesses exist, it's true. But the emancipation of impoverished communities is not measured in corner-store revenue. It's not measured in minimum-wage jobs. And no, it's especially not measured in how many black people are allowed to become police officers." Neighborhoods like those in Ferguson were not created by black people; they were created due to racist housing policies that black people had no control over. It should also be noted that Ferguson is 60% black, but has an almost entirely white police force and that the city government and school board are also almost completely white. So while they may live there, the black residents of Ferguson have little representation in the local community and are essentially living under a group of people that isn't responsive to their concerns.

With regards to the riots themselves, the larger society is asking, "why don't the protesters remain peaceful?" The answer is two-part: peace has been tried, and we are going to be condemned no matter what.

Society asks why aren't the protesters peaceful; however, we have to ask this in return: Why would you think that people would remain peaceful in the face of constant violence? Why would a people remain peaceful when their children are being killed on a seemingly weekly basis by the very people who are supposed to protect them?

Black people have tried peace before. We were peaceful in the 1960s when we were protesting for our civil rights and were met with racist mobs, fire hoses, and dogs. We had crosses burnt on our lawns, lynchings, and a bomb put in a church. During all of that time, we remained peaceful even as society enacted massive violence and repression against us. Yet, violence against the black community continues today, the only difference is that it isn't so blatant. Martin Luther King Jr. was nonviolent and died at the hands of an assassin, a violent act. Look at the Occupy protests, which were entirely nonviolent: the protesters were still met with violence, most notably in the form of a pre-dawn raid on Zuccotti Park. So, even when protesters are nonviolent, they are still met with violence.

The situation is currently such where if a black person is killed by the police, people immediately come out and find any way in which they can besmirch or blame the victim, such as with the aforementioned example involving Akai Gurley. So, they are already looking for ways to take the blame off of the authorities from day one. The situation changes, though, when oppressed people fight back. Not only is the violence denounced, but it is used as an excuse to exact massive amounts of violence against the oppressed, as we saw by the militarized police that have been used in Ferguson. When people lash out against one incident, one may be inclined to call that violence, but when violence against your community has been going on for decades and people lash out, that's no longer violence on the part of the oppressed; that's called resistance.

The question of 'why aren't there peaceful protests' is also extremely hypocritical. Many have spoken out in person and on social media condemning the riots, but at the same time they are silent on the constant police brutality that the black community deals with, and they are silent on the economic violence perpetrated against black communities, pushing them into ghettos where not only is there economic poverty, but also a poverty of expectations. On a larger scale, they are also silent when other groups riot, such as when white people rioted over pumpkins. It is extremely hypocritical to speak out against rioters, but not have a thing to say about police brutality or to ignore others who riot.

At the heart of this is how society condones state violence, but condemns violence by individuals. This mindset is a serious problem as it only gives more power to the state and consistently puts state forces in the right, while the victims of state violence are forced to prove their innocence, a situation made all the more difficult by people assuming the victims are in the wrong.

Many have pushed for peace, but peace and safety are not something that black people in America receive, whether we are just looking for help after a car accident, as was the case with Renisha McBride, or we are carrying a toy gun around, as was the case with John Crawford.

This is not the time to ask for peace. This is the time to say "No justice, no peace."

Kind of Blue
Contextualizing the Ebola Crisis, Humanitarian Imperatives, and Structural Deficits

Sonasha Braxton

Miles Davis' 1959 record release describes my passport perfectly. It's *Kind of Blue*. It's a bit faded from passing between fingers, under plastic windows, held in teeth as I've adjusted backpack straps, or tipped ungracefully into the Nile. It is so well traveled that it has begun to pale but definitely distinctly navy enough to be considered "blue." To be specific, this blue passport is not Mercosur. It is not Brazilian, Argentinian, Paraguayan or Uruguayan. Nor is it Libyan, Botswanan, or Yemeni. I wasn't born in Canada or Australia, nor Kenya, or Belarus. It's that impervious kind of blue of "vigilance and justice" that comes with the red and white stripes connoting U.S. citizenship. I would argue, that along with a few of its Western European counterparts, this is possibly one of the most benefit bearing items in the world.

With a going rate of anywhere from 300 to 10,000 USD, this blue passport allows me to enter 174 countries unannounced, to jump on a plane and go...no interviews, no green card lotteries, police clearance certificates, medical examinations, long queues, impossible evidence of financial support, a friend in the Embassy, or exorbitant fees. As symbolic of U.S. citizenship, freedom of movement, opportunity, stability, and most of all, privilege, it is in many ways invaluable. A recent observation of the beneficial nature of having this little biometric tracking device in my back pocket is that it also serves as a "get out of jail free" card, more precisely, a "get out of *Ebola Land*" card. In other words, in case of emergency, this blue passport affords you the opportunity to get evacuated, while everyone else stays behind. Take this history for example: As of November 19, 2014[1] seven individuals had been evacuated from West Africa, specifically Sierra Leone and Liberia, and taken to the United States for treatment. Dr. Kent Brantly and Nancy Writebol, U.S. health workers for missionary groups SIM USA and Samaritan's Purse, respectively, were evacuated from Liberia to Atlanta early August, treated with ZMAPP at Emory Hospital and survived. Rick Sacra, another doctor with the missionary group SIM USA, was evacuated from Liberia to Omaha, Nebraska on October 5th. There he was treated with TKM-Ebola and survived. An unidentified U.S. citizen was evacuated to Atlanta, Georgia from Sierra Leone on September 9th, and lived. An unidentified doctor was flown from Sierra Leone to Bethesda, MD on September 28th. He too survived. Freelance cameraman Ashoka Mukpo was evacuated to Omaha Nebraska, October 6th, treated and survived. U.S. permanent resident and Sierra Leonean national Dr. Martin Salia was evacuated from Sierra Leone to Omaha, Nebraska on November 15th and died after being treated with ZMAPP. The U.S. State Department did assist in evacuating to Germany two unidentified doctors from Uganda and Senegal, however, comparatively, between July and October, over 400 West African health care workers have been infected with the disease and over 200 have died. Over two months ago, President Ernest Bai Koroma's office in Sierra Leone requested that the World Health Organization (WHO) pay for the evacuation of Dr. Olivet Buck. This request was denied by WHO, as it was against their organizational policy to pay for the evacuation of non-staff. Understandably WHO was not financially equipped to begin paying for the very costly evacuation of all health care workers in West Africa infected with Ebola .[2] Yet this still looks eerily to observers, like hegemonic favoritism. While this initial discussion is colored by states' rights, organizational policy, domestic law and evacuation costs, it also serves as a basis for a more meaningful discussion entailing a deeper examination into the intersection of humanitarian priorities, the political economy of Ebola, militarized response, irresponsible journalistic coverage, and eugenics.

The Humanitarian Imperative

Far from a critique of the care and compassion of those who worked tirelessly at the risk of their own lives to assist those infected with Ebola in Sierra Leone, Guinea and Liberia, the "Western Evacuation" phenomenon has reawakened the napping giant of the U.S. role in sub-Saharan Africa's emergencies. With the colossal scope and breadth of the Syrian Crisis, and ISIS ever-looming, African crises have been put on the media back burner. With much of the initial discussion about Ebola being a "humanitarian disaster," it would seem that naturally the appropriate sequential discussion would be that of "humanitarian intervention." On the one hand, the evacuation of infected United States Citizens represents a "humanitarian act" for the affected families; and provides, for some individuals, irrevocable proof of the U.S. government as a benevolent government which demonstrates its concern and care for its citizens and residents. On the other hand, one can only imagine that, for those left behind, especially those working side by side with U.S. citizens, another message is left to reverberate in empty villages, destroyed holding facilities, overcrowded hospitals, and presidential boardrooms in Monrovia, Freetown, and Conakry. The message wrapped in a lack of pharmaceutical response is a clear one. "We Don't Value Your Lives." While this may not be the intended message, it certainly may feel like this to a population on a continent in which the feeling of being "left hanging" by the West is quite common; and for good reason. It also is not a message that hasn't been heard before. This speaks to the accepted Western-centric double standard built into our definitions of "humanitarian action." It also informs our understanding of the evacuation of foreign nationals. Case in point, during the Rwandan genocide, "the term 'humanitarian operation' was first introduced by the French representative in the informal consultations on April 9th 1994 only when France informed other Council members that a French unit of 190 troops ... would serve to evacuate only the French expatriate community and other foreigners. It had nothing to do with...the protection of Rwandan civilians.... In fact, the terms 'humanitarian operation' and 'humanitarian aim' became synonymous with the evacuation of foreign nationals..." [3]. So it should have been of little surprise that on April 9-10th the United States evacuated 50 of its nationals also at the height of the Genocide. It is arguable as to how precisely we could have predicted the degree to which this singular action was key in sealing the fate of numerous Rwandese who were left to die unprotected under the noses of the international community. As a lesson in humanitarian evacuation, for Liberia, Guinea, and Sierra Leone, what better illustration and confirmation of the U.S.'s indifference towards the lives of West African citizens and naturally the lives of African people?

According to the Central Intelligence Agency World Fact Book[4], pre-Ebola Liberia and Guinea had approximately 1.4 physicians per 100,000 people and Sierra Leone had approximately 2.2 physicians per 100,000 people. Imagine this in contrast to the United States, which has 2500 doctors per 100,000 people. Therefore even the death of a few health care workers in these countries, makes a verifiable difference. The logical question, as Rony Zachariah of Doctors Without Borders poses is, if *"you have one nurse for 10,000 people and then you lose 10, 11, 12 nurses. How is the health system going to work?"* [5] The deaths of health workers in these countries represent not only casualties of human life but movement towards the entire health care system as a casualty.

A number of doctors living in infected areas have left their respective countries to avoid becoming its victims. Many health care workers working in hospitals or clinics and seeing them overrun with the virus have correctly identified themselves as directly in the line of fire, and left. This includes President Sirleaf Johnson's own son, James Adama's Sirleaf, now living in Georgia, who told the Wall Street Journal that, "the symbolism of me going there and potentially getting Ebola when I have a nine- and a seven-year-old at home isn't worth it just to appease people."[6] But many like the latest casualty in the United States Dr. Martin Salia, did not leave. Abdullah Kiatamba, born in Liberia, heads the "Minnesota African Task Force Against Ebola", which is organizing a legation of 150 Liberian-born health care workers who have volunteered to work in Liberia, Sierra Leone and Guinea.[7]

It is impossible to weigh hearts against feathers like Maat, with family and self-preservation on one scale and nation on the other. How do we dare judge anyone who puts his or her family first? The issue goes deeper than individual decisions. The greater question is, given the impending demise of the health care systems in these countries, amongst the numerous systems already fractured, and crumbling, as an inheritance of war and colonial-induced depravity, how can the future of health care be supported?

Political Economy of Ebola

While this does not serve as an argument for the State Department to neglect its citizens, it does raise very serious issues around the moral imperatives of states, specifically Western states who have played some role in the underdevelopment of their Global South neighbors. It is reminiscent again of the exploitative relationship that the West has and continues to have with Africa in which the West takes, removes, extracts, evacuates and gives back in a way that does more harm than good, creating an altruistic façade.

A laissez-faire, blame-the-victim attitude has been adopted towards these countries' inability to manage the disease. Even WHO's early Global Alert and Response begins by discussing "negative cultural values" and "traditional beliefs" [8] as the reason for the proliferation for the disease, as if to shame backwards Black Africa for their incapacity to be "civilized" enough to control the disease. The irony lies in the context. No one dares point a finger at the "negative cultural values" like Western capitalism and greed, which fueled the colonization of these countries and created the exploitative systems under which African countries must still operate.

However dire the situation of their health systems, the rapid spread of the disease and incapacity of government must be understood within the context of (1) colonial underdevelopment, and (2) the neoliberal economic policies that have played a large role in undermining and defunding the health infrastructure.[9] The initial colonial exploitation of West Africa and resulting power struggles "post-liberation," economic decline, and war have plunged many parts of West Africa into states of volatility and poverty which have continued until today. According to the 2014 Human Development Index out of 184 countries, Sierra Leone comes in 183rd , Guinea comes in 179th, and Liberia ranks highest at 175th[10]. These three countries are among the 10 poorest in the world.

Ecologist and phylogeographer Rob Wallace made the very clear connection that historically in the region, "structural adjustment programs have been encouraged and enforced by Western governments and international financial institutions that require privatization and contraction of government services, removal of tariffs while Northern agribusiness remains subsidized, and an orientation toward crops for export at the expense of food self-sufficiency. All of this drives poverty and hunger..."[11] Further, these programs in the 1980s and 1990s also moved money away from health spending. Professor of Political Economy at Oxford University, David Stuckler, who undertook research covering health care expenditures in countries under IMF programs, found that these programs grew at half of the pace of countries not under IMF agreement. According to Stuckler, "these arrangements tied the hands of governments so that when there were disease outbreaks, they didn't have the resources in place to control them." [12] This lack of basic human needs, compounded by historically destabilized governments, which are unable to manage the spread of disease, has also burgeoned the virus's spread. While the IMF, World Bank and other international financial institutions have agreed to allow changes in how loans may be spent, provision for some emergency debt relief and grants,12 Liberia, Sierra Leone and Guinea find themselves in the same cycles, which created their initial impoverishment. Instead of mass debt forgiveness, there is a focus on loans are being redirected towards disaster management, and away from systems building and fortification. What does this mean? A culture of firefighting is being demanded and encouraged. Without working structures, governments will never fully function independently, and as the "borrowers" these countries will continue to operate at the mercy of its "leaders" and the whims of its "lenders." Therefore, Ebola is now serving to concretize in some way, economic enslavement to and dependence on the West. While this serves as just part of the discussion, context is critical. So often, in our busyness in blaming the victim, the structural milieu is ignored. Amongst the evacuations, and fear mongering, it is easy to forget that that the injury was inflicted long ago, and in this case specifically, the rapid spread of the new infection is simply proof of the gravity of the initial wound. And I'll bet my blue passport on that.

Notes

[1] https://www.internationalsos.com/ebola/index.cfm?content_id =407
[2] http://www.cbc.ca/news/health/ebola-outbreak-who-denies-request-from-sierra-leone-to-fly-out-infected-doctor-1.2765491

[3] Piiparinen, T. (2013). The Transformation of UN Conflict Management: Producing images of genocide from Rwanda to Darfur and beyond

[4] https://www.cia.gov/library/publications/the-world-factbook/fields/2226.html

[5] http://news.yahoo.com/leone-ebola-outbreak-catastrophic-aid-group-msf

[6] Wall Street Journal

[7] http://time.com/3543077/west-africa-doctor-ebola/

[8] http://www.who.int/csr/don/2014_07_03_ebola/en/

[9] http://www.commondreams.org/news/2014/10/16/assassination-public-health-systems-driving-ebola-crisis-experts-warn

[10] Development Report 2014 - "Sustaining Human Progress: Reducing Vulnerabilities and Building Resilience"" . HDRO (Human Development Report Office) United Nations Development Programme .

[11] https://www.jacobinmag.com/2014/08/the-political-economy-of-ebola/

[12] http://www.nation.co.ke/business/IMF-World-Bank-policies-may-share-blame-in-Ebola-crisis/-/996/2527938/-/6xoceyz/-/index.html

Whiteness in the Psychological Imagination

Dr. Jonathan Mathias Lassiter

"My project is an effort to avert the critical gaze from the racial object to the racial subject; from the described and imagined to the describers and imaginers; from the serving to the served"

- Toni Morrison

"Well I know this, and anyone who's ever tried to live knows this. What you say about somebody else - anybody else - reveals you. What I think of you as being is dictated by my own necessity, my own psychology, my own fears and desires. I'm not describing you when I talk about you, I'm describing me"

- James Baldwin

Imagine a person. How tall is this person? What is the gender? How does this person dress? How does this person speak? Now, imagine the skin color of this person. As you pictured this person, was it a white person? If it was, you are not alone. For many, person is synonymous with white person. However, too often little attention is given to this fact. White people just are. Their race and embodiment of whiteness is seldom analyzed or is done narrowly. Furthermore, the psychological implications of whiteness for white people remain largely unexamined. This lack of detailed and nuanced study about white people and whiteness uneases me. There is a dearth of discourse about white people as a racial subject and whiteness as a pathological system with psychological consequences for white people. This essay is an attempt to address that (dis)ease and move toward an understanding of white people and whiteness, as racial subjects and a pathological system, respectively, in the field of psychology and beyond.

I begin this essay with a discussion of definitions for terms that will be used throughout. I transition to an overview of the racial origins of psychotherapy and the subsequent erasure of those origins. The remainder of the essay will present a discussion of whiteness in the psychological imagination and its implications, first for people of color and then white people.

Terminology

It is important to have a common understanding of the three critical terms that will be used repeatedly throughout this essay. These terms include *psychological imagination, white people,* and *whiteness.Psychological imagination* is used to describe the formulations and definitions of ideas and ideals that pertain to psychology-in the mainstream-as an academic discipline, and to psychological phenomena in general. This imagination influences people who work or study in that discipline as well as those who do not. The term *white people* refers to people who, regardless of national origin or cultural background, have white skin, consider themselves to be white and/or are treated by the majority of people in society as such, and personally benefit from resources and privileges associated with whiteness. This term is used in this essay to discuss the general populace of white people in America regardless of socioeconomic status. No disclaimer should be needed but to increase the likelihood that the points of my essay are understood and not clouded by defensiveness, this author knows that not all white people embrace and actively collude in whiteness. Furthermore, it should be understood that whiteness can be and is internalized by both white people and people of color. One does not have to have white skin to perpetuate whiteness. However, the perpetuation of whiteness is only beneficial to white people. People of color, no matter their collusion or protest, are still systematically and systemically oppressed by whiteness. *Whiteness* is defined as

"a complex, hegemonic, and dynamic set of mainstream socioeconomic processes, and ways of thinking, feelings, behaving, and acting (cultural scripts) that function to obscure the power, privilege, and practices of the dominant social elite. Whiteness drives oppressive individual, group, and corporate practices that adversely impacts...the wider U.S. society and, indeed, societies worldwide. At the same time whiteness reproduces inequities, injustices, and inequalities within the...wider society" (Lea & Sims, 2008, pp.2-3).

It should be noted that whiteness is not monolithic or immutable. Its meaning is constantly shifting and being constructed through an array of discourses and practices in various arenas of society (Wray & Newitz, 1997). In this way, white people either directly or indirectly benefit from their positioning at the top of a hierarchy that preferences their ways of thinking, feelings, behaving, and acting above those of others. This positioning of whiteness is held consciously, subconsciously, and unconsciously by both people of color and white people. It is enacted in both subtle and overt ways. Too often the white human being is the person who is really being considered when one is discussing or writing about the human being. Yet, the whiteness of the human being is obscured and painted as an every (wo)man.

White-washed Psychology

Psychology, as many understand it, in the western world is grounded in whiteness. Plato's thoughts, in 387 BCE, on the brain and mental processes and René Decartes' ideas about dualism of mind and body in the 1600s are taught in most, if not all, History of Psychology courses to be some of the earliest foundational writings about psychological processes. Psychological science is thought to have its beginnings in Wilhelm Wundt's experimental laboratory in psychology at the University of Leipzig, Germany that opened in 1879. Furthermore, it is commonly taught that the origins of psychotherapy are found in Sigmund Freud's and his students' work beginning in 1886.

It should be noted that Freud, himself, was a Jewish person. His approach to conducting psychotherapy with his patients was aligned with many characteristics of Jewish culture. These characteristics included being exceedingly verbal, emotionally expressive, trusting of reputable strangers, and believing in the "expert opinion" of a professional (Langman, 1997). The Jewish traits were the underpinning assumptions of patients' behaviors in the psychotherapy room. Freud and other early members of the psychotherapy movement, such as Sandor Ferenczi, Karl Abraham, Max Eitingon, Otto Rank, and Hans Sachs taught their students to approach psychotherapy and their patients in this manner (Langman, 1997). In many ways, western psychotherapy in the early 20th century was a secularization of Jewish mysticism (Bakan, 1958). However, the ethnic foundation of psychotherapy rooted in Jewish culture was eroded with the shift toward an empirical approach ushered in by white Americans John B. Watson and B.F. Skinner with their theories of behaviorism (Langman, 1997). Behaviorism focused on objective and measurable behaviors while rejecting the subjective domains of human experiences such as thoughts and emotions. This shift was a step toward the whitening of psychotherapy in that it centralized many characteristics of white culture including rugged individualism, competition, mastery, and control over nature, a unitary and static conception of time, and a separation of science and religion (Sue et al, 1998). This shift highlights the mutability of whiteness and its tendency to leech the essence from its counterparts. British colonists were once defined by their Christianity and Europeanness but their Christianity and Europeanness became subsumed by their whiteness in the Americas. In a similar way, Jewish cultural contributions to western psychology and psychotherapy were subsumed under the whiteness of American white people.

However, more obscured than the Jewish underpinnings of psychotherapy and psychology, is its earliest ethnic foundation. The African roots of psychology predate all others. In-depth scholarly research reveals that the origins of what is now called psychology can be found in the philosophical, scientific, and mystical practices of the Anunian and Kemetic civilizations dating back to 4,000 BCE (Bynum, 2012). In these traditions, psychology is considered as the study of the human spirit (Nobles, 1986). It is the study of how people understand and define their humanness within the context of a community (Piper-Mandy & Rowe, 2010). Anunian and Kemetic psychology preferences a view of the self as primarily a spiritual entity projected into the physical realm (McAllister, 2014). Meyers (1988) proclaimed that the African worldview is an optimal one in which encompasses viewing the spiritual, mental, soulful, and physical aspects of being as one; knowing one's self through symbolic imagery and rhythm; valuing interpersonal harmony and interconnectedness; embracing self-worth as an intrinsic value that derives from one's very being; and viewing life as a plane that is unlimited (Karenga, 1993; Meyers, 1998). Life is thought to be trifold operating on three planes that are before-life, earth-life, and after-life (Fu-Kiau, 1993, 2001 as cited by Piper-Mandy & Rowe, 2010). The human spirit is thought to move through "seven moments" which are "before, beginning, belonging, being, becoming, beholding, and beyond" (Piper-Mandy & Rowe, 2010, p. 14). As can be seen, the earliest conceptualizations of psychology were not limited to the physical realm bounded by empiricism with which white-washed psychology has become identified. It was more encompassing of the seen and unseen, the before, now, and beyond. This type of psychology is a more complete assessment of the human experience that acknowledges the knowable and unknowable. (See Piper-Mandy & Rowe, 2010 for more details.) It is rooted in Africa and predates any other thought on the study of humanness. However, whiteness has recast psychology in its imagination. From this perspective, the image of the purveyors and consumers of psychology are tacitly assumed to be white or, if not white, approached in their relation to whiteness. Psychology is limited by whiteness-informed ideals of quantification, denial of the spiritual, and biomedical preoccupation.

White People and Whiteness in the Psychological Imagination

Psychology, much like all fields of human inquiry, often defines white people and whiteness in relationship to what it is not. Guthrie (2004) points out that some of the earliest studies of racial differences related to psychological abilities attempted to define white people as separate, and as members of a "higher" form of human being than people of color. For example, a series of psychological studies from as early as 1881 and 1895, reportedly "proved" that people of color, namely Japanese, American indigenous, and African-American people, had quicker reaction times to sensory stimuli and thus were more "impulsive," while white people were more "reflective" (Guthrie, 2004). The interpretation of the results of such studies is interesting. These

402

results were interpreted to imbue white people with a presumed desirable quality of reflectivity and people of color with a presumed undesirable quality of impulsivity. Other early studies conducted by white psychologists also found "evidence" of African-Americans' lack of ability for abstract thought but prowess in sensory and motor skills (Guthrie, 2004). This type of psychological imagining defines white people as mentally adept and physically underdeveloped; implicitly, and sometimes overtly, suggesting that white people's intellectual skill should be valued over the physical capacities of people of color. And thus, this intellectual value sets white people as the standard in the realm of intellectual functioning. These interpretations of research highlight that scientific findings can be used for the uplift and humanizing of people, or for their pathologizing and dehumanizing of them. Such interpretations by pioneering white scientists in the field of psychology point to an imagining of white people as superior and people of color as inferior.

One may protest that findings of early psychological studies are outdated and do not reflect mainstream contemporary psychology. I agree that such blatant racist interpretations of research findings are almost nonexistent in today's world. However, it has been replaced with a colorblind mentality that does not address these racist underpinnings and subconsciously positions white people as the default against which all others are measured. One does not have to look far to find evidence of this point. It is common practice for editors of peer-reviewed psychological journals to publish articles with titles such as *"Millennials, narcissism, and social networking: What narcissists do on social networking sites and why," "Finding female fulfillment: Intersecting role-based and morality-based identities of motherhood, feminism, and generativity as predictors of women's self satisfaction and life satisfaction,"* and *"Friendship between men across sexual orientation: The importance of (others) being intolerant"* (Barrett, 2013; Bergman, Fearrington, Davenport, & Bergman, 2011; Rittenour & Colaner, 2012). The broad language in the titles (i.e. "millennials," "female," "women," "men") of these articles suggest that the authors of these studies have recruited and conducted research with a sample of diverse participants who represent a microcosm of the diverse human family. These articles' titles suggest that the findings of the studies are, with a margin of error of course, applicable to all men, women, and millennials. A glance at the Methods sections proves otherwise. Not the least offense, the samples are virtually racially homogenous. These studies included 6.8%, 8.8%, and .08% people of color. While any findings from these studies are an addition to the understanding of psychology, they should be clearly understood as an examination of psychological concepts among white people in America, not as universal concepts or even American concepts. No journal editors required that the authors change their titles to reflect the predominantly white culture of their participants. While some readers might not understand the significance of these titles and the titling practice in psychology, the absence of reference to white people is commonplace and this small sample of studies is unfortunately representative of the type of widespread branding of the psychology of white people as the psychology of people. This type of branding obscures the culture of white people and the interplay of whiteness with psychological phenomena. It makes it hard for one to understand the essence of whiteness because this type of branding erases whiteness and elevates the psychological experiences of white people to be those of the human race. Dyer (1997, p. 2) wrote "there is no more powerful position than that of being 'just' human. The claim to power is the claim to speak for the commonality of humanity...whites are people whereas other colours are something else." In this way, white people implicitly set themselves as the arbiters of humanity and maybe even the only true embodiment of it.

From this point of view, whiteness in the psychological imagination is conflated with humanness in the psychological imagination. Therefore, whiteness is superior and centered in the psychological imagination. It is often obscured yet powerful in its organization of the field of study in a way that revolves around itself and thus maintains its power. It positions itself as the pure, unbiased presentation of scientific phenomena that explains what it means to be human. This imagining of whiteness is erroneous and dangerous.

Whiteness and Its Implications for Psychology Students of Color

Students of color often experience the psychology field as an unwelcoming and dehumanizing space. Research indicates that psychology students of color report experiencing stereotyping, alienation and isolation, cultural bias, prejudice, and challenges to their academic qualifications and merit in their educational programs (Gonzalez, Marin, Figuerosa, Moreno, & Navia, 2002; Johnson-Bailey, 2004; Lewis, Ginsberg, Davies, & Smith, 2004; Vazquez et al., 2006; Williams, 2000; Williams et al., 2005). Psychology students of color do not see themselves or the communities they represent reflected in the image of psychology. Researchers (Maton et al., 2011) found that African Americans were 12.6 times more likely, and Asian American and Latina/o American each 5.1 times more likely to report stereotypical rather than fair and accurate representation compared to white students. In turn, Asian Americans were 49 times more likely, African Americans 23.7 times more likely, and Latina/o Americans 19.9 times more likely to report that their group was not represented at all than to report fair and accurate representation as compared to white students (Maton et al., 2011). Students of color are overwhelmingly presented a curriculum that paints whiteness as humanness. They are deprived of an image of humanity that includes them and are thus dehumanized in their educational process.

Experiences of dehumanization and disempowerment in a system of whiteness leaves students insecure in their academic abilities, unsure of their sense of belonging in academia, emotionally battered by racial insensitivity, and feeling impotent to address these issues. Thus, students engage in self-censorship, assimilation to whiteness-centered academic program norms, and abandonment of scholarly pursuits of interest and use to communities of color (Gildersleeve, Croom, & Vasquez, 2011). Whiteness in psychology often leaves students of color feeling isolated and treated unjustly.

My colleagues and I are intimate with the types of experiences that the empirical research on students of color elucidates. One day during my third year in graduate school, I had an African American female, let's call her "Natasha," start crying when I asked her how she was feeling. She told me, "I don't feel like I belong here. These students say some of the most offensive, racist shit and the professors agree with them. Then when I speak up and call them out, I'm told that I should respect everyone's opinion. It feels like they don't want me to succeed." Listening to Natasha, who was a first year student, I remembered my own experience of feeling racially assaulted in academic and clinical training settings. I felt her pain and the confusion that accompanied it. Boiling with empathy, I said "it's because they *don't* want you here." Natasha looked at me with an expression of astonishment. "Look around," I continued, "how many professors of color do you see here? Don't you know that when they created the first programs in psychology, you and I were not the students they had in mind? We were not meant to be here. But we are. And it is up to you to make sure that you stay here, against all odds. The world needs your brilliance. The world needs your intelligence and the perspective that only you can offer. So cry, get mad, but use that to push you forward, to the top." While, I admit that I might have been emotional when I responded to my friend, the overall message was one of resilience. Scholarly research on the history of psychology support my statement and illuminates the struggles of people of color who were the pioneers in graduate education in psychology (Guthrie, 2004). It has often been the case that in a system of whiteness students of color have had to generate their own power from within and use adversity to propel them forward. It is an uneasy and unjust position to be in but unfortunately, often, the reality. Resilience is the cornerstone of the foundation that students of color must build upon when facing whiteness in the psychological imagination.

Multicultural sensitivity and diversity are popular topics in psychology training programs. While the American Psychological Association and many APA-accredited schools and internship training programs tout diversity on paper, many students of color find there to be little in reality. I often heard at clinical training sites that "there are several different forms of diversity and too often people get hung up on race." This is a true statement, of course. However, the tone with which it was often spoken and the number of times that it was mentioned whenever someone mentioned diversity or race highlighted an unsettling thought for me. Was this comment an excuse to not discuss race? Was this comment their get-out-of-the-race-question-free-card? In my experience, discussions about race and ethnicity were rarely undertaken in any sustained or formal manner. At one site, there was only one formal discussion of race throughout the whole year. Particularly egregious about that discussion was that an African American psychologist who was unaffiliated with the organization was engaged to conduct it. This was troubling because one of the only *two times* a psychologist of color presented a didactic was when the topic involved race and ethnic diversity. That psychologist was recruited for this one time only event. An implicit message is that the only topic people of color are qualified to discuss is race. And as evidence of the lack of diversity in the organization, it had to reach beyond its walls to find a qualified speaker on the topic. Furthermore, race and ethnicity was boiled down to one presentation and not discussed in any formal manner during the rest of the year. In addition, the focus of that site's approach race and ethnicity was limited to African Americans. I am not opposed to people of color's unique and similar experiences as human beings being highlighted in the study of psychology. It should be a foundational component of psychology education. It is the manner in which the spotlight is shined on people of color that is troublesome. People of color are often discussed in psychology as if they are outside of society and in some cases, outside of the species. People of color are presumed to diverge from the default of whiteness and thus are the special cases. They are often examined and presented in a consumable manner to onlookers who, with scientific and objective perspectives, try to understand them. If people of color are the special cases, then who are the people to whom their exotification is being explained? Who does this type of racial and ethnic diversity training serve and whom does it not serve? Furthermore, white people and their race and ethnicities are rarely included in conversations about race and ethnicity. Their racial and ethnic heritages are erased by whiteness and they are placed outside of the paradigm into a separate and implicitly elevated position. Thus, reinforcing whiteness in the psychological imagination.

"Diversity is more than race" seemed to be code for "let's not talk about race." This silence around race often seemed to come up in case presentations. I have often found myself as one of the only psychological trainees of color in organizations that served predominately people of color. Many of my white peers often presented clients of color in similar ways: "she's so angry;" "he won't talk to me." However, many never questioned how their race might be influencing the client's behavior or their conceptualization of and approach to the client. Or if they did so, it was with a "yeah, but" dismissive quality. Many of my white counterparts have tried to wish away race. During one group supervision session one colleague commented that the only way to decrease racism and fully incorporate men of color into society was to stop treating them with "kid gloves." I was unsettled by this colleague's statement and either the sheer ignorance or blatant racism that it demonstrated. I could not help but respond. I commented that men of color most often experience the exact opposite of what she was suggesting and that in fact they are treated with iron fists. "Men of color," I said, "are often subjected to punishment for behaviors that their white counterparts are not and are punished harsher than their white counterparts when they do commit crimes." This colleague responded with an expression of discomfort that proved she had no real understanding of the experience of people of color and yet all she wanted was to "help" these young men who came from unfortunate circumstances. While I don't think this particular colleague had malevolent intentions, inequality and injustice often stem from the blind spots of well meaning people. Students of color in psychology programs often experience a barrage of microaggressions and blatant ignorance that assault their racial and ethnic identities and, sometimes, their humanity.

The Scholarly and Pedagogical Centering of Whiteness in Psychology

Researchers have found that the majority of participants in research studies are citizens of western, industrialized, rich, and democratic nations and most of them are highly educated (WEIRD; Henrich, Heine, & Norenzayan, 2010). Thus, the knowledge about the psychological experiences is incredibly first-world and neglects the experiences of the majority of people on earth who do not inhabit such WEIRD spaces. Even within these WEIRD spaces, whiteness further constricts psychological knowledge. As in a previous section of this essay, many of the titles of published research papers purport to describe universal psychological phenomena but in actuality only present a white-centered description of it, as most psychological study samples are predominately composed of white people.

Three recent critical reviews of the racial composition of participants of studies published in scholarly psychology journals provide statistical information about the centering of whiteness in psychological research. In 2005, researchers found that among all the studies published in the top three counseling psychology journals from 1990 to 1999, 57% of them reported the races or ethnicities of their samples (Delgado-Romero, Galvan, Maschino, & Rowland, 2005). This means that 43% of the studies failed to present data about race or ethnicity and implied that either 1) race and ethnicity is not important enough to report or 2) that the sample was homogenous in its whiteness. Furthermore, the authors of this study found that when race was reported, it was often in relation to whiteness. For example, many studies referred to their participants' race as "white" or "other." Again, this sets whiteness and white people as the default stand-in for humanity and people of color as deviations from the norm. Among studies that did report specific racial and ethnic characteristics, overall samples were composed of 78.2% white people, 5.8% Asian Americans, 6.7% African Americans, 6.6% Latino/as, 0.9% Indigenous people, and 0.1% multiracial people (Delgado-Romero et al., 2005). Compared to the overall population of the United States, whites and Asian Americans were overrepresented and African Americans, Latino/as, and Indigenous people were underrepresented in counseling psychology research. In an analysis of the races and ethnicities of participants in studies that were published in the top six American Psychological Association journals in 2007, authors found that 60-82% of them were white (Arnett, 2008). Furthermore, 7-60% of the studies published in these journals did not report the racial and ethnic composition of their samples (Arnett, 2008). An examination of the race and ethnicity reporting in four social science/psychology journals focused specifically on ethnic and racial minorities found much more inclusion of people of color. Specifically, of participants of studies published in these journals from 1990 to 2007, 38.7% identified as Latino/a, 22.5% identified as Black, 17.8% identified as white, 9.0% identified as Asian/Pacific Islander, 1.6% identified as Indigenous, 0.4% identified as multiracial/biracial; 8.3% were categorized as "nonrespondent" (i.e., the study did not provide information), and 1.7% were categorized as "other" (i.e., individuals did not identify as any of the listed classifications) (Shelton, Delgado-Romero, & Wells, 2009). It seems that people of color are only included in the psychological literature when the topic of study is race or ethnicity. These three critical reviews provide empirical evidence of the frequent exclusion of people of color from the psychological imagination.

When race and ethnicity are included in research studies, these constructs are usually approached in three distinct ways. These include the universalist, culture assimilation, and culture accommodation approaches (Leong & Serafica, 2001). The universalist approach ignores race and ethnicity. Race and ethnicity are deemed unimportant and not worthy of incorporating in the empirical process. Research studies that use this approach do not even ask participants about race or consider how it may interact with or influence the manifestation or expression of the psychological phenomena under study. The culture assimilation approach relegates people of color to the margins and they are conceptualized as deviations from whiteness and white people. Studies that use this approach are usually comparative in nature; they assess the difference of the racial and ethnic groups on various psychological phenomena with white people positioned as the reference group. People of color are assessed based on whether or not they significantly differ from white people. Conclusions from these types of studies often focus on how people of color can or should adjust to become more assimilated with whiteness to better match the performance of white people in the psychological domains under study. The culture accommodation approach more fully considers the influence of the race and ethnicity (and how race and ethnicity influences the sociological context of people) on the expression of psychological phenomena. Studies that utilize this approach move beyond ignoring and comparing people of color to white people. They seek to understand how race and ethnicity influences how people define, experience, and make sense of psychological phenomena in a culturally specific manner. Beyond culture accommodation approaches, many psychologists of color have developed culture-specific schools of psychological thought. The advent of Asian American Psychology, Latino/a Psychology, Black Psychology, and African-centered Psychology illustrate a move away from an assimilationist stance to an indigenous focus. Specifically, these fields of study center the humanity of people of color and examine all psychological phenomena from a perspective that is inextricably tied to one's cultural context.

The centering of whiteness is engrained in the academy and those seeking to de-center it often find it difficult. When scholars try to emancipate their scholarship from the confines of whiteness, they are often met with opposition from the gatekeepers of psychology (i.e. journal reviewers and editors, funding agencies, and colleagues). There is empirical evidence of academics of color facing barriers in their universities due to racial discrimination, both at the individual and structural levels. The devaluing of scholarship that does not privilege whiteness is a particularly troubling occurrence. A recent study found that it is hard for the research of scholars of color to be funded (Ginther et al., 2011). Ginther and her colleagues found that Asian Americans and Black applicants were less likely to receive investigator-initiated research funding from the National Institutes of Health (NIH; the largest governmental funder of scientific research in the United States) compared to their white counterparts. Even after statistically holding constant differences in the applicants' educational backgrounds, countries of origin, training, previous research awards, publication records, and employer characteristics, Black scholars were still found to be at a disadvantaged in receiving funding from the NIH. If this disadvantage is found at the national level at an institution that has a long history of creating programs to increase diversity (Ginther et al. 2011), the racial disparity in research funding at other organizations (e.g. local, institution-based, or private) is likely to be greater. When scholars of color are able to conduct their research, either with or without funding, they often find that it is not deemed as scholarly legitimate or scientifically rigorous (Harley, 2008; Kameny et al., 2014; Stanley, 2007; Turner, Gonzalez, & Wood, 2008). There are many times when scholars of color find themselves at odds with journal reviewers when they attempt to publish scholarship outside of whiteness. Stanley (2007) wrote about the clash between counter and master narratives in the academy. She explains:

"A master narrative is a script that specifies and controls how some social processes are carried out. Furthermore, there is a master narrative operating in academia that often defines and limits what is valued as scholarship and who is entitled to create scholarship.

This is problematic, because the dominant group in academia writes most research and, more often than not, they are White men. Members of marginalized groups, such as women and people of color, have had little or no input into the shaping of this master narrative. Therefore, research on marginalized groups by members of marginalized groups that reveals experiences that counter master narratives is often compared against the White norm..." (Stanley, 2007, p. 14).

In contrast, counter narratives: "...act to deconstruct the master narratives, and they offer alternatives to the dominant discourse in educational research. They provide, for example, multiple and conflicting models of understanding social and cultural identities. They also challenge the dominant White and often predominantly male culture that is held to be normative and authoritative" (Stanley, 2007, p. 14). Researching and publishing the research of counter narratives that de-center whiteness and more fully embrace the diversity of humanity often requires assertiveness and perseverance. Presenting a non-pathological, non-comparative, and non-deficit representation of people of color in the scholarly literature is a revolutionary act.

One would think that in a field like psychology where so much lip service and written policy is focused on diversity this would not be the case. Research findings, which have been discussed throughout this essay, prove otherwise. Unfortunately, I have personally experienced the sting of gatekeepers who are invested in perpetuating master narratives. Recently a reviewer had this to say about a manuscript of mine that focused on an all Black sample of men who have sex with men (BMSM): "In this paper, the population of black gay men is treated almost as a universe unto itself...the author seems to make conclusions about how religious BMSM are without making explicit comparisons to white men who have sex with men or to other groups." These particular remarks from this reviewer are indicative of an investment in the centering of whiteness. When the reviewer comments that I treat the population of BMSM as "a universe unto itself," it implies that there is something inaccurate about or amiss with the notion that BMSM could possibly be of scholarly (maybe even human) value in and of themselves. He also suggested that I make a comparison between the Black men in my sample and white men and that no conclusions can be made about the religiosity of BMSM without such a comparison. His suggestion is indicative of the assimilationist approach that was explained by Leong & Serafica (2001). In other words, in his opinion, whiteness is the standard. Without whiteness to measure the experiences of people of color against, how can one know what is real? In his critique, this reviewer strips away the legitimacy, worth, and humanity of BMSM. In his imagination, BMSM cannot possibly exist in the absence of whiteness. The reviewer goes on to comment that the "...questions of how and why the relationship between religiosity and sexuality may be different among black men than among white men are indeed fascinating questions." I question, "fascinating to whom?" Too often, researchers of all races whose scholarship focuses on people of color are subjugated to journal reviewers' fascination with whiteness. Publishing and presenting research about people of color that is not pathology-focused or comparative, while not impossible, is challenging in mainstream scholarly outlets.

The Psychological Wage

Thus far the research reviewed in this essay has been persuasive in its accounting of the narrowing and repressive effects of whiteness for knowledge production and for the experiences of students and faculty of color in the field of psychology. However, it would be a mistake to believe that whiteness in the psychological imagination only has implications for people of color or only for people who work and study in the field of psychology. Taking the widespread influence of whiteness into account, the remainder of this essay seeks to explore two questions. These two questions are related to the quotes that opened this essay. The first quote is taken from Toni Morrison's groundbreaking work, *Playing the Dark:*

414

Whiteness in the Literary Imagination. In that book, she undertakes the task of trying to understand the people who have crafted the image of whiteness (and blackness) that she sees abound in American literature. In her view, whiteness in American literature is parasitical, nourishing itself on the imagined oppositeness of blackness. Whiteness is made superior by the supposed inferiority of blackness. It is made great by the degradation of its counterparts. Whiteness has the same function in the psychological imagination. It penetrates the psyches of all people, regardless of race and ethnicity, with white supremacy. White people-whether or not they internalize this cultural domination, actively engage in racism or racial microaggressions, or exploit people of color for economic prosperity-benefit from the image of whiteness in the psychological imagination. However, what does the other side of the coin look like. In other words: "What are the benefits *and* costs of whiteness in the psychological imagination for white people?" Whiteness in the psychological imagination offers white people purpose, power, and protection. It offers purpose by making white people's mental health and lived experiences foundational. White people are constructed as prototypes whose psychological experiences are the starting point from which all other people's experiences begin to be understood and the desired endpoint, which all other people must reach to be considered healthy or human. This purpose intersects with the power bestowed upon them.

Whiteness in the psychological imagination imparts an authority to and a preferencing of white people's experiences. Even when the topic of study is pathology, white people's pathology is still held as the standard for what deviations from "normative" behavior should look like. Therefore, even white people's unhealthy behaviors are considered more desirable. No matter what they do, prosocial, asocial, or antisocial, it is still considered better. Therefore, there is no way for white people to ever be in any position but at the top of a constructed psychological hierarchy. Psychology has given white people power through its empirical support for the demonization, marginalization, and stigmatization of people of color. It is a shackle for people of color and a throne for white people.

Whiteness in the psychological imagination protects white people from grappling with how their embodiment of whiteness is cancerous. It does not require them to consider the lives of people of color and the deleterious effects of whiteness. Their survival is not dependent on such knowledge. The centering of white people's experiences allows white people to be blind to the experiences of people of color. They can remain oblivious to, ignore, forget about, erase or render historical-and thus, make irrelevant-the exploitation, domination, and disenfranchisement of people of color. This privilege of ignorance perpetuates their focus on themselves and the marginalization of others. White people have the option to advance in a world delusionally believing there are no consequences for their actions.

The belief that whiteness does not scar the person who embraces it is erroneous and perverted. The costs of the psychological imbuement to whiteness of purpose, power, and protection are a sense of heightened threat/defensiveness, emptiness, and loneliness/disconnection. People at the top of a hierarchy need others to be placed beneath them. Otherwise, their status at the top is meaningless. A surplus of exploited and disenfranchised people is a necessity for whiteness to have any benefit. It is the exploited and disenfranchised people who white people measure their whiteness against. It is these people through whom they can work out their own self-image and put to work for their own financial, psychological, and social benefit. However, this positioning is tenuous and always will be, as human nature is not meant to be exploitatively hierarchal. Imbedded in whiteness is a zero-sum mentality that believes that if one person or group possesses a thing or trait the other person or group cannot also share that possession or trait. Thus, there is a heightened sense of threat that the benefits of whiteness can be taken away at any time. Defensiveness develops to guard those benefits. This defensiveness is seen in the backlash against psychological research that attempts to move away from white-centered discourses and racial comparative research to an indigenous paradigm that preferences narratives of people of color. It is seen in the psychological genocide that is carried out by whiteness in its centering of definitions and policies-in media, educational institutions, financial markets, health services, and governmental agencies-that are diametrically opposite and detrimental to peoples' of color images and interests (Kambon, 1980). A constant sense of heightened threat and defensiveness-conscious, subconscious, or unconscious-keeps people at arms-length. People with such defensiveness find themselves living a life of paranoia and hypervigilance.

The sense of purpose that whiteness in the psychological imagination provides for white people is empty. It is inextricably tied to the meaning of their whiteness. However, the centrality of whiteness is a distorted mental machination. It is a superficial prize that inflates the ego with a fictitious substance. If a purpose and identity is built upon a distortion that sets it as opposite and superior to others, what happens when whiteness is discovered to be a fraud? Again Toni Morrison's words come to mind. In an interview with Charlie Rose in 1993 she spoke about the hollowness of race and its racist use. She stated,

"But if the racist white person-I don't mean the person who is examining his consciousness and so on-doesn't understand that he or she is also a race, it's also constructed, it's also made, and it also has some sort of serviceability. But when you take it away, if I take your race away, and there you are, all strung out, and all you've got is your little self. And what is that? What are you without racism? Are you any good? Are you still strong? Are you still smart? You still like yourself?"

White people who embrace whiteness are completely dependent on it and they are seldom aware of their addiction and delusion, and if aware constantly suppressing and denying it. In its attempted cooptation of humanity, whiteness renders white people inhuman.

It transforms white people into an ideal of perfection. This ideal is unrealistic and hollow.

Whiteness in the psychological imagination deprives white people of a concept of themselves as interdependent members of a human family with many diverse members. Critical psychological elements of whiteness such as competitiveness, power-dominance drive, assertiveness-aggression, and anxiety avoidance pit them against their human brethren (Kambon, 1992, 1998). These values foster loneliness/disconnection. This is because, often, whiteness erases itself from the psyche of white people and replaces it with a universalism that centers their experiences as the only legitimate experiences. Therefore all they see are reflections or iterations of themselves. When confronted with people of color, they view these folks as people to be ignored, appropriated, or eliminated (Lorde, 1984) and not as human beings with whom to commune as equals. Whiteness in the psychological imagination alleges that people can survive on their own with rugged individualism and materialism, separated from the spiritual and psychological collective.

The second question, to be addressed in this section, is inspired by James Baldwin's quote at the beginning of this essay. Baldwin's quote highlights the reflective nature of definitions. The qualities and worth that one confers to someone else is of direct proportion to the qualities and worth one confers to her/himself. If one marginalizes another's experience, in actuality she/he is forcing something of her/his own experience (own being) out of view and possibly out of consciousness. This is a detrimental thing because it creates fractional, unhealthy human beings that are narrowed and egotistic, cut off from themselves and others. It seems, to me, that this is only remedied when one values her/himself enough to recognize the humanity of another as just as inextricably tied to her/his own and just as significant. So my second question is, "How does one go about freeing her/himself from whiteness in the psychological imagination to live a more whole, integrated life?" While, I have posed this question, I will not answer it. Too often, people of color are as asked to provide the suggestions for how white people can begin to grapple with and overcome their whiteness. I refuse to do the work for people who are afflicted (willingly or otherwise) with whiteness. I will leave that work to them.

If white people knew who they were, they would not need to define themselves in relation to others. They would not feel a need to stifle the breath of others to suck in air. They would let go of their zero-sum mentality and realize that their survival is inextricably related to the survival of all of the colored peoples of the world. White people are a statistical minority. There is no way that they can survive through sheer whiteness alone. Whiteness is a delusion that has created a race of schizophrenics separated from themselves and others. But that is because so many white people do not recognize their inherent worth. Their ideas of supremacy are grounded in the machinations of their whiteness and separateness, not their humanness or connectedness. There is no need for this. If white people can let go of their whiteness, educate themselves-and not rely on or requests that others do so-commune without ulterior motives, they can begin to embody the fullness of humanity that is based in the reality of community and not the illusion of superiority and materialism. When white people can let go of whiteness, they will recognize themselves as human and not need to dehumanize others and co-opt people of color identities, land, and cultural creations to lionize themselves. White people are not dumb; they are not evil. Whiteness, however, is evil. It is an arrogant ignorance. It is a poison that must be rejected in the psychological imagination and in the minds of all people-those with white and melanized skin.

The centering of whiteness in psychology is not only a cancer to society but also a detriment to the field of study. It renders psychology fraudulent in its claims to understand the human psyche. As discussed before, the overwhelming body of psychological research marginalizes people of color who constitute the majority of the human species. Whiteness in the psychological imagination paints an erroneous picture of psychological phenomena, limits the psychological knowledge base, and stifles a more true understanding of the complex, multifaceted experience of the human.

References

Arnett, J. (2008). The neglected 95%: Why American psychology needs to become less American.*American Psychologist, 63*, 602-614. doi: 10.1037/0003-066X.63.7.602

Bakan, D. (1958). Sigmund Freud and the Jewish mystical tradition. Princeton, NJ: D. Van Nostrand.

Baldwin, J. (1963). *Take this hammer.* Retrieved from https://*vimeo.com/13175192*

Barrett, T. (2013). Friendships between men across sexual orientations: The importance of (others) being tolerant. *The Journal of Men's Studies, 21,* 62-77. doi: 10.3149/jms.2101.62

Bergman, S., Fearrington, M., Davenport, S., & Bergman, J. (2011). Millennials, narcissism, and social networking: What narcissists do on social networking sites and why. *Personality and Individual Differences,* 706-711. doi: 10.1016/j.paid.2010.12.022

Bynum, E. (2012). *The African Unconscious : Roots of Ancient Mysticism and Modern Psychology.* New York: Cosimo Books.

Delgado-Romero, E., Galván, N., Maschino, P., &Rowland, M. (2005). Race and ethnicity in empirical counseling and counseling psychology research: A 10-year review. *The Counseling Psychologist, 33,* 419-448.

Dyer, R. (1997). *White.* New York: Routledge.

Gildersleeve, R. E., Croom, N. N. & Vasquez, P. L. (2011) "Am I going crazy?!": A critical race analysis of doctoral education. *Equity & Excellence in Education, 44,* 93-114. doi: 10.1080/10665684.2011.539472

Ginther, D., Schaffer, W., Schnell, J., Masimore, B., Liu, F.,...& Kington, R. (2011). Race, ethnicity, and NIH research awards. *Science, 33,* 1015-1019. doi: 10.1126/science.1196783

Gonzalez, K., Marin, P., Figuerosa, M., Moreno, J., & Navia, C. (2002). Inside doctoral education in America: Voices of Latinas/os in pursuit of the PhD. *Journal of College Student Development, 43*(4), 540-557.

Guthrie, R. (2004). Even the rat was white: A historical view of psychology (2nd Edition). Upper Saddle River, NJ: Pearson.

Harley, D. (2008). Maids of academe: African American women faculty at predominately White institutions. *Journal of African American Studies, 12*, 19-36. doi: 10.1007/s12111-007-9030-5

Henrich, J., Heine, S., & Norenzayan, A. (2010). The weirdest people in the world? *Behavioral and Brain Sciences, 33*, 61-83. doi: 10.1017/S0140525X0999152X

Johnson-Bailey, J. (2004). Hitting and climbing the proverbial wall: Participation and retention issues for Black graduate women. *Race Ethnicity and Education, 7*, 331-349. doi: 10.1080/1361332042000303360

Kambon, K. (1980). The psychology of oppression. In Asante & Vandi (Eds.). *Contemporary Black Thought,* pp. 95-110. Beverly Hills, CA: Sage Publications.

Kambon, K. (1992). *The African personality in America: An African-centered framework.* Tallahassee, FL: Nubian Nations Publications.

Kambon K (1998) *African/Black Psychology in the American Context: An African-Centered Approach.* Tallahasse, FL: Nubian Nation.

Kameny, R., DeRosier, M., Taylor, L., McMillen, J., Knowles, M., & Pifer, K. (2014). Barriers to career success for minority researchers in the behavioral sciences. *Journal of Career Development, 41*, 43-61. doi: 10.1177/0894845312472254.

Karenga, M. (1996). Black psychology. In K. Monteiro (Ed.). *Ethnicity and Psychology: African-, Asian-, Latino-, and Native-American Psychologies-Revised Printing*, pp. 21-39. Dubuque, IA: Kendall/Hunt. Retrieved from http://www.radford.edu/jaspelme/minority-groups/past_courses/Karenga_Black_Psychology.pdf

Langman, P. (1997). White culture, Jewish culture, and the origins of psychotherapy. *Psychotherapy,34*(2), 207-218.

Lea, V., & Sims, E. (2008). *Undoing whiteness in the classroom: Critical education teaching approaches for social justice activism.* pp. 2-3. New York: Peter Lang.

Leong, F., & Serafica, F. (2001). Cross-cultural perspective on Super's career development theory: Career maturity and cultural accommodation. In F. Leong & A. Barak (Eds.)., *Contemporary models in vocational psychology: A volume in honor of Samuel H. Osipow* (pp. 167-205). Mahwah, NJ: Erlbaum.

Lewis, C., Ginsberg, R., Davies, T., & Smith, K. (2004). The experiences of African American Ph.D. students at a predominately White Carnegie I-research institution. *College Student Journal, 38*(2), 231-245.

Lorde, A. (1984). *Sister outsider: Essays and speeches.* Trumansburg, NY : Crossing Press.

Maton, K., Wimms, H., Grant, S., Wittig, M., Rogers, M., & Vasquez, M. (2011). Experiences and perspectives of African American, Latina/o, Asian American, and European American psychology graduate students: A national study. *Cultural Diversity and Ethnic Minority Psychology, 17*, 68-78. doi: 10.1037/a0021668

McAllister, C. (2014). Towards an African-centered sociological approach to Africana lesbian, gay, bisexual, transgender, queer, and intersexed identities and performances: The Kemetic model of the cosmological interactive self. *Critical Sociology, 40,* 239-256. doi: 10.1177/0896920512455935

Meyers, L. (1988). *Understanding an Afrocentric world view: An introduction to an optimal psychology.* Dubuque, IA: Kendall/Hunt.

Morrison, T. (1992). *Playing in the dark: Whiteness and the literary imagination.* New York: Vintage Books.

Nobles, W. (1986). *African psychology: Toward its reclamation, reascension & revitalization*. Oakland, CA: Black Family Institute Publications.

Piper-Mandy, E., & Rowe, T. (2010). Educating African-centered psychologists: Towards a comprehensive paradigm. *Journal of Pan African Studies, 3*(8), 5-23. doi: Retrieved from http://www.jpanafrican.com/docs/vol3no8/3.8EducatingAfrican.pdf

Rittenour, C., & Colaner, C. (2012). Finding female fulfillment: Intersecting role-based and morality-based identities of motherhood, feminism, and generativity as predictors of women's self satisfaction and life satisfaction. *Sex Roles, 67,* 351-362. doi: 10.1007/s11199-012-0186-7

Shelton, K., Delgado-Romero, E., & Wells, E. (2009). Race and ethnicity in empirical research: An 18-year review. *Journal of Multicultural Counseling and Development, 37,* 130-140. doi: 10.1002/j.2161-1912.2009.tb00097.x

Stanley, C.A. (2007). When counter narratives meet master narratives in the journal editorial-review process. *Educational Researcher, 36*(1), pp. 14-24.

Sue, D., Carter, R., Casas, J., Fouad, N., Ivey, A., Jensen, M....&Vazquez-Nutall, E. (1998). Ethnocentric monoculturalism. In P. Pederson (Series Ed.), *Multicultural aspects of counseling series: Vol. 11. Multicultural counseling competencies: Individual and organization development* (pp. 14-25). Thousand Oaks: Sage.

Turner, C., Gonzalez, J., & Wood, J. (2008). Faculty of color in academe: What 20 years of literature tells us. *Journal of Diversity in Higher Education, 1,* 39-168. doi: 10.1037/a0012837

Vasquez, M., Lott, B., Garcia-Vazquez, E., Grant, S., Iwamasa, G., Molina, L., & Vestal-Dowdy, E. (2006). Personal reflections: Barriers and strategies in increasing diversity in psychology. *American Psychologist, 61*(2), 157-172.

Williams, K. (2000). Perceptions of social support in doctoral programs among minority students.*Psychological Reports, 86*(3), 1003-1010.

Williams, M., Brewley, D., Reed, R., White, D., & Davis-Haley, R. (2005). Learning to read each other: Black female graduate students share their experiences at a White research institution. *The Urban Review, 37*(3), 181-199.

Wray M., & Newitz, A. (1997). *White trash.* New York: Routledge.

Patchouli Oil or Maybe Weed
Black Women's Hair and the Politics of Resistance

Sonasha Braxton

E!'s, *Fashion Police* may not carry service pistols or be under intense global scrutiny for their chronic casualty infliction on innocent Black and Brown bodies, but they have brought attention to themselves recently for engaging in behaviors that, like the US's Police Force's actions, appear to be founded in prejudice and racial bias. Dr. Jason Williams, The Hampton Institute's Criminal Justice Chair states, "policing in America has always been one of color/class-consciousness...American policing at its foundation is inherently protective of the status quo" [1]. Even the most apolitical offerings of dictionary.com are happy to include amongst its definitions of policing, "regulation and control of a community".[2] Arguably, both of these definitions are also applicable to the*Fashion Police.* However, to enforce and maintain the color and class status quo, their weapons of choice are not Glock 19s, but microaggressions.

On February 23rd, 2015 the cast engaged in their normal "poking fun at celebrities in good spirit" on Oscar night. [3] The show judges A-list celebrities' sense of fashion, informed inevitably by collectively constructed Euro-centric standards of style and beauty as perceivably embraced by American culture. Veteran, Italian-American Giuliana Rancic commented on 18 year-old biracial Zendaya Coleman's choice to wear her hair in locs (dreadlocks)[4]. Giuliana's edited remarks were the following, "Zendaya is more high-fashion. The hair to me on her is making her a little more boho". The non-edited remarks continued as... "I feel like she smells like patchouli oil...or weed" pre-empting her remark with how much she normally likes the actress's short, straight hair. [5]

And the show went on. The writers wrote. The actors read and ad-libbed. The audience cheered. The co-hosts did not interject (except for Kelly, based on her friendship with Zendaya). The editors edited. The producers gave it the okay. Therefore the comments, as potentially benign as they might be argued to have been, did not reflect solely the off-brand humor of a single individual, but multi-leveled microaggressions, which Columbia University Psychologist Derald Sue defines as "everyday insults, indignities and demeaning messages sent to people of color by well-intentioned white people who are unaware of the hidden messages being sent to them". [6] While it may not represent the kind of overt racial epithet that many people incorrectly use to gauge the quantity of racism in existence, it warrants notice because such comments reflect the subtle ways in which elements of Black culture are unfailingly ridiculed and devalued. Giuliana's comments reflected not only age-old stereotypes about locs, and their relationship to "deviancy," but a wider cultural bias about Black women's hair, sanctioned the moment the cameras kept rolling and the episode aired. Navigating a world of consistent microattacks often constitutes the very regular experience of many Black women. Zendaya is biracial. Her father is Black and her mother is White. The most common identifiers of race are skin tone and hair texture. Zendaya, in her choice to wear the natural style of locs, made a statement about her "Blackness". Locs on Black people are grown through "a process of 'matting', which is an option not readily available to White people because their hair does not 'naturally' grow into such 'organic' looking shapes and strands". [7] In other words, let's be honest, locs look very different on Black and White people. While the locs were not her own, they represented the shape and texture of locs as often appear distinctly, when grown by Black people. Giuliana's statement that Zendaya was too high fashion for the look cannot possibly be misinterpreted. For her, locs and high fashion were mutually exclusive. So Black hair, in this particular representation of its original state, could not be beautiful. Zendaya looked like a young Black woman with a distinct texture of locs. While her skin tone might make her race appear somewhat ambiguous to some, her hair worn as locs, did not. They stood in confirmation of her "Blackness". Giuliana's message, coated thickly in "style- talk", was that Zendaya's natural Blackness was not fashionable, was not beautiful, and was in need of regulation and control.

For Zendaya, her choice to wear her hair in locs for the Oscars was, "to showcase them in a positive light, to remind people of color that our hair is good enough".[8] And that was an act of resistance. It was pointed. It was purposeful. When notions of beauty have been white washed, historically, anything existing outside of that norm becomes an act of resistance. Black women's hair, whether styles are chosen for aesthetic, cultural or convenience reasons, transforms into a message that we are passively or actively emitting to the world. It serves not as an obligation but an **invitation** for Black women to embrace resistance to archaic Euro-centric beauty norms.

Why Hair Matters

Many of us African-American women grew up with some conception of what "good hair" or "bad hair" was. I, for example, was never told I had bad hair, but I honestly often dreamed of having hair that would be easier to manage, that didn't hurt when

426

my mother combed or braided it. I remember using my tiny allowance to go to Sally's Beauty Supply to buy a bag of braiding hair, that I would hide in my bookbag and attach to my ponytail in the school bathroom. I begged for a relaxer because my friends had them and what was beautiful on TV was long, straight hair that would blow in the wind. Like any pre-adolescent, I wanted to be pretty. I wanted to be accepted and acceptable, and that for me, without being told explicitly, was "good", long, tossable hair. According to Ingrid Banks, Associate professor of Black Studies at UC Santa Barbara, "hair becomes a marker of difference that Black women recognize at an early age, particularly given media representations of what represents beauty".[9] In relation to what has been popular in mainstream media, we've loved our hair, hated it, cut it, fought with it, bleached it, weaved it, sewn it, braided it, cursed it, and praised it. To achieve certain looks, our hair requires upkeep, maintenance, and money. Each of us has some kind of relationship with our hair. ALL women have learned in some way, at some time, to associate beauty with the presentation of our hair; however, for Black women, those who do not have our hair have consistently defined that association. And it is often our buying in to this image of beauty, that we have not created, that has defined how we have viewed and entered into a relationship with our own hair.

Hair also exists as symbolism. "Desirable" hair, for a long time, has consisted of long, straight hair. We have achieved this with weave that is long, "Brazilian", "Indian", "Malaysian", "Peruvian". Images of Black women in the media, though they are beginning to shift, continue to be saturated with long, straight hair which is much closer in resemblance to the texture of "White hair" than "Black hair", thus espousing an ideal of beauty which is much closer to Euro-centric norms than anything else. It has been argued that adhering to such norms of beauty, by replicating these styles and images is symbolic of self-hatred; embracing and loving a constructed Euro-centric ideal of beauty instead of cultivating and acknowledging one's hair in its natural form. While this argument is certainly reflective of our collective conditioning in multiple areas around "white is right" and European beauty as better, as a lingering psychological effect of slavery (also reflected in our valuing of certain skin tones, eye color, and body types) it most certainly does not account for all personal aesthetic choice. Ingrid Banks argues that hair forms part of the social construction of the body, it takes on social meaning as it is "an important medium by which people define others, and themselves as well. In a sense, hair emerges as a body within the social body and can reflect notions about perceptions, identity and self-esteem".[10]It is at once public and personal, and thus **matters** because it is symbolic of how we view other Black women and how we view ourselves.

A VERY SHORT History of Natural Hair

Hair has always paid a central role in perceptions, identity, and self-esteem. As far back as ancient Kemet (Egypt), hair represented kinship, status, age, religion, and ethnicity. A Stone Age rock painting in the Tassili Plateau of the Sahara dating back to 3500 BCE, showed a woman with cornrows feeding her child.[11] In the early 15th century hair functioned as a carrier of messages in most West African societies. For ethnic groups such as the Wolof, Mende, Mandingo and Yoruba, for example, "hair was an integral part of a complex language system". [12] Ever since the existence of African civilizations, hairstyles have been used to indicate a person's marital status, age, religion, ethnic identity, wealth, geographic origin and/or rank within the community. The Kuramo of Nigeria could be identified by shaved heads with a single ruft of hair left on top. Young unmarried Wolof young girls often wore partially shaved heads. Hair could communicate desires, Nigerian housewives in polyamorous society created a hairstyle intended to taunt their husband's other wives called the kohin-sorogun (turn your back to the jealous rival wife).[13] Thus hair existed historically as a medium of communication for Black women.

Yet for others, hair even transcended communication with other persons, to act as communication with God. Mohamed Mbodj,

Senegal native and Chair of the African and African-American Studies Program at Manhattanville College in New York indicated the power hair held in pre-Colonial Senegal, commenting that "the hair is the most elevated point of your body, which means it is the closest to the divine", and that this relationship between hair, the body and the divine was "communication from gods and spirits...and was thought to pass through the hair to get to the soul". [14] For hundreds, if not thousands of years, prior to European colonial influence, Africa experienced the valuation of hair not just as related to the individual but the individual as he or she related to the world and to God. Similarly, Rasta philosophy and spirituality concretized hair as a mystical link or "psychic antenna", connecting Rasta with God and his mystical power, or "earth force", which is immanent in the universe. This tradition stemmed from: the biblical laws of the Nazarites that forbid cutting hair, the hair styles of Ethiopian priests and warriors, and as a symbol of the lion's mane.[15] Therefore the historical comprehension of natural hair is one, which has recognized it as being not **just** hair, but communication, personal and spiritual power.

Hair as Social Control

As natural Black hair has served as the container for communication and power it has also been manipulated institutionally to control and regulate that power. Under South Africa's racist White apartheid government, the Population Registration Act required the non-White population be classified into distinct categories to facilitate a successful "divide et impare" strategy. Under apartheid, the classes, Colored, Indian and Black were each allowed specific access to power, and those classified as "Blacks" relegated to the lowest rungs of South African society. Because race is a social construction, tests too had to be constructed as an effort to classify and separate people whose phenotypes were less stereotypically "African", into manageable groups. Race tests had the capacity to give power, or to take it away, to allow access to certain fundamental human rights or to deny them. One of these tests was the "pencil test" in which a pencil was stuck in the hair of a person whose race was considered ambiguous. If the pencil fell, the person "passed" and could be classified as White, if it fell only after shaking his or her head, that person would be classified as colored, if it stuck despite shaking his or her head, he or she was considered Black.[16] There were different versions of such racial testing, but this particular one distinctly displays how hair was used directly as a means of social control by the minority White apartheid government. It is a clear example of how the state practice of racial classification explicitly recognized the malleability and constructivist nature of race, which created the capacity for control and policing of Black bodies, class, status, and lives.

Hair used as a means of social control is ubiquitous. The history of legal and personal challenges to companies, institutions and organizations who have historically held Black people, especially women, to a European hair standard which denies their natural texture, curls and kinks, is a long one. They support the erasure of Black women's natural selves from sight, by creating policy regulations, which uphold "implicit demands that they [Black women] straighten their hair and then maintain that hairstyle through various processes". [17] Here are a few examples of the many instances of oppression of Black women's hair and of resistance:

1. **Paula Mitchell** was a hotel reservations operator working for the Marriott Hotel in 1987. She was threatened with termination if she did not remove her cornrows as braids were against company regulations falling under the prohibited "extreme faddish hairdos". Paula was given the option of wearing a wig with a "European" style hair do or taking out her cornrows. Paula did neither. As she put it, "to wear a wig under these circumstance... would be shamefully hiding a part of my cultural

identity". [18]After legal involvement, Marriott was required to change their policy.

2. **Cheryl Tatum and Cheryl Parahoo** in 1988, were employees of the Hyatt Hotel coffee shop who also wore cornrows. This was found by management to be subject to regulation, as it fell within the category of "extreme" and "unusual". The women were told to wear wigs. Only after national media attention were Hyatt's policies amended by Corporate.

3. **Janet Bello and Jackie Sherrill** in 2010 and **Markeese Warner** in 2012 were denied employment with Six Flags because of their natural locs. Six Flags' policy in a statement issued to ABC news was that *"Six Flags enforces a conservative grooming policy across all parks. The policy does not permit certain hairstyles such as variations in hair colors, dreadlocks..."(etc.)* as it is considered an "extreme" hairstyle. [19]

4. **The U.S. Army** regulations rolled out Army Regulation 670-1 released in March 2014 which prohibited women from wearing locs and twists, and restricted the size of braids to 1/4 inch. Locs were defined as "any matted, twisted or locked coils or ropes of hair (or extensions)" inclusive of "unkempt" or "matted" braids or cornrows. The language and rules were slightly amended in September 2014 which redefined locs, removing "matted" and "unkempt" and allowed female officers to wear twists.

5. January 15, 2015: The **Royal Barbados Police Department** became subject to a section of the RBPF Policy On General Appearance Of Police Officers in

431

which "Police officers are prohibited from wearing any style dreadlock or locks while in uniform or on duty in civilian attire..." [20]

6. March 2015, a friend, Sandisiwe Qweni, in South Africa posted on FB "my daughter told me a teacher told her that her short natural hair is not "wanted" in the school a couple of months ago... she tells me that they have been told that Afros and extensions are not allowed. I don't mind the extensions but Afros....the type of hair that grows out of her head is not allowed?... How do the "learned" people in my daughter's school not see that putting these restrictions and therefore forcing children to chemically or manually straighten their hair is a violation of black girls' bodily autonomy and right not to be exposed to harmful chemicals?"

As Ms. Qweni alluded to, such regulations are tantamount policing of black women's (and girls') bodies. To label what is natural to us as "extreme", "unprofessional", "unwanted" is an attempt to use power to enforce conformity to Euro-centric standards, to remove natural from the realm of beautiful, professional and high-fashion.

Natural Hair as Revolution

Black women's natural hair embodies resistance. It is resistant by nature, the same way it resists small-tooth combs. There is both beauty and strength in that resistance. An article appearing recently in The Economist featured Muthoni wa Kirima the only woman Mau-Mau fighter ranked as a field marshal. The Mau-Mau rebels in Kenya, known for their fierce anti-imperial resistance to British colonial rule became idolized in the 1960s in the hearts and minds of many freedom fighters globally. The trademark aesthetic associated with the Mau-Mau, and thus with African liberation, were locs. Ms. Kirima, still feeling shorted by the current Kenyan government said that she would not cut her floor-length locs, which she has been growing for at least 60 years, until she saw the benefits of independence from Colonial rule [21]. As an academic discourse, hair politics in Kenya has and continues to exist "as a symbol of resistance against attempts by the post-Colonial state to overwhelm intellectual and public sentiments about human rights abuse, poor governance, and indigenization of the Kenyan election system...embedded in the experiences of the Mau-Mau freedom fighters who put their lives on the line to battle British colonial rule. Their long, dreadlocked hair was and still remains a symbol of resistance to neo/colonialism..." [22] Intersected with gender and the roles traditionally women took up or were permitted to occupy in Kenya's liberation struggle, Ms. Kirima's resistance and her hair became and continue to be remarkably intertwined.

It is not simply locs, but any natural hair that defies mainstream cultural beauty norms that can be a tool of resistance. Take the 1960s for example, and the emergence of the Black Panthers, a progressive political organization formed to defend Black people against continued violent oppression of Black people in the United States. At this time Black people began to reclaim their hair's natural state as a purposefully resistant act. In 1968 Kathleen Cleaver, former Black Panther and current lecturer at Emory University School of Law described the natural hair movement at that time as the following: "we were born with our hair like this... it's a new awareness among Black people that their own natural physical appearance is beautiful ... for so many years we were told that only White people were beautiful that only straight hair, light eyes, light skin was beautiful, and so Black women would try everything they could, straighten their hair, lighten their skin to look as much like white women... but this has changed because Black people are aware now that their own appearance is beautiful and proud of it".[23] The beauty in the naturalness of the afro, for example, "symbolized a reconstitutive link with Africa, as part of a counter-hegemonic process helping to redefine a diasporean people not as Negro but as Afro-American" [24]. Natural hair served as a redefinition of identity, not just liberation from White/Colonial oppression, but from internalized inferiority.

Natural Hair as Empowerment

Precocious 18 year-old Zendaya was certainly correct. We are subliminally hit regularly with microaggressions and overt statements that tell us our hair is not good enough. Empowerment comes in choice, and it seems that more Black women are now choosing to "go natural". In August, 2013, Mintel, the self proclaimed "world's leading market intelligence agency" claimed that relaxer sales in the last 8 years were down 26%. [25] There has certainly been a noticeably stronger embrace of natural hair amongst Black women. Black women can choose when we would like our hair to be an accessory, and how we present ourselves to the world. Yet we must accept that neither our hair nor our bodies, attached to this hair escape judgment. As Black women, we can use our energy to react to and mold ourselves differently based on these judgments, or we can embrace our hair as resistant to social control, or to gender norms that state that our beauty is defined by how men judge our hair. We can use our hair as a tool of empowerment as did Halle Berry, by filing a lawsuit against her White ex-husband for manipulating her daughter's natural hair by straightening it and lightening it as an effort to erase traces of her Blackness. Our hair can demand liberation.

We can allow our hair to be revolutionary without reducing the revolution to our hair. Angela Davis in speaking on the iconoclastic legacy of her afro said, "it is both humiliating and humbling to discover that a single generation after the events that constructed me as a public personality, I am remembered as a hairdo. It is humiliating because it reduces a politics of liberation to a politics of fashion...". [26]We can learn from our elders. We can dis-allow our natural hair to simply become an acceptable mainstream fashion trend that needs the approval of or is swallowed by "mainstream society", one that is separate entirely from liberation. We can recognize the revolution of simply embracing our natural state. There is a space for Black women's hair to be revolutionary, to throw off ideals of beauty that we as Black women have been conditioned to believe were only accessible if we changed something fundamentally intrinsic and natural about who we are. We can redefine for ourselves, what is beautiful. We can choose to discontinue allowing our hair, and our bodies, attached to the hair, to be defined as "good" or "beautiful" on other's terms. We can, as Zendaya did, refuse to allow it to be policed. It may be *just hair* to some, but there are social and cultural messages about perceptions, identity, class, gender, communication, power, oppression and liberation that come with it, which we can choose to embrace as realities. As we have been historically conditioned to love and accept everyone but ourselves as beautiful, choosing to love ourselves and embrace the beauty of our natural state, truly exists a revolutionary act.

Notes

[1] http://www.hamptoninstitution.org/policing-the-blacks.html#.VQxAX5HTEpE
[2] http://dictionary.reference.com/browse/policing
[3] https://www.youtube.com/watch?v=YPEAMPfXtOw
[4] The word locs is used here in place of dreadlocks, because it is said that the etymology of the word "dreadlocks" evolved from their characterization by European colonizers as "dreadful"
[5] https://www.yahoo.com/tv/s/e-failed-giuliana-rancic-fashion-police-zendaya-debacle-053433217.html
[6] http://www.apa.org/monitor/2009/02/microaggression.aspx
[7] Ferguson, R. (1990). *Out there: Marginalization and contemporary cultures*. New York, N.Y.: New Museum of Contemporary Art

[8] http://www.huffingtonpost.com/nancy-laws/i-am-not-my-hair-zendaya-response-dreadlocks_b_6742772.html

[9] Banks, I. (2000). *Hair matters beauty, power, and Black women's consciousness*. New York: New York University Press.

[10] Ibid

[11] Willie, F. Page, ed. (2001). *Encyclopedia of African history and culture: Ancient Africa (prehistory to 500 CE), Volume 1.*

[12] Byrd, A., & Tharps, L. (2001). *Hair story: Untangling the roots of Black hair in America*. New York: St. Martin's Press.

[13] Ibid

[14] Ibid

[15] Murrell, N. (1998). *Chanting down Babylon: The Rastafari reader*. Philadelphia: Temple University Press.

[16] Rasmussen, B. (2001). *The making and unmaking of whiteness*. Durham, N.C.: Duke University Press.

[17] Onuwachi-Willig , A. (2010). Exploring New Strands of Analysis under Title VII. Retrieved from http://georgetownlawjournal.org/files/pdf/98-4/Onwuachi-Willig.PDF

[18] Ibid

[19] http://www.clutchmagonline.com/2012/07/dreadlocks-are-unacceptable-for-employment-at-six-flags-and-many-other-companies/

[20] http://www.stabroeknews.com/2015/news/regional/01/21/bajan-cops-uproar-dress-code/

[21] http://www.economist.com/news/middle-east-and-africa/21575787-female-veteran-mau-mau-laments-new-order-historic-hair

[22] Mutua, E. M. (2014). Hair Is Not Just Hot Air: Narratives about Politics of Hair in KenyaHair Is Not Just Hot Air: Narratives about Politics of Hair in Kenya. *Text and Performance Quarterly, 34(4)*, 392-394

[23] https://www.youtube.com/watch?v=cKdPUaBCTBA

[24] Ferguson, R. (1990). *Out there: Marginalization and contemporary cultures*. New York, N.Y.: New Museum of Contemporary Art

[25] http://www.mintel.com/press-centre/beauty-and-personal-care/hairstyle-trends-hair-relaxer-sales-decline

[26] Ongiri, A. (2010). *Spectacular blackness the cultural politics of the Black power movement and the search for a Black aesthetic.* Charlottesville: University of Virginia Press.

Teaching Ferguson, Teaching Capital
Slavery and the "Terrorist Energy" of Capital

Curry Malott and Derek R. Ford

Critical education harnesses the present moment, looks to history to grasp the forces determining the present, and links it with social struggles in an effort to push the configuration of the present beyond its breaking point. Given the recent non-indictments of killer cops Darren Wilson and Daniel Pantaleo, critical educators across the U.S. and the globe are bringing the pressing topics of police brutality, state violence, and people's resistance movements into the classroom. In this essay, we contribute to these efforts by arguing that the deadly and unpunished police violence against African Americans requires not only an awareness of slavery, but an analysis of the relationship between capitalism and slavery, and the subsequent subsumption of racism and white supremacy within capitalism. We use the name Ferguson in the title as a symbol of the daily occurrence of police violence that dates back to at least the end of the Civil War and the terrorist policing of newly "freed" slaves.

The purpose of this analysis is to explain and contribute to the anti-capitalist undertones that exist within the current movement against police brutality. These new street movements were generated spontaneously by the state-sanctioned police murders of Michael Brown and Eric Garner, but they are expressions of a much more generalized repression in Black, Latino, and working-class communities across the United States. According to "Operation Ghetto Storm," a 2013 report by the Malcolm X Grassroots Movement, a Black person in the U.S. is killed every 28 hours by police, security guards, and vigilantes. [i] Statistical analyses by ProPublica show that Black men are 21 times more likely to be shot by police than white men.[ii] While this rate of murder is alarmingly high, it is also the regular brutality, harassment, and degradation inflicted by police on people of color, people with disabilities, Queers, and other oppressed groups in society that has catapulted the rebellions currently taking place in the U.S. Racism and white supremacy are not surface features of U.S. society, they structural features that are engrained materially and ideologically. Indeed, Joe R. Feagin and Karyn D. MicKinney (2002) has demonstrated that racism "generates major barriers to the full health and well-being of African Americans," in that it carries "personal, psychological, and physical costs" (p. 8). Feagin demonstrates that "physical reactions to racial discrimination often take the form of all-day headaches, stomach problems, chest pains, stress diabetes, and hypertension" (p. 31).

In this article we focus particularly on the relationship between race and capitalism. What we see below is that a review of the evidence seems to suggest that the social justice movement of the 21st century must take as its center a critique of capital, which provides the larger context that informs the manifestation of bourgeois ideology from white supremacy, patriarchy, homophobia, to the blatant disregard for the health of the world's vital eco-systems.

Higher Education and Racialization

Arguing that white supremacy, racism, and the deadly devaluing and criminalization of Black life can be traced back to the long legacy of anti-Blackness propagated to justify slavery is an important, but incomplete, insight. That is, the vicious and dehumanizing racism advanced by European slavers to justify slavery became deadly, outlined below, only when cotton became an international commodity propelling slavery into the process of the self-expansion of capital. Capitalism, this analysis suggests, continues to be the force driving the deadliness of white supremacy in the contemporary context. But before capitalism exerted its deadly influence on slavery, white supremacy and anti-African sentiments were already being advanced as an apology for the actions of the *man-stealers* of Europe. Institutions of higher education, such as Harvard, were established *by* the elite *for* the elite during America's colonial era to advance this agenda of racialization.

For example, in his widely acclaimed *Ebony & Ivy: Race, Slavery, and the Troubled History of America's Universities*, Craig Steven Wilder (2013) begins his text noting that, "Harvard's history was inseparable from the history of slavery and the slave trade" (p. 3). One of the primary purposes of higher education was to continually advance the ideological justifications for slavery and train the elites who would manage the system. Explaining what this most undemocratic purpose of higher education looked like in practice Wilder's (2013) account is explicit: "The academy...popularized the language of race, providing intellectual cover for the social and political subjugation of non-white peoples" (p. 3). Harvard Anatomy and Surgery professor between 1809 and 1847, John Collins Warren, taught, "that in physical development, cultural accomplishment, and intellectual potential, black people sat at the bottom of humanity" (Wilder, 2013, p. 3). Situating this purpose of education in the larger context of the social and economic order dominated by slavery Wilder (2013) explains how "college initiated" young white male elites:

...into the slave regimes of the Atlantic world. The founding, financing, and development of higher education in the colonies were thoroughly intertwined with the economic and social forces that transformed West and Central Africa through the slave trade and devastated indigenous nations in the Americas. The academy was a beneficiary and defender of these processes. College graduates exploited these links for centuries. They apprenticed under the slave traders of New England, the Mid-Atlantic, and Europe. They migrated to the south and to the West Indies for careers as teachers, ministers, lawyers, doctors, politicians, merchants and planters...The antebellum south represented a field of opportunity, where the wealth of the cotton planters was funding the expansion of the educational infrastructure. (pp. 1-2)

It is important to note that this purpose of education did not arise spontaneously from faculty, but from the elite investor class responsible for the establishment and ongoing profitability of the colonies themselves. In other words, education was subordinated to the interests of the ruling classes.

The Marriage of Capitalism and Racism

As if the devastating and long-lasting effects of biological racism were not enough, the internal drive and spirit of capital propelled the atrocities of slavery in America into the truly horrific and genocidal. Making this point, Marx (1867/1967) notes that before the invention of the cotton-gin, a piece of labor-saving technology that dramatically increased the efficiency of the tedious work of processing cotton, which involves separating the seeds from the fibers, southern slavery was directed at "immediate local consumption" (p. 226). The cotton gin is credited to Eli Whitney, but Herbert Aptheker (1974) suggests that a skilled slave

441

constructed original schematics for the gin. Prior to the cotton gin, however, there was no incentive or gain to be accrued by working slaves to death. However, as the cotton gin dramatically reduced the value of labor with the notable decrease in the amount of slave labor hours needed to process a given quantity of cotton, the productivity of slavery skyrocketed, leading to an intensified engagement with the international market (which was initially established by the slave-trade itself). For example, the world's primary productive consumer of raw cotton at the time, England, saw an increase in the consumption of this material from 13 thousand to about 3 ½ million bales from 1781 to 1860 (DuBois, 1896/2007). British capitalists accumulated slave-labor cotton from the American south, combined it with British labor power and forced the subsequent cotton goods on India and China chiefly through military force. North American merchants began amassing fortunes as slave vendors before 1800, and built an industrial superpower off of slave cotton after 1820. The surge in wealth and potential for even more returns had the corrupting effect of further barbarizing a practice already deeply entrenched in dehumanization.

However, the labor saving technology and the forced-open international market were not the only conditions necessary for the manifestation of these developments. The ability to not only replace, but to expand his human means of production, that is, his access to new slave labor, required ever new supplies of captives. This tendency, largely unique to capitalist accumulation, is no different under wage labor as Marx (1867/1967) consistently documents: "we heard how over-work thinned the ranks of the bakers in London. Nevertheless, the London labor-market is always overstocked with German and other candidates for death in the bakeries" (p. 267). Explaining how this principle operated within slave-labor Marx (1867/1967) is instructive:

...When his [the enslaved] place can at once be supplied from foreign preserves, the duration of his life becomes a matter of less moment than its productiveness while it lasts. It is accordingly a

maxim of slave management, in slave-importing countries, that the most effective economy is that which takes out of the human chattel in the shortest space of time the utmost amount of excertion it is capable of putting forth. (p. 266)

Again, this development represents the barbaric and deadly shift that always accompanies unfettered capitalism: "it was no longer a question of obtaining from him a certain quantity of useful products. It was now a question of the production of surplus-labor itself" (Marx, 1867/1967, p. 236). As a result, the whole of the south was transformed into a vast region of cotton fields, and it became more profitable to work slaves to death than to take care of them into old age.

Yet according to bourgeois ideology, which always presents itself as a non-perspective, or as "just the way it is," capitalism is the path to freedom and equality. Given this normalized idea, which informs the view that before 1865 slavery was the only barrier to freedom in the U.S., it is not intuitive that the introduction of capitalism would lead to the escalation of atrocities within slavery. Dominant historical narratives teach us just the opposite. That is, the historical narrative American students tend to be uncritically reared on is that once slavery was abolished, capitalism could begin spreading its freedom and equality southward, gradually chipping away at the white supremacist ideological residue of a bygone era standing as a fading barrier to meritocracy. Challenging the core of this ideology Marx's (1867/1967) discussion of the internal logic of capital makes it absolutely clear that the spirit and intent of capital is a dangerous force, which continues to inform the deadliness of white supremacy.

For example, throughout volume 1 of *Capital* Marx takes great pains to highlight the true spirit and intent of capital, which is to accumulate as much value (and, specifically, surplus-value) as possible. Marx meticulously demonstrates that human labor power is the only commodity that has the ability to *produce* value. Marx therefore divides the working-day into two parts, a necessary part and a surplus part. The necessary portion of the workday is the

443

amount of time it takes for the worker to reproduce the value of her or his own labor-power (which is determined by such elements as geography, technology, and the state of class struggle). If this takes six hours of labor, then the remainder of the day is surplus (although Marx went demonstrated that necessary labor-time and surplus labor-time "glide one into the other"). From capital's perspective then, the ideal length of the working-day would be its physical limit, 24 hours. Marx (1867/1967) showed, with example after example, the results of this deadly impulse to accumulate surplus labor hours, and thus surplus value, from England and beyond. This murderous drive, Marx consistently argues, is the true spirit and intent of capital, which always appears when capital goes unregulated. For this reason Marx (1867/1967) often compares this omnipresent instinct innate to the capitalist mode of production to the mythical werewolf whose terror will always emerge given the correct conditions, that is, where production is not regulated. Today, we see this "terrorist energy" (Marx, 1867/1967, p. 286) manifesting itself throughout much of the world, especially in so-called free trade zones, in South America, the Caribbean, Eastern Europe, and in the most oppressed and criminalized areas within the U.S., especially African American working-class communities. Again, Marx (1867/1967) provides many examples of this tendency. In one instance Marx (1867/1967) notes the result of the British public, in the mid-nineteenth century, having been turned against the working-class:

The manufactures had no need any longer to restrain themselves. They broke out in open revolt not only against the Ten Hours' Act, but against the whole legislation that since 1833 had aimed at restricting in some measure the "free" exploitation of labor-power. It was a pro-slavery rebellion in miniature, carried on for over two years with a cynical recklessness, a terrorist energy all the cheaper because the rebel capitalist risked nothing except the skin of his "hands." (p. 286).

This is the true spirit and intent of capital that will always work laborers to death unless restricted by working-class resistance or state-enforced regulations. It is for these reasons that laborers have organized unions and struggled to restrict capital's insatiable appetite from extracting the maximum amount of surplus value out of each individual laborer for at least the past 200 years. Capital is therefore always seeking ways to reduce the value and thus the cost to capital of a laborer's capacity to labor. For example, restrictions placed upon the length of the working day in the nineteenth century were met with almost immediate increases in the intensity of labor by speeding up machines and watching ever more diligently the efficiency of operations. Another example is increasing the productivity of labor-power through the invention of machines, which reduces the value of labor-power by shortening the amount of labor time it takes to reproduce the value of labor-power. This necessarily increases surplus labor-time. Because the use of any given commodity belongs to the buyer rather than to the seller, the value of these products belongs to the capitalist, not to the laborer. If the laborer's labor did not produce more value than it cost to use, then the capitalist would not buy it.

Ideologically, this drive to lower the value of labor-power results in the social value of the laborer's subjective social being is devalued. This can result in low self-esteem, self-hatred, and even the worship of the ruling class by the working class. This can happen despite the fact that many of the labor-saving technologies that drive down the value of labor-power are actually produced by workers through the production process (i.e., forms of cooperation). However-and this is where education can play a pivotal role-the result among workers conscious of the capitalist system is deep resentment and either cynicism and despair, or organization and revolution. The most exaggerated example of the tendency to culturally devalue the working class are the ways anti-Black racism has been employed to justify dramatically increasing the rate of exploitation of and unemployment in Black communities. In times of crisis and recession the Black worker, consequently, is always the first to be laid off. As a result, today, generally speaking, the Black family is 22 times more likely to be in poverty than the white family. The white worker's greater access to jobs includes access to police jobs. White workers therefore tend to hold the police jobs in not only white working class neighborhoods, but in Black ones as well. With the exaggerated devaluing and demonization of the young Black male, it is not surprising that white cops kill Black youth at alarming rates with near impunity. This is a legacy that can be traced back to the era when slavery became lethal. But, serving the purpose of the necessary ideological mechanisms described above is the very process of capitalist circulation itself and the use of the money-relation. Making this point, and using slavery as a contrasting example strengthening the impact of his argument, Marx (1867/1967) explains with biting precision:

In slave-labor, even that part of the working-day in which the slave is only replacing the value of his own means of existence, in which, therefore, in fact, he works for himself alone, appears as labor for his master. All the slave's labor appears as unpaid labor. In wage-labor, on the contrary, even surplus-labor, or unpaid labor, appears as paid. There the property relation conceals the labor of the slave for himself; here the money-relation conceals the unrequited labor of the wage-laborer. (pp. 539-540)

It is no wonder why there was so much push back against a conception of freedom after the abolition of slavery in the U.S. in 1865 based upon an agrarian land reform that might be thought of as a mild form of reverse-primitive accumulation. The transition from chattel slavery to wage slavery was therefore assisted by a form of capitalist education. This was in many ways a relatively easy transition even though there was significant push back from former slaves who knew all too well that being compelled to sell their labor to their former masters represented anything but freedom. Mandatory ignorance laws, part of the Black Codes, enforced after a series of slave revolts in its deadly era of value augmentation, resulted in a deep sense amongst former slaves that education possessed some liberatory potential. The role Historically Black Colleges and Universities (HBCUs) have played in the post-Civil War struggle for liberation should therefore not be surprising. Consider:

Public HBCUs became epicenters in the struggle for human rights...shaping the destiny of America. Driven by a tenaciously segregated society, the students and faculty joined hands with religious and civic leaders and moved the entire nation toward a new level of social consciousness. The story of public HBCUs is a story of a people liberated through education [and] empowered through political action...They serve as laboratories where solutions to issues facing the Black community are addressed. (Payne, 2013, pp. 15-16)

With the official end of slavery in the U.S. in 1865 the material wealth generated by slave labor in the cotton kingdom had already been amassed and used to develop and expand the machine factory throughout the North. Former slaves were at the forefront of Reconstruction and the rise of the HBCU. Of course, the changing needs of capital as the industrial era of capital emerged, led to the Morrill Acts and Land Grant Universities charged with advancing mechanical arts, military science, and agricultural technologies, provided the incentive for the expansion of systems of higher education from the perspective of capital. However, in the hands of former slaves, it is not surprising that HBCUs came to play a central role in the Civil Rights movement. In the neoliberal era, it is equally not surprising that in the attack on public higher education HBCU's have suffered the most and the first, as a general rule. The logic moving these developments is an insatiable appetite for the accumulation of surplus value. The murder of Black youth at the hands of white cops only mirrors the ways in which the werewolf within capital has been unleashed with a savage barbarity on Black communities. The larger context, of course, is a declining capitalist economy increasingly desperate for opportunities to augment new values.

Through the bourgeoisie's doctrinal system, laborers are socialized to believe that capitalism is the true path to freedom and equality. The laws of exchange are supposed to guarantee this. That is, unlike the prejudice and bias driving aristocratic feudalism and slavery, buyers and sellers, under capitalism, meet on the market as equals. From this perspective the exchange between labor, the seller of labor power, and capital, the purchaser of labor power, is fair. Labor, after all, willingly sells her product on the market, and the capitalist purchases it for its market value. The products that are created from the commodity the laborer sells, labor power, do not belong to the seller, but to the purchaser, the capitalist. No coercion or exploitation therefore exists within this exchange, as far as the buyer is concerned. But the price of labor power is based on the value it takes to reproduce her existence for another day, as discussed above. If this value is reproduced through six hours of labor, for example, then the rest of the workday is surplus, and thus represents surplus value. From the perspective of the class conscious laborer the productive consumption of her labor power is fundamentally based on a hidden process of accumulation or exploitation. Capitalism is in fact based exclusively on this drive to augment as much surplus value as possible, and when unfettered, or unregulated, inevitably leads to the premature exhaustion and death of the laborer himself and herself. Rather than freedom and equality, outside of the freedom of the capitalist to exploit and the laborer to be exploited or excluded, what capitalism offers is social misery and degradation fueled by a slew of unmet needs and a deadly white supremacy informed by the same "cynical recklessness" and "terrorist energy" Marx (1867/1967) witnessed in the nineteenth century. The fight against the murderous white supremacy at the heart of America's bourgeois society is therefore at the same time the fight against the *terrorist* process of value augmentation unique to capitalism.

National Oppression and Resistance

Capital, as Marx constantly reminds us, is not a thing but a social relation. Resistance is thus *internal* to capital. One of the primary tasks of the critical educator is to foster this resistance, in terms of consciousness, subjectivity, and organization. What we have been witnessing in streets across the country over the past few weeks has been a tremendous display of this spontaneous resistance to oppression and exploitation. Perhaps history will show that the non-indictments of Warren and Pantaleo were small sparks that lit the prairie ablaze. There are many factors that will determine this potentiality, however. We believe that one of these factors is the way in which we understand police brutality, racism, and capitalism. If we see police brutality as accidental to the system, and if we see racism as merely a left-over from slavery, then the burgeoning resistance movement will undoubtedly exhaust itself, collapsing under the weight of ideological mystifications. If police brutality and racism are seen as endemic to the capitalist production and augmentation of value, however, then the street rebellions we are witnessing could translate into a broad-based, national mass movement striking at capital itself. In this closing section, we want to offer one final connection between capitalism and racism, one that has important implications for organizing: the concept of national oppression.

Just like every worker in the U.S. is taught that the overthrow of the slaveocracy in the south gave way to capitalism's attendant equalities and freedoms, so too every worker learns that the U.S. is a nation. Schools have students recite that the U.S. is "one nation" on a daily basis. This assertion, however, is as false as it is commonplace. The U.S. is instead a country that contains within it many oppressed nations, including the Black nation.

The national question was first broached by Marx in relation to Ireland and the struggle of Irish workers. Initially, Marx believed that Ireland would be liberated by the struggle of workers in the colonial power, England. Marx changed his position, however, after

449

taking into account the anti-Irish racism that was deep-seated in the English working-class. Instead of relying on workers in the colonizing country to liberate the colony, Marx called on English workers to support Ireland's right to self-determination. Lenin took up and advanced this line in relation to Czarist Russia which, at the time of the Bolshevik revolution in 1917, was referred to as a "prison house of nations," in that Russia contained hundreds of nationalities and languages. These oppressed nations within Russia suffered a higher rate of exploitation as well as cultural oppression. By viewing these entities as oppressed nations, Lenin and the Bolsheviks were able to move beyond the mere calls to "unite the working class," and were able to pay particular attention to particular forms of oppression. It is no coincidence, then, that racial and national relations within the Soviet Union were greatly advanced, especially when compared to the U.S. This is never mentioned in U.S. schools, of course, because it disrupts the capitalist narrative of the Soviet Union as an "authoritarian" or "totalitarian" state. While there were definitely authoritarian elements within the Soviet Union's complex history (and within any country's history, for that matter), it is crucial to acknowledge the important gains made for the majority of workers and oppressed people (See Malott and Ford, 2014).

The Marxist and Leninist conception of national oppression has visceral resonances with the situation in the U.S. today. There is, additionally, a lineage of the left that has viewed the U.S. as a multinational state-as a state, that is, that contains within it oppressed nations, including the Black nation. Black communist militant Harry Haywood was one of the most prominent figures in articulating the position of a Black nation inside the U.S. Working in collaboration with Bolsheviks, Haywood formulated the "Black Belt" thesis, which held that Blacks constituted an oppression nation within the U.S. Black people constituted a nation because they were "set apart by a common ethnic origin, economically interrelated in various classes, united by a common historical experience, reflected in a special culture and psychological makeup" (Haywood, 1978, p. 232), in addition to holding a contiguous territory stretching across the south. As such, Black people in the U.S. had a right to national self-determination. This position was eventually adopted by the entire communist movement at the 6thCongress of the Third International in 1928. As a matter of historical record, it is quite remarkable that as far back as 1928, communists and communist parties across the world were fighting for the right of Black people in the U.S. to self-determination. Yet they were not doing so out of a desire for separatism. Ultimately, they wanted all races and nations to unite on a class-basis. By emphasizing national oppression and the rights of oppressed nations to self-determination, however, communists were able to pay particular attention to the ways in which some people are super-oppressed and exploited, and to how the bourgeoisie were able to extract even more surplus labor-time from these populations. This position was also intended to combat the racism and national chauvinism engrained in white U.S. workers. And, in addition to serving as a means to agitate against calls for integration into U.S. capitalist society, it allowed Haywood to think more precisely through the relationship between reform and revolution. In *For a Revolutionary Position on the Negro Question*, written in 1958, four years after the *Brown v. Board of Education*decision, Haywood reminded the Communist Party USA of its position and railed against the CPUSA for following the NAACP's "bourgeois assimilationist" position. Haywood wrote: *While we Communists fight for every possible democratic demand of the Negro people, and welcome all advances made, we have pointed out that the Negro question is at bottom the question of an oppressed nation in the South and a national minority in the North.* Here, Haywood is saying that reform and revolution are not mutually exclusive. Yes, we should fight for judicial reforms, but we must have no illusions as to their ultimate effectiveness. Haywood went on to rail against the leadership of the CPUSA:

With the outlawing of the segregation of schools by the Supreme Court in May of 1954, the right-revisionist trend in our Party unreservedly embraced the pro-imperialist swindle of imminent,

451

peaceful, democratic "integration" of the Negro people into all aspects of American life.

This was two years after Kruschev's "secret speech," in which he denounced the entirety of Stalin's leadership, and which marked a definitive rightward turn for the international communist movement. What is most notable, however, is the way in which Haywood is able to support calls for reform while at the same time insisting upon revolution on a class basis.

As we approach 2015, the U.S. is still highly racially segregated socially, economically, and geographically. With the framework of national oppression, the images of white cops and reserve troops repressing the rebellions in Ferguson and elsewhere begin to make more sense. The ways in which the struggles against police brutality, racism, and capitalism can join together also becomes clearer in this framework. It is the duty of working-class whites not to be mere "allies," but to be *comrades* fighting for socialism and supporting the right to self-determination for Black people and all oppressed nations within the U.S. Only in this way can multinational class unity against capitalism be built, a unity that takes seriously the differences within the working class.

References

Aptheker, H. (1974). *American Negro Slave Revolts*. New York: International Publishers.

DuBois, W.E.B. (1869/2007). *The Suppression of the African Slave Trade to the United States of America, 1638-1870.* New York: Oxford University Press.

Feagin, J.R. , & McKinney, K.D. (2002). *The Many Costs of Racism*. New York: Rowman &Littlefield Publishers.

Haywood, H. (1958). *For a revolutionary position on the Negro question.* Available at http://www.marxists.org/history/erol/1956-1960/haywood02.htm.

Haywood, H. (1978). *Black Bolshevik: Autobiography of an Afro-American Communist*. Chicago: Liberator Press.

Malott, C., & Ford, D.R. (2014). Contributions to a Marxist Critical Pedagogy of Becoming: Centering the *Critique of the Gotha Programme. Part 1. Journal for Critical Education Policy Studies*, 12(3).

Marx, K. (1867/1967). *Capital: A Critique of Political Economy: Volume 1: The Process of Capitalist Production*. New York: International Publishers.

Payne, N. (2013). The Economics of Equality. In Edward Fort (Ed.). Survival of the Historically Black Colleges and Universities: Making it Happen. New York: Lexington Books.

Wilder, C.S. (2013). *Ebony & Ivy: Race, Slavery, and the Troubled History of America's Universities.*New York: Bloomsbury Press.

[i] https://mxgm.org/wp-content/uploads/2013/04/Operation-Ghetto-Storm.pdf

[ii] http://www.propublica.org/article/deadly-force-in-black-and-white

Social Economics

The Great Recession, Six Years Later
Uneven Recovery, Flawed Indicators, and a Struggling Working Class

Colin Jenkins

In July of 2014, Barack Obama boasted of an impressive recovery the US has undertaken since the Great Recession of 2008, proclaiming, "We've recovered faster and come farther than almost any other advanced country on Earth." To support this claim, the White House released a report showing that, out of 12 countries identified as "advanced" (France, Germany, Greece, Iceland, Ireland, Italy, Netherlands, Portugal, Spain, Ukraine, United Kingdom and United States), the United States is "one of only two (the other being Germany) that experienced systemic financial crises in 2007 and 2008 but have seen real (gross domestic product) per working-age person return to pre-crisis levels."

Reports such as these have become commonplace in 2014, not only from those in the White House, but also from multiple media sources. Within mainstream circles, the recovery has generally been lauded by the Democratic wing of the media (MSNBC, Huffington Post, and of course reports from the White House) and questioned by the Republican wing (Fox News, the Wall Street Journal). Since the reports stemming from these sources are almost always politically-charged, they have a tendency to be misleading in at least some manner. In the rare instance where genuine information or analysis leaks from the mainstream, it is usually the unintended result of a media spin.

Ultimately, the intended purpose of these reports are reduced to either showing Barack Obama and the Democratic Party in a good light (by focusing on seemingly positive statistics) or showing Obama and the Democrats in a bad light (by focusing on seemingly negative statistics). Often times, the same statistics may be used; however, spun differently. Neither side is interested in formulating meaningful analysis, but rather in swaying voters one way or the other. Still, in this media tug-o-war, facts are sometimes used to support political arguments, and thus may be useful from time to time if one is able to pick them out of the fray. But, even when we catch a glimpse of fairly reliable statistics, how do we cut through the politically-charged spins to give them meaning?

Take Obama's July statement for instance. It suggests that the US has experienced a strong recovery since the 2008 economic crisis, right? Well, not necessarily. What it says is that the US has experienced a better recovery than 11 out of 12 of its "advanced" counterparts that "experienced systemic crises," which (it's important to note) were handpicked by the White House. According to the International Monetary Fund, there are actually 36 countries that are considered to have "advanced economies." And considering the global nature of the economy, it's difficult to claim that 67% of them avoided systemic crisis. When compared to the 36, the US ranks 12th in GDP growth and 9th in unemployment rate recovery. Not necessarily bad, but certainly not as good as suggested.

Which brings us to some other questions: How accurate are GDP and unemployment rates when assessing the overall economic well-being of a country? Why are such macroeconomic indicators used so frequently in mainstream analyses? Do they accurately represent the well-being of the working-class majority, or do they simply represent convenient fodder used to supplement political spins? Let's take a look.

Gross Domestic Product and the Dow Jones Industrial Average

Two major indicators used to determine the overall health of the economy are the Gross Domestic Product (GDP) and the Dow Jones Industrial Average (DJIA).

US GDP growth rates over the past six years suggest a strong recovery. Since falling more than 16 percent during the Great Recession of 2008-09, the GDP has experienced growth in 19 out of 21 financial quarters.

2013 was especially successful in terms of GDP growth, averaging over 3 percent for the first time since the recession. 2014 started out slow, dropping a little over 2% in the first quarter (Q1 2014); however, this was written off as an irregularity by analysts, including PNC Senior Economist Gus Faucher, who attributed the drop to " bad weather " that "was a significant drag on the economy, disrupting production, construction, and shipments, and deterring home and auto sales." Since that time, the GDP has been growing at a rate of 4.1% over the past six months.

The DJIA has shown even bigger signs of recovery. After being cut in half between September 2007 (15,865) and February 2009 (7,923), the DJIA has experienced an almost unfathomable boom. It hit its highest point ever in November 2013, nearly five years after the recession, at 16,429, and has been breaking records ever since. Heading into November of 2014, it stands at 17, 390 - the highest point in its 128-year history.

Corporate Profits

Not surprisingly, the cumulative amount of corporate profits in the United States has paralleled the success of the stock market. American Enterprise Institute economist Mark J. Perry has illustrated a sharp correlation between the S & P 500 Index and after-tax corporate profits in the chart below:
Perry explains this phenomenon:

"Starting about 2009, a one-to-one relationship between stock prices and after-tax corporate profits has once again re-emerged, and both the S&P 500 and corporate profits have increased by the exact same 119% at the end of 2013 from their cyclical, recessionary lows. The all-time record highs for the S&P 500 Index in 2013 were being driven by record-high corporate profits as the chart shows, and it's almost certain that the ongoing bull market rally in 2014 continues to be supported by record-high corporate profits."

The corporate landscape has rarely been as conducive to generating profit as it is right now. As a result, the post-recession years have been dubbed "a golden age of corporate profits" by those in both mainstream and alternate media. Specifically, "corporate earnings have risen at an annualized rate of 20.1 percent since the end of 2008." As a percentage of national income, "corporate profits stood at 14.2 percent in the third quarter of 2012, the largest share at any time since 1950."

To put the significance of this growth in perspective, at the end of 2008, during the peak of the recession, US corporate after-tax profits totaled $671.40 Billion. At the end of June 2014, that total has nearly tripled to $1.842 Trillion.

Unemployment Rate and Job Growth

Another major indicator used to gauge the state of the economy is the unemployment rate. In October of 2009, after the residual effects of the recession had settled, the US unemployment rate officially hit 10% for only the second time since 1940 (10.8% in 1982). After hovering around 9% through 2011, the rate has steadily decreased over the past few years, dropping below 6% in September of 2014 - a level untouched since July of 2008. This new 6-year low in the rate includes 1.9 million people dropping from the ranks of the unemployed, and the number of "long-term unemployed" falling 1.2 million over the past year.

According to the US Department of Labor, "employers added 248,000 jobs in September (2014)" and "payrolls have expanded an average 227,000 a month this year, putting 2014 on track to be the strongest year of job growth since the late 1990s." The job growth rate in 2014 included a 300,000+ jump in April. And much of this expansion has been fueled by the private sector, which "has now added 10.3 million jobs over 55 straight months of growth" since the recession.

Flawed Indicators

Based on assessments which focus on macroeconomic indicators like the GDP, DJIA, and Unemployment Rate, one could reasonably come to the conclusion that not only has the US fully recovered from the "Great Recession," but it has actually surpassed pre-recession levels in economic well-being. However, this begs the question: whose well-being? And a closer examination uncovers plenty of contradictions.

The contradictions that arise from such assessments are largely due to the inherent flaws of these indicators. According to the New Economy Working Group, "Gross Domestic Product (GDP) has many deficiencies as a measure of economic well-being. Most often noted is the fact that it can only add, which means it makes no distinction between beneficial and harmful economic activity." Also, GDP analyses focus solely on total growth, and do not attempt to assess levels of wealth distribution:

"There could be complete income equality with everyone's purchasing power growing equally. Or the society may be divided between a small minority of the extremely affluent and a majority of the extremely destitute - or anything in between. GDP gives no clue one way or the other. Growth in the incomes of a few billionaires can produce impressive growth in GDP even as a majority of people starve."

In fact, during the past half-century, the DJIA has lost almost all of its credibility as a reliable indicator of economic well-being. And since the rise of globalization in the late-1990s, it has become increasingly irrelevant to economic activity on a national level. "The Dow's biggest flaw, perhaps, is that it doesn't help us to make sense of an increasingly interconnected global economy - one in which what's good for GM isn't always good for the country," explains Adam Davidson. "GE, IBM and Intel, for example, all make more than half their profits in other countries. And while this may be great for their shareholders, it means little for most Americans."

The ever-increasing gap between corporate profit and workers income has also served as a death knell to the DJIA indicator. "In the postwar boom of the 1950s, the economy was growing so fast, and the benefits were so widely shared (throughout the socioeconomic ladder), that following 30 large American companies was a solid measure of most everyone's personal economy," Davidson adds. Back then, "what was good for GM really was good for the country." In a modern economic environment that rewards CEOs 331 times more than the average worker, and 774 times more than minimum wage workers, this is no longer the case. (In 1983, this ratio was 46 to 1)

Historically, the unemployment rate has been considered a fairly weak indicator of economic well-being, and for good reason. Its two major flaws lie in its failure to gauge levels of income, and its inability to consider things like "underemployment" and "hidden unemployment."

These lost categories include "people who have given up looking for jobs or work part time because they can't find full-time position." In 2014, as unemployment statistics suggest a vast improvement in labor participation, "more than 9 million Americans still fit into these categories, about 60 percent - or 3.5 million - above prerecession levels, according to the Labor Department."

Evan Horowitz explains:

"Let's say there are 100 people either working or looking for work. If 94 of those people have jobs, and six are seeking jobs, then the unemployment rate is 6 percent.
Notice that a lot hinges on people 'working or looking for work.' Say you want to work, but the job market is bad and you decide to put off the search until conditions get better. You're still unemployed, just not counted as unemployed by the government.
To return to the example, if three of those six people looking for work get discouraged and give up, the unemployment rate would fall to about 3 percent."

Furthermore, the unemployment rate completely ignores income. In other words, even rates that are considered to represent "full employment" (4-5%) essentially mean nothing if a considerable number of jobs pay poverty wages.

State of the Working Class

Because macro-indicators like the DJIA, GDP, and unemployment rates are severely flawed in their ability to reflect standards of living and economic well-being for a population, it is important to evaluate how the majority is fairing in this so-called recovery. Since the US population throughout is largely driven by consumerism, a telling statistic is the market-based core personal consumption expenditures (PCE) price index, a measurement used to determine the amount of expendable income the average consumer possesses at a given time. According to Josh Bivens of the Economic Policy Institute, "the market-based price index for core PCE (i.e., excluding food and energy) rose just 1.3% over the past year, well below the Fed's 2% inflation target." This supports further evidence that impressive gains in GDP and corporate profits are simply not reaching (or trickling down to) a majority of Americans.

Despite recent and steady job growth, there are still 1.4 million fewer full-time jobs in the US today than there was in 2008. A recent survey conducted at Rutgers University reports that more than 20 percentof all workers that have been laid off in the past five years still have not found a new job.
When considering workers who have given up on job searches, the unemployment rate is estimated at more than 12 percent.
A more accurate indicator than the unemployment rate may be the actual employment rate. When looking at this, we see that roughly 80 percent of " prime-age workers " (those between 25 and 54) had jobs in 2007. "That bottomed out at around 75 percent during the worst of the downturn, but has risen to only 76.7 percent since." Despite steady job growth, new jobs simply do not stack up to the jobs that were lost. In sectors that experienced severe job losses due to the recession, workers are earning 23% less today. The average annual salary in the manufacturing
and construction sectors - a particularly hard hit area - was $61,637 in 2008. It has now plummeted to $47,171 in 2014. Similar adjustments to income levels imply that $93 billion in lower wage income has been created during the recovery - meaning workers, across the board, are receiving a much smaller share than they were before 2009.

A report by the United States Conference of Mayors (USCM) also showed that "the majority of metro areas - 73 percent - had households earning salaries of less than $35,000 a year," hardly a living wage for families facing ever-rising commodity prices. Despite increased productivity and corporate profits, most workers' wages have actually fallen. Biven reports, "From the first half of 2013 to the first half of 2014, real hourly wages fell for all deciles, except for a miniscule two-cent increase at the 10th percentile. Underlying this exception to the general trend at the 10th percentile is a set of state-level minimum-wage increases in the first half of 2014 in states where 40 percent of U.S. workers reside." "As a percentage of national income, corporate profits stood at 14.2 percent in the third quarter of 2012, the largest share at any time since 1950, while the portion of income that went to employees was 61.7 percent, near its lowest point since 1966," reported Nelson Schwartz in 2013. Dean Maki, chief US economist at Barclay's reports that "corporate earnings have risen at an annualized rate of 20.1 percent since the end of 2008, but disposable income inched ahead by 1.4 percent annually over the same period, after adjusting for inflation," adding that "there hasn't been a period in the last 50 years where these trends have been so pronounced."

In the midst of impressive GDP growth, the US working class is experiencing a legitimate hunger crisis that does not seem to slowing down. "As of 2012, 49 million Americans suffer from food insecurity, defined by the U.S. Department of Agriculture (USDA) as lack of access to 'enough food for an active, healthy life.' Nearly one-third of the afflicted are children. And millions of them don't even have access to food stamps, according to a new report from the anti-hunger organization Feeding America."

In May of 2014, there were 46.2 million Americans on food stamps, a slight decrease from a record 47.8 million in December 2012. According to the US Department of Agriculture, 14.8% of the US population is currently on the Supplemental Nutrition Assistance Program (SNAP). Prior to the recession, the percentage of the population requiring such assistance hovered between 8 and 11 percent.

According to the US Census Bureau, "in 2013, there were 45.3 million people living in poverty" and "for the third consecutive year, the number of people in poverty at the national level was not statistically different from the previous year's estimate." The official poverty rate is at 14.5 percent.

Conclusion

Between 2008 and 2013, the number of US households with a net worth of $1 million or more increased dramatically, from 6.7 million to 9.6 million. Households with a net worth of $5 million and $25 million respectively also increased. "There were 1.24 million households with a net worth of $5 million or more last year, up from 840,000 in 2008. Those with $25 million and above climbed to 132,000 in 2013, up from 84,000 in 2008."
The US government, or more specifically, the Federal Reserve, has been instrumental in this uneven recovery that has been characterized by massive corporate profits and booming millionaires on one side (a small minority), and falling wages, increased poverty, and frequent reliance on food stamps on the other side (a large majority).

According to a September 2014 study by the Harvard Business School, the widening gap between America's wealthiest and its middle and lower classes is "unsustainable," and "is unlikely to improve any time soon." The study points the finger at "shortsighted executives" who are "satisfied with an American economy whose firms win in global markets without lifting US living standards" for American workers, and therefore create an extremely polarized population where a majority of workers are disenfrachised from the business world.

The practice of quantitative easing (QE) - "An unconventional monetary policy in which a central bank purchases government securities or other securities from the market in order to lower interest rates and increase the money supply" - has become common during the recovery. Essentially, this practice "increases the money supply by flooding financial institutions with capital in an effort to promote increased lending and liquidity." After three bouts of QE, all occurring since the recession, the Federal Reserve has acquired $4.5 trillion in assets , while adding at least $2.3 trillion of additional currency into the economy.

Robert D. Auerbach - an economist with the U.S. House of Representatives Financial Services Committee for eleven years, assisting with oversight of the Federal Reserve, and now Professor of Public Affairs at the Lyndon B. Johnson School of Public Affairs at the University of Texas at Austin - estimates that 81.5% of this money has not been used to "stimulate the economy," but rather " sits idle as excess reserve in private banks."

Others have reported that, rather than sitting idle as Auerbach suggests, the money has actually funneled through to major corporate players, creating massive personal wealth for a select few. CNBC's Robert Frank reported just last week that "the world's billionaires are holding an average of $600 million in cash each - greater than the gross domestic product of Dominica," which "marks a jump of $60 million from a year ago and translates into billionaires' holding an average of 19 percent of their net worth in cash."

When considering the top-heavy recovery numbers, and increased misery for the working class, this comes as no surprise. And it certainly comes as no surprise to political economist Doug Henwood, who reported such trends back in 2012:

"Despite the strong recovery in cash flow, to record-breaking levels, firms are investing at levels typically seen at cyclical lows, not highs. Some cash flow is going abroad, in the form of direct investment, but still you'd think returns like these would encourage investment. Instead, they've been shipping out gobs to shareholder. Here's a graph of what I call shareholder transfers (dividends plus stock buybacks plus proceeds of mergers and acquisitions) over time:

Though not at the preposterously elevated levels of the late 1990s and mid-2000s, transfers are at the high end of their historical range. Instead of serving the textbook role of raising capital for productive investment, the stock market has become a conduit for shoveling money out of the 'real' sector and into the pockets of shareholders, who besides buying other securities, pay themselves nice bonuses they transform into Jaguars and houses in Southampton."

The Great Recession - like the 2001 recession before it, the 1990-91 recession before that, the 1981-82 recession before that, the 1973-75 recession before that, and so on - was the result of deeper systemic deficiencies. While the emergence of financialization opened the door for manipulative and predatory finance tricks (credit default swaps, mortgage-backed securities,

NINJA loans, etc...) and helped to construct an impressively profitable house of cards, it is only part of the story. Ultimately, it is the boom & bust, cyclical nature of capitalism, along with its perpetually underlined falling rates of profit (not cumulative profit), that are truly responsible, though almost always ignored.

The nature of this latest recovery suggests that the final nail in the working-class coffin, whose construction has been underway since the birth of neoliberalism, has been secured into place. Despite desperate measures used to pump massive amounts of currency into the economy through QE, virtually none has trickled down to the 99%. It's like déjà vu, all over again. And again... And again...

Zombie Apocalypse and the Politics of Artificial Scarcity

Colin Jenkins

Dystopian narratives have long been an alluring and thought-provoking form of entertainment, especially for those who take an interest in studying social and political structures. From classics like Nineteen Eighty-Four and Brave New World to the current hit, The Hunger Games, these stories play on our fears while simultaneously serving as warning signs for the future.

Their attractiveness within American society is not surprising. Our lives are driven by fear. Fear leads us to spend and consume; fear leads us to withdraw from our communities; and fear leads us to apathy regarding our own social and political processes. This fear is conditioned as much as it is natural. The ruling-class handbook, Machiavelli's *The Prince*, made it clear: "Since love and fear can hardly exist together, if we must choose between them, it is far safer to be feared than loved."

The idea of apocalypse is a central tenet of human society. We've been taught about Armageddon, Kali Yuga, Judgement Day, Yawm ad-Dīn, nuclear holocaust, the end times, the four horsemen, and the Sermon of the Seven Suns. Hierarchical societal arrangements leave us feeling powerless. Exploitative systems like capitalism leave us feeling hopeless. And the widespread deployment of fear ultimately keeps us in our place, and out of the business of those who own our worlds.

The last half-century has brought us the zombie apocalypse - a fictional world where the human race has largely been transformed into a brainless, subhuman horde of flesh-eaters, with only a few random survivors left to carve out any semblance of life they can find in a barren landscape. The emergence and immense popularity of the TV show *The Walking Dead* is the latest, and perhaps most influential, piece in a long line of narratives centered within themes of survival, human interaction, and scarcity.

Human Nature and Interaction

Behind all political battles, social critiques, and theoretical inquiries lies the most fundamental question: when left to our own accord, how will we interact with one another? How one answers this question usually goes a long way to how one perceives the world, and how issues are viewed and opinions are formed. To our dismay, potential answers are typically presented in dualities. Are we good or evil? Competitive or cooperative? Generous or greedy? Violent or peaceful?

A common theme among religion has been that human beings are "born into sin" and heavily influenced by "evil forces" to do harmful things. One who embraces this theme will tend to have less faith in humanity than one who does not. For, if we really are engaging in a daily struggle to resist the powers of evil, it is reasonable to assume that evil will take hold of many. How can we trust anyone who, at a moment's notice, could potentially lose the ability to act on their own conscience? The common theme of our dominant economic system - capitalism - is that human beings are inherently competitive and self-centered. When combined, it is easy to see how such ideologies may create intensely authoritative and hierarchical systems. After all, people who are influenced by strong and evil metaphysical forces while also being drawn toward callous, self-interest certainly cannot be trusted with free will. This lesson is drilled deep into our psyches with each episode of *The Walking Dead*, where the potential threat of flesh-eating zombie hordes become an afterthought to the clear and present danger of "evil" humans who are out to get one another. Whether it's a sadistic governor charming an entire town with violent gladiator events, an outlaw gang with the obligatory pedophile, or a pack of hipster cannibals salivating at the thought of eating their next visitor, the intended theme is clear - human beings are not capable of co-existing, even in a world where they rarely interact.

But is this idea accurate? Are we really drawn toward conflict? Must we compete with one another to survive? Is it appropriate to apply Darwin's evolutionary theories in a social sense where the "fit" are meant to gain wealth and power over the "weak"? Or are we, as Peter Kropotkin theorized in his classic*Mutual Aid*, more inclined to mimic most other species on Earth, which have been observed over the course of centuries to exhibit "Mutual Aid and Mutual Support carried on to an extent which made me suspect in it a feature of the greatest importance for the maintenance of life, the preservation of each species, and its further evolution?"

There is ample evidence that we are drawn to cooperation. "Caring about others is part of our mammalian heritage, and humans take this ability to a high level," explains neuroscientist Sandra Aamodt. "Helping other people seems to be our default approach, in the sense that we're more likely to do it when we don't have time to think a situation through before acting. After a conflict, we and other primates-including our famously aggressive relatives, the chimpanzees-have many ways to reconcile and repair relationships." Studies have shown that in the first year of life, infants exhibit empathy toward others in distress. Evolutionary Anthropologist Michael Tomasello has put "the concept of cooperation as an evolutionary imperative to the test with very young children, to see if it holds for our nature and not just our nurture. Drop something in front of a two-year-old, he finds, and she is likely to pick it up for you. This is not just learned behavior, he argues. Young children are naturally cooperative."

So, if we are truly inclined to cooperate with one another, why is there so much division and turmoil in the world? The answer to this question may be found by assessing not only the mechanisms of capitalism, but more importantly in the creation of artificial scarcity as a means to maintain hierarchies.

Capitalism and Artificial Scarcity

It is no secret that capitalism thrives off exploitation. It needs a large majority of people to be completely reliant on their labor power. It needs private property to be accessible to only a few, so that they may utilize it as a social relationship where the rented majority can labor and create value. It needs capital to be accessible to only a few, so that they may regenerate and reinvest said capital in a perpetual manner. And it needs a considerable population of the impoverished and unemployed - "a reserve army of labor," as Marx put it - in order to create a "demand" for labor and thus make such exploitative positions "competitive" to those who need to partake in them to merely survive. It needs these things in order to stay intact - something that is desirable to the **85 richest people in the world who own more than half of the world's entire population (3.6 billion people)**.

But wealth accumulation through alienation and exploitation is not enough in itself. The system also needs to create scarcity where it does not already exist. Even Marx admitted that capitalism has given us the productive capacity to provide all that is needed for the global population. In other words, capitalism has proven that scarcity does not exist. And, over the years, technology has confirmed this. But, in order for capitalism to survive, scarcity must exist, even if through artificial means. This is a necessary

471

component on multiple fronts, including the pricing of commodities, the enhancement of wealth, and the need to inject a high degree of competition among people (who are naturally inclined to cooperation).

Since capitalism is based in the buying and selling of commodities, its lifeblood is production. And since production in a capitalist system is not based on *need*, but rather on *demand*, it has the tendency to produce more than it can sell. This is called overproduction. Michael Roberts <u>explains</u>:

Overproduction is when capitalists produce too much compared to the demand for things or services. Suddenly capitalists build up stocks of things they cannot sell, they have factories with too much capacity compared to demand and they have too many workers than they need. So they close down plant, slash the workforce and even just liquidate the whole business. That is a capitalist crisis.

When overproduction occurs, it must be addressed. There are multiple ways to do this. Marx addressed three options: "On the one hand by enforced destruction of a mass of productive forces; on the other, by the conquest of new markets, and by the more thorough exploitation of the old ones." Another is through the destruction of excess capital and commodities. Whichever measure is taken, it is paramount that the economy <u>must emerge</u> from a starting point that is different from the ending point where the crisis began. This is accomplished through creating scarcity, whether in regards to labor, production capacity, or commodities and basic needs.

Maintaining scarcity is also necessary for wealth enhancement. It is not enough that accumulation flows to a very small section of the population, but more so that a considerable portion of the population is faced with the inherent struggles related to inaccessibility. For example, if millions of people are unable to access basic needs such as food, clothing, shelter, and healthcare, the commodification of those needs becomes all the more effective. On the flip side, the mere presence of accessibility - or wealth - which is enjoyed by the elite becomes all the more valuable because it is highly sought after.

In this sense, it is not the accumulation of personal wealth that creates advantageous positions on the socioeconomic ladder; it's the impoverishment of the majority. Allowing human beings access to basic necessities would essentially destroy the allure (and thus, power) of wealth and the coercive nature of forced participation. This effect is maintained through artificial scarcity - the coordinated withholding of basic needs from the majority. These measures also seek to create a predatory landscape - something akin to a post-apocalyptic, zombie-filled world where manufactured scarcity pits poor against poor and worker against worker, all the while pulling attention away from the zombie threat.

Control through Commodification

A crucial part of this process is commodification - the "transformation of goods and services, as well as ideas or other entities that normally may not be considered goods, into commodities" that can be bought, sold, used and discarded. The most important transformation is that of the working-class majority who, without the means to sustain on their own, are left with a choice between (1) laboring to create wealth for a small minority and accepting whatever "wages" are provided, or (2) starving. In The Socioeconomic Guardians of Scarcity, Philip Richlin tells us that:

"When society deprives any community or individual of the necessities of life, there is a form of violence happening. When society commodifies the bare necessities of life, they are commodifying human beings, whose labor can be bought and sold. Underneath the pseudo-philosophical rationalizations for capitalism is a defense of wage slavery. For, if your labor is for sale, then you are for sale."

We are for sale, and we sell ourselves everyday - in the hopes of acquiring a wage that allows us to eat, sleep, and feed our families. In the United States, the 46 million people living in poverty haven't been so lucky. The 2.5 million who have defaulted on their student loans have been discarded. The 49 million who suffer from food insecurity have lost hope. The 3.5 million homeless are mocked by 18.6 million vacant homes. And the 22 million who are unemployed or underemployed have been deemed "unfit commodities" and relegated to the reserve army of labor.

The control aspect of the commodification of labor comes in its dehumanizing effect - an effect that was commonly recognized among 18th and 19th century thinkers. One of those thinkers, Wilhelm Von Humboldt, when referring to the role of a wage laborer, explained "as whatever does not spring from a man's free choice, or is only the result of instruction and guidance, does not enter into his very nature; he does not perform it with truly human energies, but merely with mechanical exactness, suggesting that "we may admire what he (the laborer) does, but we despise what he is," because he is essentially not human.

The worker, in her or his role in the capital-labor relationship, exists in a position of constant degeneration. This is especially true with the onset of mass production lines and the division of labor - both of which are inevitable elements within this system. "As the division of labor increases, labor is simplified," Marx tells us. "The special skill of the worker becomes worthless. He becomes transformed into a simple, monotonous productive force that does not have to use intense bodily or intellectual faculties. His labor becomes a labor that anyone can perform." As automation and technology progress, such specialized task-mastering even seeps into what was once considered "skilled" labor, thus broadening its reach.

In this role, workers are firmly placed into positions of control within a highly authoritative and hierarchical system.

A World beyond Profit

Dystopian narratives are no longer fiction. From birth, we are corralled into a system that scoffs at free will, stymies our creative and productive capacities, and leaves us little room to carve our own paths. The constructs directed from above are designed to strip us of our inclination to care and cooperate, and make us accept the need to step over one another to get ahead. This is not our nature. Whether we're talking about Kropotkin's studies in "the wild" or Tomasello's experience with children, observable evidence tells us we've been duped.

Another world is not just possible; it is inevitable if we are to exist in the long-term. In *Post-Scarcity Anarchism*, Murray Bookchin offers a glimpse into this world not constructed on labor, profit, and artificial scarcity:

"It is easy to foresee a time, by no means remote, when a rationally organized economy could automatically manufacture small "packaged" factories without human labor; parts could be produced with so little effort that most maintenance tasks would be reduced to the simple act of removing a defective unit from a machine and replacing it by another-a job no more difficult than pulling out and putting in a tray. Machines would make and repair most of the machines required to maintain such a highly industrialized economy. Such a technology, oriented entirely toward human needs and freed from all consideration of profit and loss, would eliminate the pain of want and toil-the penalty, inflicted in the form of denial, suffering and inhumanity, exacted by a society based on scarcity and labor."

The barren landscape for which we've been placed has a future beyond Hershel's overrun farm, the confines of a prison, the Governor's creepy town of Woodbury, and the trap known as Terminus. It has a future beyond the artificial constructs of capitalism and hierarchy. Human nature is talking to us... and we're starting to listen.

Competing Visions in Economics as a Social Science
A Primer

David Fields

Economics (indeed every discipline of the social sciences) has never been, and never will be, value-free. Social scientists have always relied, and will continue to rely, on sets of elaborate positions, perceptions, and views about the ultimate nature of reality; essentially, it is the reliance on preconceived notions of how the world works, and how it should work, when analyzing manifest phenomena. Aspects of conscientiousness precede investigation and thus one cannot separate the knowing mind from the object inquiry. What constitutes a fact perceives the observation and hence the conception of what is determined as socially significant; the mind is active in constructing and determining the lens through which observation deciphers what of social phenomena is worthy of factuality.

All theorizing is based on first order principles (Lawson, 1989). Thus, what underlie all theories of human behavior are general apperceptions and ideological convictions of the relationship between the individual and society. They are epistemological foundations-what Joseph Schumpeter labeled as 'preanalytical visions'-which dictate modes of examination and inquisition. Hence, different pre-analytical visions predispose the focusing on different social and economic problems and lead to entirely different attitudes towards social settings and human actions within those settings (Hunt, 1983). Preanalytical visions have pertinent implications for normative assessments of the human condition. In economic theory, there are two distinct preanalytical visions with differing ethical implications-propositions associated with the neoclassical theory of value and those with the labor theory value. Both perspectives aim to apprehend how commodities obtain their value and where and how that value is determined and expressed in society.

The neoclassical preanalytical conception of the human being is that of the single-minded seeker of maximum utility (pleasure with respect to cost-benefit analysis and bounded rationality). This perspective perceives that the nature of individual preference orderings, with respect to consumption, is taken as given (more like taken for granted) and primary, without regard to agency and the social institutions and processes within which likes and dislikes are formed (Hunt, 1983.) The surrounding within which individual actions take place is conceived as an endless array of opportunity costs for the attainment of constrained optimization. Categorical positions such as class, gender, and race are systematically negated in favor of centering attention on the (rather fictitious) assumption that society is based upon isolated exchangers/producers maximizing pleasure with initial endowments given by the Malthusian notion of the natural lottery of life. The only way in which human sociality appears is in individual needs for other entities with whom to exchange. In this sense, all economic theory is exchange theory.

478

Neoclassical economics determines the value of a commodity on the basis of utility derived from it. The more utility that one derives from consuming a commodity, the higher would be its value. Utilitarianism is the underpinning of the theory, which holds this value to be the true value despite the fact that pleasure, is an entirely subjective feeling that varies from consumer to consumer. The theory holds that when commodity A is exchanged for commodity B, the ratio in which the exchange occurs is determined by marginal utility (MU) derived by consuming the last units of commodity A and B. The crucial point is that the origin of value lies essentially in the institution of the market since this is the arena where isolated individual exchanges occur. Hence, the successful functioning of markets reveals how the values of commodities reflect their true values because free market exchanges are seen as complete contracts.

This ideation of utilitarianism does not question the social origins of conscious human desires. The Benthamite dictum that nature places mankind under the governance of two sovereign masters-pain and pleasure-reigns supreme. The issue of whether or not desires are exclusively metaphysically given is completely ignored. Human beings are simply assumed to be sophisticated calculating maximizers of utility. Hence, it is understood that exertions of work by individuals are never undertaken without the promise (with respect to consumption) of greater pleasure or the avoidance of greater pain (Hunt, 2001: 132). Differing social and cultural contexts make no difference whatsoever.

In this sense, neoclassical economics rests on the notion that Robison Crusoe is the natural, universal, pervasive unalterable characteristic of all human beings in all societies. The aim is to demonstrate how the competitive capitalist economy automatically obtains efficient situations in which it is impossible to make one person better off without necessarily making someone else worse off whereby unique organizations of production, exchange and distribution lead to maximum attainable social welfare. Situations of conflict are defined away; situations where improving the lot of one unit is not opposed by other naturally antagonistic units are rare within this view. Since the level of analysis is on rational calculating individual units and not social units, how can changes that might make some better off without making others worse be discerned? It precludes the scientific evaluation of the degree to which existing desires reflect underlying universal human needs and the particular sets of social institutions that enhance the necessary capabilities for which these human needs can be met (Hunt, 2005).

In addition, the most essential differentiating feature of capitalism-private property-is viewed as eternal, universal, and inherently just (Hunt, 2005). It absolves capitalism of all the exploitation that is undertaken to produce and make profits. Total income of society is produced and distributed simply by some sort of 'natural law'. Thus, if workers have appropriate moral virtues and exercise responsibility, jurisprudence, self-control, and unremitting hard work, they can easily become entrepreneurs and accumulate capital.

Heterodox economics, on the other hand, examines the welfare of human beings through a lens that accentuates and exhibits interconnections. Within this preanalytical vision, it is appropriate to speak of systems of human behavior and visualize modes of productions that govern how human beings relate each other at historically specific times in the process of extracting from nature the means for human survival.

Starting with an analytical framework that invokes recognition of specific modes of production, we have the capacity elucidate the underlying processes that actually govern how the products of labor are distributed and how labor in general is assigned to specific technical processes. From this perspective, we can visualize historically specific modes of political power gives us the means that detail the apparent characteristics of social decision-making and the ordering of rights, privileges and responsibilities.

In contrast to utilitarianism of neoclassical economics, heterodox economics understands human beings distinctly as producers and focuses on the fact that the starting point of any theory is the recognition that that in all societies the process of production can be reduced to series of human exertions. It is ascertained that humans, unlike animals, generally cannot survive without exerting effort transforming natural environments into more suitable living spaces. Where utilitarianism sees humans in individualistic terms where there is no difference between exchanging with nature and exchanging with other human beings, heterodox economics sees human beings as cooperative social beings dependent on each other for human survival.

Since capitalism directs production solely for the impersonal institution of the market, interdependent labor is indirectly social. To illustrate this, Karl Marx noted:

Under the rural patriarchal system of production, when spinner and weaver lived under the same roof-the women of the family spinning and the men weaving, say for the requirements of the family-yarn and linen were social products, and spinning and weaving social labor within the framework of the family. But their social character did not appear in the form of yarn becoming a universal character exchanged for linen as a universal equivalent, i.e., of two products exchanging for each other as equal and equally valid expressions of the same universal labor time [as it w would be the case under capitalism]. On the contrary, the product of labor bore the specific social imprint of the family relationship with its naturally evolved division of labor. Or let us take the services and dues in kind of the Middle Ages. It was the distinct labor of the individual in its original form, the particular features of his labor and not its universal aspect that formed the social ties at that time. Or finally let us take communal labor in its spontaneously evolved form as we find it among all civilized nations at the dawn of their history. In this case the social character of labor is evidently not affected by the labor of the individual assuming the abstract form of universal labor...The communal system on which this mode of production is based prevents the labor of an individual from becoming private labor and his product the private product of a individual; it causes individual labor to appear rather as the direct function of a member of the social organization (cited in Hunt, 1991).

In addition,

As a general rule, articles of utility become commodities only because they are products of the labor of private individuals or groups of individuals who carry on their work independently of each other [in capitalism]. The sum total of the entire labor of these private individuals forms the aggregate labor of society. Since the producers do not come into social contact with each other until they exchange their products, the specific social character of each producer's labor does not show itself except in the act of exchange. In other words, the labor of the individual asserts itself as a part of the labor of society, only by means of the relations which the act of exchange establishes directly between the products, and indirectly, through them, between the producers. To the latter, therefore, the relations connecting the labor of one individual with that of the rest appear, not as direct social relations between individuals at work, but as...social relations between things (cited in Hunt, 1991).

Heterodox economics exposes the true nature of social organization under capitalism that leads to extraordinarily pernicious effects on workers. The capitalist market systematically prevents many from developing real conscious desires that reflect potentialities for self-realization and self-appreciation, i.e. become "emotionally, intellectually, esthetically developed human beings" (Hunt, 2002:242). Human senses are shaped and refined through working and transforming nature into useful things. It is through one's relations with what one produces that an individual achieves pleasure and satisfaction. Through visible direct interdependent social production, recognitions of one's ability, dexterity, and talent are palpable. Under capitalism, however, the scenario is quite different:

The bourgeoisie, wherever it has got the upper hand, has put an end to all [...] idyllic relations. It has pitilessly torn asunder the motley [...] ties [...], and has left remaining no other nexus between man and man than naked self-interest, than callous cash payment. It has drowned the most heavenly ecstasies of religious fervor, of chivalrous enthusiasm, of philosophical sentimentalism, in the icy water of egoistical calculation. It has resolved personal worth into exchange value (cited in Hunt, 2002: 242).

This social organization of production is not oriented to human needs and aspirations, but rather by profit calculations estimated by legally protected extortionists (capitalists, or the bourgeoisie). The effects are total and degradation and total dehumanization of working-class people where they are reduced to nothing but disconnected brutes engaged in simple animal functions, not developing freely their physical and mental capacities. Capitalism, as such, is the accumulation of wealth at one pole, and the accumulation of misery, agony of toil, slavery, ignorance, brutality, and mental degradation at the opposite pole (Hunt, 2002: 244).

Heterodox economic analysis make it apparent whether or not society meets basic human needs and are translated into realized conscious desires for higher stages of human development. It shows that with a materialist approach to the study how humans relate to each other and organize to produce what is necessary for survival one can justifiably assert whether certain systems of human behavior do, in fact, generate the conditions for social harmony.

In hindsight, it is nearly impossible (if not completely impossible) to formulate egalitarian economic and social policies based on neoclassical ontology and epistemology. Perspectives that only consider market exchange, with a reductionist sense of human desire, systematically disregard the social nature of production; in the final instance, they effectively negate clear understandings of the totality of socioeconomic inequity (Campbell, 2010).

This analysis does not cover the social nature of money; as such, it is worthwhile for the reader to refer to the following:

Bellofiore, R. 1989. "A Monetary Labor Theory of Value." *Review of Radical Political Economics* 21(1-2):1-25.

Hein, Eckhard. 2006. "Money, Interest and Capital Accumulation in Karl Marx's Economics: A Monetary Interpretation and Some Similarities to Post-Keynesian Approaches *:" *The European Journal of the History of Economic Thought* 13(1):113-40.

Hein, E. 2008. "Marxian and Post-Keynesian Theory-Similarities and Differences Part 2: Monetary Analysis in Marx and Similarities to Post-Keynesian Approaches." Berlin, Germany. Retrieved June 9, 2014 (http://www.boeckler.de/pdf/v_2008_07_27_hein_lecture.pdf).

Ingham, G. 1996. "Money Is a Social Relation." *Review of Social Economy* 54(4):507-29.

Ingham, G. 1996. "Some Recent Changes in the Relationship between Economics and Sociology."*Cambridge Journal of Economics* 20(2):243-75.

Ingham, G. 1999. "Capitalism, Money and Banking: A Critique of Recent Historical Sociology." *The British Journal of Sociology* 50(1):76-96.

Ingham, Geoffrey. n.d. "The Ontology of Money." *TWILL*. Retrieved May 3, 2014 (http://www.twill.info/wp-content/uploads/2013/03/The_ontology_of_money.pdf).

Works Cited

Arge, R. C. and E.K. Hunt. 1971. "Environmental Pollution, Externalities, and Conventional Economic Wisdom: A Critique." *Envtl. Aff.* 1:266.

Campbell, Al. 2010. "Marx and Engels' Vision of a Better Society." *Forum for Social Economics*39(3):269-78.

Foley, Duncan. 2004. "Rationality and Ideology in Economics." *Social Research: An International Quarterly* 71(2):329-42.

Hunt, E. K. 2005. "The Normative Foundations of Social Theory: An Essay on the Criteria Defining Social Economics." *Review of Social Economy* 63(3):423-45.

Hunt, E.K. 2002. *History of Economic Thought*. 2nd Ed., Armonk, NY: M.E Sharpe.

Hunt, E.K. 1991."The Role of Value Theory in the History of Thought," in Hunt, E.K and Rajani K. Kanth. *Explorations in Political Economy*. Savage, MD: Rowman & Littlefield Publishers, Inc.

Hunt, E. K. 1983. "Joan Robinson and the Labour Theory of Value." *Cambridge Journal of Economics*7:331-42.

Lawson, Tony. 1989. "Abstraction, Tendencies and Stylised Facts: A Realist Approach to Economic Analysis." *Cambridge Journal of Economics* 13:59-78.

Monopoly Capitalism in the Twenty-First Century
Neoliberalism, Monetarism, and the Pervasion of Finance

Colin Jenkins

The following is the third part of a multi-part series, "Applying Poulantzas," which analyzes the work of Greek Marxist political sociologist, Nicos Poulantzas, and applies it to the unique political and economic structures found under neoliberalism and post-industrial capitalism.

With industrial or "competitive capitalism," it was the "separation and dispossession of the direct producers (the working class) from their means of production" which created this multi-layered, class-based societal structure. [1] Globalization has resulted in a massive shift of national economies. Former industrialized nations are now considered "post-industrial" due to the ability of large production-based manufacturers to move their operations into "cheaper" labor markets. International and regional trade agreements have facilitated this shift. With post-industrial capitalism and the widespread destruction of "productive labor," or labor that produces a tangible product and is thus exploited through the creation of surplus value, it is the complete reliance on a service economy which produces no tangible value that allows for strict control through wage manipulation. The ways in which the working class interacts with the owning class has changed significantly, if only in regards to their physical worlds. In the US, financialization has replaced industrialization as the main economic driver. Alongside this shift, monopoly capitalism has effectively replaced "competitive capitalism," and globalization has ushered in the neoliberal era. These developments have rearranged the superstructure and forced capitalist states to develop new methods in maintaining a societal equilibrium that is constantly being pushed to the brink of unrest at the hands of a capitalist system that breeds concentrations in wealth and power, while simultaneously driving the working-class majority towards a state of functional serfdom.

The emergence of monopoly capitalism was inevitable. "The battle of competition is fought by cheapening of commodities," explained Marx. "The cheapness of commodities depends, ceteris paribus, on the productiveness of labor, and this again on the scale of production. Therefore the larger capitals beat the smaller."[2] Whether we are referring to technology and automation, the relation of finance and the varying degrees of access to capital, or merely the all-encompassing process of "cheapening commodities" which Marx refers to above, it all works in tandem to create a funneling effect whereas capital becomes concentrated. And with this concentration of capital comes the concentration of wealth, which in turn inevitably breeds concentrations of other forms of power, i.e. political. In this sense, what many have come to refer to as "corporatism" is more correctly viewed as a mature stage of capitalism, rather than a differentiation from capitalism. The "marriage of corporation and state" that Benito Mussolini once referred to is merely a byproduct of capitalist advancement - the natural consequence of concentrated interests relying on the state apparatus to both facilitate its progression and protect its assets. The consequent development of financialization could also be seen as an inevitable late stage of capitalism. As Paul Sweezy explains, while paraphrasing Marx, "Further, the credit system which 'begins as a modest helper of accumulation' soon 'becomes a new and formidable weapon in the competition in the competitive struggle, and finally it transforms itself into an immense social mechanism for the centralization of capitals.'"[3]

In the US, the creation of the Federal Reserve and the use of government-approved, macroeconomic policy-making has been a crucial tool in maintaining the equilibrium that is a central theme of Poulantzas' work. It has, in a sense, represented a Captain's wheel on a chaotic ship rolling over rough seas. The Keynesian model that dominated the American landscape from the late-1930s until the late-1970s relied on fiscal policy to supplement private sector instability, mainly by stimulating and supplementing this sector through infusions of money.

A shift to monetarism in the late-1970s paralleled the arrival of the neoliberal era, an intensification of privatization, and deregulation. While the all-encompassing policy-direction found under neoliberalism extended into the geopolitical realm to include "free trade" agreements and far-reaching international policies directed by the IMF and World Bank, it was this newfound reliance on monetary policy that created more ground between the standard operations of capitalist economy and the development of a "corporate-fascistic model." In other words, it allowed for greater returns on corporate profit in spite of wage stagnation, an overall degeneration of employment, increased poverty, and a consequent decline in expendable (consumer) income from within the working class. With regards to the equilibrium, direct manipulation of the money supply has allowed for a tightly-controlled mechanism that safeguards this extension and intensification of systemic inequities. Neoliberal economist Milton Friedman echoed the call for monetarism through his analysis of the Great Depression:
"The Fed was largely responsible for converting what might have been a garden-variety recession, although perhaps a fairly severe one, into a major catastrophe. Instead of using its powers to offset the depression, it presided over a decline in the quantity of money by one-third from 1929 to 1933 ... Far from the depression being a

failure of the free-enterprise system; it was a tragic failure of government." [4]

Friedman's assessment wasn't critical of the existence of the Fed, or even of the Fed's ability to manipulate the money supply, but rather quite the opposite; it was critical of the Fed's failure to increase the money supply in times of crisis. In this sense, Monetarists did not oppose the Keynesian approach of intervention, but rather the nature of that intervention -fiscal policy (government spending) versus monetary policy (Quantity Theory of Money). The former provides money to the government, which in turn creates public programs and/or increases public spending that directly affects the population. The latter provides money to the financial industry and/or government, which in turn provides money to "power players" (corporate interests, big business, bank bailouts, etc...) in the hopes that such money will make its way through the population, hence "trickle down." Modern monetarism (Post-2008 financial crisis) has intensified through multiple bouts of QE (Quantitative Easing), which has reaped tremendous growth for the financial industry and big business (see the Dow Jones Industrial Average) while having no positive effect on the population, which continues to struggle through stagnation, chronic unemployment, and impoverishment.

It is no surprise that financialization found a perfect bedfellow in neoliberalism. "The neo-liberal bias towards de-regulation, which widened the space for financialization, was more often linked to an institutional fix that relied (and still relies) on 'unusual deals with political authority', predatory capitalism, and reckless speculation - all of which have fuelled the global financial crisis," explains Bob Jessop. "As the limits to 'more market, less state' emerged, there was growing resort to flanking and supporting measures to keep the neo-liberal show on the road. This was reflected in the discourse and policies of the ' Third Way ', which maintained the course of neo-liberalization in new circumstances, and is linked to the North Atlantic Financial Crisis (witness its eruption under 'New Labour' in Britain as well as the Bush Administration in the USA)." [5]

While conducted and carried out on different spheres, and for different reasons, financialization and expansionary monetary policy have emerged in parallel to one another. Because of this, they have maintained a loose relationship in the era of neoliberalism, with one (financialization) creating massive rifts and chaotic patterns of accumulation, and the other (monetary policy) attempting to manage the aftermath of this chaos. This has added yet another element to what Poulantzas saw as the inevitable rise of the authoritarian nature of State Monopoly Capitalism (SMC), whereas the capitalist state is forced to become more and more involved in maintaining equilibrium. In the economic realm, this amounts to monetary policy; in the political realm, this amounts to steadying the superstructure (balancing austerity measures with the welfare state); and in the social realm, this amounts to increased militarization of domestic police forces and a gradual erosion of civil liberties, features that become necessary when society's equilibrium is pushed toward a breaking point (civil unrest).

In the era of finance-dominated accumulation, and especially following periodic, systemic crises, governments have extended their reach to deal with unprecedented volatility. This was seen following the financial crisis of 2008-09, as capitalist states the world over scrambled to right their ships which had been steered into a perfect storm of financialized accumulation (many guided by illegal schemes; see the mortgage-backed securities scandal). Since then, it has become commonplace for governments, through monetary policy, to "intervene periodically to underwrite the solvency of banks, to provide extraordinary liquidity and to guarantee the deposits of the public with banks." [6] This is not to suggest that government intervention in the capitalist system is a new phenomenon; only that its methods have changed as capitalism has changed. Poulantzas explains:

"In the competitive capitalist stage, the capitalist state (the liberal state) always played an economic role; the image of the liberal state being simply the gendarme or night watchman of a capitalism

490

that 'worked by itself' is a complete myth... From taxation through to factory legislation, from customs duties to the construction of economic infrastructure such as railways, the liberal state always performed significant economic functions..." [7]

With monopoly capitalism and the onset of financialization, the tendency toward extreme developments in both accumulations of the dominant classes and dispossession of the dominated classes requires higher degrees of state intervention. These interventions inevitably extend far beyond the economic base. Poulantzas contrasts this development with its former stage of 'competitive capitalism':

"If it is possible to speak of a specific non-intervention of this state into the economy, this is only in order to contrast it with the role of the state in the stage of monopoly capitalism, the 'interventionist state' which Lenin already had in mind in his analysis of imperialism. The difference between this and the state of competitive capitalism is not, as we shall see, a mere quantitative one. In the stage of monopoly capitalism, the role of the state in its decisive intervention into the economy is not restricted essentially to the reproduction of what Engels termed the 'general conditions' of the production of surplus-value; the state is also involved in the actual process of the extended reproduction of capital as a social relation." [8]

The emergence of expansionary monetary policy, most notably in the US Federal Reserve's use of Quantitative Easing, has become the go-to method of addressing the chaotic effects of financialization. This has become a necessary component for embedded capitalist interests that have taken advantage of a system that privatizes gains and publicizes losses. For the working classes, the reliance on consumer credit for not only luxury goods but necessities has illustrated how financialization has penetrated everyday life. To the former industrialized working classes (like that in the US), this is due to the emergence of both globalization and neoliberalism, which "favour exchange- over use-value" and "treat workers as disposable and substitutable factors of production," and "the wage (including the social wage) as a cost of (international) production." [9]

The permeation of this trifecta (Globalization, Neoliberalism, and Financialization) is not lost on the working classes. "Neoliberalism tends to promote financialization, both as a strategic objective and as an inevitable outcome," Jessop writes. "As this process expands and penetrates deeper into the social and natural world, it transforms the micro-, meso- and macro-dynamics of capitalist economies." [10] For the economic base and its power players, the state's use of expansionary monetary policy becomes a lifeboat, providing eternal life to corporate accumulation. For the working-class majority, whose existence is more and more precarious due to declining wages, consumer credit (often predatory) becomes a necessity to satisfy basic needs. Jessop concludes:

"The primary aspect of the wage is its treatment as a cost of (global) production rather than as a source of (domestic) demand; this is linked to re-commodification of social welfare in housing, pensions, higher education, health insurance, and so on. This leads to growing flexibility of wage labour (especially increasing precarization), downward pressure on wages and working conditions, and cuts in the residual social wage. A further result is the financialization of everyday life as the labour force turns to credit (and usury) to maintain its standard of living and to provide for its daily, life-course, and intergenerational reproduction. Combined with the increased returns to profit-producing and interest-bearing capital, this also intensifies income and wealth inequalities in the economies subject to finance-dominated accumulation, which now match or exceed their levels in just before the 1929 Crash (Elsner 2012; Saez 2013)." [11]

Monopoly capitalism in the 21st century has become ever more reliant on capitalist states to serve as facilitators, protectors, and a damage control mechanism. Former industrialized nations have shifted the remnants of "competitive capitalism" to global labor markets (which are also state-supplemented) and replaced them with service-sector economies based in finance schemes that seek to reproduce "fictitious capital" at alarming rates. Capitalist states, in adjusting to this shift, have embraced expansionary monetary policy as a means to address the ensuing chaos by supplementing and protecting financial institutions (the dominant classes in the age of neoliberalism/financialization). Will the volatility created by this shift finally bring capitalism to its breaking point? Will the prospect of automation force governments to develop radically new welfare states that include basic income guarantees? Will highly-exploited, global labor markets radicalize and collectivize, and bring the neoliberal era to its knees? The future brings many questions.

Notes

[1] Poulantzas. Classes in Contemporary Capitalism. Verso, 1978, pp. 97-98.
[2] Marx, Karl. Capital, Volume 3. Moscow: Progress Publishers, 1894.
[3] Sweezy, Paul M. "Monopoly Capital." Monthly Review, Volume 56, Issue 5. October 2004.
[4] Friedman, Milton & Friedman, Rose. Two Lucky People: Memoirs, University of Chicago Press, 1998.
[5] 'Finance-dominated accumulation and post-democratic capitalism', in S. Fadda and P. Tridico, eds, Institutions and Economic Development after the Financial Crisis, London: Routledge, 83-105, 2013.
[6] *Lapavitsas, C. (2013) Profiting without Producing: How Finance Exploits All, London: Verso.*
[7] *Classes in Contemporary Capitalism, p. 100.*
[8] Ibid. p. 100.
[9] Bob Jessop. (April 1, 2014) "Finance-Dominated Accumulation and Post-Democratic Capitalism."

http://bobjessop.org/2014/04/01/finance-dominated-accumulation-and-post-democratic-capitalism/
[10] Jessop, 2014.
[11] Jessop, 2014.

Works Cited

Elsner, W. (2012) 'Financial capitalism - at odds with democracy: The trap of an "impossible" profit rate', Real-World Economics Review, 62: 132-159.http://www.paecon.net/PAEReview/issue62/Elsner62.pdf
Saez, E. (2013) 'Striking it richer: The evolution of top incomes in the United States (Updated with 2011 estimates)', at http://elsa.berkeley.edu/~saez/.

Social Movement Studies

The Universal and the Particular
Chomsky, Foucault, and Post-New Left Political Discourse

Derek Alan Ide

Postmodern theory was a relatively recent intellectual phenomenon in 1971 when Noam Chomsky and Michel Foucault sat down to discuss a wide range of topics, including the nature of justice, power, and intellectual inquiry. At one point Chomsky, who Peter Novick suggests as an example of left-wing empiricism in post-war academia, engages the concrete issue of social activism and invokes the notion of "justice," to which Foucault asks poignantly: "When, in the United States, you commit an illegal act, do you justify it in terms of justice or of a superior legality, or do you justify it by the necessity of the class struggle, which is at the present time essential for the proletariat in their struggle against the ruling class?" After a brief period he quickly reiterates the question again: "Are you committing this act in virtue of an ideal justice, or because the class struggle makes it useful and necessary?" Chomsky attempts to situate a notion of justice within international law, to which Foucault replies: "I will be a little bit

Nietzschean about this... the idea of justice in itself is an idea which in effect has been invented and put to work in different types of societies as an instrument of a certain political and economic power or as a weapon against that power... And in a classless society, I am not sure that we would still use this notion of justice." In other words, for Foucault justice is only intelligible within a relative framework of class antagonisms. Meanings of justice may differ, but they are only understandable vis-à-vis certain class positions. Chomsky responds: "Well, here I really disagree. I think there is some sort of an absolute basis--if you press me too hard I'll be in trouble, because I can't sketch it out-ultimately residing in fundamental human qualities, in terms of which a 'real' notion of justice is grounded."[1]

Foucault's position appears correct, at least on the surface, because it is deeply rooted in the recognition of class-based power, hegemony, and contestation. Chomsky, on the other hand, has trouble sketching out any "pure form" or "absolute basis" of justice. Instead, it appears to be an abstraction to which he has some, perhaps understandably, visceral attachment. Yet, Foucault's position seems at odds with the stance that Patricia O'Brien attributes to him when she explains that, for Foucault, "culture is studied through technologies of power-not class, not progress, not the indomitability of the human spirit. Power cannot be apprehended through the study of conflict, struggle, and resistance... Power is not characteristic of a class (the bourgeoisie) or a ruling elite, nor is it attributable to one... Power does not originate in either the economy or politics, and it is not grounded there."[2] Instead, it is an "infinitely complex network of 'micro-powers,' of power relations that permeate every aspect of social life."[3]

In one way, the adoption by "critical" leftists (the proliferation of critical race theory, whiteness studies, etc. may be a reflection of this) of this notion that power is an "infinitely complex network of micro-powers" may help to explain the rise of the post-New Left vocabulary and the political orientation of those who engage in privilege discourse. Thus, institutional "oppression" as a "pattern of persistent and systematic disadvantage imposed on large groups of people" becomes sublimated by "privilege," where the criticism is centered on "set of unearned benefits that some individuals enjoy (and others are denied) in their everyday lives." Likewise, "liberation," referring to ultimate victory against systems of exploitation and oppression, is abandoned in favor of fighting for "safe spaces," where "the attempt to create occasions or locations wherein the adverse effects of privilege on marginalized people are minimized in everyday interpersonal interactions."[4] Thus, Joyce Appleby, Lynn Hunt, and Margaret Jacob characterize postmodernists as "deeply disillusioned intellectuals who denounce en masse Marxism and liberal humanism, communism and capitalism, and all expectations of liberation."[5] The persistence of postmodernist intellectual parameters on the post-New Left political discourse could not be clearer.

What O'Brien says is "most challenging of all is the realization that power creates truth and hence its own legitimation," [6] a position which seemingly aligns with Foucault's comment to Chomsky that justice is an "invented idea...put to work in different types of societies as an instrument of a certain political and economic power or as a weapon against that power." The notion that "power is not characteristic of a class" or that it "does not originate in either the economy or politics" seems far from the position Foucault takes when discussing the issue of justice and class power with Chomsky. Thus, at best one finds a level of disconnect between Foucault's position a la O'Brien and the position he seemed to be articulating vis-à-vis Chomsky. At times it seems that Foucault is even at odds with himself. Contradictions aside, others such as Daniel Zamora have posited that the very questions Foucault asks are incorrect, and have "disoriented the left." The problem for Zamora is "not that [Foucault] seeks to 'move beyond' the welfare state, but that he actively contributed to its destruction, and that he did so in a way that was entirely in step with the neoliberal critiques of the moment."[7]

Despite such contradiction and critique, one of the most recognizable transitions in history that occurred with the advent of postmodernism was the so-called "linguistic turn." Thus, as O'Brien explains, "one of Foucault's recognized contributions, which a wide variety of the new cultural historians embrace, lie in the importance he attributed to language/discourse as a means of apprehending change."[8] Clifford Geertz, albeit in a very different way, also posited the importance of linguistic and textual interpretation. For Geertz, "materialism of any kind" was "an implicit target."[9]Conversely, action is text and "the real is as imagined as the imaginary."[10] Thus, "man is an animal suspended in webs of significance he has himself spun." [11] In many ways, language and discourse came to dominate and displace discussions of power and oppression for postmodernists. This "interpretative turn," as Aletta Biersack refers to it, is a sort of hyper-hermeneutics, where etymology in essence becomes epistemology.

This linguistic turn may also have some relevance to the post-New Left discourse as well. As the radical left retreated into academia, and in the absence of social movements in the first world on a large scale, power become viewed as an infinitely complex web of micro-powers which permeate everyday life. Likewise, the political-linguistic discourse reflected a by now largely alienated intellectual leftist community. Thus, for critical postmodern left-wing academics language and every-day, small scale interactions sublimate material reality and large-scale, institutional structures. This has been explored in detail by Steve D'Arcy's "The Rise of Post New-Left Political Discourse," which asks the poignant question of whether activists from the New Left era would even find the discourse of today's left intelligible. Juxtaposing words like "oppression" vs. "privilege," "exploitation" vs. "classism," "alliances" vs. "being an ally" (a fundamental distinction!), and "consciousness-raising" vs. "calling out," D'Arcy explicates upon the seismic shift that has gripped leftist discourse.[12]Strategic alliances between oppressed groups or blocs are replaced with hyper-individualized conceptions of being an ally, economic and structural analyses associated with words like exploitation are replaced with "classism," suggesting personal prejudice against members of certain economic backgrounds, etc. This "post-New Left" lexicon is fundamentally different than the language utilized by groups and organizations spanning the New Left of the 1960s and 1970s, or even the old left of the 1930s and before. It is also a language keenly peculiar to the first world, and in particular North America and a few European states. The implications of this shift are contentious, but however one views the linguistic transition it is clear that both the political goals and results have been restructured with its advent.

More generally, poststructuralists have put forward a "theoretical critique of the assumptions of modernity found in philosophy, art, and criticism since the seventeenth and eighteenth centuries."[13]They "argue against the possibility of any certain knowledge... [and] question the superiority of the present and the usefulness of general worldviews, whether Christian, Marxist, or liberal... there is no truth outside ideology."[14] For them "no reality can possibly transcend the discourse in which it is expressed" and while scientists or empiricists may think certain practices "bring them closer to reality... they are simply privileging the language that they speak, the technologies of their own self-fashioning."[15] Thus, historical truth, objectivity, and the narrative form of history have all been targets of the postmodernist critique. Jacques Derrida, for instance, advocated deconstruction "to show how all texts repressed as much as they expressed in order to maintain the fundamental Western conceit of 'logocentrism,' the (erroneous) idea that words expressed truth in reality."[16] Since "texts could be interested in multiple, if not infinite, ways because signifiers had no essential connection to what they were signified."[17] In this way, language was a barrier to truth and precluded human capacity to know truth.

The effect this has had on history is complex. For instance, "the history of what postmodernists called 'subaltern' groups-workers, immigrants, women, slaves, and gays-in fact proved difficult to integrate into the story of one American nation."[18] Partha Chatterjee, for instance, is one of the intellectual founders and banner holders for postcolonial and subaltern studies. Chatterjee, in his study of the "nationalist imagination" in Asia and Africa, *The*

Nation and Its Fragments, cites Foucault as helping him recognize how "power is meant not to prohibit but to facilitate, to produce."[19] For Chatterjee, colonial rule created "a social order that bore striking resemblance to its own caricature of 'traditional India': late colonial society was 'nearer to the ideal-type of Asiatic Despotism than anything South Asia had seen before.'"[20]Specifically referring to search for pre-European capitalism in India, Chatterjee asserts that the "development of industrial capital in... Western Europe or North America, was the result of a very specific history. It is the perversity of Eurocentric historical theories that has led to the search for similar developments everywhere else in the world." [21] Thus, for postcolonial scholars, and implicit in the subset of subaltern studies, totalizing and universal theories are an intellectual and historical impossibility.

This has not permeated all of academia, however. There has been a spirited defense of the radical Enlightenment tradition, especially from the left, as the heated exchanges between Vivek Chibber and Partha Chatterjee have shown. Chibber, in his magnum opus *Postcolonial Theory and the Specter of Capital,* demonstrates the intellectual inconsistences and failures of subaltern studies and offers a comprehensive critique of postcolonial theory. His argument is that it is possible, indeed necessary, to posit a totalizing, universal theory without succumbing to Eurocentrism or reductionism (economic or otherwise). In his work he takes to task Ranajit Guha, Dipesh Chakrabarty and Partha Chatterjee, three scholars who he considers emblematic of postcolonial theory. Thus, the battle was pitched between Chatterjee, who rejects universal discourses, and Chibber, who asserts a nuanced and sophisticated Marxist analysis. Chatterjee laid out the battlefield in his response, suggesting that Chibber implores a "plea for continued faith in the universal values of European Enlightenment." He acknowledges that "the debate between universalism and its critics continues and will not be resolved in a hurry. The choice between the two sides at this time is indeed political." Indeed, while he claims the "greatest strength of the universalist position is the assurance it provides of predictability and control over uncertain outcomes," he argues that the critics of universalism, a category he places himself in, "argue that the outcomes are unknown, indeterminate, and hence unpredictable. They accept the challenge of risky political choices, based on provisional, contingent and corrigible historical knowledge." His main contention, then, is that "the working classes of Europe and North America and their ideologues can no longer act as the designated avant-garde in the struggles of subaltern classes in other parts of the world... Historians of Subaltern Studies have only attempted to interpret a small part of these struggles. And changing the world, needless to say, is a job that cannot be entrusted to historians."[22]

In response, Chibber argues in favor of universalizing categories when applicable, suggesting that the "motivation for my intervention was to examine a common charge that postcolonial theory levels at the Enlightenment tradition, that its universalizing categories obliterate all historical difference. They do so, we are told, because they homogenize the diversity of social experience by subsuming it under highly abstract, one-dimensional categories." Here he cites the example of Marx's concept of abstract labor, which he argues postcolonial theories have simply misunderstood. Therefore, "while it is certainly true that some universalizing categories might be problematic, it is sheer folly to insist that this is a necessary flaw in all such categories. Postcolonial theory's broadside against Enlightenment universalisms is vastly overdrawn." Instead, he argues postcolonial and subaltern studies have been an immense failure both intellectually, in understanding the actual conditions of their subjects, and politically, not only by failing to facilitate radical change in any direction but by actually constraining and enervating radical analysis and transformation of society.

Indeed, Chibber proclaims that "Chatterjee's essay [against Chibber's book] is designed to allay any anxieties that his followers might have about the foundations of their project... It is a palliative, a balm, to soothe their nerves." Not only was this meant to boost morale in the wake of political failure, however, it was also meant to be an attack on the radical Enlightenment tradition, particularly Marxism: "Subaltern Studies was not just supposed to offer a rival framework for interpreting colonial modernity; it was also supposed to have internalized whatever was worth retaining from the Marxian tradition, thereby inheriting the mantle of radical critique. For years, the Subalternists have focused just about everything they have written on the irredeemable flaws of Marxism and the Enlightenment -- how they are implicated in imperialism, their reductionism, essentialism, etc." [23] Thus, the battle between postmodernism, of which postcolonial theory and subaltern studies are intellectual legacies, and modernity are not over. This is particularly true in the realm of history, where the debate between Chatterjee and Chibber is only the most recent manifestation.

For leftists, this battle is of immense importance. The words we utilize, the discourse we construct, and the movements which both manifest from and shape our language are at stake. The political implications of these choices are dire, especially at a time when the forces of reaction are winning everywhere across the world. Yet, there are perhaps few places on Earth where the left is weaker than the first world. This is particularly true where post-modern discourse and post-new left political vocabulary has emerged victorious. Without ignoring the insights of the particular, and without exaggerating the past victories and potential of the universal, it would appear that post-new left political discourse has left our side stranded. It has failed to facilitate growth and shown itself incapable of capturing the masses, all the while forcing us to feed upon ourselves, augmenting isolation and alienation from each other. Perhaps the time for a renegotiation of this development is in order; perhaps the left requires a discourse rooted more in the universal and less in the particular.

Notes

[1] "Human Nature: Justice versus Power, Noam Chomsky debates with Michel Foucault" (1971), accessed March 15, 2014. http://www.chomsky.info/debates/1971xxxx.htm.

[2] Patricia O'Brien, "Michel Foucault's History of Culture," *The New Cultural History*, ed. Lynn Hunt (Berkeley: Univerisity of California Press, 1989), 34.

[3] O'Brien, "Michel Foucault's History of Culture," 35.

[4] Stephen D'Arcy, The Public Autonomy Project, "The Rise of the Post-New Left Political Vocabulary." Last modified January 27, 2014. Accessed March 15, 2014. http://publicautonomy.org/2014/01/27/the-rise-of-the-post-new-left-political-vocabulary/.

[5] Joyce Appleby, Lynn Hunt, and Margaret Jacob, Telling the Truth About History (New York: W.W. Norton, 1994), 206.

[6] O'Brien, "Michel Foucault's History of Culture," 35.

[7] Daniel Zamora, "Foucault's Responsibility," https://www.jacobinmag.com/2014/12/michel-foucault-responsibility-socialist/

[8] Ibid., 44.

[9] Aletta Biersack, "Local Knowledge, Local History: Geertz and Beyond," *The New Cultural History*, ed. Lynn Hunt (Berkeley: Univerisity of California Press, 1989), 75.

[10] Biersack, "Local Knowledge, Local History," 78.

[11] Ibid., 80.

[12] Steve D'Arcy, "The Rise of Post-New Left Political Discourse." http://publicautonomy.org/2014/01/27/the-rise-of-the-post-new-left-political-vocabulary/

[13] Appleby, Hunt, and Jacob, 201.

[14] Ibid., 202-3.

[15] Ibid., 204.

[16] Ibid., 215.

[17] Ibid., 215.

[18] Ibid., 217.

[19] Partha Chatterjee, *The Nation and Its Fragments* (Princeton: Princeton University Press, 1993), 15.

[20] Chatterjee, *The Nation and Its Fragments*, 32.

[21] Ibid., 30.

[22] Chatterjee Partha, "Subaltern Studies and Capital," Economic and Political Review Weekly, XLVIII, no. 37 (2013), http://www.epw.in/notes/subaltern-studies-and-capital.html (accessed March 15, 2014).

[23] Vivek Chibber, Verso Books, "Subaltern Studies Revisited: Vivek Chibber's Response to Partha Chatterjee." Last modified February 25, 2014. Accessed March 15, 2014. http://www.versobooks.com/blogs/1529-subaltern-studies-revisited-vivek-chibber-s-response-to-partha-chatterjee.

An Ideal Blueprint
The Original Black Panther Party Model and Why It Should Be Duplicated

Colin Jenkins

The rise of the Black Panther Party (BPP) in the late 1960s signified a monumental step toward the development of self-determination in the United States. In a nation that has long suffered a schizophrenic existence, characterized by a grand facade of "freedom, liberty and democracy" hiding what Alexis de Tocqueville once aptly described as "old aristocratic colours breaking through,"[1] the BPP model provided hope to not only Black Americans who had experienced centuries of inhumane treatment, but also to the nation's exploited and oppressed working class majority that had been inherently disregarded by both the founding fathers' framework and the predatory nature of capitalism.

As we grind our way through the tail-end of a neoliberal storm, it has become clear that in an age of extreme inequality, unabated corporate power, and overwhelming government corruption at all levels; we have a war on our hands. Not a war in the traditional international sense, but a domestic class war; one that has decimated our communities, our hopes for a better future, our children's educations, and our collective physical and mental well-being. The aggressors in this war are powerful - so much so that resistance often seems futile, and the opposition insurmountable. Multi-trillion dollar financial institutions and multi-billion dollar corporations pulling the strings of the most powerful politicians - Presidents, Senators, Congress members, and Governors alike - all of whom have at their disposal the abilities to print money at will, control markets through fiscal and monetary policy, deploy powerful militaries anywhere in the world, and unleash militarized police forces to terrorize our neighborhoods.

Despite this juggernaut of an enemy, working-class resistance has not subsided. And although it took a proclaimed "economic crisis" to wake many from their slumber, developments within activist and direct action circles have been positive over the past half-decade. The Occupy movement sparked much-needed discourse on income inequality and corporate/government corruption while setting up the fight for a $15 minimum wage, which has caught on like wildfire throughout the country, and especially among the most vulnerable of the working class - low-wage service sector workers. Anti-war protestors who made their presence felt during the Bush administration - only to disappear after Obama's election - have begun to trickle back with the gradual realization that nothing has changed. And anti-capitalist political parties throughout the Left, though still small and splintered, have gained momentum and membership while successfully plugging into some mainstream working-class consciousness (Kshama Sawant and Socialist Alternative's rise in Seattle; the Black Autonomy Federation's regrouping of grassroots, anti-authoritarian struggle; the International Socialist Organization's ongoing solidarity with folks like Glenn Greenwald, Jeremy Scahill, Ali Abunimah and Amy Goodman; the Socialist Party USA's growing relevance; and the Party for Socialism and Liberation's relentless battle in the trenches of anti-war, anti-police brutality, and anti-racist activism).

These developments, while positive in many respects, have ultimately been limited. Some of these limitations are due to external factors that continue to plague the American public: a general deficit in education and knowledge, a lack of class-conscious analysis, and the inundation of corporate media and propaganda, to name a few - all of which pose elements that are difficult, if not impossible, to control. Other limitations are due to internal factors which are largely controllable, such as organizational structures and approaches. It is regarding these internal shortcomings where the original Black Panther Party model becomes invaluable and should be held as a standard blueprint for all organizations and parties seeking revolutionary change.

The following is a list of attributes, both tangible and conceptual, that made the BPP an effective model for true liberty and self-determination; and, consequently, a substantial threat to the status quo of ever-strangling corporate and governmental power. Organizations and parties of today, whether through piecemeal or wholesale consideration, would do well to take this ideal mix into account.

Theoretical Foundation and Internationalism

Despite constant grumblings regarding the "inundation" and "worthlessness" of theory from within the modern Left, a glance at the operational effectiveness of the original BPP lends credence to its usefulness.

The BPP was firmly rooted in revolutionary political philosophy, most notably that of Marxism - a tool that is needed to understand and properly critique the very system which dominates us - capitalism. "Capitalist exploitation is one of the basic causes of our problem," explained one of the party's founders, Huey P. Newton, and "it is the goal of the BPP to negate capitalism in our communities and in the oppressed communities around the world."[2]

The BPP's ongoing exploration of theory allowed for the development of a crucial class component that perfectly balanced their fight against institutional racism. This helped create the notion that the fight for racial justice could not be won outside the confines of economic justice and class division, something revolutionary counterparts like Martin Luther King, Jr. and Malcolm X would also eventually realize.

Stemming from Marxism was the method of and adherence to "dialectical materialism," which "precluded a static, mechanical application" of theory and allowed the party to adapt to the constantly developing environment while maintaining a mission based in class and racial oppression. "If we are using the method of dialectical materialism," argued Newton, "we don't expect to find anything the same even one minute later because one minute later is history." [3] Regarding the party's embrace of this method, Eldridge Cleaver noted, "we have studied and understand the classical principles of scientific socialism (and) have adapted these principles to our own situation for ourselves. However, we do not move with a closed mind to new ideas or information (and) know that we must rely upon our own brains in solving ideological problems as they relate to us." [4]

The Party's belief in "international working class unity across the spectrum of color and gender" led them to form bonds with various minority and white revolutionary groups. "From the tenets of Maoism they set the role of their Party as the vanguard of the revolution and worked to establish a united front, while from Marxism they addressed the capitalist economic system, embraced the theory of dialectical materialism, and represented the need for all workers to forcefully take over the means of production." This approach was echoed by Fred Hampton, who urged all to resist fighting racism with racism, but rather with (working class) solidarity; and to resist fighting capitalism with "Black capitalism," but rather with socialism.

Through this theoretical base, "Newton and the BPP leadership organized with the intent of empowering the Black community through collective work," Danny Haiphong tells us. "Each concrete medical clinic, free breakfast program, and Panther school were organized to move community to confront the racist, capitalist power structure and embrace revolutionary socialism and communalism."

The Party's Ten-Point Program and platform, which evolved slightly over the course of several years, rested on demands that focused not only on historical roots to the daily injustices faced by Black Americans and oppressed communities, but also took on an international scope that allowed for understanding macro-systemic causes, and particularly those associated with capitalism. As Cornel West explains, "The revolutionary politics of the Black Panther Party linked the catastrophic conditions of local Black communities (with the disgraceful school systems, unavailable health and child care, high levels of unemployment and underemployment, escalating rates of imprisonment, and pervasive forms of self-hatred and self-destruction) to economic inequality in America and colonial or neocolonial realities in the capitalist world-system."[5] "It was the politics of international radical solidarity ... Because of the tremendous hostility that the Vietnam War was generating, youth organizations in Germany, France and Sweden created solidarity committees for the BPP. We would travel back and forth; and they raised money for us. There were liberation movements in Africa who read our paper and contacted us," says Kathleen Cleaver. The Party even established its own embassy in Algeria, a nation that had no diplomatic ties with the United States at the time. With a firm understanding of political economy and geopolitics, the party possessed a "big picture approach" that has become a necessity, especially in today's world of globalization, neoliberalism, and multinational corporate power.

Praxis and Direct Action

"They (the people) can do anything they desire to do," Newton professed, "but they will only take those actions which are consistent with their level of consciousness and their understanding of the situation. When we raise their consciousness (through education), they will understand even more fully what they in fact can do, and they will move on the situation in a courageous manner. This is merging your theory with your practices." [6]

The BPP didn't just talk about change, they actively pursued it. Their presence was felt in the neighborhoods for which they lived and worked. They walked the streets, talked with folks, broke bread with neighbors, and cultivated a sense of community. Their numerous outreach efforts were well-planned, beautifully strategic, and always multi-pronged - combining basic and pleasant human interaction with education and revolutionary politics. They were the perfect embodiment of solidarity, often times rejecting notions of leadership and superiority to create a radical landscape where all were on equal footing. The sense of empowerment felt by all who came in contact with them was unmistakable.

In an effort to curb police brutality and the indiscriminate murders of black youth at the hands of racist police tactics, the party regularly deployed armed citizen patrols designed to evaluate the behaviors of police officers. They coordinated neighborhood watch programs, performed military-style marching drills, and studied basic protective manuevers to ensure measures of safety and self-preservation for citizens living in oppressed communities.

In January of 1969, in response to the malnutrition that plagued their communities, the party launched a "Free Breakfast for Schoolchildren" program, which was introduced at St. Augustine's church in Oakland, California. In a matter of a few months, the program had spread to other cities across the country. In April, the Black Panther newspaper reported on its progress and effectiveness:

The Free Breakfast for School Children is about to cover the country and be initiated in every chapter and branch of the Black Panther Party... It is a beautiful sight to see our children eat in the mornings after remembering the times when our stomachs were not full, and even the teachers in the schools say that there is a great improvement in the academic skills of the children that do get the breakfast. At one time there were children that passed out in class from hunger, or had to be sent home for something to eat. But our children shall be fed, and the Black Panther Party will not let the malady of hunger keep our children down any longer.

By year's end, the program had blanketed the country, feeding over 10,000 children every day before they went to school. To compliment this, the Party "launched more than 35 Survival Programs and provided community help such as education, tuberculosis testing, legal aid, transportation assistance, ambulance service, and the manufacture and distribution of free shoes to poor people." This type of tangible solidarity and assistance is needed today. Food drives, safety programs, neighborhood watch, and basic accessibility and assistance should not represent things that are beneath revolutionary politicking.

Intersectionality

Due to their solid theoretical framework, the Party was able to deploy a proto-intersectionality that allowed them to go beyond issues of racial oppression and police brutality in order to address broad roots and common causes. In doing so, they were able to redirect the emotional rage brought on by targeted racism and channel it into a far-reaching indictment of the system. This created the potential for broad coalitions and opened up avenues for unity and solidarity with revolutionary counterparts, especially with regards to Black women.

Despite stifling elements of misogyny and sexism, the emergence of women as key figures in the Black Power movement was ironically made possible through the BPP. One of the party's early leaders, Elaine Brown, pointed to a conscious effort on the part of female members to overcome patriarchy from within party lines. "A woman in the Black Power movement was considered, at best, irrelevant," explains Brown. "A woman asserting herself was a pariah... It was a violation of some Black Power principle that was left undefined. If a Black woman assumed a role of leadership, she was said to be eroding Black manhood."[7]

Leaders like Brown, despite carrying this heavy burden of being drawn into a fight within THE fight, were incredibly important to the party's mission and became highly influential members, local leaders, fierce orators, and public representatives for the party-at-large. Brown made impressive runs for Oakland City Council in 1973 and 1975, receiving 30% and 44% of the vote respectively. In 1977, she managed Lionel Wilson's Oakland mayoral campaign which resulted in Wilson becoming the city's first Black mayor. Regarding the dynamics of sexuality and gender in the party, journalist and activist Annie Brown tells us:

The BPP had an open mind towards sexual expression as well as the roles women could play in social change organizations. The embrace of female empowerment and varied sexual identities within the party allowed for women like Angela Davis, to rise to prominent positions of power within the party while other radical organizations of the time such as Students for a Democratic Society (SDS) and The Student Nonviolent Coordination Committee (SNCC) saved leadership roles for men, and forced women to remain in the background.

After addressing these early pockets of misogyny and hyper-masculinity, the party was shaped heavily by women, to the point where it "transformed gender roles in the Black Power movement," and paved the way for similar developments in other grassroots movements in the U.S. In researching for her forthcoming book, "What You've Got is a Revolution: Black Women's Movements for Black Power," Historian Ashley Farmer found the Party's newspaper regularly "defied gender roles by depicting women as strong, gun-toting revolutionaries," while female party members were heavily involved in setting "a community-focused revolutionary agenda that supported programs for daycare, groceries, and housing." In addition to celebrating women as "tough revolutionaries," the newspaper included an "explicit focus on women's issues" throughout its publication. For years, Women Panthers assumed leadership roles and " turned toward local-level activism, providing food, housing, and health care in local black communities." The inclusion of women as active participants in the struggle was eventually, if not initially, embraced by founding members. As Historian Robyn Spencer writes, "Seale and Newton didn't exclude African-American women in their rhetoric or in their involvement. The message became: Black brothers and sisters unite for real social action."[8] This development within the party's evolution led to a membership that was majority (roughly two-thirds) female by the early-1970s, a desirable goal for a modern Left that still possesses a troublesome androcratic identity.

Discipline

Despite constant meddling from the FBI and its COINTELPRO program, which sought to "disrupt, confuse and create tension within the organization," the BPP's organizational structure was solidly built, baring a slight resemblance to that of the Nation of Islam. Some BPP chapters operated with military-like discipline, a quality that tends to be lacking on a loose and often times hyper-sensitive Left (even amongst Leninist organizations). This was accomplished with a good mix of horizontal leadership and chapter autonomy, which allowed for creativity, initiatives and actions throughout the organization, while also maintaining the discipline necessary for taking broad action and staying focused on the big picture.

The party recognized the severity of the situation for oppressed and working-class communities within a racist and capitalist system. The system's inherently predatory nature regarding social and economic issues provided a glimpse of a society based in class division, and the daily brutalization of communities of color at the hands of the police confirmed the presence of an all-out class war. In this sense, the party organized for this purpose - equipping themselves with ideological ammo, building poor and working-class armies through community outreach and education, arming themselves for self-defense, and operating their mission with a high degree of strategy and discipline.

Mao Zedong's revolutionary military doctrine, "Three Rules of Discipline and Eight Points for Attention," was highly influential in the party's daily operations. These "rules of engagement" emphasized obedience to the needs of oppressed peoples as well as conducting actions in a respectable and honorable manner (Be polite when speaking; Be honest when buying and selling; Return all borrowed articles; Pay compensation for everything damaged; Do not hit or swear at others; Do not damage crops; Do not harass females; and Do not mistreat prisoners). "There were some aspects of Chairman Mao's thought that had helpful and sensitive application for the life of the Panthers in the ghetto," explained Cleaver.[9]

In addition to Mao's "little red book," the party made Che Guevara's "Guerilla Warfare" required reading in all of its political education classes. Recognizing the similarities between the Black struggle in America and the struggle of the colonized in many parts of the world, party members studied anti-colonial resistance and Regis Debray's *foco theory of revolution*, which posited the idea that "vanguardism by cadres of small, fast-moving paramilitary groups can provide a focus (in Spanish, foco) for popular discontent against a sitting regime, and thereby lead a general insurrection." While the BPP didn't apply this in the same manner as a revolutionary peasantry would in taking up arms against an imperial force, they were able to use many points as a foundation for unity and self-defense, if not merely for inspiration in battling forces of oppression. Said Newton:

... all the guerilla bands that have been operating in Mozambique and Angola, and the Palestinian guerillas who are fighting for a socialist world. I think they all have been great inspirations for the Black Panther Party... they are examples of guerilla bands. The guerillas who are operating in South Africa (against Apartheid) and

numerous other countries all have had great influence on us. We study and follow their example."

This disciplined approach allowed the party to establish clear targets for opposition, while also dissuading reactionary behaviors that were dangerously counterproductive and counter-revolutionary. An example of this came in a message released to members through the organizational newspaper in 1968. The message was in response to news of frequent quarrels with hippies:

"Black brothers stop vamping on the hippies. They are not your enemy. Your enemy, right now, is the white racist pigs who support this corrupt system. Your enemy is the Tom nigger who reports to his white slavemaster every day. Your enemy is the fat capitalist who exploits your people daily. Your enemy is the politician who uses pretty words to deceive you. Your enemy is the racist pigs who use Nazi-type tactics and force to intimidate black expressionism. Your enemy is not the hippies. Your blind reactionary acts endanger THE BLACK PANTHER PARTY members and its revolutionary movements. WE HAVE NO QUARREL WITH THE HIPPIES. LEAVE THEM ALONE. Or - THE BLACK PANTHER PARTY will deal with you."
Such focus is crucial and should be a primary goal for a modern Left that is often intensely and frustratingly sectarian.

An All-Inclusive, Working-Class Orientation

Perhaps the most valuable of the BPP's attributes was its common acceptance and inclusion of the most disenfranchised and oppressed of the working classes - the unemployed, the poor, and those alienated by the criminal justice system through racist and classist laws and law enforcement practices. This approach stood in contrast to the overly-Eurocentric package that housed orthodox Marxism, and openly defied the highly romanticized, lily white version of working-class identity espoused by many Leftist organizations throughout history - often symbolized by the white, chiseled, "blue-collar" man wielding a hammer.

Over the years, Marx's assessment and discarding of the "lumpenproletariat" - a population that he described as "members of the working-class outside of the wage-labor system who gain their livelihoods through crime and other aspects of the underground economy such as prostitutes, thieves, drug dealers, and gamblers" - had been accepted by many on the Left. However, the BPP's familiarity with Zedong and Guevara led them away from this commonly accepted notion, and their philosophy paralleled that of Frantz Fanon, who in his ongoing analysis of neocolonialism, deemed the lumpen to be "one of the most spontaneous and the most radically revolutionary forces of a colonized people."
The BPP recognized similar dynamics within the United States - particularly the relationship between Black, poor, and disenfranchised populations and the power structure - and viewed this as a microcosm of international colonialism. In their eyes, the American "peasantry" wasn't tilling fields and cultivating crops - it was the homeless lying in the streets, the unemployed standing on the corners, the racially disenfranchised left with no options in life, and the unlawfully imprisoned masses behind bars. They saw potential in society's castaways and embraced the idea of a revolutionary class made up of displaced workers who were never given a chance to participate in the labor market.

Newton, particularly, was a firm believer in the revolutionary potential of the 'Black lumpenproletariat' in the United States, and viewed this notion as an important challenge to the "bourgeois nature" of the Southern Civil Rights movement, which he believed had become completely reliant on a reformist-minded, Black middle-class leadership that was too concessionary and did not properly represent a revolutionary working-class orientation.
Today, at a time when over 20 million able-bodied Americans have been forced into the "underground economy," and another 2.5 million are incarcerated, the idea of drawing society's castaways toward class-conscious political movements is ripe. Narratives that focus on the erosion of the "middle class" are not only insufficient,

they're irresponsible. Our true struggle lies with the multi-generational poor, the unemployed, and the imprisoned victims of the draconian "Drug War" and prison industrial complex.

A Winning Formula

The BPP model could be summed up with the following formula: (THEORY + INTERSECTIONALITY) + (PRAXIS + EDUCATION) = CLASS CONSCIOUSNESS = REVOLUTIONARY CHANGE. Like no other, the party successfully blended a heavy academic foundation with a non-academic approach, using community outreach programs to serve basic needs while also educating and promoting class consciousness. Their crucial "Survival Programs" sought to satisfy immediate Maslovian needs without losing sight of the ultimate goal of uprooting and transforming society from below.

"All these programs satisfy the deep needs of the community but they are not solutions to our problems," explained Newton. "That is why we call them survival programs, meaning survival pending revolution. We say that the survival program of the Black Panther Party is like the survival kit of a sailor stranded on a raft. It helps him to sustain himself until he can get completely out of that situation. So the survival programs are not answers or solutions, but they will help us to organize the community around a true analysis and understanding of their situation. When consciousness and understanding is raised to a high level then the community will seize the time and deliver themselves from the boot of their oppressors." [10]

The party also wasn't afraid to display physical prowess and utilize the art of intimidation in their struggle. In fact, they saw this as a crucial component necessary to counter reactionary and senseless violence from racist citizens and police officers. They provided security escorts for Betty Shabazz following Malcolm's death, and sent thirty armed members to the California State capitol to protest the Mulford Act. This approach, coupled with similar tactics of self-defense used by the Nation of Islam, proved to

be a vital compliment to the non-violent wing of the Civil Rights movement, ultimately allowing its "more palatable elements" to secure legislative victories. Furthermore, it challenged the notion that reactionary and racist conservatives had a monopoly on intimidation and violence - a notion that has gained an increasingly strong foothold over time, and should be challenged again.
The BPP's model is needed today. A firm foundation of knowledge, history, internationalism, and political economy is needed. A concerted effort to bond with and assist our working-class communities and disenfranchised sisters and brothers is needed. An infusion of authentic, working-class politics which shifts the focus from 'middle-class erosion' to 'multi-generational disenfranchisement' is needed. The blueprint is there. Let's use it.

Notes

[1] Alexis de Tocqueville, Democracy in America. Penguin Books edition, 2004: p. 58
[2] The Huey P. Newton Reader, Seven Stories Press, 2002. p 229
[3] Kathleen Cleaver and George Katsiaficas. Liberation, Imagination, and the Black Panther Party: A New Look at the Panthers and Their Legacy. Routledge, 2001, p. 30.
[4] The Huey P. Newton Reader, p 230
[5] The Black Panther Party: Service to the People Programs, the Dr. Huey P. Newton Foundation. Edited and with an afterword by David Hilliard. University of New Mexico Press, 2008
[6] The Huey P. Newton Reader, pp. 228-229.
[7] Johnnetta B. Cole, Beverly Guy-Sheftall, Gender Talk: The Struggle for Women's Equality in African American Communities. Random House, NY: 2003. p 92
[8] Robyn C. Spencer, "Engendering the Black Freedom Struggle: Revolutionary Black Womanhood and the Black Panther Party in the Bay Area, California," *Journal of Women's History*, 20 no. 1 (2008), 3.

[9] Cleaver and Katsiaficas, p. 30.

[10] To Die for the People: The writings of Huey P. Newton, City Lights Books, 2009.

Retracing Toledo's Radical History

Derek Alan Ide

It is not difficult to sense the alienation and demoralization that impinges upon so many people as they drive through the streets of Toledo, Ohio. These are streets that were constructed to be driven on and nothing else. Unlike many of the cities in Europe, or even some in the United States, it is not a walkable city. The haphazard urban planning, or lack thereof, and the complete lack of any public transit system, with the exception of TARTA buses and private cabs, combine to make Toledo more than inhospitable to those without their own private vehicle. Those who can afford it have spent the past five decades fleeing to outlying suburbs, and those who cannot remain trapped within the confines of a "Little Detroit" which, after the 1970s, has witnessed the gutting of its manufacturing base. Since 2000, Toledo area poverty has risen faster than any other U.S. city. [1] In 2009, nearly 30% of the population of Toledo lived below the poverty line. Over 11% lived below half the poverty line.[2]

In Toledo, isolation is the rule rather than the anomaly. While the Occupy Wall Street movement rocked the United States in 2011, Toledo's Occupy Wall Street was anemic and enervated. Responses exist but they are individual, small-scale, and incapable of drawing the numbers that such dire conditions warrant. Aside from a few key activists and organizers, most individuals, even those who have lived here their whole lives, have taken the state of things for granted, or at least feel powerless to change them. No mass movement exists, in spite of the abject conditions, that people can plug themselves into. Toledo, as someone recently put it, is "a hard place to love if you didn't grow up here."

This has not always been the case, however. Toledo was once a center for economic activity, a hub of material exchange through which goods and labor moved rapidly. More importantly, however, Toledo has a long and radical history, one that has often been hidden away by the quotidian drudgery and daily grind of life. From the 1934 Auto-Lite Strike to the Black Panther Party headquarters on Door St., the city has not always been bereft of a culture of resistance. This once-proud resistance was not only manifest in one of the few general strikes to every rock a major U.S. city, or in the sheer violence and force brought down against the Panthers, it was also located on the campus of the University itself. From UT's Students for a Democratic Society in the early 1970s to the Black Student Union, which spearheaded the divestment movement from South Africa in the mid-1980s, Toledo students have always been engaged in the struggles of the day. The purpose of this article is to recount these struggles, but more importantly to provide as much space as possible to the voices that engaged in them. It should be noted that while what comes below is not an all-encompassing account of every radical initiative and movement in Toledo's history, plenty of which remain to be written about and exceed the knowledge of the author, this is a brief attempt to retrace as much of Toledo's radical history as possible. It is a history that every Toledo worker, student, and citizen should know.

The 1934 Auto-Lite Strike

By 1934, Toledo was in the midst of the depression. While the crisis was astute on the national scale, in Toledo it was catastrophic. Whereas 25 percent of all workers and 37 of all nonfarm workers were unemployed in 1933,[3] Toledo faced an unemployment rate of over 50% in 1934.[4] As Rebecca E. Zietlow[5] and James Gray Pope explain:

Without an economic safety net, people literally struggled to survive. Toledoans told stories about families eating nothing but apples, and burning their furniture to warm themselves during the harsh upper Midwest winters. These conditions were devastating for those workers without jobs, but they also had a profound impact on employed workers. The managers at industrial plants such as the Auto-Lite plant treated unskilled and semi-skilled workers as fungible and disposable.

Over one-third of Toledo's population lived on meager emergency relief during the depression. Willys-Overland employed 28,000 in 1929, out of a total population in Toledo of 290,000. By 1932, it employed only 3,000 people.[6] As Willys-Overland and other automobile plants shut down or significantly reduced production, so too did auto parts manufacturers, a significant component of Toledo's industrial base.

The Electric Auto-Lite Company, an auto parts manufacturer, was the site of one of the most heroic and historic strikes in not only Toledo, but U.S. history. At Auto-Lite, workers were treated contemptuously, and supervisors exercised arbitrary power over all aspects of their work life. Although Congress had enacted the National Industrial Recovery Act (NIRA) in 1933 which, under Section 7(a), provided workers with the right to organize, Roosevelt's insertion of merit clauses "granted employers the right to establish open shops and discriminate against militants." [7] As Frances Fox Piven and Richard Cloward explain:

Early in 1934, demands for union recognition at the Electric Auto-Lite Company and several smaller firms were rejected, and 4,000 workers walked out. The workers returned to the plants after federal officials secured a commitment from the employers to "set up a machinery" for negotiations. But Auto-Lite then refused to negotiate, and a second strike was called on April 11. Only a minority of the workers joined the walkout this time, however, and the company determined to keep its plant open, hiring strikebreakers to reach full production.

Toledo was a stronghold of A. J. Muste's radical Unemployed Leagues, and the Musteites rapidly mobilized large numbers of unemployed workers to reinforce the picket lines. On April 17 the company responded by obtaining a court order limiting picketing and prohibiting league members from picketing altogether. But the Musteites decided to violate the restraining order, and some local Communists joined in with the slogan "Smash the Injunction by Mass Picketing" (Keeran, 168). A handful of militants then began picketing. They were quickly arrested, but upon their release, they returned to the picket lines, their numbers now enlarged by workers emboldened by the militants' example. More arrests and further court injunctions seemed to only galvanize the strikers, and the numbers of people on the picket lines grew larger day by day. Sympathy for the strikers in Toledo was such that the sheriff could not use the local police to protect the strikebreakers and instead deputized special police, paid for by Auto-Lite.

By May 23, the crowd massed outside the plant had grown to some 10,000 people, effectively imprisoning the 1,500 strikebreakers inside the factory. The sheriff then decided to take the initiative, and the deputies attacked. The crowd fought back, several people were seriously wounded, and a contingent of the Ohio National Guard was called in. Armed with machine guns and bayoneted rifles, the Guardsmen marched into the Auto-Lite plant in the quiet of dawn and succeeded in evacuating the strikebreaking workers. But the next day, the crowd gathered again, advanced on the Guardsmen, showering them with bricks and bottles. On the third advance, the Guard fired into the crowd, killing two and wounding many more. The crowd still did not disperse. Four more companies of Guards men were called up, and Auto-Lite agreed to close the plant. Then, with the threat of a general strike in the air, the employers finally agreed to federal mediation which resulted in a 22 percent wage increase and limited recognition for the union. [8]

The AWP skillfully utilized the language of slavery and emancipation to inspire the strikers:

Its banner equated the end of chattel slavery in 1865 with the end of wage slavery through collective action in 1934. AWP flyers produced at the time made this connection more explicit. One leaflet proclaimed, "Toledo workers will not work at the points of bayonets like craven slaves." Another declared, "[T]he workers of Toledo . . . have starved and sweated and cried in their misery while waiting for this hour. Now they have shaken off the chains of their masters." A leaflet produced by the Auto Workers Union Organization Committee agreed, "It now remains the task of completely closing this slave pen of Minniger."[9]

One of the most important elements of the strike was the influence of A.J. Muste, a leader of the American Workers Party, who helped organize the Lucas County Unemployed League.[10] Charles Bogle explains the vital importance of this development:

The strike would have ended... had it not been for the actions of a committee of Auto-Lite workers who asked for assistance from the Unemployed League. The Unemployed League, affiliated with the socialist American Workers Party (AWP), had formed in 1933 to organize mass actions by Toledo unemployed workers to obtain cash relief. More important for the fate of the Auto-Lite striking workers, the League's policy was to unify the employed and unemployed. [11]

This policy of unification was a vital component of the strike, and allowed a limited, plant-based battle to transform into one of the most important industrial city-wide struggles in U.S. history.[12] The success of the Toledo strike was a significant factor that contributed to the formation of the United Auto Workers, one of the few remaining unions of any significance in the United States. More importantly, it acted as a catalyst for passage of the National Labor Relations Act (NLRA) of 1935, which codified the legality of trade unions, collective bargaining, elected labor representation, and the right to strike. Although the plant was demolished in 1999, the entrance was left standing, with an inscription that reads: "This stone doorway will stand forever as a symbol of the Toledo Auto-Lite workers' commitment, loyalty, and solidarity, which enabled them to break with the past, and enter a better future." As Zeitlow and Pope maintain, "That future has now receded into the past, and the example of the Auto-Lite strikers affirms to a new generation that with commitment, loyalty, and solidarity, a better future can be won."[13]

National Committee to Combat Fascism (Black Panther Party)

On July 25, 1967, Door Street, dubbed "Black Mecca" for the array of black-owned shops, restaurants, and nightclubs, had been the site of a large-scale uprising that came on the heels of an even larger rebellion in Detroit two days prior.[14] One witness to the riots proclaimed "The reasons for the riots, I think, were to achieve some kind of justice - we just didn't have it all the time." [15] Three years later, an organization had arisen to politically direct the energy and frustration manifest in 1967. By 1970, the 1300 block of Dorr Street was home to the Toledo chapter Black Panther Party headquarters. The Toledo Panthers, at this time operating under the name the National Committee to Combat Fascism (NCCF), had organized a nascent Free Clothing program and [16] a Free Breakfast program, in step with other chapters across the country. Already at this time across the country, Black Panther Party headquarters had been attacked and raided, and the 21-year old martyr Fred Hampton had been pulled out of his bed and shot in the head less than a year before. In the early morning hours of September 18, 1970, a man approached Toledo Police Officer William Miscannon, stationed outside the Party headquarters at Junction and Door. The stories differ as to what happened next. One source suggests Miscannon asked the man what was going on, to which the man responded "This is what's going on," before pulling a silver handgun and shooting Miscannon in the head.[17] Yet another source suggests the man approached and shouted "Hey baby, I've got something for you!" before shooting.[18] Either way, Miscannon was killed and the murder was blamed on local Panther John McClellan. Although McClellan was charged, two different trials ended in hung juries, and no new evidence was able to be presented against him.

The Toledo Police, however, took no qualms in using the killing as a pretext for attacking the Panther headquarters. Within hours, some forty officers surrounded the headquarters and "riddled... [the] Panther headquarters with bullets during a five-hour battle," in what Mike Cross, the Panther defense minister in Toledo, called "an unprovoked attack by racist pigs."[19] The guns were apparently procured by John McClellan's brother, Larry, who took "about 20 rifles" from a shooting range at Bowling Green State University, near Toledo. [20] Sixteen year old Troy Montgomery was seriously wounded. When the ambulance arrived, the police refused to allow the black ambulance driver Leroy Hardnett to take the boy to the hospital. Hardnett reported at the time that "They told us to leave him in the streets and die."[21] The boy was eventually taken to Mercy Hospital and survived. The Panthers stockpile of weapons was confiscated by the police. The assault did not end that night, however. One Black Panther article titled

527

"Toledo Piggery Continues" detailed how "Two members of the Toledo N.C.C.F. (brothers Conrad and Kenneth) were kidnapped, while on their way to the office, and illegally held for eight days in the Toledo Pig Pen. The brothers were unable to make a phone call to let anyone know what had happened to them." [22] Although Panther operations were hampered by this attack, this was not the end of the Toledo chapter.

The thugs of the state continued their war on Toledo's Panthers. On November 28, 1970 an article entitled "The Dungeon" appeared in the Black Panther party newspaper exposing the conditions that prisoners faced in Toledo's Lucas Country jail. The report was signed by ten prisoners, five Black and five white, and immediately they faced retaliation for their political commitments to the struggle. This excerpt from the Black Panther detailing the attack deserves to be quoted at length:

The Inmates knew that their lives would be in grave danger because of this, but they felt that getting the truth to the people about what was happening in this fascist pig pen was much more important than their own personal safety. This was clearly shown in the last paragraph of the article which stated "All the men (five Black and five White) incarcerated in this jail's maximum security section have signed this report being well aware of the physical and mental repression that will follow from the jail's administration. They wish the people to know that no matter what happens to them they have stood up and are resisting as men."
Tuesday Dec. 8. 1970, under pretense of conducting a weapons search, more than 25 racist pigs and their bootlicking flunky nigger pigs, launched an unprovoked, brutal attack against the men in the maximum security section of the Lucas County Jail. When the pigs started brutalizing and beating them, the brothers righteously began to defend themselves. Within minutes the rest of the inmates on all three jail floors began to join in the resistance against the pig deputies. For 2 hours the prisoners of the dungeon resisted heavily armed pigs from the Sheriffs Dept. and city Police... 17 prisoners were beaten, stripped of their clothes and sent to the

hole (A 10' × 12' windowless room in the basement). Included among them was a sick 73 year old Black man and two members of the N.C.C.F., John and Larry McClellan. All 17 prisoners remained in this room for 2 days and were literally covered with their own wastes. The only food they received was one cup of water and one slice of bread a day per person.

...[On] Thursday Dec. 10, incarcerated N.C.C.F. member John McClellan, accused of offing racist pig Miscannon Sept. 18th, 1970, stopped a pre-trial motion in his defense to expose the conditions that he and 16 other men had been subjected to for over 48 hours in the hole. He refused to participate any further in the court proceedings until the cruel and unusual punishment was immediately ended.

Presiding Judge, Wiley, adjourned the court and visited the jail along with newsmen and attorneys, from 1:30 P.M. to 2:30 P.M. When court was re-convened he ordered that John McClellan released from the hole immediately. This brother again showed that he is a true servant of the people when he said. "The constitutional rights of the other 16 men are also being violated. I will not leave those other men in the hole to die. If we are not all released together, then I will return to the hole with my friends, many, who are sick and will die it not released immediately." Judge Wiley then ordered Sheriff Metzger to release all the men held in the hole. This racist pig Judge had seen with his own eyes, the degradation of 17 naked human beings covered with their own wastes and visibly very sick. Yet, all he could relate to was releasing John McClellan. This brother exposed the true-nature of this pig and backed him up against the wall, where in order not to show his fascist nature, he had to recognize the rights of the other prisoners held in the hole...

Now a prisoner can remain in the hole for only 12 hours at a time and then be released for 6 hours before returning again. Still this rule doesn't stop his said constitutional rights against cruel and unusual punishment from being violated. It just determines how long his rights will be violated.

A prisoner will still he stripped naked, forced to sleep on a concrete floor if its not too crowded, have no toilet facilities or running water and receive bread and water to eat. Actually, nothing has changed regarding the way the prisoners are treated in the hole. only the length of time they are to be kept in there. To end the sham. Pig judge Wiley had the nerve to dink the following statement' "This is an unsatisfactory solution, but I had to balance the necessity for security against a minimum of decency."

The pigs have always put their security and profits before the desires and needs of the people. The crimes being committed daily in the "Dungeon" are comparable to the horrendous war crimes committed by the Nazis against their victims in the concentration camps.

Today, the barbarous ruling class of America far surpasses the Nazis in Germany. They are making and implementing plans for the total extermination of Black people in America, and waging a genocidal war on the rest of the poor and oppressed in the world. We are not going to rid ourselves of the brutality and murder waged daily against the people of the world by the Nixon-Agnew-Mitchell-Hoover fascist clique, unless all people rise up and begin to wage revolutionary armed struggle within every oppressed community of the world. In essence, we must relate to the social and political ideology of inter-communalism so that all people of the world can no longer be manipulated along racial, cultural, and national lines by the fascists of America.

ALL POWER TO THE PEOPLE!
THROUGH REVOLUTIONARY INTERCOMMUNAL SOLIDARITY!
Toledo N.C.C.F.
1334 Dorr St.
Toledo, Ohio[23]

In stark contrast, *The Byran Times* presented the "disturbance" as an "attempt to free two Black Panthers." This revolt was "quelled" by the "authorities."[24] But the Panthers and McClellan were not demonized by the Black community, despite how the press sought to malign them. Indeed, in July of 1972 the Toledo NCCF held a

"Community Day of Justice." Some "6,000 people, mostly Black, attended Community Day for Justice to show support for Comrade John McClellan." The John McClellan Free Food Program distributed "1,000 free full bags of groceries (with a chicken in every bag)" and over 1,000 Sickle Cell Anemia tests were given. A "massive number" of people were registered to vote. When the bags of food arrived, "everyone felt as one beautiful, Black sister did: 'Lord knows, those Panthers are really going to do it'." [25]

Campus Activism from the Black Student Union to Students for Justice in Palestine

As the Black Panthers were organizing on Door Street, just a mile or so west students were organizing around a variety of issues on the "Toledo University" (now University of Toledo) campus. Both the Black Student Union as well as the Students for a Democratic Society became politically active at the college. Toledo's SDS, while small, ruffled a lot of feathers on campus and were even the target of extensive FBI surveillance. Recently declassified documents reveal their tactics were extremely dirty. One COINTELPRO operative, Gene Foder, recalled how he "would attend an organization's meeting and wait for speakers to denounce law enforcement, as they often did. Then, with a burst of apparent outrage, he would rise and point out his fellow undercover officers. The groups would kick out those officers and often welcome Mr. Fodor into their ranks, grateful for his watchful eye and unaware that he too was a part of the system they opposed."[26] The BSU, for its part, was also quite militant. At one point it occupied University Hall, the iconic building on campus,[27] in the aftermath of the the Jackson State shooting:

At 6:00 a.m. on Monday May 18, Black students blocked the entrances to University Hall for five hours. A crowd of about 2,000 gathered when they could not get into the building to attend classes, some angry and some supportive of the BSU. Their demands, very similar to those of Black students at San Francisco State College and Cornell, were as follows: "$200,000 for a Black studies programs, manned and directed by Blacks; the hiring of a full time coordinator of Black studies; first priority placed on hiring of Black professors in each department; a Black student enrollment commensurate with the population of Blacks in the City of Toledo; a minimum of three Black graduate students in every department" ("The Declaration," 1970, May 18). These demands arose after the BSU perceived that the UT administration did not respond to the deaths at Jackson State.[28]

The BSU continued this confident, militant approach throughout the 1980s. In 1985, at the age of 43 years old, co-founder of the Black Panther Party Huey P. Newton broke ten years of silence by addressing a crowd at the University of Toledo. He had been invited by the University of Toledo Black Student Union (BSU), which was in the midst of its struggle to get the University of Toledo to divest from its holdings in apartheid South Africa. He told the audience he had "thought BSUs had gone the way of my organization of SNCC," but instead that explained that the BSUs represented a "structure to start to build a national organization freedom." He maintained that students in general, and black students in particular, were becoming politically conscious largely through the struggle against apartheid in South Africa.[29] The BSU also brought former Black Panther, Communist Party leader, and prison scholar Angela Davis to campus. She, like Newton, engaged the issue of the divestment movement on campus: "I hear that there is a pretty strong divestment movement on this campus... Well, I think that you should keep on pushing for full and immediate divestment." [30] The BSU at UT in the 1980s was at the forefront of radical student politics with leaders like Mansour Bey who not only brought figures like Newton and Davis to Toledo, but militantly challenged the administration on issues like divestment from South Africa, even in the face of intimidation. [31]Throughout 1984 and 1985 the BSU brought anti-apartheid activists and native South Africans to campus to raise awareness and in June 1985 circulated a divestment petition. In October 1985 the BSU organized a march with over 100. Chants like "Long Live the African National Congress!" and signs such as "Apartheid is dead... may it rest in hell" characterized the march. [32] When protests alone did not accomplish their goals, the BSU erected mock shanties in protest, calling for total divestment. As The Blade reported at the time, the student action "placed TU [UT] on the crest of the biggest wave of protests on college campuses since the Vietnam War."[33] The shanty they erected was not removed until Mansour Bey, president of the BSU at the time, had secured a meeting with UT's president James McComas, who explained that UT would make its position on divestment public in three weeks.

Throughout this entire process the university administration harassed and threatened BSU leaders. As one statement explains, on the same day that they finally received a telephone call from the president in July of 1985, another call "came into the Black Student Union to tell us that campus security was investigating the records" of BSU leaders, including president Anthony Muharib and vice-president Mansour Bey. Then, Chief of Campus security Frank Pizzulo confronted Mansour Bey about some "old bench warrants" on the activists, which they claimed may "prove embarrassing if we, as student leaders were to be arrested." The BSU's July 31, 1985 remained defiant, however:

What we are concerned with here today is the double standard that prompted today's press conference [regarding divestment]. On the one hand, James [McComas] establishes a committee to study U.T.'s investments in South Africa, while on the underhand, the U.T. Security Forces launches an investigation and surveillance of those campus activists who have led the campaign to raise the political and moral consciousness of U.T.'s students and faculty... We are also very concerned with the overall implications of these police tactics which remind us of the very oppressive and inhumanitarian policies of the South African government which we are protesting against. Why these police tactics? Are they intended to intimdate all students into backing away from getting involved in controversial and unpopular issues? If so, it is not working! Therefore, we are today calling upon the support of the progressive elements of the Toledo community to stand with the Black Student Union in solidarity for our right as students and citizens of the United States to express our constitutionally guaranteed rights of freedom of speech. And furthermore, that we be permitted to continue our campaign to educate and motivate this campus to speak out on the evils and injust practices of the Botha regime in South Africa. Finally, we demand that the university's campus police forces cease and desist their harassment, investigations, and surveillance of U.T. students.[34]

In the end the University of Toledo convened an ad hoc South African Investments Study Committee that eventually called for divestment from South African apartheid. By August 1989, on the midnight hour of the apartheid regime, UT and two related private organizations completed their divestment from South Africa, totaling some $4.7 million in investments.[35]

Today the BSU is a far cry from the militant organization of the 1980s. Instead, some of the BSU's responses to the rampant murder of young black men has been paltry, acquiescent, and cowardly, not to mention their refusal to challenge US imperialism and militarism. [36] Part of this stems from the social composition of the current Black Student Union. In 2014 the BSU president refused to sign on to a statement linking the #BlackLivesMatter movement with Israel's summer assault on Gaza. The president of the BSU cited that with four of seven of their executive board members serving in armed forces via the University of Toledo's ROTC program, the BSU could not critique US policies. UT itself has recently been "recognized as a top school for military education,"[37] with one of the categories of qualification being "military culture," as can be obscenely witnessed by the disproportionate amount of students roaming the campus in their fatigues and the various training and combat simulation drills that regularly occur on campus grounds.

The BSU is not alone in this transformation from radicalism to acquiescence, however. The Latino Student Union, with radical Mexican-American working class roots, has largely devolved into a social organization that occasionally parrots US propaganda against radical states in Latin America. In 2014, for instance, the LSU become the marionette of a small but influential group of Venezuelan expats at the University of Toledo when they willingly spread vicious lies against the Venezuelan state.[38] The malicious campaign of propaganda continued in 2015, with one prominent Venezuelan student calling for US sanctions against her own country in an effort to oust Nicolas Maduro, the inheritor of Hugo Chavez's legacy, and the radical PSUV.[39] To combat this a collective of students interested in challenging the narrative of the powerful and privileged Venezuelan elites came together to form the University of Toledo Friends of Venezuela Society. Their first public statement called for "Hands off Venezuela, no to sanctions": Aside from the delusions of wealthy Venezuelan expatriates in Toledo and other U.S. cities, there is nothing the Venezuelan government has done that warrants sanctions. The primary reason they want to apply sanctions is because Chavez, Maduro, and the PSUV have threatened both the cupidity of the ruling class in Venezuela and challenged US hegemony in the region. As scholar George Ciccariello-Maher has argued in Jacobin magazine, "While the Venezuelan opposition in Venezuela is almost as delusional as the Venezuelan self-exiles in Miami [or Toledo], there's one big difference: opposition leaders on the ground have to live with the consequences of their catastrophic decisions... [Thus] while radical right-wingers in Florida [or Ohio] may be celebrating the sanctions, it would be suicidal for the opposition in Venezuela to do the same. They would simply prove what Chavistas already believe: that they are treasonous lapdogs of imperial power."

Indeed, students at UT and people of conscience should not fall for the narrative espoused by "treasonous lapdogs of imperial power." It is imperative, now more than ever, that progressive forces here in the US and around the world stand up and say "No to Sanctions!" and "Hands Off Venezuela!" Within just over a week four million Venezuelans signed a petition condemning sanctions against their country. We ought to listen to the millions of urban workers and campesinos, not the spawn of the elite here at UT. Perhaps the most important political development on UT's campus in the past few years, however, has been the advent and augmentation of the Palestine solidarity movement. Inspired by the upsurge in Palestine solidarity organizing around the country, a group of students came together to form Toledo's first organization dedicated to Palestinian solidarity in the summer of 2011. After four years of organization, education, and agitation on the issue, UT Students for Justice in Palestine led one of the most high profile divestment campaigns in the country. Calling on UT to divest from corporations that profited from the occupation of Palestine, UTSJP spearheaded an initiative modeled on the BSU's successful anti-apartheid divestment initiative. [40] In September, 2014 UTSJP paired with UT's Student African American Brotherhood to celebrate the resistance to police violence in Ferguson and the resistance to Israeli occupation in Gaza. Furthermore, they called "for the immediate end to police militarization and violence aimed at black communities in the U.S. and an immediate cessation of the $3 billion provided to Israel annually by our government to oppress the Palestinian people."[41]

By early 2015 UTSJP had pushed divestment to the forefront of campus life. In what was called "the craziest stories we've ever reported" by prominent commentator Phillip Weiss, the UT administration and Student Government originally colluded to shut down the UT Divest movement in a kangaroo court that ruled divestment "unconstitutional."[42] After a massive campaign led by a strong coalition of student groups at UT and solidarity organizations from around the country, the Student Government was eventually forced to reverse its position and voted 21 to 4 in favor of divestment on March 3, 2015.[43] Just over a month later, in late April, UT Divest won a major victory in the form of a student-wide referendum in which 57.13% of students voted to divest. Despite all of this, the university has refused to divest against the will of a majority of its students. As UTSJP's post-referendum victory letter explains, however, the struggle continues: We do not believe divestment is "contentious" or "incredibly difficult." Society's intolerable injustices do not require the search for a full consensus on what perfect justice looks like. We support divestment because we believe in human rights and international law. We believe UT should strive to actually implement its ethical and moral commitments, and adhere to its own mission statement of "improving the human condition." The majority of UT students agree with us. #UTDivest has created a movement on campus, a movement so resilient that it will continue to grow, to learn, to evolve, and to win. We will continue to work with and organize alongside all organizations that support social justice, and will struggle to ensure that UT is a place where human life is more important than profit. Consciousness has been raised, bodies have been moved, hearts and minds have been won. The arc of the moral universe is long, but it bends towards justice. #UTDivest will continue to move forward in the struggle for justice. [44]

The 2005 Toledo Rebellion and #BlackLivesMatter

One of the moments Toledo captured national media attention was in 2005 when a small group of neo-Nazis from outside of Toledo came to the city, ostensibly protest "crime." The neo-Nazis successfully utilized the state security apparatus to protect and shield themselves from mass popular resentment, invoking first amendment rights in order to acquire police protection. Hundreds of antiracists forced the city to cancel the attempted march by the neo-Nazi group, called the "National Socialist Movement," through a mostly black neighborhood in North Toledo. Instead, hundreds of residents faced off with 15 Nazis standing in "formation" on the lawn of Woodward High School. After escorting the neo-Nazis away from the anti-racist demonstration, riot police clashed with local residents angry over the neo-Nazi presence and the police protection provided by the city of Toledo. These clashes made national headlines. The city spent over $100,000 protecting the Nazis in 2005. As one local community activist, Washington Muhammad, explained at the time: "Everybody else does without a police escort. The Nazis should have had a banner behind them that said, 'Sponsored by the City of Toledo.'" [45] Anger spilled over into a small uprising, with some shops and local establishments being broken into and looted. Many of the black youth who clashed with police were arrested and sentenced, some for prison terms. In all some 114 protesters were arrested, with charges ranging from "assault, vandalism, failure to obey police, failure to disperse and overnight curfew violations." [46] The neo-Nazis were not only protected by the city of Toledo, they were successful in using the repressive apparatus of the state to arrest and then imprison black youth.

A decade later, on the tenth anniversary of their original visit, the same neo-Nazi organization, this time with a few more members, decided to attempt the same routine as before. This time, however, the city of Toledo confined them to a small section of downtown Toledo, and all of the surrounding blocks were shut down. Hundreds of on-duty, over-time, and volunteer police officers protected the small group of neo-Nazis. A highly militarized riot squad had dozens of police, some armed with assault rifles. These riot police were paired with hundreds of regular police officers. Armored vehicles were present, as well as an elaborate identification system that required facial photographs of any individual entering the area near the neo-Nazis. Although no clashes took place this time, largely due to the efforts of local organizers who held a well-attended Black Lives Matter Day in a separate location, the city of Toledo spent some $76,000 in overtime pay to protect the Nazis.[47]

Thus, the tactics of the neo-Nazi groups who came to Toledo suggest that these small extremist organizations make full use of the resources of the repressive state apparatus. The tentacles of the state not only shield the racists from popular anger, they are also used, as in 2005, to assault targeted populations and further the strategic goals of the neo-Nazis. Thus, as one local organizer proclaimed after the 2015 visit, there were around 300 fascists in Toledo that day; only 25 of them were neo-Nazis.

It is not coincidental that both visits by the Nazis were preceded by events in which the Toledo Police Department were involved in the deaths of black men. In February of 2005 TPD had electrocuted 41-year-old Jeffery Turner to death after shocking him nine times with a taser. His crime had been "loitering" near the Art Museum. Two years later a judge promptly dismissed the lawsuit his family brought against the TPD. [48] In March, 2015 34 year-old Aaron Pope died under police custody. Karen Madden, Pope's mother, explained that the police did not call for an ambulance and used excessive force against Pope. "I want justice. This has gone on too long," she exclaimed, her words not unlike those of the many mothers who have lost their sons to police violence.[49] The TPD is not alone in exercising immense state violence against black bodies. In Ohio alone many high-profile murders of black men and boys have occurred including John Crawford in Beavercreek, 12 year-old Tamir Rice in Cleveland, Samuel DuBose in Cincinnati, among others. The first two had been holding toy guns, the later was stopped in traffic for not having a front license plate. All were murdered in "unprovoked attack by racist pigs," to harp back to the language of the Toledo Panthers. In the United States a black person is murdered every 28 hours by police. By early June some 500 people had been killed by police in 2015 alone, nearly 30% of them black.[50] In response a collective of Toledo residents and long-standing community activists have formed the Community Solidarity Response Network. CSRN has been on the forefront of challenging police violence against black communities in Toledo.

Conclusion

In summation, then, Toledo is not without its radicalism. Toledo has been the site of social, economic, and political struggle for decades. From the Auto-Lite Strike to #BlackLivesMatter, the Palestine Solidarity movement to the Black Panthers, those of us residing in

Toledo have a prodigious amount of inspiration to draw from. Toledo is represents more than just social isolation and neoliberal deindustrialization. Toledo is also the Polish, Hungarian, and Italian immigrant workers who led the Auto-Lite strike, the Black prisoners and "lumpen-proletariat" that formed the Black Panthers and fought back against state repression, the activists who stood alongside their South African counterparts to end apartheid in South Africa, the Palestinian students in the diaspora who fight Israel's occupation. It is them and so much more. As the great Marxist historian and professor at the University of Toledo proclaimed in his final speech at UT: "We have the World to gain, the Earth to recuperate."[51] We in Toledo have always been and must continue to be part of the struggle to recuperate the Earth.

Notes

[1] http://www.toledoblade.com/Economy/2011/11/03/Toledo-area-poverty-rate-worst-in-U-S.html
[2] http://www.city-data.com/poverty/poverty-Toledo-Ohio.html
[3] http://www.econlib.org/library/Enc/GreatDepression.html
[4] See Zeitlow and Pope, 843.
[5] University of Toledo, College of Law.
[6] http://libcom.org/history/us-industrial-workers-movement
[7] http://www.wsws.org/en/articles/2009/05/tole-m27.html
[8] http://libcom.org/history/us-industrial-workers-movement
[9] See Zeitlow and Pope, 846-7.
[10] On the divide between the Musteites and the Communists, and the role of radical workers in the strike, see Roger Keeren, *The Communist Party and the Auto Workers Unions*.
https://libcom.org/history/communist-party-socialists-during-1934-toledo-auto-lite-strike
[11] http://www.wsws.org/en/articles/2009/05/tole-m27.html

[12] For more on the Auto-Lite Strike and other struggles during the period, see Irving Bernstein,*Turbulent Years: A History of the American Worker, 1933-1941.*

[13] See Zeitlow and Pope, 854.

[14] Patrick Dyer, http://socialistworker.org/2007-2/639/639_10_Detroit.shtml

[15] http://www.toledofreepress.com/2006/08/30/residents-recall-dorr-streets-black-mecca-days/

[16] https://iheartthreadbared.wordpress.com/2011/10/17/body-and-soul/

[17] http://www.toledoblade.com/Police-Fire/2007/02/21/Toledo-police-officer-killed-in-1970-shooting.html

[18] The Times - Sep. 18, 1970, http://news.google.com/newspapers?nid=1665&dat=19700918&id=wxsaAAAAIBAJ&sjid=iCQEAAAAIBAJ&pg=5985,3714699

[19] The Times - Sep. 18, 1970, http://news.google.com/newspapers?nid=1665&dat=19700918&id=wxsaAAAAIBAJ&sjid=iCQEAAAAIBAJ&pg=5985,3714699

[20] The Bryan Times - Dec 9, 1970

[21] The Times - Sep. 18, 1970, http://news.google.com/newspapers?nid=1665&dat=19700918&id=wxsaAAAAIBAJ&sjid=iCQEAAAAIBAJ&pg=5985,3714699

[22] http://www.negroartist.com/writings/BLACK%20PANTHER%20NEWSPAPERS/5%20no%207.htm

[23]http://www.negroartist.com/writings/BLACK%20PANTHER%20NEWSPAPERS/5%20no%2030.htm

[24] The Bryan Times - Dec 9, 1970 - http://news.google.com/newspapers?nid=799&dat=19701209&id=nVEwAAAAIBAJ&sjid=TVIDAAAAIBAJ&pg=3745,4165846

[25]http://www.negroartist.com/writings/BLACK%20PANTHER%20NEWSPAPERS/8%20no%2021.htm

[26] http://www.toledoblade.com/Police-Fire/2012/07/15/Surveillance-records-from-60s-70s-found.html#IVhTrVSb05tOu1gs.99

[27] For more on University Hall from one of Toledo's most radical professors, see Peter Linebaugh,

http://www.counterpunch.org/2014/05/16/how-did-we-get-here-university-hall-at-this-point-of-time-the-anthropocene/

[28] For more on unrest at UT in the 1965-72 period, see Matthew J. Deters, Preventing Violent Unrest: Student Protest at the University of Toledo, 1965-1972. MA Thesis, University of Toledo.

[29] Newspaper clipping, "Newton Ends 10-Year Silence With Talk at TU," Canaday Center, University of Toledo.

[30] Newspaper clipping, John Nichols, Toledo Blade, Canaday Center, University of Toledo.

[31] Add in BSU Statement here.

[32] Newspaper clipping, "Over 100 protestors march against apartheid," *The Collegian*.

[33] Newspaper clipping, Tanber, "TU Students Erect Shanty in Protest of Apartheid, Ask Total Divestitute," *The Blade*.

[34] Press Statement, Black Student Union, July 31 1985. Canaday Center.

[35] Newspaper clipping, "UT, 2 groups divest holdings in South Africa," The Blade.

[36] It should be noted that this may be shifting in the 2015-6 academic year, as the BSU is under a new leadership that appears more willing to confront this issue head-on.

[37] http://independentcollegian.com/2015/01/28/news/ut-recognized-as-a-top-school-for-military-education/

[38] http://www.hamptoninstitution.org/latino-student-organizations.html#.VcQHJPlVhBc

[39] http://independentcollegian.com/2015/03/25/opinion/letter-venezuela-benefits-from-sanctions/

[40] For a resevior of video, statements, etc. on #UTDivest, see http://utdivest.blogspot.com/

[41] http://independentcollegian.com/2014/09/16/opinion/letter-to-the-editor-solidarity-for-human-rights/

[42] http://mondoweiss.net/2015/02/divestment-officials-federation

[43] https://www.youtube.com/watch?v=SkT2RTndz-c

[44] https://www.facebook.com/UTDivest/posts/866974650049245

[45] http://socialistworker.org/2005-2/562/562_12_Toledo.shtml
[46] http://www.foxnews.com/story/2005/10/16/neo-nazi-march-causes-riots/
[47] http://www.toledonewsnow.com/story/28883577/city-neo-nazi-rally-cost-taxpayers-76767-in-overtime?clienttype=generic
[48] http://www.toledoblade.com/Courts/2012/05/16/Taser-death-suit-dismissed.html
[49] http://www.toledoblade.com/Police-Fire/2015/03/30/Family-of-Toledo-man-who-died-in-police-custody-seek-answers.html#EiPD6bCw4z4b9qHk.99
[50] http://www.theguardian.com/us-news/2015/jun/10/the-counted-500-people-killed-by-police-2015
[51] http://www.counterpunch.org/2014/05/16/how-did-we-get-here-university-hall-at-this-point-of-time-the-anthropocene/

Juxtaposing Anarchy
From Chaos to Cause

Colin Jenkins

   Anarchy is synonymous with chaos and disorder. It is a term that stands in direct contrast to the archetype of society we have become accustomed to: hierarchical, highly-structured, and authoritative. Because of this, it carries negative connotations. Merriam-Webster, the consensus source of meaning within the dominant paradigm, defines *anarchy* as: a situation of confusion and wild behavior in which the people in a country, group, organization, etc., are not controlled by rules or laws; or, a state of disorder due to absence or non-recognition of authority. The implications made in these definitions are clear - any absence of *authority*, *structure,* or *control* most surely amounts to *confusion,* *wild behavior*, and *disorder*. In other words, human beings are incapable of controlling themselves, maintaining order, and living peacefully amongst one another. So we are to believe. Far removed from the general presentation of anarchy is *anarchism*, a political philosophy rich in intellectual and theoretical tradition. Again turning to Merriam-Webster, we are told that *anarchism* is: a political theory holding all forms of governmental authority to be unnecessary and undesirable and advocating a society based on voluntary cooperation and free association of individuals and groups. Even from within the dominant paradigm, we see a wide range of divergence between anarchism, which is presented strictly as an idea, and anarchy, which is presented as the real and absolute consequence (though hypothetical) of transforming this idea to praxis. Juxtaposing these terms, injecting historical perspective to their meaning, and realizing the differences between their usage within the modern lexicon and their philosophical substance should be a worthy endeavor, especially for anyone who feels that future attempts at shaping a more just society will be fueled by ideas, both from the past and present.

While comparing and contrasting the various ways in which anarchy is deployed, we recognize three arenas: 1) Popular culture, which embraces and markets the association of chaos, wild behavior, and disorder; 2) Corporate politics, which uses the term as a pejorative, mostly to describe dominant right-wing platforms like the Tea Party and USAmerican libertarian movement; and 3) In activist and theoretical circles, where anarchism is understood as an authentic and legitimate political philosophy with roots firmly placed in the Enlightenment.

Pop Anarchy and Nihilism: Rebels *without* a Cause

The anti-authoritarian tendencies of anarchism are understandably attractive in a world that is overwhelmingly authoritative, intensely conformist, and socially restrictive. The conservative nature of American culture, which is notorious for repressing attitudes and beliefs that form outside of the dominant "white, Judeo-Christian" standard, begs for the existence of a thriving subculture that is based on rebellion, if only as an avenue of personal liberation and expression. The 1955 James Dean movie, *Rebel without a Cause*, offered a first glimpse into this nihilistic backlash against the deadening and soulless culture of conformity as it showcased the contradictory and often confusing nature of adolescence in white, middle-class suburbia.

On the heels of Dean was a baby-boomer revolution fueled by radical inquiry, hippie culture, bohemian lifestyles, and a "British Invasion." For the better part of a decade, the counterculture movement in the US that came to be known quite simply as "the '60s" boasted a wide array of meaningful causes, addressing everything from poverty to institutional racism and segregation to war. However, this brief period of revolutionary cause dissipated into a new and distinctly different counterculture through the 1970s and 80s, taking on a rebellious yet counterrevolutionary identity. In contrast to the existentialist nature of the 60s, which sought answers through philosophical exploration, the collective angst that developed in subsequent decades sought individual freedom through nihilism, self-destruction, and chronic apathy. Not giving a shit about detrimental traditions transformed into not giving a shit about anything. In turn, acts of defiance morphed from politically conscious and strategic opposition to oppressive structures to spiteful and self-destructive nothingness.

The revolutionary uprising of the 1960s, which had been stomped out by government suppression and maligned as an "excess of democracy," was effectively replaced by a reactionary insurrection bankrupt of any constructive analysis or productive goal. This nothingness was embraced by a significant counterculture that developed alongside the punk rock music scene, which flirted with anarchist politics before descending into an egoistic and narrow identity based in privilege. What followed was a brand of "pop anarchy" devoid any meaning beyond contrived images. Acts of rebellion were central, but a cause was neither constructed nor needed. The anarchist and revolutionary symbolism that screamed for meaning was reduced to shallow marketing schemes as remnants of legitimate angst were redirected into childish rants against parents, teachers, "the man," and "the system" - terms that often carried little meaning for those who used them. The exclusivity that developed made political organizing virtually impossible, and had an alienating effect on many. "Looking at the fact that most people who rear their heads at anarchist 'movement' events are roughly between 16-30 years old, with background influences of 'punk' or other 'alternative' persuasions," explains one former anarchist from the punk scene, "it is easy to understand why such 'movements' tend to alienate most people than interest them." A major problem that was exposed was demographics. "Punk primarily appealed to middle-class, staright white boys, who, thought they were 'too smart' for the rock music pushed by the corporations, still wanted to 'rock out.' It is also a culture that was associated with alienating oneself from the rest of society, often times in order to rebel against one's privileged background or parents." Because of this, "we have to admit that it was (and still is) exclusive."

By contrasting US punk culture of this time with its British counterpart, one could see the development of a counterculture that lacked revolutionary meaning or class context. As Neil Eriksen explains:

"The distinctions between US and British punk rock are based solidly on differences in the audience. In the US the counter-cultural character of punk is evident in the primary emphasis on style of dress and posturing. 'Middle class' youth can copy the style of the British punks and are afforded the economic and ideological space to make it a whole lifestyle, similar to the way the hippies dropped out, turned on and tuned in. It is primarily those who do not have to work for a living who can afford the outrageous blue, green and orange punk hair styles and gold safety pins. The working class generally cannot choose to go to work with orange hair. In England punk is much more complex, especially given the history of other sub-cultures such as the Mods, Rockers and Skinheads. British punks find in their sub-cultural expressions of music and attitudes, as well as styles, more of an organic indication of their experiences as under- or unemployed youth. In the US, punk has few organic working class roots, and it thus functions as a broad counter-cultural milieu that does not indict the system for lack of jobs, but tends toward nihilism and mindlessness."

The counterculture described above was a favorable, and almost inevitable, result of both appropriation from above and cooptation at the hands of capitalist profit. Revolutionary politics, in its authentic form, is not a profitable commodity. Instead, the radical roots of anarchist philosophy, which are briefly described in the definition of "anarchism" provided by Merriam-Webster, serve as a threat to any society that possesses extreme divisions of power and wealth. The United States - with its hierarchical governmental structure, no-holds-barred corporate landscape, and extreme divisions between the wealthy and everyone else (20% of the population owns 90% of the wealth) is no exception. For this reason, anarchism has (historically) been appropriated by the dominant culture (which is shaped by this 20%), diluted to anarchy, and served to the masses in the form of entertainment. This process has led to "gradual appearances in mainstream culture over the course of several years, at times far removed from its political origin (described bySituationists as " recuperation"). These appearances typically connected it with anarchy and were intended as sensationalist marketing ploys, playing off the mainstream association of anarchy with chaos."

The most recent form of this appropriation has come in the popular television series, Sons of Anarchy, which depicts a California biker gang inundated with drama, drug abuse, senseless murders, gun-running, and gang activity. Despite glimpses and a few mentions of the fictional founder's manifesto, which included some scattered words by genuine anarchists like Emma Goldman and Pierre Joseph Proudhon, the show clearly chooses chaos and senseless, self-serving crime as its theme. The pinnacle of this appropriation, and ignorance of the rich history of philosophical anarchism, concludes with reviews that refer to one of the show's main characters, a ruthless, murderous, and power-hungry leader by the name of Clay Morrow, as a "true anarchist."

Liberal Enablers and the Right's Appropriation of Libertarianism

In the midst of the US government shutdown in October of 2013, Senate Majority Leader Harry Reid took to the Senate floor to criticize the move. "We have a situation where we have a good day with the anarchists," Reid said. "Why? Because the government is closed." Reid's comment was meant as a jab to the Republican Party, which was largely responsible for allowing the shutdown to take place, purely as a political ploy. A few days later, Democratic Senator Elizabeth Warren referred to "anarchist tirades" and "thinly veiled calls for anarchy in Washington" coming from Tea Party members in the House as the impetus for the shutdown. Warren even went as far as equating anarchists with "pessimists and ideologues whose motto is, 'I've got mine, the rest of you are on your own,' while ironically tying in neoliberal deregulation that "tolerates dangerous drugs, unsafe meat, dirty air, or toxic mortgages," as an "anarchists' dream."

"Anarchy" has maintained its status as a pejorative in the modern American liberal lexicon, but not by choice. Borrowing from the nihilism of pop anarchy, it embraces misconceptions, ignores historical roots, and guts the term of genuine meaning. Considering that such rhetoric is coming from folks who have advanced degrees in political science, careers as political pundits, and a working knowledge of history, it can only be explained as calculated fear-mongering. The fact of the matter is that the Republican Party is just as "statist" as the Democratic Party, if only in different ways. And while the approach of political sects like the Tea Party and USAmerican "libertarian" movements present a less-statist platform than their counterparts from within the establishment, their philosophical make-ups (if you can even call them that) include a blatant disregard for the public at-large, an underlying racism that is dangerously oppressive, a love affair with capitalism, a childish refusal to recognize needs outside of privileged interests, a fanatical support for gun rights, and a narrow-minded obsession with protecting private property and personal wealth - beliefs that are more in line with the self-absorbed, reactionary nature of fascism than with the revolutionary, "cooperative individualism" of anarchism. Ultimately, the Tea Party, much like the USAmerican "libertarian" movement, is focused on one goal: protecting an embedded array of privilege and maintaining the status quo; and the means to their end (at least, theoretically) is the coercive power structure of the market, as opposed to that of the state. If and only when the market hierarchy is threatened by, say, a popular uprising, a workers strike, or a movement for civil rights, this brand of "libertarian" views the state - in the form of domestic police and military forces - as a necessary component. In other words, these so-called "anarchists" are really nothing of the sort. Instead, they are more than willing to use state power to uphold historically-based inequities related to wealth accumulation, racism, and class division.

If the cheap political jabs used by liberals were packed with historical context, they could be closer to the truth. However, this would defeat the purpose. Parts of the right-wing have, in fact, appropriated and twisted anarchist philosophy, mostly through a concerted effort to adopt an ahistorical version of "libertarianism." In his "anarcho-capitalist" manifesto, *Betrayal of the American Right*, Murray Rothbard explained this intent:

"One gratifying aspect of our rise to some prominence is that, for the first time in my memory, we, 'our side,' had captured a crucial word from the enemy. Other words, such as 'liberal,' had been originally identified with laissez-faire libertarians, but had been captured by left-wing statists, forcing us in the 1940s to call ourselves rather feebly 'true' or 'classical' liberals. 'Libertarians,' in contrast, had long been simply a polite word for left-wing anarchist; that is for anti-private property anarchists, either of the communist or syndicalist variety. But now we had taken it over, and more properly from the view of etymology; since we were proponents of individual liberty and therefore of the individual's right to his property."

Of course, like all others who claim this contradictory title of anarcho-capitalist, Rothbard either failed to recognize "how property results in similar social relations and restrictions in liberty as the state," or simply believed that "liberty" was synonymous with feudalistic ideals. As one anarchist (of the authentic variety) writer laments, the thought process of this faux-anarchism is that a "capitalist or landlord restricting the freedom of their wage-workers and tenants" is ok, but any such restrictions from "the state" is not. "It's an oddity that in the United States, the main current of libertarian thought has been twisted and inverted into a kind of monstrous stepchild," explains Nathan Schneider. "Rather than seeking an end to all forms of oppression, our libertarians want to do away with only the government kind, leaving the rest of us vulnerable to the forces of corporate greed, racial discrimination, and environmental destruction."

Since the Democratic Party's use of the term borrows from the simplistic, nihilistic version of "pop anarchy," rather than the complex, philosophical version of anarchism, it becomes useful within the modern political arena. The true right-wing appropriation of anarchism as noted by Rothbard, which is fabricated in its own right, becomes buried under the fear-mongering and falsely implied association by the likes of Reid and Warren. Historically, this same type of fear-mongering has allowed for fascist scapegoating (Reichstag Fire), capitalist scapegoating (Haymarket Affair), and unlawful state executions (Sacco and Vanzetti), all designed to exploit widespread ignorance regarding anarchist beliefs and prevent authentic libertarian movements from spreading through the populace. "The figure of the anarchist has long dominated our national imagination," explains Heather Gautney. "It's a word that conjures up the lawless, the nihilistic and even the violent. It's the image Senators Reid and Warren invoked in their talking points against the Republicans." It's also an image devoid any real meaning. By removing its substance and demonizing its association, the establishment wins.

Anarcho-Punk, Underground Hip Hop, and Conscious Chaos: Rebels *with* a Cause

While "pop anarchy" took over much of the American punk scene in the '70s and '80s, it was only part of the story. Punk culture still served what Henry Rollins once succinctly described as "the perfect expression of postmodern angst in a decadent society," creating an outlet for rebellious urges seeping from the dominant culture. It also served as a catalyst for pockets of revolutionary politics. When done right, it was the perfect combination of expression and meaning. The hard, edgy, and chaotic sounds spilling from the music represented a form of liberation that was desperately needed, while the lyrics roared against the establishment and aimed at deadening conformity and the music industry's increasingly corporatized and cookie-cutter production value. The UK provided an example of this perfection when it birthed anarcho-punk.

"From the numerous situationist slogans that graced the lyrics of early punk bands, to the proliferation of anarcho-punk bands such as Crass and Conflict in the early eighties, punk rock as a subculture has had a unique history of having a strong relationship with explicitly anarchist and anti-capitalist political content over the years," explains an anonymous Colours of Resistance blogger . "Many anarchists today, including myself, are by-products of punk rock, where most become politicized from being exposed to angry, passionate lyrics of anarcho-punk bands, "do-it-yourself" zines, and countless other sources of information that are circulated within the underground punk distribution networks. Some are introduced to punk through the introduction to the anarchist social circles. Regardless of which comes first, the correlation between the punk scene and the anarchist scene is hard to miss, especially at most anarchist gatherings and conferences."

Within the anarcho-punk movement, "the possibilities for advances in popular culture in the dissolution of capitalist hegemony and in building working class hegemony" began to surface. "The fact that punk rock validated political themes in popular music once again," Eriksen suggests, "opened the field" for the left libertarian movements. As an example, punk initiatives like "Rock Against Racism were able to sponsor Carnivals with the Anti-Nazi League drawing thousands of people and many popular bands to rally against racism and fascism" and "openly socialist bands like the Gang of Four were taken seriously by mainstream rock critics and record companies, and thereby were able to reach a broad audience with progressive entertainment."

Punk ideologies that arose from this era touched on concepts like anti-establishment, equality, freedom, anti-authoritarianism, individualism, direct action, free thought, and non-conformity - many ideas that are synonymous with historical-anarchist thought. This social consciousness naturally led to activism, and specifically, acts of direct action, protests, boycotts, and squatting. These elements represented authentic anarchist philosophy and served as a counter to nihilistic and empty "pop anarchy," while politicizing many.

Another form of "rebellion with a cause" came from American hip-hop and rap. The rise of hip-hop in the US paralleled that of the punk scene, and shared many of the same revolutionary tendencies. While not explicitly anarchist, hip-hop took on an identity that mirrored authentic anarchist philosophy. Its anti-authoritarian nature was far from nihilistic, but rather survivalist; born in response to centuries of racial subjugation, economic strangulation, and violent oppression at the hands of domestic police forces. Hip-hop's birthplace, the Bronx (NYC), characterized its development. "Heavily influenced by the economically and socially oppressed ghettoes, along with the echoes of the last generation's movements for liberation and the street gangs that filled in the void they left," Derek Ide tells us, "the South Bronx provided the perfect matrix in which marginalized youth could find a way to articulate the story of their own lives and the world around them. In this historically unique context, a culture would be created through an organic explosion of the pent-up, creative energies of America's forgotten youth. It was a culture that would reach every corner of the world in only a couple decades.."

In the end, hip-hop and gangsta rap provided endless displays of socially-conscious and revolutionary tracks throughout the '80s and '90s, and combined with the punk scene to construct a form of "conscious chaos" that provided valuable social and cultural analyses as well as revolutionary goals that sought to establish a more just world. These counter-cultural movements represented an important about-turn from the contrived nihilism and "pop anarchy" that had surfaced in response to the "excess of democracy" in the '60s, and displayed elements that echoed authentic anarchism, as a revolutionary libertarian philosophy.

Authentic Anarchism and Its Philosophical Roots

The roots of Anarchism, as a school of thought, are firmly placed in the Age of Enlightenment and, specifically, within two major themes stemming from that period: liberalism and socialism. In a sea of definitions, one of the most concise and encompassing is offered by Lucien van der Walt and Michael Schmidt in their 2009 book, "Black Flame: The Revolutionary Class Politics of Anarchism and Syndicalism." In it, they describe anarchism as "a revolutionary and libertarian socialist doctrine" that "advocates individual freedom through a free society" and "aims to create a democratic, egalitarian, and stateless socialist order through an international and internationalist social revolution, abolishing capitalism, landlordism, and the state." [1]

Anarchism's roots in the Enlightenment are undeniable. From Jean-Jacques Rousseau's "Discourse on Inequality" to Wilhelm von Humboldt's "The Limits of State Action," the libertarian strain born of this time served as the precursor to the anarchist thinkers of the

19th and 20th centuries. Their similarities are found in a philosophical examination of social inequities like personal wealth, private property, political power, and all forms of authority established within human societies - elements that are heavily scrutinized by anarchists. However, despite these roots, Schmidt and van der Walt tell us that anarchism should be considered "a relatively recent phenomenon" that emerged specifically "from the 1860s onward within the context of the modern working-class and socialist movement, within the womb of the First International." [2] For this reason, anarchism can most aptly be described as "socialism from below." In fact, the demarcation between enlightenment philosophy and anarchist thought is generally found in their distinct reactions to hierarchies created by systems of monarchy, feudalism, and theocracy (enlightenment) and hierarchies created by the exploitative nature of capitalism and the modern liberal, democratic state (anarchism).

The development and separation of anarchism from the Enlightenment was made clear by prominent anarchist thinkers at and around the turn of the 20 th century. In the years following the Paris Commune, Russian revolutionary anarchist, Mikhail Bakunin, expressed his disgust with the idea of a "purely formal liberty conceded, measured out and regulated by the State, an eternal lie which in reality represents nothing more than the privilege of some founded on the slavery of the rest," and "the shabby and fictitious liberty extolled by the School of J-J Rousseau and the other schools of bourgeois liberalism, which considers the would-be rights of all men, represented by the State which limits the rights of each - an idea that leads inevitably to the reduction of the rights of each to zero."[3] A few decades later, in a critique of liberalism, Peter Kropotkin denounced the aim of all so-called "superior civilizations," which was "not to permit all members of the community to develop in a normal way," but rather "to permit certain, better-endowed individuals fully to develop, even at the cost of the happiness and the very existence of the mass of mankind." This separation had much to do with the newly developed social constraints stemming from capitalism. As Noam

Chomsky explains, "It is true that classical libertarian thought is opposed to state intervention in social life, as a consequence of deeper assumptions about the human need for liberty, diversity, and free association..." however, "on the same assumptions, capitalist relations of production, wage labor, competitiveness, and the ideology of 'possessive individualism' all must be regarded as fundamentally antihuman" as well. For this reason, he suggests, "libertarian socialism is properly regarded as the inheritor of the liberal ideals of the Enlightenment," while it also embraces its own identity through the inclusion of a class analysis and critique of the coercive structures stemming from the capitalist hierarchy.[4]

   The socialist nature of anarchism represents a fundamental current in both its thought and process, yet is often overlooked by many who claim to be anarchists, especially in the United States. This misunderstanding is caused by both pro-market (and even pro-capitalist) "libertarian" movements that are ahistorical and seemingly blind to the authoritative structures of modern, industrial capitalism, as well as by the abovementioned "pop anarchy" phenomenon and "liberal enabling" that falsely limit anarchism to a vague and unsophisticated "anti-government" stance. Superficial dualities that have captured consensus thought, most notably that of "collectivism vs. individualism," are also largely responsible for this misinterpretation. Because of this, the virtual disappearance of class analysis from modern libertarian thought in the United States not only represents a significant departure from nearly two centuries of libertarianism, but also neglects to address a highly-authoritative and hierarchical private structure that has long surpassed its governmental counterpart. Schmidt and van der Walt explain the importance of rejecting "pop anarchy" stereotypes and maintaining this class analysis within anarchist thought: "For anarchists, individual freedom is the highest good, and individuality is valuable in itself, but such freedom can only be achieved within and through a new type of society. Contending that a class system prevents the full development of individuality, anarchists advocate class struggle from below to create a better world. In this ideal new order, individual freedom will be harmonised with communal obligations through cooperation, democratic decision-making, and social and economic equality. Anarchism rejects the state as a centralised structure of domination and an instrument of class rule, not simply because it constrains the individual or because anarchists dislike regulations. On the contrary, anarchists believe rights arise from the fulfilment of obligations to society and that there is a place for a certain amount of legitimate coercive power, if derived from collective and democratic decision making.

The practice of defining anarchism simply as hostility to the state has a further consequence: that a range of quite different and often contradictory ideas and movements get conflated. By defining anarchism more narrowly, however, we are able to bring its key ideas into a sharper focus, lay the basis for our examination of the main debates in the broad anarchist tradition in subsequent chapters, and see what ideas are relevant to current struggles against neoliberalism."[5]

When considering and rejecting both public and private forms of restriction, the most fundamental element of authentic anarchism clearly becomes cooperation. This theme was thoroughly established by Kropotkin in his 1902 classic, Mutual Aid: A Factor of Evolution, in which he pointed to "the practice of mutual aid, which we can retrace to the earliest beginnings of evolution, we thus find the positive and undoubted origin of our ethical conceptions; and we can affirm that in the ethical progress of man, mutual support not mutual struggle - has had the leading part. In its wide extension, even at the present time, we also see the best guarantee of a still loftier evolution of our race." This theme was echoed by Rudolf Rocker in his 1938 treatise on Anarcho-Syndicalism. Said Rocker, "Anarchism is a definite intellectual current in the life of our time, whose adherents advocate the abolition of economic monopolies and of all political and social coercive institutions within society" while calling on "a free association of all productive forces based upon cooperative labor" to replace "the present capitalistic economic order."[6]

Why Does this Matter?

The importance of Anarchist theory lies in its critique of hierarchies and the uneven distribution of power emanating from such. This makes this school of thought an important component as we move forward in attempting to address the pervasive ills of society, whether coming from the state or corporate structures that tower over us. The mere questioning of these "authorities" is crucial in itself. As Chomsky tells us:

"... any structure of hierarchy and authority carries a heavy burden of justification, whether it involves personal relations or a large social order. If it cannot bear that burden - sometimes it can - then it is illegitimate and should be dismantled. When honestly posed and squarely faced, that challenge can rarely be sustained. Genuine libertarians have their work cut out for them." [7]

While many socialist-oriented strains incorporate this same analysis, some do not. Essentially, regarding the formation of class-consciousness, anarchist theory of all varieties (syndicalism, mutualism, communism, etc.) act as ideal compliments to historically strong currents of Marxism, Leninism, Maoism, and Trotskyism, and should be included within all such theoretical considerations. When transforming theory to praxis, anarchism's inclusion of worker collectivization in the form of labor or trade unions prove valuable in this regard. In his treatise on Syndicalism, Rocker made a compelling argument for the usefulness of this brand of anarchism as a component to working-class emancipation. For the Anarcho-Syndicalists," says Rocker, "the trade union is by no means a mere transitory phenomenon bound up with the duration of capitalist society, it is the germ of the socialist economy of the future, the elementary school of socialism in general." He continues, "Every new social structure makes organs for itself in the body of the old organism. Without this preliminary, any social evolution is unthinkable. Even revolutions can only develop and mature the germs which already exist and have made their way into the consciousness of men (and presumably, women); they cannot themselves create these germs or generate new worlds out of nothing." [8]

Putting this philosophy into action is still of utmost importance. Creating a brand that is palatable and accessible to the working-class majority, without sacrificing its revolutionary tone and message, is also crucial. In his 2013 book, "Translating Anarchy: The Anarchism of Occupy Wall Street," Mark Bray stresses the importance of deploying a practical anarchism which avoids the esoteric idealism that so many genuine and well-intentioned anarchists get bogged down in. This pragmatic approach is perhaps most important when attempting to relay information via short interviews and sound bites. Bray points to three specific lessons he learned while interacting with mainstream media during his time at Zuccotti Park:

"First, I learned the value of presenting my revolutionary ideas in an accessible format. How I dress, the words I choose, and how I articulate them affect how I am received, so if my primary goal is to convince people of what I am saying, then it's often useful to shed my "inessential weirdness." Second, I realized the usefulness of letting tangible examples sketch the outline of my ideas without encumbering them with explicit ideological baggage. Finally, I concluded that the importance that Americans place on the electoral system dictates that any systematic critique should start with the corporate nature of both parties. Like it or not, that's where most people are at in terms of their political framework, so if you skip past the candidates to alternative institutions, for example, without convincing them of the bankrupt nature of the electoral system, you'll lose them." [9]

Essentially, anarchism is what democracy is supposed to be - self-governance. In this sense, anyone even remotely involved in the Occupy movement had the privilege, likely for the first time in their lives, to truly witness democracy (anarchism) in action. "This is not the first time a movement based on fundamentally anarchist principles - direct action, direct democracy, a rejection of existing political institutions and attempt to create alternative ones - has cropped up in the US," explains David Graeber. "The civil rights movement (at least, its more radical branches), the anti-nuclear movement, the global justice movement ... all took similar directions." And, in a country where a large majority of citizens have given up on and/or no longer believe in their representatives, a little democracy may be exactly what we need, even if it's not what our white, wealthy, slave-owning "founding fathers" wanted. "Most (of the founding fathers) defined 'democracy' as collective self-governance by popular assemblies, and as such, they were dead set against it, arguing it would be prejudicial against the interests of minorities (the particular minority that was had in mind here being the rich)," Graeber tells us. "They only came to redefine their own republic - modeled not on Athens, but on Rome - as a 'democracy' because ordinary Americans seemed to like the word so much."

In our inevitable and necessary escape from the faux democracy of America's colonists and founders, anarchist thought will undoubtedly play a role. It is, after all, the only school of thought that can be described as authentic, class-based libertarianism. Its foundation is the reasonable expectation that all structures of dominance, authority, and hierarchy must justify themselves; and, if they cannot, they must be dismantled.

This covers ALL coercive institutions - not only governments, the state, police, and military, but also cultural phenomena like patriarchy, racism, and white supremacy, and most importantly, economic systems like capitalism. Unlike modern forms of "libertarianism" in the US, which ignore racist structures and the historical formations behind them, and falsely view the labor-capital relationship inherent in capitalism as a "choice," authentic Anarchism correctly views such elements as coercive and forced; and seeks to dismantle them in order to move forward with constructing a society based on free association, where all human beings have a healthy degree of control over their lives, families, and communities.

Contrary to consensus thought (propaganda), such as those rooted in "rugged individualism" and "American exceptionalism," there is a collective and cooperative nature to true liberty. We simply cannot gain control over our lives until we learn to respect the lives of all others. This is the essence of community. And we cannot begin to do this until we deconstruct illegitimate hierarchies of wealth and power, which have been constructed through illegal and immoral means over the course of centuries. Recognizing these structures and realizing that they are NOT legitimate, and therefore do not deserve to exist, is the first step in this process. Embracing contributions from this school of thought is crucial in this regard. Fundamentally, Anarchism is a working-class ideology. Occupy Wall Street was largely influenced by it. Workers' co-ops are largely influenced by it. Any action that attempts to establish free association within society can learn much from it. Its foundational requirement of organic human cooperation and peaceful co-existence has been tried and tested throughout history - from hunter-gatherer societies across the world to Native American communities to the Paris Commune to revolutionary Catalonia to Chiapas. It provides a philosophical foundation - not a rigid blueprint - that allows for limitless potential in attempting to solve our problems, collectively, while trying to carve out a meaningful human experience for everyone. It may not provide all answers, or even most, but its foundation is worthy of building from, or at least considering. Its true value is found in its inclusion of historical formations as well as its role as a catalyst for new ideas and action - something we desperately need, moving forward.

Notes

[1] Schmidt, Michael & van der Walt, Lucien. Black Flame: The Revolutionary Class Politics of Anarchism and Syndicalism. AK Press, 2009, p. 33

[2] Schmidt & van der Walt, p. 34

[3] Guerin, Daniel. "Anarchism: From Theory to Practice." Monthly Review Press, 1970. Taken from the Preface by Noam Chomsky.

[4] *Chomsky on Anarchism* , selected and edited by Barry Pateman. AK Press: 2005, p. 122-123

[5] Schmidt and van der Walt, p. 33

[6] Rudolf Rocker, *Anarcho-Syndicalism: Theory and Practice*, 6th edition. AK Press, 2004. P. 1

[7] *Chomsky on Anarchism* , p. 192.

[8] Rocker, P. 59.

[9] Mark Bray, *Translating Anarchy: The Anarchism of Occupy Wall Street*. Zero Books, 2013.

Society & Culture

A Country Walking Dead
The Zombie as Metaphor in American Culture and Film

Sean Posey

We are currently living through the age of the zombie-zombie politics, zombie banks, zombie infrastructure, etc. Public intellectuals such as Noam Chomsky, Chris Hedges, Paul Krugman, and others have used the zombie as a metaphor for everything from our dysfunctional financial system to our alienating political institutions. The popularity of zombies among public intellectuals and its potent symbolism is best reflected in the zombie films of the past few decades, which have traced long-term problems in American society.

For over forty years, the films of George A. Romero-and now the television show *The Walking Dead*-have reflected the major failings of social institutions and community in America. Zombie films tend to wax in times of discontent and uncertainty and wane (at least in quality) in times of prosperity and quietude. Romero's films echo societal themes that are growing increasingly important and increasingly dark. And in the post-2008 era, where institutional failure is so widespread that the term "zombie' can be freely and accurately applied, we have truly entered the age of the living dead, which is best showcased by the enormous popularity of *The Walking Dead.*

George Romero's *Night of the Living Dead* introduced zombies to the mainstream public consciousness during one of the most turbulent years in American history-1968. Outside of the dark movie houses, America was tearing itself apart in the streets of the inner cities and in the massive protests against the Vietnam War. The film itself centers on a motley crew of travelers taking refuge in a farmhouse as the dead rise up around them. Filmed outside of Pittsburgh, one can't help but think of how the countryside would have seemed an appealing escape in 1968 as Pittsburgh's Homewood and Hill neighborhoods burned in the aftermath of Martin Luther King's assassination. The racially tinged power struggle that takes place in the film between Ben (Duane Jones) and Harry (Karl Hardman) mirrored the racial struggle taking place across the country and in nearby Pittsburgh in 1968.

The battle between Ben and Harry eventually sets the stage for the failure of the travelers' efforts to halt the zombie onslaught. This acts as a kind of stand-in for the inability to build the "beloved community" that Martin Luther King famously described, and which seemed to die with him. The inability of the makeshift group to pull together and the failure of the government to master the crisis-conveyed through television broadcasts-reflected the seeming impotency of the American government on both foreign and domestic fronts in the late 1960s.

The decade of the 1970s brought further crises for America that was exhibited in zombie films. Romero's 1978 zombie sequel, *Dawn of the Dead,* captured the ennui of the decade of stagflation, suburbanization, and consumerism. At the beginning of the film, a group of four survivors escape the confines of a collapsing city in a helicopter. Without food or prospects, they land atop a large suburban shopping mall. As in *Night of The Living Dead* rural areas-despite their hallowed place in the American imagination-hold little promise. Rampaging soldiers and civilians make a game out of killing zombies in the sticks. As one character puts it, "Those rednecks are probably enjoying this whole thing." [1]Instead, the mall, with its cornucopia of merchandise, becomes the mecca for the group-and for the zombies.

Dawn highlights the 'zombiefication' of the American consumer class. Even in death, hordes of former shoppers surround the mall and mindlessly wander its confines. While watching the zombies, the survivors muse on their motivations.

Fran: They're still here.
Stephen: They're after us. They know we're still in here.
Peter: They're after the place. They don't know why; they just remember. Remember that they want to be in here.

The group themselves, after expelling the undead from the mall, fall back into the familiar pattern of shopping-consumerism survives even the end of the world. And Romero's set-up mimics the geographic and societal reality of the day: Cities are "dead zones" to be avoided, and the mall is the centerpiece of American life, and in this case, also death. Even though America was reeling from high gas prices in the 1970s, it continued to build far-flung suburbs that contributed to the hollowing out of cities. The traditional downtown had been replaced as the center of civic life by the mall. [2] In the film, the group is eventually challenged for control of the mall, not by the undead, but by a marauding biker gang. Symbolically, the mall becomes a place where community goes to die. The mall, as in real life, became not a center for community, but a center for consumption-and those considered undesirable could be excluded.[3]

As the doldrums of the 1970s gave way to "Morning in America," domestic zombie films lost their hard edge.[4] Spoofs and sophomoric scripts probably seemed more natural for a frivolous decade of excess. In the middle of a long line of films like *I Was a Teenage Zombie, Redneck Zombie,* and *Hard Rock Zombies* came the third film in Romero's trilogy-*Day of the Dead.* This exceptionally dark film failed to perform at the box office, and was bested by the tongue-in-cheek *Return of the Living Dead.*

Day begins with another group of survivors surveying the now totally overrun cities. However, most of the film takes place in a claustrophobic military complex underground. Members of the military-represented as brutes and would-be fascists-and a team of scientists occupy opposite sides.

Even the pretend world of the mall in *Dawn* is no longer possible, as one character mockingly mentions: "You know the power's off on the mainland now, in case you haven't heard. And all the shopping malls are closed."[5]

In *Day*, institutional failure and the failure of community are central. Once again, the remnants of humanity are unable to pull together. The military fails, and the scientific community is ultimately rendered impotent. The zombies breach the underground complex and only a few people escape. As film scholar Robin Woods puts it, "*Day* represents an uncompromisingly hostile response to the 80s...And beyond that, the film prefigures our own dark times: *Day* is if anything more relevant today than it was when it appeared, as things have only got progressively blacker and more desperate, and events are currently escalating into a world situation of which the end of life on the planet (...the pollution of the environment) seems a not unlikely outcome."[6]

The American zombie failed to captivate audiences in the roaring 1990s. There appeared to be little place for the undead-even in jokey spoofs-in a time of credit default swaps, technological triumphalism, and nearly full employment. Yet all that changed with beginning of the twenty-first century-the dawn of the new zombie era. Some scholars have tied the rebirth of interest in and fascination with zombies to the coming of the post- 911 world. [7] There certainly is truth to that; however, some of the best films of the genre from the new century are British or from other foreign markets. Dreadful dreck like*Resident Evil* and the remake of *Dawn of the Dead* were among the biggest American hits of the immediate post-911 era.

It wasn't until 2005, when George Romero returned with *Land of the Dead*, that we saw a return to the themes of community in crisis and the failure of institutions that directly reflects what is

567

happening in America. As Roger Ebert put it, "The parallels with the real world are tantalizing." [8] Much like our society, the city where *Land* takes place is riven by vast class chasms. While most of the city's population lives in filth and misery, the wealthy elite exist in the confines of a high-rise known as Fiddlers Green. Led by Dennis Hooper-in a character directly modeled after Dick Cheney-Fiddlers Green resembles something straight out of Thorsten Veblen's *Theory of the Leisure Class*. The wealthy class relies on a series of mercenaries to do their bidding and to procure for them the luxuries they are accustomed to. However, after being rejected for membership in the Green, one of the mercenaries (John Leguizamo) sets in a motion a series of events that brings down both the rich and the impoverished as zombies breach the city's defenses.

The post-2008 era has arguably woven the living dead even deeper into the American fabric.[9]Journalism, economics, and political writing have eagerly adopted the zombie metaphor. And the zombie has come to the small screen as well. Today, the most popular show on television is AMC's*The Walking Dead*. And though George Romero has called it "a soap opera with a zombie occasionally," *The Walking Dead* sums up its time as well as any of Romero's era-defining zombie films.[10]

Walking is an unremittingly bleak show, one that would seem an unlikely hit. The desperate journey of ex-police officer Rick Grimes and his band is awesomely trying and tragic. As they stumble from one near disaster to another, Grimes' group eventually makes their home in a prison-one of the most failed institutions in modern American life. Their main nemesis becomes a man known as the "The Governor," who heads a gated community where life...almost...carries on as before, with the population largely blinded to the disaster outside the town's limits. Like the survivors trapped in the mall in *Dawn of the Dead*, the residents of Woodbury try to continue their lives of consumption and comfort. *Walking* highlights the failure of community in America, but it also eschews individualism. Almost every episode points to the importance of communal action. This is especially evident in the pointless war The Governor wages on Rick's group that eventually ends up destroying both sides. Rick's insistence on building a beloved community where ethical action and communal decision-making are paramount, clashes with the self-destructive and maniacal vision of The Governor. As in the Romero films, humans become a far more dangerous obstacle than the undead themselves.

Despite Romero's criticism of the show, *Walking* reflects his own summation of his living dead series: "All of my zombie films have been about the humans. The zombies, they could be anything.... The stories are about how people fail to respond in the proper way." [11] *The Walking Dead* is also much more about the failure of people, institutions, and community, than it is about zombies. Like the films of Romero, *The Walking Dead* acts as an allegory for our times. There is little room for hope in *The Walking Dead*, but that has not diminished its popularity.

As the American people-and American institutions--have failed to respond in the proper way, the zombie has become a more trenchant symbol of a country walking dead. The films of George A. Romero, and now the show *The Walking Dead,* best illustrate that evolution. However, unlike Rick Grimes and company, and the survivors of the Romero films, we have not yet met our apocalypse, and our institutions and communities have not fully failed us...not yet.

References

[1] *Dawn of the Dead,* directed by George Romero, United Films, 1978.

[2] Lizabeth Cohen, *A Consumers' Republic*: *The Politics of Mass Consumption in Postwar America*(New York: Vintage Books, 2003), 6.

[3] Ibid., 265.

[4] Peter Dendle, *The Zombie Movie Encyclopedia* (Jefferson, McFarland Press, 2010), 8-9.

[5] *Day of the Dead* , directed by George Romero, United Films, 1985.

[6] Robin Wood, *Hollywood from Vietnam to Reagan...And Beyond* (New York: Columbia University Press, 2003), 223.

[7] James Russell, *The Book of the Dead*: *The Complete History of Zombie Cinema* (London: Fab Press, 2005), 192.

[8] Roger Ebert, Review of Land of the Dead, 2005.

[9] See Bruce Watson, "When the Recession Bites," *The Big Issue,* November 7, 2013; David DiSalvo, Neuronarrative, "Vampires vs. Zombies: Who's Winning the War for the Recession Psyche?"*Psychology Today*, October 28, 2010 and Lance Rubin, "We are the Walking Dead: Zombie Literature in Recession Era America," in *The Great Recession in Fiction, Film, and Television*, ed. Kirk Boyle and Daniel Mrozowski (Lexington: Lexington Books, 2013).

[10] "George A. Romero: 'The Walking Dead' is Soap Opera with Occasional Zombie," *Huffington Post*, November 1, 2013. http://www.huffingtonpost.com/2013/11/01/george-romero-walking-dead-soap-opera_n_4183182.html (Accessed February 21, 2014).

[11] Jasie Stokes, "Ghouls, Hell and Transcendence: the Zombie in Popular Culture from *The Night of the Living Dead* to *Shaun of the Dead* " (master's thesis, Brigham Young University, 2010), 18.

Eternal Fascism and the Southern Ideology

Jeremy Brunger

Umberto Eco's 1995 essay "Ur-Fascism" informally outlines the most striking qualities of fascistic theory and practice. It remains one of the most popular tool-kits for intellectuals in discovering where the barbarity of fascism might once again materialize, for Eco was convinced fascism did not die at the end of the second World War. If there is an "eternal fascism" inherent to Western life, the critical observer must ask: in which groups is it most fostered? Is it limited to bald-headed neo-Nazis manufacturing methamphetamine by moonlight, the poor white lumpenproletariat of godforsaken boondocks, the aged reactionaries of the Mediterranean and the Rhine? To the chagrin of sanity, the evidence suggests otherwise: one can trace the fascist tone to one of the most politically active regions of the United States. The American South features in abundance all the tendencies of proto-fascism, from its enduring historical disadvantage following Reconstruction, reverence for the redemptive firearm and the punitive crucifix, hegemonic tendencies in matters of race and religion, and perhaps most importantly, the affinity for hero-worship. If fascism finds its formal renaissance anywhere in the twenty-first century, it will be in the Southern Ideology, which still mutters vaguely the threat that "the South will rise again," confuses faith in the God of Abraham for the will to power over man, and sees fit to solve its social ills with paranoid gun-toting, capitalist republicanism, and social excommunication rather than the humane critical understanding of the Other.

*

To begin this analysis of the Southern Ideology, it is necessary to point out that "ideology" is not identical with "culture." Culture is a metaphor quite aptly likened to the situation of a bacterium being cultured in a petri dish; the bacterium can sense nothing other than that substance in which it is being grown, and as such, does not recognize it as anything but a natural, eternal verity. To humanize the metaphor, consider ideology to be the words written on the walls of the petri dish. Then consider these words are inscribed in culture only by those who hold power. As such, all Southerners are not fascists-many, perhaps most, are well-distanced from this theory. The ideology is fostered by, and fosters, those already in power, those not citizens by default but rather citizens by assertion.

*

Eco's first tenet of "eternal fascism" has it that

The first feature of Ur-Fascism is the cult of tradition. Traditionalism is of course much older than fascism. Not only was it typical of counter-revolutionary Catholic thought after the French revolution, but it was born in the late Hellenistic era, as a reaction to classical Greek rationalism... This new culture had to be syncretistic. Syncretism is not only, as the dictionary says, 'the combination of different forms of belief or practice;' such a combination must tolerate contradictions. Each of the original messages contains a silver of wisdom, and whenever they seem to say different or incompatible things it is only because all are alluding, allegorically, to the same primeval truth. As a consequence, there can be no advancement of learning. Truth has been already spelled out once and for all, and we can only keep interpreting its obscure message.

Such a description no doubt boggles the mind of any native Southerner. Traditionalist conservatism is the dominant political form from Florida to the majority of Appalachia to Tex-Arkana. The reigning political agenda, stemming from the mid-century Republican platform onto the neoconservative administration of former President Bush, sees modernism as something to be defended against, as though the progressive agenda were intimately tied to some imaginary Red Plot. Since the 2000s, the Southern peculiarity has been nationalized. Any politician antagonizing traditional values will not be elected to office; nor will any non-Christian politician survive the culture of criticism pertaining to his religion. Tradition is seen as possessing more utility than mere historical value, while progressiveness and modernism are seen as dangerous attempts to re-instate state socialism. In the familial sphere, the traditional patriarch-submissive wife-obedient children triad still stands dominant, while non-traditional families, like homosexual or poly-amorous families, are seen as undesirable, confused, and confusing. Home ownership is viewed as a key to political participation, with proletarian and other non-propertied classes being relegated to the ideological back-burner. There is no vivid unionization movement, nor political support for the welfare state. In fact, attacking the foundations of the welfare state appears to be one of conservativism's chief weapons in his political arsenal-macroeconomics of the flunking polity is still seen as a microeconomic moral infirmity. All of these developments are seen-once again-as outgrowths of communist subversion dating from the mid-century, or as otherwise foreign intrusions into the classic Southern community. Of course, such forays into the 1950's Golden Age are based on mythological assumptions of communitarian solidarity rather than statistical analysis of real historical social relations, when broken families, impoverished districts, and moral panics defined social life as much in the past as they do in the present. Romantic histories-the gallant South, the mystical Pacific-conceal and apologize for peasant suffering.

The most obvious symptom of this ideological syncretism is the marriage of biblical Christianity and politico-economic conservatism. Especially within the Fundamentalist strain, biblical morality posits that poverty is less a moral problem than a problem in distributive justice; yet the conservative critique of poverty lays its blame on sinful individuals. That the poor ought to be supported by the wealthy does not pass muster in the conservative worldview, no matter how much it thinks itself biblically grounded. Both the communism of the early Christians and the socialism of nineteenth-century Christianity are cast aside in pursuing Christian capitalism (a distinctly twentieth-century phenomenon). These contradictions stand to Eco's reason-truths are not dialectical and do not come from debate, but rather are found in sola scriptura biblical exegesis of a characteristically conservative pattern. It does not matter that state welfare programs are categorically more effective than church services in alleviating local working-class poverty: it only matters, for the Southern conservative, that state intervention is destructive by definition. Compelling comparisons might be made of historical feudal social relations to the Third Estate and the modern status of poverty in the South, given that nobility and the clerical class-when not engaged in class warfare-saw themselves as sole paternal caregivers to the poor. Limited-government ideologies proliferate, insisting the government is not designed to care for the well-being of its people in the aggregate, but rather to bolster and maintain the property relations of its upper class and maintain their singular dominance in the most impoverished region of the country: the sprawling hills and mountains of the South.

Eco continues his critique, saying that

Traditionalism implies the rejection of modernism. Both Fascists and Nazis worshiped technology, while traditionalist thinkers usually reject it as a negation of traditional spiritual values. However, even though Nazism was proud of its industrial achievements, its praise of modernism was only the surface of an ideology based upon Blood and Earth (Blut und Boden). The rejection of the modern world was disguised as a rebuttal of the capitalistic way of life, but it mainly concerned the rejection of the Spirit of 1789 (and of 1776, of course). The Enlightenment, the Age of Reason, is seen as the beginning of modern depravity. In this sense Ur-Fascism can be defined as irrationalism.

While there is not a proper anti-technology movement in the South per se, there is a pervasive climate of anti-intellectualism and anti-scientism, as foremost expressed in the popular disagreement with the neo-Darwinian synthesis. In fact, Tennessee is home to the most aggressive anti-evolution movement of the twentieth century, while Texas is home to the most vocal opponents of the theory of environmental decline as a result of industrial activity. Darwinian-derived evolution, environmental concern, and the more worrying insights of sociology are all seen as species of false consciousness-with some even going so far as to label environmentalism a Marxist invention. The Southern Ideology forgets that, once upon a time, the parsons and the preachers were the only men of letters to be found. Beyond this, the traditionalist identification of self with land is a strong cultural current throughout the rural areas of the region, along with its inevitable accompaniment of xenophobic racism. The homeland institution wars with the anonymous drifters of the city-culture. Given that historical fascism did not, in practice, limit the excesses of capitalism, but merely aimed its roaring engine to the benefit of the state, Eco's position that fascism was not co-incident with capitalism is faulty. Nevertheless, Southern republicanism allies itself wherever possible with high capital, even if it is to the detriment of its population. From its tourist towns to its metropolises, Southern governments support capitalism enthusiastically-usually in the form of importing business for the exploitation of its cheap, half-educated labor force. The irrational practices of racism, patriarchal social relations, and misinterpreted biblical religion all link the American South to Eco's understanding of eternal fascism: just consider the Rebel Flag, a militant relic of the Civil War and reified symbol of slave republicanism, and then consider the tilted swastika of the Germano-fascist regime. The only difference is one can still see the Rebel Flag touted through township and city, pasted on university dorm walls and tattooed on shoulder blades, flashing the ancient petulance in the public eye. The Southern proletarians who exhibit this rebellion live in cramped living quarters even while supporting their betters; in mistaking the cause of the misery in multicultural initiatives and liberal movements toward equality, the poorest in the region bolster the social positions of their real oppressors and universalize squalor among their young in a nationalist delusion.

In discussing fascistic disdain for the intellectual in society, Eco writes

Irrationalism also depends on the cult of action for action's sake. Action being beautiful in itself, it must be taken before, or without, any previous reflection. Thinking is a form of emasculation. Therefore culture is suspect insofar as it is identified with critical attitudes. Distrust of the intellectual world has always been a symptom of Ur-Fascism, from Goering's alleged statement ('When I hear talk of culture I reach for my gun') to the frequent use of such expressions as 'degenerate intellectuals,' 'eggheads,' 'effete snobs,' 'universities are a nest of reds.' The official Fascist intellectuals were mainly engaged in attacking modern culture and the liberal intelligentsia for having betrayed traditional values.

There is, perhaps, no better characterization of Southern culture than Eco's description of fascism here. Southern culture is largely heteronormative, and given that it has only recently industrialized since the 1970's, it is still largely based on reproducing social relations based on athletics rather than intellect. In an economy of pure muscle, this survival might be understood as once having value; but in an Information Age economy that values thought-work over grunt-work, it has little practical utility beyond willing wage-slavery. Right-wing media is popular in the South, with its usual targets of the "liberal intelligentsia," the secular university, racial minorities, and the specter of communism issuing from all of the

576

above. Masculinity is viewed as an end in itself, with all deviations therefrom being devalued or derided. Military culture, the chief characteristic of fascist social life, is prevalent-given that much of America's standing army comes from the South, due in part to there being little opportunity for lower-middle class youth to establish a future, this is not surprising. Post-WWI German fascism came to prominence after Germany began to feel itself existentially and economically threatened after the Treaty of Versailles ruined its national vitality. Given that the South remains an economic under-achiever in the domestic arena, and that culturally it is seen as subordinate to the general Northern zeitgeist (Southern English is not standard, but is rather a basilect which hopeful emigrants quickly learn to forget), it is not surprising that, in their discourses, Southern ideologues and fascist ideologues sound startlingly similar in their aims and rhetoric. Social science dare not enter.

Eco, discussing the value of critical theory, continues:

No syncretistic faith can withstand analytical criticism. The critical spirit makes distinctions, and to distinguish is a sign of modernism. In modern culture the scientific community praises disagreement as a way to improve knowledge. For Ur-Fascism, disagreement is treason.

What better description of fundamentalist religion and socially-embedded opposition to scientific inquiry? In questioning the reigning dogmas of capitalist competition, anti-welfare government, and the nuclear family, the Southern activist is instantly marginalized or linked to the boogeyman of socialism. In the sphere of political theory, criticizing the marriage of conservatism and an essentially socialistic religion-a contradiction in terms-is sure to paint the critic as an uninformed, ahistorical dissenter. But analyzing the surface of Southern culture's conservatism by relating to its rather proletarian past reveals it to be what it is: a logical paradox unsupportable by thinking people. The philosophic tendency subordinates to the religious tendency, if not for intellectual value, then for mere social utility-Southern Christianity is a shibboleth, and as such, an entryway into power that defies the very foundations of the faith it cynically uses. The original Christians were outcasts from Roman hegemony, poor and diseased, marginal and pathetic. They were mytho-revolutionaries, not conservatives; at any rate, the early Church was awash in heresy and doctrinal battles, not unified in theoria. In the South, the only "liberation theology" extant is a variation on right-wing anarchism, while the general religion preaches the long-outdated theme of obedience. As roving bands of cash-poor Christians addicted to the fetishism of authority flock and flit from one city to the next hoping for a better turn of fate, they are categorically denied by Christians who pay their property taxes, sent to live in downtown wastelands and fret the police whose patience grows as dim as their hope for this life. Religion disintegrates when actually confronted with the moral dilemmas for which it was designed. Even the bigger cities have the small-town feel of isolation, the distinct impression their denizens have not yet left the outer bounds, and catercorner to every liquor store there are two churches which deliver much the same.

Besides, disagreement is a sign of diversity. Ur-Fascism grows up and seeks for consensus by exploiting and exacerbating the natural fear of difference. The first appeal of a fascist or prematurely fascist movement is an appeal against the intruders. Thus Ur-Fascism is racist by definition.

The Southern syncretism is globally renowned for its pathological racism. Nineteenth-century theories of racialism are still common currency in the South, as is the lay understanding of racial essentialism. Families still see fit to bar their young from interracial dating and marriage, and whiteness, as a social fact, is still viewed as a supreme value. The typical habit of denouncing foreign influences, especially with immigrant Mexican labor, melds comfortably with the denunciation of models of sexual difference. Homosexuality is mistaken for an incarnation of "Hollywood Values" rather than a natural human phenomenon and is beaten or prayed away. Diversity and the Rawlsian difference principle, in general, are decried as liberal intrusions into a primordial white capitalist paradise founded not in actual history but in the pseudo-historical imagination. Even as municipal services decline in breadth and quality, Southerners worry more of an incoming horde of Babel, a Brown Plague come to undo their immemorial caste system and expand their multicultural nightmare. Race-horror is more prevalent than the horror of war, which is why they support the second by decrying the first. In exclaiming the virtues of First World aristocratic philosophy, Southern thought closes in on itself, and ignores how much of the region resembles the underdeveloped world when exposed to realist scrutiny unsympathetic to the romance of white property.

The fascist impulse owes its prevalence to Eco's next observation: *Ur-Fascism derives from individual or social frustration. That is why one of the most typical features of the historical fascism was the appeal to a frustrated middle class, a class suffering from an economic crisis or feelings of political humiliation, and frightened by the pressure of lower social groups. In our time, when the old "proletarians" are becoming petty bourgeois (and the lumpen are largely excluded from the political scene), the fascism of tomorrow will find its audience in this new majority.*

In Germany and Italy, fascism was specifically a lower-middle class development. Fundamentalist Christianity and institutional racism do not find much expression in the Southern lower class, which tends to have more divergent religious views and more tolerant views on interracial marriage; rather, the Southern parallels to fascism find their most vocal expressions in its middle class. Especially since the financial crisis of 2007-08, the Southern middle class has returned to a thorough-going religious atmosphere centering on the family and private property, racial rhetoric is abundant even now as President Obama nears the end of his second term in office, and the decrying of socialistic policies (which are actually centrist policies according to the global political spectrum) rallies in the popular domain. Rather than recognizing that middle-class precarity depends on corporate malpractice and right-wing government, the Southern middle class understands only that it is endangered, and so sees fit to vent its worries on its classic targets: those who are different. Economic difficulties are due to the black president's corruption, not an essentially unstable national-economic way of life, just as threats to culture are due to outside influences rather than internal contradictions. To study these contradictions is to incite the charge of red-baited communism, even as accusers forget who first coined the term of their beloved capitalism. Dr. Martin Luther King was murdered in the same state that gave birth to the Klan for preaching that both the white man and the black man were exploited in common. Even in the university towns, ten-story tall crucifixes dot Alpine highways in robust mimesis of the theocratic pretension as symbols wholly antithetical to King's message: they signify authority, not inquiry. In an era of social disruption and economic change-when "all that is solid melts into air"-the eternal fascism finds its home. Eco writes

To people who feel deprived of a clear social identity, Ur-Fascism says that their only privilege is the most common one, to be born in the same country. This is the origin of nationalism. Besides, the only ones who can provide an identity to the nation are its enemies. Thus at the root of the Ur-Fascist psychology there is the obsession with a plot, possibly an international one. The followers must feel besieged. The easiest way to solve the plot is the appeal to xenophobia. But the plot must also come from the inside: Jews are usually the best target because they have the advantage of being at the same time inside and outside. In the U.S., a prominent instance of the plot obsession is to be found in Pat Robertson's The New World Order, but, as we have recently seen, there are many others.

America is no longer a white, protestant, wealthy country; those who do fall into this category, having their social identity threatened by a changing cultural climate, seek more and more intensive ideologies with which to understand the world. The politics of the American South are, still, overwhelmingly white and protestant, but many of its subjects are not. The misattribution of this change to recent developments rather than diversifying historical currents-in the Melting Pot era, the whiteness of Irish immigrants was not yet an established social fact, but became one over time-reveals that historical ignorance is one of the many vices of dominant Southern culture. The vague idea that some obscure subculture is constantly threatening American virtues (ISIS, crypto-

Marxist senators, "the Left Coasts") routinely crops up in Southern discourse, even as poverty and under-employment grows within the Southern states due to its inherent infrastructural and social deficits. Instead of Jews, Southern discourse focuses on the plots of racial, sexual, and religious minorities from nearby and abroad. In offloading responsibility to outlanders, the Southern status quo is maintained in all its contradictions.

The Southern Ideology expresses the contradiction between its opponents, its leaders, and the people who subscribe to it: *The followers must feel humiliated by the ostentatious wealth and force of their enemies. When I was a boy I was taught to think of Englishmen as the five-meal people. They ate more frequently than the poor but sober Italians. Jews are rich and help each other through a secret web of mutual assistance. However, the followers must be convinced that they can overwhelm the enemies. Thus, by a continuous shifting of rhetorical focus, the enemies are at the same time too strong and too weak. Fascist governments are condemned to lose wars because they are constitutionally incapable of objectively evaluating the force of the enemy.*

Southern discourse is pro-capitalist, but its adherents are more often than not in poverty themselves. Rather than distrusting their better-off superiors, however, the Southern conservative poor prefer to distrust East Coast liberals as symbols of wealth-a perversion of what wealth is for, the establishment of a family, or for wealth stolen through socialistic redistribution. The rhetoric of "Wall Street versus Main Street" is a populist example of this (Tea Party on the right, Occupy on the left), but the emphasis tends to lie on the idea that Main Street represents a social minority, when in fact it does not. Most Americans either live or aspire to live middle-class lifestyles, and most government attention is paid to this group, with the rest looking out for the interests of high capital and the limited interests of the working poor. Imagining that they are persecuted lends their ideology credence, given the current zeitgeist of identity politics (replacing proletarians and women with white Christian patriarchs in a muddled, illogical algebra of oppression); but they are, in reality, no more persecuted than normal people ever have been. Actual minorities have vocal defense groups defending their interests against normative onslaughts, and sensing that their own group lacks this special defense, the white Southern middle class invents one for the sickly purpose of special pleading. The idea that there is a cultural war against their lifestyle is preposterous, but leading media outlets, like Fox News, continue to insist that the typical American way of life is under threat from non-white queer Bolsheviki. Of course, the only threat to this lifestyle is the capitalist economic model it itself supports, and the rudderless antinomies the Southern Ideology preserves.

In fact, Southern political culture is rather Hobbesian in the most alarming sense of the word:

For Ur-Fascism there is no struggle for life but, rather, life is lived for struggle. Thus pacifism is trafficking with the enemy. It is bad because life is permanent warfare. This, however, brings about an Armageddon complex. Since enemies have to be defeated, there must be a final battle, after which the movement will have control of the world. But such a "final solution" implies a further era of peace, a Golden Age, which contradicts the principle of permanent war. No fascist leader has ever succeeded in solving this predicament.

In "right-to-work" states, employment is seen as a privilege rather than a right or a mere path to survival, and welfare assistance is seen as a deep taboo suggesting moral incompetence. The South overwhelmingly supported the Iraq War-elements of racism and Islamophobia aside-in the most jingoistic manner possible. Neoconservative policy has as its direct and stated aim that "democracy," an abstraction, ought to be violently spread throughout the whole world. This teleological end to history, once seen in the Jacobinite-Hegelian view of the French Revolution, finds its next expression in the economic policies of globalization, by which Washingtonian economic models are assumed to work in disparate economies the world over. In short, America assumes it

582

holds the key to global problems, and sets itself up to manage them. The most vocal applause for these globalist efforts resound from the militaristic South which, despite its native diversity, cannot imagine a world that operates according to social laws different than its own. Southern thought-leaders preach that leftism is a conspiracy theory even as they scour the doctrines of the holy book of the West's very first conspiracy theory.

In any society with vast economic divides between rich and poor, Eco suggests the eternal fascism can erupt once again in elitist terms that deride elitism:

Elitism is a typical aspect of any reactionary ideology, insofar as it is fundamentally aristocratic, and aristocratic and militaristic elitism cruelly implies contempt for the weak. Ur-Fascism can only advocate a popular elitism. Every citizen belongs to the best people of the world, the members of the party are the best among the citizens, every citizen can (or ought to) become a member of the party. But there cannot be patricians without plebeians. In fact, the Leader, knowing that his power was not delegated to him democratically but was conquered by force, also knows that his force is based upon the weakness of the masses; they are so weak as to need and deserve a ruler. Since the group is hierarchically organized (according to a military model), every subordinate leader despises his own underlings, and each of them despises his inferiors. This reinforces the sense of mass elitism.

The Southern elite are, of course, the white propertied class that views all others as inferior and subordinate-hardly worth the political time, in fact. Even where this fails, Southerners take up the mantle of nationalism: "America is the best country in the world." It isn't the best country in the world by any statistical analysis, but such mythologies are common to fascistic ideologies. When not serving in the military, they serve in intensive capitalist industries (which themselves feature militaristic labor hierarchies) that bolster their notions that everyone has a place in society. In this respect the tone turns to Calvinism, and the moral realism of poverty, for those who fail to succeed in the capitalist environment, comes to the ascendant. No scientific critique of economic failure is allowed. Only criticism of moral failure is sanctioned-and thus to be poor is to become un-American. The mid-level employee, glad to have a job, detests the entry-level employee, as though the mid-level were any less an existential penalty. Below them all exist the unemployed and under-employed who rarely even make blips on the political radar except to remind the wealthy there are barbarians concerned only with use-value circling the borders. Eco presses on one of his most salient points about everyday heroism next:

In such a perspective everybody is educated to become a hero. In every mythology the hero is an exceptional being, but in Ur-Fascist ideology, heroism is the norm. This cult of heroism is strictly linked with the cult of death. It is not by chance that a motto of the Falangists was Viva la Muerte (in English it should be translated as "Long Live Death!"). In non-fascist societies, the lay public is told that death is unpleasant but must be faced with dignity; believers are told that it is the painful way to reach a supernatural happiness. By contrast, the Ur-Fascist hero craves heroic death, advertised as the best reward for a heroic life. The Ur-Fascist hero is impatient to die. In his impatience, he more frequently sends other people to death.

American popular culture is unequivocally heroic. The most successful films in its canon feature violent farces in which the white male hero vanquishes the egghead evil genius, or the syndicalist Soviet forces, or the alien (cargo-cultish immigrant) machinations of foreign powers. The hero looks like the typical viewer of these films: white males who want to be heroes. Since the world is not a fantasy, however, these children later grow up to think of the world in embattled terms of nation and enemy, Manichean reckonings of good and evil, gun-violence and double-standard law and order. The educational system grades students according to a hierarchical ability to integrate into capitalism, graduating top-ten heroes directly into the workforce and the rest into the welfare offices. Beyond education lies the whole sports industry-football has a monolithic presence in the South, with its university teams commanding higher budgets than entire academic departments combined-in which a few gladiators, selected from among the hoi polloi, are paraded in shows of athletic feat to audiences struggling at home for the means of subsistence. The collective struggle for existence becomes the individual struggle for existence against others-who this is, it matters not, so long as there are heroes and enemies to be fought. Behind all this lies a well-spring of nihilism that disallows the everyman to merely exist and be comfortable. The American way ensures that one is always fighting, whether people or their causes, oneself or some outsider figure dreamed up in the paranoid imagination of an Old Testament demagogue. This is a general product of the American monoculture, but it finds more grizzly embodiment in the South: anti-muslim sentiment mingles with anti-secular sentiments as some twin conspiracy from beyond the national borders in a nation that was, according to the conservative myth, founded on Christo-propertarian values. Once the culture war dissipates, the military absorbs and recruits them all: long live death.

Next, Eco focuses on the culture of uber-masculinity:

Since both permanent war and heroism are difficult games to play, the Ur-Fascist transfers his will to power to sexual matters. This is the origin of machismo (which implies both disdain for women and intolerance and condemnation of nonstandard sexual habits, from chastity to homosexuality). Since even sex is a difficult game to play, the Ur-Fascist hero tends to play with weapons - doing so becomes an ersatz phallic exercise.

Southern patriarchy is the norm, with non-patriarchal families being relegated to the cultural shadows, about which popular culture frightfully whispers. The overwhelming popular distaste for homosexuality in general, and especially the idea of gay-led

585

families, speaks to the value the South places on masculinity taken to excess. A man is not his job, since most jobs there (retail, auto, maintenance, construction) are dismal: he is his sexual prowess, he is the distance between himself and the feminine. Gun culture is a massive feature of its everyday life, from its legal rulings (guns being allowed in high schools and grocery stores) to its tragedies (children shooting themselves with their parents' handguns). Gunslinging plays as large a role in Southern culture as the consumption of literature might play in other parts of the world- they are the regional past-time, taken as an extension of innocence from home protection to gift-giving. Of course, this is due in part to the crime endemic to the region's cities (caused, in turn, by poverty and political corruption) and in part to the practice of hunting in the rural hinterlands. It is not an uncommon rite of passage for a father to take his son to the shooting range, or indeed, even his daughter, for the paranoiac social climate co-extends in equal measures. The odd one out is the person who sues; the gunslinger mythos becomes universal as the South achieves an antic matrimony of the Nazarene with Sade.

Eco highlights a distinction between democratic practice and republican practice by examining the politico-theology of eternal fascism:

Ur-Fascism is based upon a selective populism, a qualitative populism, one might say. In a democracy, the citizens have individual rights, but the citizens in their entirety have a political impact only from a quantitative point of view - one follows the decisions of the majority. For Ur-Fascism, however, individuals as individuals have no rights, and the People is conceived as a quality, a monolithic entity expressing the Common Will. Since no large quantity of human beings can have a common will, the Leader pretends to be their interpreter. Having lost their power of delegation, citizens do not act; they are only called on to play the role of the People. Thus the People is only a theatrical fiction. To have a good instance of qualitative populism we no longer need the

Piazza Venezia in Rome or the Nuremberg Stadium. There is in our
future a TV or Internet populism, in which the emotional response of
a selected group of citizens can be presented and accepted as the
Voice of the People.

The South is not a democratic region- it prefers to elect
republican elements, which, by nature, do not much defer to their
Rousseauvian demos. The "common will" is filtered through
popular right-wing media and deflected against actual
parliamentary practice. It is a noted eccentricity that, in the South,
elections are decided in the churches. Its populism is one which
ignores the secular history of American politics and instead focuses
on its religious fringe. No matter that most people do not want a
President who decides which war to wage according to his prayers,
or the scattering of tea-leaves in his breakfast cup-it only matters if
the religious majority thinks it right. Right-wing pulpits condemn
minority lifestyles as being non-religious, and therefore non-
political. They ask: what use does vox Dei have for the vox populi of
the poor, or homosexuals, or immigrants? The fictive majority
aligns itself with God and his exact prescriptions, leaving the
deviants to the shadows of civilization. Horse-mouthed small
business owners refer to their own neighbors as trash as their own
children sink into hedonism; unread, uncouth mercenaries of
capital pretend to culture even as they skirt Mosaic law and
condemn the universities that wouldn't accept them. Patriarchal
ontology has not yet been dismantled by the last stages of the
Enlightenment: married man is below God, below him married
woman, below him the offspring. The dreadful rest may do as they
please provided they do not hog the political platform or scrounge
from the public trough-that is for "people who deserve it," which is
everyone, not the people who apply. The private narrative of one
alone being deserving of civilization's benefits, and all others being
thieving parasites, speaks to the Southern citizen's identification
with a personal God: they bear the burden of civilization and suffer
for it so that the sinners may frolic with their grotesque families in
abiding narcosis. They pay no heed to the actual aggregate

population; only certain of its members have a say in the community, while the rest are rabble, even when the rabble outnumber them. To the rest of the country, the highest Southern citizen casts a pale lot in a contest against their lowest citizen-a king of the hill complex-but when one lives ascendant in the New Feudalism, surrounded by stranded and illiterate people desperate even for day labor, such comparisons little matter.

Eco ends his list on an Orwellian note:

Ur-Fascism speaks Newspeak. Newspeak was invented by Orwell, in 1984, as the official language of Ingsoc, English Socialism. But elements of Ur-Fascism are common to different forms of dictatorship. All the Nazi or Fascist schoolbooks made use of an impoverished vocabulary, and an elementary syntax, in order to limit the instruments for complex and critical reasoning. But we must be ready to identify other kinds of Newspeak, even if they take the apparently innocent form of a popular talk show.

It does not take the reader long to glance through school textbooks in the South to note glaring inconsistencies, or worse yet, the home-school textbooks purveyed by its religiously-inclined companies. The lack of educational attainment in the South is nothing short of depressing, from illiteracy rates being the highest in the country (excluding immigrants who do not speak English), statistics concerning how many books households with children have (few to none), to cultural disrespect for intellectual endeavor (book-smarts are devalued as effete, while street-smarts are encouraged as masculine even in a world that has passed these values by). In fact, the Southern educational sector is the worst performing sector in the country by any relevant means of analysis. The Southern economy does not need many thinkers: otherwise, its factories would idle into rust. As for Newspeak, only the eternal fascist could think "democracy" means "American hegemony" or that "the land of the free" means "the Christian dominion." Pertaining to Eco's final remark-"even if they take the apparently innocent form of a popular talk show"-who is not reminded of Fox News, the radio butcheries of Rush Limbaugh, or the slew of political candidates wielding God and corruption with the same hand, whose respective audiences enthusiastically outnumber the populations of entire states?

*

The greatest misfortune of the Southern Ideology is that Southerners themselves suffer for it. By misplacing the blame for systemic poverty on communist specters and liberal spooks, Southern politicos impoverish their own constituents-both those who consent and those who dissent. By insisting on racist practices, unavowed but extant, white Southerners learn to distrust their own black neighbors while praising the capitalists who rent and exploit them both. In the middle of this dramatic race-to-the-bottom are children who, with under-funded educations, can expect little in the way of an agreeable future beyond the workhouse or the charities of church. Fascism by another name is not just a topic for punditry. Real, living people think and speak in its terms without the slightest idea of their affinity with the twentieth-century's darkest movement. The will to fascism, masquerading as the Southern Ideology, stands to benefit only a very select milieu of the region's population. Beyond these elect, it has such abundant victims they either live their lives in isolation or become finally convinced they must flee the South rather than fix it: because, they think, there is no fixing it. To the detriment of all concerned, reactionaries and regressives provoke this exodus with all too human satisfaction, as the project of Enlightenment moves first to dusk and concludes in night, suspending the somber South in the medieval gloom it deserves.

Shoulders Back
Combating the Consequences of Gender Stereotypes

Syard Evans

She stood, stone-faced, with her shoulders back and her chest held high. Her face was expressionless, and her chin was tucked in tight. This was her "nervous but determined stance."

I marveled at how distinctive and developed a "nervous but determined stance" could get in just 11+ years of life.

The whispers were occasionally interrupted by blurted shouts, "Look! It's a girl." As if a person possessing female genitalia had not been seen in public in the last three decades.

She cut her eyes to me and said, "So stupid," without ever relinquishing the solidity of her stance. She was firmly committed to being there, and nothing some half-pint sized little boy said was going to move her from her steadfastness. As I looked at her, I saw the three-year-old who once told me that she really liked climbing trees, but climbing trees was a "boy" thing. I responded to her then by asking, "What makes something a "boy" thing? If you like it, why can't it be a "you" thing?"

Apparently, she got my message.

Football was something she had wanted to do for the last two years; and this year, she was doing it. Right in the middle of small town, USA, in a community that, quite literally, worshiped a football deity, she stood in line, surrounded by approximately 120 boys, waiting to get fitted for her football pads, because she had the intrepidity to be a girl who played football. It did not matter if she was the best player that had ever played. It didn't even matter if she was any good. All that mattered was that she had the sound knowledge that if she was interested in something, she could at least try it, regardless of her reproductive organs.

She's certainly not the first girl who has braved the hits and tackles, not to mention the snickers and the bullying, to put on some football pads. Notables include Sam Gordon , who dominated her Utah league in 2012 as a 9-year-old, Holly Mangold , who played offensive lineman in high school and received offers to play on the collegiate level before deciding to pursue Olympic weightlifting as a member of the 2012 US Olympic team, and Shelby Osborne , who signed to play defensive back for an NAIA college in Kentucky in 2014. Girl participation on predominantly male sports teams and leagues is not limited to football, either. Mo'ne Davis blew the sports world up with her 70-mile-an-hour fast ball and complete-game shutout in a 2014 Little League World Series game. At the same time, Becky Hammon made major headlines when she was hired as the NBA's first female coach as an assistant coach for the San Antonio Spurs. And these are only a few of the more renowned examples of the many young women pursuing their non-traditional passions each year. Slowly and with much effort, female athletes throughout the country are pushing past the traditional restrictions of "girlhood" to pursue the things that interest them.

Despite these many strides toward inclusion in sports, as I stood in line with the girl who was playing football and marveled at her "nervous but determined stance," I was jarred by sadness at the thought of the thousands of little girls who will not be allowed to develop an interest in certain things, much less muster the courage to pursue those things, simply because they are girls. I thought about how those stifled interests would eventually impede career pursuits, relationship decisions, and ultimately the processes of defining self and worth, and I wanted to scream. But the more I thought about all the little girls who weren't standing in line to get fitted for football pads, the more I began to notice all of the little boys who were. And I couldn't ignore that there were a good number of boys standing in that same line who had no desire to be there at all.

Gender oppression and gender isolation are harmful for women, no doubt; however, men are traumatized by the established roles society insists they conform to as well. The expectations for men to be strong, tough, and emotionless create restrictive experiences that disallow pursuits of interests and passions outside of the accepted parameters associated with having a penis. As I watched little boys as young as 8-years-old stand in line to be fitted for football pads, I saw faces mixed within the crowd that were terrified to be there. Faces of little boys who would rather be anywhere else in the world but standing right there. And I couldn't help but think about the first big hit they would take and the responses that would come with it, "Suck it up, boy. Boys don't cry." It would be an early step in the indoctrination to manhood that prevents any emotions outside of anger and rage, and forbids vulnerability of any kind. The indoctrination to manhood that, no doubt, contributes to almost 80% of suicides in the US being completed by males in recent years, with males being far less likely to access mental health services than their female counterparts. Society assumes that the power and authority associated with male privilege are attributes that everyone desires; and, therefore, struggles to understand why anyone with a natural right to those attributes could ever desire any other lot. This is likely why many Americans can understand and embrace a woman who wears pants, t-shirts, and baseball caps, but cannot fathom a man who wears dresses. The genderization of clothing attaches the privilege of maleness to pants, t-shirts, and caps; and the disempowerment of femaleness to dresses. For many, a woman's desire to 'borrow some privilege' via clothing is understandable; however, many struggle to contemplate why a man would willingly yield the power and control associated with male privilege by putting on a dress. To foster the most productive and functional society possible, we must not only provide our girls the opportunity to suit up and hit hard when those are the things that drive them, but we must also stand with our boys as they invest their energies into learning to sew or perfecting the art of make-up. Opportunity for self-exploration and self-discovery must start at the point of interest and passion, not at the point of the pre-existing expectations attached to a child.

Here's hoping every child has opportunities to stand shoulders back and chest held high to pursue something she or he loves.

Spirituality & Religion

Lessons from *The Brothers Karamazov*
Doubt, Freedom, and the Organic Nature of Religious Truth

Ali Ahmed

If you have read Dostoevsky's *The Brothers Karamazov*, you will agree that it is one of a select few treasure-houses of literature. A classic novel of ideas, it is singular in that unlike many classics, Dostoevsky's magnum opus has only one group of readers: admirers. (There might admittedly be some dissidents here and there but, to me, they have not really read the novel) It is certainly one of the most powerful works I have ever read. While it is not as long as Tolstoy's *War and Peace*, it is still however good and lengthy. And if you haven't read it, yet, then in this two-part series, by exploring a little of the profound depths of the novel and drawing out some of its lessons, I intend to persuade you that you are worth it.

In abbreviations of the book, the novel is often boiled down to the infamous section of the Grand Inquisitor, which says a lot about the novel as that particular section does not really, at least in my estimation, move the plot. Nevertheless, readers might agree that it forms perhaps the most gripping part of the novel. By focusing on this particular chapter, we'll get a sense of Dostoevsky's understanding of the place and purpose of religion, and how he envisions the real liberation of man vis-à-vis religion.

Without getting into too much detail about the plot, allow me to briefly preface our discussion by saying that the novel is about the return of the three Karamazov brothers to their birthplace, their father's home in the town of Skotoprigonevsk. In the days that follow, their father is murdered and one of the brothers is accused with the crime. Essentially, as far as plot is concerned, the novel is a whodunit, but as we've mentioned, *The Brothers Karamazov* being a novel of ideas, Dostoevsky is infinitely more intrigued by the intricate subtleties of thought and emotion, the hundred indecisions and the hundred visions and revisions, than he is with solving the crime. Now, each of the three brothers-Dmitri, Ivan, and Alyosha, in that order-are quite different from one another and that's part of the dynamic of the story. In the chapter of the Grand Inquisitor, which takes place before the murder scene, the two younger Karamazov brothers, Ivan and Alyosha, meet at a local tavern and catch up. It's been years since they've had a chance to speak to each other. Ivan, the elder, has since been through several years of schooling, including University, and has thus become somewhat of a recognized intellectual. Alyosha, the youngest brother, chooses the path of spiritual training and has joined the monastery to become a monk. After many years of separation, the two younger brothers meet-earlier in the novel-and in this chapter, Ivan presents his thesis, his "what I believe" to Alyosha.

Ivan relates to his brother a philosophical "poem" he has written, set during the severest days of the Spanish Inquisition in the 15th century. A large crowd has gathered outside of a cathedral in Seville, just a day after a hundred heretics were burned at the stake by the Cardinal Grand Inquisitor in an auto-da-fe. The people are a scattered, miserable sight, and it is in the midst of this misery that Jesus reappears, not in the form of the spiritual lion that vanquishes falsehood at the end of times - as is prophesied - but in the same human image in which he walked on the earth fifteen centuries ago. He says nothing but the people know it is him; there is a healing power even in the touch of his garments. He cures an old man of his blindness and witnesses a funeral procession leading out of the cathedral. The mother of the dead child wails and begs him for his help. With the same words with which he had brought back the dead all those years ago, he brings the little girl back to life. She sits up in the coffin, still holding the flowers in her hand, and looks around in amazement. By this point, the Cardinal Grand Inquisitor, who had been eyeing the situation from a distance, has had enough. He is enraged at what he has seen and orders his guards to take away the meddling intruder. The people not only don't intervene, but they have been made so utterly submissive to the aged Inquisitor that they, as one body, bow down to him as Jesus is taken away to prison. In his sermon on the Dostoevsky Brothers, Robert M. Price makes a noteworthy point when he says, about Jesus, "after all, wasn't he, and doesn't he remain, the greatest of heretics?" That is indeed a common oversight, the fact that all prophets are, by virtue of their task, rebels against the status quo. But more on that another time.

"Why, then, have you come to interfere with us?" asks the Grand Inquisitor of Jesus in the cell. "Anything you proclaim anew will encroach upon the freedom of men's faith, for it will come as a miracle, and the freedom of their faith was the dearest of all things to you, even then, one and a half thousand years ago. Was it not you who so often said then: 'I want to make you free'? But now you have seen these 'free' men...this work has cost us dearly...but we have finally finished this work in your name. For fifteen hundred years we have been at pains over this freedom, but now it is finished, and well finished...these people are more certain than ever before that they are completely free, and at the same time they themselves have brought us their freedom and obediently laid it at our feet." What exactly is the aged Inquisitor babbling about? Well, Jesus had made it his priority to inspire faith freely. The faith that he demanded was born of constant thought and personal reflection in the face of doubt and disarray. "Such an experience of faith," writes Simon Critchley in his piece in the New York Times, "is not certainty, but is only gained by going into the proverbial desert and undergoing diabolical temptation and radical doubt...doubt is not the enemy of faith. On the contrary, it is certainty." The truth that sets you free is a difficult truth because it is predicated upon the constant dialectical process between certainty and doubt. Contrary to popular opinion, which is of course based on an easy and widely accepted interpretation of faith, religion does not demand a surrender of contemplation, but rather exactly the opposite. Religion is not a manual for life, as some might like to declare, with an extensive index that conveniently leads you to the solution for every situation. Those that think that religion is just that, a manual, compromise the organicism that is at the heart of faith and reduce the grand design of the human subject to the machinations of an operating system. It is only in understanding and accepting faith as a living, organic process that addresses each individual subject's search for truth in a world of "diabolical temptation" that one exercises the freedom Jesus required from the faithful.

Returning to the Grand Inquisitor, we note again, to emphasize his point, what he tells Jesus: "Was it not you who so often said then: 'I want to make you free?'...For fifteen hundred years we have been at pains over this freedom, but now it is finished." The freedom of faith that we've been discussing; the organic, dialectical process - born of contemplation - navigating between the waters of doubt and certainty, all that is finished. It is finished because this freedom has been a burden on humanity, says the Grand Inquisitor, who accuses Jesus of mistakenly believing it to be strong enough and thus demanding more than it can handle. The Grand Inquisitor says that the Church has replaced this dialectical process with the fixity of certainty (and the Inquisition-the burning of "heretics"- itself both actuates and demonstrates this shift), for that is more conducive to the happiness of mankind than the burden of free thought and free choice. So how has the Church accomplished this? "You were warned," says the Inquisitor to Jesus in the prison cell. "You had no lack of warnings and indications, but you did not heed the warnings, you rejected the only way of arranging for human happiness..." That course of "arranging for human happiness" was offered to Jesus by the devil in the account of the three temptations which, exhorts the Inquisitor, was the real miracle. But Jesus rejects each of these temptations precisely because they sacrifice human freedom. "Decide yourself who was right: you or the one who questioned you then?" asks the Cardinal Grand Inquisitor. The Church has effectively re-written the narration and thus defeated the entire trajectory of faith that Jesus had envisioned.

After a 40-day fast in the desert, Jesus is met by the devil, whose temptations come in the form of three questions. Each of these temptations the Grand Inquisitor identifies with a single word. In the first, the devil tells Jesus to convert stones into bread, not so much for his own sake, but for the benefit of the people who will, struck by the **miracle**, immediately follow him thereafter. Man cannot live on bread alone, replies Jesus, but rather on the word of God. This Palestinian Prophet has in mind something other than the contentment offered by a material appetite; he envisages a spiritual satiation. In the next question, the devil tempts Jesus to throw himself off from the top of the temple. If he is really the son of God as he claims, says the devil, he will be propped up by angels who will keep him from falling onto the ground. Not only will this prove his devotion to God, but it will force the people into faith. They will have no option but to believe, incapable as they will be of processing the **mystery**. In the final temptation, the devil takes Jesus to the top of a mountain, offering him a vista of humanity and heaven, and promises him a combined package of eternal and temporal power under one singular**authority**. All kingdoms of all peoples would answer to one single sovereign. This would ensure the happiness of humankind through unity. Dissent is a result of difference. In this new scheme, humanity would be homogenized; it would be composed of a factory-line of people. Each individual would thus be exactly like the other, hence not an individual at all. A familiar scene out of so many science fiction movies we all know. Jesus is well aware of this and thus simply rejects the final offer.

"In this you acted proudly and magnificently, like God," says the Inquisitor to his prisoner, "but mankind, that weak, rebellious tribe-are they gods? ...could you possibly have assumed...that mankind, too, would be strong enough for such a temptation? Is that how human nature was created-to reject the miracle, and in those terrible moments of life, the moments of the most terrible, essential, and tormenting questions of the soul, to remain only with the free decisions of the heart?" He accuses Jesus of setting unachievable goals for humankind, that "weak, rebellious tribe." The freedom that he wanted for them is of no consolation in the face of existential despair; hence they themselves give up their freedom for happiness. "We corrected your deed and based it on miracle, mystery, and authority. And mankind rejoiced that they were once more led like sheep, and that at last such a terrible gift, which had brought them so much suffering, had been taken from their hearts." Finally, the Inquisitor reveals that the Church, though working in the name of Christ, is actually in cahoots with the devil. "Exactly eight centuries ago, we took from him what you so indignantly rejected, that last gift he offered you when he showed you all the kingdoms of the earth." It is in working with the devil that they have "corrected" the work of Jesus and thus rewritten the entire flight plan of the human spirit that he had envisioned. "Why did you reject that last gift? Had you accepted that third counsel of the might spirit, you would have furnished all that man seeks on earth, that is: someone to bow down to, someone to take over his conscience, and a means for uniting everyone at last into a common, concordant, and incontestable anthill". This is the Grand Inquisitor's ultimate assessment of humanity: a pathetic, rebellious band of weaklings who cannot bear the burden of a conscience and thus collectively seek a higher being to fall down in front of. A higher being that can dictate their lives and free them of any accountability. They find comfort in this collective unconsciousness and hate being told that things could be arranged differently. It is out of pity for what it believes to be the human condition that the Church sets out to rewrite religion, of which it has a rather bleak view.

In rejecting miracle, mystery, and authority, Jesus had desired faith freely given, faith that was, as we've mentioned before, born of a process. The two opposing poles of doubt and certainty charge and propel man towards truth, living life in the middle-path that is faith. "If faith becomes certainty," writes Critchley, "then we have become seduced by the temptations of miracle, mystery, and authority. We have become diabolical. There are no guarantees in faith. It is defined by an essential insecurity, tempered by doubt and defined by a radical experience in freedom." This radical freedom does not make easy the most terrible moments of life, nor is it any fun to live a life tempered by doubt. The insecurity that is at the heart of faith is terribly demanding and it takes its toll on even the most mentally adept; hence the daily, new converts to the Church of certainty, the religion of the Inquisitor. And it is only the ones who are certain of themselves and their faith that can pass judgement on others - who are either coerced into conviction or annihilated if found wanting. This is why certainty demands homogeneity, for it cannot tolerate difference. Those who follow this creed have not really dealt with their internal insecurity; they have merely covered it with the blanket of blind faith. And in the darkness, their insecurity silently spreads like a plague. A toxin of the mind and soul. While Jesus founded his teachings on spiritual precepts (Man shall not live on bread alone...), the Church has effectively recalibrated it on materialistic principles, hence the emphasis on the physicality of the three temptations. It is materialistic precisely because the Church has sought power by subverting the transcendent principle of religion. As Gabriel Marcel notes in *Man and Mass Society*, "even the authentic religions may become similarly degraded in their very principle of being. They too can degenerate into idolatries; especially where the will to power is waiting to corrupt them; and this, alas, is almost invariably the case when the Church becomes endowed with temporal authority". The will to power, the ego, chokes the organicism of religion and thus do we see multiple, temporal authorities reigning and disputing over fragments of a shattered spirit. More and more splinter groups that invoke heaven with more zealousness than those before them.

"You hoped that, following you, man, too, would remain with God, having no need of miracles" says the Inquisitor. "But you did not know that as soon as man rejects miracles, he will at once reject God as well, for man seeks not so much God as miracles. And since man cannot bear to be left without miracles, he will go and create new miracles for himself, his own miracles this time..." The miracles man makes himself are the miracles of technology; the manipulation of matter. And since man had invested in faith for the sake of miracles to begin with, mastery over matter leads him to believe that he no longer needs God. As Dostoevsky himself says in the novel, commending Alyosha, for the realist, faith does not spring from miracles, but miracles from faith. Modern man belongs to the Church of White Coats, investing his faith in the idea that Physics alone reveals all; nothing stands outside of the frontiers of Physics. And Metaphysics, if it still exists, is an increasingly diminishing field as Science grows to encompass more of that which it did not know before. That is thus another reason why I believe that the Cardinal Grand Inquisitor is the prophet of materialism because a materialistic universe is essentially deterministic; the future is merely the result of all the physical data-the atoms-present in the universe. Human free will is an illusion. "It is very important for us to recognize," says Marcel, "that a materialistic conception of the universe is radically incompatible with the idea of a free man: more precisely, that, in a society ruled by materialistic principles, freedom is transmuted into its opposite, or becomes merely the most treacherous and deceptive of empty slogans." Marcel goes on to say that freedom in a society run on materialistic principles would be evanescent, it would consist of "rendering oneself sufficiently insignificant to escape the attention of the men in power...from the point of view of the individual in such a society, there is no conceivable way out at all: private life, as such, does not exist any more".

While real religion is predicated upon a self-willed process between certainty and doubt, and this process is an expression of human liberty as one chooses to face their personal insecurities and the despair of the human condition, the religion of materialism quietly rids you of your autonomy to afford you happiness. And it does this under the banner of making you free, convincing you that you've been a captive under religion. It sells you "freedom" in bulk; and what is more comforting than the freedom of certainty-freedom from self-doubt. The Church of Materialism has become so pervasive in so short a time that its principles have corrupted religions with principles of transcendence, religions that, under the increasing pressure of a secular, materialistic conception of the universe, have - unfortunately - lost ground in their "radical experience of freedom."

Apologetics Over Liberation
Same-Sex Marriage, Trans* Death, and the Role of Queer Clergy

Hillary Brownsmith

I met Ash* when I was working as a caseworker in a large men's homeless shelter and referral agency in Atlanta. Ash came to get a referral to another service agency for homeless people in town. I initially assumed she lived in a women's shelter or slept on the street. But she told me during our first meeting that she slept in a bunk upstairs, surrounded, any given night, by between 700 and 1000 men. As an adult trans woman, this was Ash's only option. Ash's situation was unbelievable. New to Atlanta and to homeless services, I couldn't trust that this men's drop-in shelter with minimal security and poorly trained staff was Ash's only possible placement. So I called around. I talked to staff at other shelters. I talked to housed trans women. I read public accommodation ordinances. I contacted a transgender right's attorney. But Ash had, of course, been right.

At that time, Atlanta had shelter for trans women under 21 and trans women who had tested positive for HIV/AIDs. Adult trans women who didn't know their status or who didn't have HIV/AIDS slept in men's shelters, like the one where I worked. Typically, these shelters required trans women to present as male to receive services. During their time in shelter, they were harassed, denied certain services, and sometimes raped by other clients.

Ash lived in the shelter off and on during my year-long contract there. She did sex work in the evening and attended a nursing program during the day. She would come by my office sometimes and tell me how things were going but the news was rarely good. At the end of my stint at the shelter and during a time when Ash was facing a particularly high rate of harassment and discrimination from shelter staff, Ash came to live with me. But her stay was short. My house was far outside of downtown, where most of her johns lived, her boyfriend still lived at the shelter, and she admitted to feeling like an imposition. So less than a month after she moved in, she asked me to drop her off back at the shelter. I did.

I called Ash regularly after that day but a year and a half passed with no word. Then one morning a mutual friend called me with news that Ash had died in Florida, where her family lived. The person on the other end of line didn't know the cause of her death. A memorial service was held for Ash in Atlanta. Bulletins from Ash's funeral in Florida sat in stacks on a table by the church basement entrance. Her parents had "taken her back"...they had picked a photo of her presenting as male for the bulletin cover and they used her birth name and male pronouns in the sparse obituary they had written for the local paper.

A string of people stood up and spoke about Ash. A young man, her chosen son, told the room not to cry because Ash's life had been painful and perilous. A local trans* activist called Ash's death at 29 of pneumonia a human rights issue. A trans* minister closed by noting that Ash had "made her final transition and now God is calling her by her true name".

In spite of the directive from Ash's son, we did cry. Ash's life was not the one-dimensional tragedy that the mainstream media portrays when documenting the lives and deaths of trans women, particularly black trans women like Ash. Ash spoke out against unfair treatment of other trans women, she gave me gardening advice, she talked about traveling the world one day, she hung out in the park and fed the ducks when the shelter got to be too much, she had friendships and partnerships that she valued, she did more than survive...she lived a life of love and resistance. When she died, all that goodness disappeared and we grieved that.

Though trans* experience is not monolithic, Ash's story points to a larger truth that mainstream LGB activists, Christian or not, appear unable to face. The story of Ash's life and death illustrates the necessity of privileging queer survival issues over the politics of inclusion currently espoused by the gay rights movement. While same-sex, civil marriage was being secured nationwide and LGB inclusion in the military was taking effect, the life and death issues of inadequate access to healthcare and housing; employment discrimination and disproportionate rates of queer (specifically youth and trans*) homelessness and imprisonment were going largely unaddressed.

In 2012, $33 million was spent to bring marriage ballot initiatives to just four states. (1) In 2013 Human Rights Campaign spent $1.6 million lobbying congress. Though the HRC is supposed to represent all issues affecting the queer community, the majority of this large sum was spent to forward the issue of same-sex, civil marriage. (2) A year later the Employment Non-Discrimination Act, introduced in almost every Congress since 1994, failed to pass once again. (3) As of 2015, only three states and the District of Columbia have outlawed reparative therapy for queer minors. (4)This month, the families of Shade Shuler, Ashton O'Hara, Kandis Capri, Elisha Walker, and Tamara Dominquez are soliciting donations for their loved ones' funeral services.

These disparities call into question the argument that multiple issues can receive equal attention or funding at the same time. As marginalized people in a myriad of movements have always known, the issues effecting the most privileged demographic in the movement; in this case, white adult gay men and lesbians in the middle and upper classes; are addressed first and the trickle down social justice they promise never arrives. Marriage equality does not lead to an end to the bullying that causes queer youth to be twice as likely as their straight classmates to drop out of high school. Military inclusion doesn't diminish the resolve of the prison system to place trans women in men's prisons.

Many radical queer activists have given greater context to the disparities outlined here. They have done rigorous research to help us all better understand the racist, classist, capitalist and cisnormative reasons that marriage equality was so heavily funded and well-publicized.(5) What has not been widely written about is the role queer clergy played in promoting issues of inclusion over issues of survival and liberation.

Believe Out Loud, an online platform for "Christian faith and LGBTQ advocacy" estimates that 5,000 U.S. churches "intentionally embrace the full inclusion of lesbian, gay, bisexual and transgender people". (6) This number is based on self-reported statuses or affiliation with "welcoming" denominations making it a conservative estimate. Many of these churches not only welcome gay members, they have or would welcome queer clergy.

Over the last few decades, the rate of LGBTQ church inclusion has moved at an ever-increasing pace. Many secular queer activists have seen LGBTQ desire to attend seminary or pursue ordination as inherently assimilationist and self-hating in light of the church's gross mistreatment of queer persons over the centuries. This critique, while built on a true history of oppression and grounded in an awareness of the corrosive nature of internalized homophobia and/or transphobia, fails to acknowledge the existence of queer liberation theology and the power of Other-ed voices in the pulpit. While the argument for civil marriage and military inclusion was about interacting with an institution "just like everybody else", being a queer minister has always had the ability to be peculiarly queer endeavor.

If queer ministers had used the lens of queer liberation theology, a theology that goes beyond "gay is ok" apologetics to assert that God views heterosexism and cissexism as sinful and has a preferential option for oppressed queer persons, the church body would arguably be interested in a different set of queer issues. After accomplishing the goals of church inclusion, a queer minister grounded in liberation theology could have taken on topics that the church has failed to properly address, making itself an uneasy fit or an unwelcome addition to many current social justice movements that focus on survival issues.

Queer ministers could have gotten their churches to talk openly about sex. These frank conversations could have pushed liberal "welcoming" churches to not merely reject the sexual rules endorsed by more conservative denominations but to develop strong, inclusive sexual ethics. While life-long sex education and classes on child sexual abuse awareness and prevention are being implemented by churches in a couple of American denominations, issues pertaining to sex; sexual violence; rape culture; and sexual consent are not often addressed from the pulpit.

White queer ministers could have made prisons and policing a constant point of study and discussion in the white church. While it is important not to detract from the particularly brutal violence black persons have experienced at the hands of the prison industrial complex, queer people are aware that policing not only works to protect white bodies and white property but also to protect white, heterosexual ideas of purity and normalcy. Naming this under-discussed function of policing and imprisonment could have dispelled the idea that unjust policing and sentencing is just an issue for black communities and called white churches into the work for prison abolition and a strong critique of policing.**

Queer ministers had the ability to reiterate and nuance the anti-capitalist economic agenda of unearned, God-given abundance. Making it clear that when we say that all God's children deserve housing, food, and medical care we should be explicitly including people with criminal records, histories of drug use, and people living with HIV/AIDS should have been straight-forward task for ministers belonging to communities where these struggles are experienced in disproportionately higher numbers.**(7)(8)(9)**During a time when the government provides less support for underserved communities and more private-sector, safety net organizations are claiming religious exemptions and complicating applications for service, this stance is particularly needed from clergy.

Certainly, there are queer ministers who have discussed these issues. But it is hard to believe that the majority of queer ministers allowed stories like Ash's to direct their ministries when the only queer issue the liberal church has felt the need to take a public stand on is marriage. Marriage not only fails to push the church to think differently about sex, it allows the church to maintain the most conservative position on romantic relationships and sexuality. Marriage equality advocates have attempted to erase the fact that queer folks are persecuted and feared because of who they have sex with and how they have sex by making this about "love"; using hashtags, campaign slogans, and photos that portray gay marriage just like monogamous, child-rearing straight marriage. Additionally, the battle for same-sex civil marriage has pitted the liberal white church against the black church, with black churches being cast as homophobic and dangerous and liberal white churches holding themselves up as safe havens with a monopoly on the words "welcoming", "affirming", and "open". Perhaps most frightening of all, is the amount of influence that queer clergy and their affiliated denominations have exerted on the government around the issue of same-sex marriage. Though activists have pointed out that conservative churches and denominations are out of line and should lose their tax exempt status for lobbying against same-sex marriage and promoting anti-gay candidates from the pulpit, this critique has not extended to liberal churches who engaged in the same practices to support same-sex marriage. **(10)**

So what happened to queer liberation theology and the power of the preaching voice of the Other? Though numerous other liberation theologies (e.g. Latin American, Black, Womanist, Korean, Palestinian) are still widely used, the concept of queer liberation theology has fallen out of fashion. Academics still discuss and write on the topic of queer theology but usually without the liberative idea of the queer person as an oppressed person in possession of God's preference. Though the reason for the disappearance of this particular lens has not been explicitly named, it is implied. The implication both in the academy and in the church is that the work of liberating the queer person is done.

This idea, while false, persists because there is no queer church to rebut it. Unlike other people who claim a liberation theology, queer people do not gather for worship in a segregated, predominately queer space. When queer people become ministers or theologians, there are not masses of organized people imploring them to write or preach a liberative word. Queer folks, scared of attending more conservative churches and not ministered to by liberal churches that merely celebrate inclusion, leave the church and join radical social justice activists outside the church who accompany the least and most maligned, the very people the church is called to care for and invite in. So queer ministers stand in the pulpit and perhaps tell their coming-out story and make a few jokes about the supposed discontinuity of being a gay Christian. But they are not reflecting back to the congregation a true understanding of the state of most queer lives in America.

Queer ministers, on the whole, are not queering ministry, they are not doing ministry for queer laity, and they are not bringing a queer lens to the pulpit. Queer ministers are "just like everybody else" in ministry. And that truth is not just a hard loss for gays and lesbians living in rural areas and conservative regions of the country, trans* folks, displaced queer youth, and those who are experiencing or are at risk of experiencing transphobic or homophobic violence. This is a hard loss for the entire Body of Christ. We need the whole Body to understand the wounding experienced by queer persons, and those stories are best conveyed by people who move in the world as queer people. We also need a queer lens to see old, supposedly settled issues in a new light. When the minister closed Ash's memorial service by saying "Ash has made her final transition and now God is calling her by her true name", she was speaking about liberation. In that church basement, the struggle for queer survival was raised up as real and difficult. The room needed to hear about freedom and God's great affection for those who are brutalized by this culture. The preacher saw those needs and ministered to them as only another queer person could. Certainly, her words were directed by the voice of God as much as they were directed by the story of a queer woman who resisted the system that eventually killed her. To hold these two voices together in ways that teach the church who it is and who it must serve; this is the work that all queer ministers must be faithful enough to undertake.

Notes

1. http://www.washingtonpost.com/blogs/the-fix/wp/2013/07/01/how-much-will-the-gay-marriage-fight-cost-over-the-next-three-years-tens-of-millions/
2. http://www.opensecrets.org/industries/background.php?cycle=2014&ind=j7300
3. http://www.washingtonblade.com/2014/12/03/house-panel-rejects-last-ditch-panel-pass-enda/
4. http://www.huffingtonpost.com/2015/05/19/oregon-gay-conversion-therapy-ban_n_7337350.html
5. For more information about the ways racism, classism, and cisnormativity played into the battle for same-sex marriage: http://www.againstequality.org/about/marriage/
For insight into the ways that corporate interests were protected by proponents of same-sex marriage: http://www.nytimes.com/2015/06/28/opinion/sunday/the-price-of-gay-marriage.html?_r=0
6. http://www.believeoutloud.com/background/christianity-and-lgbt-equality
7. http://srlp.org/wp-content/uploads/2012/08/disproport-incarc.pdf
8. http://www.cdc.gov/msmhealth/substance-abuse.htm
9. http://www.cdc.gov/hiv/group/gender/transgender/index.html
10. http://www.cbsnews.com/news/editorial-mormon-church-should-lose-tax-exempt-status-over-prop-8-support/

*Name changed to protect the privacy of other persons mentioned in this story.

**This argument assumes that unless white persons see white people mistreated by the criminal justice system they will not abandon hope in the system and its ability to reform. At this juncture in our history, the murder and mistreatment of so many black people should be enough for all Christians, regardless of race, to turn against this death-dealing, sinful institution. Unfortunately, I do not see evidence of this anti-racist, abolitionist trend in the white church. This argument also assumes a racially segregated worship community. According to a recent study by LifeWay Research, 8 in 10 churches are predominately composed of one racial group. It is also important to note here that as a white person who was raised in a white church and currently attends a white church, I can really only speak out of and critique that institution.

Reclaiming Our Prophetic Fire
From Personal Faith to Communal Transformation

P. Joshua Hatala

Pope Francis' call for action on climate change and his biting moral critique of late capitalism have been met with dismissiveness by self-professed Christian Republicans. Beyond mere political expediency and old-fashioned anti-popery, Republican leaders' responses to the Pope's encyclical are characteristic of an individualistic brand of American Christianity that has its roots in 19th-century religious revivalism and the early 20th-century triumph of consumer capitalism.

While it is easy to scoff at politicians who call upon Christian morality when it is politically advantageous, Republican insistence that religion, as Jeb Bush put it, "ought to be about making us better as people,"[1] is characteristic of an American Christianity that relegates faith to the realm of individual moral choice and subjective, often emotional, experience. This thinking runs deep in the American religious psyche and has been a feature of American evangelicalism since the early 19th century Protestant revivalism of the Second Great Awakening.

In this transformation of American religious life during the Second Great Awakening, believers privileged experience over dogma and abandoned their focus on the Hebrew Bible- a hallmark of their Calvinist (Puritan) forebears. As Stephen Prothero writes in *American Jesus: How the Son of God Became a National Icon*, the Puritans' "...covenant theology took its cues from Israel more than Galilee, focusing not on the individual's relationship with God the Son but on the community's covenant with God the Father. In 1827 Ralph Waldo Emerson would famously describe his time as 'the age of the first person singular'. Puritans lived in a world of the first person plural." [2] As a result of the disestablishment of the churches, the 19th century saw the replacement of the covenantal *community* with individualistic piety, further propelled by a burgeoning class of populist preachers and seemingly inexhaustible new forms of scriptural exegesis. Prothero writes that, "through this orgy of activism, evangelicalism became not only the dominant religious impulse in the nation but also a major cultural force", later described as the "evangelical century".[3] No longer concerned with the fate of nations and whole peoples, by the mid 1800s Jesus was understood and described as a "comforter" and is depicted in popular art as a soft-faced, loving friend.

Republican chairman of the House Committee on Natural Resources Rob Bishop's retort to the Pope that the latter's moral critique of capitalism and environmental degradation is "a political issue,"[4] reveals the extent to which faith has been divorced from the rigorous theology of American Calvinists like Jonathan Edwards and the Catholic Church's understanding of a collective and communal social justice. While Bishop describes himself as "pro-life, pro-family, and pro-Second Amendment"[5], and served for two years as a Mormon missionary (a denomination born of the Second Great Awakening), if we can take him at his word, the application of his faith to the public sphere ends where the *collective* begins. Much like the profound difference between collective covenant and individualistic Jesus piety, Bishop's religiously informed focus on *individual* restrictions and freedoms take center stage. If one's religious tradition restricts itself to internal piety then it will be ill-equipped to address contemporary moral issues like climate change.

Instead, it will focus exclusively on the *individual's* relationship to society, as is the case with the religious right's abandonment of public schools for home schools and vouchers and its insistence on regulating individuals' bodies, but not climate change or structural oppression. As Rick Santorum said, essentially calling for a relegation of morality and theology to private spheres that affect individuals but not the collective, "We probably are better off leaving science to the scientists, and focusing on what we're really good at, which is theology and morality."

Individualistic Jesus piety was bolstered by a Victorian era that saw the completion of a trend begun during the Second Great Awakening. In this era sentimentality triumphed over reason. In *The Feminization of American Culture* Ann Douglas analyzes the impact of literary women and Protestant ministers on 19th century American Victorian culture, and on each other. A battle for influence ensued between more traditional clergymen as their professional power waned as a result of disestablishment, and women authors, on the rise vocationally, who carved out their own domain, mainly in fiction. These authors began to "feminize" American culture through popular novels that raised sentimentality of above reason and doctrine. In this context, ministers and women competed for the attention of female readers and parishioners. Clergy responded in kind, tailoring their written work and tenor of their preaching to this new sentimental ethos in order to attract and retain parishioners. Grand Puritan theology was replaced by sentimental fiction that concerned itself with private and domestic life. This focus on the emotional and private life increasingly displaced the intellectual, public, and historical life of the people. Additionally, this resulted in a kind of "consumer" church life that relied on pandering to parishioners' desires that, Douglas argues, ultimately paved the way for a consumerist mentality.

In 1891 Pope Leo XIII issued an encyclical on the rights of laborers, amplifying the Catholic idea that moral principles can and should inform economic and social realities. While Pope Leo composed, American capitalism was entering a new era. William Leach writes in *Land of Desire: Merchants, Power, and the Rise of a New American Culture*:

"In the decades following the Civil War, American capitalism began to produce a distinct culture, unconnected to traditional family or community values, to religion in any conventional sense, or to political democracy. It was secular business and market-oriented culture, with the exchange and circulation of goods at the foundation of its aesthetic life and of its moral sensibility. ... The cardinal features of this culture were acquisition and consumption as the means of achieving happiness; the cult of the new; the democratization of desire; and money value as the predominant measure of all value in society." [6]

This "land of desire" was built by the labor power of a working class that was the central focus of Pope Leo XIII's encyclical, yet with the exception of a handful of "Social Gospel" preachers like Walter Rauschenbusch, or Catholic Monsignor John Ryan of Catholic University in Washington D.C. American Christianity was not prepared to raise a moral voice against worker exploitation, raw commercially driven desire, and naked greed- all of which are clearly antithetical to basic Christian teaching. Largely unchallenged, "American corporate business, in league with key institutions, began the transformation of American society into a society preoccupied with consumption, with comfort and bodily well-being, with luxury, spending, and acquisition, with more goods this year than last, more next year than this."[7] As a result, the triumph of consumerism "diminished American public life, denying the American people access to insight into other ways of organizing and conceiving life, insight that might have endowed their consent to the dominant culture...with real democracy."[8]

In 1906 John Wanamaker, merchant and owner of Wanamaker department stores, proudly coined the phrase "land of desire" to describe the emergence of a consumer culture he was helping to create. Emblematic of an American Christianity ill-equipped to challenge consumer culture, Wanamaker was a devout Presbyterian who contributed greatly to the development of the World Sunday School Movement and worked to grow the YMCA. He led parallel lives- one devoted to commercial ventures built on exploitation and the creation of artificial desire for consumer goods, and one equally dedicated to religious life. At one point, Wanamaker almost entered the ministry. The legacy of individualistic piety and sentimentalist Christianity, as Leach points out, "illustrate[s] the inadequacy of evangelical religion- and of mainstream institutional religion generally in this period- in dealing with the moral challenge of the new corporate industrial order."[9] Indeed, this inadequacy has again been illustrated by Republican leaders' responses to Pope Francis' latest exhortation, *Laudato Si'*: On the Care of our Common Home. Their responses are grounded in a lasting legacy that has its roots in the 19th century and allows sharp divisions between the sacred and the profane, social justice and individual morality, personal piety and covenantal righteousness.

While none of us wants to return to our Puritan past, nor move into a theocratic future where religious tenets govern the public sphere, we can begin to consider ways in which mainline and evangelical American Christianity can speak, to paraphrase Cornel West, with a "prophetic voice" to our social and economic crises. This voice has survived among the marginalized, thriving in many Black churches across America- one of the reasons we are again seeing Black churches burnt down throughout the south. It comes through clearly in Pope Francis' encyclical. It is reflected in the social mission of many denominations and individual believers, yet it remains marginalized, drowned out by a current of mainstream American faith that lacks socially transformative power- a faith that is unable or unwilling to speak to climate crises, economic exploitation, and all forms of injustice, preferring inner transformation and personal experience to the common good.

Walter Rauschenbusch wrote, "The Church, the organized expression of the religious life of the past, is one of the most potent institutions and forces in Western civilization. ...It cannot help throwing its immense weight on one side or the other. If it tries not to act, it thereby acts; and in any case its choice will be decisive for its own future." He went on to write that, "It is important to note, further, that the morality which the prophets had in mind in their strenuous insistence on righteousness was not merely the private morality of the home, but the public morality on which national life is founded. They said less about the pure heart for the individual than of just institutions for the nation." It's time to reclaim the prophetic fire that runs through the Christian tradition so that the "immense weight" of the social justice mission of the churches, along with their rich intellectual traditions, can be employed for the common good.

Notes

[1] Alan Neuhauser, "In Sweeping Encyclical, Pope Calls on 'All Humanity' to Halt Global Warming,"*U.S. News & World Report*, June 18, 2015, http://www.usnews.com/news/articles/2015/06/18/pope-francis-encyclical-calls-on-all-humanity-to-halt-global-warming
[2] Stephen Prothero, *American Jesus: How the Son of God Became a National Icon* (New York: Farrar, Straus and Giroux, 2003), 44.
[3] Ibid., 49.
[4] Matthew Daly and Erica Werner, "Congressional Republicans Shrug Off Pope's Climate Message,"*The Washington Post,* June 18, 2015, http://www.washingtonpost.com/politics/congress/inhofe-popes-climate-encyclical-could-harm-poor/2015/06/18/
[5] Rob Bishop For Congress, http://www.votebishop.com/meet-rob
[6] William Leach, Land of Desire: *Merchants, Power, and the Rise of a New American Culture* (New York: Random House Books, 1993), 3.

[7] Ibid., xiii.
[8] Ibid., xv.
[9] Ibid., 224.

Violence is Violence?
Inter-Generational Strife, Self-Defense, and the Black Lives Matter Movement

Hillary Brownsmith

The Bible is brimming with instances of people waiting for a prophet or movement only to have that person or mobilization arrive and go unrecognized or, worse yet, be violently suppressed because it doesn't conform to the expectations of the waiting masses.

Since I started working and/or living in radical Christian settings seven years ago, I have heard elders wax nostalgic about the civil rights movement. I have watched older folks who lived during the end of the Jim Crow era weep when discussing their own recognition of that important historical and cultural shift. I have also watched elders chastise young folks, sometimes rightfully, for failing to care about this history; the nonviolent tactics employed; and the ways hearts, minds, and institutions were forever altered. I write about a lot of issues with the marginal confidence of a generalist. But if there is an issue on which my nerve consistently fails it is on the generational tension and resulting divide as it exists in the radical Christian left. This issue of generational conflict feels close...maybe too close. I have watched the "old guard" in established Christian communities push out younger folks for misunderstandings that boil down to generational politics (i.e. democratic socialism vs. anarchism). I have watched young people leave established churches to start generationally homogenous churches of their own. And, of course, I have seen so many people under 40 leave parish ministries and take their seminary training to chaplaincy work or academia.

Wondering if perhaps there was something to our elders complaints that young folks are disrespectful and too "now focused", I decided to really seek instruction from "the silent generation". I am a member of a church with only 3 consistently attending members in their 20s (my partner and I are included in that number). I am now employed by that church. And over the last year I was part of an apprenticeship program administered by this church and five of my favorite ministers, all but one of whom is over sixty. This experience of committing to a religious community and earnestly trying to understand the stories that my generation supposedly won't hear has given me a stronger understanding of our elders' position. Naturally, greater understanding makes critique even harder. But I do hope that it gives the resulting critique the weight of a well-informed position.

We, like our Biblical ancestors, are living during an under-recognized and sometimes castigated movement. That mobilization began when Michael Brown was murdered in Ferguson, Missouri on August 9, 2014. Though it has gone uncovered by major media outlets, protests in Missouri have gone on uninterrupted since Michael's death...over 200 days of resistance against racist policing and the notion that white lives matter more than black lives. But as Tef Poe announces in his song War Cry, a song that celebrates the Black Lives Matter (BLM) movement while pointing out the systematic racism that makes the movement necessary, "this ain't your daddy's civil rights movement".

Other writers have pulled this line from Tef Poe's work and written important pieces about the ways BLM refuses to bend to

621

expectations about what racial justice movements in America should look like.**1** These writers have pointed out that folks who lived through the civil rights era take issue with the lack of a charismatic singular leader like Dr. King or are turned off by BLM's unapologetically intersectional organizing. In so many words, other articles have noted that BLM has no shortage of leadership; it is simply broad-based. It has also been articulated by multiple writers that fighting for all black lives; trans* lives, queer lives, children's lives, women's lives and men's lives; doesn't weaken or fracture the movement, it makes it relevant and life-saving to more people. These two issues have received due coverage and I have been in churches recently where these organizing differences were overcome many years ago. I have been tempted to speak too broadly and say that what sets BLM apart from the civil rights movement and what our elders take issue with is the "violence" associated with BLM. But rightly named, property destruction and physical self-defense against police are what people have a problem with. **2**

I am singularly focusing on self-defense because I have never been able to abide the way so many Christian elders back up, theologically and ethically, the prohibition against physical self-defense.**3** I know brilliant folks who have done important theological work to open the Bible as a liberative document for marginalized and brutalized peoples, making justifiable allowances for the ways that they keep themselves safe and whole. Yet those same people cite anecdotes of "creative nonviolence" every time a new story of a person of color physically resisting police comes to the fore.

There are major theological questions that left-leaning, learned Christians (both white and black) seem to have answered in favor of marginalized persons facing systematic violence until it comes to physical self-defense. In most other contexts I hear these Christians say we are called to be disciples of Christ not Christ himself, that equality of sin is not Biblically-backed (the sin of voluntarily participating in a genocide is not the same as shoplifting), and that our God is preferential and sides with the poor. But when self-defense is discussed we are suddenly all called to be led away by the Roman guard and hung on the cross so that we might save the world. Suddenly all sins are the same, "violence is violence", and the white male cop is just as victimized by the fallen order as the black child he is beating. Suddenly God loves the Egyptian as much as the enslaved Hebrew and resists sending the plagues so that the Egyptians might slowly come to understand the Hebrews' humanity and justly rule over them.

I attended a Black Lives Matter Youth Assembly in Raleigh this month where this statement was made: "Black Lives Matter means unwaveringly supporting the right to self-defense for black people to respond to the violent systems that profits off of forced nonviolence and passivity." Are we, the Church, not part of the violent system in this equation? Why do our elders continue to hold onto Walter Wink's biblically unsupported idea that institutions, like policing and prisons, "are good creations of God (as we are)...and can be redeemed (as we can be)"?[4] If cops demeaned their own credibility by publicly beating unresisting black protestors during the civil rights movement, how much more credibility have they lost by killing, with impunity, Eric Garner and Tamir Rice on film? With these situations in mind, how much more nonresistance against police brutality will black people need to participate in before we understand that cops are not being transformed by the suffering of their victims? Why can't the vast majority of Christians who oppose the use of physical self-defense understand that calling the cops to defend their lives or property is exponentially more violent than the physical self-defense they oppose? [5]

The Black Lives Matter movement is here to subvert the dominant consciousness. BLM is pointing out our deadly, racist dependence on prisons and policing. These folks are working to bring about a new day where justice and safety are attainable for everyone. And to have this new day, we must also employ new tactics, recognizing the expiration date on tactics that worked in a different era when the empire too used different mechanisms to oppress and seduce. Our theology has progressed so many times to support the last and the least. No Christian in the radical left, regardless of age, would now tell a woman to stand by her abusive husband or insist that a child passively undergo beatings from an abusive parent. It is time that our theology; our churches; and our elders, the best movement building teachers we have, acknowledge the injustice of insisting that black people sacrifice their bodies for the moralizing of the police force and this nation.

We must recognize this historical movement for what it is and what it dares to do. And just as this movement needs to be intersectional, it needs to be inter-generational. Let us all say unequivocally and believe without reservation that black lives matter.

Notes

1. Murphy, Carla. "The Hope and Burden of the Civil Rights Movement". Colorlines. January 16, 2015.
2. Armstrong, Amaryah. "On Ferguson and Property". Women and Theology. November 26, 2014. (posted to Jesus Radicals on January 9, 2015)
3. I understand that there are Christians under 60 who oppose the use of physical self-defense but I believe that younger generations are questioning this prohibition in greater numbers. I believe this is evidenced by the cohesion that exists in BLM. During the civil rights movement, King's followers were asked to refrain from physical self-defense. This request was not made by leaders of other black liberation movements working in the US at that time. In an interview featured in Black Power Mixtape, Stokley Carmichael points to one of the reasons that Dr. King opposed physical self-defense while others did not:

"Dr. King's policy was that nonviolence would achieve the gains for black people in the United States. His major assumption was that if you are nonviolent, if you suffer, your opponent will see your suffering and will be moved to change his heart. That's very good.

He only made one fallacious assumption: In order for nonviolence to work, your opponent must have a conscience. The United States has none."

Radical left Christian millennials, regardless of their position on physical self-defense, are vocal about America's lack of conscience. Additionally, the issue of self-defense hasn't created any recognizable rift in the BLM movement.
4. Wink, Walter. The Powers That Be: Theology for a New Millennium. Doubleday, 1998. Pg. 36
Later on in The Powers That Be (pg.159), Walter Wink makes a distinction between violence and force, defining force as "a legitimate, socially authorized, and morally defensible use of restraint to prevent harm being done to innocent people". His example of force is a police officer apprehending a murderer. Wink does not discuss in this book the violence perpetrated by police but does spend a great deal of time naming actions perpetrated by American soldiers in foreign nations as violence, not force.

Urban Issues

Learning from the Cleveland Model
Notes on the Next American Revolution

Sean Posey

In 2009, during the depths of the Great Recession, a small laundry opened in one of the most depressed neighborhoods in the poverty-stricken city of Cleveland. This seemingly obscure event proved to be a large salvo in what is slowly becoming a national dialogue on the future of wealth democratization in America. The Evergreen Cooperative Laundry-itself one part of Evergreen Cooperatives-is a "green" industrial laundry rooted in Cleveland's historically challenged Glenville neighborhood. Evergreen Cooperatives mission: to create worker-owned cooperative enterprises connected to a larger concept of community wealth building. Evergreen's economic experiment is part of what is called "The Cleveland Model" by its ideological father, the political economist Gar Alperovitz.

Cooperatives are not new, neither here or aboard. A departure from the traditional cooperative model, the Cleveland Model has been heralded as the start of one of the most concrete initiatives to realize a vision of an economic system beyond currently existing capitalism in America. And as income inequality, wage stagnation, and community disinvestment continues, more and more intellectuals, activists, and urban stakeholders are paying attention.

Ideological Origins

As the New Left began to collapse into rancor and recrimination in the early 1970s, noted leftist intellectuals Gar Alperovitz and Staughton Lynd began a conversation about the direction of progressive movements in the 1970s. Alperovitz, a historian and a political economist, served at high levels in Congress and the State Department before turning his attention to the possible democratic reordering of the economy.

In "Strategy and Program: Two Essays Toward a New American Socialism," Alperovitz tries to chart a course between capitalism and state socialism. By the early 1970s, the failure of the Soviet and Sino socialist models was clear. The destruction of the Soviets (local workers' councils) and the imposition of broad, centralized power in the hands of sclerotic planners had corrupted the Russian socialist model from the very beginning. The results of Maoist totalitarianism, once known, furthered the disillusion with the then currently existing state "socialist" structures.

With this is mind, Alperovitz reiterates a central question that the New Left had groped towards, but never full confronted. "We return to the basic issue: could society ever be organized equitably, cooperatively, humanely, so wealth benefited everyone without generating a highly centralized, authoritarian system?"[1] Alperovitz imagines a decentralized system of worker-owned enterprises acting in tandem with the best interests of both their businesses *and* the local community.

But this is just a first step. "... Affirm the principle of collective ownership or control of capital... and extend it, at least initially, to local communities, the sub-units of which are sufficiently small so that individuals in fact, learn cooperative relationships *in practice.* These however should be conceived only as elements of a larger solution-as the natural building blocks of a reconstructed nation of regional commonwealths." [2]

Alperovtiz's ideas are an extension of Leftist economic thinking dating back to Rosa Luxembourg. But in the wake of the collapse of the New Left, few outlets existed to promulgate such ideas. Instead, the shutdown of a steel mill in the highly industrialized city of Youngstown, Ohio, ended up providing a venue for an idea that would later blossom in the fertile soil of post-industrial Cleveland.

The Youngstown Example

On September 19, 1977, the Youngstown Sheet and Tube Company announced it would close its Campbell Works operation, just outside of Youngstown. Within a month, almost five thousand workers found themselves unemployed. This was one of the first large-scale plant closings of the era, but unlike many that came later, a concerted grass-roots effort emerged to not only keep the plant open, but to transfer ownership to the steelworkers themselves.

Within a month of the closing, the Ecumenical Coalition of the Mahoning Valley was organized to address the shutdown. Staughton Lynd and Gar Alperovitz, then director of the National Center for Economic Alternatives, converged on Youngstown to assist the Ecumenical Coalition. The approach involved direct action and intensive feasibility studies to determine how to enact a "community/worker" takeover of the mill.

With a broad array of local religious figures in the forefront, the Ecumenical Coalition led a local fundraising campaign and lobbied officials in Washington for grants and loans. The Carter Administration initially offered $100 million in guaranteed loans to back the project. Yet after a series of political setbacks, the administration ultimately reneged on the deal.

From the start, the steel companies opposed a buyout by workers. But even the United Steelworkers turned their back on the idea of worker ownership of the mills; instead, they closed down the local chapter in Youngstown.

Despite the failure of the Ecumenical Coalition's effort to buy the mill, the example set in Youngstown set the stage for the expansion of worker-owned cooperatives in Ohio. The formation of the Ohio Employee Ownership Center at Kent State University was directly inspired by the events in Youngstown, and today the Buckeye State has one of the best systems for developing cooperatives in the nation. [3] Against this backdrop came the creation of Evergreen Cooperatives in the heart of some of the most troubled neighborhoods in urban America.

Glenville and the University Circle Neighborhoods

Situated on the East Side of Cleveland, the Glenville neighborhood was once one of the finest communities in the city. During the early twentieth century it hosted summer residences for the city's wealthy along with the upscale Cleveland Golf Club and the Glenville Race Track. By the 1950s, white flight had already begun, and African Americans constituted the majority of Glenville's population by the 1960s.

In July of 1966, riots broke out in the Hough neighborhood that lasted for six days. Racial tensions increased in the city over the next two years, and despite the election of the city (and the nation's) first black mayor, Carl Stokes, in 1967, the situation continued to deteriorate.

On the night of July 23, 1968, heavily armed police-units set out on a mission to surveil black power activists in the Glenville area. Within hours a fierce firefight erupted between officers and a group led by Black Nationalist Ahmed Evans. Several civilians and police died in the nights of intense rioting that followed what became known as the "Glenville Shootout." Mayor Stokes was eventually forced to call in the National Guard. The flames died out, but the events haunt the city to this day.

"Cleveland began its steep decline" in 1968, according to long-time investigative reporter Roldo Bartimole. "...[T] he racial disturbances and animosities ingrained themselves into the fabric of the city and I don't believe they yet have worked themselves out." [4]

Today, about 70 percent of the households in Glenville are below the poverty line. The infant mortality rate is on par with Bulgaria. Nor is Glenville alone. Hough is one of the poorest neighborhoods in America, and the neighborhoods bordering University Circle are in various stages of collapse. [5]

The Cleveland Model

In 2005, the Cleveland Foundation along with some of the biggest anchor institutions, business, and civic groups in the city, spearheaded the "Greater University Circle Initiative." It was designed to stimulate real and lasting development in the ailing neighborhoods around University Circle. From this, Evergreen Cooperatives emerged in 2009.

Evergreen Cooperatives-itself a holding company-houses three businesses thus far under its umbrella: Evergreen Cooperative Laundry, a "green" industrial laundry; Evergreen Energy Solutions, which installs solar panels, other environmentally friendly home and commercial energy services; and Green City Growers, the largest hydroponic greenhouse in an American city.

Unlike the many failed efforts to use tax incentives and "empowerment" zones to attract corporations to the inner city, Evergreen draws its initial funding from a variety of corporate, government, and philanthropic sources. However, employees are hired whom will all own a stake in the businesses "over a period of time."

Evergreen shares some similarities with the Mondragon Corporation-a federation of over 250 worker cooperatives in the

631

heart of Spain. Formed in 1956 as a way to economically empower the Basque community, Mondragon is now one of the leading examples of the power of worker cooperatives. But unlike the Basque experiment, Evergreen is more planning oriented, especially in regards to creating a "culture of community." [6]
Cleveland's inner city neighborhoods, devastated by capital flight, have not benefitted from the billions of dollars being spent locally by anchor institutions in the city. Anchor institutions, often educational or medical non-profits, by their very nature are firmly rooted to a particular locality. And they have large budgets. The Cleveland Clinic and University Hospitals spend about $3 billion a year on services and goods.

Evergreen draws on this stream, providing laundry services for the Cleveland Clinic, food for hospital cafeterias, weatherization and solar installation services for other local non-profit institutions. Employees come from Glenville, Hough, and other low-income neighborhoods. These "worker-owners" and the profits they generate are then able to re-circulate into the surrounding communities. And, over time, more and cooperatives are scheduled to come on line-powered by a revolving loan fund.
A board of directors oversees the cooperatives, assuring they function not just for the workers (a problem that many cooperatives have encountered) but also for the surrounding communities. The board can also prevent any one cooperative from leaving the community, dissolving, or from selling itself to an outside entity.[7]

The broad idea is rooted in economic decentralization and the empowerment of cities and regions. It's related not only to Alperovitz's work, but also bears relation to Jane Jacob's idea that urban areas are the primary centers of successful economies. In the absence of a federal urban policy, the Evergreen initiative can be seen as a very local effort to address very systemic problems.
The Cleveland Model, though only five years old, has already attracted an enormous amount of attention. But is it the beginning of a model that can move beyond capitalism and state socialism?

Criticisms

Evergreen is not without its detractors. For all its potential, it remains unclear where small-scale developments like this could go in terms of challenging large capitalist structures and on what time scale. The environmentally friendly nature of the Evergreen Cooperatives is a crucially important aspect of the operation-one given great emphasis by Alperovitz and others. The Evergreen Cooperative Laundry, for example, uses one third the heat and water of a conventional industrial laundry. Yet, considering the dire straits we face with the continuing shift of the climate, how much longer can we afford to wait for these kinds of initiatives to spread and scale-up?

Even some socialists have gone after the Cleveland Model, dismissing the notion that it represents "municipal socialism," as Alperovitz has claimed.

The socialist publication *Workers World* states its suspicion quite clearly.

"One even has to wonder if the 'cooperative' is truly worker-owned. After three years, there are reportedly around 50 workers with a $3,000 stake in the company, which comes to $150,000. Who owns the rest of the shares? Evergreen's website encourages investment in the Evergreen Cooperative Development Fund LLC, which provides 'economic returns to Fund investors.' " [8]

As *Workers World* also mentions, the CEOS and all of the directors are white, while the vast majority of those living in the neighborhoods are African American. Not much progress from the days of Ahmed Evans.

Cecil Lee, the former CEO of Evergreen Laundry, and current president, Allen Grasa, both came from Sodexo-a company that has been boycotted at least nine times, based on their involvement in everything from anti-union campaigns to investments in for-profit prisons. [9]

The Cleveland Clinic, one of the largest anchor institutions involved in using Evergreen's services, has a notoriously poor reputation with the neighbors around it. The clinic's expansion has come at the price of small businesses and low-income neighborhoods; something that even the cooperative's "newspaper" has addressed.[10]

Noam Chomksy has been generally supportive of worker-owned cooperatives, but he also points out some of the more obvious difficulties facing their functioning and their possible expansion across the country.

"That's (the Cleveland Model) a step forward but you also have to get beyond that to dismantle the system of production for profit rather than *production for use.* That means dismantling at least large parts of market systems. Take the most advanced case: Mondragon. It's worker owned, it's not worker managed, although the management does come from the workforce often, but it's in a market system and they still exploit workers in South America, and they do things that are harmful to the society as a whole and they have no choice. If you're in a system where you must make profit in order to survive. You are compelled to ignore negative externalities, *effects on others."[11]*

And Chomsky emphasizes the likely reaction that capitalist institutions will have over time to the spread of community based worker cooperatives: "Of course they're going to be beaten back. The power system is not going to want them any more than they want popular democracy any more than the states of Middle East and the west are going to tolerate the Arab spring.... They're going to try to beat it back." [12]

These legitimate criticisms underline the need to view the one-person one-vote, worker-owned cooperative as simply one step in the democratization of the local.

The Cleveland Model (despite its problems) and initiatives resembling it, is likely to be a piece of the solution to our systemic woes-probably a large piece at that.

Land trusts (as a community-tool to fight displacement by gentrification), B-corporations, public and cooperative banking, and turning private monopolies into public ones, are all likely to become more popular ideas as the current system continues to erode. In particular, when (not if) the financial sector sparks another economic meltdown, support for turning the large banks into public utilities could possibly surge.

For now, as increasing numbers of American cities are effectively left to their own devices, more and more of them are looking towards models like the one in Cleveland. It will be, however, up to those on the Left to assure that a critical spotlight shines on efforts that simply reproduce inequality on a different scale. Communities-not just foundations and large anchor institutions-must have a real seat at the table. This will ultimately require the rebirth of radical grass roots organizations.

"Real power depends upon having a power base to operate from," according to Alperovitz. Neighborhoods, communities, cities, and regions need real economic, cultural, and political power. And it's there where the Left will have to step up, not just with rhetoric, criticism and slogans, but also with viable solutions.

References

[1] Gar Alperovitz and Staughton Lynd, *Strategy and Program: Two Essays Toward a New American Socialism* (Boston: Beacon Press, 1973), 53.
[2] Ibid.,
[3] Gar Alperovitz, *What Then Must We Do? Straight Talk About the Next American Revolution* (White River Junction: Chelsea Green Publishing, 2013), 31.
[4] Roldo Bartimole, "1968-The Year that Changed It All," *Cleveland Leader*, April 2, 2008.http://www.clevelandleader.com/node/5310 (Accessed October 21, 2014).

[5] David Wilson, *Cities and Race: America's New Black Ghettoes* (London: Routledge, 2007), 76.

[6] "The Cooperative Economy (a Conversation with Gar Alperovitz)," *Orion Magazine*, August 2014.http://www.orionmagazine.org/index.php/articles/article/8163/ (Accessed October 31, 2014). Also see Gar Alperovitz, David Imbroscio, and Thad Williamson, *Making A Place for Community: Local Democracy in a Global Era* (London: Routledge, 2002).

[7] Capital Institute, *Field Study no. 2: The Evergreen Cooperatives of Cleveland*.http://www.capitalinstitute.org/sites/capitalinstitute.org/files/docs/FS2-Evergreen%20full%20article.pdf(accessed October 22, 2014).

[8] Martha Grevatt, "Beyond Socialism? A Critical Look at the 'Cleveland Model,'" *Workers World*, April 25, 2013. http://www.workers.org/articles/2013/04/25/beyond-socialism-a-critical-look-at-the-cleveland-model/ (Accessed October 22, 2014).

[9] Mary Bottari, "Outsourcing America: Sodexo Siphons Cash From Kids and Soldiers while Dishing Up Subprime Food," *Huffington Post*, September 24, 2013. http://www.huffingtonpost.com/mary-bottari/post_5631_b_3982325.html (Accessed October 31, 2014).

[10] Toni White, "A New Perspective," *Neighborhood Voice*, February 22, 2013.http://www.neighborhood-voice.com/neighborhood-news/a-new-perspective/ (Accessed October 22, 2014).

[11] Laura Flanders, "Talking with Noam Chomsky," *CounterPunch*, April 30, 2012.http://www.counterpunch.org/2012/04/30/talking-with-chomsky/ (Accessed October 24, 2014).

[12] Ibid.,

I Wish I Was In Dixie?

Culture, Planning, and the Future of the Southern "Boom"

Sean Posey

In addressing the growth of sprawling, low-density, autocentric communities around much of America, Joel Kotkin, a 'New Suburbanist,' states the case for a new outlook:
Rather than reject such cities, we are committed to their improvement. All of our analysis of current and likely future trends reveals that sprawling multipolar cities with overwhelmingly auto dependent suburbs will continue to enjoy economic and demographic growth over the next several decades. [1]
Despite what many New Urbanists might want to believe, Kotkin - though a sprawl apologist - is likely correct. Polycentric cities will continue to grow, and they will continue to attract new residents- for now. Much of that growth will occur in the South, now the most populous region in the United States.

Ultimately, however, this is an unsustainable trend. Attempting to sustain it will have enormous portends for one of the most complicated and ecologically fragile areas of the country. The

American South, long a sparsely populated region with a unique agrarian culture and mindset, is transforming dangerously. How will it react to the potentially fatal economic, environmental, and cultural challenges presented by growth and sprawl in a time of climate flux?

A Nation within a Nation

The eighteenth-century South represented a firmly agrarian, slave-dependent system that was qualitatively different from the Northern colonies. Slavery remained a presensce in the North as well-and it would remain an important part of places like the future District of Columbia well into the next century. Yet a rising merchant class in the North felt threatened by the neo-feudal South. The Three- Fifths Compromise might have prevented Southern representatives from walking out on the Constitutional Convention, but as time passed, the regional divide between the two only grew.

Southern culture placed a heavy emphasis on honor, family, and "ease." Morris Berman views the South of this era as a historically traditional society. It was the rapidly growing and entrepreneurial North that proved to be the historical anomaly. The North, far from inspired by abolitionist rhetoric, saw the Southern outlook on life as the primary impediment to the spread of industrial capitalism.[2] According to historian Barrington Moore, "It is difficult to find a case in history where two different regions have developed economic systems based on diametrically opposed principles and yet remained under a central government that retained real authority in both areas." [3] No longer reliant on the Southern cotton economy by the mid-nineteenth century, the North viewed the opening of territories in the West as the next frontier in capital expansion; they viewed the possible expansion of slavery into those territories as an economic and cultural threat.

After the Civil War and the calamitous defeat of the Confederacy, the seed of a more urban and industrial mindset was planted in the beleaguered South. In the words of Thaddeus Stevens, this was "intended to revolutionize their principles and feelings... (to) work a radical reorganization in Southern institutions, habits, and manners."[4] With this in mind, Reconstruction ended and the North abandoned African Americans to the machinations of Jim Crow.[5]

Still, the South remained a seemingly perpetually backward region, one in thrall to racism and ignorance. Aside from a few industrial cities like Birmingham, Alabama, the region remained predominately rural in character in almost every sense. But as the industrial cities of the Midwest and Northeast entered an era of decline in the post-World War II era, the South began to rise on the rays of an ascendant 'Sun Belt.'

Atlanta: Capital City of the New South

On the eve of the Civil War, Atlanta, Georgia, resembled a township more than it did a city. Only 9,000 souls called the ramshackle city home in the years before William Tecumseh Sherman put the torch to it in 1864. The Union army also destroyed the railroad system that gave Atlanta the nickname "Terminus" and made it a hub for the shipment of Confederate goods. But despite the decimation of the Civil War, the population quickly grew by over 100 percent inside a decade. Atlanta continued to grow until technology (air conditioning) allowed a new wave of migrants to comfortably live in what became the unofficial capital of the post-war South.

Atlanta's population almost reached 500,000 in 1970, but the confluence of white flight, freeways, and a penchant for suburbanization and political decentralization changed the metro area into a sprawling ball of humanity, concrete, steel and seemingly unstoppable outward momentum. Even though the population of the city proper dropped by 40,000 from 1960 to 2010, the metro area grew into the ninth largest in the country; it's now home to 5.5 million people.

Metro Atlanta's awesome economic might made itself felt in the post-war years. Atlanta's economy grew into the seventeenth largest in the world. The city "too busy to hate" also attracted a plethora of Fortune 500 company headquarters. The seemingly ever-expanding Hartsfield-Jackson airport became the world's busiest. Atlanta even regained its important position as a railroad and shipping center.

Despite such success, several converging problems are casting a shadow on Atlanta's future. Aaron Renn, noted urbanist, sums up the immediate challenges facing the city in the second decade of the century: "With over one million new people, Atlanta added almost no jobs in the last decade. From 2001-08, its GDP per capita actually declined by 6 percent. And over that same period its per capita income declined from 109 percent of the U.S. average to 95 percent, a stunning 14-point drop that was the worst of any large city."[6] As Renn mentions, the city's freeways are inadequate; suburban roads are outdated, and public transportation funding is grossly inadequate. In 2012, residents voted down a $7.2 billion transportation plan designed to deal with the city's enormous traffic problems. A distrust of government and a fractured voting public seemed to contribute to the defeat. While Renn sees Atlanta's sagging competitive spirit as the ultimate problem, the real issue remains sustainability.

Atlanta's storm sewer system is grossly insufficient. There's a projected 60 percent increase in demand for water by 2020, at a time when the city has been unable to expand water access in any meaningful way. In 65 years the average summer temperature will be around 96 degrees with highs of around 115 degrees. Formerly tropical diseases will likely spread into the region, including yellow fever and dengue. According to researchers at Georgia Tech, business as usual will lead to "water shortages and further declining air quality, as businesses and industry decide that Atlanta's environment cannot sustain long-term operations for their companies nor provide a desirable quality of life for its employees."[7]

But the city is not an anomaly. Atlanta's rise - and its current difficulties - is also reflected in the fastest growing region of the South.

Florida: The Southern Boom State Extraordinaire

Long before America fell in love with the sub-tropical temptations of the Sunshine State, Florida was a backwater with seemingly few charms and even fewer people.
Less people lived in Florida in at the beginning of the twentieth century than live in Detroit today. Marshes, mangrove swamps, and the feared bloodsuckers-Ceratopogonidae-or 'no-see-ums,' hindered development and made much of the state deeply unpleasant for human settlement. Florida was an agricultural state, and beaches were considered frontier lands with little practical use or commercial value. Much like other parts of the South, air conditioning helped make Florida suitable for mass development. Bulldozers, retirees, and DDT spread quickly over the land in the post-war years.
Between 1970 and 1990, Florida outpaced even the massive growth of the South as a whole. By 2000, over fifteen million people lived in Florida. In 2014, the Sunshine State surpassed New York as the third largest state. After a brief pause during the Great Recession, Florida's seemingly unstoppable production homebuilders returned to churning out their barely differentiated wares all over the state's low-density developments. But Florida's rapid rise has reshaped the culture - and much more ominously - the delicate balance of its ecosystems.
Interestingly enough, Florida is the only former Confederate state where the majority of citizens fail to consider themselves "Southerners." Florida's culture could be, in this sense, divorced from the rest of the South. However, Florida, like much of the South today, revolves around small government and endless growth as its "theme, mantra, and creed."[8]

The business of growth as usual is now threatening the very future of the state's most important city. After sinking into decline in the 1970s, and after suffering one of the worst race riots in post-1960s era, Miami roared back and became the key city at the crossroads of Latin America and the US. A growing financial center and a receptacle for large amounts of foreign investment, Miami is a critical part of the Florida economy.

Accidents of geography, poor planning, and a changing climate now threaten to undo all of that. Miami is threatened by rising waters due to its proximity to sea level and by an even more difficult problem. The city itself is situated on a bed of porous limestone; seawater is coming up from below-threatening infrastructure and fresh water supplies. The *Guardian* paints a picture of city already under a slow siege:

Today, shop owners keep plastic bags and rubber bands handy to wrap around their feet when they have to get their cars, while householders have found that ground-floor spaces in garages are no longer safe to keep their cars. Only those on higher floors can hope to protect their cars from surging seawaters that corrode and rot the innards of their vehicles.[9]

The problem, as *The Guardian* points out, is that climate change deniers are running the show in Miami. Sadly, that's the case for the entire state-and much of the South in general. The current governor, Rick Scott, former governor and now presidential candidate, Jeb Bush, and Senator Marco Rubio, are all climate skeptics. While these growth obsessed misleaders fiddle, the state continues a binge of unsustainable development.

For the past two decades the Intergovernmental Panel on Climate Change has consistently underestimated global sea level rise by as much as 80 percent. [10] In Florida those effects are currently showing up in Miami, but they will soon make themselves felt in Tampa Bay, Charlotte Harbor, and in tidal rivers around the state.[11] Unlike the Florida of yesteryear, development in the past half-century focused on coastal cities, directly along eroding beaches, and on endangered barrier islands. And development continues unabated, even as the scientific evidence against it continues to accumulate.

Hurricane Katrina and the Future of Catastrophe

Florida is not the only Gulf Coast state facing serious problems. The category five-Hurricane Katrina helped reveal some of the serious structural, economic, and social weaknesses undergirding the other states of the Deep South. While Georgia, Florida, and the Southeast have economically prospered, Louisiana and Mississippi remain the poorest states in the country. The coastal areas of these states offer vacation playgrounds that belie the deep poverty that dominates the interior.

In New Orleans, inner city poverty-especially concentrated in fierce housing projects like Magnolia, formerly located in Central City-provided the dark side of Mardi Gras and the endless party of the French Quarter. That dark side came into full view when Katrina struck the Gulf.

Katrina is perhaps most remembered for the Bush administration's failure to respond to the aftermath of the storm, but state and local government also failed on multiple levels. The city government improperly implemented an evacuation procedure with the storm less than a day from landfall. Hundreds died because of that mistake, and more joined them in the hasty evacuation that took place after the storm had already made landfall. The poverty-stricken and the most helpless were left to fend for themselves as local government collapsed. The state government also neglected to issue an evacuation order within time. Perhaps most disturbing, President Bush and Governor Blanco knew of the distinct possibility that the levees would fail. Blanco insisted that a poor state like Louisiana couldn't have possibly handled such an event; however, the truth is Louisiana is poor for a reason. Like the Bush administration, the state's political culture has long viewed government and governing as the problem-an acute problem throughout the South.

Katrina also brought to the surface old racial and economic rifts that are imbedded throughout cities in the South. While hundreds of local police abandoned their posts and government officials high-tailed it out town, well-armed mercenary forces (from Blackwater and ISI) arrived, not to keep order, but to safeguard the mansions of the city's elite. In the neighborhood of Algiers Point, white homeowners armed themselves and fired on desperate African Americans trying to reach high ground in the neighborhood. Several police officers were convicted of beating and murdering a man who sought their help (they burned his remains with his car). Seven other officers were convicted of killing unarmed civilians in a case where the lead investigative officer himself was later convicted of conspiring to falsify and cover-up damning evidence.[12] Damage done in other parts of the Gulf Coast was aided and abetted by government officials and developers. As social scientists have pointed out, developers, wealthy homebuyers, and local planners share blame for wrecking the natural ecosystems that help protect coastal areas from storm surges: "Instead of leaving wetlands and swamps-natural buffers for flood prone areas-local authorities 'develop' them into residential and commercial areas and assure their residential safety through participation in the National Flood Insurance Program."[13]

The economic, social, and planning problems that were brought to the harsh light of day by Katrina have not dissipated; to the contrary, they are growing worse. Yet the environmental damage done to the Gulf Coast might pale in comparison to the next round of development that threatens the very existence of what is left of the old Southeast's rural landscape.

The Rise of Charlanta

Six of the ten fastest growing cities are already in the South. However, future development in the region could be even more rapid and all encompassing. For some years now, researches have been studying the rise of the "Charlanta" mega-region. Mega-regions, or 'endless cities,' are a global phenomenon: continuous growth pushing out from cities is creating contiguous urban areas from Hong Kong to Rio de Janeiro. These connected 'megapolises' are now driving much of global economic growth.

This appears to be the destiny of what is being called the Charlanta corridor, which consists of almost fifty metropolitan areas stretching from Charlotte to Atlanta. Between now and 2060, researchers are predicting a nearly 192 percent increase in development in the corridor. [14] Yet this future development is likely to resemble current development in the South: low density urban areas that are mainly dependent on automobiles as the major locus of transit. A model of this nature goes directly against United Nations recommendations that growing cities should be both well regulated and built around sustainable public transit.[15] The environmental costs of the Charlanta growth model, on the other hand, are likely to be extreme, according to researchers:

The changes we project would have significant and lasting effects on the region's ecosystems. The increasingly fragmented natural landscape would reduce habitat availability, suppress natural disturbance processes (such as wildfires) hinder management actions that come into conflict with urban areas, and likely eliminate existing corridors. Furthermore all these impacts could occur simultaneously, posing a particularly devastating threat to already vulnerable species and systems.[16]

The proliferation of urban heat islands, ecosystem destruction, and the forced migration of wild life; an overreliance on the automobile at the expense of public transit; and, ultimately, the erasure of the character of the Southeast's rural areas and wilderness, will be the result of business as usual development. In a call for smart growth and a reevaluation of future development in light of the revelations made by the Charlanta study, *SustainAtlanta* writes that the South's "constant connection to the environment has allowed us to enjoy the simple, important things in life and not stress about the complications of human society."[17]

Unfortunately, that statement is already outdated. Irresponsible development and an embrace of the Northern fixation on boundless growth and "industriousness" have already changed the face and character of the South.

A Question of Culture

In some real sense, Thaddeus Stevens and the North did succeed. There has been a radical reorganization in the institutions and the culture in the South. In a time where the industrial heartland of the Midwest is barely beating, the South has become a growth engine. The South as an alternative to the "hustling" culture of America-as Morris Berman views the antebellum South-is now a thing of the past. Real estate hustling, corporate culture, and even the big banking industry, is now firmly rooted south of the Mason Dixon. But the South is still the most distinctive region of the country; unfortunately, much of what makes it distinct now is unlikely to help the region deal with future challenges.

In *My Tears Spoiled My Aim, and Other Reflections on Southern Culture,* John Shelton Reed gives some glimpse into the changing Southern mindset: "And finally, individualism may be reflected in a sort of economic libertarianism that was apparently suppressed during the hard times of the past 120 years, but that seems to be coming back in our own times, at least among Southern whites."[18]

The rise of the Tea Party in the South and the election of libertarian-inspired senators like Rand Paul and former congressman Ron Paul are symptoms of that change. Nor is this a trend reserved for native Southerners. As early as the 1980s, Robert H. Freymyer showed that migrants to the South tended to be more economically conservative than native Southerners.[19] Migrants for example, have driven Florida's remarkable growth, but it remains a conservative state, despite the presidential elections of 2008 and 2012.

The South's justified reputation as the most violent region in the nation has not changed either. After Alaska, the states of Louisiana, Mississippi, and Alabama lead the nation in gun deaths per hundred thousand residents.[20] A growing body of research is showing that higher temperatures cause increased violent crime rates. Matthew Ranson's groundbreaking analysis of fifty years of monthly crime data and daily weather data for almost every county in the country gives further credence to such analysis. According to Ranson's projections - under a "business as usual" approach to controlling CO_2 emissions - the country could see an additional "30,000 murders, 200,000 cases of rape, 1.4 million aggravated assaults, 2.2 million simple assaults, 400,000 robberies, 3.2 million burglaries, 3.0 million cases of larceny, and 1.3 million cases of vehicle theft in the United States" over the course of the rest of the century. With large projected increases in summer highs in cities from Atlanta to New Orleans, and with water shortages and increasingly destructive storm systems, this could prove catastrophic for a region already burdened with inordinately high crime rates.

If Southern culture transformed over the course of the twentieth century to embrace a Northern 'grow at any cost' mentality, it surely must now change again. Cities and state governments in the South are going to have to jettison Tea Party leaders and climate denying business elites who seek to strip mine the region and cover some of the most ecologically delicate and important land in the country with blacktop and endless sprawl. At the same time, the ghosts of racism and inequality, which still haunt the Deep South, will have to be confronted. If not, the future of Dixie seems grim - and the entire country will be all the more impoverished for it.

Notes

[1] Joel Kotkin, "What is the New Suburbanism?" in *Contemporary Debates in Urban Planning,* ed. Abhijeet Chavan, Christian Peralta, and Christopher Steins (Washington, DC: Island Press, 2007), 28-31.

[2] See Morris Berman, *Why America Failed: The Roots of Imperial Decline* (New York: John Wiley and Sons, Inc., 2011).

[3] Barrington Moore, *Social Origins of Dictatorship and Democracy*: Lord and Peasant in the Making of the World (Boston: Beacon Press, 1966).

[4] C. Van Woodward, *Origins of the New South: 1877-913* (Baton Rouge: Louisiana State University Press, 1951), 142.

[5] ibid.,

[6] Aaron Renn, "Is It Game Over for Atlanta?" The Urbanophile Blog,http://www.urbanophile.com/2011/11/20/replay-is-it-game-over-for-atlanta/ (Accessed February, 7, 2015).

[7] Georgia Tech, "Local Warming: Consequences of Climate Change in Atlanta,"
2008, Judith
Curry. http://curry.eas.gatech.edu/climate/pdf/atlanta_rev.pdf (Accessed February 6, 2015).

[8] Gary R. Mormino, *Land of Sunshine, State of Dreams* (Gainesville: University of Florida Press, 2005), 16.

[9] Robert McKie , "Miami, the Great World City, is Drowning While the Powers That be Look Away,"*Guardian*, July 11,
2014. http://www.theguardian.com/world/2014/jul/11/miami-drowning-climate-change-deniers-sea-levels-rising (Accessed February 9, 2015).

[10] The Florida Oceans and Coastal Council, *Climate Change and Sea Level Rise in Florida: An Update of the Effects of Climate Change on Florida's Oceans and Costal Resources*. (Tallahassee, FL, 2010).

[11] ibid.,

[12] See A.C. Thompson, "Katrina's Hidden Race War," *The Nation*, December 17, 2008

[13] Susan L. Cutter and Melanie Gall, "Hurricane Katrina: A Failure of Planning or a Planned Failure?" in *Naturrisiken und Sozialkatastrophen,* ed. C. Felgentreff and T. Glade (Heidelberg: Spektrum Akademischer Verlag, 2008), 353-366.

[14] Terando AJ, Costanza J, Belyea C, Dunn RR, McKerrow A, et al. (2014) The Southern Megalopolis: Using the Past to Predict the Future of Urban Sprawl in the Southeast U.S. PLoS ONE 9(7): e102261. doi:10.1371/journal.pone.0102261

[15] UN Habitat, *State of the World's Cities 2008-2009* (Sterling, VA, 2008), 16.

[16] ibid., 16

[17] "The Death of the American South," SustainAtlanta,http://sustainableatlantaga.com/2014/08/19/the-death-of-the-american-south/ (Accessed February 9, 2015).

[18] John Shelton Reed, *My Tears Spoiled My Aim: and Other Reflections on Southern Culture* (New York: Mariner, 1994), 60.

[19] "Two-Party System in South Forseen," *Gadsden Times*, March 27, 1981.

[20] "Which is the Most Dangerous State?" (Interactive Map) *Rolling Stone*,http://www.rollingstone.com/feature/gun-control/map#deadPer100K (Accessed February 10, 2015).

The New Left and the City

Sean Posey

The political and cultural trauma of the 1950s brought about the beginnings of a monumental evolution of the American Left. A decade after the end of the war, the long-feuding AFL and CIO merged. A subsequent purge of leftists from the old CIO ensued as entrenched labor bosses sought to eliminate dissidents, ingratiate themselves to the political elite, and gain cover against charges of communist collusion. In 1956, the Red Army roared into Hungary to eliminate a grassroots revolution against the Stalinist government in power. Marxists in the West began to have their eyes opened to the reality of Soviet Communism, while the purges of American McCarthyism eliminated real and imagined radicals in nearly every institution of American life. The old "Labor Left," having achieved many of its bread and butter issues, appeared to be incapable of dealing with an insurgent Right. In 1960, sociologist C. Wright Mills wrote an open letter to a new generation of radicals. Entitled "Letter to the New Left," Mills' manifesto called for a rethinking and reorganizing of the America Left.

A new generation soon answered Mills. Originally known as the Student League for Industry, the Students for a Democratic Society emerged in 1962. That same year they authored an organizational manifesto known as the "Port Huron Statement," which greatly influenced much of the Left throughout the remainder of the decade. A remarkably far-sighted document, it accurately diagnosed many of the systemic issues facing the country at the dawn of the sixties. The list of deep-rooted problems addressed by SDS ran the gamut from the environment, sustainability, income inequality, and very presciently, the multiplying issues then manifesting themselves in urban areas.[1]

The drama of the sixties left American cities on the brink of ruin, and the New Left movement of the era responded to the conundrum of the city in variety of ways. When the New Left splintered in the 1970s, most major urban centers began to enter the worst phases of what became known as the "Urban Crisis." Today, as more cities begin to grow and redefine themselves in a new era of urbanism, the next generation of leftists must come to grips with the fact that cities will be the key arena for organizing movements for socioeconomic change in this century. In order to understand where that might take the Left today, it's important to grasp the history and inheritance of the New Left and the city. (I restrict my field of study here to America, although the New Left was indeed a global phenomenon. I also use an admittedly expansive definition of the New Left-one that encompasses more traditional groups like SDS and the so-called "counterculture" movement, broadly speaking.)

As the decade of the sixties dawned, the Student Nonviolent Coordinating Committee, born in the Jim Crow South, became one of the most important early groups in the New Left. SNCC took an active role in the various campaigns designed to break segregation-including the Freedom Rides, lunch counter sit-ins, and the Mississippi Freedom Summer of 1964. SNCC's influence spread far and wide among student groups. After Stokely Carmichael assumed leadership of the organization in 1966, SNCC moved in the direction of Black Nationalism, yet despite this change in philosophy (SNCC expelled white members of the organization in 1966.) the group foundered when it attempted to address issues in the broiling cities of the North; instead, much of SNCC's membership jumped ship to join groups like the Black Panther Party. While SNCC concerned itself mostly with small towns throughout the rural South, it also directly influenced the urban organizing campaigns of SDS.

In the early years of the group, SDS quickly expanded its presence on university campuses; however, in a move designed to organize around access and economic opportunity in the inner city, SDS soon established the Economic Research and Action Project (ERAP). The ERAP was promoted as an effort to build an "interracial movement of the poor."[2] SDS hoped the ERAP would help build movements to consolidate community control in northern cities and then link-up with the civil rights movement in the South. By 1964, students were moving into ERAP offices in Chicago, Baltimore, Newark, Boston, and Cleveland.

Different ERAP chapters took on different roles and even had different on-the-ground approaches. But a key strategy, often used in community organizing, involved tackling local quality of life issues and then positioning them within greater economic and political contexts. Yet contradictions soon arose. Students wanted to simultaneously allow community residents to organize around their own ideas and issues-with little input from the organizers-but they also wanted them to coalesce into larger radical movements.[3] In other words, ERAP members, many of who were plagued by guilt over their comparatively privileged class status, relinquished control over organizing while also continuing to hold very fixed notions about where such organizing should lead.

Disputes over the direction of SDS eventually broke out within the organization itself, especially between Tom Hayden-who spoke in favor of the direction taken by the ERAP-and Robert Alan Haber, the first president of SDS-who favored a return to campus organizing and activism. While the rift between ERAP and campus activists continued, ERAP's Newark Community Union Project, centered in Newark, New Jersey, grew to become the most successful venture proffered by the organization.

The NCUP primarily worked on housing issues, including rent strikes and campaigns against slumlords. The group even managed to take control of the local "War on Poverty" community board. Much of the organization's work centered on building a loosely recruited chain of contacts and resident supporters, as opposed to the more traditional membership approach.[4] They also recruited heavily from the working class, especially among black women, many of who became dedicated organizers in their own right. But the NCUP, despite making some real gains, was only marginally successful when it came to addressing or understanding issues of paramount concern to the community-like police brutality. Also, as Kevin Mumford points out, the NCUP and the SDS "did not see poverty as a cultural problem or a matter of behavior, but neither did they show appreciation for the intersection of race and class, of how deindustrialization and the rise of the suburbs had come to marginalize black urbanites." [5] But events soon ended any potential learning opportunities for activists on the ground in Newark and elsewhere.

The Free Speech Movement and the escalating war in Vietnam, along with the deteriorating circumstances facing many cities where SDS operated, ultimately sapped much of the energy behind the ERAP. The Cleveland, Chicago, and Newark groups survived until 1967. The Newark Riot and the growing Black Power movement made further interracial organizing difficult. Instead, SDS moved deeper into the world of campus radicalism, and Black Power came to the fore of New Left activity in American cities. Much of the vanguard of SNCC, along with scores of the unaffiliated, moved toward the burgeoning Black Power movement as the era of the 'long, hot summer' descended on cities from coast to coast. In particular, California's Black Panther Party for Self-Defense defined the new movement. Born in the segregated neighborhoods of Oakland, the Panthers set the stage for the confrontation between black radicals in cities across the country and local and national law enforcement officials, especially the FBI, who vowed to destroy the organization and those like it.[6] While much attention has been paid to the Panther's clashes with police and their insistence on armed self-defense, their urban community programs have received far less notice.

The Black Panther Party of the early 1970s is often portrayed as a spent force, riven by internal disputes and external attacks by the government. Yet the Panthers continued to pioneer important health programs in Oakland. Offering food and clothing assistance to urban neighborhoods was an early part of the Party's community platform, as was the Free Breakfast Program for Children. Additionally, as new Panther chapters opened across the country, each was ordered to open a community based medical clinic or PFMC. According to Alondra Nelson's research, these sites offered a multitude of services:

"At the PFMCs, Panther cadre worked with both lay and *trusted-expert* volunteers-including nurses, doctors, and students in the health professions-to administer basic preventive care, diagnostic testing for lead poisoning and hypertension and other conditions, and in some instances, ambulance services, dentistry, and referrals to other facilities for more extensive treatment. At the free clinics, the Party also administered patient advocacy; Black Panthers and volunteers helped clinic clients to navigate housing, employment, social welfare programs, and similar matters." [7]

In contrast to the War on Poverty or Model City programs, The Party's initiatives were purely local and more focused on the direct needs of black urban dwellers. The Party's much heralded sickle cell anemia initiative was a prime example.[8] The government and non-profit health groups eventually sought to co-opt the Panther's programs, especially the breakfast program and the sickle cell program, even as they sought to demonize the Party itself. As pressure on the group mounted, chapters around the country folded-leaving only the original Oakland chapter, which survived until 1982.

While Black Power spread throughout cities in the North, the movement against the Vietnam War, the hippie culture, and the broader youth movement spurred what became widely known as the "counterculture." Much of the counterculture consisted of semi-serious or outright frivolous elements; still, it did play a key role in several cities. The Los Angeles New Left, which proved particularly active, attempted to build bridges between the overtly political groups, the hippies and counterculture crowd, and the black and Latino communities of the city. While the New Left evolved a very internationalist outlook over time, the Left In Los Angeles adopted a rather local and regional outlook.[9] The Sunset Strip became one of the initial gathering points for the counterculture; the radical newspapers *The Open City* and the famed *Los Angeles Free Press* both began in the area. A strange amalgamation of dissidents merged in Hollywood and Venice to form a movement that "was an essentially New Leftist one-participating in social and racial egalitarianism, authenticity, and cultural experimentalism."[10]

During the Summer of Love, the city's New Left organized a series of interracial solidarity gatherings, though largely cultural in nature; they were also fairly unprecedented for the era. Other less successful events were held in East L.A. and Watts, which revealed the continued gap between the white counterculture and communities of color. But as Venice and Hollywood became more radical, the LAPD launched a brutal crackdown in 1968, targeting white radicals, the black community, and hippies alike. All three groups had been extremely active in fighting against a proposed freeway that would have isolated the Venice "ghetto" from the tourist areas. This "freeway revolt" would be repeated in other cities where various New Left and radical groups came together to try and defeat highway programs scheduled to bisect inner cities and to destroy neighborhoods.

The counterculture, however, proved to have deeply ambivalent feelings about cities. As historian Steven Conn points out, "Causally or coincidentally, hippies left the city at exactly the moment when civil rights and urban issues became virtually synonymous." [11] That's overstating the argument, as the aforementioned example of Los Angeles reveals, but Conn's point is not without merit. The majority of communes were actually in urban areas, though they spanned a variety of types from the strictly middle class to the radically political.[12] Many from the counterculture did end up in rural communes as the plight of cities worsened and the "back to the land" movement spread. The counterculture's touchstone film, *Easy Rider*, perfectly captures the urban anomie and the rural communes that increasingly pervaded the era as the sixties progressed.

The story of Peter Fonda and Dennis Hoppper's fictional counterculture biker duo, in many ways, pays homage to the back to the land ethos of the late sixties. The film itself plays like a vision quest, moving in a dream-like state through the largely rural areas of America. When the duo visits a commune in the Southwest, Fonda asks one of the members what city he is from. "The city? Doesn't make any difference what city," he replies. "All cities are alike. That's why I'm out here." When Hopper questions the future of the desert commune, Fonda immediately counters him: "This is nothing but sand, man. They ain't gonna make it, man. They ain't gonna grow anything here." "They're gonna make it," Fonda replies. "Dig, man. They're gonna make it." [13] The film's portrayal of the open road and dropout culture ends tragically, and it is far from clear that it glamorizes anti-urbanism, but *Easy Rider* accurately described much of the politically ambivalent Left during the Age of Aquarius.

By the beginning of the 1970s, the New Left was splintering, and America's deeply troubled cities began to enter their nadir. SDS dissolved and the Weatherman organization emerged from the pieces. Yet the Weatherman soon went underground to embark on a campaign of targeted bombing, and although they moved from city to city, they remained a hidden entity. The break-up of the Black Panthers in New York City birthed the Black Liberation Army, which launched Eldridge Cleaver's promised urban war against police before being dismantled. While these organizations went their separate ways underground, the fading counterculture, for the most part, joined their parents in suburbia. The rural communes, while surely never more than a small grouping, did influence the environmental movement and even the feminist movement, both of which grew as the New Left and the counterculture faded away.

The New Left could never quite overcome internal difficulties, external attacks, or the enormous structural problems tearing away at urban areas in the 1960s and early 1970s. Many of the most ardent leftists of the era eventually moved to suburbs, and some even became Republicans or Reagan Democrats-aligning themselves with an administration that completely turned its back on American cities. The radical Left, once so numerous in urban centers across the country, shrank to almost nothing.

Over the past decade, a kind of urban renaissance has swept cities from Los Angeles to Washington DC. But this "renaissance" mirrors the highly unequal macro-economic changes that have beset American society in general. Service sector workers and the lower class in revitalizing cities are struggling markedly with gentrification, a lack of public housing, and the privatization of public space. In 2011, The Occupy Wall Street movement bravely retook public spaces to begin voicing the demands of a generation besieged by inequity. It is fitting that Occupy began in New York, a city that has become the province of not only Wall Street financiers and the ultra-wealthy of every stripe, but also a depository for foreign capital. Evermore skyscrapers condos are going up in the Big Apple (usually investment properties for the global elite) while public housing and affordable housing for the middle class goes wanting. And while Occupy ultimately faltered, offshoot groups like Occupy Sandy and Occu-Evolve continued to do important work in New York.

Over fifty years after the Port Huron Statement accurately predicted that urban centers would form the locus of future leftist organizing, the bare beginnings of new organizing are emerging. According to David Harvey, "The current wave of youth-led movements, throughout the world, from Cairo to Madrid to Santiago-to say nothing of a street revolt in London, followed by an 'Occupy Wall Street' that began in New York city before spreading to innumerable cities in the US and now around the world-suggests there is something political in the city air struggling to be expressed." [14]As new movements form, the "New, New Left," will have to struggle with the legacy their forbearers, for both good and ill, have left them. And they will have to confront the growing citadels of inequality that are American cities today.

Notes

[1] See "The Port Huron Statement of the Students for a Democratic Society," University of Michigan,http://coursesa.matrix.msu.edu/~hst306/documents/huron.html (Accessed May 18, 2015).

[2] Jennifer Frost, *An Interracial Movement of the Poor: Community Organizing and the New Left*, (New York: New York University Press, 2001), 1.

[3] Wini Breines, *Community and Organization in the New Left, 1962-1968.* (Santa Barbara: Praeger Publishing), 126.

[4] Kevin Mumford, *Newark: A History of Race, Rights, and Riots in America* (New York: New York University Press, 2007), 91.

[5] Ibid., 86.

[6] Joshua Bloom and Waldo E. Martin Jr., *Black Against Empire: The History and Politics of the Black Panther Party* (Berkeley: University of California Press, 2013), 6.

[7] Alondra Nelson, *Body and Soul: The Black Panther Party and the Fight Against Medical Discrimination* (Minneapolis: University of Minnesota Press, 2011), 6.

[8] Ibid., 116.

[9] David McBride, "Death City Radicals: The Counterculture in Los Angeles," in *The New Left Revisited,* ed. Paul Buhle and John Campbell McMilllian (Philadelphia: Temple University Press, 2003), 114.

[10] Ibid., 127.

[11] Steven Conn, *Americans Against the City: Anti-Urbanism in the Twentieth Century* (New York: Oxford University Press, 2014), 269.

[12] Timothy Miller, *The 60s Communes: Hippies and Beyond* (Syracuse: Syracuse University Press, 1999), 144.

[13] *Easy Rider,* Directed by Dennis Hopper, Columbia Pictures, 1969.

[14] David Harvey, *Rebel Cities: From the Right to the City to the Urban Revolution* (London: Verso, 2012), 116-117.

Women's Issues

Women's Rights Activism 101

For the Busy Woman

Cherise Charleswell

Women and girls account for a slight majority of the world's population, and this is despite continued practices of female infanticide. What is female infanticide? It is an ancient phenomenon that is still practiced in the modern world in deeply patriarchal societies which place a low value on the birth of females. Thus, gender-selective deaths, which involve the killing of baby girls due to this preference for male babies, are carried out. In nations like China, girls are twice as likely to die in their first year of life as boys. So, let's be clear: women's rights are human rights. They involve treating women and girls with the same dignity that is given to men and boys. It is ensuring that all genders have their humanity acknowledged and their lives equally valued.

In keeping with the notion of value, women's rights also involve valuing the work carried out by women, and providing them equal pay for this work. Women's rights is about valuing the input and opinion of women and thus ensuring that these viewpoints are included in decision-making processes, whether they are conducted in corporate or non-profit boardrooms, professional association committee meetings, school boards, city councils, state legislatures, or the US Congress.

While feminists are actively engaged in women's rights activism, there are many women (and men) who also do this work, who do not consider themselves feminists. This is because feminism has not yet been successful in making a connection with women of color, women from/in the global south, and women who are not academics. The reasons for this disconnect are various and will not be discussed in detail at this time. However, feminists and other women's rights activists share the same goals and/or beliefs. For example, if you believe any of the following to be true, you may be a feminist:

- Female babies born have the same right to life as their male counterparts.
- You currently use or have used birth control, or do not have a problem with women using it.
- You believe that when women and men perform the same job, they should receive equal pay.
- You are against adult men marrying child brides.
- You find victim blaming of rape victims appalling, and believe that a woman/girl should not be raped regardless of what she wears.
- Last --- you are a supporter of rights and equality for women and men.

What is Activism & Advocacy?

In the most direct terms, activism is an act or a series of efforts that are carried out in a vigorous manner to promote, direct, bring about, or even impede social, cultural, political, economic, and environmental change. In short, it is simply carrying out a form of action on an issue. For example, there are times when activists want to bring about cultural change (end female genital mutilation), and then there are times when activists want to impede changes to the environment (air and water pollution resulting from fracking which affects the health of pregnant women).

There are many varying approaches to activism, and advocacy is one of the most widely used forms. The most basic definition of advocacy is that it is the act or process of supporting a cause or proposal. Thus, advocacy is a type of activism that is carried out in support of a specific cause, and it is usually done through engaging the political process. Advocates often focus on and aim to influence resource allocation and public policy, such as paid sick leave, which is not granted to many workers, especially low-income women workers. In May, advocacy efforts helped to get Assembly Bill 1522 passed, which will secure paid sick days for shift workers through the California State Assembly with a 48-20 vote (no Republicans supported the bill).

For business groups and allied lawmakers, the bill allegedly hamstrings businesses by chipping away at their bottom line. The legislation holds a spot on the California Chamber of Commerce's annual "job killers" list. Assemblywoman Gonzalez, D-San Diego, explained why women's rights advocates worked around this issue, and why this bill is beneficial to society as a whole: "Most of these workers are low wage and hourly, disproportionately women and Latinos, and they have to choose in their jobs whether to go to work sick and be able to make ends meet or lose a day's pay," Gonzalez said, adding that it would be a boon to working parents who need to take time off to care for sick children." Advocacy work can be difficult and frustrating due to the reality of a slow-moving political process, as well as the fact that advocates have to compete with lobbyists who represent moneyed-interests; and who thus have the financial resources to persuade legislators to vote in their favor. Essentially, lobbying is nothing more than legalized bribery; and the Supreme Court's decision on Citizens United only made this process of bribery and corporate-directed policy more feasible. On January 21, 2010, with its ruling in Citizens United v. Federal Election Commission, the Supreme Court ruled that corporations are persons, entitled by the U.S. Constitution to buy elections and run our government. A number of advocate groups and coalitions, including Move to Amend are working diligently to overturn this decision by amending the constitution and rejecting the idea that money is speech. Among the list of Move To Amend Endorsing Organizations is The Hampton Institute, as well as a plethora of women's rights activist groups who realize that money-interest in politics has a very negative impact on the lives of women; just consider the recent Hobby Lobby decision. Other endorsing organizations include: Detroit Women of Color, Women's International League for Peace and Freedom, Main Street Moms, Texas Democratic Women, The Women's Network, Advocates for Democratic Principles, Women Against Military Madness, and so on.

So, Why Do Women Lead Such Busy Lives?

Engaging in direct political advocacy and the building of such skill-sets can be quite time consuming, which makes it difficult for women to do so; and that is due to the very busy lives that women lead. Patriarchy is a prominent factor in why women lead such busy lives. Systems of patriarchy define what women's work is and ultimately place less value (resulting in less pay or compensation) for the work that women do.

Specifically, women lead busy lives due to the following:

- Women workers engage in unpaid labor which includes cooking, cleaning, and caring for children.
- Women workers include single women who continue to do the bulk of the housework and are again unpaid for this labor and expenditure of energy.
- Women workers are often unpaid or receive very low pay for being caregivers to the elderly and disable; particularly their relatives. This is especially true for women in nations that lack strong healthcare or pension systems.

- Then there is the issue of gender pay inequity that leaves women workers making far less than men, and often adds the burden of taking on additional jobs or finding other means of income. This is particularly true for single mothers and single women in general, who cannot rely on the additional income of their spouse.

Therefore, women are perpetually busy, because outside of our paid work and professional obligations, we do most of the care work in families; caring for children, the elderly, the sick, and the disabled. According to the U.S. Census Bureau, women devote more than 110 million hours a year to unpaid interactive child care, more than double the 55 million hours put in by their male counterparts.[1] This care work is socially and economically essential, but the fact that women do far more of this work than men will continue to be a major reason for women's disproportionate poverty.

Unpaid work, and that which has low pay, not only keeps women busy, but it also ties them into poverty and makes social mobility difficult. This is because gendered domestic labor only reinforces a patriarchal system of gender hierarchy, which limits educational and job opportunities for women and their daughters. In other words, they are too busy with these other tasks to find the time and energy to educate themselves, so that they can compete for better and higher paying jobs which will afford them greater financial independence.

During a 2013 UN General Assembly meeting of its social, humanitarian, and cultural body, Magdalena Sepulveda, a UN Special Reporter, shared these sentiments as she advocated for political and institutional changes: "Unpaid care work is at the foundation of all our societies, and crucial for economic growth and social development," she noted. "However, it has been mostly overlooked or taken for granted by policy makers. This has an enormous impact on women's poverty and their enjoyment of rights - as they carry out the majority of unpaid care ."

Why We Must Do This Work?

At this point, it should be understood that, yes, women are busy and, yes, activism will take some effort, and thus demand even more of our time. As burdensome as this may sound, we must still do this work. We must continue to challenge the structural sources of inequalities inherent in policies, laws, institutional mechanisms, and societal attitudes. Not doing so will surely result in negative consequences and taking a step back in time when gender inequality was far much greater, and women and girls had even less rights. In the US, we must engage in battle, due to the ' War on Women' that conservative interests are waging.

We must continue to do this work, to honor the work done by our foremothers in garnering the rights we now enjoy (and take for granted):

- The right to vote (Interesting enough, Colorado, the first state to legalize the use of marijuana, also happens to the be the very first state to adopt their amendment giving women the right to vote in 1893). All women in the US were not given the right to vote until the passage of the 19th Amendment in 1920.
- In 1960, the Food and Drug Administration approved the use and distribution of birth control pills --- a big win for Reproductive justice, which has not been realized for many women in the Global South; and which still represents a financial burden for women here in the US. Again, refer to the Hobby Lobby decision.
- In 1963, one of the first steps towards gender pay equity was taken with the passage of the Equal Pay Act, which made it illegal for employers to pay a woman less than a man for doing the same job. Of course, this effort was not fool proof, and the practice continues. Hence the advocacy efforts around the Paycheck Fairness Act .

- In 1973, Roe v. Wade established women's rights to safe and legal abortions. Again, many women in the global south do not have the right and access to safe abortions, and many women here in the US face intimidation when trying to practice this right or reside in states where access to safe clinics is limited. It was not until 1978 that the Pregnant Act passed, banning employment discrimination against pregnant women.

Despite these "wins," there is still much work that is left to be done domestically, and certainly globally, when it comes to women's rights and the protection of families. Just consider how the US compares on the issue of paid and protected parental leave.

Addressing Intersections

Engaging in women rights activism can be more difficult for women of color due to the other intersecting factors that impact their lives; particularly the issue of racism. Often, when calling attention to sexism, misogyny, and gender inequity, women of color are told that those issues do not exist, are a distraction, or are not as important as the collective burden of and fight against racism. In other words, they should endure and ignore blatant sexism, and devote all of their efforts, time, and attention to fighting racial oppression.

For Latina women, this means that they are not to challenge patriarchal cultural attitudes such as machismo. For women of the Muslim faith, it means speaking out against Islamophobia, all while having to protest or denounce honor killings, such as the recent stoning death of a Pakistani woman who married a man without her family's approval. For Indigenous/Native American women, this involves advocating for improved health and social conditions on reservations and in their communities, all while suffering domestic violence and physical assault rates that far exceed women of other ethnicities[2], with the Department of Justice estimating these assault rates as much as 50% higher than the next most victimized demographic.[3]

For Asian women, this revolves around the practice of masking internal tension, and with it gender activism; in order to make it seem that Asian women do not struggle with sexism. This contention is of course ludicrous when considering the patriarchal nature of many Asian societies, along with the historic stereotype of the timid, submissive, sexually available, geisha-like Asian women. Such misconceptions have spawned the #NotYourAsianSidekick hashtag, which gives a voice to and lends credence to the full lived experiences of Asian women. While activist groups like the Asian Women Coalition Ending Prostitution advocate for the rights of women and girls by focusing on and eradicating prostitution and sexual exploitation. They point out that is not a time honored cultural practice among Asians. It is, instead, a form of male violence against women. For Black women, it means they must continue with the false narrative of equality within the civil rights and Black power movements, and they must certainly not interrupt the discussion on police violence and aggression against Black men and boys by pointing out the inconvenient truth that Black women and girls are subjected to the same violence.

Ultimately, feminism provides a central framework for women's rights activism, because it seeks to remove all oppression, whether based on gender, race, ethnicity, sexuality, or income. Women of color must realize that they can and should advocate for their rights as women and as people of color; for their Full Humanity.

Building a Movement

Women, particularly women of color, continue to be impacted by gender inequality along with the socioeconomic effects of this inequality; and the end result is that these women often find themselves too busy to fully engage or figure out how they can contribute to women's rights movements. They are busy with wage-work, unpaid labor, and the list goes on. For this reason, women's rights activism should focus on building an inclusive movement, which accommodates women who may have limited financial resources and time, and who are not academics, elitist, and professionals. In her article, Gender Activism Must Be Taken Out Of Posh Hotels And Into The Mainstream , Mariz Tadros criticizes the focus on the elite and "professional" women's rights activists by pointing out critical barriers to movement building. She offered the following sentiment in this regard: "Meetings on gender development, held in five-star hotels are too elitist, sanitized and contained..... professionals who "do" gender and development have a wealth of knowledge but are incapable of communicating in ways that touch the public." Her comments echo the critical criticisms that I shared in the article Feminism Is Not Just For Academics: Overcoming Disconnect and Division.

Although feminism acts as a central framework for women's rights movements, feminism is not enough for movement building and ensuring that women and girls are given the full rights of humanity; not if it is going to be relegated to academic conferences, pop culture theorizing, and remain disconnected from the very masses that it claims it wants to uplift. Movement building is essential for activism that seeks to bring about revolutionary, political, socio-cultural, and institutional change. Having a movement behind you, with members -- other women and men-- working with you, helps to remove some of the barriers to activism for women who are busy and who may feel as if they already have too much on their plate. A movement ensures that they are not again bearing the burden of responsibilities alone. Instead, they can offer their own small contributions towards the struggle for women's rights.

Strategies

Below are a list of strategies, some requiring little effort and others requiring a little more effort and time commitment, that any busy woman can engage in to carry out women's rights work:

- Have a specific women's issue that you are concerned about? Perhaps something on the ballot or up for a committee vote? Take a few minutes to write a letter to a newspaper or an elected politician who represents your district. Simply let them know your thoughts on the issue and what you would like to be done.
- Do you have a little more time? Arrange a visit with one your elected officials.
- Unsure about what to say or do when you are on one of these visits? There are a number of women's organizations that offer free or low-cost advocacy training. These training seminars could be one-day seminars or full courses. For example, women in the Los Angeles area can enroll in the California Black Women's Health Project's (ATP) Advocacy Training Program or take advantage of the Latinas for Reproductive Justice's various community education and mobilization efforts.
- Many organizations such as Latinas for Reproductive Justice also provide Policy Advocacy Toolssuch as fact sheets, a list of priorities, research reports, action kits and more.
- Stay informed and share all you know about critical women's issues by joining mailing lists and signing up for free newsletters. Great resources include the Association For Women's Rights in Development which offers many focused newsletters, the Women of Color Network or even the HuffPost Women. Bookmark these sites, print and clip articles of interest, become an amateur archivist. And again, remember to SHARE this information.
- If you are a student, research your school's sexual assault policy and inform other students. If you will like to do more, register with the SAFER Campus Accountability project. You can do so by

registering at www.safercampus.org and submit your school's policy review form to the database. Members of the public can access this database for free.

- Take a page from the LGBTQ community and be "OUT" with your views and stance on issues that affect women and girls. Engage your family and friends on these topics. If you self-identify as a feminist, do not keep it a secret. Let it be known, and explain why.

- Utilize adornments. Integrate feminist/womanist items - t-shirts, pins, brooches, and other accessories in your wardrobe and wear them proudly.

- Digital Feminist Activism - is often referred to as the 4th Wave of Feminism, and it offers many opportunities for virtual advocacy and activism. Sign-on to an online petition around an issue that impacts women and children. If it is a topic that you feel very passionate about, be sure to customize your letter that you are submitting with your electronic signature. Join or follow the wide array of women-centered groups on Facebook and Twitter. Share and/or Re-tweet stories and posts that highlight the issues you are passionate about. Use hash-tags when possible to draw attention to an issue. Join the growing Feminist Network, which is a global online community created to be a tool that increases the networking, visibility and voice of feminists around the world. Create media for social change and distribute on social media; this can include memes, infographics, and more.

- Support feminist programming, such as Feminist Magazine on Pacifica Radio's KPFK 90.7FM, also Pacifica's Joy of Resistance, Multicultural Feminist Radio WBAI 99.5FM, or Wombanist Views a monthly radio program. Call in and be part of the discussion or contact producers with show ideas.

- Create resistance art, whether this is through poetry (spoken word and written), short stories and essays, music, theater, photography, or other forms of visual art. Get this art published in zines, blogs, websites, feminist publications, magazines, newspapers, and academic journals. Also, support this type of artistic expression. For example, New York based Price of Silence, a grassroots performing arts collective that brings the global struggle for women's rights to

life for audiences to live and breathe activism in action; performs a number of shows throughout the year. While there is the Stop Telling Women To Smile art series created by Tatyana Fazlalizadeh; which attempts to address gender based street harassment by placing eye-catching drawn portraits of women, which include captions that speak directly to offenders, in public spaces.
- Build unity by hosting sister-gatherings, sista circles, women's retreats, and collective meetings in order to support other women. These gatherings offer the perfect opportunity to build relationships, release frustrations, exchange ideas, and offer mutual encouragement.
- Donate whatever you can to organizations, websites and blogs engaged in women's rights activism, advocacy, etc. Support their efforts.
- Have a special skill? Would like to become even more involved? Volunteer. A number of organizations also have virtual volunteer programs and internships. Remember that their budgets are often diminutive or non-existent, so volunteers are a valuable and much needed resource.
- Last but not least, Vote!

Despite the progress made, particularly during the past century, women around the world - especially in the Global South as well as women of color and working-class women residing in post-industrial nations - continue to be impacted by gender inequity and all of its negative consequences. It is this need for continued progress, along with a need to combat attempts to turn-back-the-clock and erode rights that have already been gained, that makes contemporary women's rights activism and advocacy imperative. However, this is a daunting task which will require much more than theorizing, but rather mobilization of and the contribution of women activists - the professional and grassroots-from all walks of life. We must realize the gender inequity we protest against and work to eradicate also makes it difficult to mobilize these women, often leaving them too busy and overwhelmed by their day-to-day responsibilities. It is for this reason that we must develop and share

alternative forms of activism and advocacy that could be utilized by working-class women.
Please share these strategies and add to the toolkit and conversation by sharing others that you may use.

References

Nancy Folbre, For Love and Money: Care Provision in the United States (New York: Russell Sage Foundation, 2012)

Brief for National Network to End Domestic Violence et al. as Amici Curiae Supporting Respondents at 2, Plains Commerce Bank v. Long Family Land and Cattle Co., 128 S. Ct. 2709 (2008) (No. 07-411). 2

Steven W Perry, American Indians and Crime- A BJS Statistical Profile 1992-2002, Bureau of Justice Statistics, US Department of Justice, Office of Justice Programs, December 2004.

Latina Feminism
National and Transnational Perspectives

Cherise Charleswell

Women's studies and the early waves of feminism were initially dominated by the experiences of white middle-class women, thus leaving Latinas, like other women of color, feeling excluded or not fully represented. Outside of women's studies, ethnic studies also left Latinas feeling the same, in that they focused on issues of racial and ethnic oppression and cultural nationalism, while ignoring the critical issues of sexism and heterosexism. Women and women's issues were only seen as "White," thus denying Latinas and other women of color their full identity. Eventually, Latina women joined other women of color in the introduction of gender issues into ethnic studies and critical race issues in women's studies. Their actions were taking a direct stance against not only the exclusionary practices of white middle-class feminism, but also against those within other social movements. These women helped to ensure that civil rights struggles transcended the US borders, and a number of Latina women have taken on leadership roles in the struggle for human rights. Thus, Latina Feminism, just like the Latino identity, is complex, and is oftentimes transnational in

674

nature. For example, being a Latina means that one has a cultural identity and ethnicity, shared by those from or with origins in Latin America. Latinas can be of any racial group, or more likely a mix of various racial groups.

Origins of Latina Feminism

Latina Feminism in the United States really began to take shape following the Civil Rights and Black Nationalist movements, which saw all oppressed people - Gay, women, other ethnic groups - coming forward and using solidarity to spark social changes during the middle of the 20th century. Although Latina women took leadership roles in the other movements, their contributions have for the most part gone unnoticed or ignored. When scholars and community leaders speak about the legacy of these groups, they continue to excluded Latina women; and even well known iconic images do not include them.

Xicana (Chicana) Feminism

Chicana feminist thought and action really began to take shape during the late 1960s, with an increase in organizing during the 1970s. Chicana feminisms itself was an outgrowth or response to the male-dominated Chicano movements, which demanded access to education, as well as social, political, and economic opportunities and justice for Latino people; and took place primarily in the American South West. Like other women of color, Chicanas realized that discussions of women's issues, such as birth control, were being rejected, ignored, or side-lined; while mainstream White middle class feminism was also unwilling to speak out about the unique oppressions that Chicana women faced; particularly workplace exploitation or discrimination

The Women of the Young Lords

The Young Lords was a mostly Puerto Rican (African Americans and other Latinos were members) organization that was formed in the late 1960s by individuals who were primarily under the age of 20. What was so groundbreaking about this group of young people is that they redefined what is was to be Puerto Rican, openly exclaiming their pride in being Boricuans, not "Spanish", but Afro-Taino; and while fighting for basic human rights - clothing, shelter, food, access to healthcare and justice - they openly challenged machismo, sexism, and patriarchy. Women, such as Connie Cruz, Luisa Capteillo, Denise Oliver, and Bianca Canales, quickly emerged as leaders in the Young Lords. Their Ten-Point Health Program was ahead of its time, and it was clear that they understood early on that factors in one's environment (today referred to as social determinants of health by public health specialist) were important to health and wellbeing. Their Ten-Point Health Program was as follows:

We want total self-determination of all health services in East Harlem (El Barrio) through an incorporated Community-Staff Governing Board for Metropolitan Hospital. (Staff is anyone and everyone working at Metropolitan.)
We want immediate replacement of all Lindsay administrators by community and staff appointed people whose practice has demonstrated their commitment to serve our poor community.
We demand immediate end to construction of the new emergency room until the Metropolitan Hospital Community-Staff Governing Board inspects and approves them or authorizes new plans.
We want employment for our people. All jobs filled in El Barrio must be filled by residents first, using on-the-job training and other educational opportunities as bases for service and promotion.
We want free publicly supported health care for treatment and prevention. We want an end to all fees.

We want total decentralization--block health officers responsible to the community-staff board should be instituted.

We want "door-to-door" preventive health services emphasizing environment and sanitation control, nutrition, drug addiction, maternal and child care, and senior citizen's services.

We want education programs for all the people to expose health problems--sanitation, rats, poor housing, malnutrition, police brutality, pollution, and other forms of oppression.

We want total control by the Metropolitan hospital community-staff governing board of the budge allocations, medical policy along the above points, hiring, firing, and salaries of employees, construction and health code enforcement.

Any community, union, or workers organization must support all the points of this program and work and fight for that or be shown as what they are---enemies of the poor people of East Harlem.

#5 essentially calls for universal healthcare.

#7 focuses on prevention on disease and is forward-thinking in looking at addiction as not a criminal activity, but a disease.

#8 describes the need for programs to address the social determinants of health.

Unfortunately, despite their seemingly Progressive attitudes, the Young Lords was still governed by an all-male central committee and its initial 13-point platform advocated for "revolutionary machismo." The women members turned on the pressure and began to directly address this sexism, which resulted in the "machismo" line being dropped, and a new point was added to the program, stating, "We want equality for women. Down with machismo and male chauvinism"; and more importantly, attention and protest was turned to the issue of sterilization. In short, during the 1960s, Puerto Rican women were used as guinea pigs for the development of the birth control pill and later birth control and sterilization were used in some sort of twisted eugenics campaign as a tool of social policy and as a form of directed population control. Over a third of Puerto Rican women of child-bearing age were sterilized. The Young Lord's fight against this abusive practice

677

inspired Ana Maria Garcia's 1982 documentary, <u>La Operacion.</u> The Young Lord's Women's Caucus was progressive and transformative in other ways: defending a woman's right to abortion and childcare, and establishing a women's union with a publication called La Luchadora; and their efforts helped to ensure that half of the content of the Young Lords' newspaper, Pa'lante, focused on women's issues.

Pioneering Latina Feminists in the US

Although "feminist" is being used to describe these women, we must keep in mind that many of them may have not considered or referred to themselves as feminists. Their actions - advocating for women's equality and challenging patriarchy and systems of oppression - indeed made them feminists.

Nina Otero-Warren was a Chicana educator, politician, suffragist, and first wave feminist. She worked for women's suffrage in New Mexico and, in 1918, became superintendent of public schools in Santa Fe County. Later, in 1923, she became Inspector of Indian Schools in Santa Fe County, where she was able to improve the education of indigenous populations.

Jovita Idar was a pioneering Chicana activist and feminist. As early as 1910 she was writing articles for her father's newspaper, covering stories on discrimination, lynching, and other violence committed by Texas Rangers - all issues that, unfortunately, remain relevant today as we continue to witness the same type of oppression. <u>La Ligua Femenil Mexicanista</u> (The League of Mexican Women), which she formed in 1911, is now recognized as the first attempt in Mexican-American history to organize a feminist social movement. These women formed free schools for Mexican children and provided necessities for the poor.

Maria Rebecca Latigo de Hernandez was not a self-described feminist; however, she was a pioneering Xicana activist, working for the improvement of civic, educational, and economic opportunities for Mexican-Americans. In 1929, she co-founded the Orden Caballeros of America, a civic and civil organization.

Sylvia Rivera was a bisexual trans Latina activist and feminist who advocated for the inclusion of queer and transgender people who were left out of the gay-rights movement. She co-founded the Street Transvestite Action Revolutionaries (S.T.A.R.) in 1970.

Feminist scholar Gloria Anzaldua self-describes as a "Chicana/Tejana/lesbian/dyke/feminist/writer/poet/cultural theorist." Her writing focused on providing representations of women of color. Her 1987 book "Borderlands/La Frontera: The New Mestiza," her most famous work, focuses on overlapping issues of gender, race, sexual orientation, and class (factors which feminist scholar Kimberlee Crenshaw later referred to as intersections when speaking on the theory of intersectionality). Other notable works by Anzaldua include "This Bridge Called My Back: Writings by Radical Women of Color" (co-authored with Cherrie Moraga) and "Making Face Making Soul/Haciendo Caras: Creative and Critical Perspectives by Feminists of Color."

Although Cesar Chavez became the face of the United Farm Workers, has a national holiday in his honor, and was featured in the biographical film Cesar Chavez, much has been known about Dolores Huerta, labor leader, activist, feminist, awardee of the Presidential Medal of Freedom, and co-founder of the United Farm Workers. Her lobbying efforts helped to bring about the Immigration Act of 1985. Her other political achievements include: In 1961, she succeeded in obtaining the citizenship requirements removed from pension and public assistance programs.

In 1962, she was instrumental in the passage of legislation allowing voters the right to vote in Spanish, and the right of individuals to take the drivers license examination in their native language;

In 1963, she helped secure Aid for Dependent Families ("AFDC") for the unemployed and underemployed, disability insurance for farm workers in the State of California, and unemployment benefits for farm workers.

She continues her activism work as an active board member of the Feminist Majority Foundation.

Chicana second-wave feminist, Cherrie Moraga, began discussing "interlocking" oppressions early on in her activist, academic, and artistic career during the 1970s. She co-authored "This Bridge Called My Back: Writings by Radical Women of Color" with Gloria Anzaldua in 1981, and was a founding member of La Red Xicana Indigena, a network of Chicanas organizing nationally and internationally for social change, indigenous rights, and political education.

Pioneering Latina Feminists in Latin America

Leila Gonzalez was an intellectual involved in the Brazilian Black movement and is credited for being responsible for the development and practice of Black Feminism in Brazil (More to come on the topic of racial identity and Black feminism in Latin America and the US). Leila was born in 1935, just 47 years after the Lei Áurea ("Golden Act") abolished slavery in Brazil, and despite being a Black woman, she went on to earn university degrees in history, geography, philosophy, and a PhD in social anthropology. Petra Herrera was a Soldadera, a female soldier who fought along the men during the Mexican Revolution. She initially disguised her gender and went by the name "Pedro Herrera." After not being credited for valor in battle and promoted to a General, Petra left Pancho Villa's forces and formed her own all-woman brigade. In 1946, Felisa Rincon de Gautier was elected mayor of San Juan Puerto Rico, becoming not only the first woman to be elected mayor of San Juan, but of any mayor capital city in the Americas. She held this position from 1948 - 1968. She was an active participant in Puerto Rico's women's suffrage movement (won in 1932) and her efforts on child care programs inspired the United States' Head Start program.

Puerto Rican Nationalist, Blanca Canales, has been conveniently erased from history books, and is not greatly discussed in women's studies courses. She helped organize the Daughters of Freedom, the women's branch of the Puerto Rican Nationalist Party, and is one of the few women in history to have led a revolt against the United States, which was known as the Jayuya Uprising, taking place in 1950. The US government declared martial law to put down the uprising, sentencing the activists to life imprisonment and dismissing their protests as nothing more than an "incident between Puerto Ricans."

Afro-Puerto Rican poet, feminist and activist, Julia de Burgos, used her writings to openly contest the prevailing notion that womanhood and motherhood are synonymous. She courageously began challenging these notions in the 1930s.

Celia Sanchez was the woman at the heart of the Cuban Revolution, and although she was rumored to be the main decision-maker, more is known about her male counterparts Fidel Castro and Che Guevara. She was the founder of the 26th of July Movement and leader of combat squads throughout the Revolution.

Frida Kahlo was a Mexican artist born around the time of the Mexican Revolution. She is best known for her self-portraits filled with pain and passion, which mirrored her own life. She survived polio, a horrific and near-fatal bus accident, an amputation, multiple miscarriages, as well as rampant infidelity. Her work represents a celebration of indigenous traditions, as well as an uncompromising depiction of the female experience and form, the dichotomies, the personal and political, love and loss, physical and emotional pain.

Intersectionality and the Latina in the United States

For the most part, the Latina in the United States is still viewed as "The Other," a racial minority outside of the dominant White society (despite the growing Latino population), and at times as a stereotypical caricature, whether it is the Domestic or the Spicy oversexed Spanish Fly, whose presence is primarily for the pleasure and entertainment of men (Sophia Vergara's public persona and willingness to be literally put on display during the 2014 Emmy Ward s best exemplifies this caricature). This status as "The Other" has historically left Latinas having to cope with not only gender oppression, but gender and discrimination based on their ethnicity. These are the intersections that impact their lives. Further, one has to understand how these varying intersections drive Latinas to feminism in different ways than their white counterparts. For example, reproductive justice for Latinas, expands beyond the need to control reproduction and ensure that there are no unwanted pregnancies, but includes the need to safeguard the right of women of color to have children.

In a 2013 Ms Magazine interview, Latina feminist blogger, Sara Ines Calderon, explained why feminism or women's issues often go undiscussed or are not viewed as urgent matters to Latinas: "I find mainstream feminism to often be lacking in substance for myself. I can't relate to it, perhaps because to me feminism is often wrapped up with white privilege. I'm not sure why there aren't more Latinas discussing feminism online. I think one major reason is that, since Latinos are historically not the dominant class and are often immigrants, there are other, more important things that occupy their time. I know that's true for myself; I spend much more time talking about politics and structural issues in my blogging than just pure Latina feminism because I feel like, in the larger sense, it's more important."

Of course, one has to ask, why can't Latina women actively and simultaneously advocate for equality, whether it is racial, gender, or based on sexual orientation? The problem with saying that women's issues are not as important, or can wait, is that they will need to be given an opportunity to be addressed; and thus impeding any form of progress.

On Invisibility: Afro-Latinas in the US

The group often excluded from discussions about the Latina experience in North America are Afro Latinos, whose complex identities, renders them invisible. These women include actresses Rosie Perez, Rosario Dawson, Zoe Saldana, and Gina Torres. While also coping with gender inequality, Afro-Latinas also face discrimination (and racism) from other Latinos, the dominant white society, as well as African-Americans (who are often adamant that Afro-Latinos put their racial identity before their cultural or ethnic). Due to these varying degrees of invisibility and discrimination, alluding to intersectionality is not enough; instead, the experiences of Afro-Latinas can be viewed as a complex spider web.

"The Other": The Indigenous & Afro Latinas in Latin America

"I know that when I was working at the Spanish language television station, there was no one of color on television. And I knew this before, so it wasn't like I got there and I was like 'Whoa, there's nobody on TV.' You just realize that you know, when I go travel, and I go to Cuba, and I go to Puerto Rico, and I go to Peru. You go to these places and you see people who are brown, of indigenous descent. But then you look at the television and you go, 'How come what I see is not what I saw when I visited these places?'"

Kim Haas, founder of the Los Afro-Latinos, shared these sentiments during her interview for Feministing. Her statement speaks to the fact that while Latinos in North America are seen as a monolithic group, indigenous women and those of African descent in Latin America are explicitly seen as "The Other," and are marginalized. While Latinas in the Chicana movement and other Latino social movements in North America advocate for inclusion, fair representation, and civil and human rights, these marginalized groups - indigenous and Afro Latino - in Latin America have historically and continue to have to do the same. When it comes to the media, they remain invisible for the most part, and in comparison to their mestizo or "White" Latino counterparts, these marginalized groups disproportionately have higher rates of poverty and disease. Thus, indigenous and Afro Latina feminists in

Latin America have to cope with these deeply rooted intersections - discrimination, racial prejudice, marginalization, poverty, and gender inequality. It is this ironic reality that marks the difference between Latina Feminism in North America and Feminism in Latin America. A mere crossing of the United States border automatically lumps these groups, the marginalized indigenous and Afro-Latino women, with the mestizo/"White" Latinas who represent the dominant society, in the same way that Middle Class, White women in North America were accused of harboring privilege in that they were members of the dominant society.

Acknowledging and addressing this reality has proven to be difficult in Latin America. During the 20th century, Latin American nations were moving towards Democratic forms of governance. By the 1980s, many spaces for debate and political analysis began to open up for different voices from the Latin American civil society; however, these organizations were still not addressing the issue of racism. Thus, during the 5th Latin America and Caribbean Feminist Encuentero taking place in San Bernardo Argentina, different Black women from throughout the region met for the first time and discussed the reality of Black women's lives and the need for their own spaces and having their own voice in Latin America. This initial meeting led to the 1st Latin American and Caribbean Black women's Encuentro in 1992, which took place in Santo Domingo, Dominican Republic. Thus, Afro-Latin American feminism was built on the common experiences of Afro-Latinas who collectively experience gender and racial oppression.

Indigenous women, from various tribes in Latin America (Mayan, Quechuas, Quiche, etc.) have given rise to an indigenous feminism, which really began to take root in the 1990s. The Zapatista National Liberation Army (EZLN) emerged in 1994, serving as a catalyst for indigenous women's organization in Mexico, and an example of indigenous feminism for the rest of Latin America. The Zapatista women created what was called the Women's Revolutionary Law, and made it public on January 1, 1994. The 10 point law called for the following rights for indigenous women: the right to political participation and to hold leadership posts within the political system, to a life free of sexual and domestic violence, to decide how many children they want to have, to a fair wage, to choose a spouse, to an education, and to quality health services. In looking at this law and the declaration of women of the Young Lords (previously discussed), it is clear that Latina women in Latin America and in North America - and of varying racial, ethnic, and economic backgrounds - have been advocating for essentially the same rights. These issues - reproductive health, having to counteract patriarchy, having full representation, and so on, forms the basis of the commonality as feminists.

Indigenous feminists advocate not only for increased political, cultural, and civil rights, but also for a more equal society within their respective tribes. The following provides an overview of how indigenous feminism differs from the mainstream framework of feminism:

"Indigenous feminism differs from the western idea of the movement; indigenous feminist groups consider equality not just as a gender issue but also as an issue of equality between the human race and nature. Whilst the indigenous feminist groups are fighting their own battles regarding their ethnicity, class and gender, and the perceived exclusion they have experienced as both women and indigenous people, they also work within and for their own groups' overall struggles against issues such as climate change and deforestation." (Castillo, 2010)

Ultimately, ethnicity, class, and gender identity have shaped the struggle of indigenous women in Latin America, and they have opted to assert themselves into the broader struggles of their communities (against multinational organizations and the destruction of the environment and their homelands, exploitation by Latina American governments, as well as violence that accompanies the trafficking of narcotics), all while creating specific spaces to reflect on and speak out against their experiences with sexism and exclusion within their own societies.

Mobilization & Organizing

Latin-American and Latina/Chicano feminism organization continues to evolve, as an increasing number of Latinas in Latin America and North America begin to define their own forms of feminism, which are distinctive and complex. Whether it is considering the Afro-Latina in North America, whose ethnic identity is often dismissed, or the Afro-Latina in Latin America who is faced with great racial discrimination despite their ethnic identity as a Latino, or the mestiza or "White" Latina in Latin America who holds a position of privilege in the dominant society, or the mestiza/"White" Latina in North America who is viewed as "The Other" and faces the same types of prejudice and discrimination. Peasant, poor, working-class, or professional Latina women, whether in the West or Latin America, often have a myriad of concerns, those dealing with survival (escaping violence and having ready access to shelter, food, and potable water). They strive for increased political participation, representation, and socioeconomic equality, as well as safeguarding reproductive justice health and rights (including access to contraception and safe abortions, and access to education.

These transnational Latina feminisms involve different methods of women's organization and mobilization. In the 21st century, these efforts highly rely on digital media, which is often touted as the 4th Wave of Feminism. This form of mobilization is carried out through blogs (L atina Feminista,Womanisms, Los Afro Latinos), journals (Chicana/Latina Studies, Latin American Perspectives), and think tanks, social media group pages, electronic newsletters, discussion boards, and websites. However, grassroots efforts of organizing are still used, particularly in areas where women have greater economic uncertainty and may not readily have access to digital media. There are, of course, the professional conferences, symposiums, and political advocacy which bring together Latina women who engage in discussions that center on how much progress has been made towards gender equality and how much more work has to be done. They call attention to, draft needed policies, and engage legislators.

Here are various Latina Feminist Mobilization Efforts & Organizations:

Chicana por mi Raza : is an online archive project that focuses on recapturing and highlighting the contribution of Mexican American, Chicana, and Hispanic women to vibrant social, political, and economic justice movements in the United States; looking at the development of Chicana feminist thought and action from 1960 to 1990. The website will serve as a digital archive, and is set to launch later this year. Items that will be available in the archive includes: newspapers, reports, leaflets, out-of-print books, correspondence, and oral histories.

Mundo Afro Salto : A regional Black culture group, decided to profile women of African descent in Salto Uruguay, in recognition of the 2011 United Nations International Year for People of African Descent. This was done via video, where these women proclaim not only their black heritage, but touch on gender issues, declaring that house work is not only woman's work.

The Roundtable of Latina Feminism : Is a collective grounding hosted by John Carroll University, which provides a dedicated space to discuss all issues related to Latina and Latin American feminisms. These gatherings are held annually, and they represent a break from academic conferences, which founder Mariana Ortega believed prioritized competitive and agnostic discussions. Instead, the roundtable provides an example of an alternative enuentros, and centers on the idea of transnational coalition building.

Colectivo Feminista Sexualidade Saude (CFSS): is a feminist health action group based in Brazil that provides health education and training for women and professionals. They encourage self-help and also have a focus on women's mental health, violence against women, and child mortality.

CEFEMINIA : is a non-profit women's organization founded in 1975 in Costa Rica, which focuses in five key areas: violence against women, women's health, women and the legal system, as well as housing and environmental justice. The organization promotes self-help and community-based efforts, including providing needed housing.

California Latinas for Reproductive Justice : is a state-wide organization that focuses on building Latinas' power and cultivating leadership through community education, policy advocacy, and community-informed research, in order to achieve reproductive justice.

Black Women of Brazil : is a website dedicated to Brazilian women of African descent, which features news, essays, reports and interviews spanning an array of topics including race, racism, hair, sexism, sexual objectification and exploitation, affirmative action, socioeconomic inequity, police brutality, etc. intended to give a more complete view of the experiences of black women in particular, and black people in general in Brazil with a goal of provoking discussion through the lens of race.

Conclusion

Despite their distinctive characteristics, Latina Feminisms are quite similar, and this may be due to the transnational interconnections and bidirectional contacts between North America and the countries of Latin America. The greatest similarities is that Latina feminisms all differ from the Western middle-class white construct, and remain deeply rooted in social movements that impact their communities. For this reason, much of Latina Feminist organizing is non-academic, where Latinas in women's movements often do not accept the label feminist. These women are self-taught, and their actions are not shaped by academic theory, but lived experiences with sexism, racism, marginalization, and inequality; which have contributed to their awakening and activism. Latina feminists have collectively criticized white-dominated Western feminism for being too homogenous, particularly in the blogosphere, where Latina feminist issues are not believed to be discussed in a satisfactory manner on mainstream feminist blogs. However, Latina feminist blogs, websites, publications, and organizations must take their own advice and grow to be more inclusive; and create spaces for the voices of marginalized indigenous and Afro-Latina women.

Ultimately, Latina feminisms advocate for the recognition of the full humanity of women and girls, and the removal of sexism, racism, ableism, classism, and discrimination based on sexual orientation.

References

Castillo, R. A. (2010). The Emergence of Indigenous Feminism in Latin America. Chicago Journals, Vol. 35,(No. 3), 539-545.

Is There Room for Decolonial, Transnational, and Radical Feminist Discourse in Pop Culture Feminism?

Cherise Charleswell

Pop culture feminism has become the dominant form of Western feminism, and much of this has been fueled by the ease of communication and creation of viral content on social media, along with the fact that noted pop culture figures, such as Beyonce, Meryl Streep, Patricia Arquette, and so on have openly or symbolically referred to themselves as feminist. Thus, on one hand it may be viewed as an achievement for feminism, in that it garners more visibility and sparks much needed discourse; however it does not necessarily lead to an understanding of feminist thought and practice. Members of Beyonce's "bee hive" were able to witness her 2015 performance at the MTV *Video Music Awards* and catch a glimpse of her silhouette in front of the letters F E M I N I S T, and they may be able to twirl along to her music in front of a mirror; but following Beyonce's brand of feminism, which is deeply rooted in pop culture, does not necessarily lead one to understand the tenets of feminism. The bottom line is that provocative imagery does not automatically equate to activism or empowerment. Take for example Kim Kardashian's career which is filled with a plethora of provocative images. In no way does her objectification and physical transformation under the male gaze, empowering to women; especially since her public persona lacks any depth, substance, or evidence of independent decision-making. Empowerment requires "ownership" and activism requires the ability to openly and intelligently speak about various issues, such as those involved in body politics; or simply making it clear that you have more to offer than your "body."

That is essential – moving the conversation beyond women's bodies—whether it is about slut shaming, fat shaming, sexual liberation, and so on; which currently dominates pop culture. What must be kept in mind is that women globally do not hold the same sexual attitudes, have different cultural attitudes on body size, and may not desire to dress in provocative clothing. Thus, what is liberating should not be defined from a Western perspective. Further, for some women, particularly women of African descent there is a deep and problematic history that is tied to the objectification and exploitation (physically and commercially) of their bodies; and this simply points to the need to refocus public discourse around the fact that women are much more than just their bodies. They are capable beings that deserve the same opportunities of men—in terms of education, employment, and social mobility.

Therefore, feminism is about more than body image and declaring to the world that you are sexually liberated; it is an ideology that advocates for social, political, economic, and cultural equality across genders, as well as race, ethnicity, and class. In other words, it advocates on behalf of the most marginalized in a society, and thus should highlight the issues of oppression and exploitation that they experience; and much of this advocacy begins with inquiry, raising awareness and education.

Discussions and analysis on pop culture are indeed needed, given the clear reality that pop culture often hurts women through dehumanization, objectification, and dismissing them altogether, but unfortunately, pop culture feminism, which focuses on media representations of feminism and nuanced rebuttals of vile pop-culture misogyny, often only offers limited discourse on feminist issues. Essentially, simply reflecting on and responding to the statements of celebrities and politicians, televised moments, advertisements, magazine covers, and events deemed worthy enough to receive coverage by corporate-dominated media is problematic. And it is problematic for the following reasons: (1) Responses to media bias, helps to ensure that ONLY the issues selected and/or presented in media are discussed and receive widespread coverage, (2) Responses to media and pop culture does not allow a space for Agenda setting and guiding discourse. Feminist should not be chasing the story, but pointing out the stories, the lived experiences, and the injustices that are being ignored and dismissed, and deserve to be covered. Interestingly enough in the 2014 *Time* article, *How to Reclaim the F-Word? Just Call Beyoncé,* writer Jessica Bennett, asserts that "Beyonce's brand of empowerment isn't perfect, but her VMA performance on Sunday accomplished what activists could not: She took feminism to the masses". [1] Her statement, following my previous sentiments about pop culture feminism is correct, there is certainly an increase visibility, and of course celebrity may help lead to social acceptance. However, the statement is short-sighted and historically inaccurate. Women's socio-political advancements and the rights that we enjoy today were achieved by the work of activists who brought their message to the masses in order to create social change.

As a result of the nominations released for the 2015 *MTV Video Music Awards* (yes they are still running), rapper Nicki Minaj became embroiled in a very public feud with pop singer Taylor Swift, as well as Miley Cyrus due to her decision to insert herself in this feud. Black women and others, included and many pop culture feminist bloggers and academics defended Nicki's actions, and stated that her decision to take a stand to speak out against the industry's exclusion of non-white women, particularly Black women who influence pop culture, and those who have more curvy figures (even though her curves are surgically enhanced). While defending Nicki's body positive "feminism", pop culture feminists seemed to have amnesia. Nicki's persona, music and lyrics have actually been antifeminist, in that they uphold and spew colorism, texturism, and misogyny. For example, on her second album, Roman Reloaded, the first single which was a dis record, was entitled *"Stupid Hoe"*; and within the song's lyrics she called her adversaries *"Nappy headed hoes"*. Yes, a hurtful and historical slur used against women of African descent. Then there is also the matter in which Nicki Minaj referred to herself as "The female Weezy (Lil Wayne), a man who music and persona is steeped in misogynoir, and just about everything that is anti-feminist in nature. Ultimately, this points out the problem with Pop Culture feminism, the willingness to claim celebrities as feminists, despite their contradictory bodies of work and persona. And that is why a more radical and analytical perspective is needed.

Certainly celebrities and other women of privilege are readily able to garner press and interviews, but their strategies won't work for other women who do not have the same resources at hand. Their work often does not exhibit any substantial effort towards ending sexist, racial, sociopolitical, and economic oppression. For that reason, pop culture feminism, with its dominance and growing influence on social discourse, needs to ensure that the voices and issues of women who are not in positions of privilege are raised. These include women in the global south in post-colonial societies, who are still dealing with the continued assault of western imperialism which only aggravates issues of gender inequality; as well as the marginalized women of color, working class, and immigrant women in Western societies. Pop cultural feminism must make room for perspectives that are decolonial, transnational, and radical; putting forth a show of solidarity for all forms of anti-white supremacy patriarchal activism.

Broadening Perspectives

American pop culture, like American politics focuses solely on America. Americans are ignorant to current foreign affairs, history, and even geography; and this translates to ignorance and indifference that is seen in Western feminism, particularly when it comes to pop culture.

Central to all feminisms should be the understanding that male domination is universal. Further, the manner in which patriarchy manifest its self is through various interactions between economic, ideological, and cultural systems; which means that women's or feminist's means of resisting the different manifestations of patriarchy, will also be varied.

Yet, Transnational solidarity, as well as the inclusion of marginalized populations within Western societies continues to be a difficult goal to achieve because of the continued dominance of Western feminism—and its often myopic (tunnel-vision) focus on pop culture. There is a lack of self-reflexivity, as well as the inability or unwillingness to address the ways in which imperialism, the effects of colonialism, and racism continues to structure and impact the lives of women, girls, and families around the world. This willful ignorance helps to explain instances such as:

- The statements made by soap opera actress Nancy Lee Grahn during the Oscars, where she could not understand why Viola Davis needed to point out the lack of opportunities for women of color.

- Meryl Streep and the slew of white feminists not seeing the problem of adorning t shirts with the statement, "*I Rather Be A Rebel Than A Slave*" for the promotions of their film The *Suffragists*.

- Discussions about rape culture that never seem to include or make central the plight of indigenous women who have some of the highest rates of rape. [2]

- The lack of solidarity shown to Black women and girls who are victims of police state violence.

- The fact that there is virtually no coverage, hashtags, and trending topics about the plight of refugee women fleeing Syria; and the ties between U.S. government policies, the de-stabilization of Iraq and the rise of ISIL/ISIS.

- The lack of *"trending"* topics that highlight the plight of migrant workers in the United States. Now, *"slut walks"*, particularly those organized by celebrities, such as Amber Rose, garner many followers, likes, retweets, and shares.

- Amnesty International, a human rights organization, adopted a policy that calls for the full decriminalization of the sex trade; stating that the decision was made in the interest of protecting the safety and human rights of sex workers. Despite Amnesty International's unfortunate claims the fact remains that prostituted individuals often come from vulnerable populations and lack choice (Agency). [3] Also, studies have found that legalization or decriminalization actually increases human and sex trafficking. [3] Certainly there are sex workers who do have some degree of agency with their chosen profession; however the vast majority of those involved in sex work globally are forced into it by systems of human trafficking, violence, and intimidation, and there is nothing glamorous or sexually liberating about what these women, girls, and boys have to endure.

- The fact that most of the women who hold leadership positions in many of the mainstream and global women and development organizations are white, cis, women often of a privileged economic background. Just look at the leadership of The Feminist Majority Foundation, which *advocates for equality globally*, it is essentially as described.

- The many instances where women's groups based in the Global North, or funded by organizations in the Global North develop campaigns to "assist" women in the Global South, but often do not allow women from these areas to hold leadership positions, or be decision makers--- those positions goes to those who have illustrious Western education in gender studies, development, and other related social science backgrounds. Thus, far too many programs continue with this White Western savior model, that leaves communities dependent.

Conclusive Statements

Pop Culture feminism currently remains the most dominant form of Western Feminism, and the views shared by pop culture feminist are important critiques to misogynistic images in media and their impact on society. However, non-Western feminist have charged Western feminism, including Academia of spending a vast amount of time and effort nit-picking over ideologies and theories; while ignoring the dire hardships of those from marginalized communities from around the world.

Further, there is often a failure to formulate strategies to redress the problems highlighted in pop culture feminism. The focus needs to once again be primarily about gender and racial equality that will improve the lives and health outcomes of women and girls; and this must go beyond sassy memes and posts about fat acceptance (without regard for how being fat may be a luxury to some or the result of living within a food desert for healthier and nutritious food options for others), trigger warnings, and mindless debates about battle of the sexes.

What type of mindless debates and discussions?

Posts like this that have become ubiquitous on social media--- and was shared by a white cis heterosexual woman on Facebook on a Feminist group page.

> **Vent:**
> *My boyfriend is pulling the "not all men" card and called me a "man hater" because I said "men are scumbags" in reply to a comment he made about some dude doing some scumbag like shit.*
> *Anyone else encounter this or the like with a significant other?*

Perhaps there is a chance that pop culture feminist would use their influence, capabilities, and virtual networks to more frequently highlight an include the voices of feminist who are speaking from a more radical, transnational, and decolonial perspective. These perspectives may not be as sensational, and may force Western feminists to question their own role and compliancy in the exploitation and oppression of other women---particularly those in marginalized communities and the Global South. Perhaps this will lead to discussions and will allow pop culture feminism to become more informed, culturally aware, and political savvy. For, the greatest way to achieve gender equality globally is not through continuous discussion; but activism, direct advocacy, and much needed policy change.

In the end, it is not about waging the oppression Olympics, in terms of the impact and experiences with patriarchy. Gender rights, human rights, women's issues, and feminist issues are broad and multifaceted; and this should be addressed and included in the work of pop culture feminists. There is a historical debate about whether art (in all of its formats) reflect or is shaped by reality; or vice versa. One can argue that the influence is bidirectional. In this way, feminist have the opportunity to do more than react to the arts, media, etc., and can instead begin to create the news headlines that highlight the stories and voices that often go unheard.

References

[1] Bennett, J. How to Reclaim the F-Word? Just Call Beyoncé. *Time*. (Aug. 26, 2014). Retrieved from http://time.com/3181644/beyonce-reclaim-feminism-pop-star/ .

[2] *Futures Without Violence*. The Facts on Violence Against American Indian/Alaskan Native Women. Retrieved from https://www.futureswithoutviolence.org/userfiles/file/Violence%20Against%20AI%20AN%20Women%20Fact%20Sheet.pdf .

[3] *Demand Abolition*. A Brief Review of the Evidence on the Consequences of Legalizing or Decriminalizing Prostitution. Retrieved from http://prostitutionresearch.com/wp-content/uploads/2012/01/Fact-Sheet-on-Decriminalization-Demand-Abolition.pdf

Gentrification is a Feminist Issue
A Discussion on the Intersection of Class, Race, Gender, and Housing

Cherise Charleswell

An Overview: What is Gentrification?

From a socioeconomic standpoint, gentrification may be defined as a gradual process of renewal and rebuilding that involves the influx of upper-income or affluent - usually white people - into existing urban districts that are often viewed as being deteriorating areas. This process causes the displacement of the low-middle income working-class, and often long-time, residents due to the increase in rents and property values and changes in the district's overall character and culture. The "rent gap" is often noted as the underlying mechanism of gentrification. The following is an overview of the cyclic nature of this rent gap put into historical perspective:

· By the close of the Second World War there was a movement of capital to the suburbs. This movement was fueled by greater amount of open land, lower cost of land, little existing development, and opportunities for profit.

· Capital and resources left the city -- and followed urban migration (white flight) to the suburbs

· Racist housing practices, including legislation that forbid selling homes and renting to non-White residents helped to uphold de facto segregation.

· By the 1960s many of these urban areas, with the loss of capital, jobs, and so on; began to deteriorate, and property values fell.

· Currently with the higher costs of property in the suburbs and other communities, there are fewer and fewer opportunities to invest small and gain a big profit; thus making the once "undesirable" urban properties with their low property values and costs, more "desirable."

· By the 1980s gentrification was in full-swing.

· Reinvestment in the urban communities causes the cost of property to rise quickly and long-standing residents who were once able to afford to live in these once "undesirable" areas, find themselves unable to afford the higher cost of rent and home mortgages. Further, they are unable to afford to patronize the new and costly stores that have replaced the shops that they used to frequent.

This rent gap is facilitated by a number of agents and practices, and "retenanting" is a professional euphemism given to the commercial real estate agents whose job is to study a community and help to make change -- gentrification -- happen quickly. Their work involves helping to kick out commercial tenants who are paying extremely low rent, and then finding tenants who will pay higher rates for the same spaces. The following expose was released discussing the work of one of these agents working in Highland Park, a hilly area northeast of downtown Los Angeles that has been a target for gentrification for residents fleeing even higher home prices and rents in neighboring Hollywood, Silver Lake, and Echo Park. Then there was the 2012 release of the documentary film "My Brooklyn," directed by Kelly Anderson and produced by

Allison Lirish Dean, which offers detailed examples of this rent gap and an even broader analysis of the many factors behind gentrification. Brooklyn itself is home to some of the most rapidly gentrifying areas in the United States, and is among the most expensive cities to reside in.

Viewing the complex matter of gentrification through a feminist lens helps to uncover how multifaceted it is; in that gentrification involves the oppression, marginalization, displacement of vulnerable populations, particularly women and children who are often already negatively impacted by the effects of classism, sexism, and racism. Gentrification threatens to erode the communities and livelihood maintained by these women because their displacement becomes a precondition for the total transformation of the area.

When considering the complex definition and various factors involved in this process, one thing must remain clear -- it is driven by the private sector and is the result of capitalism's relentless pursuit of profit. The very sector of society that has control and influence over all levels of government in the United States, and is thus able to create policies that help to facilitate and increase gentrification in communities around the country --- as well as those outside the United States. This far-flung reach is due to the nature of multinational corporations which wield their power and influence globally. I was reminded of this while on vacation in Portugal this past Spring. As I was walking along a typically narrow, winding street in Vila Nova de Gaia, which is just South of Porto, a resident of the city pointed out how many of the original homeowners and families that lived along the street for many, many years, were becoming displaced. Their homes and shops were being bought up and replaced with hotels. Already, I could begin to see how the character of the community was changing. These new hotels used color schemes and architectural design styles that seemed completely out of place with the homes in the area, which were decorated with world-renowned, intricate and vibrant Portuguese ceramic tiles. I asked where these families went, and the response was that they were relocated to areas much further away from the city center.

And this seems to be a common theme on both sides of the Atlantic -- the lack of consideration that goes to displaced residents. Truly considering these residents would mean that factors which led them to these areas, which were previously viewed as being undesirable, should be taken into account. Thus, the argument can be put forth that gentrification may be viewed as new-wave colonialism, having economic, social, and public health repercussions for women, communities of color, and the poor. In this sense, it is a feminist issue, and should be interrogated, at least partly, as such.

Feminization of Poverty & the Cost of Housing

In the most simplistic terms, the feminization of poverty refers to the fact that women represent a disproportionate share of the world's poor. Further, the feminization of poverty is not only a consequence of lack of income, but is also the result of the deprivation of opportunities and genderbiases present in both society and government. For women of color, the loss of opportunities are also a result of institutional-level racism and discriminatory practices. It is these biases that have helped to create the gender-wage gap and all of the socioeconomic consequences of inequity.

So, how does the feminization of poverty relate to the discussion of gentrification?

For more than 30 years, women in the United States have had to deal with not only stagnant wages , where average wages have barely kept pace with inflation since 1979, but also with the persisting gender-wage gap. Even more troublesome is that these wages have remained stagnant despite an exponential growth in worker productivity.

For myself, and those born the generation after me, the 80s and 90s babies, this means that our overall standard of living is probably reduced by 50% in comparison to previous generations; and this includes college educated women who may also find it difficult to afford the loftier rental prices in gentrified neighborhoods. Salaries are simply not keeping up with the cost of living; especially the cost of housing.

Further, the gender-pay gap helps to ensure that those who are more likely to be impoverished and coping with issues of food insecurity, homelessness, etc. are women and children. Working-class and low-income women are the group who are most vulnerable to gentrification in that they live in the areas that are being targeted by this process. In essence, the sexist, racist, discriminatory and biased practices, beliefs, and policies that have helped to create the gender-pay gap also help to facilitate their removal from areas that they were once able to afford.

Having lower wages means that these working-class women will be unable to resist or withstand the process of gentrification and remain in their homes and neighborhoods. This is due to the fact that lower wages means that an increase in the amount on rent or mortgage costs is extremely difficult for women who are already dealing with wage deficits. To put this into perspective, a Latina woman who on average makes only $0.56 to a white man's $1.00 hourly, would be least likely to be able cope with a marked increase in rent, as well as the higher cost of groceries and other goods which occur when an area undergoes gentrification. In comparison, a white man, who make higher wages on average, would be more capable of remaining in a neighborhood that is undergoing gentrification.

Intersections: Communities of Color

When taking a look at the definition of gentrify, the root word of gentrification, one can readily discern what is implied, especially when considering the change in demographics of these neighborhoods:

"To change (a place, such as an old neighborhood) by improving it and making it more appealing to people who have money ."

The term "*appealing*" harkens back to the language used by banks, realtors, and others who wanted to ensure that certain neighborhoods would remain devoid of people of color. The American suburbs were actually built out due to this phenomenon of *White flight* from urban centers which, without resources and investment, were left to decay. In fact, post-New Deal communities actually received federal subsidies for home ownership, while others, that had Black residents or other people of color, did not. This process was called "*red-lining*", and it often barred any neighborhood with more than 5% of Black people/people of color from receiving subsidies for home ownership and wealth building. This process helped to keep Compton, California, the birthplace of gangster rap, completely White up until the early 1950s. This process led half a million whites to move out of Brooklyn in the 1970s.

The following statements shared by Zach Behrens in his*essay* , *Before the 1950s, the Whiteness of Compton was Defended Vehemently,* explains why these covenants manifested.
"Covenants across the country began in the late 1910s and early 1920s in response to the increasing black population in American cities, namely Northern and Western ones that saw the rise during World War I during the so-called great migration from the South. In Los Angeles, however, the move of African Americans was slow until World War II. Still, that slow growth in the 1920s was enough for white homeowners to become concerned about declining property values because of the black influx."

These discriminatory housing practices were - or continue to be -- used against other people of color around the US, and one can argue that at its roots, and according to the terminology used in its definition, gentrification is a racist practice that seeks to make a neighborhood more *appealing* to those who are deemed desirable - in other words, white people, or more specifically, wealthy white people. Women of color, particularly those who are working class and thus subjected to oppressive systems of racism, classism, ableism, and sexism, are deemed the most undesirable and are consequently marginalized. The rising cost of living, escalating rents and mortgages, stagnant wages, and gender wage-gap literally force them out of their neighborhoods, despite many having community ties for multiple generations.

Ultimately, the process of gentrification sits on a historical legacy of oppression and discrimination, and has only worsened with the shrinking of the middle class and transfer of wealth to the smallest percentage of the US population over the past 40 years. Furthermore, it has left women, especially women of color, as the most vulnerable in this process of systematic displacement. It is a matter where race, class, and gender intersect. And, for this reason, gentrification must be recognized as a feminist issue.

Notes

[i] Eduardo Porter, "The Bane and Boon of For-Profit Colleges," *New York Times*, February 25, 2014 (http://www.nytimes.com/2014/02/26/business/economy/the-bane-and-the-boon-of-for-profit-colleges.html)

[ii] Caitlin Rosenthal, "The Long and Controversial History of For-Profit Colleges," *Bloomberg View*, October 25, 2012 (http://www.bloombergview.com/articles/2012-10-25/the-long-and-controversial-history-of-for-profit-colleges)

[iii] Ibid

[iv] Emily Hanford, *A Brief History of For-Profit Education in the United States*, American Radioworks, http://americanradioworks.publicradio.org/features/tomorrows-college/phoenix/history-of-for-profit-higher-education.html

[v] Daniel L. Bennett, Adam R. Lucchesi, and Richard K. Vedder, *For-Profit Higher Education: Growth, Innovation, and Regulation*, Center for College Affordability and Productivity (July 2010), pg 9

[vi] Jeffrey Selingo, "For-Profit Colleges Aim to Take a Share of State Financial Aid Funds," *The Chronicle of Higher Education*, September 24, 1999

[vii] Tim Post, "For-Profit Colleges Fight Effort To Ban State Aid To Students," *Michigan Public Radio News*, March 25, 2009 (http://www.mprnews.org/story/2009/03/25/for_profit_schools_loans)

[viii] Judy Lin, "Most California For-Profit Colleges Lose State Grants," *San Jose Mercury News*, August 1, 2012 (http://www.mercurynews.com/ci_21208286/most-california-profit-colleges-lose-state-grants)

[ix] David J. Deming, Claudia Goldin and Lawrence F. Katz, "The For-Profit Postsecondary School Sector: Nimble Critters or Agile Predators," *The Journal of Economic Perspectives* 26:1 (Winter 2012), pg 145

[x] Steven Salzberg, "For-Profit Colleges Encourage Huge Student Debt," *Forbes*, July 12, 2015 (http://www.forbes.com/sites/stevensalzberg/2015/07/12/for-profit-colleges-encourage-huge-student-debt/)

[xi] FinAid, *90/10 Rule*, http://www.finaid.org/loans/90-10-rule.phtml

[xii] Bennett, Lucchesi, Vedder, pg 150
[xiii] Aaron Glantz, *GI Bill Funds Flow To For-Profit Colleges That Fail State Aid Standards*, The Center for Investigative Reporting, http://cironline.org/reports/gi-bill-funds-flow-profit-colleges-fail-state-aid-standards-6477 (June 28, 2014)

[xiv] Jose L. Cruz, Jennifer Engle, Mamie Lynch, *Subprime Opportunity: The Unfulfilled Promise of For-Profit Colleges and Universities*, The Education Trust (November 2010), pg 3

[xv] Clive R. Belfield, "Student Loans and Repayment Rates: The For-profit Colleges," *Research in Higher Education* 54:1 (February 2013), pgs 18, 26

[xvi] U.S. Senate, Senate, Committee on Health, Education, Labor, and Pensions, *For Profit Higher Education: The Failure to Safeguard the Federal Investment and*

706

Ensure Student Success, 112th Congress, 2nd Session, July 30, 2012 (Washington D.C.: GPO, 2012) pg 42

[xvii] Shahien Nasiripur, "Heald College Fined For Misleading Students About Job Prospects," *Huffington Post*, April 14, 2015 (http://www.huffingtonpost.com/2015/04/14/heald-college-fine-jobs_n_7067056.html)

[xviii] Hannah Appel, Astra Taylor, "Subprime Students: How For-Profit Universities Make a Killing By Exploiting College Dreams," *Mother Jones*, September 23, 2014 (http://www.motherjones.com/politics/2014/09/for-profit-university-subprime-student-poor-minority)

[xix] Blake Ellis, "My College Degree Is Worthless," *CNN*, November 2, 2014 (http://money.cnn.com/2014/11/02/pf/college/for-profit-college-degree/)

[xx] Capsee, *Employers Value For-Profit Degrees Less, New Study Finds*, The Center for Analysis of Postsecondary Education and Employment, http://capseecenter.org/employers-value-for-profit-degrees-less/ (October 6, 2014)

[xxi] Lisa Wade, "In Many Employers' Eyes, For-Profit Colleges Are Equivalent to High School," *Pacific Standard*, September 3, 2014 (http://www.psmag.com/business-economics/many-employers-eyes-profit-colleges-equivalent-high-school-89940)

[xxii] Tamar Lewin, "Government to Forgive Student Loans at Corinthian Colleges," *New York Times*, June 6, 2015 (http://www.nytimes.com/2015/06/09/education/us-to-forgive-federal-loans-of-corinthian-college-students.html)

[xxiii] For excellent resources on Roman history for this period see; Havell. H.L.. Republican Rome. 1914. Oracle Publishing, 1996. Also see; Scullard, H.H.. From the Gracchi to Nero. 1959. 5th edition. Routledge, 1982. Also see; Parenti, Michael. The Assassination of Julius Caesar. The New Press, 2003. Also see; Titchener, Frances. "To Rule Mankind and Make the World Obey". Portable Professor Series. Barnes & Noble Audio; 2004.

[xxiv] Quoted in; Parenti (2003), 61.

[xxv] For excellent resources on the life and political career of Theodore Roosevelt see; Morris, Edmund. Theodore Rex. Random House, 2002. Also see; The Roosevelts: An Intimate History. Dir. Ken Burns. PBS, 2014. Also see; Brands, H.W.. T.R.: The Last Romantic. Basic Books, 1998.

[xxvi] For an excellent history of this period, up to 1900, see Brands, H.W.. American

Colossus. Anchor Books, 2011.

xxvii See; Abbott, Elizabeth. Sugar: A Bittersweet History. The Overlook Press, 2011.

xxviii Havell (1914), 367.

xxix Colonies were a great tool for the Romans to relieve social pressure accumulating among the *Plebs Urbana* at Rome. Being re-settled in a colony gave the colonist a second chance, which many wanted, even at the cost of re-settlement far from Rome, the idea of which would have abhorred a true Roman. This was thus an easy way for politicians to win acclaim and popularity with the people.

xxx These stats come from Sunstein, Cass. The Second Bill of Rights. Basic Books, (2004): 36-38.

xxxi I mean "republican" in the classical political sense here. The republican tradition has a long history in political philosophy. Excellent modern work in this tradition has been done by Philip Petit. See Republicanism. Oxford University Press, 1997.

xxxii Sunstein (2004), 90.

xxxiii These are two of F.D.R.'s "four freedoms". See Sunstein (2004), 80.

xxxiv See; Hanson, Victor Davis. The Other Greeks. 1995. University of California Press,1999. Also see; Hanson, V.D.. Warfare and Agriculture in Classical Greece. University of California Press, 1998.

xxxv Proscription is a process whereby Roman citizens were declared 'outlaws', 'traitors', or 'criminals' by the state, i.e. the Senate. Once a citizen was declared a criminal they effectively had a bounty put out on their head. If one was a victim of proscription, one would have twenty hour hours to either flee or face trial; the outcome of this trial would not be much in doubt. In response to proscription many Roman citizens chose suicide. This was because if they either fled or were convicted in court their property would be forfeited to the state. Thus, in order to keep property in the family, many proscribed individuals chose suicide to exile or execution.

The Hampton Institute is a working-class think tank providing commentary, analysis, research and theory on a wide range of social, political, economic and cultural issues. Visit us on the web at **www.hamptoninstitution.org**.